———— FOURTH EDITION —

HISTORICAL AND PHILOSOPHICAL FOUNDATIONS OF EDUCATION

A Biographical Introduction

GERALD L. GUTEK
Loyola University Chicago

PEARSON

Merrill
Prentice Hall

Upper Saddle River, New Jersey
Columbus, Ohio

Library of Congress Cataloging-in-Publication Data

Gutek, Gerald Lee.
  Historical and philosophical foundations of education: a biographical introduction/
Gerald L. Gutek.--4th ed.
    p. cm.
  Includes bibliographical references and index.
  ISBN 0-13-113809-X
  1. Educators--Biography. 2. Education--History. 3. Education--Philosophy. I. Title.

LA2301.G88 2005
370'.82'2--dc22   2004045175

Vice President and Executive Publisher: Jeffery W. Johnston
Executive Editor: Debra A. Stollenwerk
Editorial Assistant: Mary Morrill
Production Editor: Kris Robinson-Roach
Production Coordination: bookworks
Design Coordinator: Diane C. Lorenzo
Cover Designer: Bryan Huber

Cover Image: Reproduced from the collections of the National Archives; courtesy of Library of Congress
Photo Coordinator: Lori Whitley
Production Manager: Susan Hannahs
Director of Marketing: Ann Castel Davis
Marketing Manager: Darcy Betts Prybella
Marketing Coordinator: Tyra Poole

This book was set in Janson Text by Pine Tree Composition. It was printed and bound by R. R. Donnelley & Sons Company. The cover was printed by Phoenix Color Corp.

Photo Credits: Corbis/Bettmann: p. 62; courtesy of the Library of Congress: pp. 11, 49, 94, 108, 122, 135, 150, 174, 196, 214, 237, 256, 274, 294, 313, 331, 378, 398; reproduced from the collections of the National Archives: pp. 31, 77, 353; and courtesy of the Instituto Paulo Freire, Paulo Freire Archives: p. 423.

Pearson Education Ltd.
Pearson Education Singapore Pte. Ltd.
Pearson Education Canada, Ltd.
Pearson Education—Japan

Pearson Education Australia Pty. Limited
Pearson Education North Asia Ltd.
Pearson Educación de Mexico, S.A. de C.V.
Pearson Education Malaysia Pte. Ltd.

10 9 8 7 6 5 4 3 2 1
ISBN: 0-13-113809-X

For my granddaughter, Claire Elizabeth,
and her parents, Andrew and Laura Swiatek

Historical and Philosophical Foundations of Education: A Biographical Introduction developed from my more than three decades of teaching the history and philosophy of education at Loyola University Chicago and as a visiting professor at Northern Michigan University, Otterbein College, and the University of Glasgow in Scotland. Over time, the identification of the biographies and development of the chapters were stimulated by discussions with my students. The book reflects my belief that educational biography is a valuable, powerful, but too-often neglected medium for preparing teachers, administrators, and other professionals in education. I hope the book's fourth edition will continue to focus more attention on the use of educational biography in professional education programs.

Organization and Coverage

As the book's title indicates, I have organized its contents around three broad themes: major movements in world history, the biographies of leading educators, and the philosophies and ideologies that came from their ideas. As a historian, I have been intrigued by the interaction of individuals in their historical contexts and how they create meaning from their transaction with the cultural situation of living at a given time and place.

As a teacher of the history and philosophy of education, I decided to organize the book around the major movements in world and western history: the age of Confucius in ancient China, the classical periods of ancient Greece and Rome, the Middle Ages, the Renaissance, the Protestant Reformation, the Enlightenment, the age of revolution, the foundations of the United States, the Industrial Revolution, the rise of ideologies, the progressive movement, the end of imperialism in the postcolonial world, the rise of African American consciousness, and the development of liberation pedagogy. This kind of periodization around broad historical currents helped me to construct a cognitive map on which I could locate people and events and give myself a perspective on the past. However, I also determined that this kind of periodization should not simply be chronological but should be enlivened by lives that represented the efforts, the trials and errors, and achievements of those who shaped the history and philosophy of education.

My interest in biography—the stories of lives—provided a means to give the great movements of educational history a personal face. Biography enables us to see ourselves through the lives of others. For each of the great movements in history, I identified an important contributor to educational philosophy and method. For ancient China, there was Confucius, an educator whose philosophy exerted a powerful force on Asian culture; for ancient Greece and Rome, there were Plato, the founder of idealism; Aristotle, the founder of realism; and Quintilian, an exemplary teacher of rhetoric. Medieval Christianity was epitomized by the great theologian Thomas Aquinas. Erasmus was the ideal representative of Renaissance humanism. John Calvin and Johann Amos Comenius represented two different ways of interpreting the educational changes produced by the Protestant Reformation. For the Enlightenment and post-Enlightenment eras, the figures of Jean-Jacques Rousseau and Johann Heinrich Pestalozzi stood out in bold relief. For the age of revolution and republicanism three persons—Thomas Jefferson, Mary Wollstonecraft, and Horace Mann—were leading characters. Jefferson made the intellectual connection between the Enlightenment's rationalism and the republican impulse in North America. Mary Wollstonecraft undertook a revolution for women's rights. Horace Mann was a strong voice for creating public education for the new American republic. Educational responses to the Industrial and Darwinian revolutions came from such theorists as Robert Owen, a utopian socialist; John Stuart Mill, a liberal; and Herbert Spencer, a social Darwinist. Early twentieth-century progressivism is exemplified by Jane Addams, founder of Hull House, and John Dewey, America's leading Pragmatist philosopher. The rights of children were asserted by Friedrich Froebel, founder of the kindergarten, and Maria Montessori, who created her own version of early childhood education. The attack on colonialism came from Mohandas Gandhi, who won India's independence by nonviolent resistance. W. E. B. Du Bois's commitment to equality of persons signaled a rising African American consciousness that would lead to pan-Africanism. The liberation pedagogy of Paulo Freire encompassed important strands in contemporary educational criticism such as neo-Marxism, existentialism, postmodernism, and critical theory.

At various times in my academic career, I have taught courses in philosophy of education. As I examined the lives of the great educators in their historical contexts, their views on philosophy of education—what constitutes the educated person—surfaced and came into perspective. I found that my students, too, gained deeper insights into philosophy of education by making connections with founding figures. For example, an examination of Plato's ideas leads to a consideration of philosophical idealism, Aristotle's ideas to realism, Thomas Aquinas to Thomism, Erasmus to humanism, Comenius to Pansophism, Rousseau to naturalism, Dewey to Pragmatism, and Freire to liberation pedagogy.

I found that the lives and ideas of certain key figures provided students with an understanding of ideology and how ideology influences educational policy. Here, Robert Owen provides insights into utopianism, Mary Wollstonecraft into feminism, John Stuart Mill into liberalism, Herbert Spencer into social Darwinism, Jane Addams into progressivism, and W. E. B. Du Bois into pan-Africanism.

Although the various major historical, philosophical, and ideological currents are rich and complex, how the world's leading educators interacted with the context of their lives to create their own meanings of education cuts across this complexity. Because an individual's life is multifaceted, biography becomes a tool that provides a clear, interdisciplinary way to look at the development of educational ideas. Each educator treated leads us to a broader and more generous appreciation of our educational heritage, and often illuminates current challenges.

Format

The book provides students with an interesting and personal but structured way to examine the historical and philosophical foundations of education. The first chapter examines how educational biography can be used in teacher and professional education programs. The following sections are included in each of the subsequent 24 chapters:

- The *Historical Context* that places the educational thinker in the historical, cultural, and philosophical situation of her or his time.
- A *Biography* of the educational thinker that analyzes the formative persons and events that shaped his or her educational philosophy or ideology.
- An *Analysis of the Educational Thinker's Philosophy or Ideology* that identifies the theorist's principal ideas about truth and value, education and schooling, and teaching and learning.
- A *Conclusion* that assesses the educational contributions and significance of the theorist.
- *Questions for Reflection and Dialogue*, intended to stimulate personal reflection and group discussion, that relate the educational thinker to her or his time in history and illuminate current issues and controversies in education.
- *Projects for Deepening Your Understanding* that encourage a further engagement in reading, research, and field work and that help to stimulate readers to apply history and philosophy to educational issues and controversies.
- *Suggestions for Further Reading* that include both long-standing and recent books.

Features

Historical and Philosophical Foundations of Education: A Biographical Introduction, Fourth Edition, offers the following features:

- An examination of the historical, philosophical, and ideological foundations of education through the study of the biographies of the world's leading educational thinkers.
- An examination of the history and philosophy of education in a single book that is especially useful in courses that integrate these fields.
- A solid grounding in the historical and philosophical foundations of education based on sustained teaching experience.
- *Questions for Reflection and Dialogue* and *Projects for Deepening Your Understanding*.

New to This Edition

It is not easy to choose the major figures to treat in a book such as this. Every professor of history and philosophy of education has his or her own favorites. After consultation with professors who used the third edition, I determined to again feature the 21 theorists, philosophers, and educators who were treated in that edition. The fourth edition includes two new chapters, Chapter 2 on Confucius and Chapter 24 on Paulo Freire. I decided that a discussion of Confucius would broaden the book into more of a world history and philosophy of education by examining an educator whose ideas were—and remain—a powerful force in Chinese and Asian culture and education. A discussion of Freire provided the opportunity to not only examine liberation pedagogy but also to conclude the book by commenting on new trends in educational philosophy such as neo-Marxism, existentialism, postmodernism, and critical theory. I have included my ongoing research on Maria Montessori and her method in a revised Chapter 21.

The fourth edition has been updated and the suggested readings revised to include recent publications in the field. In particular, biographies of Mary Wollstonecraft, Jane Addams, John Dewey, Maria Montessori, and Mohandas Gandhi have been expanded to reflect new biographical treatments of these people. Chapter 13 on Wollstonecraft has been revised to position her more firmly as a pioneer in feminist theory of education. Chapter 19 on Addams includes more insights about her struggle against the conventional Victorian restrictions on women's freedom to make career and life choices. Chapter 20 on Dewey, examining his early life and education, portrays him as a person who responded to his times emotionally as well as philosophically. Chapter 21 on Montessori includes more discussion of her conception of a science of education, her orientation to educational psychology, and her broader social theories. Chapter 22 on Gandhi places him more deeply in the South African and Indian contexts in which he formulated his philosophy of nonviolence.

Acknowledgments

My biographical and historical interests were developed by my graduate education at the University of Illinois in Urbana. Professors J. Leonard Bates, Arthur E. Bestor, Jr., and Norman Graebner were masters in developing for their students the importance of people in historical contexts. My study with Professor Harry Broudy emphasized that educators benefited from having a perspective on the development of educational ideas over time. The experimentalist theme of people interacting within their contexts owes much to the introduction to John Dewey that I received from William O. Stanley and Joe Burnett. Archibald Anderson, my major professor, provided the insights that placed the history of education in its broad cultural context. It was Professor Anderson who encouraged me to write my first biography of an educator, my doctoral dissertation on George S. Counts. My discussions with my friend and colleague Steve Miller, Loyola University Chicago, about the philosophy of education have always been thought provoking and a stimulus to my writing.

I appreciate the advice, support, and patience of Debbie Stollenwerk, my editor at Merrill/Prentice Hall, who encouraged me to prepare a fourth edition. I want to thank Kris Roach, my production editor, and freelance copyeditor Terry Andrews for working with me to bring this fourth edition to publication.

I also want to acknowledge the insights provided by my colleagues in the history and philosophy of education who reviewed the book and made excellent suggestions that guided my revisions: Malcolm B. Campbell, Bowling Green State University; Richard L. Farber, The College of New Jersey; Louise Fleming, Ashland University; Tracy Ann Scholl, Minnesota State University, Moorhead; and Robert E. Vadas, State University of New York.

I want to acknowledge how my grandchildren—Claire, Abigail, Mills, and Luke—each at their own stage of development and education, have given me fresh insights into the work of the educational thinkers treated in this book. I especially want to thank my wife, Patricia, for her love and for her support of my research and writing.

EDUCATOR LEARNING CENTER:
AN INVALUABLE ONLINE RESOURCE

Merrill Education and the Association for Supervision and Curriculum Development (ASCD) invite you to take advantage of a new online resource, one that provides access to the top research and proven strategies associated with ASCD and Merrill— the Educator Learning Center. At **www.EducatorLearningCenter.com** you will find resources that will enhance your students' understanding of course topics and of current educational issues, in addition to being invaluable for further research.

How the Educator Learning Center will Help Your Students Become Better Teachers

With the combined resources of Merrill Education and ASCD, you and your students will find a wealth of tools and materials to better prepare them for the classroom.

Research

- More than 600 articles from the ASCD journal *Educational Leadership* discuss everyday issues faced by practicing teachers.
- A direct link on the site to Research Navigator™ gives students access to many of the leading education journals, as well as extensive content detailing the research process.
- Excerpts from Merrill Education texts give your students insights on important topics of instructional methods, diverse populations, assessment, classroom management, technology, and refining classroom practice.

Classroom Practice

- Hundreds of lesson plans and teaching strategies are categorized by content area and age range.
- Case studies and classroom video footage provide virtual field experience for student reflection.
- Computer simulations and other electronic tools keep your students abreast of today's classrooms and current technologies.

Look into the Value of Educator Learning Center Yourself

A four-month subscription to Educator Learning Center is $25 but is **FREE** when used in conjunction with this text. To obtain free passcodes for your students, simply contact your local Merrill/Prentice Hall sales representative, and your representative will give you a special ISBN to give your bookstore when ordering your textbooks. To preview the value of this website to you and your students, please go to **www.EducatorLearningCenter.com** and click on "Demo."

CONTENTS

Part IV

PART

I

CHAPTER 1

Educational Biography and the Historical and Philosophical Foundations of Education

Historical and Philosophical Foundations of Education: A Biographical Introduction is designed to introduce teachers, prospective teachers, and other educational personnel to the history and philosophy of education by examining the life stories, the biographies, of the leading figures who shaped educational theory and practice. Its focus is the theme that key people, by interacting with the cultural contexts in which they lived, developed ideas about education that continue to affect us today. Some of these figures were professional educators, others were philosophers and ideologists who were concerned with issues in education. By examining the lives, ideas, and contributions of these leading personalities on the world scene, this book seeks to illuminate the connection between education and the great transforming events and trends that have shaped our world.

Overview

This book is a historical narrative that describes the context, times and situation, and biography of each world figure examined. In addition, we analyze the educational ideas and practices that each person developed and consider their contemporary meaning and significance.

The narration begins in Chapter 2 with Confucius, a philosopher and teacher whose ethical theory became highly significant in China and throughout Asia. Chapter 3 examines Plato, who in ancient Athens established the philosophical foundations of the Western cultural and educational heritage. Chapter 4 continues to explore the Greek context by examining Aristotle's philosophical and educational ideas. Chapter 5 examines the educational theory and practices of Quintilian, the Roman rhetorician, who elaborated on the ideal of rhetoric education that had originated in ancient Greece with the Sophists and Isocrates. The educational philosophies of Plato, Aristotle, and Quintilian illuminate the Graeco-Roman contribution to the Western cultural and educational heritage and are used as the point of departure in our study of educational history and philosophy.

Chapter 6 examines Thomas Aquinas's construction of theistic realism. Using the context of the Medieval synthesis, the chapter describes how Christian theology and classical Graeco-Roman philosophy, especially that of Aristotle, were integrated in Western education. Chapter 7 carries the reader from the Middle Ages to the Renaissance by examining the Christian humanism of Erasmus of Rotterdam. In Chapter 8, the important events generated by the Protestant Reformation that stimulated universal education and literacy are examined as the backdrop of the life and ideas of the Protestant reformer John Calvin. Chapter 9 considers the life and educational ideas of Johann Amos Comenius, whose philosophy of Pansophism sought to heal the wounds of religious intolerance and nationalist antagonism.

Educational reform is the underlying theme in Chapter 10, on Jean-Jacques Rousseau, and Chapter 11, on Johann Heinrich Pestalozzi. Rousseau, a prophet of the Enlightenment, exemplified the motifs of naturalism and child permissiveness in education. Pestalozzi, a nineteenth-century Swiss educational reformer, implemented the new way of thinking about nature by emphasizing the need to relate both affective and cognitive development in schools.

In Chapter 12, the narrative moves from Enlightenment Europe to the American social and political context by examining Thomas Jefferson's ideas of republican civic education. Chapter 13, on Mary Wollstonecraft, examines an early feminist who infused revolutionary thinking into her quest for equality between women and men. Chapter 14, on Horace Mann, the "father of the American common schools," explores his work in creating public schools and in forging partnerships between the states and local districts. Through the ideas of Jefferson and Mann, the political, economic, and cultural origins of U.S. public education in the early republican and early national periods are presented.

Chapter 15, on the life and ideas of Robert Owen, the early nineteenth-century communitarian socialist, points up a new concept in educational theory—the use of education as a means of social change and reconstruction. Chapter 16 treats Friedrich Froebel, the educator who used idealism as the kindergarten's philosophical foundation.

Chapter 17, on John Stuart Mill, examines the English philosopher's rendition of utilitarian liberalism and defense of the freedom of ideas. Chapter 18, discussing Herbert Spencer, examines the reformulation of liberalism, a potent ideology in Anglo-American politics and education. Using Darwin's evolutionary theory, Spencer reaffirmed classical liberalism by giving it a scientific rationale based on survival of the fittest. Spencer's social Darwinism, which had a pervasive influence on U.S. social attitudes and policies, was later attacked by John Dewey in the twentieth century.

In Chapter 19, the narrative focuses on Jane Addams, the pioneering social worker and founder of Chicago's Hull House. Addams's articulation of the philosophy of "socialized education" and the historical context in which she worked illustrates how urbanization and immigration transformed the United States from a rural-agrarian to an urban-industrial-technological society.

Chapter 20 examines John Dewey, the United States's leading twentieth-century philosopher of education. By placing his philosophy in its broad historical and cultural context, Dewey's pragmatic instrumentalism, or experimentalism, can be seen as stimulating a major reconceptualization of learning and teaching in the United States. Dewey's pragmatic and progressive liberalism challenged Herbert Spencer's social Darwinism.

Chapter 21 examines the work of Maria Montessori. Her theories and practices of early childhood education had an international effect, expanding our views of the child and the processes by which children learn.

The story of Mohandas Gandhi, in Chapter 22, shows how one person challenged the might of a great empire to win freedom and independence for his people. In educational history, Gandhi's life and philosophy of nonviolent resistance to oppression marked the beginning of the end of colonialist exploitation. The discussion of Gandhi's educational ideas is particularly useful for portraying the foundations of education in an Asian cultural context.

Chapter 23 treats the life, ideas, and significance of W. E. B. Du Bois, a sociologist and historian who was a determined activist for African American civil and educational rights and progress. To fully appreciate Du Bois's struggle, it is necessary to understand the effect of the Reconstruction period in U.S. history and the accommodationist philosophy of Du Bois's principal rival, Booker T. Washington.

Chapter 24, the concluding chapter, examines the life and work of Paulo Freire, a Brazilian educator who formulated the philosophy of liberation pedagogy. Emphasizing that education always takes place in a ideological context, Freire argued that genuine education should strive to liberate individuals, especially members of marginalized groups, from exploitation and domination by ruling elites. Freire's liberation pedagogy has been especially influential on the contemporary educational philosophy of critical theory.

Organization

I use four structural devices in treating the impact of these selected significant figures on the historical and philosophical foundations of education: (1) historical contexts, (2) educational biographies, (3) the development of educational ideas, and (4) an assessment of significance. Each chapter establishes the historical context in which the particular person lived and worked and then examines how the person's interaction with his or her historical context or environment stimulated that individual to reflect on education and to formulate ideas about education or, in some cases, to develop a complete philosophy of education.

Because people generate ideas within a cultural context, we examine the general historical context to present the setting and situation in which the educator, theorist, or ideologist lived. Each context illustrates how educational ideas in the past as well as in our own times were responses to challenges—political, social, economic, religious, and intellectual. For example, Plato was responding to the cultural and political decline of the Greek *polis*. Jane Addams faced the dilemma of dealing with new immigrant Americans in an urban and industrial society. John Dewey addressed the need for a new social consensus in a society where social and economic change was eroding the inherited foundations of democracy. W. E. B. Du Bois struggled against persistent racial discrimination that relegated African Americans to the status of second-class citizens.

Using the historical context as an organizing theme illustrates the point that educational ideas originate in particular situations and in a particular time and place. Even though these educational ideas may emerge from a particular context, they often have a larger meaning and value that we may apply in many other contexts. However, we are each our own historian and philosopher of education. The larger meaning that we can gain from studying the lives of educators depends on the challenges we face today. New challenges in different times create the need to revisit and study anew the shaping ideas of our educational heritage.

For students of the historical and philosophical foundations of education, the use of contexts is designed to develop a sense of historical perspective and continuity with our educational past. This past, however, is not to be viewed as completed, or isolated from our educational present. Rather, the varying contexts in which leading educators, philosophers, and ideologists interacted with their environments are viewed as episodes in an ongoing educational experience. It provides us with a historical, philosophical, and ideological map or grid on which we can locate ourselves as educators today. Such a map of the mind helps us to avoid the rootlessness and presentism that today often characterizes too much of the rhetoric about education, teaching, and learning.

Students of education—prospective teachers, teachers, curriculum specialists, administrators, and policy makers—can benefit professionally by becoming sensitive to the theme of contexts. What takes place in the school as a formal educational setting does not occur in a cultural vacuum. The world outside of the school's walls determines much of the power—or futility—of the teaching and learning taking place within. Contemporary educators soon come to recognize that social problems, political issues, and cultural change affect the school's efforts to instruct children. The changing fortunes of the economy obviously determine the extent to which the public will support schools financially. Incidences of violence in the society will enter schools.

Although few question that the contemporary context of education affects schooling, professional programs for preparing educators have not sufficiently used the theoretical power of understanding educational contexts. Critics allege that many teacher education programs are intellectually shallow, lacking a sense of historical and cultural perspective. Without a historical memory, U.S. educators are often victims of an all-consuming "presentism." Without this collective remembrance, they may be "culturally illiterate" to the great ideas and heritage of their own profession. In this book I seek to contribute to restoring the memory of our educational past in a way that illuminates the present and points to the future.

A second key element, or organizing theme, is the use of educational biography, an exploration of those events of an educational nature that helped to form a person and shape her or his intellectual or educational worldview. Biographies consider how people confront and resolve the challenges of their lives. By focusing on important world personalities such as Calvin, Jefferson, Addams, and Gandhi, the narrative examines how a significant person, through contextual interaction and challenge, developed insights into educational theory and practice. It examines how significant persons have constructed educational philosophies by searching for meaning in their own experiences, their own interactions, within the context of their lives.

A highly useful discussion of the interaction of an educator in relationship to her or his context occurs in Jay Martin's excellent biography, *The Education of John Dewey*. Reflecting on his interpretation of Dewey's life, Martin found that he not only had to write about ideas but also needed to probe his subject's mode of thinking, especially how Dewey's thinking often originated "through his emotions." Turning to context, Martin found that Dewey "actively responded to the character and condition of the time in which he lived."[1] The interpretation of Dewey's life requires the biographer to examine the inner resources of his subject in relationship to the problems and possibilities of the context in which he lived. Martin's reflections on writing biography can be used to guide us in our study of the lives and times of the world's leading educational thinkers. For example, we can ask: What process did the person use to formulate her or his ideas about education? How were these ideas a response to the problems, issues, and possibilities of their historical context? We can also turn these questions to our own self-examination, asking, How do I formulate my ideas? How are my ideas a response to the problems and possibilities of my context—my own time and place?

Craig Kridel, a scholar on educational biography, argues, "Biographical inquiry provides a fresh perspective on and new possibilities and dimensions for education."[2] Barbara Finkelstein, a highly recognized historian of education, finds biography useful to (1) "explore intersections between human agency and social structure"; (2) "stabilize or transform the determinancies of cultural tradition, political arrangements, economic forms, social circumstances and educational processes into new social possibilities"; and (3) "view the relationships between educational processes and social change."[3]

Like Kridel and Finkelstein, I believe that the study of biography and autobiography, while providing fascinating insights into human behavior, is useful for educators. If we pause for a moment, we can reflect on and construct our own educational autobiography. The primary sources of this autobiography are the formative influence of parents, siblings, friends, adversaries, peers, teachers, politicians, clergy, and others on what we have become and how we view the world. The curriculum—the formal courses—we studied in school, and how our teachers taught these courses are also important sources for us. Our involvement with and participation in informal educational agencies, such as churches and the clergy, media and news commentators, libraries and librarians, workplaces, and employers and employees, are important in forming us and our attitudes.

In addition to those people and agencies that shape our educational autobiographies, key events in our lives have a special power over our interpretation. How we perceive these events shapes our perspective of reality in its various dimensions—politically, economically, religiously, socially, intellectually, aesthetically, culturally, and educationally. In particular, the key events of childhood and youth take on a special significance, becoming almost like lenses through which we establish a personally meaningful vision of our own lifetime. For those who came to maturity during the Great Depression of the 1930s, the stock market crash, the specter of unemployment, reduced family circumstances, and the personality of Franklin D. Roosevelt supply the lenses to interpret what has occurred to them. For the generation of the 1960s, the Civil Rights Movement, sit-ins, freedom marches, protests over the Vietnam War, and the power and effect of John Kennedy, Robert Kennedy, and Dr. Martin Luther King, Jr., illuminate their vision of subsequent events. For those who come to maturity in the first decade of the twenty-first century, the war on terrorism, especially the images of hijacked planes crashing into the twin towers of the World Trade Center in New York City on September 11, 2001, is likely to shape their view of the world.

We examine events in the childhood and youth of the key personalities in this book—Pestalozzi, Wollstonecraft, Froebel, Montessori, Jane Addams, and John Dewey—to try to find the lenses through which they glimpsed the sweep of history. Often these key events, those happenings of war and peace, affected the development of their educational philosophies.

From the interaction of context and biography comes the development of educational ideas. It is the body of educational ideas that forms what we can take from one time and situation to another. Although all educational ideas have contextual origins, some ideas are powerful enough to transcend their time and place. For example, Plato's idealism, Aquinas's Thomism, Erasmus's humanism, Rousseau's naturalism, Jefferson's republicanism, Owen's communitarianism, Spencer's social Darwinism, and Dewey's instrumentalism were powerful bodies of ideas that have shaped our worldview and our thinking on human nature and on education. Ideas come to constitute a philosophy of education to answer such questions as, How did the particular theorist conceive of truth, human nature, society, social change, education, schooling, the curriculum, teaching, and learning?

The book's final organizing device deals with the question of historical and educational significance or meaning. A theory's relevance, significance, or meaning depends to a large extent on our own educational context, or situation, and the challenges, issues, and problems that it presents to us as educators. As our educational problems and challenges change, so does the meaning we acquire from studying the lives and contributions of the great thinkers on education. When issues of early childhood education assume a larger importance in today's educational context, then the careers and theories of Pestalozzi, Froebel, and Montessori assume a heightened significance for us. When contemporary critics allege that our schools no longer convey the Western cultural heritage to the young, then a reexamination of the philosophies of Plato, Aristotle, Aquinas, and Quintilian provide a useful perspective on our intellectual and educational origins. As U.S. schools assume the responsibility for educating new immigrants, reexamining Jane Addams's ideas on assimilation helps us understand the current debates over multiculturalism. When ethnic and religious tensions erupt and bring violence to people merely because they are members of a particular group, then Comenius's call for ecumenical education and understanding takes on a new resonance. When acts of terrorism take the lives of innocent people, many of whom are noncombatant women and children, then Gandhi's plea for nonviolence becomes an urgent matter for all of us.

Educational ideas—philosophies, ideologies, and theories—are considered in their broader relationship to education in its formal and informal aspects and to schooling in its more particular institutional setting. The author believes that educational ideas need to be examined and juxtaposed with those found in literature, politics, history, philosophy, and other areas in the humanities. It is important to keep extending the frame of reference to the larger world of scholarly inquiry.

To this end, the *Questions for Reflection and Dialogue* and the *Projects for Deepening Your Understanding* are designed to lead the reader to broader considerations of educational issues. The *Suggestions for Further Reading* also includes selections from history and philosophy as well as education.

To examine the large organizational themes of historical and cultural contexts, educational biographies, educational theories and philosophies, and historical and educational significance discussed in this book, you may use the following questions as guides:

1. How did the context and the life of a particular theorist shape his or her ideas on education?
2. How did the people presented in this book either reflect or reconstruct the cultural and educational forces and trends that were present in their historical and cultural contexts?
3. Were the people examined in this book agents of educational continuity or change?
4. How did the ideas of key people influence educational policy formulation during their own time and in later history?

Questions for Reflection and Dialogue

1. Identify the key personalities of the current cultural context. How do these individuals shape attitudes and values?
2. Accept the validity of the proposition that key events during one's childhood and youth provide the lenses through which one sees later events. What are the key events that shaped your vision of the world? What are the key events that have shaped the collective vision of the students in this course?
3. Discuss the concept of educational autobiography. If you were to write your own educational autobiography, what questions would you ask yourself?
4. Discuss the concept of educational biography and assume that you are planning to prepare an educational biography of another student enrolled in this course. What questions would you ask in an oral history interview?
5. Examine the current cultural context in which we live. What are the major issues, problems, and challenges in the context that face education and educators?
6. Identify one educational event in your life. Why is that event significant?

Projects for Deepening Your Understanding

1. Go to a bookstore or to your library and do a survey of biographies that have been published in the past year. Prepare an analysis of the general categories of biography, the people treated, and how many of them relate to education formally and informally.
2. Is there a particular person who is a model for you? In an essay, explain why that person is a model.
3. Write your own educational autobiography.
4. Write an educational biography of a student in this course.
5. During the time that you are enrolled in this course, keep a diary or a log of the significant educational events that have occurred. At the end of the course, prepare a summary that indicates which of them remain significant and why.
6. The following journals deal with biography: *Vitae Scholasticae: The Bulletin of Educational Biography* and *Biography: An Interdisciplinary Quarterly*. Read several issues of these journals. Select and review an article on the nature or problems of biography.
7. Visit the library of an elementary school and examine its collection of biographies. What kind of biographies appear to be in the library holdings?

Notes

1. Jay Martin, *The Education of John Dewey: A Biography* (New York: Columbia University Press, 2002), 3–4.
2. Craig Kridel, ed., *Writing Educational Biography: Explorations in Qualitative Research* (New York: Garland, 1998), 4.
3. Barbara Finkelstein, "Revealing Human Agency: The Uses of Biography in the Study of Educational History," in Kridel, *Writing Educational Biography*, 46–47.

Suggestions for Further Reading

Adamson, Lynda G. *Notable Women in World History: A Guide to Recommended Biographies and Autobiographies.* Westport, CT: Greenwood Press, 1998.

Andrews, W. I., ed. *African American Autobiography.* Upper Saddle River, NJ: Prentice Hall, 1993.

Batchelor, J., ed. *The Art of Literary Biography.* Oxford: Clarendon, 1995.

Bender, Thomas. *Intellect and Public Life: Essays on the Social History of Academic Intellectuals in the United States.* Baltimore, MD: Johns Hopkins University Press, 1993.

Ducharme, E. R. *The Lives of Teacher Educators.* New York: Teachers College Press, 1993.

Evans, Fanny-Maude. *Changing Memories into Memoirs: A Guide to Writing Your Life Story.* New York: Barnes & Noble Books, 1984.

Freedman, Diane P., and Frey, Olivia. *Autobiographical Writing Across the Disciplines: A Reader.* Durham: Duke University Press, 2003.

Garis, Robert. *Writing About Oneself: Selected Writing.* Boston: Heath, 1965.

Goodson, I. F., and Walker, R. *Biography, Identity and Schooling.* London: Falmer, 1991.

Howe, Daniel W. *Making the American Self: Jonathan Edwards to Abraham Lincoln.* Cambridge, MA: Harvard University Press, 1997.

Kass, Amy A. *American Lives: Cultural Differences, Individual Distinction: An Anthology of American Autobiography.* Amawalk, NY: Golden Owl Pub. Co., 1995.

Kridel, Craig, ed. *Writing Educational Biography: Explorations in Qualitative Method.* New York: Garland, 1998.

Krupat, Arnold. *Native American Autobiography: An Anthology.* Madison: University of Wisconsin Press, 1994.

McEntyre, Marilyn Chandler. *A Healing Art: Regeneration through Autobiography.* New York: Garland Pub., 1990.

Middleton, Sue. *Educating Feminists: Life Histories and Pedagogy.* New York: Teachers College Press, 1993.

Morton, Marian J., and Duncan, Russell. *First Person Past: American Autobiographies.* St. James, NY: Brandywine Press, 1994.

Reinier, Jacqueline S. *From Virtue to Character: American Childhood, 1775–1850.* New York: Macmillan, 1996.

Sanders, Valerie. *Records of Girlhood: An Anthology of Nineteenth-Century Women's Childhoods.* Aldershot, Hampshire; Burlington, VT: Ashgate, 2000.

Sayre, Robert F. *American Lives: An Anthology of Autobiographical Writing.* Madison: University of Wisconsin Press, 1994.

Stine, Peter. *Autobiography: Special Issue.* Farmington Hills, MI: Oakland Community College, 1991.

Smith, Glenn L., and Smith, Joan K., eds. *Lives in Education: A Narrative of People and Ideas.* New York: Lawrence Erlbaum Associates, 1995.

Van Patten, James J., ed. *Academic Profiles in Higher Education.* Lewiston, NY: Edwin Mellen, 1992.

Wagner-Martin, L. *Telling Women's Lives: The New Biography.* New Brunswick, NJ: Rutgers University Press, 1994.

Ward, Martha Coonfield. *A Sounding of Women: Autobiographies from Unexpected Places.* Boston, MA: Allyn & Bacon, 1998.

West, Elliot, and Petrik, Paula, eds. *Small Worlds: Children and Adolescents in America, 1850–1950.* Lawrence, KS: University Press of Kansas, 1992.

CHAPTER 2

Confucius: Proponent of Educating for a Harmonious Society

We begin our study of the impact of biography on educational philosophy, policy, and practice with an examination of the life and ideas of Confucius (551–479 B.C.E.). For many people, especially those of China and East Asia, Confucius is esteemed as the world's foremost and greatest philosopher. Regarded as the source of perennial good sense, Confucius is invoked as the leading moral authority and the source of universal proverbial wisdom. Confucianism has had a significant impact on the philosophical, ethical, political, and social ideals of world culture. For more than two thousand years, the Confucian ethical code, with its emphasis on personal discipline, the central role of family, and the need for harmonious social and political relationships, has shaped Chinese civilization. To understand Confucianism's origin and development, we focus on China, one of the world's earliest and most enduring civilizations. Chinese culture and learning, especially Confucian philosophy, was carried to the peoples of Korea, Vietnam, and Japan, where it stands as an enduring cultural legacy and a powerful educational force.

This chapter examines how Confucius developed his philosophy of education in response to a time of social unrest and political turmoil. We shall see him as an educator who sought to restore calm and harmony from the existing chaos. By examining his philosophy of education, we can understand the impact it has had on millions of people over the centuries and assess its significance today.

To organize your thoughts as you read this chapter, focus on the following questions:

1. What were the major trends in the historical context of ancient China in the time and situation in which Confucius lived?
2. How did Confucius's educational biography shape his philosophy and practice of education?
3. What are the essential themes of Confucianist education?
4. How did Confucius's educational philosophy influence educational policies and practices in later centuries?
5. What has been the enduring impact of Confucius's educational ideas?

The Historical Context of Confucius's Life

To understand the historical context of Confucius's life and career as an educator, we turn to the culture and society of ancient China. Our knowledge of the history of ancient China dates from the Shang state in the fourteenth century B.C.E. Archeological findings indicate that the Shangs had developed a sophisticated civilization. The Shangs were conquered by the Chou people, who established the Chou dynasty. From about 1050 to 222 B.C.E. the Chou dynasty ruled China. The Chou king controlled his realm through a feudal system of political relationships by which he appointed trusted subordinates to control the kingdom's provinces; in return for their appointments, these officials pledged their fealty and loyalty to the king. In this hierarchical political system, the subordinate officials exercised considerable autonomy in administering their provinces but were to give their paramount loyalty to the king, regarded as the realm's father figure. The Chou system embodied two related principles, paternalism and hierarchy, which would become very important in the philosophy that Confucius was to develop. The principle of paternalism portrayed the king, or the ruler, as a benevolent father figure whose subjects owed him their loyalty and commitment. As a fatherlike ruler, the king was to be concerned with the welfare of his subjects, who were regarded as his political children. Political control was exercised by the use of a hierarchy in which power flowed downward from the king, to his appointed officials, to the common people. At each level of the downward flow of authority, there were obligations, duties, and responsibilities. The king was to be a good, benevolent, kindly ruler who looked out for the welfare of his people; the subordinate officials were responsible for executing the king's orders with fairness, justice, and kindness; the common people were to respond by being law-abiding citizens and paying taxes to support the general welfare of their country. While the flow of authority in this hierarchical system was essentially downward from the king at the summit, there was also an upward flow of loyalty from the common people to the officials, ultimately reaching the king. The concept of hierarchical relationships was analogous to a ladder; each rung of control depended on the one above and below it. The ethical base of the system required each official at each rung of the administrative ladder to accept the authority of the one who ranked above him. The system functioned according to the principle that the harmony of hierarchical rule gave security and peace to all its participants. Confucius would develop an ethical system that enshrined the principles of benevolent rule and the sanctity of hierarchical relationships.

One of the leading figures of the Chou period was the legendary figure Chou Kung, the Duke of Chou, the younger brother of King Wu, the dynasty's founder. After King Wu's death, the Duke acted as regent for Wu's son Ch'eng, who was too young to rule on his own authority. Although the Duke had lived some five hundred years before the time of Confucius, Confucius used the Duke as a model of everything that was good and benevolent in a ruler. He used the Duke to portray how a wise, enlightened, learned, and noble counselor advised the king but never attempted to seize power for himself.

The Duke developed the concept of the "Mandate of Heaven," according to which the king is entitled by Heaven to rule as long as he is concerned with and promotes the people's welfare. Should the king neglect or abandon his mandated role, Heaven will withdraw the decree and bestow it on another king who is more worthy to rule. Heaven, in Chinese philosophy, is defined as a force that has the power to control events on Earth. The Chinese concept of the Decree of Heaven differed from the European idea of the "divine right of kings," according to which a king, whether good or bad, was placed on his throne by God. If the king was a good man, his subjects enjoyed his rule. If he was evil, however, his subjects had no choice but to endure his rule.

Confucius found much merit in the Duke's style of statesmanship and diplomacy. The Duke sought to preserve and perpetuate the best traditions of the past. Seeking to avoid an abrupt rupture from the past, the Duke applied the wisdom of the cultural heritage to contemporary issues to guarantee smooth continuity between past and present. The Duke embodied what would become the Confucian values of respect for knowledge and learning, law and order, and social harmony and integration.[1]

During the Chou dynasty, certain ways of behaving that required showing respect for one's ancestors, elders, and rulers were elevated to rituals, the correct way of acting in a particular situation. These rituals, known in Chinese as *li*, acquired a profound significance in ancient China. In his own teaching, Confucius would emphasize the proper performance of these rituals to his students.

By the sixth century B.C.E., the Chou empire was showing symptoms of internal social stress and political instability as the hierarchical system began to disintegrate. The king's centralized authority weakened as once-loyal subordinates seized power in their own districts, ignored the Chou court, and became warlords who vied with each other for power. Clearly, the Chou court had lost the Mandate of Heaven as China disintegrated into rival warring states. The once-harmonious political landscape became a treacherous quagmire as warlords struggled against each other, using cunning, duplicity, and brute force to gain dominance. Treaties were made and then ignored; bribery was an accepted means of obtaining favors; assassinations were commonplace.

In his *Spring and Autumn Annals*, Confucius chronicled the Chou decline, referring to it as the periods of "Spring and Autumn" (722–481 B.C.E.). Confucius was repelled by the chaos of political turmoil and social unrest during which traditional values and customs were challenged, ignored, and disregarded.[2] Reacting against this instability, Confucius looked to what he regarded as the "golden years" of peace, stability, and law and order epitomized by the Duke of Chou. He developed a social, ethical, and educational philosophy designed to return China to this idealized past. In the ethical system he developed, Confucius sought to restore a harmonious, stable, centralized, and orderly system, ruled by a single paramount benevolent political and moral authority. Confucius died in 479 B.C.E. but his ideas were disseminated by his students.

In 221 B.C.E., a new dynasty, the Ch'in, conquered China; its leader, the King of Ch'in, proclaimed himself Shih Huang Ti, the "First Emperor." He took that title because he envisioned himself as the first in an unending line of emperors descended from him. Shih Huang Ti destroyed the remnants of the feudal states, replacing them with new administrative provinces, headed by his own appointed loyal governors.[3] The Ch'in emperor established a uniform and authoritarian state that sought to eliminate all dissent. He espoused a philosophy called Legalism that gave the emperor's decrees the force of unquestioned law whose violation brought punishment and even death. The Ch'in rulers and their Legalist advisers imposed a tight censorship on the expression of ideas and attempted to root out Confucianism. Unable to maintain its succession to the throne, the Ch'in dynasty was replaced by the Han dynasty under the Emperor Han Kao Shu, "the High Ancestor." The Hans, who ruled China from 207 B.C.E. to 220 C.E., established Confucianism as the dominant philosophy throughout the empire. The Han emperors were followed by the Manchu dynasty. The Confucian system, set in place during the Han dynasty, remained as the dominant philosophy until 1912, when the empire was overthrown and replaced by the republic.

Confucius: The Life and Career of a Philosopher-Educator

Although Confucius formulated a philosophy that has endured for more than twenty-five hundred years, few details are known about his life. While a short outline of his life is available, the known facts have been shrouded by legends and myths.

Confucius was the son of Shu Liang He, a court official in the state of Sung. After the assassination of the Duke of Sung, Shu's family fled to and found safety in Lu, a small neighboring state, where they took up residence in the town of Tsou. K'ung Ch'iu, to be known in the West by his Latinized name Confucius, was born in 551 B.C.E.[4] A serious and studious youth with a reverence for custom and tradition, Confucius was drawn early in his life to the scholar's pursuit of knowledge. He most likely received a traditional education with lessons in literature, poetry, music, and etiquette. He especially enjoyed music, learned to play the lute, and took part in group singing. Even in his youth, his interest in rites and rituals motivated him to undertake an extensive study of them. He was concerned with learning about the origin and meaning of traditional rituals and their correct transmission and application to contemporary life. In ancient China, rites and rituals, since they were observed and practiced in the home, were learned directly by the young.

Early in his career, Confucius sought to pursue two goals: gaining appointment as a government official and being a teacher. His first school, established in Lu, had the mission of preparing young men for government service. For a short time, he served as police commissioner (commissioner to prevent crime) of Lu. In 497 B.C.E. Confucius journeyed from Lu, traveling, as Aristotle did in ancient Greece, to study the traditions, customs, and forms of government of other places. (See Chapter 4 for Aristotle.) This kind of knowledge, he believed, would provide him with the necessary background to pursue his goals of government service and teaching. On his travels, Confucius hoped to meet a benevolent ruler who would invite him, like his hero the Duke of Chou, to serve as his trusted advisor.

As he journeyed though the kingdoms of ancient China, Confucius, already esteemed for his wisdom, consulted with the leading officials at the various courts. He carefully studied the places he visited, researching their social and political traditions and institutions. However, he did not secure an appointment as a government official. After more than a decade of traveling, he returned to Lu, where he opened his second school in 484 B.C.E. Confucius now integrated his goals of government service and teaching into one pursuit—educating others to become skilled, ethical, competent, and trusted government officials like his model, the Duke of Chou.

Confucius believed that the officials he would prepare needed to recognize the importance of knowledge in performing their offices. In ancient China, there was no clear-cut demarcation of authority between executive, legislative, and judicial offices as in the United States. The mandarins, those entrusted to rule in the king's name, often combined all these roles. They had to implement the decrees that came down to them from the emperor. These decrees were often framed in very general terms and had to be interpreted and applied justly and fairly. As they were interpreting decrees, the mandarin officials were often creating law. They had to settle legal disputes and, in effect, were judges. Because of their far-reaching powers, Confucius believed that the officials had to be steeped in knowledge. They especially needed to be informed of the traditional wisdom and how it might be applied in the present. Confucius believed that the way to prepare officials was through careful study of the Chinese classics. He advised his students that studying and holding office were inseparable. There was great emphasis on the doctrine of preparation—getting ready for office by studying.

Confucius designed an educational program to prepare good men as ethical administrators. For him, it was of crucial importance that the administrator he was preparing not only be efficient but also be an ethical and benevolent person. Such an official would take responsibility for his actions and not fall back on the pretext that he was merely carrying out the orders of a superior. He asked his students, "What has one who is not able to govern himself to do with governing others?"[5] As a teacher, Confucius was highly motivated by what he saw as the need to reestablish law and order in a war-ravaged China. Saddened by the bloody strife being waged about him, he refused to believe that war was society's natural order. Rather, he believed that it was normal, indeed desirable and necessary, for people to cooperate with each other for the common good. A truly good ruler would seek to advance the welfare and happiness of his people rather than personal power and wealth. To further his goal of bringing peace, security, and stability to China, Confucius sought to educate officials who were virtuous, capable, and prudent. The state, he believed, needed to be continuously administered by officials of the highest ethical standards, carefully prepared for careers in government service, and devoted to pursuing the people's general welfare.[6]

To examine Confucius as a philosopher, educational statesman, and teacher, we first turn to his general philosophy of education and then to his work as a teacher.

Confucius's Philosophy of Education

Confucius's philosophy of education is primarily an ethical theory intended to guide people into leading the benevolent—the good—life, by doing what is right. Although he respected religion, especially religious rituals, Confucius did not get highly involved in theological questions of the human being's relationship to God, nor did he concern himself with metaphysical questions about the nature of ultimate reality. He urged observance of rituals, many of which had religious origins, however. He did refer to heaven, which for him was a kind of impersonal intelligence that governed the universe and that in Chinese tradition was the abode of the gods and the ancestors. Human life and action, however, in the Chinese cosmology were not determined or predestined by a supernatural God as in Western religions. Confucius did not speculate about the possibilities for rewards or punishments in the afterlife. He believed it was difficult enough to examine the conditions of living without delving into unanswerable otherworldly matters.

According to Confucius, there are some things that we can control and take responsibility for and others that are beyond our control. For example, we cannot control the family, rank, and station into which we are born, nor can we control the length of our life and the time of our death. We can control, however, our moral relationships and responsibilities to other people. Ethical behavior, then, which we can control, should be our major human endeavor. Confucius asserted the sole human purpose is to become as good, as benevolent, as ethical as possible. This goal is pursued for its own intrinsic value.

In the ancient Chinese tradition, human beings are composed of matter, which is arranged into a pattern. The most desirable and beautiful of the personality and character patterns is called *wen*. Confucius believed that human beings had the power to create a beautiful pattern of their humanness through education. Thus, he gave education the highest priority in his philosophy. Educational attainments included physical grace and bearing and athletic skills; cultural skills such as reading and writing; and the mastery of intellectual bodies of knowledge such as literature, mathematics, and music. The beautiful and harmonious character, however, also included a person's bearing, deportment, and refinement. Underlying all these qualities was the sense of ethics—knowing what was good and right and doing it.[7]

The central theme in Confucius's philosophy is *tao*, the Way, which means the road to take, a guide to conduct, and following a course of action. For Confucius, the Way embraces all that we know about the universe and how human beings should relate to it. The Way tells us the right path to take and, importantly, it is not a mystery but can be taught by a rightly informed teacher to students. Further, the Way is the most important part of the cultural heritage and it can be transmitted from generation to generation. Individual persons and governments should follow the Way, which contains the high ethical and moral standards that lead to peace, justice, and mutual cooperation and to a world free of hatred, suspicion, turmoil, strife, and war. Following the Way means leading a life of virtue.

While virtue is partially a gift from heaven, benevolence, the most important moral value a person can achieve, depends largely on one's own efforts. The key to benevolence is to "not impose on others what you yourself do not desire" and to know what other people wish or do not wish done to them.[8] Closely related to benevolence are wisdom or intelligence, *chih*, and courage, *yung*. According to Confucius, the wise person is certain and not plagued by doubts about what is good or bad, or right or wrong. However, a person who lacks wisdom can easily mistake the specious for the genuine. This can happen with borderline cases where the application of a rule or definition is uncertain, especially in moral cases. To keep on the right path, it is important to follow the *li*, the rites and rituals, about the rules of proper behavior, especially in relationships and the performance of duties. Closely related to wisdom is the ability to distinguish good from bad character in human beings. The most difficult thing in predicting the future lies in the human being's unpredictable nature. Thus, the study of human character gives a hope of predicting and controlling human events—what is going to happen based on what has happened. This is especially important for the ruler who needs to be able to choose his advisors from men of wisdom and good character.

Courage, the fortitude to see a moral purpose through to its end, is indispensable for a gentleman. He has to pursue his moral purpose fearlessly. According to Confucius, "Faced with what is right, to leave it undone shows a lack of courage." While a benevolent man will possess courage, a courageous man may not necessarily possess benevolence. In the benevolent person, courage refers to the will necessary to achieving what is good. In the evil person, however, it is the means to realizing wickedness. It is important that courage be guided by *li*, the rites, otherwise it becomes unruly. Courage to be a virtue must serve benevolence without fear.[9]

Reliability, *hsin*, means that a person's word is good; that he will do what he promises to do. Reliability concerns fulfilling promises, pledges, and resolutions about future conduct. It means not to make empty promises and fail to live up to one's word. Reverence, *ching*, means that a person is aware of the responsibility to promote the common welfare and fears the failure of doing so.

Respectfulness, *kung*, refers to the manner in which one observes rituals. A person should be respectful in dealing with others so that he will be treated with respect himself. If a man is respectful to others, he will not be treated with insolence or humiliated by others.[10]

Confucius defined wisdom as "when you know a thing, to recognize that you know it, and when you do not know a thing, to recognize that you do not know it."[11] He believed that wisdom came to human beings in three ways: some are born with an innate wisdom; others acquire wisdom through their intrinsic love of study; and still others come to wisdom by seeking the knowledge that can solve their problems. Confucius believed that he could prescribe the studies that would lead his students to the knowledge that was at the base of wisdom. The study of the past, for him, was the rich source of a guiding kind of knowledge. Our quest for knowledge came out of our past experience and it was important that our individual lives, our individual autobiographies, be connected with the larger cultural heritage—the accumulated wisdom that is carried by tradition. He did not say that we should remain solely wedded to the past but should relate the ongoing events of our life to the backdrop provided by the past.

Confucius distinguished between learning and studying. Learning has a practical or applied result such as learning how to swim or read. In learning something new, a person improves himself. A learner either acquires a new skill or becomes more proficient in an old one. To study something is more theoretical; it means that a person is engaged in research that focuses time and energy on a subject to know it as a body of knowledge. In learning, the focus is on the learner; in studying, the focus is on the subject. In studying, a person acquires knowledge that is intrinsically valuable but need not make any practical difference.[12]

The ideal moral character for Confucius is the gentleman, a person of cultivated moral character achieved through concerted study, effort, and self-cultivation. For Confucius, education's paramount goal is to develop a noble character; over time and by earnest study, the person gains wisdom and leads an ethical life. This ideal man is humane, wise, and brave. His character embodies a sense of benevolence and he is in accordance with the rites and rituals. In contrast to the person who seeks personal power and material wealth, the person of noble character acts on moral and ethical standards. The ultimate virtue is *ren*, being humane in all relationships, which is the ethical source for all other values.[13]

A highly important aspect of Confucius's philosophy relates to the proper performance of the rites, or *li*—the rules or procedures that govern how one is to behave in performing sacred rituals, ceremonies, manners, and etiquette. The rites are the processes of civility that govern action in every aspect of life. For Confucius, the rites are the repository of past insights into morality that have been rendered into a way of acting. For Confucius, human relationships and interactions should be guided by the observances that have taken on a semireligious aspect because of their enduring role in Chinese life.

Although contemporary society is much less ritualized than that of ancient China, some examples may clarify the meaning of ritual and how we are educated to observe certain ritualized behavior. The death of a family member or friend is a personally disturbing event. There is a body of rituals that have developed on the proper way to observe a person's death and burial. These last rites have to do with funerals and the behavior that is appropriate to attending a funeral. The saying "I am sorry at your loss" is expected by the bereaved family members. Religious services are often conducted, and tributes are made about the deceased. Often memorial services are held to commemorate the life of the person. When a young person is a victim of violence, classmates construct small altars with candles, flowers, and other remembrances. The purpose of these acts is to get us through a difficult time by channeling our grief into a specific and acceptable way of behaving. Much learning, both in and out of school, has to do with learning to perform the rituals, the accepted behaviors of life. Consider the common phrase often used by teachers—"His (or her) behavior is unacceptable." This means a certain way of following a ritualized behavior is being violated.

In Chinese culture, sacred rituals had to do with the respect for the deceased ancestors and the honoring of their memory in ceremonial remembrance. In the United States, one can observe Memorial Day tributes to deceased veterans of military service, such as the president placing a wreath at the Tomb of the Unknowns. When a ritual is performed, it is done in much the same way each time it is performed. Those who perform it know what to do and those who participate are clear about their expected roles. The ritual reduces the possibility for mistakes and accidents to occur. It reduces awkwardness.

Confucius gave great attention to ritual in his philosophy of education. Knowing how to observe and perform the rituals of life meant that actions would be governed by civility. It was particularly important that future government officials know how to perform the rituals and ceremonies of state and diplomacy.

A ritual is a set of procedures done in basically the same way each time it is performed. The *li* to which Confucius referred originated in ancient times and were passed on as an inheritance to each new generation. Confucius realized that for rituals to have force they needed to be understood and respected by the person performing them. If they became empty forms, they would lose their significance. Yet they occasionally needed adaptation to fit changing circumstances. It was also important for the person performing the ritual to do so with the right disposition. Confucius advised his students, "Unless a man has the spirit of the rites, in being respectful he will wear himself out, in being careful he will become timid, in having courage he will become unruly, and in being forthright he will become intolerant."[14]

Confucianism is primarily an ethical system in which values and virtues center on human relationships rather than on metaphysical speculation about ultimate truth or theological prescriptions and proscriptions. Confucius asserted that all human relationships should be based on good faith, genuine understanding, and respect for others. This kind of good faith requires that the participants in human relationships know and share the same moral and ethical standards, requirements, and expectations. Such ethical knowing and sharing rests on locating relationships in a clearly defined hierarchy. The concept of hierarchical relationships can be viewed as an ethical ladder; each person has a connection with the person on the rung above or below. In Confucius's philosophy, the concept of a hierarchy is a recurrent theme. The idea of an ethical hierarchy is considered necessary to creating and maintaining social harmony: everyone standing on the social ladder will know her or his place, duties, and responsibilities and the proper way of performing these duties.

Confucius identified the major roles and corresponding duties and responsibilities in the Five Relationships: between parent and child, elder brother and younger brother, husband and wife, friend and friend, and ruler and subject. Each relationship carries with it specific roles and responsibilities. Parents are responsible for giving their children nurturing and care, moral formation, and education; a child, in turn, owes a parent respect, obedience, care and support in old age, and loving remembrance after death. The parent-child relationship establishes the foundation for the other relationships. Harmonious and stable families, Confucius argues, lay the foundation for social and political harmony. A husband and wife are to support and care for each other. The husband is responsible for supporting and protecting the wife. The elder brother is responsible for caring and guiding younger siblings who owe him deference and respect. The relationship between the ruler and the subject parallels that of parent and child. The ruler is to provide care, guidance, and protection to the subject, who, in turn, is to be respectful, obedient, and loyal. Friends are to be loyal and considerate of each other. Friendship is the only relationship that can be between people of equal rank and age. In all the other relationships, ranking comes into play, with one member of the relationship being older than the other, having authority over the other, and having a status that is higher in the hierarchy. Although persons in subordinate positions owe their superiors obedience and deference, those of superior rank also have personal, social, and ethical responsibilities to those dependent upon them. The subordinates—a good son, a worthy wife, and a loyal minister—have an ethical obligation to remonstrate against unethical behavior in their superior.[15]

The Five Relationships and the ethical hierarchy based on them had profound implications for Chinese society and government. Recall that Confucius was developing and teaching his philosophy during a time of great social unrest and war. The hierarchical pattern of ethics based on relationships was to be a remedy for this upheaval and the key to developing social and political harmony. Confucius's strategy was to identify those elements in China's tradition that emphasized hierarchy and to reinforce them by giving them prominence in his philosophy. Highly important elements in this strategy were to make the family into a conservative bastion resistant to radical change and to recreate the Chinese empire on the basis of extended family-like relationships.

The foundation for ethical behavior was established in the family, which Confucius regarded as the cornerstone for the whole social and political structure. The two most important relationships within the family were between father and son, and elder and younger brother. If a man followed the requirements of family relationships, he could be counted on to behave correctly in society. As Confucius said, "Being good as a son and obedient as a young man is, perhaps, the root of a man's character." If being a good son makes a good subject, being a good father makes for a good ruler. Love for people outside one's family is looked upon as an extension of the love of one's own family members. Confucius especially emphasized filial piety, children's whole-hearted devotion and obedience to their parents. Most important was the relationships between father and son. The respect for the family was reinforced by *li*, ritual observances based on respect for one's ancestors. Thus, a ritualistic connection between the living and the dead members of the family reinforced loyalty to the family as a sacred duty.[16] Behavior was guided by the admonition that one should not bring disgrace upon one's family and ancestors.

As an educator, Confucius was most concerned with preparing officials as administrators, officers, and magistrates in the Chinese empire. In his ethical system, he made a connection between the harmonious family and the well-governed, harmonious political state. It was of crucial importance that the political state be governed wisely, prudently, and according to traditional rules and expectations. Political rule is an extension of personal ethics and morality. If the ruler is benevolent, the government will work for the good of the people. It is important that the emperor personify benevolence, appoint and follow the advice of wise counselors, and, by promoting peace and security, win the affection of his people through benevolent government. This mutual trust, especially people's confidence in their ruler, is necessary for the well-run state.[17]

Confucian ethics are especially important in government. The emperor, as sovereign, is to be the paramount virtuous father-figure for his subjects. His guiding principle is to secure and maintain the general welfare, happiness, and security of all his subjects who constitute a large extended family. The emperor can achieve this aim only when the empire is administered by the most capable, most ethical, and most benevolent officials. Thus, Confucius embarked on an educational program designed to prepare such ethical officials. Although strongly enamored of tradition, Confucius was a moderate reformer. He rejected the view that officials should come from a hereditary elite who inherited their positions. Rather, he argued that those who governed in the emperor's name should be knowledgeable and ethical persons. He further believed that wise teachers could provide knowledge and instill virtue in their students.[18]

The concept of hierarchical ethical relationships has important implications for education. The idea of a hierarchy that puts individuals into relationships that are superior and subordinate is very different from the idea that human relationships are based on equality. In conditions of equality, the individuals engaged in a relationship are continually redefining the relationship, creating new openings to each other, and often establishing or reestablishing boundaries. The relationship is flexible; the ethics tend to be fluid. Character education in situations of equality tend to be based on how individuals relate to and treat each other. Often, the ethical prescription is that we should treat each person as an equal, respect how they differ from us, and even value such differences. In contrast, Confucianist ethics set up well-defined patterns of behavior that are definite rather than flexible or fluid. The person is respected because of her or his position, status, and achievements. The conditions of the relationship are well known to the participants. Education is designed to fulfill ethical expectations rather than to create them. Since the person is defined as a father, mother, brother, sister, ruler, or subject, much of Confucianist ethical or character education is learning the appropriate behaviors associated with the person's role and rank. Character education means learning and knowing one's roles in the network of relationships that form the community and fulfilling the designated role behaviors that ensure social harmony. Since change, novelty, and innovation can bring about what is unexpected, Confucius based his ethical system on tradition. If a certain practice or behavior contributed to maintaining peace, security, and tranquillity in the past, then it is worthy of being encased in a ritualized way of behaving and transmitted to and practiced by people in the present. For Confucius there is only one true way, not many paths to truth.

Confucius's School: The Philosopher as Teacher

Confucius was both an educational philosopher and an educational practitioner. He was a teacher who founded and conducted a school. He established goals for his students and developed a curriculum and a method of instruction.

Confucius held up before his students the ideal of *shih*, a term that once meant knight but was redefined to mean educated gentleman. Just as the knight had a military mission, the gentleman had a mission defined in cultural and ethical terms. The gentleman pursues his mission by being benevolent and ethical and by holding steadfast to the proper course—the Way.

Enjoying a reputation as a wise and learned teacher, Confucius's strong intellectual qualities and force of personality attracted students who were preparing for government positions. They sought admission to his school because the quality of his instruction was highly esteemed. He was known to be a teacher of great integrity who insisted on high intellectual and ethical standards. At any particular time, it is estimated that Confucius enrolled 70 students in his school.

Applicants to Confucius's school had to demonstrate their academic ability, their sense of ethics, and especially their zeal to devote sustained time and energy to their studies. Confucius did not admit his students on the basis of their social status or wealth but rather on their aptitude for serious academic study and their willingness to apply themselves to their work. Since he was preparing students from all social classes for government positions, he had to teach them the forms of polite behavior, court etiquette, and ceremonies. However, he wanted them to be men of good character rather than polished puppets who performed meaningless rituals that they mimicked but did not understand.

Requiring his students to apply themselves diligently to their lessons, Confucius dismissed those who lacked the necessary seriousness. He constantly urged his students to study intensively and to practice self-cultivation and self-control so that they would learn how to become worthy officials and administrators. Like other truly effective teachers throughout history, Confucius held high expectations for his students. He told them the demands he placed on them were not to satisfy his own need but rather to impress on them that they alone were responsible for making the most of their opportunity to study and to shape their future.

A dignified person with a commanding personality, Confucius was at ease with his students and self-confident as a teacher. His students recalled that as a teacher he maintained the proper distance but was approachable. In China, the rules regarding teacher-student relationships were carefully observed. Students were to hold their teachers in high regard and respect. Confucius's students remembered him as a patient listener and a temperate, gentle, informal, and cheerful mentor.[19] He corrected and criticized his students in a positive and constructive way. As with Socrates in ancient Greece, mentoring and discipleship were important elements in Confucius's philosophy of education. His students referred to him as "the master." This kind of respect became an important characteristic of education in China and in east Asia where Confucianism became a major intellectual and educational force. Many of those who studied with Confucius became ardent disciples, dedicated to perpetuating and disseminating his teachings. Many of his students obtained important administrative posts in the imperial government. Their success attracted more students to seek a Confucianist education.

Confucius's method of instruction was informal and largely conversational; using tutorial methods, he conversed with his students individually or in small groups. Sometimes he gave short lectures, led discussions, and asked and answered questions. He assigned the passages they were to study, identifying and commenting on key points, and worked with the students to arrive at the major ethical principle they conveyed.

To individualize his method, Confucius trained himself to be a good listener so that he could know his students well. Making them feel comfortable in his presence, he encouraged them to identify their goals and expectations and asked them what they hoped to learn to implement them. He assessed students individually, noting their strengths and weaknesses. After analyzing students' personalities and characters, Confucius tailored the lessons to reinforce their strengths and help them overcome their weaknesses.[20] Should a student be inclined to act too quickly or impulsively, he counseled him to defer action until he had reflected on the consequences his actions were likely to have and to seek the advice of wise persons before acting. However, if a student was overcautious and reluctant to act, Confucius urged him to act quickly and take decisive action.

Like Socrates in ancient Greece (see Chapter 3), there are no extant writings of Confucius. Our knowledge of him as an educator is based on the *Analects*, notes of his lectures and comments recorded by his students. Confucius was also a scholar who most likely edited and commented on such early Chinese classics as the *Book of Poetry*, the *Book of History*, the *Record of Rites*, and the *Spring and Autumn Annals.*

Living during a time of military conflict and cultural change, Confucius wanted education to serve as an agency of creating social stability. He was suspicious of those who claimed they possessed new knowledge or innovative methods. Rather he believed that knowledge formed a continuum in which what appeared to be a new idea actually came from an already existing body of knowledge and was really an extension of that knowledge. The teacher was a guardian of the cultural heritage whose main role was to transmit it to the younger generation, so that there would be continuity in the culture. For him, education was a process of transmitting the cultural heritage, from one generation to the next, in order to perpetuate it and guarantee its continuity over time. The role of the teacher was to act as an agent of transmission of the great truths of the past, the classics, and to analyze how this stable body of knowledge was to be interpreted for the present situation.[21] This did not mean that the teacher should seek to preserve the status quo without adaptation but rather that there should be no sharp break or cultural gap between the past and present. According to Confucius, "A man is worthy of being a teacher who gets to know what is new by keeping fresh in his mind what he is already familiar with."[22]

Confucius designed a curriculum that emphasized literature, poetry, music, the study of rites and ceremonies, and the practice of civility.[23] As part of the students' study of literature, Confucius used the *Odes*, a literary anthology. It was expected that every educated person should be knowledgeable about the *Odes*, which in China provided an intellectual and cultural frame of reference much like Homer in ancient Greece or the Bible in eighteenth- and nineteenth-century America. Quotations from the *Odes* were used in public speaking, formal proclamations, and diplomacy. A well-chosen quotation from the *Odes* could be used to convey one's meaning in polite or delicate situations, especially diplomatic negotiations. It was also a delicate and veiled kind of speech that made it possible to criticize a ruler and his government indirectly—by using a quotations that made a point through someone else's words.[24]

To teach poetry, Confucius used the *Book of Poetry*, a collection of poems by various authors. He believed that poetry, in addition to its intrinsic aesthetic qualities, was a valuable study because it stimulated the intellect, enlarged the sympathies, and moderated the opinions. Conveying allegorical and metaphorical meanings, poems were often quoted by diplomats. Parties involved in negotiations were expected to know the meaning and symbolism of the poems.

Confucius emphasized the importance of music. He played a stringed instrument similar to a lute and enjoyed singing. Music was important for its ceremonial uses as well as personal enjoyment. Many official court ceremonies were accompanied by music. Music was also used in performing some of the rites contained in the *li*. Confucius's emphasis on the importance of music in a person's education was similar to the approach of Plato and Aristotle in ancient Greece; music was accentuated as a part of moral education and for its power in bringing about harmonious sensitivity. For Confucius, music was not only for personal enjoyment; it was also an affair of the state. Like Plato, he regarded some forms of music as beneficial to the state and others as simply harmful.[25] (For Plato and Aristotle, see Chapters 3 and 4.)

At the core of Confucius's character education is the *li*, which he called "the guiding principle of all things great and small."[26] Confucius's teaching centered on learning the meaning and significance of the *li*—the rituals and ceremonies—that were handed down by tradition. (The significance of the *li* in Chinese culture is discussed earlier in the chapter.) It was important students acquired the proper psychological and emotional disposition, the reverence, for the rites as well as the correct method of performing them. Confucius equated reverence for the *li* with good character formation and proper conduct. It was important that the overt performance of a ritual became internalized in the student's psyche to create a general respect for the past and for tradition. In the educated person, the *li* functioned to channel behavior into socially accepted and useful channels. Observing and correctly performing the *li* was a way of avoiding impulsiveness and awkwardness in situations by providing a known and acceptable means of expressing the emotions. Through learning rituals, the individual avoided being taken by surprise by any sudden and unexpected event, situation, or crisis, and could act appropriately. Confucius advised his students, "Courtesy, if not regulated by *li*, becomes labored effort; caution, if not regulated by *li*, becomes mere timidity; courage, if not regulated by *li*, becomes unruliness; frankness, if not regulated by *li*, becomes effrontery."[27] A man may be inclined to show respect toward another, but unless he knows the code of behavior on how to express it, he may either fail to express it or express it in an unacceptable manner. Good intentions, while necessary, are insufficient unless accompanied by the knowledge of how to express and carry them out in a culturally and socially acceptable way.

The educational outcome that Confucius hoped to achieve through the study of literature, poetry, music, and ritual was the gentleman, a person who was versed in and refined by studying the arts. This kind of person possessed *ren*, the humane qualities and character of goodness and benevolence.[28]

Confucianism in Chinese Culture

After Confucius's death, his disciples traveled throughout China; several of them gained appointment as government officials and others became influential teachers. Their chief rivals were a group of scholars called the Legalists, who argued for an authoritarian, orderly, and disciplined rule. The Legalist philosophy was accepted and used as the rationale of the Ch'in empire in the third century B.C.E. The Ch'in rulers were expansionist and set about to conquer the smaller Chinese kingdoms. Legalism justified the use of force and conquest as the means to establish state control. The people were regarded as instruments to achieve the ruler's wishes. The ruler was to monopolize all power and to keep his subjects in a state of fear, afraid to question his authority. According to Legalism, speech, opinion, and activity that deviated from the ruler's will was to be quickly and rigorously suppressed. By 221 B.C.E., the Ch'in had conquered all of China and Legalism became the official philosophy of the empire. In the name of efficiency, laws and regulations were made uniform throughout the country.

The Legalists set out to eradicate the Confucianist philosophy as a rival system. Under their influence, the Han emperor ordered the burning of all books except those on medicine, divination, and agriculture. In particular, the Legalists sought to destroy the literature related to Confucius, especially the *Book of Poetry* and the *Book of History*, which they alleged were being used to undermine the Ch'in dynasty's authority. The Legalists claimed that the books' references to a harmonious and prosperous golden age in the past were being used to cast doubts on the legitimacy of Ch'in rule.[29]

The Legalist supremacy was not to last, however. The first Ch'in emperor's rule was short, from 221 B.C.E. until his death in 210 at age 50. His eldest son, out of favor with his father, had committed suicide. His younger second son, a weak boy, succeeded him but was dominated by a manipulative court official. A popular rebellion arose against the Ch'in, who in Chinese tradition had lost the "Mandate of Heaven." With the rebellion's success came the overthrow of Legalism and its replacement by Confucianism.

The rebellion led by Han Kao Tsu succeeded and he became the new emperor. As his armies occupied Ch'in territories, he repealed the Ch'in laws, counseled with village elders, and tried to win popular support by vowing to end Ch'in tyranny. Han Kao Tsu's style of leadership followed the principles of Confucius. Claiming that he was acting for the good of the people, Han Kao Tsu stated that as emperor he would select and supervise highly competent officials who would govern in his name. He sought out and selected Confucianist scholars, who advised him on Confucius's ethical principles.

Wen, Han Kao Tsu's son, succeeded his father as emperor. Wen elevated Confucianism to the official state philosophy. He put such Confucianist political ideas into practice as reducing taxes, allowing criticism of government policies, and taking measures for famine and flood relief. Confucianist scholars were appointed to office throughout the empire, creating a cultural and intellectual Confucianist establishment through which aspirants to office had to pass to attain recognition and position. Among the leading interpreters of Confucius was Mencius (374–289 B.C.E.). Mencius, who was born after Confucius's death, studied the master's works with those who had been trained by him. He reaffirmed essential Confucianist principles: the people are the most important constituent of the state, and government should be entrusted to virtuous and capable scholars. Even more than Confucius, Mencius emphasized that when a ruler failed to bring about the public good, it was the duty of the people to rebel and replace him. Mencius's philosophy asserted that scholars should have the greatest respect and highest position in the empire. A teacher's relationship to a pupil resembled that of a father to a son.

From this time, emperors turned increasingly to China's scholarly tradition, especially to Confucian philosophy. Scholars were encouraged to edit the ancient texts and reopen their schools. This led to the development of the Confucian canon—the elevation of Confucianist literature to authoritative texts.

At the core of Confucianist education were the "Five Classics" and the "Four Books." The Five Classics were the *Classic of Change*, the *Classic of Documents*, the *Classic of Poetry*, the *Record of Rites*, and the *Spring and Autumn Annals*. Each of the Classics emphasizes the importance of wisdom, harmony, and order, and encourages self-cultivation and self-discipline. In particular, the *Classic of Change*, examining the practice of divination, deals with the connections between the human and natural worlds. Confucius is credited with writing several commentaries on the *Classic of Change*. The *Classic of Documents* records important historical events, citing case studies of good government and ethical behavior. The *Spring and Autumn Annals*, which studies the Chou dynasty, provides a guide to be used by future rulers. The *Classic of Poetry*, a collection of poems, ranges from courtly to folk poems and songs. Many of the poems are allegorical commentary on good and bad government. The *Record of Rites* is a didactic manual on how to properly observe the *li*—the rituals and manners of etiquette needed for good behavior and self-cultivation. Confucius is credited with writing the *Spring and Autumn Annals* and with editing the other classics.[30]

The Four Books, summations of Confucius's teachings, were used as the official core texts of Confucian education from 1313 to 1905 C.E. The Four Books consist of Confucius's *Analects*, the *Mencius*, the *Great Learning*, and the *Doctrine of the Mean*. The *Analects*, which were recorded as notes by his students, contain Confucius's own prescriptions for creating a harmonious society and a just and benevolent polity. The *Mencius*, written by a famous disciple, elaborates and comments on Confucius's doctrines as expressed in the *Analects*. The *Great Learning* puts forth the argument that personal self-cultivation is the necessary condition for creating and maintaining a harmonious society. The *Doctrine of the Mean* connects the cosmos, heaven, with humanity.[31] In particular the *Great Learning* emphasizes the need to diffuse knowledge as far as possible through education.

Confucianism came to permeate the entire Chinese educational system during the imperial period. Throughout China, academies and schools based on Confucianism were established. The curricular core was the study of Confucius's principles and the interpretations of later Confucianist scholars.

Primary schools used simplified manuals to teach young children the basics of Confucius's ideas, which were presented in stories and proverbs. Popular books featured examples and homilies to teach his ethical doctrines. The Confucian classics and works were studied and memorized by every aspiring student and formed the basis of the civil service examinations, necessary to enter government service. Only those who passed these rigorous examinations were eligible for the sought-after and prestigious government positions.

Under the system of imperial examinations, the candidates who had earned their "bachelor's" degrees in local academies assembled at the provincial capital for the examinations for the "master's" degree. Each candidate spent the days required for the examinations in one of a vast collection of cells, guarded by monitors, who made sure that there was no cheating. Essay questions, to be answered eloquently, tested the candidates' knowledge of Confucius's philosophy and classical literature. In particular, candidates were required to apply Confucianist principles to administrative and judicial issues of government. The highly competitive examinations were passed by a select few, known as the *shih*, who became the administrators and managers of the vast Chinese empire.[32]

Conclusion: An Assessment

To attempt a conclusion and assessment about the influence of Confucius is difficult. To do so, we turn to how Confucianism entered into Western thought and then consider its significance throughout Asia.

The first introduction of Confucianism to the Western world came from the Jesuits, the Society of Jesus, a Roman Catholic religious order of priests that entered China around 1600 C.E. As members of a highly trained and intellectual religious order, the Jesuits gained entry to the Chinese imperial court and Chinese intellectual circles. Several were even honored with appointments as advisers to the imperial government. The Jesuit entry into China's ruling elite corresponded well with the Jesuit missionary strategy to concentrate their efforts on the upper classes, where they believed their influence would be most effective. The Jesuits wrote reports about what they found in China and sent them to the head of their order in Europe. Included in their reports were comments on Confucius's philosophy. The leading Jesuit scholar on China was Matteo Ricci, who praised Confucius's philosophy as rational and "not inferior" to Western philosophy.[33]

During the eighteenth-century Enlightenment, philosophers such as Voltaire rediscovered the earlier introduction of Confucius by the Jesuits. The Enlightenment theorists found Confucius's ethical principles to be highly compatible with their thinking. There was conformity between their ideas and Confucius's: society and government should be based on natural ethical principles that could be known through human experience.

Modern Western thought has shown a pronounced attraction to Eastern or Oriental philosophy. Along with Buddhism, Confucius's philosophy attracts individuals who are seeking ways to examine their lives and find greater personal meaning and serenity. Confucianism is a many-layered philosophy. It can be approached as a kind of conventional wisdom—a Chinese version of Benjamin Franklin's *Poor Richard's Almanac*—or as a deeper search for the Way, the true path to take in life.

Confucius's philosophy has had a profound impact on Asian society and culture. It has been such a powerful influence that it is part of a person's social and cultural identity. It exerts a considerable influence on family, social, and economic structure and relationships. The Confucian ethic of filial piety lies at the heart of many Asian families.[34]

Confucianism entered Korea and Vietnam as a consequence of Chinese invasions during the Han dynasty. Afterward, Confucian philosophy and education continued to exercise a profound influence on Korean and Vietnamese culture, society, and politics. For example, the Korean kingdom adopted a Chinese-style government, bureaucracy, and educational system. Confucianism was carried to Japan through the Japanese policy of importing Chinese culture. In particular, Confucianist ethical and political ideas were well fitted to the Japanese monarchy's goal of creating a centralized and uniform state.[35] Modern Singapore is particularly noteworthy for its systematic character education program, which rests largely on Confucian ethics. The Singapore school program emphasizes such traditional Confucianist principles as social harmony between ethnic groups, working for the common good, and taking personal responsibility for contributing to the economic growth of the island nation.

In modern China, the position of Confucianism has had an interesting history. In the People's Republic of China (PRC), Confucianism's emphasis on tradition was attacked during the Cultural Revolution (1966–1976) as causing the country's political and military weaknesses. Mao Tse-tung encouraged children and students to denounce the traditional authority of elders and teachers as counterrevolutionary. Despite attacks by Mao and other Communist leaders, Confucianism has survived and remains a cultural force in the PRC. In many respects, the style that Communist leaders have used resembles Confucianism, which emphasized working for the good of the state, party, or collective and submitting to its authority.

Confucius developed his ideas as a response to the chaotic and calamitous period of the "warring states" in China. His philosophy was designed to recreate stability out of chaos. To do so, he turned to what seemed to have worked in the past and applied these lessons to his contemporary society. His philosophy did not seek a utopian remaking of the social order but rather the application of what he regarded as the "commonsense" means by which society might prosper in a peaceful world.

In the twenty-first century, the modern world finds itself in another "warring states" period. However, the chaos comes not so much from rival nation-states but from disruptive forces that are at work within nations and internationally. Within countries, rival and antagonistic ethnic groups wreak havoc on civilians, especially innocent women and children. Internationally, terrorist organizations cause death and destruction. These modern agents of chaos disrupt civility and stability throughout the world. Perhaps an examination and reflection on Confucius's principles can provide a commonsense response to the trials and uncertainties of modern times.

Questions for Reflection and Dialogue

1. Confucius gave great importance to the meaning and practice of the *li*, the rituals. Can you think of some ritualized behaviors that are important in American culture and society? Have you observed situations when people are either comfortable or ill at ease with ritual performance?
2. Reflect on the great emphasis that Confucius placed on appropriate and proper relationships. Today, it is common to talk about "having a relationship" or "being in a relationship." How does the modern sense of relationship compare and contrast with that of Confucius?
3. Some critics of Confucianism contend that it is a philosophy that reinforces convention and tradition rather than bringing about needed social change. Do you agree or disagree with their assessment? Why?
4. Reflect on the respect that teachers have in American society. In your opinion, do teachers enjoy respect? How might Confucius react to the status and prestige of American teachers?
5. Reflect on the contemporary American family. How is the family defined today? How might Confucius react to your definition?
6. Reflect on the role that examinations have in contemporary American education. Consider the role of standardized testing in the Standards Movement and the SAT and ACT in college admissions. Compare and contrast the emphasis on examinations today with that of the imperial examination system during the Chinese empire.

Projects for Deepening Your Understanding

1. In your classroom clinical experience, observe and note how students learn rituals. In a log, record and analyze the kinds of rituals learned in schools.
2. In school situations, some behaviors are regarded as appropriate and others are inappropriate. Make a list of appropriate and inappropriate behaviors and indicate why a certain kind of behavior is so designated. Determine how students learn to make distinctions between the appropriate and the inappropriate. Then, hypothesize about how Confucius might evaluate your list of appropriate and inappropriate behaviors.
3. Interview several international students from Asian countries about the impact of Confucianism on their lives and thinking. Report your findings to the class.
4. Read and review a selection from Confucius's *Analects*.
5. Develop a short paper that portrays the teacher-student relationship from a Confucianist perspective.

Notes

1. Arthur Cotterell and David Morgan, *China's Civilization: A Survey of Its History, Arts, and Technology* (New York: Praeger Publishers, 1975), 26.
2. Conrad Schirokauer, *A Brief History of Chinese Civilization* (New York: Harcourt Brace Jovanovich Publishers, 1991), 28–29.
3. Cotterell and Morgan, *China's Civilization*, 47–49.
4. D. C. Lau, "Introduction," *The Analects*, trans. D. C. Lau (New York: Penguin Books, 1979), 9.
5. Herrlee G. Creel, *Confucius and the Chinese Way* (New York: Harper & Row, 1960), 76.
6. Creel, *Confucius and the Chinese Way*, 2, 29.
7. Lau, "Introduction," *The Analects*, 38.
8. Lau, "Introduction," *The Analects*, 15–16.
9. Lau, "Introduction," *The Analects*, 24.
10. Lau, "Introduction," *The Analects*, 26–27.
11. Creel, *Confucius and the Chinese Way*, 138.
12. Lau, "Introduction," *The Analects*, 44–45.
13. Conrad Schirokauer, *A Brief History of Chinese Civilization*, 31.
14. Confucius, *The Analects*, Book VIII, in D. C. Lau, "Introduction," *The Analects*, 89.
15. Jennifer Oldstone-Moore, *Confucianism* (Oxford and New York: Oxford University Press, 2002), 55–57.
16. Schirokauer, *A Brief History of Chinese Civilization*, 31.
17. Schirokauer, *A Brief History of Chinese Civilization*, 31.
18. Creel, *Confucius and the Chinese Way*, 165–66.
19. Creel, *Confucius and the Chinese Way*, 57–58.
20. Creel, *Confucius and the Chinese Way*, 79.
21. Schirokauer, *A Brief History of Chinese Civilization*, 30–31.
22. Confucius, *The Analects*, Book II, in D. C. Lau, "Introduction," *The Analects*, trans. D. C. Lau (New York: Penguin Books, 1979), 64.
23. Creel, *Confucius and the Chinese Way*, 76.
24. Lau, "Introduction," *The Analects*, 42.
25. Creel, *Confucius and the Chinese Way*, 88.
26. Oldstone-Moore, *Confucianism*, 54.
27. Creel, *Confucius and the Chinese Way*, 86.
28. Oldstone-Moore, *Confucianism*, 54–55.
29. Creel, *Confucius and the Chinese Way*, 211–17.
30. Oldstone-Moore, *Confucianism*, 35–37.
31. Oldstone-Moore, *Confucianism*, 37–38.
32. Cotterell and Morgan, *China's Civilization*, 56–58.
33. Creel, *Confucius and the Chinese Way*, 257–60.
34. Oldstone-Moore, *Confucianism*, 98–99.
35. Oldstone-Moore, *Confucianism*, 20–21.

Suggestions for Further Reading

Ames, Roger T., and Rosemont, Henry, trans. *The Analects of Confucius: A Philosophical Translation.* New York: Ballantine Books, 1999.

Bahm, Archie J. *The Heart of Confucius: Interpretations of Genuine Living and Great Wisdom.* Fremont, CA: Jain Pub., 1998.

Chu, Hsi. *Learning to Be a Sage.* Berkeley: University of California Press, 1990.

Cleary, Thomas F. *The Essential Confucius: The Heart of Confucius' Teachings in Authentic I Ching Order: A Compendium of Ethical Wisdom.* Edison, NJ: Castle Books, 1998.

Confucius. *Springs of Oriental Wisdom.* Johannesburg: S. N. M. Publications, 1967.

Creel, H. G. *Confucius and the Chinese Way.* New York: Harper & Row, 1960.

Fingarette, Herbert. *Confucius: the Secular as Sacred.* Prospect Heights, Ill.: Waveland Press, 1998.

Gardner, Daniel K. *Zhu Xi's Reading of the Analects: Canon, Commentary, and the Classical Tradition.* New York: Columbia University Press, 2003.

Ivanhoe, P. J. *Confucian Moral Self-Cultivation.* Indianapolis, Ind.: Hackett Publishing Co., 2000.

Lau, D. C., trans. *The Analects.* London: Penguin, 2003.

Legge, James. *The Wisdom of Confucius.* Hoo: Grange Books, 2002.

Ni, Peimin. *On Confucius.* Belmont, CA.: Wadsworth, 2002.

Oldstone-Moore, Jennifer. *Confucianism.* Oxford and New York: Oxford University Press, 2002.

Palmer, Joy. *Fifty Major Thinkers on Education: From Confucius to Dewey.* London: Routledge, 2001.

Pound, Ezra. *The Great Digest of Confucius.* Port
        Townsend, WA: Copper Canyon Press, 1978.

Reid, T. R. *Confucius Lives Next Door: What Living in
        the East Teaches Us About Living in the West.*
        New York: Vintage Press, 2000.

Selover, Thomas W. *Hsieh Liang-tso and the Analects
        of Confucius: Humane Learning as a Religious
        Quest.* New York: Oxford University Press,
        2003.

Shigeki, Kaizulka. *Confucius: His Life and Thought.*
        Mineola, N.Y.: Dover Publications, 2002.

Slingerland, Edward G. *Confucius' Analects.*
        Indianapolis, Ind: Hackett Publishing Co.,
        2003.

Slote, Walter H., and De Vos, George A.
        Confucianism and the Family. Albany, N.Y.:
        State University of New York Press, 1998.

Strathern, Paul. *The Essential Confucius.* London:
        Virgin, 2002.

Tu Wei-ming. *Confucian Thought: Selfhood as Creative
        Transformation.* Albany: State University of
        New York Press, 1985.

Van Norden, Bryan W. *Confucius and the Analects:
        New Essays.* Oxford and New York: Oxford
        University Press, 2002.

Wilson, Thomas A. *On Sacred Grounds: Culture,
        Society, Politics, and the Formation of the Cult of
        Confucius.* Cambridge, Mass.: Harvard
        University Asia Center, 2002.

Yao, Xinzhong. *An Introduction to Confucianism.* New
        York: Cambridge University Press, 2000.

Plato: Idealist Philosopher and Educator for the Perfect Society

This chapter examines the life, educational philosophy, and contributions of Plato (427–347 B.C.E.), one of the leading contributors to the development of philosophy in the Western world. Plato was a founding figure in establishing the intellectual foundations of Western civilization, and his philosophical works are still the point of departure for analyzing many educational issues that face us today. For example, Plato speculated on the nature of the universe in which we live, commented on the process by which human learning takes place, and constructed an argument for establishing the good society. Contemporary educators still grapple with similar questions about the nature of education and the goals and purposes that give it substance and direction.

In this chapter, we analyze Plato's influence on Western and U.S. education in terms of the historical context in which it originated and its enduring impact on educational philosophy and policy. First, we examine the social, political, economic, and intellectual contexts of the ancient Greek society in which Plato lived. Second, we study Plato's biography, education, and career to trace the development of his ideas about education. Third, we analyze the continuing effect of Platonic thought on Western philosophy and education.

Plato's contributions are most interesting to us as educators because of their multidimensional nature. He sought to answer the basic human question: What is good, true, and beautiful? This enduring question goes to the heart of our concern for educating people who possess a knowledge of reality, are ethical in their behavior, and live lives that are balanced and aesthetically harmonious.

To help you to organize your thoughts as you read the chapter, consider the following focusing questions:

1. What were the principal cultural currents in the historical context of the ancient Athenian society in which Plato lived?
2. How did Plato's life shape his philosophy of education?
3. How did Plato's educational philosophy shape his educational proposals, policies, and practices?
4. What is the enduring impact of Platonic philosophy on Western education?

The Historical Context of Plato's Life

You may ask why we begin our study of the history and philosophy of education with ancient Athens and Plato. What fascination do the ancient Greeks hold for us today? What can we learn from them that will illuminate our concerns about society and education?

The ancient Greek world, located on the southern tip of the Balkan Peninsula and on the many islands in the Aegean and Ionian seas, was the setting of a remarkable and varied civilization. Though all spoke Greek, society and politics were expressed differently in the various city-states.[1] The Greeks lived in separate, autonomous, independent city-states, or *poleis*, each of which exhibited both cultural similarities and also distinctive differences. By briefly examining the Greek lifestyle and culture we come to the important questions that Plato sought to answer in his philosophy of education. We might say that many Greek thinkers, including Plato, were on an intellectual journey to find the meaning of life and of human existence.

Our exploration of Plato's historical and cultural context begins with the theme of the search for meaning. In the history of Western civilization and education, ancient Greek culture signaled a dramatic cultural shift from the earlier despotic Egyptian and Persian empires that existed at the time.

In the ancient world, the great "Oriental empires" that developed in the fertile crescent of the Tigris and Euphrates rivers of Mesopotamia, such as the Assyrian and Persian, and the Egyptian in the Nile River valley were ruled by powerful emperors who claimed divine origin and godlike powers. Despotically controlling vast empires, these rulers allowed their subjects little or no freedom to make their own choices. According to the belief systems in these empires, the emperor or pharaoh was placed on Earth as a semidivine ruler over his subjects, who were to live in abject submission. A priesthood that was part of the ruling elite gave religious sanction to the political status quo. This world was to be accepted in a fatalistic way by those who lived in it; they were not to question but to obey. The temple priests said this was the way it had always been and the way it would always be.

In such a closed system of thought, it is easy to set educational goals. Education's overriding purpose, both formally in schools and informally in society and work, was to transmit the beliefs and values that sustained tradition from one generation to the next. This educational process of cultural transmission deliberately avoided questions that might challenge the prestige and status of the ruling elite. Learning consisted of memorizing sacred texts or lists of prescriptions and imitating the values that marked one's position in a hierarchical society.

The ancient Greeks, especially those who lived in Athens, took a sharply different view of society, politics, and education than did the inhabitants of the despotic Persian and Egyptian empires. Although some Greeks were content with the transmission of traditional religious beliefs, cultural forms, and political institutions, others—especially in Athens—who found that tradition did not answer all their questions began to search for the meaning and purpose of life. This Athenian quest involved creating the kind of education that would assist in that search. Once the Athenians embarked on the search for meaning there were no limits to their inquiry. In the minds of the Greeks, the one answer to life found in the despotic empires was not only inadequate but also undesirable.

As the Greek philosophers probed life's meaning, many possibilities emerged. Plato, one of these philosophers, was both invigorated and disturbed by the intellectual ferment of ancient Athens. He rejected the irrational ordering of society in the despotic empires but he feared that the Greeks, lacking a stable and consistent view, might fall into intellectual and social anarchy and disorder.

For the ancient Greeks, the place in which one lived had important consequences for how one's life was lived. (Throughout this book we follow the idea that a person's *context*, which includes place, is highly important in shaping one's ideas about education.) For the ancient Greeks, the meaning of place carried with it a sense of social, political, cultural, and educational organization. This organized place, called a *polis*, meant for them a self-governing political unit, or city-state. Among the Greek poleis were Thebes, Corinth, Delos, and the great rivals Athens and Sparta. Although the polis involved political organization, its meaning involved much more than politics. It referred to a particular city-state's total culture as expressed in philosophy, religion, art, music, law, literature, architecture, and education. While the Greeks in common embraced this large and integrative comprehension of the polis, each polis worked out its own cultural life differently.

An illustration of how varied the Greek polis could be is evident in comparing Athens and Sparta, which had diametrically opposed political, social, and educational institutions and processes.[2] Sparta was a semifascist, military polis whose citizens were considered state possessions. At a male child's birth, Spartan leaders determined if he was strong and healthy enough to be trained as a soldier. Infants regarded as unfit were left to perish. Spartan citizens were expected to be soldiers who would collectively defend their polis against foreign foes and keep the majority of "noncitizens," the slave population of helots, under subjugation. The education of Spartan males was directed almost exclusively to military drill, training, and gymnastics. Spartan girls were educated to become mothers of future soldiers. Spartan education, designed to transmit the military tradition and train citizen-soldiers, was closely censored so that ideas from the outside would not present cultural alternatives. Sparta was like the anthill or the beehive in which the citizens sacrificed their individuality for what had been defined generations earlier as the civic good.

Athens, which went through various stages of historical development, was a thoroughgoing democracy at its cultural zenith, the age of Pericles. Its citizens pursued varying interests and occupations, but were also to be involved in the total life of their polis. When Athens was threatened, they were expected to rise to its defense. They were to participate in the assembly that made law and to serve on juries that adjudicated disputes. The art and architecture of temples and public buildings reflected an aesthetic sense of harmony, the ideal of Athenian life. In Athens, a rich life of the mind developed as a succession of philosopher-teachers, including Protagoras, Socrates, Plato, Aristotle, and Isocrates, examined the questions of human life and meaning with their students.

A core Greek belief was the expectation that each citizen would participate in the city's civic life. While they agreed that to be uninterested in civic responsibilities diminished human potentiality, they disagreed about what kind of sociocultural organization best encouraged the full development of citizens. Should citizens be educated according to Sparta's one-dimensional military model or on the multidimensional humanistic perspectives found in Pericles's Athens? Single-minded training fulfilled the Spartan purpose, whereas the realization of the Athenian purpose required generally and liberally educated citizens. It was in this cultural context that Plato sought to answer questions of political organization and education.

Closely related to the sociophilosophical issue of the nature of the polis was the question of what constituted its good citizen. Throughout the Greek city-states, the commonly shared cultural and educational tradition had been derived from Homer's epics, the *Iliad* and the *Odyssey*. In these epic poems, transmitted in an oral tradition to Greek youth, an image of the heroic figure emerged. The Greek warrior-knight portrayed in these epics was courageous, cunning, and resourceful in the struggle against Trojan adversaries and eloquent in the councils of his lord, the king Agamemnon. The educational question at the time of Plato was whether the message and values of Homer's epics were still relevant for Greek society.

Greek philosopher-educators, especially in Athens, debated the nature of the good human being and the kind of education needed to develop him. For Athenian culture, the good man possessed and exhibited *arete*, defined as generalized excellence in all those characteristics that comprised human nature. For more cerebral theorists, such as Plato and his student Aristotle, the good man was most excellent in rationality, the power of reason that defined the human being.

Not all the theorists and educators of Athens shared Plato's propensity for the primacy of reason. A group of itinerant teachers, the Sophists, who taught for a fee, challenged the intellectual conception of the good man. Responding to the economic growth and prosperity that was transforming Athenian society, the Sophists asserted that there were many answers, rather than one, to the question of what made a man good.[3] For example, what made a man a good political leader? What made a man a good speaker? What made a man a good soldier? According to the Sophists, the answers to these questions depended on the situation in which one found oneself. Asserting a theory of *cultural relativism*, the Sophists claimed they could educate people to be successful and popular in a variety of circumstances. In Athens, where the ability to persuade people in the assembly and in the courts was the key to power, the Sophists concentrated on teaching the skills of public speaking, or rhetoric. Their version of rhetorical education supplied students with a repertoire of information, psychological insights, and public-speaking skills that would make them persuasive, successful, and powerful. Much of Plato's educational philosophy was designed to counter the Sophists' appeal.

Plato as an Idealist Philosopher

In examining Plato's life and career, we will concentrate on those events and experiences that stimulated him to formulate an idealist philosophy of education and an organic theory of society.[4] Pursuing the Greek search for meaning, Plato established a way of thinking that located a meaningful life in the cosmos as part of the universal order of unchanging reality. The place to lead the good life was in an idealized and unchanging polis, the republic.

Although he lived in Athens, a polis renowned as the cradle of Western democracy, Plato resisted many of democracy's egalitarian tendencies. His resistance may have been influenced by his aristocratic Athenian family origins or it may have come from his antagonism to the cultural and ethical relativism that he saw as a consequence of popular democracy, especially its tendency to level human differences.

Plato's father, Ariston, claimed to be a descendant of Codrus, the last king of Athens before the establishment of democracy. Perictione, his mother, was a descendant of Solon, the famous lawgiver of ancient Athens. Plato was the youngest of four children. In his *Republic*, he briefly mentions his brothers Glaucon and Adeimantus. His sister, Potone, was the mother of Speusippus, his successor as the leader of the Academy, the school of philosophy that Plato established in Athens. According to some accounts, Plato's real name was Aristocles, and the name Plato was actually a nickname that referred to his broad shoulders.[5]

During Plato's youth and adulthood, Athens experienced a period of political turmoil and acute social change. After Athens' defeat by Sparta, a conservative pro-Spartan regime was installed. Critias, a cousin of Plato's mother, was the leader of the 30 tyrants who then ruled Athens. In the minds of the democratic majority in Athens, the tyrants were merely Spartan puppets.[6] When the democratic faction returned to power, the conservatives who had cooperated with the tyrants were deposed and their families and associates purged from state positions. Plato, who resented his family's fall from political power, resisted the democratization of Athenian life that threatened their favored social and political status. Because of his family's fall, a political career was closed for Plato. Disenchanted with the vicissitudes of everyday politics, Plato turned increasingly to speculation and theory.[7]

Plato's educational conceptions were shaped by his own education as well as by his family background. As a child and youth, Plato received a conventional Athenian education. In primary school he learned to read, write, and compute. He went to the *palaestra* for gymnastics and physical education. In the school of the *citharist*, where he studied instrumental music, dancing, and singing, he learned the oral tradition of Greek literature that had been stressed since Homer's time. When he was 18, Plato performed his year of required military service in the cavalry.

Plato's real education, however, came as a young man when he joined a group of students who were searching for the meaning of their own lives in particular and the meaning of life in general. This quest brought Plato, then 22, into the company of Socrates. As is true of many educators, Plato was influenced by his teacher, Socrates (470–399 B.C.E.). Frequenting the *agora*, the Athenian marketplace, Socrates and his students pursued basic questions about goodness, truth, and beauty. Socrates' principal premise was that knowledge is the source of the virtuous or reflective life. Unlike the Sophists, who claimed they could transmit knowledge and virtue to their students, Socrates did not believe that a teacher could pour knowledge into a student's mind. He argued that knowledge comes from within each person's mind. The teacher's task, Socrates said, was to ask stimulating and challenging questions that caused the student to think critically, deeply, and reflectively. Through the Socratic method, the instructional strategy named for its originator, the teacher challenges and prods students to think, raising to consciousness ideas already in the mind. The critical thinking process, encouraged by Socrates, involves the critical examination of beliefs, including those that are traditional and current or popular. Important to learning is to unlearn and cast off false beliefs and opinions.

Through this process of inquiry, Socrates challenged not only the old order of traditional beliefs but also the newer method of the Sophists, who claimed they could teach students to present a positive public image and manipulate public opinion by the clever use of fact, myth, crowd psychology, and speech technique. Claiming to be a midwife of ideas, Socrates, an iconoclast, shattered many traditional images of Athenian society.[8]

Charged with impiety to the gods and corrupting the youth of Athens, Socrates was brought to trial, convicted, and sentenced to death by the Athenian court. He was sentenced to take his own life by drinking hemlock, a poison.

Socrates' trial and death made a deep impression on Plato, who wrote about it in his dialogue, *Crito*.[9] Socrates' case was one of the earliest and most famous of a long line of cases involving academic freedom—the right of a teacher to teach and of a learner to learn without interference from either arbitrary political authorities or a countervailing public opinion.

Plato's dramatic account of Socrates' last hours indicates the power that the event had on his thinking. In Plato's dialogue, Crito and other students urge Socrates to save his life by fleeing from Athens or recanting his beliefs. Socrates resists his students' entreaties, maintaining that he must be true to himself and follow the dictates of reason that shaped his knowledge and conscience. Socrates claimed that once a person's reason has grasped truth, that person must follow where reason takes him. Socrates explains to Crito that life's true end is not simply to survive but to live the good life guided by truth. A truly wise person, he asserts, both knows and does what is true. To flee and desert his beliefs, Socrates claims, would be to escape one evil by doing another—denying the right to seek the truth for oneself and one's students.

Because of his association with Socrates, Plato, too, was a suspect person. He left Athens on a journey that took him to the cultural centers of the Aegean and Mediterranean worlds. At Megara, a city on the isthmus that links the Peloponnesus with mainland Greece, he studied with Euclid, the famous scholar of geometry. Megara was a prosperous polis with a population estimated at between 25,000 and 40,000. Because of its political stability and economic wealth, Megara had become a cultural center, which explains Plato's attraction to the area.[10]

In Egypt, he encountered the Pythagoreans, a group of scholars who studied mathematics. As his own philosophy evolved, mathematics, with its power of pure reasoning, continued to intrigue Plato. He later emphasized mathematics in the curriculum he developed to educate philosopher kings, the rulers of his idealized republic. In Egypt, Plato may have also encountered Oriental philosophy. His theory of reminiscence remarkably resembles the Hindu belief in reincarnation, and the socioeducational structure of *The Republic* parallels the Hindu caste system (see Chapter 22).

In Sicily, an important outpost of Greek culture, Plato studied the government of Dionysius I, who as ruler of Syracuse had organized a strong city-state. Plato questioned the strong personal power that Dionysius wielded in the region. He also became close friends with Dion, whose sister was married to Dionysius. Plato incurred the displeasure of Dionysius I, who had him arrested and sold into slavery. Fortunately for Plato and for Western philosophy, Plato's friend Anniceris purchased his freedom. Plato then returned to Athens.[11]

Influenced by Socrates' search for meaning, Plato immortalized his old teacher by writing about him and by continuing his own quest for truth. Like Socrates, he became a philosopher-educator. Unlike his mentor, who wandered through the agora, Plato taught in an institutional setting. In 387 B.C.E., Plato founded the Academy, an institution of higher education located in a shady grove near the public gymnasium in Athens. The Athenian government recognized the Academy, which had its own governing regulations, as a legal entity.

Although it is uncertain if the students who studied with Plato had to pass an entrance examination, they did have a probationary period during which they had to demonstrate their seriousness of purpose and intellectual ability. Recall that Confucius also required his students to demonstrate their seriousness and steadfastness of purpose if they were to continue in his school (see Chapter 2). Many students were residents at the Academy, where they studied arithmetic, geometry, astronomy, and harmonics, subjects designed to prepare them to study dialectics.[12] After completing these introductory courses, Plato's students rigorously pursued philosophical questions dealing with metaphysics, the study of ultimate reality; epistemology, the study of the theory of knowledge; and axiology, the examination of values.

Although Plato would argue in *The Republic* that women should have the same educational opportunity as men because they possessed an equal intellectual capacity, students in the Academy were males, as was customary in Athenian education. Women in Athens, with the exception of the heterae, a group of courtesans, were generally secluded from public and educational life. Although Plato was an intellectual, social, and political conservative, his view of women's education was more liberal than other Athenian theorists. Today we can extrapolate the ideas of Plato and the other theorists presented in this book to the education of women. However, during many of the historical periods treated here, education, especially schooling, was dominated by males and often restricted to them.[13]

While directing the Academy, Plato wrote his leading philosophical works, *The Republic*, *The Apology*, and *Phaedo*. His philosophical insights were sharpened by dialogues with his students and by preparation of lectures. Plato remained at the Academy teaching, working with students, and writing until his death in 347 B.C.E.

Plato's Philosophy of Education

In this section, we examine Plato's major philosophical doctrines for their educational implications. We begin with some situational observations on Plato's background as a possible catalyst for his ideas, concentrating on those larger concepts that have shaped Western thinking.

As Plato probed the meaning of life with his students, several trends of thought from his past converged to shape his philosophical outlook. Plato resented the fact that his family and other families of the old aristocracy had lost their influence to the newly emergent and rising commercial class. Socioeconomic rivalry, which contemporary sociologists of education call *conflict theory*, was a factor in Plato's theory of education as well as in the theories of many later educators. Indeed, it would remain a continuing factor in Western education. Existing educational institutions and arrangements reflect the belief system and values of the dominant political, social, and economic group or class that benefits from maintaining the status quo. These favored classes seek to maintain control of the institutions and processes, especially the educational ones, by which a person is prepared for positions of power and influence. (For a philosophy of education that deliberately seeks to minimize the importance of social conflict in education refer to Confucius in Chapter 2. For a philosophy that sees the school and curriculum as areas of social conflict, see Chapter 24 on Paulo Freire.)

In Plato's day, the conflict was provoked by the appearance of a new commercial class that wanted the political power and social status they believed their wealth had earned for them. The Sophists developed an educational curriculum that promised the new class access to positions of power and prestige in Athens. Arguing that everything is relative and depends on circumstances, the Sophists promised to provide their clients with the public image that made a person successful. The Sophists claimed they could create a public image for their students by teaching them the needed leadership skills, style of speech, and effective behavior patterns.[14] Thus the Sophists, who claimed their lessons would enable their students to win friends and influence people, were much like modern image makers who create a media persona for political candidates. For Plato, these "new people" with their fake public images not only undermined the old order but were unprincipled opportunists. In the assembly and in the courts, the new people argued a case to win rather than to establish the rightness or wrongness of their cause by finding the truth. They were manipulators, who, skilled in using psychology and argumentative techniques, would do anything to win and gain power.

Plato's aversion to images appeared continually in his philosophical and educational thought. For him, an image was something that had to be penetrated to reach the underlying reality. An Athenian political figure, like a modern-day politician, might appear to be an attractive candidate and deliver speeches with popular appeal, but it was necessary to penetrate the image or facade to determine if the person was really good and true. Plato's probing of these fundamental issues, as a form of civic education, related to the very system of justice in the polis.

At the Academy, Plato and his students sought to penetrate through images and appearances to find the underlying truth that explained reality. Plato's search culminated in his development of a philosophy known as idealism, which asserts that reality is nonmaterial or spiritual. For Plato, what was truly real existed in an eternally stable and unchanging realm of ideas, or pure concepts.

All ideas came from a superior, higher, and all-encompassing idea, called the form of the good.[15] The objects that we sense—that we see, touch, smell, and hear—are but imperfect representations of the perfect ideas of these objects located in the general form of the good. For example, human beings are of different heights, weights, races, ethnic groups, and languages but they are all human beings. To be a human being means that these persons' defining characteristics are found in the idea of the human being, which, in turn, is comprised in the all-encompassing higher-level concept—the form of the good. This common humanity gives people their "humanness." The same pattern of reality is true of other objects that we sense. We may sense a variety of trees such as pines, oaks, elms, and lindens, but they are what they are, trees, because they share the concept of "treeness."

The key to knowing reality is to go beyond the sensory image and reach the true realm of being, the world of ideas. Most important in Plato's version of reality is the human intellectual power to generalize and to abstract. The clearer our knowledge of these concepts, the closer we are intellectually to the form of the good and the more accurate our knowledge of reality.

In our discussion of Plato's metaphysics or conception of reality, we have been discussing knowledge of objects of which we have some sensory experience. It is also possible to use the same general metaphysical strategy for examining questions of virtue, the values prescribing ethical and aesthetic behavior. These ethical issues were the important concerns of Socrates, and Plato also explored them. What is it that makes a particular human action ethical? Or, what makes a man or woman a good person?

For the Sophists, answers to these questions were relative and depended on the consequences of a particular situation. The question of what is a good lawyer could be answered by saying that a good lawyer is a person who has the knowledge and skills to win a case. Similarly, a good general is a person who has the military knowledge and strategic skills to win a battle.

For Plato, as for Socrates, such answers were only the beginning points of the learning dialogue rather than the end. Plato would have asked, Is there a moral common ground that applies to both the good lawyer and the good general? Is not the real question what makes a good human being—what makes a good man or good woman? People and their actions are virtuous and ethical as they conform to the universal values found in the form of the good. Plato argued that values are universal regardless of place, time, and circumstances. There are universal standards of moral behavior that have applied across the centuries of human history and they apply equally to people living in different geographical places. What is ultimately good, true, and beautiful does not depend on where you live or when you live. Goodness, truth, and beauty are found in the nature of the universe.

For Plato, then, there is a true intellectual self within and superior to the material human body. There is also a true conceptual world of ideas within and above the material world of time, place, and things that we experience through our physical senses. He explained our search for this true world of ideas through his famous allegory of the cave. Prisoners, confined in the cave, are chained with a fire behind them so they cannot see real objects but merely their shadows cast on the cave wall before them. In this analogy, objects in the material world such as men, animals, and trees are mere reflections of the idea of the perfect object, like shadows on the wall of a cave. The virtues of human beings are incomplete reflections of the ideal virtues of which the highest is the idea or form of the good. The purpose of life is to strive for knowledge of ultimate and perfect ideas, the form of the good from which all other ideas are derived.

By interpreting the allegory of the cave and Plato's other works, we can analyze his epistemological theory, which deals with knowing. How do we know what we know? Epistemological theories are of crucial importance for teachers in that they examine the process by which we come to know. Closely related to theories of knowledge are the issues of how we learn and how we should teach. If our teaching methods follow the way human beings learn, then there is a better chance that they will be effective. In turn, both teaching and learning are parts of the more general question of how human beings know.

For Plato, the process of human knowing is "reminiscence," recalling the knowledge that one knew before the soul was encased in a physical body. Before birth, the soul existed in the world of pure ideas or forms and knew these universal and perfect concepts. At birth, knowledge of these concepts is retained but the shock of being born causes them to be locked away in the unconscious mind. Once the mind is in the body, we are driven by impulses that result from physical needs. The material world and our sensations of it fill us with images. Living in a society that is often based on materialism fills us with opinions, many of which are false. To really know what is real, we must penetrate these sensations and opinions to find the truth.

The search for the truth is an interior search to recall ideas latently present in our minds. Through dialogue and the Socratic method, searching questions are asked that cause us to examine our beliefs and values.[16] The interior search for the truth within us may be painful in that it may lead us to abandon conventional beliefs or reject popular public opinions.

The shared dialogue of the symposium is one process used to rediscover the truth, but not the only one. Because the truth is within each of us, it is found deeply within the recesses of the human mind or psyche. The ultimate discovery may require one to overcome sensory and materialistic distractions and in solitary introspection find the interior truth, as Henry David Thoreau at Walden Pond would do many centuries after Plato.

As indicated, Plato's metaphysical and epistemological doctrines directly challenged the Sophists' relativism. Was education to cultivate the liberal culture of the person as a generalist or was it to sharpen technical expertise? Here, Plato and his philosophical adversaries launched the debate over liberal and technical education that still goes on today.

Plato presents his defense of education for general liberal culture in his dialogue, *Protagoras*. Socrates' adversary in the dialogue, Protagoras, was a famous Sophist and a teacher of rhetoric, or oratory, who insisted that "man is the measure of all things." Protagoras promises that his method of education will make those who study with him better people. Socrates pursues the point by demanding to know what there is about the Sophists' education that will make a person more ethical and a better human being. When Protagoras answers that the teaching of political and rhetorical skills will make the student better, Socrates—Plato's mouthpiece in the dialogue—leads him into a discussion of whether a particular kind of skill is the same as general knowledge and virtue, which all men should possess. The dialogue concludes with a victory for Socrates, who argues that a genuinely and generally educated person will choose that which is the best. When knowledge is faulty and incomplete, we choose other than the best. What Socrates accomplishes is the integration of knowledge and virtue. If we know the good and the true, we will choose it. Intellectual education and moral preferences are linked in a truly liberal and liberating education.[17]

Plato's *Protagoras* presents the major issues in the debate over liberal versus technical education. For the proponents of technical education, the skill acquired by technical training will make the student a well-paid and valuable contributor to society. Knowledge and skill that come from technical education are not only relevant to social and economic needs but also are personally rewarding in a financial sense. Plato's objections in many ways remain the arguments of contemporary proponents of general education. Genuine knowledge is the knowledge that everyone should have because they are human beings. Those who possess such general knowledge will be able to make informed decisions and choices because their actions can be placed in a general context and transferred and applied to the kinds of situations that arise in life.

Plato's Republic: An Organic Society

Our examination of the historical context in which Plato lived indicated that the polis was the focal and integrative point in Greek culture. Plato and other Greek theorists sought to develop theories about the kind of polis that would renew and reintegrate Greek life. Plato, who opposed the changes taking place in his native Athens, grappled intellectually with the question, What kind of polis would enable human beings to realize their human potential and live meaningful lives? Plato answered the question by designing an ideal society in *The Republic*, his major work on politics and education.[18]

Metaphysically, Plato saw ultimate reality consisting of perfect ideas or concepts that were derived from the form of the good. Among these perfect metaphysical concepts was the idea of the perfect polis, or political society. It was this perfect city that Plato described in *The Republic*, presenting a plan for the ideal place to live, a utopian design for the good society. Although never implemented, *The Republic* is useful for educators to study because it presents a critique of society and suggests the social, political, and educational structures needed to create the good life on Earth. Those who analyze existing social and educational institutions engage in the kind of social criticism Plato employed in fashioning his idealized design for a polis. The plans for creating new institutions, structures, and processes that are part of policy designs are not unlike what Plato was attempting to do in his classic work. (For the possibilities in using utopian imagining as an instrument in creating educational designs, see Chapter 15.)

The Republic is also useful for educators because it clearly points out the intimate connection between education and citizenship. True to the Greek conception that citizens should be totally integrated into the life of their polis, Plato established relationships between the political institutions and responsibilities of citizens and the kind of education that prepared one to fulfill the requirements of citizenship.

Plato's *Republic* is an organic society in which the sociopolitical-educational institutions are interrelated and serve the common purpose of maintaining and enhancing the life of the polis.[19] In the same way, the three castes or classes that Plato identified were to function as interrelated and necessary parts of the body politic. Just as the human body is an organism composed of interrelated parts that contribute to its ongoing life, the republic is an organism in which its parts contribute to its survival, well-being, and happiness. Educators who subscribe to an organic theory of society tend to see schools as functioning parts of a total society. Their contribution to the well-being of society gives schools their mission and function.

Plato regarded the social, economic, and political changes that were taking place in Athens not as signs of progress but rather as signs of the disintegration of society. He also saw the egalitarianism and social mobility that the Sophists offered as part of their new educational design to be undermining genuine values and debasing learning. Plato took an essentially conservative stance in *The Republic*. Like contemporary conservatives in education, he wanted to reassert the kind of knowledge he considered most valuable and restore what he regarded as genuine values. Once these tasks had been accomplished, it was to endure forever. Plato's position in *The Republic* raises the major issue of what educators should do about social change—ignore it, oppose it, or encourage it.

To escape the discord of social change, Plato proposed an eternal and unchanging city, a perfect polis, that would eliminate the turmoil of the imperfect world. Plato based his perfect city on the principle of justice. Because the state existed to cultivate justice in its citizens, Plato reasoned, the state itself had to be organized according to the principle of justice. In the just society, every citizen was to do what he was suited to do by his nature.

Using the model of the organic society, Plato identified three constituent classes that would perform the necessary functions of the political organism or body. Membership in these three classes—the guardians or philosopher-kings, the defenders or the military, and the workers—was based on the person's capacity to perform the role appropriate to the particular class.

The guardians, with the greatest capacity for intellectual activity, were interested in ideas and pursuing truth. True to Plato's belief that the highest human activity was the power to reason, these people occupied the highest status in *The Republic* and exercised the greatest role. Constituting the republic's "brain trust," they would be the governors, legislators, and policy makers. In the same way the mind thinks for the human being, the philosopher-kings would think for the political body. Again, recall that Confucius, too, saw the intellectuals as occupying the top rung of decision-making in imperial China.

In second position in *The Republic* were the defenders, members of the armed forces who possessed the greatest capacity for physical courage and bravery. The defenders were assigned the responsibility of protecting the republic from its enemies. Just as the body's arms protected the human body, the defenders would serve as the armed forces of the political organism.

In third place were the workers, those who possessed the greatest capacity for economic production. The workers grew the food and provided the goods and services needed to sustain the economic life of the republic. As the human body's digestive system provides nutrients to sustain life, the workers would satisfy the economic needs of the society.

Plato believed that selecting individuals for particular assignments based on their natures or capacities was an act of justice. Each would perform the assignments for which their nature had prepared them. The principle of justice was fulfilled by the harmonious relationship of all classes in the republic. The socially integrated society, organized on the basis of intellectuality, is a just society. Justice in the individual consisted of the harmonious integration of the rational, volitional, and appetitive in the human soul, and the social soul of the polis should be likewise integrated.[20] The society that Plato outlined in *The Republic* was hierarchical, based on intellectual capacity. Just as the mind should govern the body and its physical appetites, Plato reasoned, the mind of the polis, the philosopher-kings, should govern those of lesser intellectuality.

The selection of individuals for positions within the hierarchy of society was an important issue for Plato. How people are selected for certain kinds of education and for positions following that education remains a crucial policy question today. For Plato, the issue was the relationship of the mass of population to the selected elite, the many to the few. Plato himself came from one of the original elite groups of Athens. In some ways, his philosophy and theory of the organic society is a philosophical rationale for elitism. The elite that would rule the *Republic* was an intrinsically disinterested minority who expected no personal profit from their positions but would use their positions for the good of the polis. From their philosophical orientation in seeking the good, the philosopher-kings were interested only in solving problems, not in their own special interests.

Critics of Plato's *Republic* have argued that it is an antidemocratic design for the totalitarian society. The republic was patterned after a version of Sparta but with the important difference that Plato substituted intellect for raw physical stamina and courage. Unlike his rivals the Sophists, who proclaimed the equality of persons and ideas, Plato countered that individuals were not equal in intellectual ability. The possession of this intellectual ability, or the potential to think abstractly, was not an inherited or ascribed position. Those who were intellectually inferior to the class of their birth were relegated to the class that was appropriate for them. Those who were born into a lower class in the hierarchy but who possessed intellectual acumen would be placed in a higher class. Plato reasoned that those who had the most highly developed minds should be the policy makers of society.

Plato's System of Education

In the broad sense of education as *paideia*, the word the Greeks used for the total cultural formation of the person, Plato's ideas examined in the preceding sections were educational. They were based on his philosophical idealism and his epistemological doctrine of reminiscence. The teacher's task is to effect a kind of intellectual conversion experience in the learner that redirects the person from the sensory world of appearances, images, and opinions to the realm of ideas. Whereas knowing can occur only in the mind of the person, the teacher creates the proper environment and asks the questions that will stimulate learning.

Plato believed that early childhood was a crucial stage in the total education of the person. In a child's early years, the attitudes and values—the cultural, social, and intellectual predispositions—of later life were formed. In *The Republic*, Plato specified that state-operated nurseries should be established to rear children from birth to age 6. These nurseries were to be a purified environment free of social evils and the corruptive influences of families who possessed the wrong values. These state nurseries had the following specific functions:

- Cultivate a general communal or social disposition that would be supportive of life in the republic.
- Form the proper habits or emotional predispositions to the good life so that when children grew up, they would want the knowledge valued in the republic.
- Provide a curriculum of stories, music, games, and dramas that would be models of the good life that children could imitate.
- Begin the process of identifying those who possessed keen intellectual abilities.

Plato was among the earliest of the educator-philosophers to recognize the importance of childhood in forming predispositions or attitudes that would be conducive to a particular concept of society. Theorists of later eras, such as Jean-Jacques Rousseau in *Emile* and Robert Owen in his *New Moral World*, would stress the need to shape children in preferred ways in their earliest years.

After spending their first six years in state nurseries, children from 6 to 18 were to attend schools where the curriculum consisted of music, literature, mathematics, and gymnastics.[21] Music, taught according to the broad Greek sense of the term, was designed to create the proper moral spirit. Under the heading of literature, children first learned to read and write and then studied the approved Greek classics. Literature was an important source of character formation in that it provided models that students could imitate. Mathematics, Plato's favorite subject for cultivating abstract reasoning, was an important part of the curriculum. Included in mathematics were geometry and astronomy. Gymnastics promoted character building and physical development, skill, and strength. For Plato, the proper blending of gymnastics and music encouraged a well-balanced and harmonious character. Particular exercises included fencing, archery, javelin throwing, using the sling, and horseback riding.

When they had achieved their level of capacity, students left the school to enter occupations and trades. Those who possessed the capacity to enter the ranks of the military defenders or the philosopher-kings continued for two more years, from ages 18 to 20, to pursue physical and military training. Plato believed the military defenders needed additional training because it related directly to their assigned functions in the republic. The philosopher-kings needed this training because they would be making the overall strategic decisions for the republic.

The education of the future philosopher-kings would continue for 10 more years as they studied mathematics, geometry, astronomy, and music. Combining the pursuit of mathematics and philosophy, they would search for underlying principles. Their overarching objective would be to reduce the seemingly vast array of knowledge to the one great unifying principle contained in the form of the good. When they reached age 30, the selection procedure would again be used as those with lesser intellectual powers were assigned to subordinate administrative and educational responsibilities.

For five years after that, the philosopher-kings would concentrate their education on the higher philosophical study of metaphysics, which in Platonic terms is the search to understand the form of the good. In pursuing truth, this select group of students would use the dialectic process, the examination of propositions of truth through critical discussion. At age 35, the philosopher-kings would go into the republic and actually administer and supervise the affairs of state. When they reached age 50, they would become the ruling elite—the most select of the selected ones—and become the policy makers and decision makers of the republic.

Conclusion: An Assessment

Plato remains one of the great thinkers in the history of Western thought and education. Whether we agree or disagree with him—and many disagree—Plato's basic issues of education still engage us today. Although philosophical idealism is not one of the dominant contemporary philosophies, Plato's searching questions about the nature of the good, true, and beautiful remain the continuing human quest. Should not today's teachers seek to cultivate truth, beauty, and goodness in their students?

Although Plato's republic may not appeal to democratic sensibilities today, his issues about the nature of the polis and its citizens still are relevant to education for citizenship in our schools. Public education in the United States is committed to educating citizens who will participate in the political life of their nation. But after this general commitment has been stated, precisely what should be the nature of citizenship education? Is it to nurture a patriotic love of the country and its traditions and values? Is it to be based on a critical examination of issues even if this process leads students to question inherited values? Although Plato's educational adversaries are no longer with us in the form they took in ancient Greece, what is the educational role of the media? What should teachers in classrooms do about the dynamic and vivid impressionism of television? Although conventional citizenship education is intended to encourage our participation in the political processes of our country, what is the nature of critical thinking when the processes are infused by the dynamic "packaging" of candidates and issues?

In *The Republic,* Plato raised the issue of continuity and change in culture, society, and education. Although few today are likely to endorse Plato's rejection of change, the question remains as to the degree to which schools and teachers should be conservators of the cultural heritage or agents of social change. Is the role of the schools to introduce the young to their cultural heritage by teaching them to read, write, and compute—stressing a stable curriculum of mathematics, history, science, language, and literature as is recommended by the Council on Basic Education? Should the schools incorporate current issues and new technology, such as computer literacy, into the curriculum? Should teachers boldly seek to help end poverty, pollution, and racism by actively working to build a new social order?

Plato raises the issue of identifying and selecting persons of intellectual promise to lead society. What is the role of teachers in this selection? Should they group students homogeneously? When they do, are they promoting the selective process? Should students be grouped into tracks on the basis of their academic ability, as Plato suggested in *The Republic*? Or, should educational arrangements promote equality rather than separatism? Should colleges use the SAT and ACT in their admission processes?

As we pursue questions raised by Plato, we can also think about the hidden factors that modern sociology tells us influence the processes of selection and admission such as gender, race, ethnicity, socioeconomic status, and place of residence. Plato's stress on selection also brings us to the major dilemma facing U.S. education: Is it possible to have excellence and equity in our schools at the same time?

Questions for Reflection and Dialogue

1. Identify and examine the educational issues faced by the ancient Greeks. Are these issues relevant to today's education? If so, why? If not, why not?
2. How did the concept of the *polis* shape Greek attitudes about education? Is there an American polis? If there isn't one, should one be created? If there is an American polis, do our contemporary programs of civic education adequately prepare citizens?
3. How did Plato's family background and early education shape his views on society and education?
4. How did Plato's association with Socrates influence the development of his philosophy of education? Examine your own education and determine if any of your teachers have had such an effect as a mentor.

5. Who were the Sophists and why did Plato oppose their social and educational doctrines and methods? Who would win the debate over education in contemporary American education, Plato or the Sophists? Why?

6. Identify and analyze the arguments for both liberal and technical education in both ancient Greek and contemporary American culture.

7. Examine Plato's republic as an organic society. What are the characteristics of education in such a society? How well do these characteristics fit contemporary U.S. society?

8. Compare and contrast the process of social and educational selection, or sorting and grouping of students, in Plato's republic with arrangements operating in contemporary U.S. society. For example, consider such items as affirmative action, SAT scores, and standardized testing as part of the standards movement.

9. Compare and contrast the major social, political, and educational issues of Plato's Athens with those of the contemporary United States. Be sure to consider the following: terrorism and violence, the problems of urban society and schools, changes in family structure, and the rise of technology.

Projects for Deepening Your Understanding

1. Identify the three major issues that you believe face American education. Then write an opinion paper in which you analyze them from a Platonic orientation.

2. In a position paper, argue for or against the following proposition: American education should identify the country's most intellectually gifted students and design a curriculum that challenges them to perform to their greatest potentiality.

3. Prepare a design for a school and curriculum that exemplifies Plato's philosophy of education.

4. Write a commentary that analyzes the campaigns of candidates for political office in the United States today according to both Sophist and Platonic criteria.

5. Examine contemporary proposals for educational reform in the United States. In an essay, determine if these reflect a liberal or technical approach to education.

6. In an essay, identify at least two significant social changes in contemporary U.S. society. How would Plato react to these changes? Do you agree or disagree with Plato?

7. From the Platonic perspective, prepare a review essay of two available books on instructional methods.

Notes

1. D. H. F. Kitto, *The Greeks* (Baltimore: Penguin, 1962), remains an excellent introduction to Greek civilization.

2. Gerald L. Gutek, *A History of the Western Educational Experience* (Prospect Heights, IL: Waveland, 1995), 41–48.

3. Harry S. Broudy and John R. Palmer, *Exemplars of Teaching Method* (Chicago: Rand McNally, 1965), 15–30.

4. Biographical and philosophical commentaries on Plato include Alfred E. Taylor, *Plato: The Man and His Work* (London: Methuen, 1966); and Robert W. Hall, *Plato* (London: Allen & Unwin, 1981).

5. Plato's life is discussed in G. C. Field, *Plato and His Contemporaries* (London: Methuen, 1962), 1–39. Also see Paul Shorey, *What Plato Said*

(Chicago: University of Chicago Press, 1968), 1–57.

6. L. Glenn Smith, ed., *Lives in Education* (Ames, IA: Educational Studies Press, 1984), 16.

7. Edward J. Power, *Evolution of Educational Doctrine: Major Educational Theorists of the Western World* (New York: Appleton-Century-Crofts, 1969), 55–56.

8. For the life and philosophy of Socrates, see W. K. C. Guthrie, *Socrates* (Cambridge, UK: Cambridge University Press, 1971). Also see Robert S. Brumbaugh, *The Philosophers of Greece* (Albany: State University of New York Press, 1981).

9. Eric H. Warmington and Philip G. Rouse, eds., *Great Dialogues of Plato*, trans. W. H. D. Rouse (New York: New American Library, 1956), 447–59.

10. Ronald P. Legon, *Megara: The Political History of a Greek City-State to 336 B.C.* (Ithaca, NY: Cornell University Press, 1981), 21–24.

11. Field, *Plato and His Contemporaries*, 16–17.

12. Power, *Evolution of Educational Doctrine*, 81–83.

13. Commentaries on Plato's views of the education of women include Christine A. Gorside, "Plato on Women," *Feminist Studies* 2 (1975), 131–38;

Arlene W. Saxonhouse, "The Philosopher and the Female in the Political Thought of Plato," *Political Theory* 4 (1978), 195–222.

14. Taylor, *Plato: The Man and His Work*.

15. W. D. Ross, *Plato's Theory of Ideas* (Oxford: Oxford University Press, 1951).

16. Plato, "Meno," in *The Dialogues of Plato*, trans. B. Jowett (Indianapolis: Liberal Arts Press, 1949), 37–45.

17. Power, *Evolution of Educational Doctrine*, 62–68.

18. Among the many editions of Plato's *Republic* are *Plato, The Republic*, trans. Allan Bloom (New York: Basic Books, 1968); *The Republic*, trans. G. M. A. Grube (Indianapolis: Hackett, 1974); *The Republic*, trans. B. Jowett (New York: Random House, 1941).

19. R. M. Hare, *Plato* (Oxford: Oxford University Press, 1982), 60–68.

20. S. J. Curtis and M. E. A. Boultwood, *Short History of Educational Ideas* (London: Tutorial, 1965), 1–29.

21. Robert S. Brumbaugh and Nathaniel M. Lawrence, *Philosophers on Education: Six Essays on the Foundations of Western Thought* (Boston: Houghton Mifflin, 1963), 40–43.

Suggestions for Further Reading

Barrow, Robin. *Plato and Education*. London: Routledge & Kegan Paul, 1976.

———. *Plato, Utilitarianism, and Education*. London: Routledge & Kegan Paul, 1975.

Benardete, Seth, trans., with commentaries by Bloom, Alan and Benardete, Seth, *Plato's Symposium*. Chicago: University of Chicago Press, 2001.

Brumbaugh, Robert S. *The Philosophers of Greece*. Albany: State University of New York Press, 1981.

Bryant, Joesph M. *Moral Codes and Social Structure in Ancient Greece: A Sociology of Greek Ethics from Homer to the Epicureans and Stoics*. Albany: State University of New York Press, 1996.

Cohen, David. *Law, Violence, and Community in Classical Athens*. New York: Cambridge University Press, 1996.

Emlyn-Jones, C. J., ed. *Crito*. London: Bristol Classical Press, 1999.

Jowett, Benjamin, trans. Introduction and revision by Pelliccia Hayden, *Selected Dialogues of Plato: the Benjamin Jowett Translation*. New York: Modern Library, 2001.

Kennell, Nigel M. *The Gymnasium of Virtue: Education and Culture in Ancient Sparta*. Chapel Hill, NC: University of North Carolina Press, 1995.

Klagge, James Carl, and Smith, Nicholas D. *Methods of Interpreting Plato*. Oxford: Clarendon, 1992.

Nettleship, R. L. *The Theory of Education in Plato's Republic*. New York: Teachers College Press, 1968.

Plato. *A Guided Tour of Five Works by Plato: with Complete Translations of Euthyphro, Apology, Crito, Phaedo (The Death Scene), and "Allegory of the Cave."* Mountain View, CA: Mayfield Pub. Co., 2001.

———. *Plato: the Banquet*. Percy Bysshe Shelley, trans. Provincetown, MA: Pagan Press, 2001.

————. Goldstein, Yael, ed. *The Republic: Plato*. New York: Spark Pub., 2002.

Plato, Aristotle, et al. *Great Philosophers of the Ancient World*. London: Folio Society, 2003.

Quincy, Keith. *Plato Unmasked: Plato's Dialogues Made New*. Spokane, WA: Eastern Washington University Press, 2003.

Reeve, C. D. C., Meineck, Peter, et al., eds. *The Trials of Socrates: Six Classic Texts*. Indianapolis: Hackett Pub. Co., 2002.

Reydams-Schils, Gretchen J. *Plato's Timaeus as Cultural Icon*. Notre Dame, IN: University of Notre Dame Press, 2003.

Rouse, W. H. D., trans., Warmington, E. H. and Rouse, Philip G., eds. *Great Dialogues of Plato*. New York: Signet Classic, 1999.

Scolnicow, Samuel, trans. *Plato's Parmenides*. Berkeley, CA: University of California Press, 2003.

Stalley, R. F. *An Introduction to Plato's Laws*. Oxford: Basil Blackwell, 1983.

Stokes, Michael, ed. and trans. *Apology of Socrates*. Warminster, U.K.: Aris & Phillips, 1997.

Wilson, John F. *The Politics of Moderation: An Interpretation of Plato's Republic*. Lanham, MD: University Press of America, 1984.

Aristotle: Founder of Realism

In this chapter we examine the life, educational philosophy, and contributions of Aristotle (384–322 B.C.E.), a philosopher of ancient Greece who developed the theory of Natural Realism. Aristotle, like Plato, is regarded as a founding father of Western philosophy. In a commentary, Barnes wrote that Aristotle "bestrode antiquity like an intellectual colossus. No man before him had contributed so much to learning. No man after him could hope to rival his achievements."[1]

In this chapter, we examine Aristotle's influence on Western thought and education in its historical context and in terms of its enduring impact. First, we explore the general historical context of a Greece undergoing transition from a collection of small city-states to the Hellenistic empire. We next analyze Aristotle's life, his education and career, to identify the forces that influenced the development of his philosophical and educational ideas. Third, we identify and examine the key elements in Aristotle's philosophy of Natural Realism. Fourth, we describe his ideas on schooling. Finally, we assess Aristotle's historical and contemporary significance. By this historical examination, we seek to illuminate those events and factors that contributed to the formulation of one of the Western world's most significant systems of thought.

To help you to organize your thoughts as you read the chapter, consider the following questions:

1. What were the major trends in the historical context, the time and situation, in which Aristotle lived?
2. How did Aristotle's life—his educational biography—shape his philosophical and educational perspective?

3. How did Aristotle's philosophy shape his educational ideas and practices?
4. What has been the enduring impact of Aristotle's contributions on Western educational theory and practice?

The Historical Context of Aristotle's Life

During Aristotle's time, three major features of Greek culture were of special significance:

1. Basic intellectual concepts
2. The continuing decline of the *polis* as a vital cultural focus
3. The rise of the Hellenistic civilization associated with Alexander the Great

In addition, many of the characteristics and trends present in Plato's life, discussed in Chapter 3, were still present.

Aristotle's philosophy of education reflects the Greek intellectual tradition that emphasized human reason as that which gives definition, meaning, and purpose to life. While there was also a sense of destiny or fatalism in Greek religion that saw the human being as a toy of the gods, the gods were seen to embody particular human qualities. In contrast to the view that human beings were subject to irrational forces outside of their experience, Aristotle exemplified Greek thinkers who saw human beings' rational powers as the proper focus of choice and decision-making. The human being, a person of individual character, was part of a universal frame of being. Aristotle moved away from a capricious universe governed by irrational forces to a purposeful world governed by rationality.

Like his mentor Plato, Aristotle's thought embodied the concept that *arete*—human excellence in all things—was an important goal that should direct human purposes. For Aristotle, that excellence ideally exemplified the defining quality of human nature, the pursuit of reason.

Attracted by science and believing that the universe could be explained, Aristotle drew on, refined, and extended the Greek worldview. From Thales of Miletus, Aristotle accepted the concept that the physical universe operated rationally and in a way that was knowable to human beings. From Anaximander, Aristotle took the view that a balance of force existed in nature that made things what they were. Aristotle was also knowledgeable about the atomic theory of Parmenides, who saw objects as the coming together of material particles. Like Heraclitus, who asserted that everything is constantly changing, Aristotle was intrigued by the question of what was stable and what was changing. These early Greek scientists contributed to Aristotle's intellectual quest to examine and explain reality.[2]

Aristotle was also heir to the Greek educational tradition, especially as it was practiced in Athens. The Greeks were intellectual system builders who tried to incorporate the parts of their experience—their drama, art, architecture, law, sports, and politics—into a whole. Trying to place bits of experience into a comprehensible whole was part of their desire to explain the universe in rational terms. The educational content and style they developed reflected the desire for relationship, harmony, and balance.

Greek education, especially for Athens and excluding Sparta, stressed the concept of the liberal arts—studies that were for free men. Except for the militaristic state of

Sparta, Greek education was reserved for males. Aristotle shared this gender prejudice, which was common during his time. Important subjects in Greek higher education were grammar (the study of language), rhetoric (persuasive speaking), mathematics, philosophy, and music, which included literature and poetry. Aristotle embraced the Greek version of the liberal arts curriculum. Intrigued by science, his curiosity led him to the natural sciences, to biology, botany, physiology, and zoology, areas that he emphasized in his own teaching and writing. In his quest to develop a theory that explained reality, Aristotle studied philosophy. He pursued metaphysical issues in his attempt to discover the nature of ultimate reality; he studied epistemological questions in his search to find out how human beings come to know. He developed a system of logic, of deductive reasoning, as the formula for argument. Aristotle was thus the product of the intellectual context that made ancient Greece an important point of origin in the Western educational tradition.

During Aristotle's life, from 384 to 322 B.C.E., the Greek city-states, which embodied the old order of life, were in a process of disintegration. The conviction that the civilized person was an individual who participated in the politics, art, and law of the city-state was yielding to other desires and impulses. Plato had tried to formulate an ideal political-cultural-social state in his *Republic*, which would provide citizens with the needed sense of personal and cultural integration. For Plato, the outline of the perfect republic came from the mind's power to speculate.

Aristotle took a different approach to political organization. He traveled about the Greek world visiting city-states that had different kinds of government and political organization. As the founder of political science, he described actual forms of government—monarchies, oligarchies ruled by elites, and democracies—pointing out their various features and implications for human life.

Aristotle's educational theory was a systemization of the ideas he had developed as he studied various forms of government. *Paideia*, the Greek term for the taking on of culture, had by Aristotle's time changed from meaning the education of children to meaning the cultivation of human character and behavior. In his desire to restore the vitality of the declining polis, Aristotle developed his educational philosophy.

Aristotle's life also coincided with a basic transition in Greek political life from the era of free city-states to the Macedonian empire. In 338 B.C.E. Philip, king of Macedon from 359 to 336 B.C.E., defeated the armies of the city-states at the battle of Chaeronea. Two years later, Philip was assassinated and his son, Alexander, came to the throne. Aristotle had tutored Alexander, who in the brief period from 336 to 323 B.C.E. would conquer the known world. Despite his interest in philosophy and literature, Alexander the Great is best known for his military genius and bold use of tactics and strategy.

After putting down a rebellion by some Greek city-states, Alexander extended his empire by conquering the Ionian Greek settlements and the large Persian empire. His conquests extended into the Middle East and reached northern India.

To rule his vast empire, Alexander used Greek governors and settled Greek colonists in key areas. These transplanted Greeks were aided by local non-Greek officials. The end result of the process was to Hellenize, or give a Greek cultural veneer to, the ruling elites in Syria, Egypt, Persia, and other parts of Alexander's empire. Although his reign was brief, the empire Alexander established continued after his death at age 33 in 323 B.C.E.

By the time Aristotle died, in 322 B.C.E., the Greek political world of proud, independent city-states had undergone significant change. The polis, which had long been disintegrating as a vital cultural center, had been radically altered by Alexander and his successors. The new world order, while ruled by a Greek-speaking elite, was far different from that of Pericles, Socrates, and Plato.

In the Hellenistic world created by Alexander, his successors were more interested in storing knowledge than in creating it as Socrates, Plato, and Aristotle had done. The great library in Alexandria, Egypt, was such a storehouse of knowledge. On more than one-half million rolls of papyrus, its collection preserved the literature and philosophy of ancient Greece. While there were advances in science, mathematics, and the arts during the Hellenistic period from Alexander's death until the rise of Rome, inquiry followed purely academic paths rather than pursuing the vital issues of truth, justice, and the meaning of life.

Aristotle's Life and Career

Aristotle was born in Stagira, in the northern Greek kingdom of Macedonia, where his father, Nichomachus, was court physician to King Amyntas II. His mother was named Phoestis, but little is known about her background. As was the custom, the court physician not only treated the members of the royal court but also maintained a collection of scientific specimens. As a boy, Aristotle also was attracted to collecting and cataloguing specimens from natural history—minerals, plants, and animals. (Alexander, who studied under Aristotle, is believed to have sent various plant and animal specimens to his old teacher as his armies marched through Asia Minor.) Aristotle's interest in science and medicine continued throughout his life and is reflected in his philosophy of education.[3] Intrigued by natural phenomena, Aristotle sought to catalogue and categorize the objects around him. From his attempts at categorization would come the learned and scientific disciplines that study the various dimensions of reality.

When he was 17, Aristotle left Stagira to go to Athens, the center of Greek intellectual life. He studied with Plato, the renowned philosopher who had been a student of Socrates (see Chapter 3 for a discussion of Plato's educational ideas). For the next 20 years, from 367 to 347 B.C.E., Aristotle studied with Plato at his philosophical institute, the Academy.

Plato had developed a highly speculative philosophy whose metaphysics asserted that reality was ultimately spiritual or nonmaterial. To understand the real nature of things, Plato argued, one had to transcend the senses and popular opinion and intellectually reach the world of perfect forms or ideas. Plato also emphasized a rigorous intellectual methodology, the Socratic dialogue, in which students examined propositions logically and critically. Aristotle held Plato in esteem and learned much from him, particularly the importance of logical and critical thinking. Aristotle would eventually join Plato and Socrates as a member of that triad of great Greek philosophers who are linked together in Western educational history.

As he developed as a philosopher, Aristotle became more than the lengthened intellectual shadow of Plato. Aristotle accepted his mentor's concept of form, but disagreed with Plato's metaphysical doctrine that reality was ultimately nonmaterial. Aristotle postulated a hylemorphic or dualistic position that viewed reality as composed of matter and form. Early in his career, Aristotle combined his scientific curiosity about the natural world around him, learned at his father's side, with the Platonic speculative quest to find a world of truth that existed beyond the senses. While Plato's worldview rested on a perfect and unchanging view of reality that could be glimpsed by those trained in philosophical speculation, Aristotle began his inquiries with his senses. What would intrigue the young philosopher was a desire to know how things developed and changed. After Plato's death, Aristotle set out to reconcile Plato's theory of perfect forms or ideas with the data of natural development.[4]

In 347 B.C.E., Aristotle set out on a educational tour of Asia Minor to study the geography, climate, politics, flora, and fauna of the lands east of Greece. Further, he had at this time no home to which to return; during the conquest of Macedonia, Philip of Macedon had sacked and burned Stagira.

Traveling in Asia Minor, Aristotle lived for several years in the small kingdom of Assos, ruled by King Hermias. He joined a small circle of scholars whom Plato had sent earlier to establish a school. The bright young philosopher attracted the attention of Hermias, who engaged him as a tutor and adviser. Aristotle, made a member of the court, married Hermias's niece Phythias. They had a daughter, also named Phythias. While at Assos, Aristotle studied botany and biology. He also traveled to nearby islands where he studied the political institutions, social customs, and plant and animal life.

In 343 B.C.E., Aristotle was asked by Philip of Macedon to join his court to tutor his son, Alexander. He accepted the assignment and was Alexander's tutor for seven years. In 336 B.C.E., after Philip was assassinated and Alexander became king, Aristotle returned to Athens.

Following in Plato's footsteps, Aristotle established a school in Athens, the Lyceum. Because Aristotle was a *metic*—a resident alien rather than an Athenian citizen—he could not own land, so the Lyceum happened to be wherever Aristotle was with his students rather than a building in a permanent location. He conducted his school in the public walkways and gathering places. Aristotle taught and wrote in Athens until 323 B.C.E. He acquired a reputation as a commanding intellectual and philosopher, but he was always regarded as a foreigner and was never quite accepted in Athens.

Reflecting the many interests of their teacher, the Lyceum students pursued the natural sciences, politics, metaphysics, and ethics. By most accounts, Aristotle was a demanding teacher whose lectures were carefully organized and followed a logical progression. He was a good speaker who was capable of including witticisms with his generally profound topics.

It was at the Lyceum that Aristotle developed a theory in which natural phenomena were organized in a hierarchy. At the base of the hierarchy were lifeless minerals. Somewhat higher were plants, which while alive were limited in their potential. Higher in the chain of being, or order of life, were the animals. At the summit of the hierarchy came human beings, who possessed the power of rationality.

Aristotle was a prodigious scholar and writer, and most of his treatises began as lectures to his students. For students of education, important sources include his *Metaphysics*, which puts forth his theory of reality; his *Nicomachean Ethics*, which examines the nature of virtue; and his *Politics*, which includes a commentary on schooling. Aristotle wrote on many other subjects, including *On Justice, On the Soul, On the Sciences, The Art of Rhetoric, On Animals,* and *On Plants.* His lectures and writings dealt with a range of subjects: logic, the arts and sciences, psychology, physiology, political science, mathematics, zoology, botany, biology, law, metaphysics, epistemology, and astronomy.[5]

As a scholar-philosopher-teacher, Aristotle enjoyed a prestigious reputation but was not immune to the political events taking place in Greece. After Alexander had conquered Athens, Aristotle enjoyed his support and protection. Antipater, Alexander's governor in Athens, saw to Aristotle's personal safety. That protection, however, produced a negative reaction among the Athenian patriots who regarded themselves as captive people. Aristotle, who noted the hostility, advised Alexander to exercise tact and diplomacy in dealing with his Athenian subjects.[6]

After Alexander's death in 323 B.C.E., the Athenians revolted against Macedonian rule. Aristotle was accused of impiety by the faction that had come to power in Athens. Recalling Socrates' fate on a similar charge, he decided to leave Athens. He retired to Chalcis in Euboea, where he lived with a slave girl, Herpyllis (his wife had died many years earlier). Herpyllis bore him a son, Nicomachus. Aristotle died in 322 B.C.E.

Aristotle's Philosophy of Education

For Aristotle, the world in which we live is the world that we experience through our senses. Unlike those who followed the philosophical idealism of his mentor Plato, Aristotle believed that we live in an objective order of reality, a world of objects that exist external to us and our knowing of them. Through our senses and our reason, human beings can come to know these objects and develop generalizations about their structure and function. Truth is a correspondence between the person's mind and external reality. Theoretical knowledge based on human observation is the best guide to human behavior, Aristotle said.

Central to Aristotle's metaphysics was his matter-form hypothesis. Aristotle structured reality into two parts: matter and form. All the objects we perceive through our senses are composed of matter. Matter, however, is arranged according to different designs that Aristotle referred to as *form*. Without the element of matter, nothing can exist. However, matter requires a form to become something. For Aristotle, matter carries with it the *principle of potentiality*, which means it has the potential of becoming something but must take a form or structure. Aristotle referred to taking a form as the *principle of actuality*.

Throughout his philosophy, this essential dualism was present. All objects, the specimens of minerals, plants, and animals that he collected and studied, could be analyzed according to their matter and their structure. Human beings, too, were made up of matter—tissue, bone, muscles, and sinew—but they possessed the form of the human being. For Aristotle, the power that raised the human being above the brute world was rationality. Education, as he conceived of it, was designed to enable human beings to live socially, politically, and economically in a real world of flesh and blood in addition to enabling the higher purpose of developing rationality to its highest level.

As a scientist, Aristotle was intrigued by the developmental question of how matter moved from the state of potentiality to actuality. He explained this process of change through his theory of the four causes: material, formal, efficient, and final. Every object that exists has a *material cause*, which is the matter from which it is made. For example, the chair on which you are sitting may be made of wood, which in Aristotelian terms is the material cause of the chair. The *formal cause* is the form the object has; it defines the object. Note that the wood of which the chair is composed could have been made into a desk or a bookcase. It could have been given a different form. The *efficient cause* refers to the agent that brought about the change from the material to the formal. In the case of the chair, it is the woodworker who made the wood into the chair. The *final cause* is that purpose for which the action is done. For the woodworker, the final cause is making the chair so a person can sit on it.

Aristotle's conception of causation, the movement from potentiality to actuality, rested on his view that the universe is purposeful. What goes on in reality, in the patterns of the universe, is meaningful and is tending to an end. Nature is not an accident of atoms coming together by chance. Nature has a symmetry in which every object—every mineral, plant, and animal—has a definite role in the great chain of being.

Aristotle's principle of causation and purpose, like his matter-form hypothesis, has implications for education. It means that human life is meaningful rather than meaningless. It means that human beings, by using rationality, have the power to shape or define themselves by making choices. The meaning of human life in Aristotelian terms is the pursuit of happiness. *Happiness* is defined as the fulfillment of all human potentiality, especially the power and quality of reason. Aristotle said the purpose of education is to cultivate, to develop, and to exercise each child's potentiality to be fully human.

In analyzing the process of change through the four causes, Aristotle determined that we again have two qualities with which to deal: substance and accident. *Substance*, that which exists by itself, is the stable element while *accident* is the variable quality. To illustrate Aristotle's distinctions of substance and accidence, you might think of yourself. Your special identity as a person, that which makes you who you are, is your substance. However, you have changed over time in appearance and in human development. While you are essentially the same person you were as an infant, you have grown taller and older. Your appearance has changed (accidence), but you are still you (substance).

Aristotle believed education should deal at its highest level with the unchanging elements of human nature. Note that he asserts human beings have an underlying nature that makes them human. Regardless of the historic period or their geographical location, human beings share an essential sameness. For example, all people regardless of race, ethnicity, and culture have the power to reason. While they may speak different languages, all human beings have the power of communication. Thus, it is possible for Aristotelian educators to design curricula according to that which is universal to members of the human race. At the same time, they can also provide subject matter that is pertinent to a given time and place.

In *De Anima*, Aristotle wrote about the power of the human mind in epistemological and psychological terms. The mind, through the active intellect, has the power to abstract information from sensory data, and through the receptive intellect to store this information in the form of concepts. Just as he had divided reality into two parts, form and matter, Aristotle's epistemology was dualistic in that it involved two phases, sensation and abstraction. *Sensation* is the process by which the human being acquires sensory data from the material of the object; *abstraction* is the process by which the mind sorts out sensory information and arrives at concepts based on the form of the object.[7]

According to Aristotle, we inhabit a world of objects, and our knowledge of these objects begins with our sensory experience of them. Our eyes, nose, ears, tongue, and fingers are the body's physical organs for coming into contact with objects. Our senses, perceiving the matter of the object, carry information about the object's size, color, hardness or softness, sound, and other data to the mind. Somewhat like a computer, the mind sorts out information into the qualities or conditions that are always present, or necessary to the object, as distinct from those that are occasionally found in the object. The necessary conditions are those that are the basis of a concept. Aristotle defined a *concept* as based on the formal or essential qualities abstracted from an object. These are the qualities that it shares with other members or individuals of its class but with no other objects.

To illustrate Aristotle's process of abstraction and conceptualization, we can use the human being. People come in a variety of sizes, heights, and colors and speak different languages. Underlying these differences that appear to the senses, the mind is able to abstract a common set of conditions that are necessary to being human. These are common characteristics that people share, regardless of the place and time in which they live. This universal sense of humanness distinguishes human beings from other animate and inanimate objects.

The human powers of sensation and abstraction come to play on all the objects that exist. We see all sorts of trees—pine, palm, fir, apple, and elm, for example—as individual members of a category. These different trees share a commonality—treeness—that makes them part of the general category.

Aristotle's epistemology has important educational implications for both learning and knowledge. If we come to know through our senses and abstraction, then how we learn should follow this pattern of knowing. Instruction—teaching and learning—should provide occasions for students to examine, observe, and deal with objects. It should provide situations in which students create categories of objects that share certain essential characteristics and recognize objects that are similar and different. Later, in the early nineteenth century, Pestalozzi's object lesson, which we examine in Chapter 11, followed an essentially Aristotelian epistemological approach.

Aristotle, one of the founding figures of Western science, also pioneered in categorization of objects. From the basic categories of animal, vegetable, and mineral, a highly specialized schema of classification was established. For example, the animal category could be divided into an immense array of subcategories. The information derived from the study of these subcategories could be classified into biology, zoology, anthropology, anatomy, physiology, and so on. In the Aristotelian system, everything that exists can be categorized and classified.

Aristotle's system of classification of objects and of creating bodies of information about them contributed to the organization of knowledge into the arts and sciences. It is possession of these bodies of knowledge that make a person liberally educated or free to make rational choices. Aristotle believed the human being possesses the defining quality of rationality. Through the power of sensing and abstracting, the human mind acquires concepts. Over time, one may build vast arrays of related concepts into a storehouse of knowledge, a kind of intellectual map of reality. To be free and to act rationally, the human being needs to form, weigh, and act on alternatives of action. The human mind is informed by knowledge about the world and how the objects in the world interact and behave according to their structure and function.

The Aristotelian process of liberalization through knowledge can be illustrated by an example. At certain stages in life, people make career choices that shape both their current situation and their future. The list of choices is broad and varied—baker, lawyer, gardener, physician, physicist, computer programmer, teacher, pilot, politician. To rationally make decisions, people need to possess knowledge about these various careers and the preparation needed to enter that particular career. They can go to the library to find information about a particular career, and also investigate institutions and schools that offer programs for particular careers. Using all this information, people can assess their interest and potential for the given career.

In Aristotle's view, while human beings have various careers, they all share the most important factor, the exercise of rationality. Reason gives human beings the potential of leading lives that are self-determined. To assist in the process of human self-determination, education should provide the knowledge upon which rational decisions and actions are made.[8]

Congruent with his metaphysical and epistemological perspective, Aristotle in the *Nicomachean Ethics* developed his ethical theory. He portrayed the good life as that of happiness, or *eudaimonia*. He believed the ultimate good for the human being is happiness, activity in accordance to virtue. The virtuous life is one in which actions are part of a consciously formulated plan that takes a mean, a middle course, avoiding extremes. For example, true courage would be a mean that avoids the extremes of cowardice and rashness. What decides the right course to take is *phronesis*, the virtue of prudence, or practical wisdom.[9] The goal of human life is to live a life governed by reason.

The exercise of virtue is the means of attaining happiness. Aristotle categorized virtues, or values, as either moral or intellectual. *Moral virtue* is a habit by which the individual exercises a prudent choice, one that a rational person would make. Moral virtues tend to moderation, falling between excess and inhibition. For example, the prudent person would develop a balanced diet based on the consumption of foods that promote physical health and well-being. Gorging oneself is debilitating to health. At the other extreme, starving oneself into a state of anorexia inhibits what is natural and necessary for health.

The *intellectual virtues* contribute to the perfection of the human intellect or power of reason. Through science, inquiry, and the search for first principles, each of us develops a theory that arises from observation of the world. This kind of theory has explanatory power in that it tells us about the structure and function of this world. This kind of theory is our surest and best guide to conduct.

Although Aristotle's philosophy of education emphasized the development and cultivation of the individual's intellectual potentiality, he also related the cultivation of rational excellence to the well-being of the polis, thus integrating personal and sociopolitical development. Aristotle believed cultivation of both intellectual and ethical virtues takes place in the human community. In the polis, the Greek locus of the human community, shared perceptions of human life arose. The city-state, Aristotle argued, existed so that its inhabitants would have a place to experience happiness, or to live well. The constitution and laws of the city-state should be designed to foster virtue. It is education that creates a commonality among the residents of the city.

Aristotle and Schooling

In addition to the general features of his philosophy of education, Aristotle also held opinions about schooling. Although his philosophy has greater meaning for contemporary education, his views of schooling, positioned in the Greek situation of his day, also have implications for us today.

Aristotle believed the purpose of education is to cultivate human excellence.[10] The human being's psyche, or soul, possesses the rational potentiality that education should develop. The psyche, the locus of human cognitive or reasoning powers, enables people to develop generalizations about the world and its functions. It also enables the mastery of technical skills needed for political, social, and economic survival. Along with developing rationality, education has the function of forming the human being's ethos, or ethical character.

Aristotle believed education is a general process of formation that takes place informally outside of institutions as well as formally in schools. Education in schools is planned deliberately to achieve prescribed outcomes supportive of the human quest for happiness. In structuring the school curriculum, Aristotle would begin the educational process by forming the characters of the young with dispositions favorable to the rational and ethical life. After correct habits are formed, the curriculum turns to theory, which explains the universal principles that govern reality. A lower priority would be given to technical skills that relate to the performance of specialized human functions.

Aristotle divided schooling into three stages: primary schooling, which centered on the development of skills that had generative power and the cultivation of moral predispositions conducive to the later life of reason and moderation; secondary schooling, which led from the essential skills and habit formation of the primary years to the intellectual development of higher studies; and higher education, which was almost exclusively intellectual.

Aristotle advocated a system of compulsory schools supervised by state authorities. His belief in compulsory education differed from the general practice in the Greek citystates, where, with the exception of Sparta, schooling was private and voluntary. In Aristotle's plan of school organization, children from the ages of 7 to 14 would attend primary schools. The curriculum would consist of gymnastics to develop coordination, grace of movement, and courage; letters (the study of reading and writing) to develop literacy necessary for later learning; music, which also included poetry, literature, and drama; arithmetic; and drawing. Students would have direct experience with elementary skills, especially music and drawing, so that they could practice the appropriate techniques. While these skills required technique, they also were generative in that they led to greater appreciation and enjoyment of literature, music, drama, and other art forms and had the power to draw students into other more complex and profound areas of learning.

Secondary schooling, in Aristotle's plan, was designed for young men from ages 14 through 21. These youths would continue their studies of music including literature, poetry, drama, choral music, and dancing. These studies were to immerse the young in the sources of Greek culture and civilization. The last four years of secondary education were to be spent in military drill, tactics, and strategy that would be useful in defending the polis from attack by its enemies.

As a scientist and philosopher who conducted his own school, Aristotle was most concerned with higher education. Higher studies began at age 21 and continued as long as a student was interested and capable of pursuing more abstract study. The purpose of higher education was the cultivation of reason and character. More specifically, Aristotle saw higher studies as providing an advanced liberal education for citizens; these good citizens would form an elite who would lead the polis. Higher education, like the other areas of the curriculum, was reserved for male citizens. Women, he believed, were not intellectually capable of abstract studies. Those who were not free citizens were to be trained in performing vocational functions rather than receive a liberal education.

Conclusion: An Assessment

Aristotle, like Plato, is regarded as one of the founding figures of Western philosophy. Courses in Western history and philosophy invariably contain commentaries, sections, readings, and citations related to Aristotle, the founder of Natural Realism. To assess Aristotle's significance, we can look to his influence on later historical development and to the meaning of his philosophy for contemporary education.

After the collapse of the Roman empire in the West, Aristotle's philosophy suffered a temporary decline. His logic, used in some schools in the early Christian era, found its way into the *compendia*, the small books written to codify the liberal arts. However, the dominant philosophies during Rome's imperial period were Epicureanism and Stoicism rather than Aristotle's. In the early Christian era, study of the Scriptures, theology, and religious studies dominated the curriculum.

In the late twelfth and thirteenth centuries, Aristotle's philosophy was rediscovered by Western scholars and educators. The reentry of Aristotelian ideas came by way of Arab scholars who had translated Aristotle's works; as Christians came into contact with the Arabic world during the Crusades, they rediscovered the ancient Greek philosophers. Scholastic educators of the Middle Ages, especially those in the Medieval universities, began to study Aristotle's philosophy and incorporate it into their teaching and writing. Of particular importance in reincorporating Aristotle's philosophy into Western culture is Thomas Aquinas, the founder of Thomism (discussed in Chapter 6). Following some initial debate about the prudence of giving an important role to a non-Christian, or pagan, philosopher, Aristotle's philosophy became an important part of the education of those who attended the Medieval universities. Since his rediscovery by the scholastic educators, Aristotle has been regarded as a major influence on Western philosophy and education.

Aristotle is meaningful for contemporary education. His assertion that the human being is endowed with a defining rational nature continues to inspire educators who see the cultivation of the intellect as the primary purpose of education. Educational proposals such as the "Great Books" curriculum and the "Paideia" proposal rest on Aristotelian principles.

Aristotle's argument that human beings should be liberally educated remains a great rationale in support of higher education stressing the liberal arts and sciences. That people should be educated in the liberal arts so they can frame and choose between rational alternatives is regarded as crucial to the freedom of human choice and self-determination. Much of our worldview is the product of Aristotle's quest to find out what things are and how they work. His quest to discover the structure and function of reality has shaped Western thought and education.

Questions for Reflection and Dialogue

1. Describe and analyze the mentor-student relationship that existed between Socrates and Plato and Aristotle. Do you believe that mentoring is a useful educational method? How might mentoring function between an experienced and a beginning teacher?

2. Compare and contrast the processes of teaching and learning for Plato and Aristotle. How would they react to such contemporary American learning strategies: learning how to succeed on standardized tests, maintaining a portfolio, constructivism, searching the Internet?
3. How did the Greek intellectual milieu influence the formation of Aristotle's ideas?
4. Compare and contrast Plato's idealism and Aristotle's realism.
5. What are the educational implications of Aristotle's view of a purposeful universe? Do you believe that the universe is purposeful or purposeless?
6. Examine the role of knowledge according to Aristotelian freedom of choice. Do you think most Americans make their choice on an Aristotelian or on some other philosophical base?

Projects for Deepening Your Understanding

1. Design a lesson plan for teaching a particular skill or subject based on Aristotle's philosophy.
2. Based on Aristotle's philosophy, write a defense for liberal arts education.
3. In an essay, examine the relevance of Aristotle's philosophy of education for the contemporary United States. Consider who would be likely proponents and likely opponents of applying Aristotle's philosophy to contemporary schooling.
4. Assume that you are an Aristotelian principal of a modern school and are hiring a teacher. Write a job description of the position based on Aristotle's philosophy of education.
5. Assume that you are establishing a charter school that will operate according to Aristotelian educational principles. Prepare a short prospectus designed to attract potential students.
6. Aristotle made a distinction between theory and practice and between the liberal arts and technical training. In a position paper, argue either for or against his distinction.
7. Examine the liberal arts and science requirements in your degree program. In a position paper, determine what Aristotle's reactions would be to these requirements.
8. Examine and analyze current proposals for educational reform. In a position paper, indicate if these proposals conform to or differ from Aristotle's philosophy.

Notes

1. Jonathan Barnes, *Aristotle* (New York: Oxford University Press, 1982), 1.
2. H. D. F. Kitto, *The Greeks* (Baltimore: Penguin, 1962), 169–94.
3. G. E. R. Lloyd, *Aristotle: The Growth and Structure of His Thought* (Cambridge, MA: Cambridge University Press, 1968), 3.
4. E. W. F. Tomlin, *The Western Philosophers* (New York: Harper & Row, 1967), 62.
5. Barnes, *Aristotle*, 2–3.
6. D. J. Allan, *The Philosophy of Aristotle* (London: Oxford University Press, 1970), 4.
7. John Wild, *Introduction to Realistic Philosophy* (New York: Harper & Brothers, 1948), 441–68.
8. Harry S. Broudy, *Building a Philosophy of Education* (Upper Saddle River, NJ: Prentice Hall, 1961), pp. 61–67, 125–26.
9. Anthony Kenny, *Aquinas* (New York: Hill & Wang, 1980), 20–21.

10. H. I. Marrou, *The History of Education in Antiquity* (New York: Mentor, 1964), 76–136.

Suggestions for Further Reading

Ackrill, J. L. *Aristotle: the Philosopher*. New York: Oxford University Press, 1981.

Aristotle. *The Basic Works of Aristotle*. Richard Peter McKeon, ed. New York: Modern Library, 2001.

———. *De Anima*. David Ross, ed. Oxford: Oxford University Press, 1999.

———. *Ethics*. J. A. K. Thomson, and Hugh Tredennick, eds. London: Folio Society, 2003.

———. *Nicomachean Ethics*. Trans. Terence Irwin. Indianapolis: Hackett, 1985.

———. *The Philosophy of Aristotle: A Selection*. Renford Bambrough, ed. New York: Signet Classic, 2003.

———. *The Poetics*. Buffalo, NY: Prometheus, 1992.

———. *Politics*. Richard Kraut, ed. Oxford: Clarendon Press, 1997.

———. *On Rhetoric: A Theory of Civic Discourse*. New York: Oxford University Press, 1991.

Broadie, Sarah. *Ethics with Aristotle*. New York: Oxford University Press, 1991.

Chambliss, Joseph J. *The Influence of Plato and Aristotle on John Dewey's Philosophy*. Lewiston, NY: E. Mellen, 1990.

Davidson, Thomas. *Aristotle and Ancient Educational Ideals*. New York: Burt Franklin, 1969.

During, Ingemar. *Aristotle in the Ancient Biographical Tradition*. New York: Garland, 1987.

Edel, Abraham. *Aristotle and His Philosophy*. Chapel Hill, NC: University of North Carolina Press, 1982.

Evans, John D. G. *Aristotle*. New York: St. Martin's, 1987.

Freese, John Henry. *The "Art" of Rhetoric*. Cambridge, MA: Harvard University Press, 2002.

Irwin, Terence. *Aristotle's First Principles*. Oxford: Clarendon, 1988.

Johnson, Curtis N. *Aristotle's Theory of the State*. New York: St. Martin's, 1990.

McKirahan, Richard D. *Principles and Proofs: Aristotle's Theory of Demonstrative Science*. Princeton, NJ: Princeton University Press, 1992.

Pangle, Lorraine Smith. *Aristotle and the Philosophy of Friendship*. Cambridge: Cambridge University Press, 2003.

Rankin, Kenneth. *The Recovery of the Soul: An Aristotelian Essay on Self-Fulfillment*. Montreal: McGill-Queen's University Press, 1991.

Reeve, C. D. C. *Practices of Reason: Aristotle's Nicomachean Ethics*. New York: Oxford University Press, 1992.

Salkever, Stephen G. *Finding the Mean: Theory and Practice in Aristotelian Political Philosophy*. Princeton, NJ: Princeton University Press, 1990.

Spangler, Mary M. *Aristotle on Teaching*. Lanham, MD: University Press of America, 1998.

Swanson, Judith A. *The Public and the Private in Aristotle's Political Philosophy*. Ithaca, NY: Cornell University Press, 1992.

Verbeke, Gerard. *Moral Education in Aristotle*. Washington, DC: Catholic University of America Press, 1990.

White, Stephen A. *Sovereign Virtue: Aristotle on the Relation Between Happiness and Prosperity*. Stanford, CA: Stanford University Press, 1992.

CHAPTER 5

Quintilian: Rhetorical Educator in Service of the Emperor

This chapter examines the life, educational philosophy, and contributions of Marcus Fabius Quintilianus, known as Quintilian (35–95 C.E.), a prominent teacher of rhetoric in the Roman Empire. Quintilian's development of rhetorical education is historically significant in that it incorporated important Greek concepts about the education of the orator with a theory of service to the Roman Empire.

In this chapter, we discuss Quintilian's educational contributions in terms of their origins in the historical context of the Roman Empire and in terms of their significance to educational thought. First, we describe the social, political, and cultural context in which Quintilian lived and worked. Second, we examine Quintilian's biography, education, and career to trace the evolution of his ideas. Third, we assess Quintilian's significance as a contributor to Western educational thought. Following the pattern of organization used in the other chapters in this book, we examine the interrelationships of the dynamics of educational history and philosophy. Quintilian lived during a period of social change when the last vestiges of republican Rome had been replaced by imperial rule. Nevertheless, his educational ideas contain elements of continuity, based on transmission of the educational heritage, and of change, based on the altered character of Roman political and social life. Our analysis uses the concepts of continuity and change, which are important for analyzing curriculum, teaching, and education at any time.

To organize your thoughts as you read Chapter 5, focus on the following questions:

1. What were the major trends in the historical context, the time and situation, in which Quintilian lived?
2. How did Quintilian's life, his educational biography, shape his philosophy of education?
3. How did Quintilian's educational philosophy determine his educational policies and practices?
4. What is the significance of Quintilian's contributions to Western education?

The Historical Context of Quintilian's Life

The history of Rome as a republic and as an empire covers almost 1,000 years of the human record. We shall not attempt to deal with the many political, social, and economic events in this important millennium. Rather, we shall concentrate on certain key concepts and trends that shaped the Roman outlook on life, society, and the world, indicating how this worldview shaped the Roman educational vision. We shall then see how Quintilian himself was shaped by that outlook and how he helped to reshape it.

Although Quintilian lived in imperial Rome, certain patterns of Roman life were established during the republican era, from about 450 to 27 B.C.E. The Rome of 450 B.C.E. was a small city-state in central Italy in the vicinity of the present-day Italian capital. The early Romans were primarily an agricultural people who were conservative in their values but assertive in their behavior. Growing restive under the domination of a ruling non-Roman Etruscan elite, they rose up, deposed their rulers, and established their own republic.

During the republic's early years, when contact with non-Romans was minimal, a schema or set of values was developed and prized. These values had weakened and largely eroded by Quintilian's time, but residues remained. Quintilian and other educators would harken back to the need to restore the cherished traditional values that had made Rome a great empire.

Early Roman society, its knowledge and values, and the education that helped sustain it were originally agricultural. As is true in most agricultural societies, property was emphasized—especially land tenure and ownership. The values of this rural agrarian society were inherited and traditional and sought to maintain the status quo. The tendency in education, which was largely informal and in the hands of parents, called for maintaining tradition and passing it on to the younger generation.

Early Roman republican education, primarily taught by the father as head of the household, was designed to train children, especially sons, to revere their family ancestors and to be aware of their duties to family, the state, and the gods. According to this pattern of values, the good Roman was self-controlled and self-disciplined, respected family ancestors and traditions, maintained property in good order, was thrifty and temperate, and patriotically and courageously performed the military and civil duties needed by the state. Children learned these values by imitating their parents, who were expected to be exemplars of Roman virtues. These basic values were also reinforced by religious rituals and were encoded in the Laws of the Twelve Tables, which every Roman boy was expected to memorize.

During Rome's early years as a republic, these essential values were transmitted in Roman families. When the primary school, the *ludus*, and the secondary school of the *grammaticus* were established in the third century B.C.E., the family's direct role in inculcating these values was shared with these educational agencies. However, the essential values of duty, honor, and patriotism remained dear to the Roman heart and psyche. During the conquests that created its vast empire, Romans encountered greater learning in its captive peoples. The more culturally sophisticated Greeks, for example, caused a weakening of traditional values for some Romans. As we shall see later, the cultural interchange between Greece and Rome affected the continuity of these traditional values in Roman education.

Socioeconomic and status conflicts existed throughout the history of the republic. Rome's two major classes were the patricians, members of the old aristocracy who held title to large landed estates, and the plebeians, who had lower economic and social status. The patricians controlled the Senate, the deliberative and policy-making body of Rome. They also elected two consuls, who implemented the Senate's military and civil decisions and administered Rome. Much of Rome's political history documents the struggle of the plebeians to gain more of a voice in the affairs of the republic. They gradually gained more rights from the patricians as concessions in return for military service. Over time, some plebeians accumulated fortunes in commerce and bought their way into the ruling circles of the Roman republic.

The Roman Senate was the key institution for wielding influence, debating policies, and making decisions. As in the Congress of the United States or in any deliberative body charged with examining and shaping policies, effective members needed to demonstrate several skills:

1. The ability to formulate an agenda to present to the other members of the assembly or body.
2. The ability to win the support of colleagues. Support was won by tradeoffs, in which members agreed to support each other's programs, or by using influence or exerting pressure.
3. The power of speech and effective argument. Members had to be able to debate to persuade others to support their point of view and program.

What emerged in Roman political life in the republic was a recognition of the practical power of oratory or public speaking as a means of influencing people and shaping events. A similar sense of the importance of oratory was found in ancient Greece. In this early stage of the history of Rome, public speaking and its power were appreciated. Cicero, a leading Roman senator, and later Quintilian, among others, would formulate a theory of rhetoric for educating effective public speakers. The important point is that there was a tradition in Rome, from the days of the republic, that prized and valued oratory and Quintilian would embrace it.

Rome was an expansive republic. Roman legions marched out and consolidated Rome's power on the Italian peninsula. After a series of wars with Carthage, Rome became the master of the lands bordering the Mediterranean Sea. Rome even extended its control as far north as modern Germany and present-day England. In its march to power, a significant event occurred that affected Rome's cultural life. In 272 B.C., Rome defeated the Greek armies in the battle of Tarentum. Although Rome conquered Greece militarily, it was heavily influenced by Greek culture. This cultural interchange was significant for Roman education, especially the rhetorical version of it that was Quintilian's life's work.

Not only Greece but much of the eastern Mediterranean region that Rome now ruled had earlier been influenced by Greek culture. The conquests of Alexander the Great had spread Hellenic culture well into Asia Minor. In this region Greek had become the language of the former ruling elites. After the region's conquest by Roman soldiers came Roman governors and officials who were to administer the vast empire. These Roman officials as well as important segments of Rome's aristocracy came to recognize Greek as the language of culture, refinement, and diplomacy in much the same way that French was regarded as the international language in the nineteenth century. Greek slaves were prized as the tutors of the children of well-born Romans, and young Romans of promise made the grand tour of Greece.[1]

As a result of their cultural interchange with Greece, Romans encountered the Greek emphasis on rhetoric originally developed by Plato's educational adversaries, the Sophists (see Chapter 3). The Romans already knew the practical value of oratory in winning Senate debates or in inspiring troops in battle. Now they encountered a people who had refined oratory into an art and developed a well-structured theory of rhetorical education.

Foremost among the Greek rhetoricians who would be studied and cited by the Romans Cicero and Quintilian was Isocrates (436–338 B.C.E.).[2] A well-regarded teacher of rhetoric in Athens, Isocrates wrote *Against the Sophists*, which described his school and criticized the methods used by his rivals the Sophists; and *Antidosis*, a detailed treatise on rhetorical education. Rejecting the techniques of the Sophists as shallow gimmicks, Isocrates wanted to educate an orator who was both a rational human being and an effective communicator. Such an orator, he reasoned, would be liberally educated in the arts and sciences, would be morally and ethically sensitive, and would be an excellent and effective public speaker. These orator-statesmen, Isocrates believed, would be both visionary and practical leaders who could direct the course of Athenian and, perhaps, Greek life.

Although Isocrates wanted to educate leaders of vision, men who could see events and frame policies in a broad perspective, he rejected Plato's version of the philosopher-king as being too fanciful, speculative, and unrealistic. Neither did Isocrates accept the merely practical approach to oratory in which the Sophists stressed mastery of techniques as being adequate for the statesmanship qualities he saw as necessary to genuine leadership.

When Roman educational theorists such as Quintilian encountered Isocrates' ideas, they found a theory that seemed tailor-made for the preparation of the leaders and officialdom of Rome. Isocrates' stress on the need for liberal education and ethical sensibilities had the potential of raising the level of rhetoric in the Roman Senate. Further, Isocrates' emphasis on the orator as a person who exercised an active function in policy formulation and decision making was well suited to the Roman sense of utility and practicality.

Isocrates' contributions to the history of Western educational ideas have been overshadowed by Socrates, Plato, and Aristotle. However, his ideas on the education of the orator, which significantly contributed to refining the Roman ideal of oratory, also had a long-term effect on the development of rhetorical education in the West. For example, Isocrates redefined *philosophy* as the practical interpretations that make sense of life and give order to it. A true leader should possess the ability to estimate a situation accurately as it really exists. Such an accurate appraisal would contribute to the formulation of alternatives of action.

The leader who used practical philosophy to guide actions needed, according to Isocrates, a background in the liberal arts.[3] The orator-statesman needed a command of language—of grammar, composition, and literature—which was indispensable in understanding and interpreting the past and assessing the present. He needed a background in geography, mythology, history, archaeology, and politics, because these areas created the contexts of informed discussion. To cultivate ethical sensibilities that would lead to ethical behavior, the orator-statesman needed to study philosophy, jurisprudence, and ethics. With such a background, the student of oratory could then proceed to rhetoric, oratory, debate, and declamation—subjects and skills necessary for the rational and effective communicator that Isocrates hoped to educate.

One of the Romans to make contact with Greek culture, particularly rhetorical education, was the famous senator Cicero (106–43 B.C.E.). Cicero's encounter with Greek culture contributed significantly to the historical and educational context that helped shape Quintilian's ideas. A theme introduced in this section to interpret the Roman context is continuity and change. Cicero, a political conservative from a patrician background, tried to preserve the old Roman values of honor, duty, and service that were part of the legacy of virtue from the early republic. Although some conservative Romans wanted nothing to do with Greek culture, Cicero was impressed by Greek advances in philosophy and rhetoric. He sought to integrate old Roman virtues with those of Greek learning and create a synthesis of educational ideas. In a similar fashion, Thomas Aquinas would attempt a synthesis of Aristotle's philosophy and Christian theology in the Middle Ages. (See Chapter 6.) Today's educators who seek to formulate educational philosophy and policy can learn much about the skills of theoretical integration of the past and the present as they deal with the problems as well as the possibilities of continuity and change.

Cicero, a well-born and advantaged Roman youth, spent four years, from 80 to 76 B.C.E., on a "grand tour" of Greece, where he studied philosophy and rhetoric. On his return to Rome he entered the Senate, where he supported conservative interests and resisted the erosion of republican institutions and values. In 44 B.C.E., he was implicated in the assassination of Julius Caesar.[4] Cicero believed Caesar was undermining the republic and seeking to create a personal dictatorship. As he sought to flee Rome, Cicero was killed in retribution for his association with conspirators against Caesar. Although Julius Caesar was assassinated to preserve the republic, the republic gave way to the Roman Empire. Augustus, Julius Caesar's nephew, became the first emperor in 27 B.C.E.

In 55 B.C.E., at the height of his political power and influence, Cicero wrote *de Oratorio*, or *About Oratory*, a treatise on the education of the ideal Roman orator. Written to instruct the younger generation of Rome, the book was a skillful blending of old Roman values with the newly encountered Greek philosophy and rhetoric. Cicero admonished parents to make certain their children were adept in using Latin and conversant with its literature. In addition, young Romans should understand and appreciate their cultural heritage, its history, traditions, and values. Like Isocrates, who Cicero called "the master of all rhetoricians," the Roman senator envisioned a liberally educated orator who had studied law, philosophy, ethics, psychology, political science, military strategy, geography, literature, and history. With this background, the student of oratory could turn to rhetoric and declamation. The educated orator, a skilled speaker who possessed a keenly developed ethical sense, should in Cicero's view manifest a variety of skills. He should be subtle in logic, profound in philosophy, clear in diction, poetic in expression, and have the lawyer's command of precedent.[5] Above all, the orator had to be eloquent and forceful, possessing the power to move his listeners on the course that he wanted them to take.[6]

From our foregoing discussion of the historical context that helped shaped Quintilian, certain trends or characteristics emerge. Among them are the following:

1. The Romans, a practical people, recognized the importance of oratory as a means of winning and exercising political power.
2. They inherited a well-defined set of values. These values, which were essentially conservative, were challenged and eroded by the forces of change engendered by the transformation of Rome from a small agricultural city-state to a large empire.
3. The Roman encounter with Greek philosophy and rhetoric had a pronounced effect on their views of culture and education, particularly rhetorical education.
4. The republican institutions of Rome were being subverted by what would become imperial Rome.

Quintilian as a Proponent of Rhetorical Education

In this section, we analyze Quintilian's life, career, and educational ideas. He was born in 35 C.E. in the provincial town of Callagurris, a Roman city on the Ebro River. Quintilian's birthplace is now the modern Spanish city of Calahorra.

Quintilian's introduction to oratory came from his father, who taught rhetoric. Quintilian's study with his father followed the ancient tradition that had originated in the republic: the father, as the first influence on his son, should incline him in the desired direction. Following his father's career, Quintilian became a rhetorician. When he was 16, Quintilian went to Rome, where he worked as an assistant to Domitius Afer, a distinguished rhetorician and lawyer. His legal and rhetorical apprenticeship with Domitius followed the old Roman tradition of the *tricinium fori*, the year a young man spent working with a distinguished person. The goal of this internship was to expose the young man to the knowledge and virtues that had contributed to the patron's success. After completing his rhetorical study, he became a lawyer and worked as an assistant to Domitius. When Domitius died in 58 C.E., Quintilian returned to Callagurris to practice law.

Ten years later, Quintilian returned to Rome to establish his own rhetorical school. Among his students was Pliny the Younger (62–114 C.E.), who earned a reputation as a poet and author. Quintilian also taught two grandnephews of the emperor Domitian. His skill as a master rhetorician earned Quintilian an outstanding reputation that brought him to the attention of the emperor Vespasian.

Vespasian (9–79 C.E.) was Rome's emperor from 70 to 79 C.E. Known for the simplicity of his court, Vespasian devoted himself to stabilizing the political conditions in Rome. He also embarked on a building program that led to the construction of the Temple of Peace and the Colosseum. He recognized Quintilian's talents and appointed him in 72 C.E. to the imperially endowed chair of Latin rhetoric, a position he held for 20 years.[7]

Quintilian's most important book on the education of an orator was *Institutio Oratoria* (*Institutes of Oratory*) written between 93 and 95 C.E. In stating his educational purpose and adhering to the philosophical orientation of Isocrates and Cicero, Quintilian announced that the orator he intended to educate would be "a good man" and a "perfect orator." Such an orator would possess "an excellent power of speech" and "all the moral virtues as well."[8]

Quintilian's book, like that of Isocrates, is a thorough exposition not only of rhetorical education but of general education as well. He begins with a commentary on human nature and psychology. Human beings possess the power of cognition, which enables them to know and form ideas. They also are emotional and volitional in that they have impulses, needs, and desires. Both thought and action need to be governed by human reason. Thus, at the onset of his work, Quintilian allies himself with rationalism and would have his orator be a reason-governed person.

Because the character needed by the good orator was a product of long-term development, Quintilian reasoned that attention should be paid to early childhood education: From birth to age 7, children are primarily governed by their instincts and impulses. The cognitive powers are present but are unorganized, and reason is not operative. It is most important that children's early years be devoted to creating the positive attitudes that facilitate later learning. Parents were to exercise great care in selecting the child's nurse, tutor, servants, and companions. Quintilian advised that the nurse and the tutor be selected carefully, with particular attention devoted to their speech and behavior. Concerned with the boy's total process of early socialization, Quintilian advised parents to carefully supervise his free time. It was important that his playmates be the "right type" of companions.[9]

Quintilian recognized and accepted the importance of Greek language and culture in rhetorical education. The boy he would prepare to be an orator should be bilingual, learning both Greek and Latin. Greek servants in the household were to use their language correctly so that the boy's use of language was correct. That Quintilian was writing for a wealthy audience is clear from his references to servants and tutors. In addition, he clearly is committed to the acceptance of Greek culture and education.[10]

At age 7, children begin to use their senses to develop ideas of the world about them. They also are highly imitative of adult behavior. Now, the boy goes to the *ludus*, where he learns reading, writing, and calculating.

Quintilian advised upper-class Roman parents to send their sons to school rather than having them tutored at home. Schools, he observed, provided opportunities for socialization and peer-group interaction. They also provided the competition needed by orators. In selecting a school, Quintilian advised parents to make sure the teacher was an interesting person of good character who was skilled in instruction. Also, Quintilian was far in advance of his day in opposing corporal punishment.

At age 13, the boy should go to the school of the *grammaticus*. At the time Quintilian's book appeared, Roman boys attended two grammar schools that were parallel to each other; one emphasized Greek grammar and literature, whereas the other specialized in Latin grammar and literature. In addition to grammar and literature, Quintilian recommended studying music to develop the voice and geometry to develop mental training.

After completing his studies with the *grammaticus*, the young man, if he had the aptitude and readiness, could proceed to the rhetorical school. Following the liberal arts approach stressed by Isocrates and Cicero, the curriculum of the rhetorical school included literature, poetry, drama, history, law and jurisprudence, philosophy, and the study of orators and their orations. Of course, the theory and practice of rhetoric, debate, and elocution that were so indispensable to the effective orator also were emphasized. Quintilian identified declamation as the most useful study in the rhetorical school because it provided systematic exercise in public speaking.

Conclusion: An Assessment

Quintilian's conception of the ideal orator was shaped by Roman ethical traditions and by the influence of Isocrates. Quintilian's orator was a moral leader whose ethics reflected the Roman values of honor, responsibility, and duty to the state. Like Isocrates, Quintilian believed that the good orator also needed to be a good human being. His goal was to perfect the human power of speech into eloquence, its highest and noblest expression. Although eloquence had its own value, Quintilian wanted this human excellence to be used for good and noble purposes rather than for selfish interests.

Quintilian's theory of rhetorical education can be assessed in three dimensions:

1. As an educational theory using its own internal criteria
2. In terms of its congruence with the actual realities of Roman political and social life
3. In terms of its enduring significance for the history of Western educational ideas

When judged on its own internal criteria, Quintilian's theory of education, particularly as expressed in the *Institutio Oratoria*, was remarkable for its anticipation of later education. His learning theory identified stages of human development, with an appropriate kind of education for each stage. With each stage came a readiness for a certain kind of learning. Quintilian's prescriptions on the importance of early childhood education were prophetic of contemporary research and practice. He recognized, as does the modern early childhood educator, that the child's earliest years are among the most important. This is the time in which habits and predispositions are formed, and they should be correct ones.

After early childhood comes the stage of growing to cognitive and physical maturity. For Quintilian these years were a time of developing literary skills, learning subjects, and being socialized with the right kind of peers. In the last stage of formal education, in the school of rhetoric, Quintilian stood firmly in the tradition of the liberal arts, which he regarded as essential in forming the properly educated human being.

In developing his educational theory, Quintilian was able to formulate a body of ideas that integrated the continuity of the Roman past with Greek culture. He desired to transmit what he regarded as the value-laden elements in the Roman heritage as a part of moral education. He was well versed in the theory that had been articulated before him, particularly that of Isocrates. As a coherent body of educational doctrines that applied to curriculum and methodology, Quintilian's ideas about education held together and were consistent.

Although Quintilian followed the oratorical model devised by Isocrates, the political changes that had transformed Rome from a republic to an empire also affected rhetorical education. During the republic, oratory could be used as an instrument of power to shape policies. Cicero's death in 43 B.C.E. marked the end of the republican conception of the orator as a statesman who would dynamically influence public opinion and policy. With the coming of imperial rule, actual power shifted to the emperor. In some situations, real power resided with those who advised, influenced, or actually controlled the emperor. As the Roman Empire began to decline and near its end, power often gravitated to the military and its leading generals, relegating the emperor to more of a figurehead position.

Just how congruent was Quintilian's educational theory with the realities of Roman political life? The question of how well formal education relates to a society's political, economic, and intellectual realities is always serious and difficult for educational policy makers. This question is just as important for our assessment of the adequacy of contemporary U.S. education as it was for Quintilian's Rome. To answer the question for Rome, we can reflect on the consequences of rhetorical education for the determination of policy, for the expression of eloquence, and for administrative service to the state.

In imperial Rome, actual decision making no longer rested with the Senate. Rather, it was lodged in the emperor or the imperial circle or in the army, depending on the situation. Traditional political institutions remained in the formal sense but had lost their dynamic quality. For instance, the Senate still met, but its functions were changed. Instead of debating and formulating policy, the Senate became a more ceremonial body that met to praise the emperor or to commemorate state triumphs and occasions.

Rhetorical education also remained but was growing formalized. For example, Quintilian constantly stated that students of rhetoric should concentrate on real situations and actual life and avoid the fictitious or the imaginative. These continual admonitions show that rhetorical studies were losing their immediate relationship to society and growing more into a classroom or academic study. Rhetoric remained an important preoccupation of the educated Roman elite during the imperial period but the meaning of public service had changed.

Although Quintilian might deny it, his conception of the orator had changed. The use of eloquence as an instrument of persuasion in the public forum had changed to speech that commemorated and ornamented occasions. Like today's commencement and graduation speakers, who rarely shape public policy by their addresses, the Roman orator graced public occasions. As public debate lost its power to influence events, Rome's orators became more stylized, ornamental, and formally eloquent.

The work of Quintilian and Isocrates had an important consequence in that it broadened the concept of the orator from strictly a public speaker to a more generalized public servant. The orator, educated in the rhetorical tradition, was a person prepared for many areas of public service, such as teaching, civil administration, and law. In particular, the empire needed civil administrators to represent its interests throughout the Mediterranean world. The kind of education that Quintilian offered was not unlike that of the civil servants who staffed the far-flung British Empire in the nineteenth and early twentieth centuries. Such individuals were educated in the liberal arts to give them a breadth of knowledge. This body of knowledge that originated in the past carried a sense of traditional culture. The logic and organizational skills that made an orator effective at the podium could be recast by the civil servant and effective administrator.

Finally, we come to the enduring significance of Quintilian in the evolution of the history of Western educational ideas. The reconstructed concept of the orator as civil servant and administrator would slowly turn rhetoric into the art of writing as well as the art of speaking. In the Medieval era, the art of writing came to dominate rhetoric and gave it a different educational meaning.

Quintilian was one of those educators who helped shape and transmit the bodies of knowledge known as the liberal arts. These areas of human knowledge survived the fall of the Roman Empire. After much debate, they became part of the educational preparation of the Medieval scholastics. Quintilian's ideas on education, along with those of Isocrates, would surface again during the Renaissance when humanist educators such as Vittorino da Feltre and Erasmus looked to the classical traditions of Greece and Rome to guide their efforts at reviving literary humanism. Once they became part of the classical humanism of the Renaissance, they found their way into the preparatory and advanced education of the Reformation and continued onward in the select secondary schools of the post-Reformation era.

Quintilian's efforts to develop a coherent doctrine of rhetorical education remain useful in illustrating several enduring educational issues. In trying to integrate traditional Roman values and the new Greek learning, he had to deal with continuity and change. Educators today face similar problems of integrating cherished values with new ideas and technologies. Quintilian was in many ways the complete educational theorist in that his ideas on education formed a coherent body of doctrines that covered the human life span, from early childhood to maturity. In dealing with Greek culture and education, Quintilian integrated valuable transcultural elements into his conception of education. If Quintilian faced this problem and possibility in the days of limited communication of ideas, just think of how important such integration is today in a world of rapid communication. Finally, in terms of his educational theory, Quintilian was both a victim and victor of changing political and social circumstances. In one way, Rome's political changes made rhetorical education formal and irrelevant, yet in another way gave it a new relevance. Today, the issue of what makes education meaningful and relevant to U.S. society remains a perennial question.

Questions for Reflection and Dialogue

1. How relevant was rhetorical education for Rome's social and political context? Is it relevant for the contemporary United States? Consider your answer in terms of how candidates campaign for political office.
2. How did rhetorical education form an intellectual bridge or means of integrating Greek and Roman educational ideas?
3. Using the educational ideas of Plato and Aristotle as a frame of reference, critique Quintilian's theory and practice of rhetorical education.
4. Is the theory of rhetorical education applicable to contemporary education?
5. As a theorist of education, what were Quintilian's most useful contributions?
6. Examine the rhetorical or oratorical styles of important contemporary speakers. Do you find any similarities between Quintilian's theory and their styles of oratory?

Projects for Deepening Your Understanding

1. Attend a political debate or discussion or watch one on television. Analyze the speaker's use of language, humor, and examples. Then write a critique of the speaker's style according to Quintilian's theory of rhetorical education.

2. Attend a convocation or commencement at your college or university. Analyze the speaker's use of language, humor, and examples. Then write a critique of the speaker's style according to Quintilian's theory of rhetorical education.

3. View several commercials on television. Determine how the commercial is designed to attract your attention and motivate you to buy the product. Does a theory of rhetoric underlie the commercial? Write an analysis of your impressions of the packaging of commercials on the contemporary media.

4. Visit several classes in elementary, secondary, or higher education and listen to the teacher's talk. How does the teacher use language to get attention, to motivate students, to present a lesson, and to elicit a response from students? Analyze your findings and determine if a theory of rhetoric or public speaking is present.

5. Assume you are enrolled in Quintilian's school of rhetoric and required to make a speech persuading high school graduates to become teachers. Record your speech, play it back, and then analyze it according to Quintilian's style of rhetoric.

6. In an essay, critique rhetorical education from the Platonic perspective.

Notes

1. H. I. Marrou, *A History of Education in Antiquity* (New York: Mentor, 1964), 325–41.

2. Costas M. Prousis, "The Orator: Isocrates," in Paul Nash, Andreas Kazamias, and Henry Perkinson, eds., *The Educated Man: Studies in the History of Educational Thought* (New York: John Wiley & Sons, 1966), 54–76.

3. Edward J. Power, "Isocrates: A Theory of Literary Humanism," in his *Evolution of Educational Doctrine: Major Educational Theorists of the Western World* (New York: Appleton-Century-Crofts, 1969), 25–54. Also see Gerald L. Gutek, *A History of the Western Educational Experience* (Prospect Heights, IL: Waveland, 1995), 52–54.

4. L. Glenn Smith, ed., *Lives in Education: People and Ideas in the Development of Teaching* (Ames, IA: Educational Studies, 1984), 30–32.

5. J. J. Chambliss, *Educational Theory as Theory of Conduct: From Aristotle to Dewey* (Albany, NY:

State University of New York Press, 1987), 37–38.

6. Miriam Brody, "The Vindication of the Writes of Women: Mary Wollstonecraft and Enlightenment Rhetoric," in Maria J. Falco, ed., *Feminist Interpretations of Mary Wollstonecraft* (University Park, PA: Pennsylvania State University Press, 1996), 107.

7. Power, *Evolution of Educational Doctrine*, 87–90. Also see George Kennedy, *The Arts of Rhetoric in the Roman World: 300 B.C.–A.D. 300* (Princeton, NJ: Princeton University Press, 1972), 487–514.

8. Aubrey Gwynn, "Quintilian," in *Roman Education from Cicero to Quintilian* (New York: Russell & Russell, 1964), 180–241.

9. Power, *Evolution of Educational Doctrine*, 91–92.

10. Kingsley Price, *Education and Philosophical Thought* (Boston: Allyn & Bacon, 1963), 81–109.

Suggestions for Further Reading

Bonner, Stanley F. *Education in Ancient Rome.* Berkeley, CA: University of California Press, 1977.

Chambliss, J. J. *Educational Theory as Theory of Conduct: From Aristotle to Dewey.* Albany, NY: State University of New York Press, 1987.

Cicero, Marcus Tullius. *Cicero's Caesarian Speeches: A Stylistic Commentary.* Chapel Hill, NC: University of North Carolina Press, 1993.

———. *On Duties.* New York: Cambridge University Press, 1991.

Fuhrmann, Manfred. *Cicero and the Roman Republic.* Oxford, UK, and Cambridge, MA: Blackwell, 1992.

Gwynn, Aubrey. *Roman Education from Cicero to Quintilian.* New York: Russell & Russell, 1964.

Habicht, Christian. *Cicero: The Politician.* Baltimore, MD: Johns Hopkins University Press, 1990.

Horne, Herman H. *Quintilian on Education.* New York: New York University Book Store, 1936.

Kennedy, George A. *The Art of Rhetoric in the Roman World: 300 B.C.–A.D. 300.* Princeton, NJ: Princeton University Press, 1972.

———. *Classical Rhetoric and Its Christian and Secular Tradition from Ancient to Modern Times.* Chapel Hill, NC: University of North Carolina Press, 1980.

———. *Quintilian.* New York: Twayne, 1969.

Kerferd, G. B. *The Sophistic Movement.* Cambridge, UK: Cambridge University Press, 1981.

Marrou, H. I. *A History of Education in Antiquity.* New York: Mentor, 1964.

Mitchell, Thomas N. *Cicero: Senior Statesman.* New Haven, CT: Yale University Press, 1991.

Murphy, James J., ed. *Quintilian On The Teaching of Speaking and Writing.* Carbondale, IL: Southern Illinois University Press, 1987.

Nash, Paul, Kazamias, Andreas, and Perkinson, Henry, eds. *The Educated Man: Studies in the History of Educational Thought.* New York: John Wiley & Sons, 1966.

Power, Edward J. *Evolution of Educational Doctrine: Major Educational Theorists of the Western World.* New York: Appleton-Century-Crofts, 1969.

Quintilian. *The Major Declamations Ascribed to Quintilian.* Lewis A. Sussman, trans. Frankfurt am Main; New York: Verlag P. Lang, 1987.

———. *The Minor Declamations Ascribed to Quintilian.* Michael Winterbottom, ed. Berlin; New York: De Gruyter, 1984.

———. *Quintilian on Education.* William Mitchell Small, ed. New York: Teachers College Press, 1969.

———. *Quintilian on the Teaching of Speaking and Writing: Translations from Books One, Two, and Ten of the Institutio Oratoria.* James Jerome Murphy, ed. Carbondale: Southern Illinois University Press, 1987.

Smith, L. Glenn, and Smith, Joan K., eds. *Lives in Education: A Narrative of People and Ideas.* Mahwah, NJ: Lawrence Erlbaum Associates, 1995.

Vasaly, Ann. *Representations: Images of the World in Ciceronian Oratory.* Berkeley, CA: University of California Press, 1993.

PART

II

Thomas Aquinas: Scholastic Theologian and Creator of the Medieval Christian Synthesis

This chapter examines the life, educational philosophy, and contributions of Thomas Aquinas (1225–1274), a prominent theologian and philosopher of the Middle Ages. Aquinas created a theological and philosophical synthesis that incorporated Christian doctrines with the inherited tradition of classical philosophy, especially Aristotle's Natural Realism. Aquinas's synthesis of Aristotelian philosophy and Christian faith was of great educational importance for Medieval times and for later decades as well.

We will examine Aquinas's contributions to theology and philosophy in the historical context of the Middle Ages and in terms of their enduring effect. First, we describe the cultural, religious, and intellectual context in which Aquinas lived and worked. Second, we explore Aquinas's biography, education, and career in terms of the evolution of his ideas. Third, we assess the continuing significance of Aquinas's contributions to Western education. In the case of Aquinas, we shall see the interrelated dynamics of theology, philosophy, and education. With Aquinas, as well as the educational theorists of the Reformation who we will examine in later chapters, we examine a way of thinking—theology—that we consider for the first time in this book. *Philosophy* can be defined in its broadest terms as speculation about the human being's relationship to the universe or the cosmos; *theology* refers to speculation about the human being's relationship to God. Aquinas grappled with both philosophical and theological issues before devising his theistic realism, which blends both dimensions of human thought.

To organize your thoughts as you read Chapter 6, focus on the following questions:

1. What were the major trends in the Medieval historical context in which Aquinas lived?
2. How did Aquinas's life, his educational biography, shape his philosophy and theology of education?
3. How did Aquinas's theology and philosophy determine his educational policies and practices?
4. What is the significance of Aquinas's contributions to Western education?

The Historical Context of Aquinas's Life

In discussing the Medieval context in which Aquinas lived, we shall view the thousand years historians call the Middle Ages as one great historical mosaic. In this perspective, the vast temporal landscape is composed of people, events, and situations. Our purpose is not to render a detailed chronology of the Middle Ages but rather to probe the major currents that shaped Aquinas's worldview. The Medieval centuries, 500 to 1400 C.E., are also designated the *Middle Ages* because they lie between the end of the Roman Empire and the onset of the Renaissance.

For educational historians, the Roman empire's collapse marks the closing of the Graeco-Roman classical period as a dynamic era in the origin of educational ideas. Although it lost many of its dynamic characteristics, the influence of classical learning has persisted in the Western educational heritage to the present. With the Renaissance would come a revitalization of classical learning in the West.

To understand the Medieval psyche that Aquinas shared, it is necessary to identify the following currents that shaped the time:

1. The entry of Christianity into the West and the Medieval reformulation of that religion
2. The destabilization of the Roman political and economic order and its replacement by feudalism and manorialism
3. The hierarchical organization of Medieval thought and institutions into a theological-philosophical synthesis
4. The scholastics' role in the culture of Medieval universities

Christianity, based on the teachings of Jesus of Nazareth, entered the West from Judea as the new religion's disciples, such as St. Paul, evangelized the Graeco-Roman world. Although early Christians had internal disagreements, they generally agreed on such basic doctrines as the following:

1. Jesus, the Son of God, who came to Earth as a man, possessed both a human and a divine nature.
2. Jesus' appearance on Earth occurred in Judea, at a given historical time and place, in fulfillment of the Hebrew scriptures, particularly the books of the Old Testament.
3. Jesus was crucified and died to atone for human sin, especially the original sin of Adam and Eve.

4. He rose from the dead, reappeared to his apostles, and then ascended into heaven.
5. By his death and resurrection, Jesus redeemed a fallen humanity and promised those who followed in his way supernatural salvation in heaven.
6. His apostles, disciples, and converts to the new faith were to preach the gospel, the story and message of Jesus as recorded by the Evangelists, to people throughout the world.

The early Christians were *proselytizers*, or convert seekers, who energetically preached the new religion throughout the Roman empire.

For these early Christians, the true God was a supernatural creator, a supreme and perfect being, not like the Roman emperors, who, although claiming divinity, fell from power and perished like other mortals. There was one God only, not the polytheistic pantheon of the traditional religions of ancient Greece and Rome. The purpose of life on Earth was to merit the eternal reward of the supernatural life that came after the body's death. Service to the emperor and the state was secondary to this higher and otherworldly purpose. The Roman imperial establishment saw the early Christians as subversive radicals who threatened Rome's political authority and traditional values. Christians were persecuted by Roman officialdom, with the severity of the persecution depending on the emperor's personality and the state of imperial problems and politics. Despite their adversities, Christians made converts and advanced from being a persecuted small sect to being tolerated, finally becoming declared the state's official religion.

Although it would come to be encoded in a complex theology, early Christianity's ethical principles simply enjoined believers to love God and each other. The new religion's teachings were found in the Gospels of the New Testament in which Jesus spoke to his followers in parables. Additionally, there were the sermons and letters that the leaders of the new Church addressed to congregations of believers throughout the empire. As the Christian church gained respectability and acceptance, church councils met in which the bishops clarified doctrines. The milieu in which Aquinas functioned as a theologian, philosopher, and educator was shaped by these currents in the Christian worldview.

The Mediterranean and Aegean worlds in which the Christians lived already possessed a well-developed intellectual and educational heritage that had been articulated by philosophers such as Plato and Aristotle and rhetoricians such as Isocrates, Cicero, and Quintilian (see Chapters 3, 4, and 5). At the core of this cultural inheritance was the body of knowledge known as the liberal arts. For the early Christian leaders, the presence of this pre-Christian knowledge posed serious educational questions related to the issue of continuity and change. Classical learning, particularly the philosophies of Plato, Aristotle, and other thinkers, formed a major part of the continuum of knowledge. The important element of change came from the new religious belief system, the doctrines of Christianity. For the Christians, the question was whether this pre-Christian, pagan literature was harmful or beneficial to believers' faith and morals. Some church fathers, declaring its effects pernicious, wanted it destroyed. Others, seeing it as a legacy from the past, wanted it preserved but not made part of Christian education, lest it confuse the faithful. Still other church fathers insisted that classical literature, especially the liberal arts, should not only be preserved but also form an integral part of a Christian's higher education.

Although many church leaders debated the relevance of the liberal arts in Christian education, St. Augustine (354–430), the bishop of Hippo, played a preeminent role.[1] Augustine's life, education, conversion to Christianity, and rise to prominence as a theologian illustrate the intellectual tensions found in early Christianity. Educated in the liberal arts, Augustine, the son of a Roman official, had studied rhetoric. Before his conversion to Christianity, Augustine was intrigued by Manichaeanism, a philosophy that portrayed the universe as locked in a continual struggle between good and evil, and skepticism, which though asserting thought to be a human's highest pleasure, denied that it was possible to know anything completely. After rejecting these philosophies, Augustine studied Neoplatonism, which stressed Plato's themes of the existence of an intellectual order in the universe, that goodness was related to intelligence, and that the chain of universal being led upward to the supreme and highest good, the ultimate object of human knowledge. These Platonic themes related well to Augustine's eventual conversion to Christianity at age 34. He was ordained as a priest and subsequently made a bishop. A learned father of the church, Augustine wrote *The Confessions, On the Trinity, The City of God, On Christian Doctrine*, and *de Magistro*, a treatise on education.

Convinced the liberal arts were essential in forming educated Christians, Augustine designed a cultural and intellectual bridge between classical and Christian civilizations. The liberal arts of classical Greece and Rome—grammar, logic, rhetoric, arithmetic, geometry, music, and astronomy—provided a corpus of necessary studies for higher education. Aided by the spiritual power of grace—the interior light of the mind—the liberal arts, because of the intellectual discipline they provided, led the person onward to seek a higher truth. They led to a philosophy by which humans speculated about their relationship to the universe. Philosophical pursuits had the power of leading the mind still farther upward to the higher study of the Christian Scriptures. The revealed word of God, Augustine believed, leads the inquirer—aided by faith—to theology, the discipline by which humans systematically search for divine truth and reflectively examine their relationship to God.[2] Thus, Augustine argued successfully that the liberal arts, inherited from classical Greece and Rome, should be part of the intellectual formation of the educated Christian. Aquinas would construct his theological and philosophical synthesis on the foundations of Augustine's earlier work.

In addition to these intellectual developments, the Middle Ages was a time of political and economic destabilization caused by Rome's fall. When the Roman empire disintegrated, the imperial government's political control also disappeared. With the demise of the empire's central authority, political control gravitated to the various provinces and localities that had once been under imperial jurisdiction. During the Medieval millennium, local rulers—kings, dukes, counts—asserted themselves as political authorities. In the feudal system that evolved, these rulers became overlords to vassals who owed them fealty and support. Thus, a decentralized political system emerged.

Without imperial support, the transportation and trade networks that had linked the Roman world also disintegrated. Economic production and consumption, like political life, devolved to the locality. The large Roman estate, the *latifundia*, devolved into the manor, a self-contained and largely economically self-sufficient unit of land. In this localized political and economic situation, land ownership became the means of survival and the basis of power. The Medieval knights, the lords and their vassals who held secular political power, became the great landowners. The serfs, those who worked the land, although not slaves in the sense of old Rome, were nevertheless bound to lifelong labor for their masters.

The Medieval social, political, and economic order was a fragile balance that, though not far in time from what had been the grandeur and order of imperial Rome, was always perilously close to degenerating into barbarism. In this period of political and economic disintegration and reintegration, the Christian church in the West—the Latin or Roman Catholic Church—rose as the most prominent and often most powerful institution. The church's institutional authority extended to education, within which Thomas Aquinas and other scholastic philosophers worked.

In the West, the church emerged as the sole institution to claim a universal authority that transcended the Medieval world's localism and provincialism. The bishop of Rome, located in the old imperial capital, became the pope, the supreme pontiff and visible head of the church on Earth. In many ways, church administration paralleled that of the old Roman imperial government. The pope became a kind of spiritual emperor and the curia, his administrative and theological advisers, acted as a kind of senate. Although the popes consistently asserted spiritual authority, the degree to which they exercised temporal, or political, authority varied with the leadership style of the particular pope and the degree to which the kings of the various realms sought to challenge him.

The church as it evolved in the Middle Ages came increasingly to stress the concept of *hierarchy*, in its broadest sense, an order or ranking to reality, to ideas, and to people. (Recall that Plato, too, used the concept of hierarchy when he structured social order in *The Republic*.) Dominating Medieval thought, the concept of hierarchy was integral to the Medieval synthesis in which Aquinas operated. The existence of a hierarchy means that not everything and everybody are equal. Depending on the organizational basis, some ideas, people, and things are higher and, perhaps, even better than other ideas, people, or things.

During the Middle Ages, the church came to be governed by organized bodies of ecclesiastical officials arranged in successive and subordinate ranks. At the hierarchy's summit was the pope, who held supreme authority over the church. Next were the bishops, who, subject to the pope, held authority in their dioceses, or ecclesiastical districts. At the local or parish level were the priests, who celebrated the liturgy and administered the sacraments to their congregations. The pope, advised by the curia and councils of bishops, determined doctrine and filled appointments when a bishopric fell vacant. The bishops ordained priests, whom they assigned to local parish churches.

In the Medieval period, the church exercised control over education and schools. At the parish level, there might be a school in which the parish priest or his assistant taught reading, writing, simple arithmetic, and the chants and hymns used in the mass, or liturgical service. The bishops maintained cathedral schools that taught the *studia generalia*, the general liberal arts, and the special studies that prepared a young man for the priesthood.[3] It should be mentioned that only a small minority of the male population attended these schools. The majority of the people—the serfs—were illiterate and unschooled.

In addition to the "secular clergy," so named because they were not members of specific religious communities, were the "regular clergy." The members of the regular clergy included those who lived as monks in monastic communities, such as the Benedictines, who followed the order of St. Benedict (480–543). There were also communities of religious women who followed the monastic way of life and lived in seclusion from the world. By the time of Aquinas, mendicant orders such as the Dominicans, founded by Dominic de Guzman (1170–1221), and the Franciscans, founded by St. Francis of Assisi (1182–1226), had been established. The mendicant orders were not monastic but ministered among the people. Differing somewhat on their specific patterns of organized religious life, the orders of priests, brothers, and nuns followed the particular religious rules established by their founder. They, too, were subordinate to the pope as head of the church. The religious orders performed a variety of educational services. The monasteries became centers for preserving and copying classical and religious texts and conducted monastic schools that taught basic skills along with the pattern of religious life unique to the community. Of importance for Aquinas was the *regula*, or rules, of the Dominicans, the order he joined. Known as the "order of preachers," the Dominicans became recognized experts in theology, and Aquinas became the most renowned of these theologians.

Although the principle of hierarchy was most evident in the organization of the church, it also influenced how people thought. The Middle Ages was one of the periods in history in which human concerns focused on religion. Those ideas, interests, and issues that were spiritual took priority over those that dealt with the natural order. For Medieval scholastics, the supernatural and the natural orders, although distinct, were complementary. The supernatural was the appropriate sphere for the soul, whereas the natural was that appropriate for the body. Although the two orders were complementary, the spiritual was clearly superior because the life of the soul would be eternal and destined for heaven.

The world of ideas in which Aquinas worked formed an all-embracing, overarching synthesis in which everything was related and ranked. Presiding over this worldview that encompassed the spiritual and physical dimensions of life was the church—the guardian of religious truth and morals. While theological issues within the doctrinal synthesis were intensely debated, dialogue was confined within the context of the first principles that sustained it. To leave the synthesis meant heresy and loss of the church's protection.

The Medieval university was the immediate context of Aquinas's scholarly and educational activities. The rise of Medieval universities, especially the University of Paris, which was Aquinas's intellectual home, represents the institutionalization of the major intellectual currents of the twelfth and thirteenth centuries. The development of Medieval higher learning was stimulated by the increased contact with Arabic scholars between 1100 and 1200, by the revival of urban society and economy, and by increasing demands for such learned specialists as theologians, jurists, and physicians.[4] Especially important for Western higher education was the intellectual conduit provided by Islamic scholars, who had made important original contributions to mathematics and medicine and who had preserved works of classical Greek authors hitherto lost to Western scholars. From the intellectual interface with Arab scholars, certain texts of Aristotle, Euclid, Ptolemy, and the Greek physicians entered the West.

In the thirteenth century, the rediscovery of many of Aristotle's works and their entry into scholastics' libraries posed a problem of reconciling authorities analogous to that faced earlier by Augustine. Some Christian scholars opposed Aristotle's philosophy because of its inadequacy in explaining the origin of human life as the creation of God. So fearful were some churchmen of the negative effect of Aristotle on the faith of believers that the bishop of Paris condemned several of the Greek philosopher's texts. Like Augustine before him, Aquinas found the task of reconciling Christian doctrine and classical philosophy to be an immense challenge. It was one that he would accomplish in his great synthesis.

In addition to establishing contact with the Arabic intellectual world, the Christian Crusades to capture the Holy Land stimulated a commercial revival. This economic revitalization helped support institutions of higher learning such as the universities.

The twelfth and thirteenth centuries marked the zenith of scholasticism as the preeminent method of inquiry during the Middle Ages. The Dominicans included prominent scholars whose lectures attracted large numbers of students. Abelard, the popular author of *Sic et Non*, drew hundreds to Paris to hear his lectures.

This complex of forces—new learning from Arab scholars, the revival of economic life, and the vitality of the scholastic educators—produced the Medieval universities. The existing institutions, such as the cathedral and monastic schools, though inadequate to process and analyze the expanding body of knowledge, provided the foundations for this educational expansion. From the cathedral schools, the corpus of fundamental knowledge organized in the liberal arts would remain at the intellectual core of the universities. To this would be added professional schools and specialized knowledge for theology, law, and medicine. For example, the University of Paris developed from the cathedral school of Notre Dame.[5]

Medieval universities were really corporations or guilds of masters, who were the professors, and students. As a guild, the faculties of the Medieval universities were preparing students to become teachers. The university professors were organized into faculties of liberal arts, law, medicine, and theology. Each faculty was empowered to teach, conduct examinations, and grant degrees. The possession of the *licentia docendi*, the forerunner of today's master's and doctoral degrees, meant the recipient had completed the required courses, had written and defended a dissertation, and was competent in the subject. The early universities were cosmopolitan and international in character in that students came from many lands. Because the language of instruction was Latin, these students could communicate with each other and follow their professors' lectures.

The University of Paris received royal recognition from King Philip Augustus of France in 1200 when he gave masters and students the privileged position of being under jurisdiction of special clerical rather than harsh secular courts. In 1231, papal recognition allowed it to establish its own regulations governing lectures and disputations.

The University of Paris became renowned as the authoritative institution for theology. Not only did it prepare theologians and future doctors of the church, but the faculty of theology was often consulted for its expert opinion on doctrinal issues. For Aquinas and other scholastics, theology was the major arena of scholarly inquiry. Characterized by the phrase, "I believe in order that I may know," Medieval scholastic thought was framed by the boundaries of Catholic doctrine. Although doctrinal essentials were to be accepted without question, their interpretation made for lively and often controversial debate. As a result of the "new knowledge" from the Arab scholars, the scholastics ventured into the problematic area of reconciling this new element with authoritative theological dogma. The work of the Medieval scholastics, especially in theology and philosophy, became so sophisticated and exacting that it produced a body of specialized knowledge. In a worldview that located theology at the summit of the hierarchy of knowledge, theological specialization attracted the best minds of the Medieval world, one of whom was Thomas Aquinas.

Thomas Aquinas as a Scholastic Theologian and Philosopher

In this section we examine Aquinas's life, career, and educational contributions. Aquinas was foremost a theologian and a philosopher. To appreciate his ideas on education, it is necessary to see them as a manifestation of his work on theology and philosophy.

Thomas Aquinas, the seventh son of Count Landulf of the wealthy feudal house of Aquino and his wife, Theodora, was born in 1225 in the family's castle of Roccasecca, near Naples in Italy.[6] Both parents were well educated according to the standards of the day. Theodora was Landulf's second wife. The family was large, consisting of nine children plus three sons from Landulf's first marriage.[7]

Landulf enrolled Thomas at the age of 5 in the monastic school of the famous Benedictine abbey at Monte Cassino, located in central Italy, east of the Rapido River. The ancient monastery, founded by St. Benedict in 529, located on a hill overlooking the town of Cassino, was noted for its large library of books on theology and philosophy, especially the writings of the early church fathers. Thomas studied in the monastery school from 1231 to 1239.[8]

In 1239, Aquinas went to the University of Naples, enrolling in its *studia generalia*, or liberal arts course. In Medieval universities, the study of the seven liberal arts of grammar, logic, rhetoric, arithmetic, geometry, music, and astronomy was preparatory to professional study. For example, the University of Naples offered the liberal arts program and three professional programs in theology, medicine, and law. Its academic strength, however, was in law.

Aquinas began his studies at age 14 and completed them in 1243 when he was 18. His program emphasized the study of texts, or *lectio*; disputations, or *disputationes*; and repetition, or *repetitiones*. Among the texts Aquinas studied were Aristotle's *Organon*; Boethius's commentaries; Priscian's *Institutiones*, a compendium on grammar; Donatus's *Ars Minor* and *Ars Major*; Cicero's *de Inventione*, on rhetoric; Euclid's *Elementa*, a geometry text; and Ptolemy's *Almagest*, on astronomy. Thomas thus was educated in the liberal arts, the intellectual and educational legacy from ancient Greece and Rome. His study at the University of Naples introduced him to Aristotle's logic and philosophy, which were emphasized at this southern Italian university, whose location made it accessible to intellectual currents from both Greece and the Arab world. His encounter with Aristotle's philosophy led him to devise his grand plan to create a comprehensive work, or *summa*, that united Aristotelian philosophy with Christian doctrine.[9]

At Naples, Aquinas in 1244 announced his intention of joining the Dominicans. Ranked among the most academically talented scholars in the Christian church, the Dominicans specialized in theology. His family, especially his mother, strongly opposed his decision to enter the Dominicans. She did not object to his entry into religious life, but preferred that he enter the Benedictines. As a Dominican, he could not control the family's wealth. Plotting his abduction from Naples, his mother and brothers confined him to the family castle at Roccasecca for a year. Unable to change his mind about becoming a Dominican, the family reluctantly released him. Thomas returned to the Dominicans in 1245.[10]

Aquinas's Dominican superiors, recognizing his intellectual giftedness, determined that he should pursue advanced studies. He was sent to the Dominican monastery of the Holy Cross in Cologne, Germany, where, studying under Albert, the Great, he remained until 1252. Here the Dominicans prepared members of their order intellectually in the liberal arts and in the *regula* established by St. Dominic. While at the monastery of the Holy Cross, Aquinas was ordained a priest. He also wrote one of his early essays, *On Being and Essence*.

Thus far in the education of Thomas Aquinas, the Medieval orientation to learning is clearly visible. His elementary education was under the religious auspices of the

Benedictines. His secondary education and the beginning of his higher education, too, were heavily shaped by the Dominicans, who directed him toward theological study. Most importantly, for a young man of intellectual promise like Aquinas, the life of the mind was directed to the spirituality that permeated the Medieval worldview.

Attracted to Europe's preeminent theological institution, Aquinas in 1252 entered the University of Paris. At this point in his career, he had already earned his bachelor's degree and had published his essay *On Being and Essence*. Like successful professors in contemporary colleges and universities, Aquinas possessed promising academic credentials and publications. Accepted for advanced graduate study leading to the *licentia docendi*, he was made an instructor. His academic situation was similar to a graduate teaching assistant in a large modern university who teaches general courses while studying for his or her doctorate, the degree needed to become a professor.

As an instructor at the University of Paris, Aquinas lectured in dogmatic theology, a course that emphasized the truths of revelation. He used Peter Lombard's *Libri Quator Sentiiarum*, or *Book of Sentences*, as a text. Lombard's book was considered an important text because it compiled writings of leading fathers of the church. Lombard was among the earliest proponents of the scholastic method that characterized instruction in the Medieval universities. In teaching the course, the lecturer began with a revealed truth as a premise and then argued rationally to a conclusion based on it.

In the scholastic method of teaching, the instructor lectured on the text, reviewed the arguments pro and con, provided explanations, and drew conclusions. The method was essentially book centered and relied on the lecture format. Aquinas published his interpretations on Lombard's work as *Commentary on the Sentences*. In 1256, the 30-year-old Aquinas was awarded the *licentiate*. Now a fully approved professor, he lectured on the Bible.

Devoting himself to scholarship and teaching, Aquinas wrote *Summa Contra Gentiles*, the *Summa Against the Gentiles*, which defended Christian doctrines against opposing views. *Summa Contra Gentiles*, used as a manual of Christian teaching, was divided into four topics: God, creation, providence, and salvation.[11] In this book, Aquinas challenged how Arab scholars such as Averroes had interpreted Aristotle. While Averroes suggested that Aristotle's concept of the intellect was a power shared by the whole human race, Aquinas developed the counterargument that each person, who had an individual soul, also possessed an individual intellect.[12] Although the issue of the intellect might seem obscure, Aquinas's interpretation moved to make the case of Aristotle's compatibility with Christian doctrine. Aquinas continued his efforts of reconciling Aristotle's philosophy with Christianity, writing line-by-line commentaries on Aristotle's works *De Interpretatione*, the *Posterior Analytics*, *Metaphysics*, and the *Nicomachean Ethics*.[13] Aquinas's efforts would lead to his most comprehensive theological work, the *Summa Theologiae*. Additionally, he wrote about education and teaching in *de Magistro*.

From 1259 to 1269 Aquinas was away from the University of Paris, working at other assignments for the Dominicans. He returned to Italy where he attended Dominican provincial chapter meetings. Most of the time, however, he resided at Santa Sabina in Rome. Encouraged and supported by Pope Urban IV, Aquinas continued working on the *Summa Theologiae*. In 1269, he returned to the University of Paris, where he completed this major work and continued teaching and writing until his death in 1274.

Aquinas and Theistic Realism

Thomas Aquinas was one of those commanding scholars who was able to reconcile ideas and construct an all-embracing intellectual synthesis. In building his synthesis in the *Summa Theologiae*, Aquinas sought to integrate into the Christian intellectual heritage two great principles: the importance of divine revelation as the ultimate source of truth and the validity and efficacy of human reason. Rather than condemn Aristotle's ideas, Aquinas determined to use them. For him, Aristotle's natural sciences, ethics, and politics commented on an intelligible natural order that could be raised to a higher dimension by faith. Aristotle's natural virtues, when infused by grace, could become supernatural virtues.

Thomism, as Aquinas's philosophy is known, was a variety of religious or theistic realism. Like Aristotle, who saw reality divided into form and matter, Aquinas conceived of reality in two dimensions: the supernatural and the natural orders. Based on these dualistic conceptions, human nature has a spiritual dimension located in the soul and a physical dimension grounded in the body. The human being is an "incarnate spirit," or a "spirit in the world."[14] True to the Christian conception of human nature, Aquinas held that this soul, or spiritual essence, remained after the body's death. Through the spirit, human beings are related to their creator.

Aquinas, like Aristotle, recognized that the body positioned human beings in the natural order where they shared many characteristics with animals such as instincts, appetites, sexuality, and locomotion. These physical tendencies were raised to a higher dimension by reason and spirituality. All of the earthly tendencies were to serve man but were related to the purpose of existence—the ultimate spiritual goal for which human beings had been created.

Also like Aristotle, Aquinas argued that human ideas originated through the senses, which experienced an external world of objects. The mind, in turn, formed concepts as it extracted the form of the objects as conveyed with sensory data. Added to this natural power of cognition or conceptualization was the truth God revealed through Scripture. These scriptural truths and the doctrines of the church added to and completed the knowledge that humans developed through their reason.

The human being was endowed by God with free will—the power to make choices. The power of intellect enabled human beings to frame, weigh, and to choose and act on alternatives. This power of rationality was essentially as Aristotle had framed it. However, human beings who believed in Christianity had immense assistance in making correct choices from illumination provided by divine revelation and the guidance of the church.

Aquinas was primarily an academic who explored theological and religious themes in his research and writing. He established a conception of human nature possessing complementary spiritual and physical dimensions. Because of their common creator and their underlying spiritual nature, human beings shared a common human nature. Aquinas's conception of human nature held importance for educational theory. Because every individual person had a soul and intellect, it was possible to frame general educational goals. Each person possessed a supernatural soul that, if the person cooperated with grace, was destined to experience the beatific vision of God in heaven. For Aquinas, human life and destiny were purposeful in that there was meaning to existence in this God-created universe. A curriculum based on these core principles should emphasize religious and theological studies that cultivated human spirituality.

Believing that a human being's highest and defining power was reason, Aristotle argued that a person's greatest pleasure was in cultivating rational excellence, activity in accordance with intellectual virtue. Aquinas agreed with Aristotle that reason was a highly important distinguishing human power that inclined one to the truth. Reason, however, needed faith, which endowed human beings with the acceptance of revealed and doctrinal truth. Although Aquinas concurred with Aristotle on the importance of reason, he believed the greatest pleasure human beings could experience came from the supernatural life of the soul in the vision of God after death. The emphasis Aquinas gave to reason encouraged the study of philosophy and the liberal arts that were preparatory to it.

To Aquinas, the human person was a spirit or soul within a body. Although the spiritual side of human nature was of great importance, the physical side was not to be neglected. Each person on Earth inhabited a place at a given time and had a geographical relationship to the Earth and their own biography that was part of human history. Because people were communicators, endowed with powers of speech and hearing, language studies were important. Because human beings sustained themselves by work and economic activities, these practical endeavors were important. What emerged in the Thomistic curriculum was a hierarchy of studies, with religious studies at the summit, moving gradually downward to those that cultivated rationality, finally reaching those bounded by space and time that dealt with earning a livelihood and the economic sustenance of society.

Although Thomistic education gave priority to theological and philosophical studies, Aquinas recognized that human beings, endowed with intelligence and free will, could and should act to transform their environment and make it as hospitable as possible. Although religious, the Thomistic view was not fatalistic. Human beings, guided by faith and reason, were to use their powers to formulate plans and actions to improve life on Earth.

Thomas Aquinas can be described either as a philosopher who dealt with theological issues or as a theologian who philosophized. He also taught and wrote on educational themes. In *de Magistro*, he developed a theory of education that complemented his broader philosophical and theological work. From his view of human nature, certain themes emerge in Aquinas's philosophy of education:

1. Education, like life itself, is purposeful; it is a means to an end. Human beings' ultimate destiny is the beatific vision of God, and education should contribute to realizing that goal.
2. Reality exhibits two dimensions, one spiritual and one physical. Education relates to both dimensions of human nature: the soul and the body. It should prepare the human being for what needs to be done on Earth and what will contribute to the salvation of the soul.
3. Reality—both supernatural and natural—is hierarchically structured as is society, both secular and religious. Because not all things are equal, education, especially the curriculum, should be structured hierarchically with the most important areas of study receiving the greatest priority.

In true scholastic fashion, Aquinas made some important definitions and distinctions relating to education and schooling. Education, broadly construed, contributed to the human being's total formation of the state of excellence or virtue.[15] As the process of total human formation, education encompassed schooling but was much more than formal instruction. Aquinas recognized that many agencies—the family, church, and society—played educative roles.

Aquinas referred to formal education, or schooling, as *disciplina*, when a teacher teaches some knowledge or skill to a learner.[16] This teaching involves three necessary elements: a skill or body of knowledge, a teacher, and a learner.

Aquinas combined a basic Aristotelian strategy in structuring instruction with the scholastic method used in the Medieval universities. The subject matter of instruction was *scientia*, an organized body of knowledge that contained (1) principles, (2) systematic logical development that supported these principles, (3) analogies and examples that illustrated them, and (4) conclusions. This particular format of instruction was well suited to theology and philosophy.

Aquinas's model teacher was a person who integrated knowledge and virtue as two interpenetrating elements of professional life. A person was "called" to teaching in a way that was similar to the priest's vocation, or call to service. The teacher's service to humanity was an act of love. Although the sense of loving service was necessary in the character of the good teacher, the force of personality was insufficient in itself. Teaching means that the teacher possesses a body of knowledge and the instructional skills to transmit it to students. In the Thomistic conception of instruction, teachers needed to possess rhetorical skills so that they could use language with facility; they also needed logical skills to organize their instruction according to the premises that organized the body of knowledge.

To Aquinas, a teacher's life was highly integrated in that the various elements of teaching fused harmoniously. First, becoming a teacher meant the person had a commitment to a life of service. Second, through diligent study, the teacher came to possess a body of knowledge. These elements contributed to a life that was both contemplative and active. For Medieval priests, monks, and nuns, contemplation was an important aspect of religious life. It meant they could isolate themselves from the pressures of everyday life and, in quietude, reflect on the truly important matters that give purpose and meaning to existence. Contemplation was also important for Plato's preparation of philosopher-kings in *The Republic*. Preparation for teaching also involved contemplation in that a teacher needed to study and reflect on sources and texts to incorporate them in lessons. Much of this preparation was done alone in libraries. Although contemplation was necessary in preparing to teach, instruction was active in that the teacher was deliberately transmitting a body of knowledge to learners. Knowledge was organized and presented so that students could grasp it.

In the Thomistic worldview, all things and all actions are purposeful in that they lead to an ultimate end. Teaching has as its proximate or earthly end the education or formation of students. It is to convey knowledge that will help them attain fulfillment on earth and salvation in heaven. In the Thomistic view of instruction, teachers can lead students to knowledge but only students have the power to acquire it. Students need to be ready to receive, study, and appropriate knowledge. The Thomistic school is a place of disciplined and purposeful activity directed to acquiring knowledge while recognizing the importance of spiritual grace in inclining students to truth.

Based on this conception of teaching and learning, it is possible to extrapolate some ideas about a school that reflects the Thomistic orientation. Educated in monastic schools and universities, Aquinas was educated in highly religious and highly academic environments. The Thomistic school, resting on definite theological and philosophical foundations, would emphasize structured teaching and disciplined learning. The school's climate would be charged with religious elements that reflected Christian faith and doctrine. Schooling would have a moral purpose in nurturing the habits, dispositions, and outlooks that inclined students to a purposeful life of faith and reason. In such an environment, teachers were to be models of virtue that students could imitate.

Conclusion: An Assessment

Our assessment of Aquinas's philosophy of education can be illuminated by examining certain features of Thomism that contribute to its viability as well as those features of contemporary U.S. society and education that might limit its applicability. Certain aspects of Thomism—its origin, development, and terminology—make it decidedly Medieval. Thomistic educational philosophy is most compatible with a hierarchically arranged society, which, in turn, reflects a hierarchical conception of the universe. The Medieval hierarchical structure is out of character with much of the American experience and outlook. When Europeans colonized North America, the Medieval era had already ended. The ideas and institutions the European colonists brought to the New World were more products of the Renaissance and the Protestant Reformation than the Medieval world. Although residues of Medievalism, especially in its aristocracy, persisted in Europe, North America was virtually free of it. When the American Revolution ended colonial rule, the United States was a nation conceived in the spirit of the eighteenth-century Enlightenment, not a product of Medievalism. The secularism and republicanism of the revolutionary generation of Americans were antagonistic to Medieval ideas.

In the history of U.S. public education, Medieval ideas and institutions were largely absent. The common school was a product of the twin forces of republicanism and Evangelical Protestantism. Progressive historians, including those who interpreted the history of U.S. schooling, tended to regard the Medieval centuries as "Dark Ages," devoid of those propensities that would contribute to a progressive future for humankind.

If Thomism found an intellectual home in the United States, it was in the schools, colleges, and universities established by Roman Catholic immigrants. Separating themselves educationally from what they regarded as Protestant-dominated institutions, Catholics created alternative schools. For a church whose governance was hierarchical and whose liturgy was largely celebrated in ceremonies that were Medieval in origin, Thomism, with its blending of theology and philosophy, provided a congenial intellectual perspective. Throughout the centuries, the Catholic Church continued to refer to St. Thomas Aquinas as the "philosopher" and the "angelic doctor."

Thomism dominated the philosophy of Roman Catholic colleges and universities in the United States, and generations of their students were intellectualized and socialized in the worldview it provided. Other philosophies were judged in terms of their conformity or divergence from Thomism.

In 1962, Pope John XXIII convened a church council, known as Vatican II, that brought significant changes to the Roman Catholic outlook on the world.[17] Vatican II, with its ecumenism, inaugurated an opening to the non-Catholic world. It brought about a number of liturgical changes, such as the celebration of the mass in the vernacular rather than the traditional Latin. One effect of the church council was to reduce the Medievalism that had characterized Roman Catholicism and to reassert what were claimed to be the practices of the early church. Although the philosophy of Thomas Aquinas might retain its esteemed position in the church and in Catholic colleges and universities, other philosophies challenged its supremacy.

Although Thomism can be assessed in terms of its compatibility with the U.S. historical experience and its role in shaping the intellectual outlook of Catholics in the United States, we may also examine it in terms of its continuing effect on the history of Western educational ideas. Aquinas developed one of the great syntheses in Western educational thought by integrating Aristotle's philosophy of natural realism with the doctrines of the Christian church. This synthesis, which fused the Greek and Roman classical intellectual heritage with the new cultural dynamic of Christianity, provided continuity between the past and the present. For centuries, the Roman Catholic Church carried forward both the classical Aristotelian emphasis on reason and the Christian emphasis on faith.

Aquinas's dualism, built on Aristotle's ideas, dichotomized life and learning into two dimensions: the spiritual and the corporeal. From this basic categorization came the extension of the spiritual into the intellectual dimension of theory and the corporeal into practice. This structuring of education into the theoretical and the practical characterized education long after Aquinas. This Aristotelian-Thomistic dualism would drive John Dewey to attack separations of thought and practice. Despite Dewey's criticism, the theory-practice distinction has remained an important characteristic of Western education.

Aquinas's emphasis on the rational, the intellectual, and the theoretical did not encourage human beings to be disembodied intellects. He recognized the importance of the corporeal or physical element of life as proper to the natural order. Rather than seeing spirit and body locked in perpetual war, he was a reconciler who saw the supernatural and natural orders as compatible and complementary. Perhaps the Thomistic worldview that saw the supernatural and the natural as compatible contains possibilities for ongoing synthesis in the modern world, which often sees the spiritual and the material dimensions of human nature at war with each other.

Questions for Reflection and Dialogue

1. How did and how does religion influence education and schooling? Consider such issues as the debate between evolution and creationism in the curriculum, prayer in schools, meetings of student religious groups on school property, and the posting of the Ten Commandments in schools. How might a Thomist react to these issues?
2. Aquinas argued that teaching is a vocation, a special calling to service. Do you agree or disagree? Are there differences between a vocation and a profession or are both concepts compatible?
3. Is there a difference between teaching a religion and teaching about religion? How might Aquinas reply to this question?
4. How did the Medieval context influence Aquinas's theology and philosophy of education?

5. How did Aquinas's theistic realism incorporate both Christian theology and Aristotelian philosophy?
6. Analyze the meaning of the term *hierarchy* and how it might be applied to the governance of educational institutions and to curriculum organization. If you are engaged in clinical experience or student teaching or are an inservice teacher, do you find any evidence of an institutional hierarchy functioning in your school?
7. Compare and contrast Plato and Aquinas on the concept of the *hierarchy*.

Projects for Deepening Your Understanding

1. Interview several experienced teachers on their decision to become teachers. For example, ask them: When did you decide to become a teacher? What motivated your decision to become a teacher? Would you encourage others to become teachers? What personal qualities are needed to be a competent teacher? Do you find teaching a satisfactory and fulfilling career? Then analyze your findings and determine if they support Aquinas's contention that teaching is a vocation.
2. Read the U.S. Constitution and determine what it says about religion and the federal government. How does separation of church and state and free exercise of religion affect American education? Write an opinion paper that examines teaching and religion in American public schools.
3. In a position paper, either support or oppose the following proposition: The United States is a country that is founded on Judeo-Christian principles.
4. In an essay, characterize the Medieval outlook and compare and contrast it with that of the contemporary United States.
5. Design a lesson plan to teach a subject or skill according to Thomistic educational principles.
6. In a paper, outline a curriculum organized on Thomistic educational principles.
7. In a paper, examine the concept of *dualism* and describe its educational implications.

Notes

1. Henry Chadwick, *Augustine* (New York: Oxford University Press, 1986).
2. Pearl Kibre, "The Christian: Augustine," in Paul Nash, Andreas Kazamias, and Henry Perkinson, eds., *The Educated Man: Studies in the History of Educational Thought* (New York: John Wiley & Sons, 1965), 96–112.
3. For the role of cathedral schools, see C. Stephen Jaeger, *The Envy of Angels: Cathedral Schools and Social Ideals in Medieval Europe, 950–1200* (Philadelphia: University of Pennsylvania Press, 1994).
4. Olaf Pedersen, *The First Universities: Studium Generale and the Origins of University Education in Europe* (New York: Cambridge University Press, 1997), 133–38.
5. The Medieval university is treated in Gordon Leff, *Paris and Oxford Universities in the Thirteenth and Fourteenth Centuries: An Institutional and Intellectual History* (New York: John Wiley & Sons, 1968); and Charles H. Haskins, *The Rise of Universities* (Ithaca, NY: Cornell University Press, 1957).
6. Anthony Kenny, *Aquinas* (New York: Hill & Wang, 1980), 1.
7. James A. Weisheipl, O.P., *Friar Thomas d'Aquino: His Life, Thought, and Work* (New York: Doubleday, 1974), 3–9.
8. John W. Donohoe, S.J., *St. Thomas Aquinas and Education* (New York: Random House, 1968), 23–57.
9. Donahoe, *St. Thomas Aquinas*, 26–31.

10. Donohoe, *St. Thomas Aquinas*, 27–33.
11. Thomas Aquinas, *On the Truth of the Catholic Faith*, trans. Anton C. Pegis (Garden City, NY: Image, 1955), 17.
12. Kenny, *Aquinas*, 18–19.
13. Kenny, *Aquinas*, 19.
14. Aquinas, *On the Truth of the Catholic Faith*, 62–96.
15. Donohoe, *St. Thomas Aquinas*, 58–96.
16. Donohoe, *St. Thomas Aquinas*, 58–96.
17. Giancarlo Zizola, *The Utopia of Pope John XXIII* (New York: Orbis, 1978), 255–84.

Suggestions for Further Reading

Aquinas, Thomas. *Saint Thomas Aquinas: The Treatise on Law*. Notre Dame: University of Notre Dame Press, 1993.
———. *Political Writings*. ed. R. W. Dyson. Cambridge, UK; New York: Cambridge University Press, 2002.
———. *Selected Writings*. ed. Ralph M. McInerny. New York: Penguin Books, 1998.
———. *A Shorter Summa: the Most Essential Philosophical Passages of St. Thomas Aquinas' Summa Theologica*. ed. Peter Kreeft. San Francisco: Ignatius Press, 1993.
Blanchette, Oliva. *The Perfection of the Universe According to Aquinas: Teleological Cosmology*. University Park, PA: Pennsylvania State University Press, 1992.
Brown, Peter. *The Rise of Western Christendom: Triumph and Diversity, AD 200–1000*. Cambridge, MA: Blackwell, 1996.
Chadwick, Henry. *Augustine*. New York: Oxford University Press, 1986.
Collins, Joseph Burns. *Catechetical Instructions of St. Thomas Aquinas*. Fort Collins, CO: Roman Catholic Books, 2000.
Crombie, A. C. *Science, Art and Nature in Medieval and Modern Thought*. Rio Grande, OH: Hambledon, 1996.
Davies, Brian. *The Thought of Thomas Aquinas*. New York: Oxford University Press, 1991.
Donohoe, John W., S.J. *St. Thomas Aquinas and Education*. New York: Random House, 1968.
Dunn, John. *Aquinas*. Cheltenham, UK; Lyme, NH: E. Elgar Pub., 1997.
Elders, Leo. *The Metaphysics of Being of St. Thomas Aquinas in a Historical Perspective*. Leiden and New York: E. J. Brill, 1992.
Fatula, Mary Ann. *Thomas Aquinas: Preacher and Friend*. Collegeville, MN: Liturgical Press, 1993.
Gilson, Etienne. *The Christian Philosophy of St. Thomas Aquinas*. Notre Dame, IN: University of Notre Dame Press, 1994.
Guagliardo, Vincent A., Hess, Charles R., et al. *Commentary on the Book of Causes*. Washington, DC: Catholic University of America Press, 1996.
Hall, Pamela M. *Narrative and the Natural Law: An Interpretation of Thomistic Ethics*. Notre Dame, IN: University of Notre Dame Press, 1994.
Jaeger, C. Stephen. *The Envy of Angels: Cathedral Schools and Social Ideals in Medieval Europe, 950–1200*. Philadelphia: University of Pennsylvania Press, 1994.
Kaufman, Peter I. *Church, Book, and Bishop: Conflict and Authority in Early Latin Christianity*. Boulder, CO: Westview, 1996.
Kenny, Anthony J. *Aquinas*. New York: Hill & Wang, 1980.
———. *Aquinas on Mind*. New York: Routledge, 1992.
Klauder, Francis J. *A Philosophy Rooted in Love: The Dominant Themes in the Perennial Philosophy of St. Thomas Aquinas*. Lanham, MD: University Press of America, 1994.
Leff, Gordon. *Paris and Oxford Universities in the Thirteenth and Fourteenth Centuries: An Institutional and Intellectual History*. New York: John Wiley & Sons, 1968.
McInerny, Ralph M. *Aquinas on Human Action: A Theory of Practice*. Washington, DC: Catholic University of America Press, 1992.
———. *A First Glance at St. Thomas Aquinas: A Handbook for Peeping Thomists*. Notre Dame, IN: University of Notre Dame Press, 1990.
Nelson, Daniel M. *The Priority of Prudence: Virtue and Natural Law in Thomas Aquinas and the Implications for Modern Ethics*. Washington Park, PA: Pennsylvania State University Press, 1992.

Pedersen, Olaf. *The First Universities: Studium Generale and the Origins of University Education in Europe*. New York: Cambridge University Press, 1997.

Piltz, Anders. *The World of Medieval Learning*. Totowa, NJ: Barnes & Noble, 1989.

Porter, Jean. *The Recovery of Virtue: the Relevance of Aquinas for Christian Ethics*. London: SPCK, 1994.

Richter, Michael. *The Formation of the Medieval West: Studies in the Oral Culture of the Barbarians*. New York: St. Martin's, 1994.

Shuster, George Nauman. *Saint Thomas Aquinas*. Norwalk, CT: Easton Press, 1985.

Selman, Francis J. *Saint Thomas Aquinas: Teacher of Truth*. Edinburgh, Scotland: T & T Clark, 1994.

Small, Brad. *War and Peace: the Just War Theory*. Houston, TX: Communican, 1993.

Woznicki, Andrew N. *Being and Order: The Metaphysics of Thomas Aquinas in Historical Perspective*. New York: Peter Lang, 1990.

CHAPTER 7

Desiderius Erasmus: Renaissance Humanist and Cosmopolitan Educator

This chapter discusses the life, educational philosophy, and contributions of Desiderius Erasmus (1466–1536), one of the leading classical humanist critics and educators of the Renaissance, the period of Western history known for the revival of humanist studies. The Renaissance is important in the history of Western educational ideas because it established patterns that shaped secondary education in both Europe and the United States.

We discuss Erasmus's influence on Western education in its historical context and in terms of its effect on educational philosophy and policy. First, we describe the general intellectual, social, and educational context in which Erasmus lived and worked. Second, we analyze Erasmus's education and career to determine the evolution of his ideas. Third, we assess the continuing effect of Erasmus's contributions to Western education. By examining this educator's life, we shall determine how the major historical transition from the late Middle Ages to the Renaissance shaped the educational culture of the times. For example, Erasmus developed his educational philosophy as he confronted the waning of Medieval scholasticism (discussed in Chapter 6) and the evolution of the new cultural dynamic of Renaissance classical humanism. As is true of the theorists examined earlier, Erasmus grappled with the problems of educational continuity and change.

To organize your thoughts as you read this chapter, focus on the following questions:

1. What were the major trends in the historical context of the Renaissance, the time and situation in which Erasmus lived and worked?
2. How did Erasmus's educational biography shape his philosophy of education?
3. How did Erasmus's educational philosophy determine his educational policies and practices?
4. What is the enduring impact of Erasmus's contributions to Western education?

The Historical Context of Erasmus's Life

Historians call the period from the late fourteenth through the early sixteenth centuries the Renaissance. As is true of most historical eras, historians disagree about the period's precise beginning and ending. Erasmus's life, however, squarely locates him in the Renaissance.

The term *renaissance* is used to designate a revival, a rebirth, or a renewal of interest in the humanist dimension of life and culture. The Renaissance marked the beginning of a "this worldly" view of life in contrast to the "otherworldly" perspective of the Middle Ages. For their sources of inquiry and inspiration, Renaissance humanist scholars and educators such as Erasmus looked back to the classics of ancient Greece and Rome. For Erasmus and the humanists, the Renaissance denoted the recovery of the pure Greek and Latin literature, free from the errors of the Middle Ages.[1] The Renaissance signaled a shift of emphasis from the predominantly spiritual orientation of the Middle Ages to a more humanistic perspective and a renewal of interest in the Greek and Roman classics as commentaries on human life.[2]

The Renaissance, marking the onset of the modern era, was a complex period of social, intellectual, and economic change. These economic changes not only altered the material foundations of society but also had important implications for intellectual life and for artistic and literary innovations. By the late Middle Ages, western Europe was enjoying economic revival and growth. Thriving commercial trade had stimulated the revitalization of cities. Because of their flourishing trade in the Mediterranean area, Italian principalities such as Venice and Florence were becoming centers of art and literature. German merchants, organized in the Hanseatic league, carried on a brisk trade in northern Europe. The revival of commercial life brought economic surpluses and stimulated new ideas. In what was called the "southern Renaissance" in the Italian states and principalities, part of the new wealth was channeled into subsidizing new patterns of art, architecture, literature, and education. Northern Europe, too, experienced a renaissance in art, architecture, and literature. Somewhat different from the southern Renaissance, that of northern Europe retained a religious emphasis as humanist scholars not only examined classical texts but turned their critical attention to scriptural and dogmatic works as well. Erasmus, for example, was a Christian humanist who believed that the revival of interest in the classics and classical style would contribute to a reexamination of the Bible as the pure source of God's revelation, free from the accretions of Medieval scholasticism.

The critical religious scholarship of northern European humanists such as Erasmus coincided with a weakening of the pope's authority. As the kings of nation-states consolidated and augmented their power, they came to resent papal interference in their realms. Disputes between the papacy and the French king grew so intense that King Philip IV invaded Italy, seized Pope Boniface VIII, and imprisoned him. A weakened papacy was moved to Avignon where, from 1309 to 1377, it functioned under the close scrutiny of the French king. During this period, rival popes claimed to hold authority in Rome. It was not until 1409 that the Council of Pisa ended these disputes.

The Renaissance, as a transitional period, was marked by highly significant changes in cultural and intellectual perspective, but these alterations were not uniform throughout Europe. The powerful spiritual and religious concerns of the Medieval era continued, diminished in some areas and redirected in others. In the southern Renaissance, creative artists, architects, and educators, subsidized by wealthy patrons, moved from religious to more humanistic themes and styles. Often, the architectural subjects were still churches and cathedrals but the ascetic styles of the Medieval era yielded to grandiose and palatial edifices. Art forms such as painting and sculpture, too, might still depict religious motifs but the figures and themes were often more earthly than ethereal. Inroads into what once had been dominated by the spiritual continued until a secular or romance literature carved out its own genre. For example, Dante (1265–1321) wrote his *Divine Comedy* in the Italian vernacular rather than in Latin. A writer whose outlook was poised between the Medieval and Renaissance worlds, Dante included figures from the classical period but put them in a Christian setting. Petrarch (1304–1374) was a classical scholar who preferred to write his sonnets in Italian.

If religious concerns were diminished among some scholars and educators, they were redirected for others into two areas: critical scholarship and active reform. Some individuals, primarily clerics preaching against corruption in the church, urged institutional and personal reformation. John Wycliffe, a professor of theology at Oxford University in England, preached against the growing materialism in the church. Urging a return to the early church's primitive simplicity, Wycliffe argued that the Bible should be the sole source of authority for Christians. In Bohemia, Jan Huss, preaching religious reformation, challenged papal and civil authorities. Huss was seized, tried, and condemned to death. These early attempts to reform the church anticipated the coming Protestant Reformation.

There were critical humanist scholars, like Erasmus, who favored religious reforms but wanted them to remain within the institutional and theological framework of a universal Christian church. Especially in the areas touched by the northern Renaissance—the Netherlands and the Low Countries, the German states, and England—religious issues were still a dominant but redirected set of interests. Just as they examined the ancient Greek and Latin texts, the classical humanists critically scrutinized Medieval works on Scripture, dogma, and doctrine with an eye for detecting errors.[3] These critical inquiries were directed against what was called the Medieval synthesis (see Chapter 6). The critical scholarship of the northern Renaissance would stimulate the Protestant Reformation. (The Protestant Reformation is treated separately in this book; some historians link it, however, directly with the Renaissance.)

At this point, we can consider the revival of the critical function of the educator. During all periods of history, educators transmit the cultural heritage, the legacy of the past. They also work within the institutional and ideational contexts of the period in which they live. Should educators transmit the heritage or should they attempt to change or reform the culture? Is it possible to do both? Socrates and Plato, dissatisfied with cultural changes in ancient Athens, tried to reverse them; Socrates criticized the popular opinions of his day and so did Plato. Medieval scholastics were concerned with transmitting the religious and doctrinal heritage. Although they might be critics, their major emphasis was on the synthesis rather than the deconstruction of ideas.

Renaissance humanists transmitted the classical heritage but were also severe critics. Erasmus, in particular, was a caustic critic of people, institutions, and ideas. Renaissance humanists operated as critics in several ways. First, they became experts in translating and interpreting the ancient Greek and Latin texts. Second, as recognized authorities, they made judgments about the authenticity and interpretation of these texts. Not always agreeing with each other, like modern professors, they carried on intense intellectual and academic debates. They also tended to write for those who shared their expertise rather than for a large popular audience. They became an intellectual elite, a select group of connoisseurs who regarded themselves as protectors and guardians of knowledge. Most of the time, the cultural criticisms of the humanist scholars stayed within their own academic circles. At other times, particularly when engaged in institutional criticism, their critiques entered the larger society, stimulating questions, raising doubts, and eroding established authorities.

Along with the economic and intellectual transformation of Western society during the Renaissance, a shift occurred in political identities and loyalties. The political decentralization of the Medieval era was replaced by centralizing tendencies in key parts of western Europe. In England, France, Spain, and Portugal the modern nation-state emerged. In these countries, monarchs represented the nation in a personal yet symbolic way. The nation and its monarch became the focus of loyalty, commitment, and identity for its citizens. The rise of nation-states, national monarchies, and nationalism itself set in motion tendencies that eroded the universal authority once held by the Christian church and the pope.

In the Italian peninsula, the German states, and eastern Europe, nationalist impulses also were being felt but were deflected by Medieval feudal residues. In the myriad German states, nationalist sentiments were present but submerged by the rule of the Holy Roman Empire. Italy was the location of a number of small states, duchies, and principalities, each with their own ruler who was constantly involved in intrigues, alliances, and counteralliances. Niccolo Machiavelli (1469–1527) wrote *The Prince*, a treatise on power politics, to guide his patron in gaining, using, and maintaining power. Machiavelli viewed human beings as weak but greedy individuals who followed their own self-interests. Such individuals needed to be kept in line by a strong ruler whose primary goal was to preserve, maintain, and extend his power. Using the doctrine that the end justifies the means, Machiavelli's strategy of political manipulation revealed shifts in political power.[4]

The rise of nation-states and their ruling dynasties had educational consequences. A new educated person appeared on the scene in the guise of the courtier—one who served at the royal court. Baldesar Castiglione described the *courtier* as an educated and intellectually versatile gentleman equally effective in statecraft, diplomacy, or poetry, depending on the situation.[5] Generally well-educated, the courtier, as an educational paradigm, was more versatile than the Medieval scholastic who concentrated on studying religious doctrines. At times, courtiers served as tutors to the children of the king or the lesser nobility. They might be advisers on affairs of state or serve as diplomats for the king.

Once the power of nation-states had been established internally, they began to look outward. Coastal nations such as Spain, France, England, Portugal, and the Netherlands sent navigators on voyages of exploration. The conquest of Constantinople by the Turks in 1453 had closed trade routes to the east and sent navigators sailing westward. Spurred by visions of wealth or the conversion of heathen peoples, these nations established trading colonies in Africa, Asia, and North and South America. These colonies marked the beginnings of the diffusion of western European culture across the Earth.

The educational situation of the Renaissance also can be considered in terms of continuity and change. The various schools associated with the church—the monastic, parish, and cathedral schools, and the universities—continued to function, as did the scholastic teachers within them. These older institutions were joined by a new one, the classical humanist school, and a new type of educator, the classical humanist. The educational currents of the Renaissance can be examined in terms of particular humanists and educational institutions. Some of the humanists functioned in institutional settings, whereas others operated independently. Often highly individualistic, the classical humanists should be seen as unique personalities who operated within a shared but loosely structured frame of reference. Among these humanist educators were Thomas Elyot (1490–1546), who, by translating the works of Isocrates, promoted the entry of Greek learning into England. Elyot's *The Boke Named the Governour*, addressing the appropriate education for the statesman, laid out a curriculum of Latin, Greek, the liberal arts, and the ancient classics. Louis Vives (1492–1540), who had been a student of Erasmus, served as a lecturer at Oxford and wrote *de Institutitione Feminae Christianae*, a treatise on educating noblewomen in the classical tradition. Roger Ascham (1515–1568), the tutor of Queen Elizabeth I, wrote *The Scholemaster*, which stressed the importance of Cicero and writing according to Ciceronian style (see Chapter 5).

Some humanist educators developed a new kind of educational institution—a school that stressed a curriculum based on the Greek and Latin classics. These classical humanist schools combined both a secondary and a preparatory function. They were secondary schools in that some of the older students had completed the primary branches of instruction, although some younger students entered the humanist school after mastering the basics of their own vernacular and simple arithmetic. The classical humanist schools were preparatory institutions that readied some of their students for admission to colleges and universities. These classical humanist schools—the Latin grammar school in England, the *gymnasium* in Germany, the *lycée* in France, and the *liceo* in Italy—developed into institutions that prepared the children of the upper classes, primarily if not exclusively males, as Europe's educated elite. This type of school was brought to North America in the form of the Latin grammar school in the Massachusetts Bay Colony.

One of the outstanding classical humanist schools was established by the Italian educator Vittorino da Feltre, who conducted a court school for his patron, the duke of Mantua.[6] The school was established to educate the children of the duke and his court officials in the classical languages and literatures. A few children from the lower classes also were admitted. Vittorino, following the basic guidelines of humanist education, sought to prepare well-rounded and generally educated persons who could assume leadership positions as civil servants, administrators, and diplomats. The way to accomplish this broad educational objective, he believed, was through the classics, which were the source of ethics, history, morals, and all other kinds of wisdom. Looking back to the

Greek and Roman past, Vittorino used Quintilian's treatises to guide curriculum and instruction.

John Collette, an English humanist, was impressed by his visit to a classical humanist school in Italy. When he returned to England, he established St. Paul's. This school, which originated as a Latin grammar school, became one of England's leading preparatory schools. On his sojourn to England, Erasmus visited Collette, and wrote a Latin grammar for use at St. Paul's.

The Renaissance was a time of intellectual ferment as Western culture moved from the Medieval to the modern world. Although there were new political, economic, and aesthetic developments, the greatest effect on education came by way of classical humanism. To illustrate an exemplarly classical humanist, we now turn to the life of Desiderius Erasmus.

Erasmus: Classical Humanist Educator

The following section examines the life, career, and contributions of Desiderius Erasmus. Although it is generally established that Erasmus was born in 1466, many of the events surrounding his birth are shrouded with controversy. The exact situation of his birth and family have been disputed.

He was born on October 27, 1466, either in Gouda or in Rotterdam, in the Netherlands. He is alleged to have been the illegitimate child of Gerard, a priest, and Margaret Rogerius, his housekeeper. Trying to conceal his illegitimate birth, Erasmus never disclosed his father's last name. In 1497, he added the name Desiderius and later adopted the name of the city of his birth, Rotterdam.[7] Sensitive about his illegitimacy, Erasmus attempted to create an appearance of legitimacy by altering his birthdate. He later claimed that his father was not ordained until after his mother's death.[8]

Erasmus began his schooling at age 6. He first attended a primary school at Gouda, then went to the cathedral school at Utrecht, and after that to St. Lebwin's school at Deventer, which was operated by the Brethren of the Common Life, a religious association. Founded by the Dutch religious reformer Gerhard Groote (1340–1384), the Brethren were not a conventional religious order but were rather an organization of individuals who followed a common devotional life, dedicated to performing charitable and educational good works.[9] The Brethren's elementary schools offered the usual primary subjects of reading, writing, arithmetic, and religion. The religious studies in the schools emphasized the Gospels, writings of the church fathers, and the lives of the saints. The unique characteristic of the Brethren's schools was their strong moral tone that emphasized charity in the imitation of Christ rather than formal theology.

Erasmus, in the school at Deventer for nine years, from 1475 to 1478, was identified early as an intellectually gifted student. However, in reminiscing about his school days, he found much to criticize about the Brethren, whom he felt had pressured him unduly into becoming a priest. He contended that the Brethren were more concerned with empty rituals, their own self-importance, and in keeping strict discipline rather than with encouraging genuine learning. Although finding little that was commendable about his teachers, his later writing would emphasize themes stressed by the Brethren such as the harmony of learning and religion and of reason and revelation.[10] Despite an aversion to some of his teachers, Erasmus esteemed teaching as a vocation. He would write that teaching was the "noblest of occupations" by which dedicated and skilled teachers had the opportunity of embuing the young with "the best literature and the love of Christ."[11] The importance of good literature, which to him was the Greek and Latin classics, and true Christian morality were persistent themes in Erasmus's philosophy of education.

In 1487, Erasmus entered the Augustinian priory at Steyn, where he continued advanced studies. He was still associated with the Brethren of the Common Life, who were supervised by the Augustinians. St. Augustine, for whom the order was named, had defended the compatibility of Greek and Roman knowledge with Christianity. At Steyn, he wrote *On the Contempt of the World*, a treatise defending monastic life. On April 25, 1492, at age 23, Erasmus was ordained as a priest under the jurisdiction of the Augustinian religious order.[12]

Identified as a promising young man of intellectual talent, Erasmus in 1495 entered the famous University of Paris for further studies in languages and Scripture. While at Paris, he supported himself by tutoring younger students in Latin grammar and rhetoric, subjects that would engage him throughout his life. His work as a tutor excited his interest in teaching. He wrote Latin exercises, in dialogue form, to teach his pupils correct Latin. Although published later, it is generally believed that his work as a tutor motivated Erasmus to write his *Colloquies*, which was subtitled *Formulas of Familiar Conversations by Erasmus of Rotterdam, Useful Not Only for Polishing a Boy's Speech But for Building His Character.*[13]

The *Colloquies* featured conversational dialogues in which participants engaged in intellectual discussions. The characters in these dialogues used correct patterns and styles of speech and also exhibited proper moral values. The *Colloquies* demonstrated Erasmus's conviction that good literature and morality reinforced each other. Another important theme in the *Colloquies* was the educational power of conversation. Erasmus believed that the free interchange of ideas between informed and cultivated people provided an exciting way to learn.

While at the University of Paris, Erasmus became a close friend of William Blount, an English aristocrat. Blount, in the Renaissance style, became a patron who subsidized Erasmus's journey to England. In England, Erasmus located at Oxford University. He became a member of a circle of humanist scholars including John Collette, dean of St. Paul's Cathedral and school, and Thomas More, the gifted jurist and diplomat. Eramus wrote a Latin grammar for use at St. Paul's school. He began a lifelong friendship with More, with whom he regularly corresponded. More, called a "man for all seasons," rose to become the chief chancellor of King Henry VIII. When he refused to support the king's divorce from Catherine of Aragon, More fell into disfavor, was tried for treason, convicted, and executed.

After his trip to England, Erasmus engaged in frequent travel, which he found to be highly educational. His journeys took him to the intellectual centers of France, Italy, and the Low Countries, where he engaged in lively conversations with Europe's leading humanist scholars. His travels enabled him to sharpen his language as well as his intellectual skills. A cosmopolitan scholar who felt at home in the company of other scholars, he believed that one could learn by associating with other learned persons, listening to them, reading their books, and discussing their ideas with them.[14] He especially treasured a Europe that was open to discourse that transcended national boundaries and sectarian barriers. When he saw religious warfare brewing between

Catholics and Protestants, Erasmus feared that the end of Europe's cosmopolitan dialogue was approaching.

A critic of what he considered to be abuses and corruption in the Catholic Church, Erasmus believed that the church had retained too many Medieval residues, especially in its formalism and ceremonies. He urged a return to the early church's simplicity and purity. He believed its educational endeavors were bogged down in the scholastics' preoccupation with metaphysical and theological subtleties rather than with biblically based ethics. However, Erasmus was convinced that the necessary reforms needed to take place within the Catholic Church. On the matter of internal reforms, he challenged Luther, Calvin, and others who determined that true religious renewal was possible only in reformed churches outside of the Catholic Church.

Erasmus was a prodigious scholar and author. He produced editions of such Fathers of the Church as Jerome, Cyprian, Hilary, Irenaeus, Ambrose, Augustine, and Origen. He prepared an edition of the New Testament in Greek. He wrote numerous moral, religious, political and educational commentaries, essays, and homilies.

In 1499, Erasmus published *Adages*, or *Familiar Quotations from the Classics*, a book on his favorite theme of combining literary models with moral instruction. In 1511, his distinguished reputation won him an appointment as a professor of divinity and Greek at England's Cambridge University. The next several years saw a steady stream of publications from Erasmus's pen.

In *Encomium Moriae*, or *The Praise of Folly*, Erasmus turned his pen against those whose arrogance and pomposity interfered with true humanist scholarship and teaching. He attacked teachers of grammar and dialecticians as engaged in fighting over hairsplitting trivialities rather than substantial learning. Lawyers, who assigned themselves to the highest rank in the learned, he accused of "stringing together six hundred laws in one breath," no matter how irrelevant. Sparing neither philosophers nor theologians from his critical barbs, Erasmus charged many supposedly learned philosophers with building imaginary "castles in the air" and disagreeing "violently and irreconcilably among themselves." Instead of working to resolve the conflicts in Christianity, Erasmus accused theologians of spinning intricate dogmatic webs in which to trap their unsuspecting victims.[15]

While a professor at Cambridge, Erasmus continued research and writing in two areas in which he specialized: the teaching of classical languages and biblical scholarship. In 1512, he published *de Copia*, a compendium of Latin words, phrases, and idioms designed to aid students in enlarging their vocabularies. Four years later, he completed his Greek version of the New Testament.

Erasmus's great work on political philosophy and education, *The Education of the Christian Prince*, appeared in 1516.[16] In this work, Erasmus, like Machiavelli, prescribed the political education of those who were born to rule. His advice to future rulers was far different from that of Machiavelli, who urged manipulation and subterfuge if necessary to maintain power. Instead of Machiavellian power politics, Erasmus drew an idealized portrait of a prudent, gentle, and humane ruler. If Machiavelli's treatise put forth one version of policy making, Erasmus offered the Christian prince an alternative.[17]

Erasmus advised the Christian prince to acquire a solid grasp of history and geography. He should make every effort to know thoroughly his subjects and his realm, including the location, economy, and demography of its provinces and cities. By studying history, the prince would learn the traditions and customs of each part of his realm.

Knowledge of geography and history would give him a sense of time and place and a familiarity with his people.

The Christian prince should be educated in the humanities and the principles of religion. A classical background would make the prince into an educated person able to deal with other educated people. Knowledge of religion would provide an ethical context for policy formulation and decision making. In addition to informing and guiding his own ethical conduct, a classical humanist education would help him judge the character of others. The prince who governed with a sense of justice could do so only if he was able to appoint competent and honest advisers, administrators, and diplomats who would conduct the affairs of state fairly and honorably for the good of all the people of the kingdom.

Although the Christian prince would not be a schoolmaster, he had an important educational role to play in his kingdom. As a personification of the good and ethical life, the Christian prince should serve as a role model for his subjects. Because the long-term health and prosperity of the realm depended on the proper education of children, he should provide and supervise schools and teachers. Erasmus advised the prince to exercise "greatest care" over teachers and schools so that children were taught by "the best and most trustworthy instructors." They were to "learn the teachings of Christ and that good literature which is beneficial to the state."[18] Such an education, Erasmus asserted, would incline the population of the realm to right conduct and lessen the need for coercion on the part of state officials.

In *Education of the Christian Prince*, Erasmus was developing a theory of education for peace and international education. He feared that the storm clouds of war, fueled by religious sectarianism and nationalism, were darkening Europe's horizons. He counseled the Christian prince to study the art of peacekeeping to avoid war. How ironic it was that priests should be blessing contending armies bent on killing fellow Christians in the name of religion! War carried myriad perils for the health and safety of the Christian realm. Even if war appeared to be for just causes, the entry into hostilities had deleterious effects. For Erasmus, even limited wars tended to escalate into larger ones. He admonished that war was like a plague that spreads from place to place. The costs of war were great in human and material resources that could be spent in human betterment rather than in human torment. When disputes among nations threatened to break into violence, Erasmus urged peaceful adjudication by international tribunals composed of wise and impartial arbitrators.

Erasmus on Education and Teaching

Although Erasmus saw intrinsic value in studying and commenting on ancient Greek and Roman texts, he also believed these works were of immense educational value in forming educated and moral persons. Along with the classical texts, Erasmus, as a Christian humanist, believed biblical study was needed to form the educated person. Encompassing both Christianity and the classics, Erasmus's educational philosophy was broadly conceived as a total formation, a Christian *paideia*, of the educated person. Concerned with language education, Erasmus also commented on specific aspects of instruction.

Like his humanist colleagues, Erasmus concentrated on teaching the ancient Greek and Latin languages and literature, which he believed contained almost everything worth knowing.[19] In particular, he believed that Latin, the language of international discourse during the Renaissance, was indispensable for the educated person. Classical literature, he believed, was the intellectual wellspring of Western culture, where all the knowledge of vital importance to humankind could be found.

Relying on Quintilian as a guide, Erasmus believed teachers needed to be well-educated individuals who, although scholars, avoided mindless pedantry (for Quintilian, see Chapter 5). Teachers should focus carefully on the quality of the literature selected as texts. It was imperative that classical humanist teachers possess a commanding knowledge of their subjects so that they could recognize and choose the best authors.[20] Not only did they need expert knowledge in the classical texts, they also needed to know such fundamental disciplines such as archaeology, astronomy, history, and mythology, which were of use in interpreting and explaining sources and references.

Again following Quintilian, Erasmus believed that instruction of children in correct speaking should begin at an early age. Because young children can learn to pronounce any language, they should begin with Greek and Latin along with their vernacular. In instructing children in language, the teacher, as a model, should speak as clearly and correctly as possible and encourage his students to imitate him.

Although Erasmus stressed memorization as did most humanist teachers, he also emphasized the importance of understanding content, theme, and meaning. He delineated a method of presentation structured around six objectives:[21]

1. Discuss the biography of the classical author whose text was being studied.
2. Identify the genre or type of work.
3. Discuss the theme or plot, especially the representation of time, place, and events.
4. Comment on the author's writing style.
5. Comment on the moral applications of the literary piece.
6. Extrapolate the cultural and philosophical implications of the work.

Although these objectives were to guide instruction, Erasmus did not want teachers to instruct their students in a rigid, lockstep fashion. He believed intellectual conversation in which students and teacher discussed ideas, content, and style of literary works was highly effective educationally. Complementing conversation, Erasmus recommended that students engage in the frequent writing of essays, poems, and stories to improve their expression and mastery of style. Another aid to learning he recommended was systematic note taking, a skill still practiced by successful students, especially those in college.

Conclusion: An Assessment

An assessment of Erasmus as an educator can be approached only in terms of the spirit of Renaissance humanism. Erasmus excelled in the qualities of scholarship and education that marked this era of Western history. He also exhibited its limitations. The criteria of excellence that marked Renaissance humanism called for knowledge of the ancient texts of Greece and Rome. Erasmus's prodigious record of scholarly research, criticism, and publication demonstrates his mastery of this repository of the Western cultural heritage. It also reveals a detached absorption in scholarship that caused him and other humanists to look backward to a "golden age" rather than forward to a more open universe of inquiry. Erasmus believed that to understand the present it was necessary to understand the past. An understanding of the past required knowledge of the ancient Greek and Roman contributions in literature, art, law, and philosophy. A thorough knowledge of the classical heritage could come only as educated persons studied primary sources, particularly the literary works of antiquity.[22]

These documents were written in Greek and Latin, which required the humanists to master these ancient languages. One of the humanist assumptions was that knowledge was generally found in a book, usually written in a classical rather than vernacular language. Secondary and higher education in the Western world was shaped by the belief that knowledge of Greek and Latin and their literatures was indispensable to the educated person. The entrance requirements and the curricula of secondary schools and colleges reflected this predilection to classical languages until the end of the nineteenth and the beginning of the twentieth centuries. Although Renaissance classical humanism was once a fresh and vital educational force, its long shadow fell over secondary and higher education in the succeeding centuries. Many educational reformers of later years—Rousseau, Pestalozzi, Owen, and Spencer—would challenge the deference that educators accorded the classics.

Like most Renaissance humanists, Erasmus was an elitist who saw himself as an expert guardian and interpreter of the classical heritage. Expertise was not something that could be shared by all, but was a prize won by serious and careful scholarship. Not every interpretation of the classics was equal; merit depended on the authenticity and genuineness of the text and the degree of interpretive expertise that the scholar brought to analyzing it. The humanist scholar and educator was a critic, a commentator, and an interpreter who stood between the body of knowledge and the public. Not everyone was suited by temperament or prepared educationally to be a humanist. Thus, classical humanist education carried a notion of selectivity and elitism rather than a desire to universalize and diffuse knowledge to the masses. Classical humanists believed in excellence but not in equity.

Erasmus and his humanist colleagues reasserted the conception of the educated man as a generalist, a leader who was versatile, knowledgeable in many subject areas, and comfortable in a variety of situations. The Renaissance man was not a specialist. Not everyone could possess the gift of educated versatility or be a critic of society and its institutions. However, it was possible to have an elite of educated generalists who in the spirit of genuine impartiality could be just, fair, and humane leaders of nations, arbiters of morals, and guardians of knowledge.

Although he could be a biting satirist and unrelenting critic, Erasmus was not a man of violence. Well read and well traveled, he believed that human beings, though living in various times and places, possessed a universality and a commonality. Erasmus had a cosmopolitan attitude acquired in the company of learned books and learned colleagues. Although a purist in scholarship, he was a compromiser in human affairs. Keen in his own self-knowledge, he knew he was not meant to be, nor did he wish to be, a charismatic leader, a hero, or a martyr. He was not the type of man to challenge authorities and to state unequivocally, as Luther did, "Here, I stand; I will not and cannot recant," nor the type to die for a moral principle as did his friend, Thomas More. Nor was he a zealot who would plunge humankind into warfare. For Erasmus, the educated person was urbane and witty, a conversationalist who enjoyed the world of books and found in their pages truth, knowledge, virtue, and pleasure.

Questions for Reflection and Dialogue

1. Reflect on the content and methods used in literature courses that you are taking or have taken. How might Erasmus react to the content and method used in the course?
2. Consider your own education. How much of it was based on reading, studying, analyzing, and explaining texts? How might Erasmus react to the literary aspects of your education?
3. Apply Erasmus's parody *In Praise of Folly* to individuals in your school or college. What types of people would be appropriate candidates for such a book?
4. Consider the military doctrine of a preemptive military attack from the perspective of Erasmus's *Christian Prince*.
5. Compare and contrast the cultural and educational ideas of the Medieval and Renaissance periods.
6. How did the intellectual context of the Renaissance shape Erasmus's ideas on education?
7. How was Erasmus a cultural and educational critic?

Projects for Deepening Your Understanding

1. Read a book review section of a major newspaper. Write an opinion paper on what makes a good reviewer or critic. Determine if Erasmus agrees with your analysis of a literary critic.
2. Assume you are a member of a committee that is charged with designing a core curriculum that includes 10 highly significant books. What are these 10 books? Would Erasmus agree with your selection?
3. A leading approach in teaching literature is deconstruction. Do some reading and research on deconstruction. Then write a paper determining if Erasmus would favor or oppose this method.
4. Assume you are writing a modern version of *In Praise of Folly*. Prepare a brief outline that identifies the leading contemporary candidates for inclusion in your book.
5. Read and review a biography of a leading Renaissance figure such as Erasmus, Thomas More, Machiavelli, Vittorino da Feltre, Petrarch, Dante, or Boccaccio.
6. In an essay, examine the concept of the educator as critic. What role would such a person perform in contemporary education?
7. Reflect on your own educational biography. In a paper, examine the extent to which your education reflects either continuity or change.

Notes

1. Erasmus, *Ten Colloquies*, trans. Craig R. Thompson (New York: Macmillan, 1986), ix.
2. For a useful general history of the Renaissance, see De Lamar Jensen, *Renaissance Europe: Age of Recovery and Reconciliation* (Lexington, MA: D. C. Heath, 1981).
3. Representative Renaissance humanists such as Petrarch, Thomas More, and Castiglione are treated in Robert Schwobel, ed., *Renaissance Men and Ideas* (New York: St. Martin's, 1971).
4. Schwobel, *Renaissance Men and Ideas*, 54–65.

5. Baldesar Castiglione, *The Book of the Courtier,* trans. Charles S. Singleton (New York: Doubleday, 1959). Also see Peter Burke, *The Fortunes of the Courtier: The European Reception of Catiglione's Cortegiano* (University Park, PA: Pennsylvania State University Press, 1996).

6. William Woodward, *Vittorino da Feltre and Other Humanist Educators* (New York: Teachers College Press, 1963).

7. Albert Hyma, *The Youth of Erasmus* (New York: Russell & Russell, 1968), 51–53, 55–56, 59.

8. Christopher Hollis, *Erasmus* (Milwaukee: Bruce, 1933), 4–6.

9. Theodore P. Van Ziji, *Gerhard Groote, Ascetic and Reformer, 1340–1384* (Washington, DC: Catholic University of America Press, 1963), 31–39.

10. Erasmus, *Ten Colloquies,* xi.

11. Hans J. Hillerbrand, ed., *Erasmus and His Age* (New York: Harper & Row, 1970), 92.

12. J. Huizinga, *Erasmus of Rotterdam* (London: Phaidon, 1952), 9–16.

13. *The Colloquies of Erasmus,* trans. Craig R. Thompson (Chicago: University of Chicago Press, 1965).

14. *The Colloquies of Erasmus,* 459.

15. Erasmus, *The Praise of Folly,* trans. Clarence H. Miller (New Haven, CT: Yale University Press, 1979), 85–87.

16. Erasmus, *The Education of the Christian Prince,* trans. Lester K. Born (New York: Columbia University Press, 1936).

17. Gerald L. Gutek, *A History of the Western Educational Experience* (Prospect Heights, IL: Waveland, 1995), 122–26.

18. Robert Ulich, *Three Thousand Years of Educational Wisdom: Selections from the Great Documents* (Cambridge, MA: Harvard University Press, 1954), 253.

19. Craig R. Thompson, ed., *Collected Works of Erasmus: Literary and Educational Writings 2: De Copia/De Rationae Studii* (Toronto: University of Toronto Press, 1978), 667.

20. Thompson, *Collected Works of Erasmus,* 672.

21. Gutek, *History of Western Educational Experience,* 123–24.

22. Erasmus, *Ten Colloquies,* xiv.

Suggestions for Further Reading

Augustijn, C. *Erasmus: His Life, Works, and Influence.* Toronto: University of Toronto Press, 1991.

Bainton, Roland H. *Erasmus of Christendom.* New York: Scribner's, 1969.

Burke, Peter. *The Fortunes of the Courtier: The European Reception of Castiglione's Cortegiano.* University Park, PA: Pennsylvania State University Press, 1996.

Erasmus. *Adages.* Craig R. Thompson, trans. Chicago: University of Chicago Press, 1962.

———. *The Colloquies of Erasmus.* Trans. Craig R. Thompson. Chicago: University of Chicago Press, 1965.

———. *Controversies.* Toronto: University of Toronto Press, 1993.

———. *Ten Colloquies.* Trans. Craig R. Thompson. New York: Macmillan, 1986.

———. *The Education of the Christian Prince.* Trans. Lester K. Born. New York: Columbia University Press, 1936.

———. *The Erasmus Reader.* Toronto: University of Toronto Press, 1990.

———. *The Praise of Folly.* New Haven, CT; London: Yale University Press, 2003.

———. *Christian Humanism and the Reformation: Selected Writings of Erasmus, with His Life by Beatus Rhenanus and a Biographical Sketch by the Editor.* John C. Olin, ed. New York: Fordham University Press, 1987.

———. *Erasmus on Women.* Erika Rummel, ed. Toronto; Buffalo: University of Toronto Press, 1996.

———. *Poems.* Clarence H. Miller and Harry Vredeveld, eds. Toronto; Buffalo: University of Toronto Press, 1993.

Gordon, Walter E. *Humanist Play and Belief: The Seriocomic Art of Desiderius Erasmus.* Toronto: University of Toronto Press, 1990.

Halkin, Leon E. *Erasmus: A Critical Biography.* Oxford, UK, and Cambridge, MA: Blackwell, 1993.

Hyma, Albert. *Erasmus and the Humanists.* New York: F. S. Crofts, 1980.

———. *The Youth of Erasmus.* New York: Russell & Russell, 1968.

Jardine, Lisa. *Erasmus, Man of Letters: The Construction of Charisma in Print.* Princeton, NJ: Princeton University Press, 1993.

McConica, James. *Erasmus.* Oxford, UK, and New York: Oxford University Press, 1991.

Nash, Paul, Kazamias, Andreas, and Perkinson, Henry, eds. *The Educated Man: Studies in the History of Educational Thought.* New York: John Wiley & Sons, 1965.

Rummel, Erika. *Erasmus and His Catholic Critics.* Nieuwkoop, Netherlands: De Graaf, 1989.

Schoeck, Richard J. *Erasmus of Europe: The Making of a Humanist, 1467–1500.* Savage, MD: Barnes & Noble, 1990.

———. *Erasmus Grandescens: The Growth of a Humanist's Mind and Spirituality.* Nieuwkoop, Netherlands: De Graaf, 1988.

Thompson, Craig R., ed. *Collected Works of Erasmus: Literary and Educational Writings 2: De Copia/De Rationae Studii.* Toronto: University of Toronto Press, 1978.

Van Ziji, Theodore P. *Gerhard Groote, Ascetic and Reformer, 1340–1384.* Washington, DC: Catholic University of America Press, 1963.

Woodward, William. *Vittorino da Feltre and other Humanist Educators.* New York: Teachers College Press, 1963.

John Calvin: Theologian and Educator of the Protestant Reformation

This chapter examines the life, theology, and educational philosophy of John Calvin (1509–1564), a leading figure of the Protestant Reformation. The reformed theology developed by Calvin had momentous significance not only in the history of religious ideas but for society, economics, and education in Europe and North America. Calvin devised a system of religious doctrines known as Evangelical Protestantism. Calvinism, with its sanction of industriousness and economic development, appealed to the rising professional and business middle classes. Relating a righteous earthly life and salvation to knowledge of the Bible, Calvinism also stimulated the tendency to universal literacy and education.

We examine Calvin's influence on Western and U.S. education in the historical context of the Protestant Reformation of sixteenth-century Europe. First, we describe the social, political, economic, and religious context in which Calvin developed his educational ideas. Second, we analyze Calvin's biography, education, and career to observe the evolution of his ideas. Third, we examine the transference of Calvin's theology of Evangelical Protestantism to North America, especially to New England. Fourth, we assess the continuing significance of Calvinism on education. By this analysis, we shall determine the relationship of Calvin's reformed theology to educational policy and practices. His theology, which was articulated in the midst of the Protestant Reformation, had a long-range effect on economic and social policies as well as religious doctrines, beliefs, and practices.

To organize your thoughts as you read Chapter 8, focus on the following questions:

1. What were the major trends of the Protestant Reformation, the time and situation in which Calvin lived?
2. How did Calvin's educational biography shape his philosophy of education?
3. How did Calvin's reformed theology determine his educational policies and practices?
4. How did Calvinism influence the development of education in the United States?
5. What is the enduring impact of Calvin's contributions to Western and U.S. education?

The Historical Context of Calvin's Life

In the sixteenth and seventeenth centuries, Western culture experienced a period of intense religious interest and activity. Historians have designated this period the Protestant Reformation and the Roman Catholic Counterreformation. Although the tendencies of this period were overtly religious, events were played out against a backdrop of social, political, and economic changes that worked to destroy the Medieval synthesis already enfeebled during the Renaissance.[1]

Political centralization had created strong monarchial states in England, France, Spain, and Portugal. Smaller countries such as the Netherlands were also seeking to assert their own political and economic identity. A growing sense of nationalism was surfacing in the divided German states. In England, Henry VIII threw off any allegiance to the pope of Rome and established himself as head of the church. In Germany, Martin Luther successfully challenged papal authority. The rise of strong monarchial states and the growing currents of nationalism would unleash new trends that would reshape Western attitudes.

By the sixteenth century, European nationalism had become one of the most potent political and ideological forces in modern Western history. It provided the ideological cement that would unite and hold a people together. In its simplest meaning, *nationalism* was centered on the nation, a political entity or territory, usually populated by those who were alike in ethnicity, language, and culture. In sixteenth-century Europe, these territorial nations were governed by kings who personified the nation to their people. The rise of nationalism and national states weakened loyalty and commitment to transnational figures and institutions such as the pope and the Roman Catholic Church. Primary loyalty was to the nation as people began to define themselves as English, French, Spanish, and so on.

The religious movements of the Reformation contained a nationalist element. In the German states, there was a seething resentment that an Italian pope should attempt to assert authority over Germans and draw off money to support projects outside of Germany. In England, a similar feeling arose when the pope would not agree to Henry VIII's plans to divorce Catherine of Aragon. Of equal importance to King Henry was the possibility that he could use the expropriation of church property, particularly the extensive monastic holdings, to finance his plans to make England into a commanding European power.

While the rise of nationalism had obvious political importance, it also redirected educational institutions. The sense of national identity, loyalty, and commitment was something that had to be acquired or learned. The new schools that developed during the Reformation began to emphasize nationalism and national identity. In later years, nationalism would accelerate and gain a further hold on schooling.

Economic development was still another conditioning influence of the Protestant Reformation. By the sixteenth century, new economic structures had emerged in Europe such as banking, issuance of stock, money exchanges, and credit and interest. Ownership of stock created a powerful new business class. This new class, the bourgeois or middle class, seeking to win a place of status in the European social structure, would eventually challenge the dominant landed aristocracy. Possessing wealth, the middle class would create and support educational institutions that reflected their views of knowledge and value.

It was against the backdrop of the nation-state, rising currents of nationalism, and economic change that the Protestant Reformation occurred. Although nationalism eroded and destroyed the remains of European political unity, the Reformation shattered the already debilitated Medieval Christian synthesis. The groundwork for the Protestant Reformation had been laid by John Wycliffe (1320–1384), an Oxford theologian, who condemned the church's ownership of property and preached against papal interference in English affairs. Wycliffe translated the Bible into English and urged the formation of a national English church. Although he attracted some support, the time was not ripe for his ideas to flourish.[2] The Reformation's first success would be in Martin Luther's Germany.

Like John Calvin, Martin Luther was one of the Protestant Reformation's towering personalities.[3] In fact, Luther is often cited as the person who precipitated the Reformation by posting his *Ninety-five Theses* on the door of the Court Church at Wittenberg. An Augustinian monk, Luther was a lecturer at the University of Wittenberg. Growing increasingly restive in his religious order, Luther had become disenchanted with Catholic practices such as the earning of indulgences and the veneration of the saints. His study of and lecturing on the Bible brought him to assert the doctrine of "justification by faith alone," which challenged the traditional Catholic teaching that salvation was by faith and the performance of good works. According to Luther, the justice of God was the righteousness by which God's grace and mercy justified human beings through their faith that Jesus Christ was their savior.[4]

What brought matters to the breaking point for Luther was the sale of indulgences. The issue occurred when Albert of Brandenburg, who was seeking to become the archbishop of Mainz, gave Pope Leo X a contribution to build the new St. Peter's basilica in Rome. The pope, in turn, gave Albert the privilege of dispensing indulgences. (An *indulgence* is the remission of temporal punishment, usually in purgatory, due for sins that had been forgiven through the sacrament of penance.) Tetzel, a Dominican monk, was engaged by Albert to urge the faithful to purchase indulgences. Luther, who objected strenuously to the sale of indulgences, nailed his *Ninety-Five Theses* to the door of the church at Wittenberg on October 31, 1517. In his theses, he denied the power of the pope to reduce the penalties of purgatory and rejected the efficacy of indulgences. Luther's theological objection also received a favorable hearing from Germans who opposed the interference of Rome in their internal affairs and also opposed sending German money to Rome.

After his initial objections to the sale of indulgences, Luther began to challenge other doctrines of the Catholic Church. He contended that the pope's claim to supreme authority was historically rather than scripturally based and that the pope and the church councils were capable of error. After a series of debates, Luther was condemned as a heretic by the pope. Not accepting the pope's judgment, Luther refused to recant. Instead of exiling him, several German princes protected him. Luther and his supporters circulated his theological writings throughout Germany, and Luther became the leader of the Reformation in Germany.

Luther's ideas spread across northern Germany, gaining the support of two influential groups. Members of German nobility, especially Ulrich von Hutten and Franz von Sickingen, who represented the growing German nationalism, protected Luther and helped disseminate his reformed theological doctrines. Luther also won the support of some humanist scholars and educators.

An able intellectual and educational ally of Luther was Philip Melanchthon (1497–1560), whose support demonstrates the relationship between the Protestant Reformation and the northern Renaissance. Melanchthon, a professor of Greek at the University of Wittenberg, encountered Luther teaching Scripture at the university. Luther concurred with Melanchthon's efforts to reform the university curriculum, and Melanchthon agreed with Luther's challenge to the Catholic Church.[5]

A brief look at some of Luther's ideas on education provides an overview of the Reformation's effect on education. Luther believed that if the reformed creed was to be sustained after the initial impetus of the Reformation had passed, it needed to be institutionalized in the instruction provided by schools. The young needed to attend school to learn to read so that they could read the Bible in their own language. They also needed religious instruction so they could defend their faith against sectarian rivals. In "A Letter to the Mayors and Aldermen of All Cities of Germany in Behalf of Christian Schools," Luther urged these officials to establish schools for religious, political, and economic reasons. Such schools would enable people to read the Bible in their vernacular language and educate citizens who would know and respect the laws of the civil state. Schools would instill habits of industriousness and productivity that would promote the state's economic prosperity.[6]

Melanchthon helped the rulers of various states of Germany establish primary schools to instill literacy and the reformed religion in their young subjects. As a humanist, he stressed the need to support classical humanist schools as secondary institutions that would prepare a leadership cadre to be ministers of the church and officials of the state. Because rival denominations were contending for converts, it was necessary to ensure that teachers instructed their students in the correct religious doctrines. To make sure that teachers taught the tenets of the reformed creed, various German states, with Melanchthon's assistance, prepared school codes that established guidelines for the schools' curriculum and governance.[7]

The care that leaders of the Protestant Reformation such as Luther gave to school supervision added a new dimension to education. Often given aid by political authorities, Protestant religious leaders encouraged these civil officials to support and control schools. In countries dominated by new Protestant churches, civil authorities came to exercise a large educational role. This tendency was also supported by the rise of nationalism.

In addition to Lutheranism, other Protestant denominations emerged during the Reformation era. A significant number of denominations—the Reformed, Congregational, and Presbyterian churches—followed John Calvin's theology. In England, Henry VIII established a national church, the Church of England. Pietist denominations such as the Anabaptist, the Moravian, and smaller religious groups emerged to practice religion in their own way. (See Chapter 9 for a discussion of pietism in the ideas of Comenius).

The period of the Protestant Reformation and Catholic Counterreformation, a time of intense religious conflict, was neither an ecumenical age nor one of religious tolerance. Contentious religious denominations and nation-state rivalries unleashed an era of religious warfare.

Before examining John Calvin as a religious and educational reformer, we shall consider the dominant educational ideas and institutions that formed the context for his work. Although education had exhibited a strong religious orientation during the Middle Ages and a somewhat diminished one during the Renaissance, the renewed religious impulses that had an effect on education in the Reformation had a new dimension—the defense of the faith against erring or heretical Christian rivals. Each church, be it Roman Catholic or Protestant, saw other churches as rivals following erroneous doctrine. Much of the education of the young was devoted to instilling religious doctrines certified as correct by the parent church. Young members of the particular denomination were prepared to defend their faith against rival antagonists.[8] To this end, the catechism became a popular teaching device. Constructed as a series of questions and answers, the catechism's responses contained religious principles. Students were to memorize the catechism, thereby instilling in their minds correct religious dogmas.

The assertion by Protestant reformers that people should read the Bible in their own language required an extraordinary effort to create a literate populace. The Protestant Reformation was a powerful force in bringing about the extension of primary or elementary schooling to larger sections of the population. Although primary schools had existed in the form of parish and monastic schools, a larger number of such schools were established and a larger attendance resulted from the Reformation. Primary schools were founded by a range of authorities, such as the various churches, towns, or districts. Civil authorities either established schools or helped support those established by the churches. The basic curriculum of the primary schools included religion, reading, writing, singing, and arithmetic. Primary schools were designed to educate a literate laity for the reformed churches and a law-abiding citizenry for the civil state. They were the schools for the masses, and did not lead to secondary or higher education.

Many of the Protestant reformers, including Luther, Melanchthon, and Calvin, had been nurtured intellectually by the currents of the northern Renaissance.[9] They retained a belief that classical humanist education was the best means of preparing a leadership elite for service to church and state. Studying Greek and Latin languages and literatures provided the linguistic tools ministers needed. The religious doctrines of the reformed churches were added to the classical languages. These classical humanist schools combined a secondary and preparatory function as young men of promise, typically from the upper and middle classes, were prepared for entry to colleges and universities. Mainstream Protestant denominations such as the Lutherans and Calvinists insisted that an educated ministry was needed to lead a literate laity.

John Calvin as a Protestant Reformer and Educator

John Calvin (Jean Chauvin in French), was born on July 10, 1509, in Noyon in the province of Picardy, France. He was the second son of Geurard and Jeanne Calvin. Of his three siblings, only Charles, his older brother, lived to adulthood.[10] Calvin's mother died when he was 6. His father remarried.

Geurard Calvin was the son of a cooper in the city of Pont-l'Eveque, near Noyon. Geurard's education was sufficient to launch him on a career as a civil servant. In 1480, Geurard received an appointment as a government registrar and clerk in Noyon's ecclesiastical Court. Noyon, located on the River Verse 58 miles from Paris, was known for its religious institutions. It was the seat of a bishopric and boasted a cathedral, two abbeys, and four parishes.[11] His father's position in the town placed Calvin socially in the ranks of the bourgeoisie or middle class. The attitudes and values that John Calvin stressed as a religious reformer and leader epitomized middle-class mores.

John Calvin's childhood was shaped by his father's position as an official of the ecclesiastical court, a religious institution. His father's work, which was semiadministrative and semilegal, was to influence Calvin in similar directions. Although Calvin was a theologian who would shape the basic doctrines of Evangelical Protestantism, his outlook contained a juridical and legalistic element.

Geurard Calvin's position brought the family into the circle of Charles de Hangest, the bishop of Noyon. The bishop, who recognized young John Calvin's intellectual talent, helped subsidize his education at the College des Capettes. Young Calvin was judged by his teachers to be a promising student, especially in religion and the humanities.

When he was 12, Calvin was sent to live with the Montmors family, where he received special instruction from the family tutor. He would later claim that he owed a special debt of gratitude to the family for introducing him to the intellectual riches of the arts and humanities.[12]

In 1521, John Calvin went to Paris to attend the College de la Marche. He enrolled in the grammar course, which was preparatory to studying for the arts degree. This grammar course was designed to provide the student with proficiency in Latin so that he could study the arts, which were conducted exclusively in Latin. John Calvin studied under Mathurin Cordier, who was recognized as one of France's preeminent Latin scholars.

At 14, John Calvin began the arts course at the College de Montaigu, which was famous for preparing young men to become priests. The college, under the direction of Jean Standonck, was known for its orderliness, academic rigor, and strict discipline. These were important characteristics in the lifestyle the religious followers of Calvin would choose.

Although Calvin showed a keen aptitude for the humanities and theology, he left his studies at the College de Montaigu on his father's recommendation. He enrolled at the University of Orleans to study civil law, apparently to follow in his father's profession. He applied himself intensively to his studies, displaying the discipline that would characterize his life as a religious reformer. The intensity that he applied to academic work may have caused the stomach disorders that plagued him throughout his life. Once again, he achieved academic distinction. He excelled in debate and even substituted for instructors when they were absent from their classes.

Calvin's education in letters, the humanities, theology, and law took place during the time that Europe was being swept by the intellectual and religious currents of the Reformation. Although France was still securely Roman Catholic, the religious Reformation had reached its academic institutions. Educated Europeans were discussing Martin Luther's challenge to papal authority and the Roman Catholic Church. While a student at the University of Orleans, Calvin came into contact with those who were familiar with Luther's work. An associate, Melchior Wolmar, a German student, introduced Calvin to Luther's reformist theology.[13]

Calvin completed his study of law and received his licentiate degree. Even before he had completed his legal studies, Calvin's mind kept returning to his earlier and persistent theological interests. His quest for spiritual truth led him to examine the Bible and the writings of the fathers of the early church. He approached his scriptural study like a lawyer. In his mind, he constructed a legal and theological brief that found the Roman Catholic Church to be in conflict with his interpretation of divine law.

During the midst of his scriptural investigations, Calvin had an intense religious conversion experience. This personal experience, he said, illuminated his thought "like a flash of light."[14] As a result, he claimed to recognize the irresistible power of God and the need to submit to the "Divine Majesty."

Calvin returned to Paris, where he published his commentary on Seneca's *de Clementia*. This publication showed him to be a man of many interests—theology, law, and humanist studies. He encountered a number of intellectuals who supported Luther in his struggle against the Catholic Church. He also began to speak at meetings of persons who were moving in the direction of Protestantism. At one of these meetings, on November 1, 1533, Calvin addressed the assembly on the importance of the liberal arts and philosophy. Moving from his academic theme, he struck a theological note when he proclaimed salvation by faith alone, putting him squarely in the Protestant camp. Although cautioned to be moderate and to not directly challenge the Roman Catholic Church, Calvin took a position similar to Luther's refusal to recant his beliefs. Comparing the Catholic Church to a decaying structure, Calvin asserted, "The building is too rotten to be patched up. It must be torn down and instead a new one must be built."[15]

In 1536, Calvin's *Institutes of the Christian Religion* was published and recognized as the definitive statement of the Evangelical Protestant doctrinal position.[16] *Institutes* was a forceful and lucid theological exposition that broke completely with the Roman Catholic hierarchical system of ecclesiastical governance, organization and ceremonial rituals. Calvin also asserted that people who would be saved were predestined for salvation by God's grace, not through their own actions. This predestined elect would lead disciplined and purified lives according to the laws of the Scriptures.

Calvin claimed that the Evangelical church was the true successor of the early Christian church. In his letter to King Francis I of France, which introduced the *Institutes*, he called upon the French monarch to disband the Catholic Church and to make Evangelicalism the official state church. Unlike the German princes who supported Luther, the French king upheld Catholicism as the official church of France and began a persecution of Evangelical and other Protestants.

Faced with this persecution by the French government, Calvin fled his native land and sought refuge in Switzerland. He located in Geneva, a city already predisposed to the Protestant Reformation. The famous author of the *Institutes* was given a warm welcome by the Protestant ministers and townspeople of Geneva. They asked him to stay in their city and help build a new and reformed church. Calvin eagerly accepted his assignment in Geneva and reshaped the city into a citadel of Evangelical Protestantism. He wanted to create a theocratic city where the religious and civil authorities worked together to enforce a scriptural *paideia*.[17]

Using his theological and legal skills, Calvin prepared a "confession of faith" to proclaim the true beliefs that were to guide the adherents of reformed Christianity.[18] The confession emphasized the authority of the Bible, the importance of personal guilt for sin, and the need to be reconciled to God through the redemptive act of Jesus Christ. Calvin's proclamation of the Bible as the only infallible rule of faith and life contrasted with the Roman Catholic emphasis on the dual authority of the Scriptures and the tradition of the church. The confession of faith was presented to and accepted by the Council of Two Hundred, Geneva's ruling legislative body. This document would provide the theological basis for the Heidelberg Catechism, which was widely used in the reformed churches.

As a Protestant reformer, Calvin believed that it was not only necessary to purge the corruptions of Catholicism from Christian practice, but that young members of the new church had to be instilled with correct doctrine. Like other reformers, such as Luther, Calvin turned to the catechistic method to impress the correct version of Christianity on the minds of the young. He condensed the religious principles of the *Institutes* and the confession into an abbreviated version in a catechism that could be studied by children in school.[19]

Reforming religion and life in Geneva did not go smoothly for Calvin, however. There were those in the city who resisted his efforts to remake Geneva into a city governed by the law of the Scriptures. In 1538, Calvin's opponents, dubbed the "libertines" because they opposed the social controls that he imposed on the city, won control of the city council and exiled Calvin from Geneva.

During this exile, Calvin traveled and preached in other Swiss cities before locating in Strasbourg, where he remained until 1541 as the pastor of a church established by Protestant exiles from France. Here, he met and married Idelette de Buren. During the nine years of their marriage, which ended with Idelette's death, the couple had three children, all of whom died shortly after their birth.

Never given to idleness, Calvin used his time in Strasbourg to refine his theological doctrines. He published an expanded edition of the *Institutes* and wrote treatises on the Last Supper and on St. Paul's Epistle to the Romans. His growing fame as a theologian of the Protestant Reformation brought him into contact with Philip Melanchthon, Luther's associate. Calvin and Melanchthon shared a commitment to humanism and religious reformation, and they corresponded with each other. Despite their mutual admiration, they were unable to resolve theological differences between Calvinism and Lutheranism.

During Calvin's absence from Geneva, Pierre de la Baume, the Catholic bishop who had been exiled from the city, returned and attempted to restore Catholicism. A strong reaction occurred against the bishop's efforts. Calvin's supporters regained control of the city council and recalled him to Geneva. In 1541, Calvin made a triumphal return and resumed his efforts to make Geneva into a solidly Evangelical Protestant city. He remained in Geneva until his death 23 years later on May 27, 1564.

Calvin and Education

In this section, we shall examine the implications of Calvinist theology for education. Calvin's Evangelical Protestantism emphasized the importance of proclaiming the Scriptures through preaching, writing, and reading. Based on the authority of the Bible, this religion strongly emphasized the need for the faithful to be literate, to read the Bible, and to govern their lives, their church, and their city according to its laws. The schools of Geneva reflected the Calvinist relationship between education, religious orthodoxy, civil order, and economic prosperity. Geneva's city council required all children to attend school. Parents who failed to comply with the law were fined. Further, the children of the poor were educated at the expense of the city. In Calvin's Geneva, a complete school system was created. Students attended an elementary school called the *schola privata* until age 16. The advanced school was called the *schola publica*, which later became the University of Geneva. Its original mission was to prepare clergy for the reformed churches. Its curriculum included theology, Hebrew, Greek, philosophy, mathematics, and rhetoric. The university attracted leading scholars, theologians, and classicists. In Europe and North America, the various Calvinist churches valued and emphasized education. Schools were necessary in establishing and maintaining the reformed Christian religion.

Because the Bible was the sole religious authority, it was essential that it be translated into the various European vernacular languages and be made accessible to the people. The invention of the printing press made relatively inexpensive editions of the Bible available to more people.[20] Indeed, Protestant reformers urged there be a Bible in every Christian home. Calvinist as well as Lutheran ministers wanted the members of the church to be literate so they could read their Bibles. They established primary schools to teach basic literacy and religion. This meant that the common people were to learn to read as well as the traditionally educated elites. Thus, a strong beginning was made in the direction of mass systems of primary schools in both Europe and North America.

Although Calvin and other reformers moved in the direction of universal primary schooling, they remained committed to the classical humanist education developed in the Renaissance. Calvin, like Melanchthon, was a committed humanist. Ministers of the Reformed Church were to study the Scriptures and preach the Gospel from an informed and educated perspective. A call to ministry was insufficient unless combined with scriptural and doctrinal studies. For Calvin, the Hebrew, Greek, and Latin languages and literature provided the foundation of knowledge and skills for scriptural study. The classical humanist schools were a secondary educational track for the educated elites of the Reformation period. The common people would be made literate in primary schools where instruction was conducted in their own vernacular. The religious leaders would be educated in the classics and the Scriptures in humanist schools and in colleges and universities.

Calvinism in the United States

As a religious creed, Calvinism appealed to the middle classes of western Europe. These loosely defined classes, which had emerged with the economic changes of the Renaissance, did not fit neatly into the social structure inherited from the Middle Ages.

As their name suggests, the people who composed the middle classes were positioned between the aristocracy of birth and the agricultural peasant masses. They included small tradespeople and artisans, businesspeople and bankers, and lawyers and other professionals. Although some had earned great wealth, others were merely making a living. What was different about the middle classes was that they had earned their way into the Western scheme of economic and social life rather than benefiting from inherited status.

In the areas of Europe where the middle classes existed, Calvinism attracted adherents. In Switzerland, the Calvinist church was the Reformed Church, in the Netherlands it was the Dutch Reformed Church, and in Scotland the Presbyterian Church. Of great importance in the settlement of North America were English Calvinists known as Separatists and Puritans. Their settlement in the British colonies in New England, especially at Massachusetts Bay, would exercise a profound effect on U.S. culture and education.

When the Separatists landed at Plymouth and the Puritans at Massachusetts Bay in 1620, they brought with them strongly held religious beliefs. Just as Calvin had sought to establish a heavenly city in Geneva, so did his English followers in Massachusetts seek to establish a godly commonwealth in the wilderness.[21] The Puritans of Massachusetts Bay Colony enacted some of the earliest ordinances requiring education in North America. The laws of 1642 and 1647 required civil authorities to make sure that children learned to read, write, and know the principles of religion and laws of the commonwealth. In particular, the law of 1647 required larger towns to provide a Latin master who would instruct promising youth in classical languages so that they might attend Harvard College. The significant aspect of these early laws is that they demonstrated the great importance the Puritan settlers in North America gave to education.

The Calvinist religious beliefs that the Puritans had planted in North American soil developed in the late eighteenth and nineteenth centuries into Congregationalism. As a church, Congregationalism grew out of Calvinist theology and the unique pattern of settlement that characterized New England. New towns on the westward-moving frontier were settled by Congregationalists.

In the Congregational Church, each congregation was governed by its own elected trustees. Although Congregational churches had a large degree of autonomy in their governance, they were united by their adherence to Calvin's doctrines. The Congregationalist pattern of local control extended into political organization and education. As political units, New England towns had their own elected boards of trustees. In the governance and control of schools, the pattern was repeated with the residents of districts electing school boards to establish, support, and maintain schools.

Calvinism affected how American towns and schools were governed, and also greatly influenced how people viewed each other socially and economically. Resting on the doctrine of predestination, the elect were to exhibit righteous and productive lives. The economic wealth that was the mark of the middle class was not an obstacle to salvation but rather an outward sign of membership in the elect. The possessors of wealth had to use it in the right way, for good purposes and for uplifting human beings. Wealthy people were to act as stewards of the economy in much the same way that the good steward in the Bible invested and multiplied the money that his master had given him. Modern stewards were to invest profits to make more profits; in turn, wealth could be used for churches, schools, libraries, and other institutions that ennobled and uplifted life and helped create the Christian commonwealth on Earth. By providing the political and social environment in which Christian men and women could live their lives according to the laws of Scripture, they would be prepared to enter the heavenly city for eternity.

Calvinist religious doctrines, with their emphasis on socially and economically productive lives, came to be known as the "Protestant ethic." In the United States, the Protestant ethic had a great formative effect on the institutions of the late eighteenth and nineteenth centuries. The generalized Evangelical Protestantism that was so important to American institution building exemplified Calvinist views of knowledge and values.

The ethic of Evangelical Protestantism in the United States strongly encouraged the establishment of common or public schools that would prepare a literate, law-abiding, Bible-reading, and economically productive citizenry. Common schools were to prepare responsible citizens who could intelligently elect their representatives to office and instill a basic knowledge of and respect for law and order into the young. Skills and values conducive to economic productivity would be stressed along with reading, writing, and arithmetic. Values such as a sense of the importance of time, being diligent in one's work, the need to achieve, the deferring of immediate gratification for long-term success, and other attitudes that made for effective work and management skills in factories, shops, and stores were emphasized in the common schools (see Chapter 14).

By the late nineteenth and early twentieth centuries, the attitudes and values taught in the common schools helped to shape the public philosophy. Although the religious sectarianism of their Calvinist origins had diminished, they were part of a generalized Protestant ethic. In popular literature, Horatio Alger wrote many novels in which young men, possessed of the right values, conquered all kinds of adversity. By the merits of their own talents, the heroes of the Alger narratives applied themselves so successfully that they gained the wealth and position they so deserved. A "captain of industry," like Andrew Carnegie, who in Alger-like manner rose from shop boy to industrialist, fulfilled the role of economic stewardship. In his own statement of philosophy, *The Gospel of Wealth*, Carnegie told of an economically prosperous America where modern stewards endowed libraries, universities, and schools.[22]

Conclusion: An Assessment

Calvin's theology, with its stress on literacy and education, cast a lengthened intellectual as well as religious shadow over Europe and North America. His connections among religion, civil society, and economic life forged a way of thinking, a religious worldview, that became known as the Protestant ethic.

During his own lifetime, Calvin established a strong intellectual basis for reformed Protestant theology. Education became a partner in the effort to design a commonwealth on Earth modeled along the lines of Calvin's reformed doctrines. The "New Jerusalem" was to be a city in which the inhabitants followed a code of civil behavior prescribed by the Bible.

Calvinism also signaled a modernization of Christianity to fit the new economic situation, especially the rise of the middle class. Calvin's doctrines of a righteous people engaged in industrious undertakings that benefited the commonwealth and the church suited the modernizing trends of an emergent capitalism. The Calvinist stress on literacy as a tool of salvation fulfilled both religious and economic objectives. As conceived by Calvin and his followers, the school became an institution that emphasized the moral formation of those who attended it.

In the New World, Calvinism would find a setting in which it bore institutional fruit. New England colonies, then states, became the cradle of a transplanted version of Calvinism. The common school movement incorporated the intellectual and moral objectives of a civic culture infused with a sense of religious mission.

Questions for Reflection and Dialogue

1. Analyze the relationship that Luther and Calvin saw existing between the good citizen and the good Christian. Identify and examine the motivation of groups who favor and oppose such a relationship in contemporary American society.
2. Explore the differences and similarities between a theology and a philosophy of education.
3. In your opinion, what would be Calvin's position on the following issues: added security to control violence in schools, prayer in public schools, multiculturalism, vouchers for nonpublic schools, and the posting of the Ten Commandments in public schools?
4. Reflect on several courses in education that you have taken. Has there been an emphasis on the values of hard work, effort, and diligence as desirable values in these courses? How might Calvin react to these courses?
5. What elements in the historical and cultural context provided the setting for the Protestant Reformation?
6. Why did education become such an important force in Calvin's religious outlook? In turn, is religion, especially religious values, an important force in American education?
7. What is the historical and educational significance of Calvin's reformed theology, especially in the American experience?

Projects for Deepening Your Understanding

1. With the instructor's permission, interview several of your classmates on their opinions about separation of church and state and the free exercise of religion. Prepare a paper that analyzes your findings. Would Calvin tend to agree or disagree with your findings?
2. Christian schools are one of the most rapidly growing sectors in American private schooling. Do some research on this subject and attempt to determine why they are enjoying this growth.
3. Examine a third- or fourth-grade reader and identify the values that are exemplified in the text. Would Calvin approve or disapprove of these values? Why?
4. Prepare a research paper that examines the Calvinist influence in the New England colonies and in later U.S. history.
5. Prepare a research paper that examines the influence of Evangelical Protestantism on the common school movement.

6. In a paper, discuss the effect of the Protestant ethic on U.S. life, especially the attitudes toward productive work, use of leisure, and social service.
7. In a paper, examine the role of the public school as a transmitter of moral values.

Notes

1. A useful general history of the Protestant Reformation is De Lamar Jensen, *Reformation Europe: An Age of Reform and Revolution* (Lexington, MA: D. C. Heath, 1981).
2. Matthew Spinka, ed., *Advocates of Reform: From Wycliffe to Erasmus* (Philadelphia: Westminster, 1953), 22–23.
3. Biographies of Luther include Roland Bainton, *Here I Stand: A Life of Martin Luther* (Nashville: Abingdon, 1959); E. G. Schwiebert, *Luther and His Times: The Reformation from a New Perspective* (St. Louis: Concordia, 1950); Richard Friedenthal, *Luther: His Life and Times* (New York: Harcourt Brace Jovanovich, 1967); and Bernhard Lohse, *Martin Luther: An Introduction to His Life and Work* (Philadelphia: Fortress, 1986).
4. Bainton, *Here I Stand*, 39–51.
5. Hans Engelland, *Melanchthon on Christian Doctrine: Logi Communes, 1555*, trans. Clyde L. Manschreck (New York: Oxford University Press, 1965), xxv–xxvii.
6. Robert Ulich, ed., *Three Thousand Years of Educational Wisdom: Selections from Great Documents* (Cambridge, MA: Harvard University Press, 1971), 218–38.
7. Gerald L. Gutek, *A History of the Western Educational Experience* (Prospect Heights, IL: Waveland, 1995), 141–43.
8. John H. Leith, ed., *Creeds of the Churches: A Reader in Christian Doctrine from the Bible to the Present* (New York: Doubleday, 1963).
9. For the interrelationships of the Renaissance and Reformation, see Lewis W. Spitz, *The Renaissance and Reformation Movements* (Chicago: Rand McNally, 1971); and Lewis W. Spitz, *The Religious Renaissance of the German Humanists* (Cambridge, MA: Harvard University Press, 1963).
10. Williston Walker, *John Calvin: The Organizer of Reformed Protestantism* (New York: Shocken, 1969), 23.
11. Thomas H. Parker, *John Calvin: A Biography* (Philadelphia: Westminster, 1975).
12. Parker, *John Calvin*, 4.
13. Walker, *John Calvin*, 49.
14. Emanuel Stickelberger, *Calvin*, trans. David G. Gelzer (London: James Clarke, 1959), 16–17.
15. Stickelberger, *Calvin*, 23.
16. John Calvin, *Institutes of the Christian Religion*, trans. Henry Beveridge (Grand Rapids, MI: Eerdmans, 1933).
17. William R. Estep, *Renaissance and Reformation* (Grand Rapids, MI: Eerdmans, 1986), 235–42.
18. John Calvin, *Tracts and Treatises on the Doctrine and Worship of the Church*, Vol. 2, trans. Henry Beveridge (Grand Rapids, MI: Eerdmans, 1958), 137–62.
19. Calvin, *Tracts and Treatises*, 340–57.
20. For the relationship of the printing press to Protestant education, see Carmen Luke, *Pedagogy, Printing and Protestantism: The Discourse on Childhood* (Albany: State University of New York Press, 1989).
21. Sheldon S. Cohen, *A History of Colonial Education, 1607–1776* (New York: John Wiley & Sons, 1974), 29–69.
22. Andrew Carnegie, *The Gospel of Wealth and Other Timely Essays* (Cambridge, MA: Harvard University Press, 1962).

Suggestions for Further Reading

Bainton, Roland. *Here I Stand: A Life of Martin Luther.* Nashville, TN: Abingdon, 1959.

Benedict, Philip. *Christ's Churches Purely Reformed: A Social History of Calvinism.* New Haven, CT: London: Yale University Press, 2003.

Calvin, John. *Calvin's Ecclesiastical Advice.* Louisville, KY: Westminster/John Knox, 1991.

———. *Institutes of the Christian Religion.* Trans. Henry Beveridge. Grand Rapids, MI: Eerdmans, 1933.

———. *Tracts and Treatises on the Doctrine and Worship of the Church.* Trans. Henry Beveridge. Grand Rapids, MI: Eerdmans, 1958.

Estep, William R. *Renaissance and Reformation.* Grand Rapids, MI: Eerdmans, 1986.

Friedenthal, Richard. *Luther: His Life and Times.* New York: Harcourt Brace Jovanovich, 1967.

Godfrey, W. Robert. *Reformation Sketches: Insights into Luther, Calvin, and the Confessions.* Phillipsburg, NJ: P&R Pub., 2003.

Gorski, Philip S. *The Disciplinary Revolution: Calvinism and the Rise of the State in Early Modern Europe.* Chicago: University of Chicago Press, 2003.

Graham, W. Fred. *The Constructive Revolutionary: John Calvin and His Socioeconomic Impact.* Richmond: John Knox, 1971.

Jensen, De Lamar. *Reformation Europe: An Age of Reform and Revolution.* Lexington, MA: D. C. Heath, 1981.

Kittelson, James M. *Luther the Reformer: The Story of the Man and his Career.* Philadelphia, PA: Northam: Fortress: Roundhouse, 2003.

Lohse, Bernhard. *Martin Luther: An Introduction to His Life and Work.* Philadelphia: Fortress, 1986.

Luke, Carmen. *Pedagogy, Printing and Protestantism: The Discourse on Childhood.* Albany: State University of New York Press, 1989.

McGrath, Alister E. *A Life of John Calvin: A Study in the Shaping of Western Culture.* Oxford, UK: Cambridge, MA: Blackwell Publishers, 2000.

Nestingen, James Arne. *Martin Luther: A Life.* Minneapolis, MN: Edinburgh: Augsburg, Alban, 2003.

Nohn, Frederick. *Luther: Biography of a Reformer.* St. Louis, MO: Concordia Publishing House, 2003.

Parker, Thomas H. *John Calvin: A Biography.* Philadelphia: Westminster, 1975.

Peterson, Rebecca C. *Early Educational Reform in North Germany and its Effects on Post-Reformation German Intellectuals.* Lewiston, NY: E. Mellen Press, 2001.

Schreinter, Susan E. *The Theater of His Glory: Nature and the Natural Order in the Thought of John Calvin.* Durham, NC: Labyrinth, 1991.

Spinka, Matthew., ed. *Advocates of Reform: From Wycliffe to Erasmus.* Philadelphia: Westminster, 1953.

Spitz, Lewis W. *The Religious Renaissance of the German Humanists.* Cambridge, MA: Harvard University Press, 1963.

———. *The Renaissance and Reformation Movements.* Chicago: Rand McNally, 1971.

Towns, Elmer L., ed. *A History of Religious Educators.* Grand Rapids, MI: Baker Book House, 1975.

Van Til, Henry R. *The Calvinistic Concept of Culture.* Grand Rapids, MI: Baker Academic, 2001.

Wellman, Sam. *John Calvin: Father of Reformed Theology.* Ulrichsville, OH: Barbour, 2001.

Johann Amos Comenius: Pansophist Educator and Proponent of International Education

Chapter 9 examines the life, educational philosophy, teaching methods, and contributions of Johann Amos Comenius (1592–1670), an early pioneer in reforming schools. A post-Reformation figure, Comenius lived during a time of intense religious intolerance and persecution. The Moravian Brethren, the small religious denomination that he led, was persecuted by the larger churches. For Comenius, the general enlightenment that resulted from a genuine education was a means of creating a more understanding, tolerant, and humane social order.

In this chapter, we examine the development of Comenius's ideas on education in their historical context and in terms of their continuing significance for teaching and learning. First, we describe the general social, political, and intellectual context of seventeenth-century Europe, in which Comenius lived and worked. Second, we analyze Comenius's life to determine its effect on the evolution of his educational ideas. Third, we explore Comenius's contributions to an enlightened concept of childhood, a more humane school environment, and effective methods of teaching. Fourth, we assess the significance of his educational contributions.

To organize your thoughts as you read this chapter, focus on the following questions:

1. What were the major trends in the historical context in which Comenius lived?
2. How did Comenius's educational biography shape his ideas on education?

3. How did Comenius's educational philosophy determine his educational policies and practices?
4. What has been the enduring effect of Comenius's contributions to education?

The Historical Context of Comenius's Life

Comenius's life coincided with the period of intense religious and nationalistic conflict that swept Europe during the Thirty Years' War. Pitting Catholic against Protestant, the sectarian conflict devastated Europe. In addition, the various Protestant denominations were so divided on theological issues that they were unable to unite against their adversaries.[1]

We must consider Comenius's life and educational contributions against this background of European religious, political, and military history, especially the Thirty Years' War. A brief examination of the war is helpful in understanding the dilemmas and motivation encountered by educators such as Comenius, who sought to develop a theory of international education as a means of bringing about understanding and peace among nations and people. The events of the Thirty Years' War demonstrate the difficulties of keeping conflicts localized, and reveal how wars escalate and grow out of control.

The war began over religious hostilities, but also was a power struggle by Europe's great powers to gain supremacy. At various times, the Holy Roman Empire ruled by the Catholic Hapsburg dynasty was pitted against the Protestant kingdoms of Denmark and Sweden. The German states were arrayed on both sides. France, although a Catholic country, fought against the Hapsburgs. The interplay of big power politics and religious hostility took its toll on the smaller states of central Europe, especially Bohemia and Moravia.

The conflict began in Bohemia, part of the Holy Roman Empire, ruled by the Hapsburg Emperor Ferdinand II, a zealous Catholic.[2] An underlying cause of the war was Ferdinand's policy of attempting to reverse the Protestant Reformation and restore Catholicism to his empire. Added to his religious motive was Ferdinand's diplomatic and strategic goal of controlling central Europe.[3]

The specific event that precipitated the war was the "Defenestration of Prague" on May 21, 1618, when Bohemian Protestant rebels seized the palace and threw Ferdinand's governor and representatives from its windows. Although they fell unharmed into a manure pile, the event unleashed a conflict that would devastate central Europe.

A decisive battle occurred at White Mountain in 1620. Ferdinand II's army, supported by his relatives, the Spanish Hapsburgs, were commanded by the master strategists Count Johan Tilly (1559–1632) and Duke Albrecht von Wallenstein (1583–1634). In 1620, the emperor's armies, the so-called Catholic League, defeated the Protestant army at the Battle of White Mountain. With the Protestant forces routed in Bohemia, the Brethren and other Protestant denominations were persecuted by the Hapsburg authorities. At this point Denmark, led by King Christian IV (1577–1648), entered the war on the Protestant side. Christian, who personally led his armies, enjoyed a great popularity with the middle classes of Norway and Denmark. In 1626, his armies were defeated at the battle of Lutter-am-Barenburg by the Catholic armies of Tilly and Wallenstein.

Fearing a total Hapsburg victory, Sweden, a Lutheran bastion, joined the Protestant cause under the leadership of its king, Gustavus Adolphus II (1594–1632), an astute military strategist.[4] Sweden's armies, now the hope of the Protestant cause, turned the tide in several battles in the German states. At this point Comenius tried to enlist Swedish help in gaining religious recognition and toleration for his church. However, the diplomatic intrigue and territorial objectives of the European great powers became even more complicated and obscured the events that had caused the conflict in the first place.

France, a largely Catholic country whose foreign policy was directed by its wily prime minister, the Roman Catholic Cardinal Richelieu, entered the war against the Catholic Hapsburgs in 1643. France's entry into the war was for strategic rather than religious reasons.

In 1648, the Treaty of Westphalia, a negotiated settlement, ended the war, which had begun in 1618. The treaty weakened the position of the Austrian Hapsburg emperor from the exalted position of Holy Roman Emperor to the status of another European monarch. The treaty gave the various German princes the right to determine the religion of their subjects. The major powers, such as France, gained some territory. The Calvinists were accorded religious recognition and toleration along with Catholics and Lutherans. However, there was no improvement in the situation of the smaller churches such as Comenius's Brethren.

Along with the Thirty Years' War, Comenius's educational ideas also must be examined in the theological context of his times, especially that of his church. The theology of the Unity of the Brethren, Comenius's small church, was based on the teachings of John Huss. The church's membership was predominantly in Bohemia and Moravia, then part of the Holy Roman Empire and now part of the Czech Republic. Huss (1369–1415) was a Bohemian religious reformer and critic.[5] He was condemned as a heretic by the Council of Constance and burned at the stake on July 6, 1415. After his death, small communities of religious reformers kept his ideas alive. One of these groups was the Unity of the Brethren, which Comenius would lead as a bishop. The name of the church was based on the strong belief that all Christians should be united in one faith rather than torn apart by denominational tensions, rivalry, and war. The Brethren believed in Christian unity, but did not believe that salvation came from a single set of theological doctrines and practices. Rather, they took an ecumenical position that the belief in Christ should unite all believers. The age in which Comenius worked and wrote was an intensely religious one. Religion and education went hand in hand. Most of the schools that existed were conducted under the auspices of religious denominations.

After the defeat of the Protestant forces at the Battle of White Mountain, the victorious Hapsburgs restored Roman Catholicism as the official religion in Bohemia and Moravia. The Brethren became a people in diaspora. To escape persecution in their native Bohemia and Moravia, the Brethren took refuge in other countries in Europe. Some like Comenius fled to Poland, while others went to Hungary and Germany. To understand Comenius's work in education, we must see him as an exile seeking a safe haven. When he could find no particular country to call his own, his vision grew to encompass a worldwide home.

The Brethren's revival sprang from a group of church members who, fleeing Moravia, were given refuge by a pietistical German nobleman, Count Zinzendorf (1700–1760), on his estate in Silesia. Members of the Brethren on Zinzendorf's estate established a community named Herrnhut. In 1727, a revival revitalized the community and missionaries of the Moravian Brethren came to North America to work among the Native Americans. Their settlements and schools in North Carolina, Pennsylvania, and Ohio bore the imprint of Comenius's educational work.

Comenius's Life and Career

Comenius was born on March 28, 1592, in Moravia. The Komensky family (Comenius's family name) lived in the town of Uhersky Brod, where Johann went to primary school. His parents died in 1604 when he was 12 years old. However, he was able to continue his education and eventually attended the universities of Herborn and Heidelberg. After completing his higher education, he returned to Moravia, was ordained a minister in the Unity of the Brethren in 1616, and was appointed pastor to the congregation at Fulnek in 1618, where he also served as principal of the local parish school.[6]

In 1620, the year of the Battle of White Mountain, a series of tragedies began for Comenius, his family, and his church. After their defeat at White Mountain, Protestant leaders were hunted down by the Imperial forces. Comenius's home was burned and he barely escaped with his life. For the next seven years, from 1620 to 1627, Comenius and his family hid at various locations in Bohemia. During this time his wife and two small children died, victims of plague. During this dark period of his life, Comenius wrote *The Labyrinth of the World* and *The Paradise of the Heart*. Arising from his experiences as a hunted exile and a victim of war, Comenius's *Labyrinth of the World* describes the tortuous path of a pilgrim, an exile like himself, who seeks but fails to find peace and security in the world. The pilgrim's quest is satisfied only by union with Christ.[7]

In 1628, Comenius fled across the border into Poland to begin 42 years of exile from his native Moravia. He located in the city of Leszno, some 40 miles south of the larger city of Poznan, where he ministered to his flock, wrote, and taught. In 1632, he was elected a bishop of the Brethren. In the same year, he also published his *Janua Linguarum Reserata*, which put forth his method of language instruction. Once again, he and the Brethren were victims of war. During an enemy raid on Leszno, his home, including his library of manuscripts and books, was burned.[8]

In 1641, Comenius visited England as a guest of the educational reformer Samuel Hartlib (1596–1662), an associate of Oliver Cromwell. While in England, he met with people who were interested in educational and religious reform. Once again war interfered with his educational work; this time the English Civil War between King James's supporters and Cromwell's republicans caused him to leave England in 1642.

Comenius moved to Elbing in Prussia. He continued his efforts to persuade the Swedish government, under Chancellor Oxenstierna (1583–1654), to act as protector of the interests of the Brethren and secure their right to resume their lives in Bohemia and Moravia. By this time, Oxenstierna, weary of central European affairs, was more concerned with reforming Sweden's politics and improving its economy. Comenius's efforts to enlist Swedish military and diplomatic assistance were unsuccessful. He returned to the Polish city of Leszno, the site of his first exile.

In 1650, Comenius, once again on the move, located in Saros-Patak in Hungary, which bordered Bohemia and Moravia and brought him close to his native land. Here he organized schools and wrote his religious treatise, *Lux in Tenebris*.

In 1656, Comenius accepted an invitation to locate to Amsterdam, in the Netherlands, where he attracted the interest and sympathy of Ludovicus de Geer, who became his financial benefactor. Under de Geer's patronage, Comenius was able to complete his major educational work, *Opera Didactica*, published in 1657. In 1658 he published his famous illustrated textbook, *Orbis Pictus*.

In 1668, Comenius published *Via Lucis, The Way of Light*, in which he presented a plan of international understanding and reconciliation by which Europe's warring churches and nations would come to live in peace. His various works on education were published as *Opera Didactica Omnia* from 1657 to 1668. Throughout his life Comenius worked on a comprehensive treatise that would encompass all the world's knowledge. Introductory volumes in this massive project, titled *Panergesia* and *Panaugia*, were published but he never completed the entire work he had planned.[9]

During his life, Comenius was a renowned educator, and his advice on education was sought throughout Europe. He continued his research, writing, and educational and religious work until his death in 1670.

Comenius and Pansophist Education

As an educational theorist, Comenius's educational philosophy embraced the broad, overarching goal of Pansophism. Literally meaning "all knowledge," Comenius's Pansophism was a synthesis of principles derived from theology, philosophy, and science.[10] Comenius based his theological principles on the tradition of Protestant reformist thought, especially the doctrines preached by John Huss. His philosophical underpinnings were in the mode of realism; there were real objects that could be known by human beings through their senses. Influenced by Francis Bacon, Comenius saw science as an instrument that was complementary to the Bible in providing human beings with knowledge of God's universe.[11]

Pansophism promised universal knowledge, which was to lead the knower to God, the source of all truth and goodness. Such knowledge was intrinsically valuable to the knower in that it was truth in its purest form. As the fund of knowledge of the human race, it was a valuable and indispensable cultural legacy. It was also instrumentally valuable in that the objects of knowledge could be used to secure a better and more peaceful life. Pansophism's claim of providing humankind with universal knowledge was both a way of knowing God and of achieving worldwide peace. Comenius regarded the Bible as an unerring guide to human conduct, and believed that human knowledge, refined in a structured and orderly way in the various sciences, also came from God. As human beings acquired knowledge of the sciences and humanities, they gained greater insights into God. God was all-knowing and hence possessed all knowledge that was revealed to humankind both through scholarly and scientific investigation and by Holy Scripture.

Comenius believed that the turmoil, trouble, and conflicts of his age were caused by ignorance. Ignorance, a condition of either not knowing or falsely knowing, caused intolerance, discrimination, and prejudice. Both he and the Brethren, the displaced people or refugees of the seventeenth century, were the victims of intolerance. Complete knowledge, Comenius believed, would bring people closer to God and to each other. Thus, Pansophism, an early form of international or peace education, was an argument for universal knowledge and education.

As an international or peace educator, Comenius fully anticipated the creation of a new world order of peacemaking and peacekeeping institutions. To create these new institutions, the leaders of the existing institutions—the churches, states, and schools—had to reconstruct or redesign them from rival and contentious institutions into cooperative ones.[12] Further, schools were to be transformed from agencies that indoctrinated children with a sense of their particular church or state's superiority into agencies that cultivated an ecumenical vision of a peaceable kingdom in which all could live in mutual respect.

Through his experiences as an educator, Comenius developed important insights into child nature, psychology, and development. These psychological insights were applied to classroom instruction. Unlike those who regarded childhood as a time of life to be lived through rather than enjoyed, Comenius saw it as a crucial part of the whole plan of human growth and development. In drawing his conclusions about childhood, Comenius looked to nature. This tendency to relate child development to nature and its processes can also be observed in the work of such educational theorists as Rousseau, Pestalozzi, and Froebel, whose ideas we explore in later chapters.

Unlike later naturalistic educators such as Rousseau and Spencer, who emphasized the natural over the supernatural, Comenius viewed the supernatural and natural orders as complementary. Nature, the physical and visible world that human beings observe through their senses, expresses the divine design of its creator. From his reflections and observations of nature, Comenius developed a set of principles for the use of educators. Among them were (1) nature has an appropriate time for growth and development, (2) natural operations are orderly and sequential, (3) nature proceeds gradually and completely, and (4) nature completes whatever it begins.[13]

An important concept, drawn from Comenius's observations, was that in the growth of plants and animals, nature has its own intrinsic timetable. Nothing can be hurried to grow unless it is ready to do so. Readiness that cooperates with natural forces and stimuli makes healthy development possible.

Further, based on the concept of readiness, childhood can be reduced to important developmental phases. Each phase has appropriate learning experiences. It was important for teachers to know the stages of development and base their teaching on these stages. The goal of tying instruction to child growth and development was to make both teaching and learning efficient and effective.

Given Comenius's premise that complete knowledge was both possible and desirable, instructional time had to be used efficiently. The lesson needed to be appropriate to the child's readiness and ability to learn as determined by the particular developmental stage. Effectiveness meant the child would succeed in mastering the skill or body of knowledge that was being taught. Comenius's stress on efficiency and effectiveness of instruction did not mean that teaching should be performed in a mechanical and impersonal manner. Rather, he wanted schools to be warm, emotionally secure, and satisfying environments for children. Indeed, schools that were suited to children's nature and development would be effective learning centers. For Comenius, schools were made for children rather than children being made for schools.

As a former school principal and educational theorist, Comenius in *The Great Didactic* turned to school reform. Based on his concept of readiness for learning and natural stages of human growth and development, Comenius designed a sequential system of schools. In *The School of Infancy*, he put forth his ideas on early childhood education, which today would be called *parenting education* or *home learning*. From birth until age 6, children were to be educated at home by their parents, especially by their mother, the first and best teacher. Anticipating the work of Piaget and Erikson by almost 300 years, Comenius argued that the first six years were crucial for children's later development.[14] The home should be a loving and secure environment where parents embody the values and ethics worthy of imitation by children. Unlike those who saw play as idleness, Comenius advised parents to encourage play activities where children exercised their muscles, renewed themselves, and imitated adult behavior.

The next six years, from age 6 through 12, was the period of attending primary school. Here, children would become literate and skilled in their native language, the vernacular spoken in their home and community. The primary school curriculum included reading, writing, religious education, mathematics, history, geography, music, art, and crafts.[15]

In his advice on the management of primary schools, Comenius was an early proponent of what is now called "effective schooling." He especially wanted to end the domination of instruction by exclusive reliance on recitation. According to the recitation method, each child, waiting her or his turn, would come before the teacher's desk and recite a previously memorized lesson.[16] Rather than using children's spontaneous curiosity, the recitation was a cut-and-dried monotonous recital. The process of having each child recite individually also was an ineffective use of instructional time. In place of the recitation, Comenius stressed grouping children so they could work on the same lesson simultaneously and interact cooperatively. To facilitate grouping, Comenius developed a design for school organization in which children were clustered in grades or levels.

Comenius also took a radical stand against the corporal punishment and psychological repression commonly practiced in seventeenth-century schools. For him, such schools were "slaughterhouses of the mind." Teachers were to be gentle and persuasive and instruct children without blows, threats, and ridicule. Discipline was to be fair and administered without anger.

After six years of primary school were completed, students would continue for another six years in the Latin grammar school, a secondary institution, which they attended from age 12 to 18. Here, the curriculum consisted of Greek, Latin, and Hebrew, languages then part of a conventional secondary education. Comenius's Latin school curriculum, reflecting his Pansophist ideology, was much enriched over that of conventional grammar schools. It included mathematics, geometry, physical and natural sciences, astronomy, history, ethics, rhetoric, music, and theology.[17] Along with these formal studies, opportunities for recreation were included to refresh the students.

Comenius developed his educational theories at a time when language learning, especially Latin, dominated much of secondary schooling. Like other educators of the period, Comenius continued to stress the importance of learning one's own language as well as the classical languages of Greek and Latin. In his conception of Pansophist knowledge, language learning was a necessary instrument in acquiring knowledge. Thus Comenius did not attack verbalism to the degree that Rousseau did in the eighteenth century and Pestalozzi did in the nineteenth. However, he was moving away from teaching that was dominated exclusively by words. He recognized that instruction could be made more realistic and meaningful to children by introducing objects or pictures of objects into the classroom. His book, *Orbis Pictus*, or *The Visible World*, was an innovation in textbooks. The illustrations it provided were a new way of teaching languages.[18]

To complete his system of schools, Comenius developed the idea of the Pansophist university, an institution of higher learning to be attended by the most intellectually gifted students. Here, students would study the entire range of knowledge embraced in the Pansophist philosophy of education. Learned professors would teach classes, lecture, and prepare scholarly books.

Comenius sought to develop strategies for educational effectiveness and efficiency. Concerned with losing valuable instructional time, he urged that the processes of schooling not waste that precious commodity. His work as a textbook writer and pedagogical innovator was directed toward getting the most out of the time allotted for schooling. Although concerned with using time effectively, Comenius also believed this should not diminish the humanitarian concern of the teacher for children. During his life he had seen enough of war, torment, and coercion. In the school he envisioned, children were to be liberated to use their senses and not be repressed. Above all, the Comenian ideal in education stressed the mutual respect of teacher and learner.

Conclusion: An Assessment

Perhaps to us who live in a world characterized by the explosion of knowledge, Comenius's vision of Pansophism or the possibility of attaining universal knowledge is naive. The modern world is characterized by ever-increasing new developments in science, medicine, and technology. Modern science and technology is characterized by specialization. Indeed, much of modern education is designed to prepare specialists who have expertise in a limited area of knowledge. Little of modern education is geared to cultivate the generalist who seeks to integrate all knowledge, as Comenius prescribed.

On reflection, however, the Comenian vision is not as naive as it appears. Although Comenius thought of organizing all knowledge in books, today's information technology might make his vision more a reality in the twenty-first century than was possible in his own time. Computers, with their ability to store and retrieve masses of data and information, may make universal knowledge a reality.

If Comenius were alive today, he would undoubtedly endorse the effectiveness and efficiency of computer-based instruction. The graphics that computerized learning makes possible are but a new version of the *Orbis Pictus*. He would endorse the efficient use of time that educational technology makes possible.

At the same time that Comenius would be receptive to educational technology and computer-based instruction, he would remind us that schools were made for children and not vice versa. Regardless of the technology and its efficiency, the child's nature, development, and readiness must always underlie instruction.

Comenius was an ecumenical educator who happened to live and work in a decidedly unecumenical age. Seventeenth-century schools were conducted under church auspices at a time when various denominations were in conflict. Schooling was catechetical and designed to instill the dogmas of the particular religion in an exclusionary way. Children were to learn the doctrines of their particular religion so they could defend their faith against religious adversaries. Comenius, in contrast, believed it was possible to have value-oriented religious education that reflected both denominational uniqueness as well as commonalities. While each could practice religion according to his or her denominational creed, all could feel unity in the commonality of Christian belief. In advance of his age, Comenius argued for a Council of the World's Churches.[19] In the twentieth century, the world's great religions entered into ecumenical dialogue. Thus, Comenius was a prophet of ecumenism and ecumenical education.

Comenius's world was torn by sectarian contention and nationalistic ambitions. The Thirty Years' War devastated Europe. In many parts of the world, war and senseless killing continue today. Just as Comenius and the Brethren were refugees in the seventeenth century, the twenty-first century still has its victimized men, women, and children. Modern displaced people, the homeless, and refugees remain the people that an education based on the principles of Comenius seeks to restore to wholeness and dignity. Comenius would weep over the acts of terrorism and violence that grow increasingly commonplace today. For him, knowledge and education would still be the road humankind must take to reach the peaceable kingdom.

Questions for Reflection and Dialogue

1. How did the context of the Thirty Years' War provide the background for the development of Comenius's educational theory?
2. Was the historical context in which Comenius lived and worked a continuance of the Protestant Reformation and Catholic Counterreformation or was it a new development?
3. How did the key events in Comenius's life shape his outlook on the world and his view of education?
4. Identify and examine the elements of continuity and change in Comenius's educational theory.
5. Debate the relevance of Comenius's Pansophism for contemporary international or peace education, especially conflict resolution between contending racial, ethnic, and religious groups.
6. How was Comenius an exponent of children's rights? How would he react to the violation of children's rights as a result of ethnonationalist conflicts and exploitation in the global industrial economy?
7. How would Comenius react to the incidence of violence among students in contemporary American schools and society?

Projects for Deepening Your Understanding

1. Review the literature on effective schools. Do you think Comenius would endorse effective schools?
2. Review the purposes of UNESCO. Do you think Comenius would endorse the educational activities of the United Nations?
3. If your college or university offers a program or course on peace education, obtain a copy of the program description or course syllabus. Do you think Comenius

would endorse the program or course? How might he revise the program or course?

4. Review the literature on ways to prevent violence in schools. How would Comenius react to current programs of conflict resolution and other programs designed to prevent violence in schools?

5. Research situations in the world where war, terrorism, and ethnic and religious conflict are taking place. What is the effect of war, terrorism, and ethnic and religious conflict on children? How do you think Comenius's plans for peace education would be received today?

6. In an essay, examine the key elements in Comenius's Pansophism and apply them to contemporary schools.

7. If it is available in your library, review Comenius's *Orbis Pictus.*

Notes

1. Among the histories of the Thirty Years' War are David Maland, *Europe at War, 1600–1650* (Totowa, NJ: Rowman & Littlefield, 1980); and Josef V. Polisensky, *War and Society in Europe, 1618–1644* (Cambridge, UK: Cambridge University Press, 1978).

2. Robert Bierley, S.J., *Religion and Politics in the Age of the Counterreformation: Emperor Ferdinand II, William Lamormaini, S.J. and the Formation of Imperial Policy* (Chapel Hill, NC: University of North Carolina Press, 1981).

3. Randy Petersen, "The Thirty Years' War," *Christian History* 6 (1987), 17.

4. Charles R. L. Fletcher, *Gustavus Adolphus and the Struggle of Protestantism for Existence* (New York: G. P. Putnam's Sons, 1894).

5. Ezra H. Gillett, *The Life and Times of John Huss: The Bohemian Reformation of the Fifteenth Century* (New York: AMS, 1978).

6. Eve Chyhova Bock, "Seeking a Better Way," *Christian History* 6 (1987), 7.

7. Bock, "Seeking a Better Way," 8.

8. Bock, "Seeking a Better Way," 7.

9. Josef Smolik, "Comenius: A Man of Hope in a Time of Turmoil," *Christian History* 6 (1987), 16.

10. Paul Heidebrecht, "Learning from Nature: the Educational Legacy of Jan Amos Comenius," *Christian History* 6 (1987), 23.

11. Heidebrecht, "Learning from Nature," 23.

12. Smolik, "Comenius," 18.

13. Heidebrecht, "Learning from Nature," 23.

14. Jerome K. Clauser, "The Pansophist: Comenius," in Paul Nash, Andreas M. Kazamias, and Henry J. Perkinson, eds., *The Educated Man: Studies in the History of Educational Thought* (New York: John Wiley & Sons, 1965), 165–88.

15. Heidebrecht, "Learning from Nature," 35.

16. Heidebrecht, "Learning from Nature," 35.

17. Lois Le Bar, "What Children Owe to Comenius," *Christian History* 6 (1987), 19.

18. Gerald L. Gutek, *A History of the Western Educational Experience* (Prospect Heights, IL: Waveland, 1995), 152–56.

19. Smolik, "Comenius," 18.

Suggestions for Further Reading

Cach, Josef, and Neubert, Ladislav. *Homage to J. A. Comenius: {Sbornik}.* Praha: Karolinum, 1991.

Comenius, Johann Amos. *Comenius' School of Infancy: an Essay on the Education of Youth During the First Six Years.* Will Seymour Monroe, ed. Boston: D. C. Heath, 1983.

———. *The Great Didactic of John Amos Comenius.* Maurice Walter Keatinge, ed. Kila, MT: Kessinger Pub. Co., 1991.

———. *The Labyrinth of the World and the Paradise of the Heart.* New York: Arno, 1971.

———. *The Orbis Pictus of John Amos Comenius.* Syracuse, NY: C. W. Bardeen, 1887.

Davies, Ron. *A Heart for Mission: Five Pioneer Thinkers.* Fearn: Christian Focus, 2002.

Jakubec, Jan. *Johannes Amos Comenius.* New York: Arno, 1971.

Maland, David. *Europe at War, 1600–1650.* Totowa, NJ: Rowman & Littlefield, 1980.

Murphy, Daniel. *Comenius: A Critical Reassessment of His Life and Work.* Blackrock Co. Dublin; Portland, OR: Irish Academic Press, 1995.

Van Vilet, P., and Vanderjagt, Arie Johan. *Johannes Amos Comenius (1592–1670): Exponent of European Culture?* Amsterdam; New York: North-Holland, 1994.

PART

III

Jean-Jacques Rousseau: Prophet of Naturalism

This chapter discusses the life, educational philosophy, and contributions of Jean-Jacques Rousseau (1712–1778), one of the most intriguing, paradoxical, and iconoclastic of the theorists who provoked a revolution in educational thinking and practice. Rousseau's life coincided with what historians have called the Age of Reason, or the Enlightenment, of the eighteenth century. Although Rousseau was a figure of the Enlightenment, he also anticipated the romanticism of the early nineteenth century. In Rousseau's ideas on education, we can feel the tension between reason and romanticism.

In this chapter, we discuss Rousseau's influence on Western and U.S. education in the historical context of the eighteenth-century Enlightenment and in terms of its enduring effect on educational philosophy and policy. First, we describe the general intellectual, social, and political context in which Rousseau lived and worked. Second, we analyze Rousseau's biography, education, and career to observe the evolution of his ideas. Third, we assess the continuing effect of Rousseau's contributions to education. In this analysis, we shall see how Rousseau's ideas on education, especially as expressed in *Emile*, shaped educational philosophy and instructional methods in the nineteenth and twentieth centuries. Of special interest is Rousseau's influence on child-centered educational practices.

To organize your thoughts as you read this chapter, focus on the following questions:

1. What were the major trends of the historical context of the Enlightenment of the eighteenth century, the time and situation in which Rousseau lived?
2. How did Rousseau's educational biography shape his philosophy of education?
3. How did Rousseau's educational philosophy influence educational policies and practices in later centuries?
4. What has been the enduring impact of Rousseau's educational ideas?

The Historical Context of Rousseau's Life

Rousseau's life coincided with the century of Western history known as the Enlightenment. Although earlier periods in Western history have had their intellectual revivals, the Enlightenment unleashed the intellectual and cultural trends that created a modern worldview.[1] In many respects, Rousseau helped to break down some of the inherited beliefs and introduce new ideas that would shape the future.

One of the major trends of the Enlightenment was a new way of thinking about nature and the human being in a natural universe. Since the early Christian era, Western thought and culture had been shaped largely by the supernatural order. The worldview of the Middle Ages, the Medieval synthesis, rested on a dualistic conception of reality in which the natural order was viewed as inferior to the supernatural. The age of the Reformation saw a reawakening of human interest in and awe of the supernatural order. The Enlightenment era saw theorists looking to nature to find clues on how life should be lived. Education was important in that, in the minds of the Enlightenment *philosophes* (philosophers), it prepared people to live according to the principles of nature.

For many of the thinkers of the Enlightenment, including Rousseau, it was important that human beings stop gazing upward to heaven and begin to look at the natural world about them. They should observe and study natural phenomena and from their observations extract the principles needed to operate in the "real world." The principles of the natural universe could be discovered, the Enlightenment theorists believed, by using the scientific method.

The scientific method, as the *philosophes* conceived of it, was a systematic and careful way of observing natural phenomena. Through careful and consistent observation, it was possible to discern the laws or principles that made the universe work, such as the patterns of the revolution of the planets around the sun, the rotation of the Earth, the growth of plants, and the circulation of blood in the body. There was no end to what humans could discover about their world if they applied themselves to the task correctly. For the Enlightenment generation, science meant actual observation and recording of phenomena and not the study of what the ancient Greek and Roman philosophers had written about nature. In the Enlightenment perspective, nature was "out there" waiting to be discovered.

For these theorists, the scientific method was designed to investigate whatever was observable to the senses, or empirical. The lenses of scientists' telescopes and microscopes were but special extensions of the senses that improved human sight. In the

Enlightenment view, the world of objects took on a new meaning and new significance. Truth and meaning were found in the world of things and of people, not by contemplating ideal forms as Plato had insisted or in the spiritual dimension as Aquinas had written. Nor was the Bible the sole authority as Calvin had preached. No, the truth could be found by anyone who used the right approach—the scientific method.

The general intellectual strategy of Enlightenment *philosophes*, including Rousseau, was to demystify. Although earlier thinkers such as Augustine, Aquinas, and Calvin had emphasized the importance and reverence that men and women should accord to their unanswerable questions, to the mysteries of life, the *philosophes* tried to explain everything. All questions—if they were valid—could be answered. After the Enlightenment there were two different approaches to viewing reality and organizing education, one assumed that the greatest and most powerful ideas rested on the mystery of life and the other that there were no real mysteries.

In the worldview of the Enlightenment, nature in the physical sense was all that was out there. This outward world, which human beings experienced through their senses, was orderly in that it manifested and followed certain patterns. Night followed day, the seasons of the year followed each other, the tides rose and fell with a regularity that could be plotted, measured, and predicted. The human body, too, went through stages of observable growth, as did plants and animals. For the Enlightenment mind, nature was something of which human beings were a part. The natural universe was like a great world machine or clock that was in perpetual, rhythmic movement. Unlike the opinion of modern scientists, the great world mechanism that the *philosophes* saw as the natural universe was not relative or evolving. It was a beautiful and grandiose but stable world machine.[2]

Since the early Christian era, Western thought—through the Middle Ages, the Renaissance, and the Reformation—had exalted in an idea of a Supreme Being, a divine Creator, a personal God who intervened in world and human affairs. Although most Enlightenment theorists continued to believe in a source or origin or creator of some sort, to them this force was impersonal. For many of the Enlightenment thinkers, called *deists*, this original force was a kind of point of origin that got the universe started and then left it to function on its own perfect mechanism.

The philosophers of the Enlightenment, like the humanists of the Renaissance, tended to be an initiated and educated elite. Although the Enlightenment theorists moved in a secular direction, the vast majority of the residents of Europe and the Americas continued to attend their churches and to read and follow their Bibles. Christianity in its Catholic and Protestant creedal formulations continued to be the source of truth and meaning for most people. However, there was an element about the Enlightenment *philosophes* that was different from the Renaissance classical humanists. Whereas the humanists regarded themselves as the guardians of truth, the *philosophes* saw themselves as the discoverers and disseminators of truth. Further, their truth was not meant to be merely deposited in libraries, it was intended to remake or reconstruct society along natural principles.

Although preceding eras—the classical Greek and Roman, the Medieval, the Renaissance, and the Reformation—looked to the past to find truth, beauty, and wisdom, the Enlightenment theorists looked neither to ancient texts nor sacred books. Enlightenment *philosophes* were forward looking and believed that they could shape human destiny. They believed that they could reconstruct or redesign social, political, and economic conditions to get the kind of consequences they desired. In other words, the human future could be made progressively better than the human past. The thinkers of the Enlightenment had a strong belief in the progress of the human race.

The basic strategy that the *philosophes* designed to make progress a reality was derived from their view of nature and the scientific method. If natural laws could be discovered by observing and identifying the patterns in physical nature, they reasoned, the same was true of society. By observing social, political, and economic interactions, it would be possible to discover the laws that governed human society. However, there was a problem. The intellectual and cultural baggage inherited from the prescientific past created institutional and attitudinal obstacles to social reform. For progress to take place, it would be necessary to purge or remove these obstacles.

Although the social theorists of the Enlightenment agreed that progress was a possibility, they differed on the form of the society of the future and the process that should be used to establish that society. These different views of social change marked the beginning of the age of ideologies. Initially coined by a group of French theorists called the ideologues, the term *ideology* meant a science of ideas. It was an alternative to the earlier metaphysical concepts that had preoccupied social theorists. What would emerge in the eighteenth, nineteenth, and twentieth centuries would be not one ideology but a number of competing ideologies.[3]

Although the Enlightenment theorists might debate the desired social organization of the future, they generally agreed that established churches and absolute, inherited monarchies blocked social progress. Further, the educational institutions supported by these inherited residues were agencies of miseducation. For example, the Catholic Church in France and Spain and the Orthodox Church in Russia were regarded as institutions based on unscientific dogmatic doctrines that suppressed scientific inquiry. Schools established and maintained by the established churches were agencies of indoctrination rather than genuine education. For true progress, it would be necessary to disestablish official churches and free schools from their domination. In the political realm, absolute, hereditary monarchies in which kings or queens ruled by the "grace of God" without checks or balances were also regarded as impediments to progress. What was needed were new forms of government. New philosophies of civic education needed to be created that would prepare people to establish and maintain new governments.[4]

In the political realm, the inherited monarchies were in place, buttressed by aristocracies of birth. Some of the monarchs, such as Maria Theresa and Joseph of Austria, Catherine of Russia, and Frederick of Prussia, the "enlightened despots," talked about limited reforms but did little. In the British colonies of North America and in France, full-scale revolutions would replace monarchical rule with republican government.

The Enlightenment held great importance for the future course of education. The emphasis on nature turned the interests of Enlightenment educators to the study of human nature as a means of establishing the content and method of education. Instead of looking to ancient texts for guidance, theorists such as Rousseau urged people to look to the growth and development of the human being. By observing children, it was possible to identify and plot the course of development. Educators merely needed to identify and use the activities that were appropriate to a particular stage of human development.

This emphasis on nature and discovery of natural laws through science also had important implications for learning theory and teaching methods. Enlightened educators such as Rousseau and Pestalozzi, and later the American progressive educators, would emphasize the role of the senses in learning. Children would learn most effectively and efficiently by using their senses in observing and experiencing the natural objects of their environment.

Although certain key educational reformers such as Rousseau argued for following nature and learning through the senses, the inherited educational institutions were generally resistant to change. The catechism, the classics, and the authority that came from books dominated learning for years to come. Indeed, political, economic, and social changes often preceded changes in education.

Rousseau as an Educational Theorist of the Enlightenment

This section examines the life and educational ideas of Jean-Jacques Rousseau, a leading personality, critic, and author of the Enlightenment.[5] Rousseau's autobiographical confessions reveal how his own experiences in early childhood shaped his later views on life and education. The son of Suzanne Bernard and Isaac Rousseau, a watchmaker, Jean-Jacques was born in Geneva, Switzerland, the city where John Calvin once preached the doctrines of the Protestant Reformation. Rousseau's mother died when he was 9 days old. Presumably his mother's death contributed to his choice of an orphan boy as the principal character in his educational novel, *Emile*. Jean-Jacques was reared by his father and an aunt. Rousseau claimed that his father favored him over his brother, who ran away from home to escape neglect. He claimed that he was overindulged by his highly emotional, impulsive aunt and his irresponsible, pleasure-loving father.[6]

Rousseau wrote that his father was his first tutor. Together, father and son read widely into the late hours of the night from an ill-sorted collection of books. The reading, ranging from romantic novels to such classic works as Ovid's *Metamorphoses* and Plutarch's *Lives of Famous Men*, stocked his mind with images far removed from reality. In *Emile*, Rousseau warned against introducing books too early in a child's life. It was much better, he advised, that children acquire a stock of direct experiences of their immediate environment before reading about abstract concepts about which they know little or nothing. Although his relationship appears to have been close with his father, it was brief. When Rousseau was 10, his father had an altercation with an army officer and fled Geneva to avoid imprisonment, thus ending their close relationship. Rousseau was then placed in the care of his uncle, Gabriel Bernard, and received a conventional primary education.

Rousseau went through two apprenticeships, first with a notary and then an engraver. Neither was satisfactory. The notary dismissed Rousseau, whom he charged with neglecting his duties. He left the service of the engraver, whom he claimed treated him unfairly and harshly. Early in his life, Rousseau showed he had difficulty in working as a subordinate and would flee from unpleasant situations.[7] Rousseau left Geneva in 1728 and went to Turin, Italy, where he found short-term employment as a footman for a wealthy family.

The next stage in Rousseau's odyssey took him to Chambery, in Savoy, where he lived with his paramour, a wealthy widow, Madame de Waren. She provided the money that enabled him to acquire a classical education and a knowledge of music. Under her tutelage, he was converted to Catholicism, a religion he would later abandon.

In 1739, when he was 27, Rousseau took a position as tutor to the two sons of M. de Mably. He disliked the actual practice of teaching but was intrigued by the broad issues of education. His experience as tutor in the de Mably household stimulated him to write his first treatise on education, the *Project of the Education of M. de Sainte-Marie.*[8]

In 1741, Rousseau, still searching to establish a place for himself, went to Paris, where he earned a living by copying music. Paris was then the center of the intellectual ferment of the Enlightenment. Here, Rousseau was attracted to the circle of *philosophes* of the Enlightenment. Rousseau then received an appointment as secretary to the French ambassador in Venice. Although the appointment could have been the beginning of a diplomatic career, it was not; Rousseau quarreled with his superiors and lost his position.

Rousseau once again returned to Paris. Here, he began a love affair with Therese Levasseur, an illiterate servant. The couple had five children, all of whom were placed in foundling homes shortly after their births. She later became his common-law wife. Readers of Rousseau's educational novel, *Emile*, find it ironic that Rousseau, an early proponent of child permissiveness, abandoned his own children.[9]

Established again in Paris, Rousseau renewed his association with the *philosophes* and the encyclopedists such as Diderot and d'Alembert. In 1749, Rousseau won a contest for the best essay with, "Has the Progress of the Arts and Sciences Contributed More to the Corruption or Purification of Morals?"[10] Unlike the defenders of the arts and sciences over the centuries, Rousseau answered that the arts and sciences tended to corrupt rather than liberate. He wrote articles for Diderot's *Encyclopedia;* his essay, "Discourse on Political Economy," appeared in 1755.[11] Rousseau next returned to Geneva, renounced Catholicism, reconverted to Protestantism, and regained his rights as a citizen of Geneva.

Once again, Rousseau returned to Paris, where he had an affair with the Comtesse d'Handetot. In his novel, *La Nouvelle Heloise*, published in 1761, the countess served as a model of the new woman. Rousseau's influential political commentary, *The Social Contract*, was published in 1762, the same year that he published *Emile.*[12]

Rousseau next went to England, as the guest of philosopher David Hume. Here, he started to work on his autobiographical confessions. However, his persistent tendency to quarrel with his friends occurred once again. He imagined Hume was conspiring against him and quickly left England. In 1767, Rousseau was back in France. He completed the confessions in 1770. At the invitation of Count Wielhorski, Rousseau wrote a constitution for Poland, *The Government of Poland*, in 1772.[13]

On July 2, 1778, Rousseau died of uremia at Ermenonville, some 30 miles from Paris. He was buried on the Girardin estate. On October 11, 1794, his remains were transferred to the Pantheon in Paris.

Rousseau's Educational Writing

Although many of Rousseau's essays and books have educational implications, his didactic novel, *Emile*, is most significant for education. It exhibits several general features of the Enlightenment, especially the emphasis on nature and naturalism. Those who read Rousseau's *Emile* rarely leave the book in an objective frame of mind. For some readers, it is a challenging argument for education that is completely child centered. Others reject it as a wildly utopian book divorced from educational reality.

Like Plato's *Republic*, Rousseau's *Emile* has broad social and political as well as educational implications. Rousseau most likely did not intend that his educational ideas in *Emile* be taken literally. Rather, he wanted the story told in the novel to illustrate certain major principles about education. Foremost among these principles is Rousseau's belief in the original goodness of human nature. The book begins, "Everything is good as it leaves the hands of the Author of Things; everything degenerates in the hands of man."[14] Here, Rousseau is attacking the Calvinist doctrine of human depravity and the Catholic belief in the spiritual deprivation caused by original sin. For Rousseau, human beings are not initially evil or imperfect. Infants, although not moral beings, are intrinsically good. Human beings, Rousseau believed, are corrupted by their socialization in a corrupting society and their education in an artificial culture. For example, children are not born as liars, cheats, thieves, or murderers. They learn these vices in an unnatural and corrupt society. Their intrinsic natural goodness is spoiled by corrupting adults and their institutions. For Rousseau, the challenge is to place Emile in a natural environment in which his intrinsic natural goodness will grow and develop without being tainted by a corrupt society. If this can be accomplished, the child's self-identity can be formed around the natural instinct of *amour de soi*, or self-esteem. Rousseau contrasts *amour de soi* with *amour propre*, or selfishness, by which a person learns to manipulate others for his or her own purposes. If Emile is educated naturally, perhaps, as the new Adam of the Enlightenment he will be the father of a new, naturally educated race of men and women. In a world inhabited by naturally educated and uncorrupted persons, it might be possible to create social, political, and economic institutions that also function naturally.

The educational challenge for Rousseau is how to educate the new race of human beings. The inherited educational institutions and practices offer no solution. Most of the existing primary or elementary schools were church related. Their educational philosophy, based on theological premises, saw children as inherently corrupt creatures who needed to be disciplined by authoritarian teachers. Secondary schools, too, were agencies of miseducation. They stressed a book-centered, classical curriculum that ignored nature and science.

In his novel, Rousseau tells the story of the total upbringing or education of a boy, from infancy to young manhood, by a tutor. The tutor has the sole responsibility for Emile's moral, mental, and physical development. Further, Emile is the only student in that environment. It is in this educational setting that several important themes or elements in Rousseau's theory emerge.

The first element is the location where education takes place. Conventionally, children are educated in schools, institutional settings staffed by teachers and designed specifically to educate. Historically, the school curriculum focused on learning languages, one's own and others. Further, books were regarded as the authoritative sources of knowledge. For Rousseau and other naturalist educators, the conventional school setting was wrong and even miseducative. Child-centered educational reformers sought to replace the conventional school classroom with the "prepared environment." For Rousseau, Emile's prepared environment was a country estate where the growing boy could experience nature directly. Other educational reformers who have followed in Rousseau's theoretical footsteps have tried to redesign schools to be more "natural" settings.

It should be remembered that, although naturalistic reformers such as Rousseau see the conventional school as coercive and argue for greater freedom for the child, the prepared environment can be equally limiting on freedom. A prepared environment is designed to elicit certain outcomes. The person structuring the environment is creating a design that governs behavior in less direct ways than the conventional school but in no less a controlling manner.

The second element in Rousseau's education of Emile concerns appropriateness in education. In the eighteenth century as well as in later periods education was closely related to one's socioeconomic class. Although the middle class was a rising new class, the class structure was still based largely on ascription—the status one inherited by birth. In other words, children of an aristocrat were born to rule and enjoy the luxuries of wealth and status. Education was designed to prepare them for specific future roles. The same was true of the children of peasants, who were destined to be agricultural laborers. Although there are many signs that Emile is receiving an education that only a child of the upper classes could afford to receive, Rousseau introduces a new meaning to appropriateness in education—something that nature provides.

As a true son of the Enlightenment, Rousseau's worldview saw nature as the sensible reality that human beings inhabited. He saw human nature functioning in parallel terms. In the various dimensions of nature—in plant and animal life—there were stages of development. In human life, too, there were clearly defined stages of development. In the human life span, individuals are born, go through infancy and childhood, come to maturity, reach old age, and eventually die. For each stage of development, there are appropriate kinds of activities and learning that come naturally from the conditions of the developmental stage. Although Rousseau was not the first theorist in the history of education to refer to stages of development, he did so in a dramatic way. Emile was experiencing the natural stages of human development without the intrusion of social and cultural variables.

We now turn to the stages of development that Rousseau identified in *Emile*. What Rousseau calls infancy, the earliest stage of human life, begins with birth and extends until age 5. During the first months of infancy, the child is helpless and everything must be done for him. The nurturing process is directed to building a strong, healthy body; the diet consists of simple country food. Although the child is not allowed to harm himself, he is otherwise given freedom of movement so that his muscles are developed. In the early months of life, the infant has only vague feelings of pleasure and pain, rather than ideas. By moving and touching objects, he learns to distinguish himself from objects other than himself. Because ideas are products of data that come from the senses, the child's encounters and experiences with objects are important for learning about the environment. In his earliest years, the child experiences only pleasure and pain that come from the objects encountered in his exploration of the environment. At this stage, memory and imagination are inactive.

In infancy, the young child is like an unspoiled primitive person who is close to the original state of nature. If we want to discover the natural person, the clues to his identity can be found in simple, unaffected, childlike behavior. Education should be based on this behavior. Rousseau's discussion about education for infancy has implications for parenting. He advised parents to love their children, to avoid coercing them physically and emotionally, and to give them as much freedom as possible within a secure environment.

Rousseau emphasizes the mother's role in providing the child's early formative educational experiences.[15] It is through the mother's influence on her child that a general reform of morals will take place. Once women become good and loving mothers, then men will become good husbands and fathers. When the book moves to its conclusion and Emile is about to marry Sophie, her importance in exercising a gentle influence on her husband is stressed.

Like Rousseau, Emile lost his mother in infancy and is a well-to-do orphan. Emile is a strong and healthy boy of average intelligence. To avoid conflict with other adults over how Emile should be raised, the tutor is given complete control over his education.

Rousseau defined the second stage that Emile experiences as boyhood, the period from ages 5 through 12. During these years, the boy's physical strength has increased and he is able to do more for himself.[16] It is at this stage that Emile becomes more aware of his personal self-identity and is becoming conscious of happiness and unhappiness. It is at this stage that Rousseau develops the two concepts of moral development, *amour de soi* and *amour propre*. *Amour de soi* arises from a person's natural and instinctive self-interests. Natural virtues that arise from *amour de soi* should be cultivated. *Amour propre* is based on social relationships that either make the person a manipulator of other people or an other-directed person. It is important that Emile's educational environment be nonsocial. The tutor should maintain an even temperament in dealing with Emile and should maintain a balance between excessive severity and excessive indulgence.

Rousseau reminds us that children are still amoral and nonreasonable until age 12. It is a waste of the tutor's time and effort to try to reason with Emile or to give orders and commands. Rousseau's warning against trying to instill morality through preaching essentially attacks the notion that concepts of good and bad and right and wrong can be instilled verbally. What is important is that Emile learn that his actions have consequences. Some actions will bring pleasure and others will bring pain.

Rousseau warns us about the "youthful sage," the boy or girl who is able to memorize and recite dates from history, poetry, or literary passages. Those who praise such children have misconstrued words and their recitation with genuine knowledge. Such children adjust their behavior to meet adult expectations. Neither is the child who has memorized the commandments in the catechism necessarily a good person. The youthful sage, although appearing to be intellectually precocious, is not living as a child lives but rather is forcing her or his behavior to fit patterns of performance to please adults.

Rousseau warns against the premature introduction of books. Children should not be pressured into reading. Emile will read when he is ready and needs to read. Rather than verbal learning, Rousseau argues that Emile needs more sensory and physical training. Emile observes the objects in the environment and comes to experience the effects of these objects. Most important at this stage is continued sensory training in which the various senses are used to check each other in estimating the size, shape, and dimensions of objects.

Rousseau defined the third stage in Emile's education as taking place from ages 12 through 15.[17] An important object during this stage is to introduce the concept of *utility*, or purpose. What are the uses of objects? Although nature studies have been an important aspect of Emile's education, they receive special emphasis during this period.

Emile observes natural phenomena and asks questions about them. He learns natural science by observing what he sees about him on walks with his tutor in the forest and by planting vegetables in the garden. Geography, too, is learned firsthand from the study of the immediate environment rather than by studying maps and globes. Emile also learns a manual skill, such as carpentry, to learn the correct combination of mental and physical labor. He gets his first book, *Robinson Crusoe*, which tells how Crusoe, who is shipwrecked on a tropical island, survives in a natural setting. Along with experiencing the tale of survival, Emile learns about the concept of mutual dependence that arises between Crusoe and Friday.

Emile's next stage of development might be termed adolescence, or the years between ages 15 and 18.[18] Emile now develops sexual interests and requires special guidance. When he has a question about sex, the tutor answers him directly, without mystery or coarseness. Emile is also becoming increasingly aware of social relationships and the needs and concerns of others. He is taken on short trips, where he sees people who are in less fortunate circumstances than his. At this point, he develops an awareness of the sufferings of others but is not overexposed to them lest he become insensitive to them.

Emile's next stage of development, from ages 18 to 20, is referred to as the "age of humanity."[19] It is at this rather advanced stage that Emile enters the moral sphere and becomes involved in moral relationships. Justice and goodness come from the intrinsic primitive affections with which people are endowed at birth. In Rousseau's perspective, these primitive affections are not abstract moral principles created by the intellect but grow and are nurtured throughout the process of development.

It is in the age of humanity that Emile begins to develop a cultural perspective or distance from the immediacy of his environment to broader issues and concerns. He now studies history as a vehicle for examining the human being's basic goodness and the corrupting influence of society. Rousseau warns against the academic historian's narrative of the past that stresses what is bad rather than what is good about human nature. Further, he states, historians often distort history through interpretations that reflect their own prejudices.

Rousseau, who had been both a Catholic and a Protestant, commented on the role of religion in Emile's education. In his own religion, Rousseau eventually reached what could be called a naturalistic deist position. He believed there was a creator, a God, but God was approached via nature. Recommending a naturalistic approach to religion, Rousseau warned against the dogmatic catechetical approach in which words, expressed as questions and answers, were regarded as conveying moral principles. He also admonished against the emphasis on mysteries that shrouded the human mind from natural truths. Further, the images formed during childhood about God were carried forward throughout life, often remaining at the level in which they were formed.

At age 20, Emile reaches the age of manhood and he meets and falls in love with his future wife, Sophie.[20] An interesting inconsistency is revealed in Rousseau's treatment of Sophie. She is the person who, through the natural family, will bring Emile into a natural society. However, much of Rousseau's description of Sophie reflects his male chauvinism. Men, he says, by their nature are active and strong; women are passive and weak. A woman's education is dependent on her relationship to a man. She is to win a man's affection and esteem, to give him companionship, affection, consolation, and counsel. In describing Sophie's character, Rousseau writes that she was of a "good nature" and pleasing appearance.[21] Sophie "loves virtue" but has "little experience of the practice of society but she is obliging and attentive, and she puts grace in everything she does."[22]

Before marrying Sophie, Emile travels for two years, taking the "grand tour," visiting foreign nations and studying their people, languages, forms of government, and customs. As the book ends, Emile informs his tutor that he plans to educate his children as he was educated.

Conclusion: An Assessment

An assessment of the significance of Rousseau's educational contributions can examine only a few selected themes. Rousseau was a far-ranging but undisciplined theorist who was sometimes inconsistent and contradictory in his writing. In the broad sense, however, Rousseau can be seen as a general social, political, and educational theorist who was pointing in his own way to a new but undefined society. Rousseau was tentatively suggesting a society governed by the general will of all citizens in a pervasive consensus. He raised the question of whether it would be possible to replace the artificial social and political orders with a new republic of men and women who lived in a natural relationship to each other.

The operations of the general will that Rousseau discussed in *The Social Contract* are difficult to pin down. At one end of the political continuum, they might take the form of a primitive and egalitarian society. However, at the other end, the concept of the general will could lead to a kind of totalitarian society as it did in the reign of terror under Robespierre after the French Revolution. To be sure, the Rousseauean expression of the general will is very different from John Locke's and Thomas Jefferson's political concept, in which there was rotation in office and elections decided by majority rule.

When considered as a political and social document as well as an educational one, *Emile* suggests the possibility that a new race of people might be educated that could create a society based on their extended but natural relationships. The family that Emile and Sophie are establishing in the book might be the first of many families that will create a new society.

It is in terms of education that Rousseau's educational works, particularly *Emile*, have had their greatest effect. Along with other educational theorists such as Comenius, Pestalozzi, and Froebel, Rousseau argued that childhood was a necessary and desirable stage in the human life span. Indeed, childhood experiences often pointed the way to adult behavior, ethics, and values. This sharply contrasted with earlier views that childhood was something to get through as quickly as possible. Rousseau believed that childhood was so important that its stages should take as long as a person needed to fulfill its possibilities. What came from Rousseau's work was a thrust for permissiveness—letting children follow their needs and interests as far as possible. Child-centered educators who have followed Rousseau have consistently viewed childhood as a precious and important period of human growth. These educators have designed learning environments that permit the greatest expression of children's freedom.

Although there were educators such as Quintilian and Comenius who outlined learning based on stages of development, Rousseau made a clear statement for the importance of relating appropriate learning activities to the child's development stage. Today educators ask the question, "What learning is the child ready to do?" Readiness for learning is an important theme in modern education. Teachers consider children's readiness as a key element in planning and implementing successful instruction. The importance that Rousseau gave to readiness based on natural stages of development was a warning against rushing or pushing children into forced learning, often of an intellectual nature, for which they were not ready.

Rousseau conceived of a broad and enriched learning environment that went far beyond the four walls of the book-focused conventional classroom. Just as Emile and his tutor explored the hills, valleys, streams, and gardens of a wooded country estate, contemporary teachers and students use field trips to study nature and society.

At the same time that Rousseau is significant for his child-centered perspective, his work is known for its departure from the long Western cultural tradition that stressed the liberal arts. Plato, Aristotle, Quintilian, Aquinas, Erasmus, and Calvin all strongly endorsed the tradition of the liberal arts and sciences. This tradition remains one of the enduring aspects of the Western educational heritage. The concept of a liberal education was brought to the United States, where it has been implemented and maintained in higher education. The subject matter curriculum of secondary education, too, is based on the liberal arts tradition.

Critics of Rousseau, both in his day and today, find an anti-intellectual element in his ideas. His doctrine of child permissiveness suggests that children should be the guide to their own learning. Critics of this notion argue that there are structures of reality and that the liberal arts are the tested and accumulated thinking about this reality. Defenders of liberal education say that it should form the core of an education at the secondary and higher levels and that elementary education with its stress on literacy and mathematical computation should lead to that core. Since the day of Rousseau, this tension between child-centered permissive education and subject matter education remains a point of conflict.

Rousseau was an iconoclast, a breaker of customs, conventions, and traditions. He was a quarrelsome person and an erratic and inconsistent theorist. He advocated child love and permissiveness but placed his own children in orphanages. Nevertheless, Rousseau earned a place among the great theorists and educators of the Western world. His books are still read today and his influence has extended into our times.

Questions for Reflection and Dialogue

1. What elements of cultural change during the Enlightenment contributed to Rousseau's educational theory?
2. How did key events in Rousseau's life shape his personality?
3. Compare and contrast the concepts of *supernaturalism* and *naturalism* in education.
4. Analyze Rousseau's concept of a *stage of human development* and indicate its implications for education. How important is this concept in contemporary educational psychology?
5. What were the important stages in the education of Emile?

6. What was Rousseau's theory of negative education? Is the theory of negative education applicable to contemporary American society and education?
7. What kinds of knowledge and attitudes was the tutor seeking to develop in Emile? How well does Emile's tutor fit the contemporary model of the American teacher?

Projects for Deepening Your Understanding

1. Prepare a research paper on the Enlightenment that examines how this period of history differed from preceding eras.
2. In an essay, develop a character analysis of Rousseau.
3. Read *Emile* and develop a paper that outlines his education.
4. In an essay, analyze the educational dynamics that took place between Emile and his tutor. Then, examine the relevance of these dynamics for contemporary American schools.
5. In an essay, examine the concept of *permissiveness* in education. Assess the degree to which American society and schools are permissive.
6. Select and do a content analysis on at least two books used in teacher education courses, especially those dealing with early childhood education or methods of instruction. Do you find evidence of a Rousseauean point of view?
7. Review the arguments given for national standards, especially as assessed by standardized tests. How do you think Rousseau would react to the standards movement?

Notes

1. Robert Anchor, *The Enlightenment Tradition* (New York: Harper & Row, 1967), 34–38.
2. Gerald L. Gutek, *A History of the Western Educational Experience* (Prospect Heights, IL: Waveland, 1995), 164–67.
3. Gerald L. Gutek, *Philosophical and Ideological Perspectives on Education*, 2d ed. (Boston: Allyn & Bacon, 1996), 139–57.
4. Education during the Enlightenment is examined in Harvey Chisick, *The Limits of Reform in the Enlightenment: Attitudes Toward the Education of the Lower Classes in Eighteenth-Century France* (Princeton, NJ: Princeton University Press, 1981).
5. For his autobiography, see Jean-Jacques Rousseau, *The Confessions*, trans. J. M. Cohen (Baltimore: Penguin, 1954). Biographies of Rousseau include Jakob H. Huizinga, *Rousseau: The Self-Made Saint* (New York: Grossman, 1976); George R. Havens, *Jean-Jacques Rousseau* (Boston: Twayne, 1978); and Gavin R. De Beer,

Jean-Jacques Rousseau and His World (London: Thames & Hudson, 1972).
6. William Boyd, ed. *The Minor Educational Writings of Jean Jacques Rousseau* (New York: Teachers College Press, 1962), 7–23.
7. Boyd, *Minor Educational Writings*, 20.
8. Boyd, *Minor Educational Writings*, 24–38.
9. William Kessen, "Rousseau's Children," *Daedalus* 107 (Summer 1978), 155–64.
10. Jean-Jacques Rousseau, *The First and Second Discourses*, ed. Roger D. Masters (New York: St. Martin's, 1964).
11. Jean-Jacques Rousseau, *The Political Writings of J. J. Rousseau*, ed. C. E. Vaughan (Oxford, UK: Basil Blackwell, 1962).
12. Jean-Jacques Rousseau, *The Social Contract*, trans. Maurice Cranston (Baltimore: Penguin, 1969).
13. Jean-Jacques Rousseau, *The Government of Poland*, trans. Willmoore Kendall (Indianapolis: Bobbs-Merrill, 1972).

14. Jean-Jacques Rousseau, *Emile: or On Education*, trans. Allan Bloom (New York: Basic Books, 1979), 37.
15. Rousseau, *Emile*, 37–74.
16. Rousseau, *Emile*, 77–163.
17. Rousseau, *Emile*, 165–208.
18. Rousseau, *Emile*, 211–355.
19. Rousseau, *Emile*, 357–480.
20. Rousseau, *Emile*, 357–406.
21. Rousseau, *Emile*, 393.
22. Rousseau, *Emile*, 398.

Suggestions for Further Reading

Boyd, William, ed. *The Emile of Jean-Jacques Rousseau.* New York: Teachers College Press, 1966.

———. *The Minor Educational Writings of Jean-Jacques Rousseau.* New York: Teachers College Press, 1962.

Butler, Melissa. *Rousseau on Arts and Politics: Autour de la Lettre à d'Alembert.* Ottawa: North American Society for the Study of Jean-Jacques Rousseau, 1997.

Compayre, Gabriel. *Jean-Jacques Rousseau and Education from Nature.* New York: Burt Franklin, 1971.

Cranston, Maurice W. *Jean-Jacques: The Early Life and Work of Jean-Jacques Rousseau, 1712–1754.* Chicago: University of Chicago Press, 1991.

———. *The Noble Savage: Jean-Jacques Rousseau, 1754–1762.* Chicago: University of Chicago Press, 1991.

———. *The Solitary Self: Jean-Jacques Rousseau in Exile and Adversity.* Chicago: University of Chicago Press, 1997.

Cullen, Daniel. *Freedom in Rousseau's Political Philosophy.* De Kalb, IL: Northern Illinois University Press, 1993.

Ferrara, Alessandro. *Modernity and Authenticity: A Study in the Social and Ethical Thought of Jean-Jacques Rousseau.* Albany, NY: State University of New York Press, 1992.

Havens, George R. *Jean-Jacques Rousseau.* Boston: Twayne, 1978.

Hoffmann, Stanley and David P. Fidler. *Rousseau on International Relations.* Oxford; New York: Clarendon Press; Oxford University Press, 1991.

Huizinga, Jakob H. *Rousseau: The Self-Made Saint.* New York: Grossman, 1976.

Jackson, Susan K. *Rousseau's Occasional Autobiographies.* Columbus, OH: Ohio State University Press, 1992.

Leigh, A., ed. *Rousseau: After Two Hundred Years.* Cambridge, UK: Cambridge University Press, 1982.

Melzer, Arthur M. *The Natural Goodness of Man: On the System of Rousseau's Thoughts.* Chicago: University of Chicago Press, 1990.

Miller, James. *Rousseau: Dreamer of Democracy.* New Haven, CT: Yale University Press, 1984.

Misenheimer, Helen E. *Rousseau on the Education of Women.* Washington, DC: University Press of America, 1981.

Noble, Richard. *Language, Subjectivity, and Freedom in Rousseau's Moral Philosophy.* New York: Garland, 1991.

O'Brien, Karen. *Narratives of Enlightenment: Cosmopolitan History from Voltaire to Gibbon.* New York: Cambridge University Press, 1997.

Perkins, Merle L. *Jean-Jacques Rousseau on the Individual and Society.* Lexington, KY: University Press of Kentucky, 1974.

Roosevelt, Grace G. *Reading Rousseau in the Nuclear Age.* Philadelphia: Temple University Press, 1990.

Rosenblatt, Helena. *Rousseau and Geneva: From the First Discourse to the Social Contract, 1749–1762.* New York: Cambridge University Press, 1997.

Rousseau, Jean-Jacques. *Discourses on the Origin of Inequality.* Indianapolis, IN: Hackett, 1992.

———. *Discourses on the Sciences and Arts: First Discourse and Polemics.* Hanover, NH: University Press of New England, 1992.

———. *The First and Second Discourses.* Roger D. Masters, ed. New York: St. Martin's, 1964.

———. *The Government of Poland.* Willmoore Kendall, trans. Indianapolis, IN: Bobbs-Merrill, 1972.

———. *The Political Writings of J. J. Rousseau.* C. E. Vaughan, ed. Oxford, UK: Basil Blackwell, 1962.

———. *The Religious Writings of Rousseau.* Ed. Ronald Grimsley. London: Clarendon, 1970.

———. *Confessions.* Angela Scholar and Patrick Coleman, eds. Oxford; New York: Oxford University Press, 2000.

———. *Emile: Jean-Jacques Rousseau; Translated by Barbara Foxley; Introduction by P. D. Jimack.* London; Rutland, VT: J. M. Dent; Charles E. Tuttle, 1993.

———. *His Educational Theories Selected from Emile, Julie and Other Writings.* R. L. Archer, ed. Hauppauge, NY: Barron's Educational Series, 1989.

———. *Meditations of a Solitary Walker.* Peter France, ed. London: Penguin Books, 1995.

———. *The Social Contract and the First and Second Discourses.* Susan Dunn and Gita May, eds. New Haven; London: Yale University Press, 2002.

Strong, Tracy B. *Jean-Jacques Rousseau: the Politics of the Ordinary.* Thousand Oaks, CA: Sage, 1994.

Sutton, Geoffrey V. *Science for a Polite Society: Gender, Culture, and the Demonstration of Enlightenment.* Boulder, CO: Westview, 1995.

Trachtenberg, Zev M. *Making Citizens: Rousseau's Political Theory of Culture.* London and New York: Routledge, 1992.

Weiss, Penny A. *Gendered Community: Rousseau, Sex, and Politics.* New York: New York University Press, 1993.

Johann Heinrich Pestalozzi: Proponent of Educating the Heart and the Senses

This chapter describes the life, educational philosophy, instructional methodology, and contributions of Johann Heinrich Pestalozzi (1747–1827), a Swiss educational innovator whose development of a natural method of education brought significant changes to teaching and learning. Pestalozzi's educational philosophy and teaching method shaped education in both Europe and the United States.

In this chapter, we discuss Pestalozzi's philosophy of natural education, with its holistic emphasis on both cognitive and affective development, in terms of its historical origins in early nineteenth-century Switzerland, its diffusion to other countries, and its continuing significance for contemporary education. First, we describe the historical context in which Pestalozzi lived and worked. Second, we examine Pestalozzi's biography as an educator to see how his educational ideas were formed by certain key events in his life. Third, we analyze the crucial phases in the Pestalozzian philosophy of education—the general method, which required creating an emotionally secure learning environment for children, and the special method, emphasizing object lessons with form, number, and name units. Fourth, we assess Pestalozzi's continuing significance as an educator. By this analysis, we shall see how Pestalozzi's interaction with the important economic, political, and social events and changes of his time contributed to the development of his philosophy and method of education.

To help you organize your thoughts as you read this chapter, consider the following questions:

1. What were the major trends in the historical context in which Pestalozzi lived?
2. How did Pestalozzi's educational biography shape his philosophy and method of education?
3. What were the key elements in Pestalozzi's philosophy of education?
4. What are Pestalozzi's continuing contributions to education?

The Historical Context of Pestalozzi's Life

An examination of the general historical context of early nineteenth-century Switzerland helps us to understand the cultural climate in which Pestalozzi developed his philosophy and method of education. At this time Switzerland was experiencing the social, political, intellectual, and economic currents sweeping the post-Enlightenment Western world. With its French-, German-, and Italian-speaking cantons, Switzerland was divided on linguistic as well as religious lines. In Zurich, Europe's leading Evangelical Protestant reformers, Zwingli and Calvin, had articulated their theologies. However, other Swiss cantons, resisting the Protestant Reformation, remained staunchly Roman Catholic.

Zurich, Pestalozzi's birthplace, was an important cultural and economic center for German-speaking Swiss. Although Zurich's government appeared to be representative, it was in fact ruled by a small oligarchy of aristocratic families. Supported by the clergy of the reformed church, these leading upper-class families controlled the city politically and economically. Citizenship, the right to vote, was an inheritance these favored families passed on from father to son.[1]

Pestalozzi's family, though citizens, were not part of Zurich's power structure. As a youth, Pestalozzi came to sympathize with the poor farmers of the countryside surrounding Zurich, who, lacking political power, were exploited by the corrupt bailiff system. Rural communities were administered by bailiffs, officials appointed by Zurich's cantonal government. Pestalozzi would write a didactic novel, *Leonard and Gertrude*, which portrayed life in a fictional rural community, Bonnal, that is nearly brought to ruin by a dishonest bailiff.

Pestalozzi's career coincided with the French Revolution, beginning in 1789, and leading to the empire created by Napoleon, which came to an end in 1815. For a time, Pestalozzi believed the slogan of French Revolution, "liberty, equality, fraternity," would bring positive political, social, and economic changes to Europe. Enthusiastic about the revolution's declaration of the "rights of man," he applauded the French revolutionary government's abolition of primogeniture, freeing of serfs, confiscation of church lands, and establishment of free trade.

When the French National Assembly made him an honorary citizen of the republic along with such notables as George Washington, Thomas Paine, and Jeremy Bentham, the elated Pestalozzi offered his educational services to the republic. While expressing interest in his educational ideas, the French committee on public instruction was too preoccupied with the rapidly changing political situation to give Pestalozzi's pedagogy serious consideration. When the radical Jacobins seized power from the more middle-class liberal Girondists and commenced the Reign of Terror, Robespierre's excesses disheartened the gentle Swiss educational reformer. When Robespierre was overthrown in 1795 and replaced by the more moderate Directory, Pestalozzi again looked hopefully to France as the source of European reform. When Napoleon came to power as France's first consul in 1799, Pestalozzi believed the general-turned-politician could perform a civilizing mission in Europe. Napoleon, however, preferred empire building to educational reform.

As in the rest of Europe, the revolutionary currents sweeping outward from the French borders reached Switzerland. Encouraged by the French invasion of Switzerland in 1790, the country people of Zurich forced concessions from the ruling elite. These concessions, however, did not satisfy the French, who demanded that the Swiss abolish their old government and create a new one on the French model. Facing external threat and internal pressure, the Swiss capitulated to the French demands and established the pro-French revolutionary Helvetian republic in 1798.

Although not an active revolutionary, Pestalozzi, like other liberal Swiss supporting enlightened revolutionary principles, rejoiced in the ruling oligarchy's fall from power. Once the pro-French Helvetian republic had been established, Pestalozzi volunteered his educational services. Pestalozzi's friends and allies in the new republic gave financial and political support to his educational plans. With the patronage of P. A. Stapfer, the Helvetian minister of education, Pestalozzi wrote several pamphlets supporting the new regime and was rewarded with educational positions at Stans and Burgdorf.[2]

Switzerland's political climate remained unsettled. The middle-class liberals who controlled the new Helvetian government faced internal discontent, French interference, and financial difficulties. Many Swiss regarded the Helvetian republic as a French puppet. The old elite who had been displaced resented losing power and prestige. Peasants, especially in the Roman Catholic cantons, opposed the Helvetian regime as antireligious.

When Napoleon came to power in France, the Helvetian government dispatched Pestalozzi to Paris as a member of a delegation to win the future emperor's support. Napoleon, however, decreed the Mediation Act of 1803, which restored political autonomy to the 19 Swiss cantons.[3] The return to political decentralization weakened Pestalozzi's political influence.

Napoleon's declining military fortunes after 1812 and his eventual defeat at the battle of Waterloo in 1815 again affected Swiss politics. The coalition armies who opposed Napoleon, especially the Austrians, invaded Switzerland and annulled the Mediation Act. The Swiss factions disagreed on a new political structure, with conservatives wanting a weak confederation of autonomous cantons and liberals wanting centralization. Thus, Swiss politics remained in an uneasy truce between conservative federalists and liberal centralists during the last decades of Pestalozzi's life.

Intellectually, Pestalozzi's ideas were influenced by the rationalism of the eighteenth-century Enlightenment and by romanticism. Both rationalists and romanticists looked to nature as the source of truth and for the laws that governed human development. The rationalists believed that human beings, through their reason, could discover natural laws and use them to reform society and education.

John Locke's *An Essay Concerning Human Understanding* (1690) and Isaac Newton's *The Mathematical Principles of Natural Philosophy* (1687) were important sources of Enlightenment theory. These works, as well as those of Rousseau and the French physiocrats and encyclopedists, contributed to the climate of opinion that shaped Pestalozzi's educational ideas. Locke, who rejected Plato's belief in the existence of innate ideas, asserted that ideas originated in the individual's sensory experience of external objects and were formed into concepts by the mind's power of cognition.[4] Pestalozzi's *anschauung* principle (discussed later in this chapter), according to which the mind formed concepts, closely resembled Locke's epistemology. Both Pestalozzi and Locke concurred that the human mind initially is a *tabula rasa* that gradually acquires ideas from impressions carried to it by the senses.

According to Newton's physics, the universe was a great world machine that functioned according to its own built-in dynamics. Advocating the scientific method, Newton argued that human beings could discover the natural laws that kept the planet in order and motion. Further, it was possible to express these natural laws mathematically. Although Newton wrote as a natural scientist, Pestalozzi and other like-minded social and educational theorists believed scientific inquiry was applicable to examining social, political, and educational institutions and processes.

The Enlightenment's outlook contributed to a paradigm shift from a supernatural and theocentric worldview to a naturalistic and humanistic orientation. Rejecting the traditional Christian view of the human being's inherent sinfulness, Enlightenment philosophers contended that people are naturally good and could perfect themselves through reason. Buttressed by their optimistic belief in human rationality, Pestalozzi and others, inspired by the Enlightenment, believed that human institutions, including schools, could be reformed according to nature's laws. Although the quest to develop a natural system of education was not his alone, Pestalozzi was so enthused by the Enlightenment's promise of a better human future that he devoted his life to this cause.

Along with rationalism, Pestalozzi, an eclectic educator, also experienced the evolving force of romanticism. One of the most potent influences on Pestalozzi came from Jean-Jacques Rousseau, whose *Emile* (1762) incorporated elements of both rationalism and romanticism (for Rousseau, see Chapter 10). Like Rousseau, Pestalozzi looked to nature to provide clues to the child's development and distrusted authoritarianism and verbalism in education.[5]

Referring to Rousseau's *Emile*, Pestalozzi said, "My visionary and highly speculative mind was enthusiastically seized by this visionary and highly speculative book."[6] Rousseau believed the human being is born good but is corrupted by social institutions, traditions, and conventions. In *Emile*, Rousseau tells the story of a child educated in such a natural way that his natural goodness develops free of the influence of a pernicious society.[7] Free of conventional schooling, Rousseau's fictional pupil, Emile, is educated according to nature. Many of Rousseau's educational principles were embraced by Pestalozzi, who included them in his own novel, *Leonard and Gertrude*, and in his educational experiments at Neuhof, Stans, Burgdorf, and Yverdon. Although Pestalozzi followed Rousseau's injunction against the unnatural and artificial, he did not reject society's role in education nor did he endorse a completely naturalistic religion. The following Rousseauean principles most profoundly influenced Pestalozzi's educational ideas:

1. Children are naturally good.
2. The source of evil lies in a distorted and corrupt society rather than in human nature.

3. The right kind of education can curb the contagion of a malfunctioning society and stimulate children to develop according to the good impulses of their nature.
4. Human growth proceeds gradually according to well-defined stages.
5. Sensation rather than verbalism is the true source of ideas, and healthy emotional experience rather than moral preaching is the true source of morality.
6. The natural environment is a fruitful scene of educative experiences.

Pestalozzi's economic ideas were shaped by the Enlightenment climate of opinion, especially the doctrines of Francois Quesnay and the French physiocrats, who held land to be the sole source of wealth and agriculture the only means of increasing wealth. Disputing mercantilism, Quesnay, like Adam Smith, the liberal English economist, opposed government interference with the natural law of supply and demand. In 1767, Pestalozzi studied with the physiocratic French agriculturalist Tschiffeli. These economic ideas prompted Pestalozzi to include a strong element of vocational training, especially agricultural and handicraft production, in his educational theory.

Although the Enlightenment was influencing many European and American intellectuals, the power and authority of the various churches remained strong. Their influence was particularly pronounced in schools. During Pestalozzi's life, the established state churches in Europe retained their prerogatives, which had been either reaffirmed or won during the Protestant Reformation and the Catholic Counterreformation. In Italy, Spain, France, and the Holy Roman Empire (the Hapsburg empire), the Roman Catholic Church maintained its privileged status. In France, Catholicism's fortunes as the state church depended on the policies of the faction holding power. With Napoleon, Catholicism was restored as the empire's official religion. In England, Anglicanism was officially established as the state church. On the European continent, the major Protestant denominations, Lutheranism and Calvinism, were recognized as state churches in non-Catholic countries. For example, the Scandinavian countries and some of the north German states were Lutheran; the Netherlands, Scotland, and some of the Swiss cantons were Calvinist. The religious establishment was a dominant feature of life in eighteenth- and early nineteenth-century Europe.

In Switzerland, the various cantons were either Roman Catholic or reformed Protestant according to the theology of Zwingli and Calvin. Geneva, which had been the home and workplace of John Calvin, had acquired the reputation of being a kind of Protestant Rome (for a discussion of Calvinism, see Chapter 8). In Zurich, where Pestalozzi was born, the Zwinglian-Calvinist church was supreme.

Pestalozzi was familiar with Calvinism, and was also influenced by pietism, new theological current in European Protestantism. Following a "religion of the heart" rather than an intellectualistic theology, these new churches—Moravian, Janssonist, Harmonist, Dunker, Mennonite, Hutterite, and Inspirationist—sought to reaffirm simple and primitive Christian principles (see Chapter 9 for the relationship between the Moravian Brethren and the educational theory of Comenius).

In Zurich, the officially sanctioned reformed Protestant Church emphasized doctrinal and theological conformity, whereas the pietists stressed an inner religious experience based on the direct message of the Bible. Although the Zwinglian and Calvinist Protestants saw material prosperity as a sign of God's approval, the pietists, who stressed the simple life, attached no spiritual significance to wealth.[8] Pietism's affirmation of the religion of the heart and the spiritual importance of the good-hearted person coincided with Pestalozzi's emphasis on the role of emotional-moral values in human development and education.

It is difficult to identify precisely Pestalozzi's religious persuasion. Educated in the tradition of reformed Protestantism, Pestalozzi did not break completely with his religious heritage. Like Rousseau, he was influenced by the naturalism of the Enlightenment. Pestalozzi's religious and moral outlook was an amalgamation of the reformed Christianity of his youth, pietism, the natural religion of Rousseau, and the philosophies of the Enlightenment. As a result, Pestalozzi was a naturalistic Christian humanist who held that, although the powers of human nature were God given, it was each person's responsibility to cooperate with nature and strive for personal and social regeneration.

Pestalozzi's life coincided with the onset of western Europe's transformation from an essentially agrarian to an industrial economy. In Switzerland, cottage work, or handicraft production, a step in the process of economic change, could be found along with agriculture and new industries. Believing these new economic conditions required concerted vocational education, Pestalozzi incorporated agricultural and craft activities in his schools. He wrote,

> The means to be employed for the salvation of the fatherland seemed clearly discernible and practicable. I believed that I could neutralize the most oppressive consequences of the evils of the feudal system and of the factory system through renewed effort for the education of the people to increased productivity in home and farm work and to a greater degree of self-respect.[9]

Pestalozzi's adherence to Enlightenment naturalism and physiocratic economic theory caused him to see agriculture as a major human occupation that brought people close to nature. His earliest educational venture at Neuhof was essentially agricultural, and gardening always was a highly rated activity in his schools. In the early nineteenth century, however, farming could no longer support a growing population and the rural agricultural classes were becoming impoverished. The physiocratic doctrines of "land wealth" to which Pestalozzi subscribed promised that scientific agriculture could restore prosperity.

Although agriculture remained important to Pestalozzi, he was well aware of the Industrial Revolution. The initial phase of that revolution, from 1770 to 1850, increased economic productivity but also brought about exploitation of the working classes. Pestalozzi, who deplored the tendency to dehumanize the poor, sought to stimulate economic recovery through education.

Among the major dehumanizing trends of the early factory system was the routine, mechanical, and monotonous nature of work. The factory's specialized routine destroyed the sense of pride in craftsmanship that had characterized handicraft production and the artistry of the older master–apprentice relationship. Although industrialization had some negative consequences for the working classes, it was slowly improving the quantitative conditions of life. Pestalozzi did not believe that the Industrial Revolution could or should be reversed. Rather, he felt that, with more money and more consumer products available, the working classes needed an education that would enable them to benefit fully from these economic changes.

Early industrialization was especially debilitating to family stability. To earn a livelihood, whole families—fathers, mothers, and children—worked as factory laborers. As the factory replaced the home as the workplace, child abandonment and neglect increased. The growing rates of parental neglect and child delinquency reinforced the prejudice that the working class was inherently vicious and depraved. The long-standing doctrine of child depravity that Pestalozzi struggled to overcome now had a dual rationale: the Calvinist concept that children, because of their inheritance of original sin, were born corrupt and the idea that the working classes, as the dregs of society, produced offspring who were vicious and mean.

Following Rousseau's lead, Pestalozzi, opposing the doctrine of innate human depravity, proclaimed that children were naturally good. Realizing that children were being physically, mentally, and morally malformed by the factory system, Pestalozzi believed that unwholesome human behavior was caused by environmental factors that greedy and exploitive employers forced on workers. With natural education, all children could develop into morally respectable, economically productive, and socially useful adults.

The intellectual, political, religious, and economic trends of the early nineteenth century formed the context in which Pestalozzi developed his theory of natural education. One of his goals was to reform conditions in schools. During the early nineteenth century, schools were generally unresponsive to the intellectual currents unleashed by the Enlightenment. Although the ideas of Locke, Rousseau, and Newton stimulated European intellectuals, primary schools still emphasized denominational indoctrination and rote memorization. Although reformers pleaded for pedagogical innovation, schoolmasters persisted in stressing highly verbal and catechetical instruction. Many schools still remained the "slaughterhouses of the mind" that Comenius had condemned in the seventeenth century (see Chapter 9).

Primary vernacular schools, often under church control, stressed basic literacy, writing, singing, arithmetic, and religious conformity and practice. The various Christian denominations were still engaged in doctrinal disputes arising from the Reformation. Children were admonished to defend their particular religion by memorizing catechisms, psalters, primers, and creeds. Schoolmasters were still school keepers rather than teachers and were hired because of their religious orthodoxy and prowess as disciplinarians. Heavy-handed, incompetent bigots were often preferred over educated people for teaching positions.

The various secondary schools—the German *gymnasium*, the French *lycée*, and the English grammar and public schools—were slightly more receptive to the Enlightenment than were elementary schools. But here, too, traditionalism generally held the curriculum captive. The secondary school curriculum was designed to prepare an elite group of boys for entry to the universities by instilling in them the languages and literatures of the ancient Greek and Latin classics. In higher education, in the universities, a selected few young men studied to become members of the three professions of theology, law, and medicine.

Pestalozzi was touched by the major political, intellectual, religious, economic, and educational currents that formed the context of his life. He was part of that political climate of opinion that experienced the French republican revolution with its slogan of "liberty, equality, fraternity." He knew both the rationalism of the Enlightenment and the emotionalism of romanticism and pietism. Despite the upheavals of his time, he retained an unshakable optimism that human beings were capable of self- and social perfection. It was this conviction that inspired Pestalozzi to work among the poor, develop an educational theory, and devote his life to human betterment.

Pestalozzi: The Life of an Educational Reformer

In this section we examine the biography of Johann Heinrich Pestalozzi, the Swiss educational reformer who had an effect on schools and teaching in both Europe and America.[10] Pestalozzi, the son of Johann Baptiste Pestalozzi, a physician, and Susanna Hotz Pestalozzi, was born on January 12, 1747, in Zurich. The Pestalozzis were a middle-class Protestant family of Italian ancestry. Pestalozzi's father died in 1751 at age 33, leaving three surviving children, Johann Baptiste, Anna Barbara, and Johann Heinrich, then 5 years old.[11]

According to his reminiscences, Pestalozzi grew up in a household dominated by women. His mother seems to have left the daily management of the household, which often had to struggle to make ends meet, to a trusted servant, Barbara Schmidt, a controlling figure in young Pestalozzi's life. His grandfather, Andreas Pestalozzi, a minister in the village of Hongg in the rural area of the canton of Zurich, was an important influence during young Pestalozzi's formative years. When he reached adulthood, Pestalozzi claimed that the example of his grandfather's ministry to the poor influenced him to devote his own life to the education of the economically disadvantaged. In particular, Johann Heinrich recalled driving with his grandfather to visit the poorest members of the parish.

Pestalozzi's memories of his childhood were not particularly happy. Although Babeli, as Barbara Schmidt was called by the family, and his mother were concerned and caring, Pestalozzi believed he was overly protected and isolated from the peer-group contacts that were normal for a child of his age. Lacking interaction with other children, he claimed that he knew nothing of children's games and activities. He grew up a socially inept and physically uncoordinated youth. It is interesting to note the similarity in the reflections of Pestalozzi and Friedrich Froebel, the founder of the kindergarten, on their unhappy childhoods.[12] Although Pestalozzi found his own childhood and family to be inadequate, when he developed his educational theory, he based it around a loving mother figure, Gertrude, who presided over a secure and loving household.

Because of the economies practiced in managing the household, Pestalozzi's family was able to finance his education. From 1751 to 1754 he attended a local primary school, conducted in the vernacular German spoken in Zurich, where he studied the conventional reading, writing, arithmetic, and religion. In 1754, he began his Latin and Greek studies at the Schola Abbatissana and then transferred to the Schola Carolina, a more advanced classical preparatory school that resembled the humanist *gymnasium*. He then entered university studies at the Collegium Humanitatis, where he studied Latin, Greek, Hebrew language and literature, rhetoric, philosophy, and theology. When he was 17, Pestalozzi entered the Collegium Carolinum, where he concentrated on languages and philosophy.

Pestalozzi's college years provided an exciting release from the introspective shyness of his childhood. He became a member of a circle of young men who, influenced by their professor, Jean Jacques Bodmer (1699–1773), dreamed of restoring their native Switzerland to its past greatness. Bodmer, a historian and literary critic, preached that the revitalization of Swiss life would come from imitating the rugged spirit and simple virtues of the Swiss mountaineers.

Under Bodmer's direction, his followers, organized as the Helvetic Society, intended to lead a rebirth of Swiss life. The young Helvetians, who in addition to Pestalozzi included Johann Caspar Fussli, Caspar Schulthess, Johann Bluntschili, and others who would become lifelong friends, marched off into the mountains to study peasant life and to collect folk stories and songs that represented the virtuous life, uncontaminated by modernity and materialism. Bodmer's emphasis on Swiss folk culture was similar to early nineteenth-century movements elsewhere such as that of the Grimm brothers and Ludwig Jahn in Germany, who combined romanticism and nationalism to find in the purity of the mythical past the key to happiness in the future.

To disseminate its views, the Helvetic Society established a weekly publication, *The Monitor*, which in urging reforms along the lines advocated by Bodmer, criticized Zurich's public officials. The officials suppressed publication of *The Monitor* and briefly jailed Pestalozzi and others who had contributed to its pages.

Pestalozzi's foray into political activism and journalism was an exhilarating experience for the young man. He had made some close friends for the first time in his life, and had a cause. In reflecting on these days, Pestalozzi wrote,

> Our only wish was to live for freedom, beneficence, sacrifice and patriotism; but the means of developing the practical power to attain these were lacking. We despised all external appearances such as riches, honour, and consideration; and we were taught to believe that by economising and reducing our wants we could dispense with all the advantages of citizen life. We cherished but one aim namely, the possibility of enjoying independence and domestic happiness, without having the strength to acquire and maintain them.[13]

The impressionable Pestalozzi now sought a career that would fulfill his mission of improving life for the less fortunate. His education in the classics, humanities, and religious studies gave him the academic background for the religious ministry. However, he lacked the skill of preaching. His attempt to preach a trial sermon was such an embarrassment that he abandoned religious work. For a while, he toyed with the idea of becoming a lawyer but realized that he was unsuited temperamentally for such a career. In addition, he was regarded as radical because of his association with the Helvetic Society.

In searching for a meaningful career, Pestalozzi chose agriculture. It would enable him to live the simple life of pure Swiss values that Bodmer had emphasized. Further, Pestalozzi had also become an avid disciple of Rousseau. What could be more natural than the life of a farmer? However, because he knew little about farming, he determined to study scientific agriculture with Johann Rudolf Tschiffeli, a well-known agricultural expert who had a model experimental farm near Kirchberg in the canton of Berne. Here, under Tschiffeli's tutelage, Pestalozzi studied to be a scientific farmer.

Pestalozzi married Anna Schulthess, the daughter of an upper middle-class Zurich family and the sister of his close friend Caspar. Anna, described as an attractive, patient, and capable young woman, was eight years older than her husband. Her family, who regarded Pestalozzi as an eccentric dreamer, reluctantly consented to the marriage.

With his wife's dowry and money borrowed from friends, Pestalozzi purchased a 60-acre farm near the village of Birr in the canton of Berne. Here, he built his home, which he called Neuhof, and began his experiment in scientific farming and education.

Pestalozzi's only child, whom he named Jean Jacques after his literary hero Rousseau, was born in 1770. Jean Jacques was a sickly child who suffered from "violent rheumatic attacks," which may have been epilepsy. Pestalozzi decided to use *Emile* as a guide for his son's education. Keeping a journal of Jean Jacques's progress, Pestalozzi wrote,

> Whatever you can teach him from the nature of things themselves, do not teach him by words. Leave him to himself to see, hear, find, stumble, rise again, and be mistaken. Give no word when action, or deed is possible. What he can do for himself let him do. Let him be always occupied, ever active, and let the time when you do not worry him be by far the greatest part of his childhood. You will come to learn that nature teaches him better than men.[14]

Pestalozzi followed Rousseau closely in educating his son. When Jean Jacques had difficulty in learning to read and write, Pestalozzi decided that although Rousseau was on the right educational track, the method needed to be systematized and based on psychological principles. Jean Jacques eventually married and had a child. He died at age 30.

In 1774, Pestalozzi determined education would be his life's work. Still seeking to uplift the poor economically and morally, he turned Neuhof into an agricultural and educational experiment. His plan was for Neuhof to become a self-supporting farm and handicraft school, where the sale of the children's work would support their education. This plan bore some resemblance to Gandhi's Wardha plan for basic education in India (for Gandhi's educational plan, see Chapter 22).

At Neuhof, Pestalozzi accepted orphan children as pupils and invited poor families in the vicinity of Birr to send their children, both boys and girls, to him for an education. At its peak, Pestalozzi's school at Neuhof enrolled 50 children. Often, the children came in filthy and ragged clothes. He provided them with clean new clothes, put them up in dormitories, and fed them. In summer, the children performed agricultural chores; in the winter they did cotton and wool spinning and weaving and made handicraft items. Pestalozzi taught them reading, writing, and counting by using a group method he called "simultaneous instruction." Aside from his enthusiasm for Rousseau's principles of natural education and his own memories of schooling, Pestalozzi was still searching for a method of education.

Despite his own satisfaction with Neuhof and support from friends, Pestalozzi's educational venture was a serious financial drain. Of the 50 children at the school, who ranged in age from 6 to 18, only 14 were able to work in any concerted fashion. The situation was further complicated by some parents, who would withdraw their children after Pestalozzi had provided them with food and clothing. Further, despite his humanitarian altruism, Pestalozzi, unskilled as an administrator, was especially inept at balancing accounts and keeping the school operating at a profit. In 1779, financial pressures forced Pestalozzi to close his school. However, he now knew that he had found his true vocation. He was determined to be an educator.

Pestalozzi turned to writing both to earn a living and to disseminate his educational ideas. Deeply impressed with Rousseau's success in diffusing his ideas on natural education through the didactic or teaching novel, Pestalozzi decided to write such a story.

In 1781, Pestalozzi's widely read *Leonard and Gertrude* was published.[15] In this novel, Gertrude, the heroine, is portrayed as educating her children according to the principles of natural education. Her success is so great that natural education is used to regenerate the fictional economically depressed village of Bonnal.

In *Leonard and Gertrude*, Pestalozzi developed a cast of characters that personified his views on social and educational change. Gertrude, the devoted mother of a large family, is determined that her children, despite poverty, would grow to be morally, physically, and intellectually well-developed persons. Her husband Leonard, well meaning but weak, is a stonemason by trade. Because of the village's economic depression, Leonard, like most of the men, is frequently unemployed and idles time away in the village tavern, owned by the corrupt bailiff Hummel, who exploits the village economy for his own gain. The land around the village is owned by Squire Arner, a well-meaning but absent landlord, who is unaware of the deteriorating quality of life in Bonnal.

Through a series of episodes, Pestalozzi tells the story of the good mother-teacher, Gertrude, whose actions change life in the village for the better. Each day, Gertrude gathers her children about the table where they work together spinning and weaving. As they work they recite prayers, say the alphabet, and count. The children are working and earning to support the family while they are learning. If there is sickness in the other families in the village, the kindly, compassionate, and patient Gertrude is there to help. Gertrude's household and her children become an educational model for the village.

Although managing to raise and educate her children through careful economy and natural education, Gertrude realizes that her family is part of the larger village community. Mustering her courage, she goes to Squire Arner's estate and tells him of the deplorable situation in Bonnal. True to the pattern of early nineteenth-century fiction, the good squire pleads innocence. He does not know his appointee, Bailiff Hummel, is violating his trust and responsibility. Outraged, Squire Arner accompanies Gertrude to the village where he dismisses Hummel. Together with Gertrude, Squire Arner embarks on a program of educational, social, and economic reform.

An important part of the reform program is to build a school where Gertrude's method of education can be implemented. Leonard and some of the unemployed village men are employed to build the school. The program of village reconstruction provides work and restores the economy. A teacher is hired whom Gertrude trains in the natural method of simultaneous instruction. As a result, Bonnal becomes a shining example of community renewal and humanitarianism. Pestalozzi's principal message is that education can bring about more general social reform.

Through the pages of *Leonard and Gertrude*, Pestalozzi made his first attempt to articulate his philosophy of education. His basic educational principles were the following:[16]

1. A genuine education will develop each person's intellectual, moral, and physical powers in a harmonious and integrated fashion.
2. To be successful, education needs to unite the home with the school and the school with the whole community.
3. Despite ignorance, economic depression, and moral deprivation, human beings can be uplifted and regenerated through education.
4. True social reform will result from peaceful education rather than violent revolution.

5. Education, conducted humanely, will lead to the development of a humanitarian society.

Pestalozzi's *Leonard and Gertrude* was a best seller. It was republished in numerous editions and brought recognition to its author. The novel won the gold medal awarded by the Economic Society of Berne.

Pestalozzi wrote essays and books on education. His articles, "Essays on the Education of the Children of the Poor," appeared in *Ephemerides*, a Swiss journal. In 1782, Pestalozzi wrote a sequel to *Leonard and Gertrude*, titled *Christopher and Elizabeth*. The book consisted of dialogues in which Christopher led his family in discussions of *Leonard and Gertrude*. The book failed to attract a wide readership.

Between 1782 and 1784, Pestalozzi published his own newspaper, *Ein Schweizer Blatt (The Swiss News)*, which stressed the importance of the home as an educational force, pointed to the need for a new system of education based on natural principles, and attacked existing schools as too mechanical and verbal. In 1783, Pestalozzi's *On Legislation and Infanticide* appeared, which condemned the practice of killing or abandoning unwanted children. He also examined the broader social and economic causes of crime and indicated how education could be a force in reducing crime. Pestalozzi also wrote children's books, such as *Illustrations for My ABC Book* (1787) and *Fables for My ABC Book* (1795).

In 1797, Pestalozzi attempted to establish a theoretical foundation for his educational ideas in his *Researches into the Course of Nature in the Development of the Human Race*. Although harshly criticized as confusing and highly abstract by its reviewers, *Researches* represented Pestalozzi's early efforts in the sociology of education. In the spirit of the Enlightenment, Pestalozzi stated that human progress would be advanced by education that cultivated inherent human powers. Not limited to children's schooling, education was society's agency for advancing human beings to the state of harmony, morality, and happiness.

In 1799, Pestalozzi, now recognized as an educational authority because of his publications, was called into educational service by the new Swiss government, the Helvetian republic. Battles between the French and the Austrian armies had been waged in some Swiss cantons. French armies had raided the conservative Roman Catholic cantons of Schwyz, Uri, and Unterwalden, which had opposed the pro-French Helvetian republic. Several of Pestalozzi's university friends were officials in the Helvetian government, and they secured his appointment as head of an orphanage in the village of Stans. At age 59, on January 14, 1799, Pestalozzi resumed active work as an educator. He found himself in charge of 80 children, some of whom had been orphaned as a result of war. His funds were limited, he had the assistance of only a housekeeper and cook, and the residents in the surrounding countryside were hostile. He wrote of his experience at Stans:

> I united in my person the offices of superintendent, paymaster, steward, and sometimes chambermaid, in a half-ruined house. I was surrounded with ignorance, disease, and with every kind of novelty. The number of children rose, by degrees to eighty; all of different ages; some full of pretensions; others inured to open beggary; and all, with a few solitary exceptions, entirely ignorant.[17]

At Stans, Pestalozzi reached some important educational insights. He found that, because of their harmful experiences, the children were suspicious, frightened, and often emotionally withdrawn. To make any progress in their more formal instruction in reading and arithmetic, Pestalozzi realized he first needed to win their affection. He needed to create a home-school atmosphere in which the children's material and emotional needs were satisfied. Only then could he concentrate on their intellectual education. He began to act as a father figure for the children, living with them and providing the security of a caring and loving adult.

In his work at Stans, Pestalozzi developed an important principle that undergirded his whole educational philosophy: The affective side of human nature, emotional growth, was as important as cognitive development. Neither could proceed in isolation from the other. Further, the creation of an emotionally secure environment necessarily preceded cognitive learning. Hungry, scared, withdrawn children would have great difficulty in academic learning until their basic emotional needs were met.

Slowly Pestalozzi set about the task of creating in his orphan children at Stans feelings of self-worth and esteem. Gradually, he brought order to disordered lives. Unfortunately, his work at Stans was brought to an abrupt halt July 8, 1799, after only six months of operation. Opposing French and Austrian armies had set up their battle lines in the vicinity, forcing the orphanage to close.

In July 1799, the Helvetian government found a position for Pestalozzi as an assistant to Samuel Dysli, the village schoolmaster of a working-class primary school in Burgdorf. What unfolded next was a conflict between the old, personified by Dysli, and the new in education, represented by Pestalozzi. Dysli, a shoemaker, combined his trade with school keeping, a term that aptly describes Dysli's teaching method. He would repair shoes, while each child stood before his bench to recite the lesson assigned the previous day. The children memorized the alphabet, which they recited in sing-song fashion. Then they went on to simple phrases. The goal was to have them memorize the catechism, and learn to read and to count. While one child was standing before Dysli and reciting, the others would wait their turn. A slap across the hand with a rod punished those who had failed to memorize their lessons or were disobedient.

Almost immediately on arriving at Burgdorf, Pestalozzi was at odds with Dysli. First, he opposed using corporal punishment to instill fear in children; such an environment, he believed, gave merely the appearance but not the substance of learning. Second, Pestalozzi opposed Dysli's emphasis on memorization of the catechism and passages from the Bible and other books. To Pestalozzi, this approach required children to mouth words they did not really understand. Rather than parroting words, Pestalozzi believed that children should begin their learning by exploring their immediate environment and those objects close at hand.

Thrown together by circumstances in the same classroom, Dysli and Pestalozzi quarreled. Dysli believed that his so-called assistant was really trying to usurp his position. Pestalozzi felt that Dysli was ill prepared as a teacher and was miseducating the children. Soon the quarrel left the school and factions developed around the two men. Dysli spread the word that Pestalozzi was antireligious. The conflict ended with Pestalozzi leaving the position.

Once again, friends in the Helvetian government intervened on Pestalozzi's behalf. They arranged for him to head a new educational institute located in Burgdorf castle. From 1800 to 1804, Pestalozzi directed the Burgdorf Institute, which included a boarding school for students and a program for teaching interns. His years at Burgdorf were significant. Here, he developed his educational ideas into a philosophy and method of education. By establishing a teacher education program, he ensured that his method would be disseminated in Europe and the Americas.

At Neuhof and Stans, Pestalozzi learned that it was of vital importance to create an educational climate of emotional security. Now he developed his theory of sensory learning based on the concept of *anschauung*, a German word meaning forming a concept or a clear idea from sense impressions. Human beings, he said, inhabited a world that contains a multitude of physical objects. People learn by having sense experiences with these objects; they see, feel, smell, taste, and hear them. Their eyes, ears, and other senses convey sensory data to the mind, which then sorts them out and arranges them into concepts or ideas. Only after the concept is clearly present in the mind is a name, a word that designates it, given to it. If this is the way people learn in life, why not use this method in schools? Teachers had traditionally taught words about which children did not have direct experience. Without understanding these words, children are forced to memorize and recite them.

At Burgdorf, Pestalozzi designed his famous *object lesson* in which children, guided by teachers, examined the form, the shape, and the quantity, the number and weight of objects, and then learned to name them. To provide children with direct experience with the many objects in the environment, Pestalozzi organized nature study field trips into the surrounding countryside. They observed and collected plants and minerals and studied animals and birds. Geography lessons did not focus on distant oceans and continents but on the immediate vicinity, moving outward from the schoolyard into the neighborhood and then into the countryside.

While at Burgdorf, Pestalozzi in 1801 finished his most systematic book on education, *How Gertrude Teaches Her Children.*[18] In this book, he articulated his philosophy of the two interrelated phases of education: the general method, which involved creating a climate of emotional security, and the special method, which stressed the object lessons of form, number, and sound or name.

At Burgdorf, Pestalozzi trained a number of assistants in his method. Among them were Johann Georg Tobler, Johann Christopher Buss, Herman Krusi, and Joseph Neef. Neef introduced the Pestalozzian method to the United States in the early nineteenth century. Several teachers, including Friedrich Froebel, came to Burgdorf from other countries to be prepared in the Pestalozzian method (see Chapter 16). As his fame spread and his books were translated and published in other languages, Pestalozzi's institute at Burgdorf attracted visitors who observed his method. The U.S. common school leaders Horace Mann and Henry Barnard and the scientist-geologist-philanthropist William Maclure were among those who came to observe the Pestalozzian method of education.

In 1804, a more conservative federal government replaced the liberal Helvetian regime that had supported Pestalozzi. The canton of Berne repossessed Burgdorf castle, forcing Pestalozzi to relocate his institute. The municipality of Yverdon offered him use of the local castle without cost. From 1804 until he retired in 1825, Pestalozzi continued his educational work at Yverdon. Here, he continued to write, prepare teachers, and educate students. In 1827, Pestalozzi died at Neuhof, the site of his first school.

The Pestalozzian Philosophy of Education

Pestalozzi's philosophy of education was based on his theory of natural education, influenced by Rousseau, by his emphasis on sensory-based education, and by his own experiences as a teacher and teacher-educator.

Pestalozzi expounded a conception of human nature according to which each person possessed inherent intellectual, moral, and physical powers. In this tripartite view of human nature, the mind was the source of intellectual power, the will of moral power, and the body of physical power. It was important, he reasoned, that the three powers be cultivated and developed harmoniously and simultaneously. Conventional schooling emphasized developing the intellectual but neglected the moral and physical powers. Those who succeeded in conventional schools were often clever individuals in mastering words and language but not necessarily moral persons. Ignoring physical development, conventional schooling did not provide vocational education, and many individuals, especially children of the poor, left school to join the ranks of the unemployed. It was vitally important that a truly natural method of education be introduced that developed each person's threefold powers—the intellect, the will, and the body—simultaneously and harmoniously.

For Pestalozzi, an individual's education was closely related to the well-being of society. A genuinely natural education that cultivated the three elemental powers of human beings would be the means of correcting crime, injustice, poverty, and other social ills.

Pestalozzi's theory of instruction was organized into two related phases: the general and special methods. The general method, intended to create schools characterized by a pervasive climate of emotional security, was necessary and preceded the special method. Organized around object lessons, the special method, based on Pestalozzi's *anschauung* principle, and emphasized sensory learning and concept formation.[19]

Pestalozzi's general method originated from his observations of children's behavior and his memories of his own childhood. The origins of the general method went back to the first impressions of infancy, especially to the mother–child relationship. The infant had basic needs of food, warmth, and affection that the good and loving mother responded to and satisfied. This interaction between mother and child created a bond of love, a circle of positive emotion, between them. This attachment, arising from the satisfaction of natural human instincts, was necessary to rearing an emotionally secure child.

Emotional security, the positive development of the affective domain, then proceeded through circles of development that extended outward from the initial loving relationship to the larger world. If the mother–child relationship was positive, then the emotionally secure child would respond to other people with love, trust, and affection. The next circle involved other members of the immediate family of origin. The harmoniously functioning family, like Gertrude's family in Bonnal, was one of love and security.

Moving outward from the family circle, the child's sense of security was extended to the people of the local community. Following the premise that was foundational to all of his educational theory and practices, Pestalozzi believed that human growth and education moved, by extension, from what was immediate, direct, and simple to that which was more distant, remote, and abstract. Here, Pestalozzi conjectured that the development of psychological-emotional security originated in the immediate closeness of the family and then extended to the more remote and abstract social, economic, and political relationships of the larger community and society.

The next stage in emotional development saw the person moving forward to a still larger and more abstract concept of the nation. If life in the more immediate village or town community was characterized by conditions of emotional trust, this positive attitude could be extended to the people of the nation. Moving even further outward in time and place, Pestalozzi saw the nations of the Earth united in an international circle of humanity. People of different nations, ethnicities, and languages were members of an international human community. If the essential trust and security that had originated in the mother–child relationship were nurtured and developed, then they could be extended, at a more comprehensive and mature level, to the relationships between peoples and nations.

Slowly, gradually, and surely, the circles of secure human relationships were broadened and extended outward from the person to the society and to the world. These broadening circles of love then took on a religious significance. By loving human beings, the person was led to the love of God, the father and creator of all life.

At the vernacular school in Burgdorf, Pestalozzi had argued with Dysli over religious instruction. The conventional teaching of religion in European and U.S. schools in the nineteenth century based instruction on the doctrines of the religious denomination or church that controlled the school. Depending on the particular denomination, children learned to be Roman Catholics, Lutherans, Calvinists, and so on. They learned religious principles by memorizing a catechism that structured each religious principle into a question and an answer. Pestalozzi opposed the catechetical method as a verbal approach to religion in which children memorized words they did not understand. Further, the traditional method, emphasizing doctrinal conformity, generated religious intolerance. In contrast, Pestalozzi's approach to religious instruction, resembling pietism, was based on affective human relationships that led to God.

Pestalozzi applied his concept of the genesis of human emotional security and morality to education and schools. Like Comenius, Pestalozzi found that conventional schools were not places of loving and trusting relationships (see Chapter 9). Rather, children in many schools were treated as ignorant savages who needed to be shaped into docile "civilized" subjects by psychologically and physically coercive teachers who ruled their classrooms through corporal punishment. These schools needed to be made into environments where the general method, with its emphasis on love and emotional security, guided classroom management.

Pestalozzi had created an ideal model for the development of emotional security, which he knew was absent in many families and situations. As was true of the orphan children that he taught at Neuhof and Stans, he realized that the mother–child circle was broken by a mother's death or by families' dysfunctionality. Instead of growing up emotionally secure, many children, victims of neglect and abuse, grew up distrustful of others, socially withdrawn, or deviant in their behavior. For these child victims, the emotionally healthy Pestalozzian school would serve as a restorative agency, recreating the positive conditions that children should have experienced in a loving home.

Pestalozzi criticized conventional schooling for its overemphasis on verbalism, especially its preoccupation with memorizing and reciting set passages from books. Memorizing catechism questions and answers and passages from the classics and from Scripture masqueraded in these schools as intellectual development. Successful children in conventional schools were really little pedants who, though appearing to be highly intelligent and academically adept, were "word people" whose emotional and physical powers were often stunted.

Pestalozzi's concern for creating an emotionally secure school climate added an important new dimension to teaching. To create this positive environment for children, teachers themselves needed to be emotionally healthy. Teachers in existing conventional schools were most often hired because of their conformity to religious doctrines or for their ability to maintain orderly classrooms rather than for their emotional wellness. For Pestalozzi, true teachers, emulating Gertrude, would create a homelike environment in their classrooms. Pestalozzi himself shared meals and recreation with the children in his schools; he accompanied them on their field trips and excursions and expected those preparing to be teachers to follow his example.

Once children felt they were in an emotionally secure environment with teachers whom they trusted and loved, then the second phase of Pestalozzi's plan of education, the special method, was implemented. At the special method's pedagogical center was Pestalozzi's principle that human beings acquired knowledge through their senses. Pestalozzi's emphasis on the role of senses in bringing information to the mind resembled Aristotle's Natural Realism (Aristotle's realism is examined in Chapter 4). For sense realists, such as Pestalozzi, two elements are of utmost importance—the human senses and the objects found in the world. Through the senses—seeing, hearing, tasting, smelling, feeling—information, or sensory data, is conveyed to the mind, which converts it into concepts or ideas that refer to a class of objects.

At this point in his learning theory, Pestalozzi's important principle of *anschauung* came into play.[20] Using romantic imagery, Pestalozzi asserted that the world appeared at first glance like a forest shrouded in morning mists. *Anschauung*, like rays of sun, dissipated the mist, bringing each tree in the forest into the clear vision of the mind's inner eye.

Because human beings come to know the objects in their environment through their senses, Pestalozzi reasoned that instruction also should use sensation. His special method consisted of a series of object lessons in which children, with the teacher's guidance, observed, examined, and analyzed objects found in their immediate environment. By using object lessons, children could examine minerals, plants, and animals of the natural order as well as artifacts made by human beings.

Each object was to be studied through a series of "form, number, and name" lessons, which Pestalozzi believed were the proper beginnings of education rather than the traditional reading, writing, arithmetic, and catechism lessons.[21] Every object had a form, design, or structure that could be studied by observing and touching it. In their drawing exercises, children could trace the outlines of small objects or sketch the shape or design of larger ones. Through these exercises, they abstracted the form of the object and created the concept that referred to its class of objects. By collecting and tracing the outlines of the leaves of trees, for example, children developed the concept of *leaf*.

Concurrently with form lessons, children learned about arithmetical processes and the quantities of objects through number lessons. In conventional schools, children learned to count by reciting numbers; although they could call the numbers off, the numbers they recited often remained mere words in their minds. In fact, Pestalozzi admitted that he had made this mistake in teaching his son. It was important, Pestalozzi stated, that children connect objects in their environment with the quantity of objects present. To develop this skill, Pestalozzi, who always stressed beginning with the immediate and the concrete, had children collect marbles, stones, or peas and arrange them in groups, beginning with one object, then two objects, three objects, and so forth. Thus, they learned that the number sign referred to a corresponding number of real objects. After they had mastered the skill of counting real objects, they were taught that a dot could be used to represent the object. On paper, they developed a sequence of groups of dots that represented objects. After they had mastered the ability to represent objects with dots, a kind of pictograph, they replaced the dots with number signs so that $1 = \bullet$ and $2 = \bullet\bullet$ and so on. Moving from the skill of counting, Pestalozzi used tangible objects to develop the basic computational skills of adding, subtracting, multiplying, and dividing.

Together with form and number lessons, Pestalozzi developed a series of name or sound exercises. Each object had a name and children were taught to say that name. Each object also had qualities, such as color, hardness, and softness, and children were taught to say these qualities. The names were said slowly and often broken down into simple syllables that were repeated over and over until mastered. The names of the objects and verbs were used to construct sentences whose development followed the pattern of going from simple to complex.

It was only after children had thoroughly mastered the form, number, and name lessons that Pestalozzi proceeded to the reading, writing, and arithmetic conventionally taught in schools. He believed the tracing and drawing exercises that were part of the form lessons naturally led to writing. The name lessons, with their emphasis on breaking down large words and sentences into their smaller parts, led to reading and to clear speaking. The counting exercises led to mathematical computation. With a store of clear ideas or concepts in their minds, children were led into literacy and computation.

Natural science and geography were taught in an integrated way in direct relationship to the environment. Led by their teachers, children would go on excursions, hikes, and field trips through the surrounding countryside. Their first excursions led them out from the school to the village and its immediate surroundings. They were introduced to the local world of work by visiting and observing the shoemaker, blacksmith, shopkeeper, weaver, and so forth. They then journeyed into the landscape around the village and, following the streams, learned how rivers flow and drain the nearby fields. They collected plants, stones, and other natural objects that they brought back to the school and arranged as a small natural history museum. As they walked, they observed the local geography—the location of the streams, hills, roads, and buildings. Returning to the school, they created a model of the local geography by using clay, sand, paper, and wood. Then, drawing their model on paper, they created a map. Pestalozzi believed that learning was more effective when children had direct experience with geographical places rather than memorizing the names of distant and often remote oceans, continents, and countries. Learning was more relevant when children actually saw people at work rather than memorized the principal products of various countries.

A strong methodological consistency ran through Pestalozzi's general and special methods. Both cognitive and affective growth were stimulated by children's sensations. Learning began with objects found in their immediate environment. Progressing slowly, gradually, and cumulatively, without haste or force, learning did not enter a new stage until children had mastered the preceding one. Lessons always began with concrete objects in the immediate environment before moving to those that were more abstract and remote in children's experience. Just as the cognitive form, number, and name lessons moved from the immediate, direct, and concrete to the distant and abstract so did children's moral development. They learned morality by experiencing it directly.

Not only did Pestalozzi bring about innovation in instruction, he also brought change in how children were organized in schools. The conventional approach to instruction was to have all children in one room and to have one child at a time come before the teacher to recite a previously assigned lesson. Pestalozzi believed this inefficient use of time failed to promote socialization. Instead, he developed the group process of simultaneous instruction to replace the individual recitation.

Thus, the somewhat eccentric Swiss educator, Johann Heinrich Pestalozzi, who failed at being a farmer, a minister, and a lawyer, succeeded in bringing about a significant revolution in education. Many of his innovations are now a regular part of modern education.

Conclusion: An Assessment

Pestalozzi's effect on education can be examined in terms of its diffusion from its origin to other places and times. We also may assess it in terms of its enduring significance for educational philosophy and teaching and learning.

After his death in 1827, Pestalozzi's educational philosophy and method were carried throughout Europe and North America by those who had studied with him at Burgdorf and Yverdon to be teachers. In addition, leading European and American educators who had visited the institutes at Burgdorf and Yverdon brought the Pestalozzian methodology back to their own countries. Because Pestalozzi's educational philosophy and method were so complex, some of his interpreters glimpsed only a part of his total educational edifice.

In assessing Pestalozzi's influence, it should be remembered that the most crucial phase of the general method requires creating an emotionally secure educational environment. Although eccentric, Pestalozzi was a gentle father figure to the children who attended his schools at Neuhof, Stans, Burgdorf, and Yverdon. Unfortunately, not all of those who sought to emulate Pestalozzi were suited temperamentally to be father figures. Because the object lesson was the most visible part of Pestalozzi's method, many followers did not fully comprehend the importance of the less tangible but theoretically necessary general method. They often failed to appreciate that the full success of the Pestalozzian method required an emotionally healthy school environment before proceeding to the special method's object lessons. As has often been the case with educational innovations, the particular innovation loses some of its meaning and vitality when put into practice by those who are distant from the time and place of the innovation's origin.

Despite the difficulty that some of Pestalozzi's disciples had in adequately implementing his method, it was nevertheless widely diffused in Europe and in North America. Because Pestalozzi spoke and wrote German, the German states were a natural place for transplanting his method. In the nineteenth century Prussia, the leader among the German states, introduced the Pestalozzian method. In his *Addresses to the*

German Nation in 1808, the Prussian philosopher Johann Gottlieb Fichte urged his nation to adopt the Pestalozzian system. Fichte believed that Pestalozzian education could help revitalize Prussia, which had been defeated by Napoleon's armies. The Prussian government incorporated aspects of Pestalozzianism in its educational reforms of 1809. In England, Pestalozzi's ideas were first introduced with the publication of his correspondence with the English educator J. P. Greaves.[22] Charles and Elizabeth Mayo used the Pestalozzian method at their school at Cheam Surrey, but accentuated the object lesson to the neglect of the general method. They organized the Home and Colonial School Society in 1836 to promote Pestalozzianism and prepared several books for teachers that featured the Pestalozzian form, number, and sound lessons.[23] The School Society also established a model school to demonstrate the Pestalozzian method and a training school to prepare teachers in Pestalozzian pedagogy.

In the United States, Pestalozzi's philosophy and method found a receptive audience. Here, Pestalozzianism experienced three distinct phases:[24]

1. The method's initial introduction by William Maclure and Joseph Neef
2. Concerted efforts by Henry Barnard, the common school leader, to publicize the method
3. Edward A. Sheldon's development of a full-scale program of teacher education at the Normal School at Oswego, New York

In the early nineteenth century, William Maclure, a world traveler and a pioneering geologist, while on one of his many scientific expeditions to Europe visited Pestalozzi at Burgdorf. Strongly opposed to traditional classical education, Maclure wanted to diffuse useful scientific knowledge to the U.S. farming and working classes. He determined that the Pestalozzian method would be useful in accomplishing his goal. He was so impressed by his visit to Pestalozzi's institute at Burgdorf that he recruited Joseph Neef, an assistant of Pestalozzi's, to immigrate to the United States to introduce the method.[25] Neef, who received a subsidy from Maclure, came to the United States in 1806 and located near Philadelphia, where he established a Pestalozzian school. To introduce Pestalozzian education to a wider U.S. audience, Neef wrote *A Sketch of a Plan and Method of Education* (1808) and *The Method of Instructing Children Rationally in the Arts of Writing and Reading* (1813).[26] After Neef had established schools in Pennsylvania and Kentucky, Maclure called him to New Harmony, Indiana, in 1824. Maclure had joined Robert Owen's experiment at creating a communitarian society at New Harmony (for Owen and communitarianism, see Chapter 15). Neef was one of several Pestalozzian educators who conducted schools in the Owenite community. Maclure believed that New Harmony could be an important center for scientific research and publication and Pestalozzian education. Even after Owen had abandoned his utopian experiment, the New Harmony school press continued to publish scientific and educational works.[27]

A second phase in U.S. Pestalozzianism came with Henry Barnard's efforts to promote the method. A highly distinguished educator, Barnard served as the Connecticut commissioner of common schools, editor of the *Connecticut Common School Journal*, the first U.S. commissioner of education, and the editor of the *American Journal of Education*. In his popular lectures at numerous teachers' institutes and in his many articles on common schooling, Barnard was enthusiastic about the Pestalozzian method. In 1862, Barnard's essays on Pestalozzi along with excerpts from Pestalozzi's works were published as *Pestalozzi and Pestalozzianism*.[28] Barnard encouraged his colleagues in the common school movement, such as Bronson Alcott, William C. Woodbridge, and William Russell, to incorporate Pestalozzian principles in their educational activities.[29]

The work of Edward A. Sheldon (1823–1897) and his associates at the Oswego Normal School in New York State constituted the third major phase of Pestalozzianism in the United States.[30] Sheldon, superintendent of the Normal School, made the Pestalozzian object lesson a centerpiece in his teacher education program. Sheldon and his associates Margaret Jones, who had been a teacher at the Mayo's Home and Colonial Training School in England, and Herman Krusi, Jr., the son of one of Pestalozzi's teaching assistants, developed an extensive number of object lessons on form, number, and name that became the methodological core of Oswego's program. Many of these lessons were published and used at other normal schools throughout the country. The Oswego version of Pestalozzianism was widely used by teachers. A report of the National Teachers' Association, issued in 1865, gave a strong endorsement to object teaching:

> Whenever this system has been confined to elementary instruction and has been employed by skillful, thorough teachers, in unfolding and disciplining the faculties, in fixing the attention and awakening thought, it has been successful.[31]

The teacher education program at Oswego Normal School, particularly the Pestalozzian object lesson, improved methods of instruction in elementary schools. The object lesson approach provided a structure that gave teachers more power to enliven their teaching. However, the Oswego program, though notable, concentrated on the object lesson and neglected the affective aspects of the general method.

The spirit of Pestalozzi also could be found inspiring U.S. progressive educators in the late nineteenth and early twentieth centuries. These progressives struggled against the continuing residues of formalism and verbalism in many schools. Although only one of many influences on progressivism, Pestalozzi's general method sparked the American progressive's emphasis on children's interests and needs. William H. Kilpatrick's project method and Harold Rugg's child-centered school reflected Pestalozzi's focus on the child and on activities as the basis of learning. Unfortunately for Pestalozzi in the nineteenth century and for the progressives in the twentieth, the traditional school proved to be a mighty fortress. Rather than ushering in a sweeping educational revolution, Pestalozzi and the later progressives brought about incremental changes that were incorporated slowly into the school's curriculum. The greatest contribution of these educational reformers was to set in motion forces that led to the gradual transformation and liberation of schools.

For education today, Pestalozzi's major contribution was developing a philosophy of natural education that stressed children's dignity and the importance of a child-centered curriculum. His rejection of child depravity, based on his view of a benevolent human nature, meant that he saw childhood as a uniquely important and special period of human growth. Early childhood education, in particular, was crucial in nurturing attitudes and dispositions conducive to later development. Pestalozzi's general method anticipated modern child psychology. The contemporary doctrines of the child-centered school and child permissiveness had their beginnings with Pestalozzi at Neuhof, Stans, Burgdorf, and Yverdon.

The value of Pestalozzi's special method rested on its relationships to children's experience. Pestalozzi anticipated Dewey in insisting on the importance of maintaining a child's continuity of experience. His stress on the need to maintain this continuum caused him to examine and to use the learning possibilities found in children's immediate environments. When used in such an experiential context, Pestalozzi's instructional strategies of "from the simple to the complex" and "from the near to the far" were valuable contributions to educational methodology.

Pestalozzi also was a pioneering theorist in the sociology of education. For him, education had important social implications. Despite his own admission that he had a sentimental and visionary disposition, Pestalozzi was able to interpret the broad educational importance of the political and economic trends of his time.

In terms of the ethical dimension of education, Pestalozzi sought to develop persons whose intellectual, moral, and physical powers were harmoniously developed. Fearing the dehumanizing effects of industrial specialization, he sought to educate persons who were morally sensitive to other human beings. His goal of educating the integrated person in a moral society is desirable and defensible for our age as well as his.

Pestalozzi exhibited a basic humanitarianism. As a lover of all humankind, he made love the center of his educational theory and practice. Mother love, the loving family circle, and love of God were persistent themes in his writing. In our age, Pestalozzi's emphasis on the human being's need to be a lover and to be loved may sound simplistic and platitudinous. However, Pestalozzi's philosophy of education was essentially a "love message," in which "Papa Pestalozzi" told children simply to love one another.

Questions for Reflection and Dialogue

1. Identify and analyze the major events in Pestalozzi's life that shaped his educational ideas.
2. Explain and analyze Pestalozzi's general and special methods.
3. To what extent was Pestalozzi a disciple of Rousseau?
4. Trace the diffusion of Pestalozzi's educational ideas.
5. What is the influence of Pestalozzi on the contemporary child-centered classroom and on constructivism?
6. Reflect on the problems of teasing, bullying, and gang violence in or near schools. How do these problems affect children's ability to learn? How do you think Pestalozzi might react to these problems?
7. Reflect on the problems that children encounter in families and neighborhoods with alcohol and drug abuse problems. How do these problems affect children's ability to learn? How do you think Pestalozzi might react to these problems?
8. Through introspection on your own education, reflect on the kind of teachers who created an emotionally secure learning environment. Share your reflections with other students in the course and determine if you can arrive at a profile of the teacher who best creates this kind of learning environment.

Projects for Deepening Your Understanding

1. Write a character sketch of Pestalozzi.
2. Develop a lesson plan to teach a subject or skill based on the Pestalozzian method.
3. In an essay, profile a Pestalozzian teacher as you would envision her or him.
4. In a position paper, either support or refute the statement that Pestalozzianism represents the successful transmission of an educational innovation from Europe to the United States.
5. Visit a primary school classroom. Do you find any evidence of Pestalozzi's method?
6. Observe several teachers and classrooms. Can you detect from your observation what makes an educational situation emotionally secure or insecure? How do you think Pestalozzi would react to the situations you have observed?

Notes

1. Kate Silber, *Pestalozzi: The Man and His Work* (London: Routledge & Kegan Paul, 1960), 1–2.
2. Silber, *Pestalozzi*, 108–9.
3. Silber, *Pestalozzi*, 155–56.
4. John Locke, *An Essay Concerning Human Understanding*, ed. Alexander Fraser (New York: Dover, 1959). Also see John Dunn, *Locke* (New York: Oxford University Press, 1984).
5. Gerald L. Gutek, *Pestalozzi and Education* (Prospect Heights, IL: Waveland, 1999), 10–12.
6. Johann H. Pestalozzi, *How Gertrude Teaches Her Children* (London: Swan Sonneschein, 1907), xvii.
7. Stanley E. Ballinger, "The Natural Man: Rousseau," in *The Educated Man: Studies in the History of Educational Thought*, ed. Paul Nash, Andreas M. Kazamias, and Henry J. Perkinson (New York: John Wiley & Sons, 1965), 225–46.
8. Silber, *Pestalozzi*, 2.
9. Johann H. Pestalozzi, "Views and Experiences," in *Pestalozzi*, ed. Lewis F. Anderson (New York: McGraw Hill, 1931), 101.
10. Biographies of Pestalozzi include Robert B. Downs, *Heinrich Pestalozzi: Father of Modern Pedagogy* (Boston: Twayne, 1975); Gutek, *Pestalozzi and Education*; and Silber, *Pestalozzi*.
11. Gutek, *Pestalozzi and Education*, 21–51.
12. For Pestalozzi's influence on Froebel, see Norman Brosterman, *Inventing Kindergarten* (New York: Harry N. Abrams, 1997), 18–22.
13. Roger de Guimps, *Pestalozzi: His Aim and Work* (Syracuse, NY: C. W. Bardeen, 1889), 6–7.
14. De Guimps, *Pestalozzi*, 20–23.
15. Johann H. Pestalozzi, "Leonard and Gertrude," in *Pestalozzi and Pestalozzianism*, ed. Henry Barnard (New York: F. C. Brownell, 1862).
16. Gutek, *Pestalozzi and Education*, 35.
17. Johann H. Pestalozzi, "Pestalozzi's Account of His Own Educational Experience," in Barnard, *Pestalozzi and Pestalozzianism*, 674.
18. Johann H. Pestalozzi, *How Gertrude Teaches Her Children* (Syracuse, NY: C. W. Bardeen, 1900).
19. Gutek, *Pestalozzi and Education*, 101–56.
20. Gutek, *Pestalozzi and Education*, 88–89.
21. Gutek, *Pestalozzi and Education*, 93–98.
22. Johann H. Pestalozzi, *Letters on Early Education Addressed to J. P. Greaves* (London: Sherwood, Gilbert, & Piper, 1827).
23. Elizabeth Mayo, *Lessons on Objects as Given to Children Between the Ages of Six and Eight in a Pestalozzian School* (London: Seeley & Burnside, 1835), 5–6.
24. Thomas A. Barlow, *Pestalozzi and American Education* (Boulder: Este Es Press, University of Colorado Libraries, 1977).
25. Gerald L. Gutek, *Joseph Neef: The Americanization of Pestalozzianism* (University, AL: University of Alabama Press, 1978).
26. Joseph Neef, *A Sketch of a Plan and Method of Education* (Philadelphia: Author, 1808); Neef, *The Method of Instructing Children Rationally in the Arts of Writing and Reading* (Philadelphia: Author, 1813).
27. Arthur E. Bestor, Jr., *Backwoods Utopias: The Sectarian and Owenite Phases of Communitarian Socialism in America, 1663–1829* (Philadelphia:

University of Pennsylvania Press, 1950). Also see Josephine M. Elliott, ed., *Partnership for Posterity: The Correspondence of William Maclure and Marie Duclos Fretageot, 1820–1833* (Indianapolis: Indiana Historical Society, 1994).

28. Barnard, *Pestalozzi and Pestalozzianism.*

29. Will S. Monroe, *History of the Pestalozzian Movement in the United States* (Syracuse, NY: C. W. Bardeen, 1907), 147–55.

30. Ned H. Dearborn, *The Oswego Movement in American Education* (New York: Teachers College Press, 1925).

31. Monroe, *History of the Pestalozzian Movement,* 183–84.

Suggestions for Further Reading

Anderson, Lewis F., ed. *Pestalozzi.* New York: McGraw Hill, 1931.

Barlow, Thomas A. *Pestalozzi and American Education.* Boulder: Este Es Press, University of Colorado Libraries, 1977.

Bestor, Arthur E., Jr. *Backwoods Utopias: The Sectarian and Owenite Phases of Communitarian Socialism in America, 1663–1829.* Philadelphia: University of Pennsylvania Press, 1950.

Biber, Edward. *Henry Pestalozzi and His Plan of Education.* Bristol: Thoemmes Press; Unifacmanu, 1994.

Dearborn, Ned. H. *The Oswego Movement in American Education.* New York: Teachers College Press, 1925.

DeBoer, George E. *A History of Ideas in Science Education: Implications for Practice.* New York: Teachers College Press, 1991.

De Guimps, Roger. *Pestalozzi: His Life and Work.* Bristol: Tokyo: Thoemmes Press; Maruzen, 1999.

Downs, Robert B. *Johann Heinrich Pestalozzi: Father of Modern Pedagogy.* Boston: Twayne, 1975.

Elliott, Josephine M., ed. *Partnership for Posterity: The Correspondence of William Maclure and Marie Duclos Fretageot, 1820–1833.* Indianapolis: Indiana Historical Society, 1994.

Gutek, Gerald L. *Joseph Neef: The Americanization of Pestalozzianism.* University, AL: University of Alabama Press, 1978.

———. *Pestalozzi and Education.* Prospect Heights, IL: Waveland, 1999.

Heafford, Michael R. *Pestalozzi: His Thought and Its Relevance Today.* London: Methuen, 1967.

Jedan, Dieter. *Johann Heinrich Pestalozzi and the Pestalozzian Method of Language Teaching.* Bern: Peter Lang, 1981.

Pestalozzi, Johann Heinrich. *The Education of Man—Aphorisms.* New York: Philosophical Library, 1951.

———. *How Gertrude Teaches Her Children.* London: Swan Sonnenschein, 1907.

———. *Leonard and Gertrude.* Trans. Eva Channing. Boston: D. C. Heath, 1891.

———. *Letters on Early Education.* Taipei, Taiwan: Bristol, England: Unifacmanu; Thoemmes Press, 1994.

Silber, Kate. *Pestalozzi: The Man and His Work.* London: Routledge & Kegan Paul, 1960.

Wild, Rebecca. *Raising Curious, Creative, Confident Kids; the Pestalozzi Experiment in Child-based Education.* Boston: Shambhala; U.S. distribution by Random House, 2000.

CHAPTER 12

Thomas Jefferson: Advocate of Republican Education

Chapter 12 examines the life, political philosophy, and educational ideas of Thomas Jefferson (1743–1826), American statesman and the third president of the United States. Jefferson continues to hold an esteemed position in the "symbolical architecture" of the United States, a "civilized man" with many interests and achievements.[1] Joseph Ellis, in his biography of Jefferson, states that "working on Jefferson was like entering a crowded room" in which several lively conversations were taking place.[2] Jefferson's general philosophy of education, his plans for establishing a system of elementary and secondary schools in Virginia, and his role in founding the University of Virginia reveal a political leader who developed a broad conception of education's role in republican society. An examination of Jefferson's educational philosophy highlights the necessary role of civic education in the newly created U.S. republic. In the broad expanse of Western educational history and philosophy, Jefferson is an especially illuminating figure because of his insights in relating politics and education. Gordon Lee, commenting on Jefferson's educational significance, notes that "many of the most influential considerations of educational theory . . . have been basically political."[3]

In this chapter, we discuss Jefferson's influence on education in the early republic in its historical context and in its enduring importance for civic education in the United States. First, we examine the general political climate in which Jefferson lived and worked. Second, we analyze Jefferson's biography, his education and career as a political leader and Enlightenment thinker, to determine the evolution of his ideas. Third, we explore the continuing impact of Jefferson's contributions to U.S. education, especially to the civic formation of citizens. This analysis illustrates the interrelationships between political and educational philosophy. For example, Jefferson's educational plans were part of his use of political strategies to make government by the people, through representative institutions, a reality. Although his educational ideas originated in the climate of the American Revolution and the early republic, Jefferson addressed issues of excellence and equity in education still unresolved but crucial to fulfilling the American dream.

———————————

To organize your thoughts as you read Chapter 12, focus on the following questions:

1. What were the significant ideas and trends in the historical context, the times and situation, in which Jefferson lived?
2. How did Jefferson's life and his educational biography shape his philosophy of education?
3. How did Jefferson's political philosophy shape his educational policies and practices?
4. What is the enduring legacy of Jefferson's contributions to U.S. education?

The Historical Context of Jefferson's Life

Jefferson's contributions to creating the United States as an independent and sovereign nation, a republic governed by representative institutions, can best be assessed within the larger Euro-American intellectual movement of the eighteenth-century Enlightenment. Although Jefferson gave an American rendition to the Enlightenment's ideological currents, he was intellectually well aware of the more general political and scientific trends in the Age of Reason. By applying the ideas of the Enlightenment philosophers to his political context, Jefferson was able to turn his ideas into political reality.

In his highly influential history of the Enlightenment, progressive historian Carl L. Becker uses the concept of the "climate of opinion" to analyze the Age of Reason's intellectual ferment.[4] The Enlightenment's underlying intellectual thread was that human beings, by using their reason, possessed the possibility of improving life on Earth. For Becker, the Age of Reason—the age that shaped Jefferson and that he shaped in turn—was continuous with but also broke from the past. For example, the theologians of the Medieval and Reformation eras construed the universe to be orderly, as did the Enlightenment's philosophers, but their explanations of this cosmic orderliness relied on different sources of authority. For the theologians of the earlier periods, the universe's order was caused by the creative act of God, a supreme supernatural being, who, taking a fatherly concern in the lives of human beings, revealed His word to them in the Bible and intervened in human history at certain crucial periods. For the Enlightenment *philosophes* and ideologists, the universe and its governing natural laws were products of an impersonal deity, a mechanistic first cause or prime mover.

Such earlier theologians as Thomas Aquinas and John Calvin recognized the Bible as the principal authority for explaining the universe and educating people about it (see Chapters 6 and 8). For both Catholic and Protestant educators, the needed explanations of life and how to live came from biblical and theological sources. The curriculum of educational institutions under denominational control was stocked with religiously based knowledge, practices, and values. In contrast, Enlightenment theorists such as Rousseau, Voltaire, Diderot, Condorcet, and Condillac in France and Jefferson and Franklin in the United States took a decidedly different path in searching for knowledge that explained how the universe functioned.[5] For these Enlightenment philosophers, human reason rather than divine revelation was the key to understanding. Human beings, through their rational powers, could discover the necessary truths that explained the laws of nature and the principles that should govern human society. Human reasoning, however, for them, was not a purely speculative game of intellectual hypothesizing that was disconnected from political and social realities, but arose from careful scientific research.

Jefferson and his Enlightenment colleagues believed that science and the scientific method provided the data that most accurately informed human reason.[6] Believing that human beings inhabited an observable natural and social world, they argued that people, educated according to the scientific method, could use their reason to observe nature and discover its operations and inner workings. From their careful observations, systematically recorded and analyzed, they could discover patterns. These patterns would reveal natural laws such as those of gravity, planetary revolution, Earth's rotation, the flow of blood in the body's circulatory system, the cycles of plant and animal growth and development, and so on. In the Enlightenment concept of science, the universe functioned according to an intrinsic and rather mechanical design, like a perfect clock that, once it began to tick away seconds, minutes, and hours, would do so perpetually. The reoccurring patterns of this stable universe were not subject to relativity, variation, change, and evolution as later scientists such as Darwin and Einstein would assert.

Looking to nature and examining it scientifically held immense educational possibilities. Those who dealt with *epistemological* (the theory of knowledge and of knowing) questions, such as Etienne Condillac in France and John Locke in England, concluded that ideas originated in the human sensory experience of objects that existed outside of the mind. From these sensory perceptions—the raw data of experience—humans derived their ideas. Education, based on nature and science, losing bookishness and verbosity, would become more directly based on human experience of the real world. It was in this intellectual current of the naturalism of the Enlightenment that Jefferson's political philosophy proclaimed that the people's political rights were grounded on natural law.

In their investigations of the natural world, the *philosophes* were vitally preoccupied in collecting scientific information about the world. Their enthusiasm for scientific research led them to develop such natural sciences as geology, chemistry, botany, zoology, and physics. They also had an explorer's curiosity about different places and peoples. For example, Thomas Jefferson, as U.S. president, commissioned Lewis and Clark's expedition to explore the western regions across the Mississippi River.[7] Seeking a return to nature, some *philosophes* turned to anthropology in their search for the unspoiled, simple, primitive human being who lived life according to nature's laws. This passion for scientific research and information had profound educational implications. Wherever they could wield influence, as in Condorcet's plan of education in revolutionary France or Jefferson's curricular designs for the University of Virginia, they emphasized the role and power of the natural sciences.

The struggles of Enlightenment thinkers to win a place for the natural sciences in the curricula of schools and colleges faced many serious obstacles. Educational institutions historically have lagged behind in incorporating new knowledge into their curricula. Traditionalists, who staunchly defended Latin and Greek as the core of knowledge, opposed the natural sciences' entry into the curriculum. Domination by the classics was not the only obstacle, however. When the Enlightenment ideology came on the intellectual scene, most educational institutions were still controlled by the churches. Clerics who headed and taught in these institutions believed that the principles that gave them their authority came from the Bible and from their particular church's theology.

Climates of opinion are pervasive in that ideas from one area of inquiry seep into and eventually permeate other areas of thought. The general Enlightenment reliance on scientific inquiry in the natural sciences as generating the most authoritative knowledge also permeated social, economic, and political questions. If natural laws governed natural phenomena, did they not also govern human society? Could not political science tell us how to govern ourselves properly? Could not economics provide the principles to bring order to trade, commerce, production, and consumption? Could not anthropology and sociology tell us how human beings lived and should live in mutual association? In their enthusiasm, the *philosophes* optimistically believed that a new social order, undergirded by natural laws, could be created by enlightened human beings. However, general enlightenment, through some form of popular education, was needed to create a new society in which people could live unshackled by ignorance, prejudice, and superstition.[8]

Now, not only could people observe the planet's revolution, but they possessed the possibility of creating a new society on it. Throughout the eighteenth, nineteenth, and twentieth centuries, the new social sciences were developed and struggled for a place in the schools' curriculum. For certain *philosophes*, these social sciences would provide the designs for a new social order.

With the sciences and social sciences regarded as instruments in creating a new society, some Enlightenment theorists, such as Jefferson, began the journey from philosopher to activist and from ideologue to revolutionary. Although Enlightenment philosophy proclaimed with certainty that human nature could be perfected, Catholic and Protestant theologians discounted the possibility of creating heaven on earth. Because of original sin, human beings had a fallen and weak nature that needed the guidance of strong authority figures in church and state. Further, the claims of the new social sciences challenged the theological sanction that gave established educational authorities their legitimacy.

The political status quo was another obstacle to creating an enlightened commonwealth of reasonable men and women. Europe was governed by hereditary monarchs, most of whom claimed that, because they ruled by the grace of God they were responsible to no one, neither the people nor their representatives. As an impasse developed between the old inherited political order and what promised to be the new, those inspired by Enlightenment ideology embarked on a revolutionary course in France and in Britain's 13 American colonies. One of the significant leaders of this revolution in America was the New World philosopher Thomas Jefferson.

From these general patterns of Enlightenment thought, it is possible to become still more specific in establishing the context of Jefferson's thinking. Although highly conversant with the ideas of the French *philosophes*, Jefferson felt a special intellectual kinship with the political ideology developed in England by John Locke (1632–1704), the theorist of the revolution of 1688, which replaced the Stuarts with the more constitutional monarchs William and Mary. An important work in the English Enlightenment, Locke's *An Essay Concerning Human Understanding* (1690) expressed the Enlightenment's propensity for science and empiricism.[9] His *Second Treatise on Government* (1688) expressed the principles of representative government that would shape Jefferson's political ideology and educational philosophy.[10]

Locke's *Essay*, which examined the origin of ideas, challenged the Platonic epistemology that ideas were latently present in the mind. Rather, Locke argued that the mind's processes worked, in almost a computerlike fashion, on information that came to it by the senses. The mind organized this crude sensory data into simple ideas. In turn, these simple ideas could be combined into compound and complex ones.

Locke challenged Plato's hierarchical stratification of people based on their intellectual abilities (for Plato's epistemology, see Chapter 3). While Locke did not claim that everyone knew everything equally, his theory posited that all people possessed an equal possibility of knowing. However, he did not claim that all people would use this possibility to equal effect. Drawing from Locke's epistemology, a case can be made that the provision of more educational opportunities for more people will create a more general and equitable diffusion of knowledge.

While Locke's *Essay Concerning Human Understanding* bolstered the position of those who emphasized sensation and empiricism as the foundations of knowledge, his *Second Treatise of Government* was particularly meaningful for Jefferson's political philosophy, especially to his writing of the Declaration of Independence.[11] Challenging hereditary monarchs' political supremacy, Locke contended that government arises from the consent of the governed, who to protect their natural rights of life, liberty, and property unite in mutual association and elect a government of their representatives. These representatives—divided into a lawmaking or legislative branch, an adjudicative or legal branch, and a law-enforcing or executive branch—govern the political commonwealth with the consent of the governed. Unlike absolute hereditary monarchs and aristocrats of birth, members of the government are elected or appointed for a limited term of office. On completing their term, they return to the people from which they came. To protect property rights, taxes are to be levied only with the consent of the governed. Jefferson would incorporate these Lockean principles into the Declaration of Independence in 1776 and the framers of the U.S. Constitution would be guided by them in 1788 and 1789.

The Lockean and Jeffersonian emphasis on representative government was based on the principle of election by the people and service by elected officials. Simply stated, votes cast by citizens determine results of elections. In such an electoral process, candidates winning the majority of votes would be elected and those who garnered only the votes of a minority would be defeated. Although counting votes is a simple political procedure, it holds important meaning for republican government and for civic education. It means that voters should be educated so that they cast their ballots intelligently. Like the tenure of elected officials, it means that majorities and minorities are temporary coalitions. Today's majority may be tomorrow's minority. Members of the majority are to respect the dissent of the minority. The civic education required to make elective representative institutions function must engender knowledge of the system and a value commitment to it as well. Citizens of a representative republic need a body of knowledge on which to base decisions, they need to be familiar with the political process, and they need to have the attitudes and demonstrate the behaviors that contribute to its effectiveness.

Locke and Jefferson, proclaiming the individual's naturally ordained sovereignty, stated their version of human rights as negative proscriptions that no government should violate. Among such proscriptions were that government should not interfere with freedom of speech, press, assembly, and religion.[12] Locke boldly asserted and Jefferson concurred that revolution was justified when a government violated the individual's rights of life, liberty, and property. The people had the right to rise and overthrow a repressive government. Jefferson's statement of human rights in the Declaration of Independence as "life, liberty, and the pursuit of happiness" closely paralleled Locke's identification of human rights. Locke, Jefferson, and other Enlightenment theorists saw government as the most likely violator of human rights because they lived in a time when absolute monarchies, established churches, and hereditary aristocracies reigned supreme. (Locke's and Jefferson's philosophy on limited government anticipated the rise of liberal ideology, discussed in Chapter 17 on John Stuart Mill.)

In addition to the need for civic education for republican citizens, Locke's and Jefferson's political philosophy held important implications for academic freedom, the freedom to teach and to learn. The right to information meant that teachers should have the academic freedom to teach and students the freedom to learn without government or institutional censorship of ideas, information, or books. It also implied that teachers and students had the right to raise questions without interference from agents of the church or state. When Jefferson stated that the government that governs best governs least, he was arguing for limited government. When he argued against church control of higher education, he was attempting to remove what he regarded as sectarian limitations on freedom of inquiry.

The context of the age of Jefferson included, along with the Enlightenment, the momentous events of the American Revolution and the foundational years of the early republic. Because of a series of repressive economic and political acts by the British crown, such representatives of discontented Americans as John Adams, Patrick Henry, Richard Lee, and George Washington met as a Continental Congress in 1774 to determine a course of action against British repression. In 1775, actual fighting began between British troops and colonial rebels in the Massachusetts towns of Lexington and Concord.

Thomas Paine's (1737–1809) widely circulated pamphlet, *Common Sense*, expressed in revolutionary rhetoric, urged the colonists to free themselves from the tyranny of absolute monarchy. Condemning hereditary monarchy, Paine ripped into George III as a "royal brute" whose arbitrary rule violated Americans' natural right to liberty.[13]

On July 2, 1776, the Continental Congress, voting to separate from British rule, commissioned Thomas Jefferson to draft the Declaration of Independence. Congress President John Hancock signed it on July 4 and the document was officially proclaimed two days later. For five years, the struggle went on between Great Britain and its former colonies. On October 19, 1781, the surrender of British General Cornwallis at Yorktown ended hostilities. In 1783, a peace treaty was signed.

Although the American colonists won the military struggle for independence, the challenge of founding a new republic remained unfinished. Until 1787, the United States stayed a loose confederation of states associated through the Articles of Confederation. In that year, Congress authorized convening a Constitutional Convention in Philadelphia.

Among the convention's 55 delegates were such prominent patriots as George Washington, James Madison, Robert Morris, Benjamin Franklin, and Alexander Hamilton. Jefferson, on a diplomatic mission in Europe, was not present.

After long debates, the convention institutionalized the revolutionary process into formal government structures. Following Enlightenment ideology, they devised a three-fold division of powers in a federal government, composed of an elected legislative branch (the bicameral Congress), an indirectly elected chief executive, and an appointed judiciary. Power was further divided between the federal and state governments. Between 1787 and 1788 the federal Constitution was ratified by 11 states and became the document that set the processes for governing the new republic.

In 1791, the states ratified the first 10 amendments to the Constitution, a statement of rights in the mode of Enlightenment liberalism. The Bill of Rights, as these 10 amendments were called, guaranteed the freedoms of assembly, speech, religion, and the press, preserved the people's right to keep and bear arms, and prohibited unreasonable search and seizure. The tenth amendment, which was especially significant for education, states that those "powers not delegated to the United States by the Constitution, nor prohibited by it to the States, are reserved to the States respectively, or to the people."

Although the new republic's political foundations had been laid with the Constitution, it still needed the institutions and processes to educate its citizens. Still in place but in disrepair were the inherited schools and colleges of the prerevolutionary colonial period. In New England were the locally controlled town and district schools and Latin grammar schools that still reflected much control by religious denominations. In Rhode Island and the Middle Atlantic states of New York, New Jersey, Pennsylvania, and Delaware, the schools, generally of the parochial type, were tied to religious denominations. School structures remained weaker in the South, where the dominant class of white plantation owners provided tutors for their own children but little for less economically favored groups. At the summit of the hierarchy of educational institutions were the church-affiliated colleges.

If the schools and colleges in the new republic were weak structurally, they were even less suited to the nation's republican ideology. Although educational institutions continued to function as they had before the revolution, political and educational theorists such as Benjamin Rush, Robert Coram, and Samuel Smith argued for creating a new system of educational institutions, imbued with republican ideology.[14] These theorists, later joined by Jefferson, were engaged in what today might be called strategic planning, or "brainstorming," and developed plans for a new U.S. educational system that embodied Enlightenment ideology, civic education, and a new element—cultural nationalism. Calling for a mental revolution to make Americans culturally independent, they wanted education to emphasize the following:

1. The knowledge and values needed for civic participation in a republic
2. The inclusion of scientific knowledge, method, and temperament in curriculum and instruction
3. The creation of a unique and distinctive United States culture

It is this context of the times, the philosophy of the Enlightenment and the rise of revolutionary American republican ideology, that we may study Thomas Jefferson.

Thomas Jefferson as a Political and Educational Statesman

In this section, we turn to Thomas Jefferson's life and career. Our goal is to identify those events in his life that made him a political and educational statesman and the personification of America's most cherished values. The third of 10 children, Thomas Jefferson, a promising son of prominent parents, was a member of one of Virginia's most economically advantaged and socially prestigious families. He was born on April 13, 1743, at Shadwell to Peter Jefferson (1708–1757), owner of a large plantation in Virginia's Albemarle County, and Jane Randolph (1720–1776), a daughter of one of Virginia's most socially prominent families. Shadwell, the Jefferson family's plantation estate in the foothills of the Blue Ridge Mountains, was located near the Rivanna River in Virginia's fertile Piedmont region.

Peter Jefferson, a leading figure in Virginia's plantation-owning elite, owned nearly 10,000 acres of land, more than 60 slaves, and large numbers of livestock. Active in politics, he served at various times as a county sheriff, surveyor, and justice of the peace.[15] Jefferson also served in the House of Burgesses, Virginia's elected colonial assembly. Peter Jefferson's commitment to public service made him a model his son Thomas could emulate. Although involvement in politics was an expected part of a plantation owner's social role, Thomas, like his father, made it a lifelong commitment. In the case of the son, commitment to public service would lead to the presidency of the republic.

Thomas Jefferson's early educational experiences were directed by his father. When his son was 5, Peter Jefferson engaged a tutor who taught Thomas reading, writing, and arithmetic. Employing a tutor was typical of the plantation-owning class of Virginia and the other Southern states. Unlike the residents of New England's Massachusetts, Connecticut, and New Hampshire who established town schools, the Southern gentry regarded education as a private family matter rather than a community responsibility.

When he was 9, Thomas was enrolled in a Latin grammar school conducted by the Reverend William Douglas, minister of St. James parish in Goochland County. Anglican clergymen like Douglas often maintained preparatory schools. Because the school was located some distance from the Jefferson plantation, Thomas boarded there. For the next five years, he studied at Douglas's school, where he pursued the typical curriculum of Latin and Greek. He also studied French, a language that would serve him well during his diplomatic mission to France.[16] Although he did not consider Douglas an inspired teacher, Jefferson learned classical Greek and Latin, considered indispensable for the educated person. Throughout his life, Jefferson read the classics in their original languages rather than in translations.

When Thomas was 14, his father died and he returned to the family plantation at Shadwell. Despite the loss of his father, Jefferson, continuing his education, enrolled in a school conducted by the Reverend James Maury, an Anglican minister at Fredericksburg, located 12 miles from Shadwell. From Maury as well as Douglas, Jefferson learned the doctrines of the Church of England. Although interested in religion, Jefferson as an adult was skeptical that the doctrines of Christianity were divinely inspired. Maury, esteemed as one of Virginia's most learned scholars, stressed the traditional Latin and Greek classical curriculum, a necessary preparation for college admission. In addition to the classics, Jefferson studied English literature and history and enjoyed the opportunity to use Maury's large library.[17] As a complement to his formal schooling, Jefferson also learned to dance, ride, and hunt, skills appropriate to the well-rounded Virginia gentleman.

At 17, Jefferson was admitted as a student to the College of William and Mary in Williamsburg. Here, in Virginia's capital of 1,500 people, he received a formal education at the college and an informal political education by observing the General Court and the House of Burgesses. When Jefferson enrolled in 1760, William and Mary registered 100 students in its three branches—the grammar, the Indian, and the philosophy schools. Because he already had a preparatory education, he enrolled in the philosophy school, where he studied mathematics, physics, metaphysics, logic, ethics, rhetoric, and literature.[18] Jefferson's educational encounter with the Western classical tradition shaped his intellectual outlook.

William and Mary's faculty consisted of seven professors, six of whom were Anglican ministers. The seventh professor, Dr. William Small, who taught mathematics and natural sciences, was Jefferson's adviser.[19] Small encouraged Jefferson's interest in science. He fondly recalled Small as "a man profound in most of the useful branches of science, with a happy talent of communication, correct and gentlemanly manners, and an enlarged and liberal mind."[20]

Jefferson was an extremely earnest student, often devoting 15 hours each day to his studies. His favorite study method was to take extensive notes on his reading, often copying whole passages from books. He would then revise the passage to include his opinions and style. As a result, he became a skilled writer, careful in using the phrase that best conveyed his ideas. His study skills, learned as a student, carried over into his life and his service as governor, diplomat, and president. Ellis, in his biography of Jefferson, calls him a "textual president," who made decisions in much the same way that he revised texts.[21] Jefferson also showed his abilities in studying foreign languages. He was facile in Latin, Greek, French, and Italian. Jefferson, who benefited from his own self-education and took readily to instruction by others, completed his program in the liberal arts and graduated from William and Mary in 1762.

Determined to study law, he read in that subject with George Wythe, a learned and influential Williamsburg attorney. Although law was a recognized academic discipline at the large European universities, the general practice for becoming a lawyer in the colonies was to read law, an apprenticeship in which the aspiring young man would join the office of an established practicing lawyer as an intern, with access to his mentor's library and experience. Jefferson was very fortunate to have Wythe as his legal mentor. Wythe, a member of the House of Burgesses, enjoyed a positive reputation throughout Virginia. Jefferson studied with Wythe for five years. During this time, he read the great legal classics such as Sir Edward Coke's *Institutes of the Laws of England* and Lord Henry Kames's *Historical Law Tracts*.[22] In addition to his reading of law, Jefferson continued his historical research, reading Paul de Rapin's *History of England* and John Dalrymple's *History of Feudal Property in Great Britain*. Based on his legal and historical studies, Jefferson was convinced that the rule of law, based on the primitive Anglo-Saxon values of self-government, could best be recreated in the new world of North America.[23] The well-read Jefferson was admitted to the practice of law in Virginia in 1767.

When he was 21, Jefferson assumed the role of plantation owner, managing 5,000 acres in Albemarle and adjacent counties. He, like other plantation owners, used enslaved Africans as the agricultural workforce. A participator in the slave system, Jefferson questioned slavery but took no actions against it, a gross inconsistency with his natural rights principles.[24]

Jefferson, who studied the architectural works of James Gibbs and Robert Morris, implemented his ideas of design in building Monticello, the name he gave to his mountaintop mansion retreat. Throughout his life he redesigned and added to Monticello—the center of his life, a place of family domesticity, quiet contemplation, and lively sociability. Interested in horticulture, he planted landscape gardens to grace his country estate. On January 1, 1772, Jefferson married Martha Wayles Skelton (1748–1782) who, like Jefferson, was from an influential Virginia family. Jefferson and his wife had seven children but only three survived to adulthood. In May 1782, the Jeffersons' seventh child, Lucy Elizabeth, was born. Martha, in delicate health, did not recover from the baby's delivery and died on September 6, 1782.[25] Jefferson, who was deeply in love with Martha, went into a long period of grieving and suffered a deep depression that lifted only very slowly.

By birth, education, and cultural association, Jefferson was prepared to be a member of the gentlemanly Southern elite who, along with the New England Yankee, would shape the new republic's course when the revolution brought independence. Versed in law and politics, he continued to read widely, especially in books that provided the theory of what would become the revolutionary ideology. He read Locke's *Second Treatise on Government*, Jean Jacques Burlamaqui's *Principes du Droit Naturel*, Anthony Ellys's *Tracts on the Liberty, Spiritual and Temporal, of Protestants in England*, and Adam Ferguson's *An Essay on the History of Civil Society*.[26] He also analyzed the works of Charles Montesquieu, who applied Enlightenment ideology to such questions as inequality, law, and the social compact.[27] A widely read man who valued books, Jefferson spent time and money assembling a large library.[28] Although Jefferson enjoyed the educational opportunities brought by wealth and social status, he applied himself indefatigably to a lifelong learning that went beyond his formal schooling. A person of wide-ranging intellectual interests, Jefferson was knowledgeable about philosophy, political theory, archeology, architecture, horticulture, religion, and education. His presidency was marked by a conception of that office that combined the attributes of the scholar, teacher, and leader. As a political leader, Jefferson was skilled in employing the often-contradictory idioms of enlightened scholar and popular democrat.[29]

Jefferson's actual political career began with his election to the House of Burgesses in 1769. When he arrived at Williamsburg to take his seat, the Burgesses were protesting the taxes imposed by the Townshend Acts. For the next decade, Jefferson supported the colonial cause against Great Britain. In 1773, he served as a member of the Committee of Correspondence that coordinated colonial strategy against British domination. In 1775, he was elected as one of Virginia's representatives to the Continental Congress in Philadelphia. Along with John Adams, Benjamin Franklin, Robert Livingston, and Roger Sherman, Jefferson was named to the committee charged with drafting a statement of independence that detailed the colonists' grievances against England. The committee delegated the drafting of the Declaration of Independence to Jefferson, who was its principal author. In drafting the Declaration, Jefferson envisioned himself as a voice of the people, expressing in words what Americans thought.[30] Embodying Lockean and Enlightenment political ideology, Jefferson's original draft of the Declaration of Independence stated the following:

> We hold these truths to be sacred & undeniable, that all men are created equal &
> independent, that from that equal creation they derive rights inherent & inalienable,
> among which are the preservation of life, & liberty, & the pursuit of happiness; that
> to secure these ends, governments are instituted among men, deriving their just
> powers from the consent of the governed; that whenever any form of government
> shall become destructive of these ends, it is the right of the people to alter or to
> abolish it, & to institute new government, laying its foundation on such principles
> & organizing its powers in such form, as to them shall seem most likely to effect their
> safety & happiness.[31]

In October 1776, Jefferson returned to Virginia to take his place in the state's general assembly, where he proposed legislation that clearly demonstrated his liberal Enlightenment political philosophy. He sought reform of Virginia's legal code, seeking abolition of primogeniture, the mandatory right of inheritance of the firstborn son, and restrictions on the use of the death penalty. He also sought to increase the number of voters in the state by reducing property qualifications. His efforts to reform political institutions and processes in Virginia portray the essence of what would become Jeffersonian republicanism. Jefferson's career in state government is especially illuminating for his concept of civic education.

Influenced by the Enlightenment's general religious attitude, Jefferson, a "deistic humanist," contemplated God abstractly as the "master mind, the supreme artificer, the Creator," rather than in the Judeo-Christian tradition of the Supreme Being as a personal, caring, or lawgiving God.[32] Adhering to Lockean principles, Jefferson opposed officially sanctioned state churches, such as the Church of England, which was established as the official church of Virginia. Intellectually, he believed that religious dogmas interfered with the free pursuit of knowledge. Strongly advocating separation of church and state, Jefferson introduced a "Bill for Establishing Religious Freedom" in the Virginia Assembly in 1779, which contained the words, "God . . . created the mind free, and manifested his supreme will that free it shall remain by making it altogether insusceptible of restraint." Opposing religious tests as a requirement for citizenship, Jefferson insisted that "civil rights have no dependence on our religious opinions."[33] A strong statement for separation of church and state, Jefferson's bill was enacted in 1786, affirming that

> no man shall be compelled to frequent or support any religious worship, place, or
> ministry whatsoever, nor shall be enforced, restrained, molested, or burthened in his
> body or goods, nor shall otherwise suffer, on account of his religious opinions or be-
> lief; but that all men shall be free to profess, and by argument to maintain, their
> opinions in matters of religion, and that the same shall in no wise diminish, enlarge,
> or affect their civil capacities.[34]

Jefferson's bill for religious freedom represented the founding fathers' belief in separation of church and state. In the nineteenth and twentieth centuries, the U.S. Supreme Court would uphold the concept of separation between church and state and between the church and public education.[35] However, controversies regarding the degree and extent of separation of church and state continue to arise today over issues of state-supported vouchers for pupils attending private schools, creationism versus evolution in the curriculum, and prayer and religious observances by students in public schools.

Throughout his life, Jefferson opposed the influence of religious denominations over schools and colleges as inimical to freedom of inquiry. Although Jefferson was effective in disestablishing a state church in Virginia, in other states, especially those of New England, the relationship between religious denominationalism and schooling remained close until the early nineteenth century.

In 1779, Jefferson introduced his bill "for the more general diffusion of knowledge," designed to create a state system of schools in Virginia. Although not passed by the Virginia General Assembly, the bill, an important landmark in U.S. educational history, asserted the state and local community's responsibility to establish and maintain public schools. Because of its historical significance, we examine Jefferson's bill later in this chapter.

From 1779 to 1781, Jefferson, serving as Virginia's governor, was preoccupied with coordinating the war effort against the British. In 1783, he helped draft Virginia's new constitution. His next assignment for the new American republic took him to France in 1786, where he served until 1789 as ambassador at the court at Versailles. As the representative of his country in France, Jefferson displayed his often paradoxical impressions of Europe. He was interested in and learned all he could about French ideas, politics, architecture, literature, and art. At the same time, he found France and Europe to be locked in superstition, greed, poverty, and inequalities.[36] In other words, Americans could learn from Europe how to become a different kind of people.

Because of his competency as a diplomat, he was named secretary of state, serving from 1789 to 1793. Together with Benjamin Franklin and John Adams, Jefferson was one of the early architects of U.S. foreign policy.[37] As a diplomat, he worked to gain the European nations' recognition of the United States's independence and sovereignty. He also sought to keep European nations from interfering in the internal affairs of the United States so that the new republic could consolidate its revolution by creating stable institutions. At the same time, however, he believed that the United States would one day shine throughout the world as the republican beacon.

Though his scientific interests brought him into correspondence with Europe's leading intellectuals, Jefferson believed that the United States needed to develop its cultural as well as political identity as an independent nation. He encouraged Americans to seek knowledge of the intellectual, scientific, and cultural developments in other countries, but firmly believed the American experience in the New World environment was creating a new and different people with their own unique cultural identity. Unlike the conservative traditionalists, Jefferson affirmed the prerogatives of each generation to be independent of preceding ones and unfettered by chains of custom in determining its own destiny.[38] However, constructing one's own destiny did not occur in cultural isolation.

In 1780, Jefferson began working on a manuscript that grew out of inquiries made by Francois Marbois, the secretary to the French minister, about the topography, climate, population, flora, and fauna of Virginia.[39] Marbois was conducting a survey of all the American states and Jefferson was responding for Virginia. Jefferson's manuscript, later published as *Notes on the State of Virginia*, is considered one of the most significant of the early scientific and political books published in the United States.[40] In *Notes*, Jefferson disputed the thesis of the French naturalist Georges de Buffon, who contended that North America's people, plants, and animals were steadily degenerating and were inferior to those of Europe.[41]

Jefferson's far-ranging *Notes* encompassed such topics as Virginia's minerals and soils, its river system, the conditions of Indians, slavery and African servitude, and the state's constitution, laws, and politics. The book, revealing Jefferson's intellectual acumen, provided evidence of his preference for political arrangements resting on freeholding, independent farmers and his general reluctance to consider large urban settings a positive influence on the country's future.[42]

Substituting "pursuit of happiness" for Locke's natural right of "property," Jefferson argued that all men, not only property holders, had political rights. *Notes*, which examines the condition of Virginia's schools and colleges, also includes Jefferson's ideas on education. He manifested his faith in the possibility of educating a "aristocracy of virtue and talent" that was not defined by property.[43] Jefferson revealed his moral equivocation about slavery. He argued for terminating the slave trade and the gradual ending of slavery in the United States.[44] At the same time that he expressed his forebodings about slavery's pernicious effects on both slave owner and slave, he continued to own slaves.[45]

Jefferson's scientific contributions were recognized in both Europe and the United States. In 1797, he was elected president of the American Philosophical Society, an organization that sponsored cultural and scientific endeavors and explorations.

As the United States entered the nineteenth century, new political coalitions organized to form the American political party system. Those who favored a strong central government, with limited powers to the states, organized the Federalist party. Including such prominent leaders as Alexander Hamilton and John Adams, the Federalists saw the federal government as the leading force in developing the new nation. The Federalists' opponents gathered in a loose coalition known as the Democratic-Republicans, led by Thomas Jefferson. Also known as Jeffersonians, they favored limited federal power and championed states' rights. Suspicious of concentrating political power in the hands of vested special interests, Jefferson envisioned a popularly based government with power residing in the hands of freeholders, the owners of small farms.

The rival Federalist, or Hamiltonian, and Jeffersonian parties, which took opposing positions on national political policy, differed on educational policy as well. The Hamiltonian position, which resurfaced later in the Whig and then the Republican parties, gave the federal government a paramount position in national, especially economic, development. Later, the Whigs, a successor party to the Federalists, would encourage "internal improvements" by which the federal government would subsidize certain industries such as canal and railroad building. In the nineteenth century, first the Whigs and then the Republicans generally supported common or public schools as a means of national development. (See Chapter 14 on Horace Mann for the Whig role in the common school movement.) Although Jefferson was committed to education and to the provision of schooling, his philosophy rested on an ideology of civic education that was tied more to local and state initiatives.

In 1803, President Jefferson's administration successfully negotiated the $15 million Louisiana Purchase from France. The addition of the vast territory more than doubled the size of the United States and carried the national boundaries far beyond the Mississippi River.[46] In 1804, President Jefferson commissioned the transcontinental explorations of Meriwether Lewis and William Clark. The expedition, which took the two explorers from St. Louis, Missouri, to the Pacific Ocean, was intended to provide scientific and geographical information about the territory.[47] In one of history's great paradoxes, Jefferson, who was so firmly devoted to the principle of limited government, used his presidency to not only increase the nation's size but also its future development. Jefferson's bold initiative in purchasing the Louisiana Territory was driven by his vision of the importance that the West, an immense area of natural resources and land, would play in the destiny of the United States.

After leaving the presidency, Jefferson returned to his estate at Monticello to pursue his intellectual interests. In 1814, he made another educational contribution to his country by offering his library to Congress to replace the collections of the Library of Congress, which had been destroyed during the British attack on Washington in the War of 1812. Jefferson's large library of 6,487 volumes was sold to Congress for $23,950. In the last years of his life, Jefferson energetically devoted himself to founding the University of Virginia. We discuss his role in planning and establishing the new university in the following section.

Jefferson on Education

Jefferson envisioned education as a necessary foundation for a free people who governed themselves democratically through representative institutions. His political role in the new republic as well as his own personal intellectual sensitivity to learning generated a deep and sustained interest in educational institutions and processes. Resting on his political philosophy, rooted in Enlightenment rationalism, Jefferson conceived of three broad goals for civic education in the new republic:

1. State-supported and locally controlled schooling should provide the people with a basic literary, mathematical, and historical education.
2. Schools should be agencies of identifying, selecting, and preparing the most talented persons for leadership positions by providing access to higher education.
3. Popular education should advance human liberty and freedom by safeguarding the individual's natural rights.

In 1779, as a member of the Virginia legislature, Jefferson introduced a bill for "the more general diffusion of knowledge," which was designed to establish a state system of elementary and secondary schools.[48] Although the bill did not become law then nor in subsequent efforts by Jefferson, it demonstrates his early commitment to public schooling as a component of republican citizenship and as a state responsibility. The bill was not only one of the educational plans of the revolutionary republican generation but it raised highly significant issues about equity and excellence in education that have been recurring debated questions in the United States.

The question of excellence asks to what degree educational institutions have a special responsibility in identifying the most academically gifted students and in cultivating their intellectual abilities. This query assumes that intellectual ability is unevenly distributed and that the academically talented are a minority of the population. Expressed by both Plato in ancient Greece and Confucius in ancient China, the idea that a gifted intelligentsia, an aristocracy of intellect, should be specially educated to rule has had long standing in history (see Chapters 2 and 3). In Europe, the belief in the concept of a gifted minority was institutionalized in the general population's limited access to secondary and higher education. Although Plato maintained that potential philosopher-kings could be found throughout the population, access to secondary and higher education throughout most of history was limited to males from the upper socioeconomic classes or the aristocracy who, then, had a favored opportunity to occupy leadership positions. Because of circumstances of birth, gender, and class, the majority of people were denied this kind of educational opportunity.

With the more egalitarian revolutionary ethic in the new republic, the issue of equality of access to educational institutions emerged. Although it would take two centuries to equalize the educational opportunities of women, ethnic and other minorities, and the handicapped, Jefferson saw the dimensions of the excellence and equity issue. He also realized that general knowledge, a kind of civic literacy, was indispensable if the new republic's representative institutions were to function effectively.

According to Jefferson's plan for the diffusion of knowledge, each of Virginia's counties was to be divided into "hundreds," the Anglo-Saxon name for a local district. In each hundred, a conveniently located elementary school was to be built and maintained at public expense. These hundred schools were to enroll all free boys and girls, who could attend for three years. The elementary school curriculum would feature the basic primary level skills of reading, writing, and arithmetic as well as the history of Greece, Rome, Great Britain, and North America. Although the first three years of elementary schooling were to be at public expense, children could continue at their parents' expense. By contemporary standards, Jefferson's proposal was only a modest effort to provide some degree of equity to Virginia's free children. Jefferson's proposal excluded slave children.

Jefferson's proposal included establishing 20 grammar, or secondary, schools, where promising youngsters could continue their education and prepare for entry to college. The projected grammar school curriculum included Latin, Greek, English, geography, and advanced mathematics.[49] Students who could pay their own tuition were allowed to attend. For those who could not pay, Jefferson devised a kind of merit scholarship program. From clusters of 10 elementary schools, the most academically gifted students whose parents could not afford to pay tuition were eligible to receive a merit scholarship to attend a grammar school. After one year of attendance, one-third of the lower-ranking scholarship students would be dropped. At the end of the second year, another selection would be made, with only the most academically talented merit scholars remaining.[50] In each grammar school for each class, the most intellectually able scholarship student would continue for an additional four years, thus completing the six years of grammar school. After the projected system was in place, in any given year 20 state-supported merit scholars would complete grammar school. Of these 20, the top 10 were to be admitted to the College of William and Mary. The lower 10 would become grammar school teachers or enter public service.[51]

Although Jefferson's plan would have made elementary education available to all free children, he assigned a highly selective role to secondary schooling. The plan did provide an opportunity for a small number of economically poorer students to receive a secondary education, but the thrust was for selectivity. However, Jefferson's principle of selection was not based on membership in a socially or economically advantaged class. Jefferson's compromise between excellence and equity was an uneasy one. The question remains, however: Is it possible for education to be equal and academically excellent at the same time? Although not enacted, Jefferson's bill anticipated the promise of public education that would come with the common school movement in the nineteenth century (see Chapter 14 on Horace Mann).

Throughout his life, Jefferson worked to establish a complete system of educational institutions for Virginia that encompassed elementary, secondary, and higher education. When he found his efforts to establish state-supported elementary and secondary schools frustrated by a reluctant state legislature, Jefferson turned his attention to higher education. Concerned with the educational development of his state, he had at first tried to build an educational system from the primary level upward. Now, changing his strategy, he determined that, if an excellent state university could be established, the momentum might flow downward to the lower schools.

Higher education had long been an interest of Jefferson, who had in 1779 proposed a reorganization of the College of William and Mary. When the Virginia legislature failed to act on his proposed reforms, Jefferson, as a member of the board of visitors, worked with William and Mary's president, the Reverend James Madison, on an internal reform of the College. The professorships in the grammar and divinity schools were converted into chairs of medicine, law, and modern languages. However, the more traditionally minded board of trustees undermined Jefferson's changes.[52] Jefferson then abandoned his plan to make William and Mary the apex of his educational system.

After leaving the U.S. presidency, Jefferson began his work to create the University of Virginia. As was consistently true of his leadership style, Jefferson first did his research, collecting information about existing colleges and universities of Europe and the United States. Although he appreciated the role that such universities as Oxford and Cambridge had played in preserving and transmitting knowledge, he believed their emphasis on ancient languages and literatures made them inadequate models for United States universities. The new republic, an experiment in representative government with vast expanses of underdeveloped territories, needed institutions of higher learning that were open to change and scientific in outlook. Nor did New England's Harvard and Yale, still rooted in denominationalism, present the desired paradigm. Jefferson's vision of a modern university would be state established and publicly supported and controlled. Its excellent academic character and superior facilities would attract the most able students and the finest faculty. Even before the Virginia legislature authorized a state university, Jefferson was planning the facilities of what was to be an "academical village" of attractive classrooms, libraries, and residences for professors and students.

In 1816, the Virginia legislature authorized establishment of what was called the "Central College," which eventually became the new university. The board of visitors, or trustees, of the college included Jefferson; James Madison, another former president; James Monroe, the current president; and three other prominent Virginians. In 1818, Jefferson's plan for the University of Virginia moved forward. Governor James P. Preston appointed a commission to recommend a location for the university. On August 1, 1818, meeting at Rockfish Gap in the Blue Ridge Mountains, the commission, after electing Jefferson its chairman, voted to locate the new university at Charlottesville.

The Rockfish Gap Report, embodying Jefferson's plan for the University of Virginia, included his specifications on the architectural design and location of the buildings, the curriculum, and the appointment of professors.[53] Wanting the institution to provide the useful knowledge that the republic's development required, Jefferson identified the university's mission to be the promotion of scientific inquiry and instruction. The buildings' classical architectural design would reflect the purest style of ancient Greece. By 1819, Jefferson had been elected the first rector of the University of Virginia and building construction was under way.

A search commenced to find the finest scholars in Europe and America as the university's founding faculty. Professors were appointed to teach natural science, mathematics, ancient and modern languages, anatomy and medicine, and natural and moral philosophy. As rector, Jefferson drafted the university's governing bylaws, specified requirements for examinations and degrees, and even established the class schedule.[54]

The educational principles that would guide the University of Virginia reflected Jefferson's commitment to academic freedom. Jefferson, who believed that restrictions on freedom of inquiry came most often from religious creed, made sure that the new university was without denominational affiliation; indeed, it would not even have a department of theology. Further, he insisted that the institution reflect republicanism by eliminating the typical distinctions among freshmen, sophomores, juniors, and seniors. Students were free to elect their subjects; there would be no required subjects. The board of trustees would establish the general policies, and actual day-to-day governance of the university would reside in a model of shared responsibility between faculty and students.[55]

On March 7, 1825, the first class of 30 students entered the University of Virginia, which Jefferson dedicated to the search for truth. The institution would encourage the "illimitable freedom of the human mind. For here we are not afraid to follow truth wherever it may lead, nor to tolerate any error so long as reason is left free to combat it."[56]

Jefferson died on July 4, 1826, the day marking the 50th anniversary of the signing of the Declaration of Independence.

Conclusion: An Assessment

By the standards of his own time as well as those of today, Thomas Jefferson was an exceptional person. A statesman in the most complete sense of the word, he articulated many of the enduring political principles embodied in the institutions of the new republic. Jefferson clearly understood that a free people needed a system of accessible schools in order to maintain representative government. Thus, his proposals for the "more general diffusion of knowledge" and for establishing the University of Virginia were efforts to create the educational means to enlighten a politically free people.

Jefferson's model of the political leader, the president, provides a noteworthy exemplar of leadership. He was a mentor to two of his successors to the presidency, James Madison and James Monroe. Jefferson was a well-read, scholarly person who based his policies on principle and research. His intellectual inquiries led him to many areas of scholarship—philosophy, science, political theory, anthropology, history, literature, horticulture, geography, religion, architecture, and education. An informed generalist, his comprehensive knowledge enabled him to form a generous vision of what the new nation could be.

Jefferson, who organized a political party and served in several appointed and elective offices including the presidency, was a practitioner as well as a theorist. Although he was unable to win passage of his bill for the "more general diffusion of knowledge," Jefferson did succeed in creating the University of Virginia. His success in founding the new state university provides an excellent example of Jefferson as a policy formulator and implementor. Jefferson researched the problem by going to the theoretical foundations of higher education and examining relevant aspects of its history, philosophy, and governance. He then used this theory to devise a policy for a public, state-supported and -controlled university that would advance both general and scientific knowledge. Through a series of political steps—his service on the board of the Central College and as a member of the commission on the state university—Jefferson secured passage of the legislation that established and funded the new university.

The United States and its educational system has had a number of founding figures, each of whom brought a special and often different meaning to the philosophy of education for the republic. Jefferson, in particular, contributed to its civic education. For him, education was to be general for all people to provide them with the basic skills needed to participate as citizens of a nation with representative institutions. Although it had the egalitarian component of providing popular enlightenment, Jefferson also saw American education exercising a selective role in identifying and educating the intellectually gifted for positions of special responsibility. Early on, he recognized and tried to reconcile the continuing paradox in U.S. education between the apparently opposing demands of equity and excellence.

Above all, Jefferson believed in the freedom of human reason from arbitrary impediments. He especially opposed authoritarian government and state-supported churches that controlled educational institutions as setting up impediments to the liberty of thought and inquiry and to the academic freedom of teaching and learning. He was an early proponent of the principle of separation of church and state, which has come to be a characteristic of U.S. education. Free of arbitrary restraints on reason and thoughtful action, Jefferson believed it possible to create a harmonious political order that maximized human happiness.[57]

As a representative of the Enlightenment in North America, as a founding father of the republic, and as architect of the University of Virginia, Thomas Jefferson is a commanding figure in U.S. political and educational history. A study of his life, career, and activities is particularly illuminating as a historical and biographical exemplar in educational policy, illuminating the relationships between theory and practice.

Questions for Reflection and Dialogue

1. What currents of Enlightenment thinking were especially influential in shaping the ideas of Jefferson and others of the American revolutionary generation?
2. Examine the political and educational ideas of Jefferson as a part of an intellectual transatlantic interaction between Europe and America.
3. How did Jefferson's educational philosophy deal with the issues of equity and excellence? How do these issues still manifest themselves in American education?
4. Examine Jefferson's work in founding the University of Virginia as a modern rather than a classical institution of higher learning.
5. Analyze Jefferson's concept of *civic education* and examine its applicability to the contemporary political socialization of American children and adolescents.

6. Analyze Jefferson's concept of the president as a *mentor of the people* in terms of contemporary styles of leadership in politics and education.
7. How do you think Jefferson would react to current church-state controversies in the United States such as prayer and the posting of the Ten Commandments in public schools?
8. Reflect on Jefferson's view of the role of science in education. How do you think he would react to the controversy over the teaching of creationism versus evolution in the curriculum?

Projects for Deepening Your Understanding

1. Select at least two books used in courses in U.S. history at the secondary level. In a paper, analyze and compare Jefferson's treatment in them.
2. Prepare a paper that analyzes Jefferson's style of leadership and compares it to contemporary leaders in politics and education.
3. Identify Jefferson's major political and educational principles. In a position paper, determine the relevance of these principles for contemporary U.S. society and education.
4. In a paper, examine Jefferson's use of science as an instrument of national policy and consider the relevance of his ideas to the contemporary situation.
5. Organize a panel discussion to examine the following issue: Should student financial aid be determined by academic merit or financial need? After participants have expressed their opinions, consider their views in the light of Jefferson's educational philosophy.

Notes

1. Peter S. Onuf, "The Scholar's Jefferson," *William and Mary Quarterly* 50 (October 1993), 671.
2. Joesph J. Ellis, *American Sphinx: The Character of Thomas Jefferson* (New York: Alfred A. Knopf), x.
3. Gordon C. Lee, ed., *Crusade Against Ignorance: Thomas Jefferson on Education* (New York: Teachers College Press, 1961), 1.
4. Carl L. Becker, *The Heavenly City of the Eighteenth Century Philosophers* (New Haven, CT: Yale University Press, 1932).
5. Douglas L. Wilson, "Thomas Jefferson's Library and the French Connection," *Eighteenth Century Studies* 26 (Summer 1993), 669–85.
6. I. Bernard Cohen, *Science and the Founding Fathers: Science in the Political Thought of Jefferson, Franklin, Adams, and Madison* (New York: W. W. Norton, 1995), 132.

7. Kathleen Tobin-Schlesinger, "Jefferson to Lewis: The Study of Nature in the West," *Journal of the West* 29 (January 1990), 54–61. Also see Inguard H. Eide, *American Odyssey: The Journey of Lewis and Clark* (Chicago: Rand McNally, 1969).
8. R. R. Palmer, *The Improvement of Humanity: Education and the French Revolution* (Princeton, NJ: Princeton University Press, 1985).
9. John Locke, *An Essay Concerning Human Understanding*, ed. Raymond Wilburn (New York: Dutton, 1947).
10. John Dunn, *Locke* (Oxford, UK: Oxford University Press, 1984), 22–59.
11. Garrett W. Sheldon, *The Political Philosophy of Thomas Jefferson* (Baltimore, MD: Johns Hopkins University Press, 1991), 2–3, 45.
12. Alan L. Golden and James L. Golden, "Thomas Jefferson's Perspectives on the Press as an Instrument of Political Communication," *The*

American Behavioral Scientist 37 (November 1993), 194–99.

13. Thomas Paine, *Common Sense on the Origin and Design of Government in General, with Concise Remarks on the English Constitution; Together with the American Crisis, 1776–1783* (New York: G. P. Putnam's Sons, n.d.).

14. Allen O. Hansen, *Liberalism and American Education in the Eighteenth Century* (New York: Macmillan, 1926).

15. Robert D. Heslep, *Thomas Jefferson and Education* (New York: Random House, 1969), 31–32.

16. Noble E. Cunningham, Jr., *In Pursuit of Reason: The Life of Thomas Jefferson* (New York: Ballantine, 1987), 4.

17. Harold Hellenbrand, *The Unfinished Revolution: Education and Politics in the Thought of Thomas Jefferson* (Newark, NJ: University of Delaware Press, 1990), 120.

18. Cunningham, *In Pursuit of Reason*, 4.

19. Ludwell H. Johnson III, "Sharper than a Serpent's Tooth: Thomas Jefferson and His Alma Mater," *Virginia Magazine of History and Biography* 99 (April 1991), 145.

20. Heslep, *Thomas Jefferson and Education*, 34.

21. Ellis, *American Sphinx*, 38–39, 193.

22. Edward Coke, *The Second Part of the Institutes of the Laws of England; Containing the Exposition of Many Ancient and other Statutes* (London: E. & R. Brooke, 1799); Lord Henry Kames, *Historical Law Tracts* (London: n.p., 1758).

23. Ellis, *American Sphinx*, 32.

24. Onuf, "The Scholar's Jefferson," 675.

25. Ellis, *American Sphinx*, 66.

26. Jean Jacques Burlamaqui, *Principes du Droit Naturel* (Yverdon, Switzerland: n.p., 1768); Anthony Ellys, *Tracts on the Liberty, Spiritual and Temporal, of Protestants in England* (London: W. Bowyer, 1765); Adam Ferguson, *An Essay on the History of Civil Society* (London: n.p., 1767).

27. Charles de Secondat Montesquieu, *The Spirit of the Laws*, ed. David Wallace (Berkeley, CA: University of California Press, 1977).

28. Arthur E. Bestor, Jr., David C. Mearns, and Jonathan Daniels, *Three Presidents and Their Books* (Urbana, IL: University of Illinois Press, 1955).

29. Onuf, "The Scholar's Jefferson," 680.

30. Onuf, "The Scholar's Jefferson," 681.

31. "Jefferson's Original Rough Draught of the Declaration of Independence," in *The Papers of Thomas Jefferson*, vol. I, ed. Julian P. Boyd et al. (Princeton, NJ: Princeton University Press, 1950, 545–47), quoted in Lee, *Crusade Against Ignorance*, 46.

32. Lee, *Crusade Against Ignorance*, 10–11.

33. Thomas Jefferson, "A Bill for Establishing Religious Freedom," in *The Papers of Thomas Jefferson*, vol. II, ed. Julian P. Boyd et al. (Princeton, NJ: Princeton University Press, 1950, 545–47), quoted in Lee, *Crusade Against Ignorance*, 66.

34. Jefferson, "A Bill for Establishing Religious Freedom," in Lee, *Crusade Against Ignorance*, 68.

35. Roger P. Magnuson, "Thomas Jefferson and the Separation of Church and State," *Educational Forum* 27 (May 1963), 417–21.

36. For Jefferson's views of the French Revolution, see Conor Cruise O'Brien, *The Long Affair: Thomas Jefferson and the French Revolution, 1785–1800* (Chicago: University of Chicago Press, 1996).

37. Robert W. Tucker and David C. Henrickson, *Empire of Liberty: The Statecraft of Thomas Jefferson* (New York: Oxford University Press, 1990).

38. Onuf, "The Scholar's Jefferson," 681.

39. Cunningham, *In Pursuit of Reason*, 76. Also see Thomas Jefferson, *Notes on the State of Virginia*, ed. William Peden (Chapel Hill, NC: University of North Carolina Press, 1954).

40. John C. Greene, *American Science in the Age of Jefferson* (Ames, IA: Iowa State University Press, 1984), 409.

41. Gisela Tauber, "Notes on the State of Virginia: Thomas Jefferson's Unintentional Self-Portrait," *Eighteenth Century Studies* 26 (Summer 1993), 637.

42. Tauber, "Notes on the State of Virginia," 635.

43. Tauber, "Notes on the State of Virginia," 645.

44. Ellis, *American Sphinx*, 6.

45. For a critique of Jefferson's views on slavery, see Ronald Takaki, *A Different Mirror: A History of Multicultural America* (Boston: Little, Brown, 1993), 68–76.

46. James K. Hosmer, *The History of the Louisiana Purchase* (New York: D. Appleton, 1908); and Lois Houck, *The Boundaries of the Louisiana Purchase* (New York: Arno, 1971). Also see Dan

L. Flores, ed., *Jefferson and the Southwestern Exploration: The Freeman and Custis Accounts of the Red River Expedition of 1806* (Norman, OK: University of Oklahoma Press, 1984).

47. Tobin-Schlesinger, "Jefferson to Lewis." Also see Donald Jackson, ed., *Letters of the Lewis and Clark Expeditions, with Related Documents* (Urbana, IL: University of Illinois Press, 1978).

48. Thomas Jefferson, "A Bill for the More General Diffusion of Knowledge," in *The Papers of Thomas Jefferson*, vol. II, ed. Julian P. Boyd et al. (Princeton, NJ: Princeton University Press, 1950, 526–33), quoted in Gerald L. Gutek, *An Historical Introduction to American Education*, 2d ed. (Prospect Heights, IL: Waveland, 1991), 46–52.

49. Jefferson, in Gutek, *An Historical Introduction to American Education*.

50. Merle Curti, *The Social Ideas of American Educators* (Paterson, NJ: Littlefield, Adams, 1959), 34–49.

51. Cunningham, *In Pursuit of Reason*, 59.

52. Johnson, "Sharper Than a Serpent's Tooth," 145.

53. "Report of the Commissioners Appointed to Fix the Site of the University of Virginia," in Lee, *Crusade Against Ignorance*, 114–33.

54. Cunningham, *In Pursuit of Reason*, 337–45.

55. Ellis, *American Sphinx*, 280–87.

56. Cunningham, *In Pursuit of Reason*, 344.

57. Ellis, *American Sphinx*, 9.

Suggestions for Further Reading

Ambrose, Stephen E. *Meriwether Lewis, Thomas Jefferson, and the Opening of the American West.* New York: Simon & Schuster, 1996.

Banning, Lance. *Jefferson and Madison: Three Conversations from the Founding.* Madison, WI: Madison House, 1995.

Burstein, Meyer L. *Understanding Thomas Jefferson: Studies in Economics, Law and Philosophy.* New York: St. Martin's, 1993.

Cohen, I. Bernard. *Science and the Founding Fathers: Science in the Political Thought of Jefferson, Franklin, Adams, and Madison.* New York: W. W. Norton, 1995.

Cunningham, Noble E., Jr. *In Pursuit of Reason: The Life of Thomas Jefferson.* New York: Ballantine, 1988.

de Mooy, Kees. *The Wisdom of Thomas Jefferson.* New York, London: Citadel, Turnaround, 2003.

Dunn, John. *Locke.* Oxford, UK: Oxford University Press, 1984.

Ellis, Joseph J. *American Sphinx: The Character of Thomas Jefferson.* New York: Alfred A. Knopf, 1998.

Fliegelman, Jay. *Declaring Independence: Jefferson, Natural Language & the Culture of Performance.* Stanford, CA: Stanford University Press, 1993.

Gordon-Reed, Annette. *Thomas Jefferson and Sally Hemings: An American Controversy.* Charlottesville, VA: University Press of Virginia, 1997.

Greene, John C. *American Science in the Age of Jefferson.* Ames, IA: Iowa State University Press, 1984.

Hellenbrand, Harold. *The Unfinished Revolution: Education and Politics in the Thought of Thomas Jefferson.* Newark, NJ: University of Delaware Press, 1990.

Heslep, Robert D. *Thomas Jefferson and Education.* New York: Random House, 1969.

Honeywell, Roy J. *The Educational Work of Thomas Jefferson.* Cambridge, MA: Harvard University Press, 1931.

Jefferson, Thomas. *Autobiography.* Keswick, VA: The Thomas Jefferson Society, 2000.

———. *In His Own Words: Thomas Jefferson on Politics & Principles; With an Introduction by Douglas L. Wilson.* New York: Gilder Lehrman Institute of American History, 1998.

———. *Jefferson Abroad.* New York: Modern Library, 1999.

———. *Patriot from Virginia: the Autobiography of Thomas Jefferson and Selective Works.* Salem, MA: Nova Anglia Company, 1999.

———. *Jefferson Himself: the Personal Narrative of a Many-sided American.* Bernard Mayo, ed. Charlottesville: University Press of Virginia, 1998.

———. *Jefferson on Jefferson.* Paul M. Zall, ed. Lexington: University Press of Kentucky, 2002.

———. *Notes on the State of Virginia: with Related Documents.* David Waldstreicher, ed. Boston: Bedford/St. Martin's, 2002.

———. *Thomas Jefferson: A Chronology of His Thoughts.* Jerry Holmes, ed. Lanham, MD: Oxford: Rowman & Littlefield, 2002.

———. *Thomas Jefferson: An Anthology.* Peter S. Onuf, ed. St. James, NY: Brandywine Press, 1999.

———. *Thomas Jefferson, His Words and Vision.* Nick Beilenson, ed. White Plains, NY: Petter Pauper Press, 1998.

———. *Thomas Jefferson, Political Writings.* Joyce Oldham Appleby and Terence Ball, eds. New York: Cambridge University Press, 1999.

Jefferson-Hemings Scholars Commission. *Jefferson-Hemings Scholars Report on the Jefferson-Hemings Matter, to the Thomas Jefferson Heritage Society, Thomas Jefferson Foundation, and the Monticello Association.* Charlottesville, VA: Thomas Jefferson Heritage Society, 2001.

Lee, Gordon C., ed. *Crusade Against Ignorance: Thomas Jefferson on Education.* New York: Teachers College Press, 1961.

Lehmann, Karl. *Thomas Jefferson: American Humanist.* Charlottesville, VA: University Press of Virginia, 1985.

Lerner, Max. *Thomas Jefferson: America's Philosopher-King.* Robert Schmuhl, ed. New York: Transaction, 1996.

Malone, Dumas. *Jefferson: The Virginian.* Boston: Little, Brown, 1948.

Manent, Pierre. *Tocqueville and the Nature of Democracy.* John Waggoner, trans. Lanham, MD: Rowman & Littlefield, 1996.

Mapp, Alf J., Jr. *Thomas Jefferson: Passionate Pilgrim—the Presidency, the Founding of the University, and the Private Battle.* Lanham, MD: Rowman & Littlefield, 1991.

Mayer, David N. *The Constitutional Thought of Thomas Jefferson.* Charlottesville, VA: University Press of Virginia, 1994.

Meltzer, Milton. *Thomas Jefferson, the Revolutionary Aristocrat.* New York: F. Watts, 1991.

Miller, Charles A. *Jefferson and Nature: An Interpretation.* Baltimore, MD: Johns Hopkins University Press, 1988.

O'Brien, Conor Cruise. *The Long Affair: Thomas Jefferson and the French Revolution, 1785–1800.* Chicago: University of Chicago Press, 1996.

Onuf, Peter S., ed. *Jeffersonian Legacies.* Charlottesville, VA: University Press of Virginia, 1993.

Peterson, Merrill D. *The Jefferson Image in the American Mind.* Charlottesville, VA: Thomas Jefferson Memorial Foundation: University Press of Virginia, 1998.

Randall, William S. *Thomas Jefferson: A Life.* New York: Holt, 1993.

Sheridan, Eugene R. *Jefferson and Religion.* Charlottesville, VA: Thomas Jefferson Memorial Foundation, 1998.

Sheldon, Garrett W. *The Political Philosophy of Thomas Jefferson.* Baltimore, MD: Johns Hopkins University Press, 1991.

Tucker, Robert W. *Empire of Liberty: The Statecraft of Thomas Jefferson.* New York: Oxford University Press, 1990.

CHAPTER 13

Mary Wollstonecraft: Proponent of Women's Rights and Education

This chapter describes the life, writings, and social, political, and educational ideas of Mary Wollstonecraft (1759–1797), a remarkable English woman. Her biography holds a special importance for students of education. She had a rare literary gift and the ability to translate the events of her personal life into a social and educational philosophy that stands as a groundbreaking work in feminist theory. Not content to surrender to the patterns that controlled women's lives in the late eighteenth century, Wollstonecraft struggled for her own freedom as well as for the rights of all women.

To help you organize your thoughts as you read this chapter, focus on the following questions:

1. How did Mary Wollstonecraft react to the major trends of the historical context in which she lived?
2. How did Wollstonecraft's educational biography shape her philosophy of women's education?
3. How did Wollstonecraft's theories about human nature, women, and power shape her educational ideas and practices?
4. What is the enduring significance of Wollstonecraft's contributions to women's education?

The Historical Context of Wollstonecraft's Life

Mary Wollstonecraft lived in the second half of the eighteenth century, a momentous epoch in European and American history. It was a revolutionary era, marked by the American Revolution in 1776 and the French Revolution in 1789.

These initially political revolts against absolutism, aristocracy, and monarchy unleashed significant social and economic movements that sought to construct new societies where people could freely determine their own destinies. Although revolutionary change was eroding the old established order, for people such as Wollstonecraft the forces of change were moving too slowly. Largely untouched were the social and economic traditions, conventions, and laws that still relegated much of humanity to a subordinate position. For example, in England, according to the law of coverture, when a woman married she was no longer a legal person. In a marriage, there was only one legal person, the husband, who controlled the wife and family's income and property. A married woman could not hold title to her previously own property or earnings and could not be a legal guardian for their children.[1] The subordination of women in a male-dominated society was especially onerous to an enlightened woman such as Wollstonecraft.

The late eighteenth and early nineteenth century was a period of conflicting ideologies. Spawned by the revolutions in America and France, contesting ideologists sought to develop the social, political, and economic blueprints for the coming social order. Wollstonecraft was a committed liberal who believed in liberty for all persons, the power of reason, the desirability of change, and the possibilities of progress. Education was, for liberals such as Wollstonecraft, the great instrument for creating a just and equitable society. For her, the promises of liberalism were for all people, women as well as men.[2] Thus the new social order should be one in which inherited aristocratic ranks and privileges that denied human rights and equality were to be struck down. Conservatives such as Edmund Burke presented the counterargument that traditional institutions—monarchy, aristocracy, church, and family—provided the moral foundations that kept a weak human nature in check. These institutions, conservatives asserted, preserved cultural continuity between the generations and protected humankind against the ruthlessness of a rootless mob. Wollstonecraft, challenging Burke, perceived these institutions as oppressive agencies of conformity.

For Wollstonecraft and her associates, the French Revolution marked the beginning of a new epoch in human history. Although she rejected the revolution's excesses, especially the bloody purges of the Reign of Terror, Wollstonecraft believed the revolution would bring about a new and better political and social order.[3]

Enthusiastic that the French Revolution's "Rights of Men" should be in place everywhere, Wollstonecraft and her intellectual circle interpreted the political document as a bold humanizing text. For her, it was imperative that the "rights of man" be generalized into human rights that included women. She battled against the sexist conventions of her day that denied women the right to own property and that gave the firstborn male of each family, through primogeniture, the sole privilege to inherit that property. She also struggled against the pervasive conventions of the day that ascribed women's social role as subordinate in a patriarchal, male-dominated society.

As she worked to extend women's rights in a politically revolutionary era, Wollstonecraft began to understand that important socioeconomic changes were in progress. Her life coincided with the beginning of the Industrial Revolution and the rise of the European bourgeois and English middle classes. While the social and educational roles of the aristocratic and peasant women had long been established, the emerging positions of middle- and working-class women were still being defined. Women's struggle to create their own self-definitions would be long and tortuous. Rousseau, whose ideas Wollstonecraft challenged, had recognized that the bourgeois posed a new and potentially disruptive moral threat. Driven by profit, the restless bourgeois male needed to be tamed, said *Emile's* author, by the love of a woman who created a natural family for him to lean on and support. Unlike Rousseau, Wollstonecraft did not envision the middle-class woman as a taming influence but rather saw her as an intellectual equal to her male counterpart. For her, educated men and women, as educated persons in their own right, would advance the cause of progress. However, middle-class women had to be educated out of their trivial and subordinate positions. While Rousseau and Wollstonecraft both analyzed the social and moral change heralded by the appearance of the middle class, the question of the education and role of middle-class women remained open. Even in the twentieth century, Jane Addams was a restive seeker for a career that would fulfill her aspirations to do something of significance for humanity (see Chapter 19).

Educationally, Mary Wollstonecraft was struggling against the long-entrenched doctrine of educational appropriateness, by which a particular kind of education was designed to prepare a person to discharge one's station in life. In a society of rank and privilege, each rung in society has an education appropriate to it. This meant the prince would receive the education appropriate to one who would be king; the aristocrat would receive the education suited to the ruling class; the laborer that of a producer of goods. For women, the doctrine of educational appropriateness was particularly limiting. Because conventional society held that the vast majority of women were to be wives and mothers, the appropriate education was training to be homemakers and caregivers. Outside of these conventionally ascribed roles, a few women might be governesses or teachers of small children. Higher education and alternative careers were closed to them according to conventional wisdom.

Unwilling to be confined by the conventions that subordinated women in eighteenth-century Europe, Wollstonecraft mounted an attack on gender-based restrictions. She challenged the traditions that conservatives cherished about the sanctity of established customs, traditions, and institutions. She attacked the stereotypic view of women that portrayed them as "pretty, vain, jealous, fickle creatures." She condemned the traditional female education that reinforced women's intellectual trivialization.[4]

Mary Wollstonecraft: Biographical Sketch

Mary Wollstonecraft was born on April 27, 1759, in Spitalfields in London, the second of seven children of Edward and Elizabeth Dickson Wollstonecraft. Her grandfather's financial success as a silk weaver made it possible for his son Edward to acquire land and attempt what proved to be an unsuccessful career as a gentleman farmer. Mary's untalented father was unable to maintain his position in the gentry. As his economic fortunes declined, he and his family moved frequently across England and Wales, searching for unrealized better fortunes. Turning more and more to alcohol, he grew abusive and domineering with his wife and family. Mary, as an adolescent, desperately sought to shield her battered and passive mother from her alcoholic father's abuse, often throwing herself between them to take the blows. She, too, was often a victim of his abuse.[5]

The effects of growing up in a violent, dysfunctional family exercised a powerful influence over her life. Even as a child, however, she resisted rather than yielded to the conditions that made her mother such an abject victim of male dominance and rage.[6] She determined that she would not be a passive victim, nor ever dependent on a man. Her adult writing reflected her unhappy childhood memories. Her portrayals of marriage and family life in her writings would range from idealized situations to those of abject dysfunctionality.[7]

As both child and adult, Mary Wollstonecraft faced the realities of a male-dominated society. According to the doctrine of primogeniture, which was both customary and legal in eighteenth-century England, the firstborn male inherited the family property. The Wollstonecraft family fortunes, albeit limited, were invested in Mary's eldest brother, Edward. In addition, Mary presumed that Edward was her mother's favorite child, a preference she resented. At this point, Mary was rebelling against a family that gave sons preference over daughters and a society that gave men control over women. Mary's early self-identity was shaped by the largely negative influences of opposition to a mean-spirited and abusive father, to a brother who was favored over her, and to a passive mother who accepted being a victim.[8] From these early family influences, she developed a larger sense of alienation against a biased system of gender discrimination.

Although the Wollstonecrafts moved frequently to avoid creditors or to seek their fortune, they did locate for six years in Beverley in Yorkshire. Here, Mary spent her formative years, from age 9 to 15. She attended the local school and made friends with children and young people outside her family. Even with her peers, she was trapped emotionally in the behavior patterns that she had experienced in her family. She tended to feel friendships and other social relationships in terms of domination and submission.[9]

When Mary was 15, the Wollstonecraft family moved again, locating in 1774 at Hoxton, near London. Here, Mary made a close and lasting friendship with Fanny Blood, a young woman two years older than she. Although Fanny's family was impoverished, Mary saw her new friend as possessing a character worthy of great admiration. In Fanny, Mary found an idealized heroine who would inspire her later writing.

Edward Wollstonecraft's financial reverses had an effect on the course of Mary's life. As a daughter of a middle-class family, Mary would have received a dowry to enable her to marry or an allowance to provide for her expenses. However, neither dowry nor allowance came to her and she had to search for employment. For young women of her class, her opportunities were limited to that of being a lady's companion, a primary school teacher, or a governess.[10]

In 1778, at the age of 19, Mary left home to take a position in Bath as a companion to Mrs. William Dawson, a wealthy widow. Never comfortable in situations of subordination, she found her position uncomfortable and anxiety provoking. Mrs. Dawson, who had run through a number of companions, was not an easy employer.[11] Mary experienced intense feelings against being "in service" to another, which meant more domination and control. Further, she disliked the social inferiority her position carried. Her employment, however, broadened her outlook by providing insights from outside her family. From her peripheral social position, she carefully observed the behavior of people of higher social and economic status.

After working as Mrs. Dawson's companion for two years, in 1781 Mary was called back to her family to care for her terminally ill mother, who was suffering from edema. Again, she experienced mixed emotions—the call to duty expected of a daughter but also resentment against the mother whom she felt had neglected her. After her mother's death she left her parents' home. Her father married his housekeeper and returned to Wales.

Mary went to stay with the Blood family in Walham Green after her mother's death, but again a crisis brought her back home. Mary, who resented her elder brother, Edward, took no interest in him or his family. However, she took a protective role towards her younger sisters, Eliza and Everina, and her young brothers, James and Charles. This time, her sister Eliza, who had just borne a child and was suffering severe postpartum depression, had grown to detest her husband, Meredith Bishop. Mary, seemingly prone to impulsivity, which she herself called her "incendiary" behavior, likely a consequence of growing up in an alcoholic household, decided that she and her sister would escape the situation by leaving child, husband, and extended family behind. Sometime in January 1784 they left to go it alone in London, where they lived under assumed names. Eliza's child died several months later. Mary's course of action was rarely taken by women in the late eighteenth century.[12]

Facing the prospect of supporting her sisters and herself, Mary, after considering several possibilities, decided to open a school. In 1784, with her sisters Eliza and Everina and Fanny Blood, she opened a school at Newington Green, just north of London.[13] Although the school had but a brief existence, closing in 1786, Mary's residence at Newington Green marked a clear departure in her intellectual development. She encountered a group of liberal thinkers who dissented from the Church of England and from the traditional institutions and customs of the period. In late eighteenth-century England, dissenters, though Protestant, faced political and educational disabilities. They were denied the vote and could not attend Oxford or Cambridge universities. In response, the dissenters, many of whom were England's leading intellectuals, took a proactive stance, often establishing their own schools and academies.[14] In many respects, the dissenters confronted some of the same restrictions that women suffered. The dissenters were led by Dr. Richard Price, a Presbyterian minister who, inspired by the French Revolution, espoused liberal reformist ideas. Price had an important formative influence on Wollstonecraft's intellectual development. Becoming more assertive intellectually and politically, Wollstonecraft began to develop a perspective that enabled her to relate her personal experiences to a larger worldview. She began to relate her search for self-definition to the larger context of socioeconomic and political change.[15]

On February 24, 1785, Mary's closest friend, Fanny Blood, who was suffering from consumption, married her fiancé, Hugh Skeys, who was residing in Portugal. Fanny went to Lisbon to live with her husband, hoping the milder Portuguese climate would ease her illness. Fanny soon became pregnant and Mary determined to be present as her friend gave birth. Fanny gave birth to a son and died of complications on November 29. Her baby died soon after.[16]

During Mary's six-week stay in Portugal, the school at Newington Green deteriorated and was closed. Left in a desperate financial situation, Wollstonecraft turned to writing to earn money. Her book, *Thoughts on the Education of Daughters*, quickly written in March and April 1786, was published by a leading dissenter, Joseph Johnson, in 1787.[17] Her own unhappy family experiences and a growing resentment against social and legal conventions that relegated women to subservient status shaped her first book. She was beginning to reflect on the struggle women faced to maintain emotional equilibrium in a situation over which they had little or no control. Wollstonecraft, however, at this stage in her intellectual development, though rebelling against the status quo, still accepted the traditional women's roles of wife and mother as essential points of references in her narrative.

To augment her small royalty from *Thoughts on the Education of Daughters*, Wollstonecraft from 1786 to 1787 took a position as governess to the three eldest daughters of Lord and Lady Kingsborough at the family estate near Mitchelstown, County Cork, in Ireland. At that time, the occupation of governess, a live-in tutor for wealthy young women, was one of the few occupations open to unmarried middle-class women. Wollstonecraft disliked being a governess, a position which again placed her in a subordinate position in a wealthy household. However, the salary of 40 pounds would enable her to pay off her debts and accumulate a small savings.[18] She especially resented Lady Kingsborough's idle, aristocratic lifestyle. She believed upper-class women such as Lady Kingsborough led undistinguished and trivial lives devoted to self-amusement. Lady Kingsborough represented, for Wollstonecraft, the thoroughly mis-educated and misdirected woman. She exemplified the "woman of sensibility," the "weak woman of fashion," prized among the English aristocracy, who sought admiration of males but neglected her own intellectual development.[19] As an outlet for her hostility, she turned again to writing, completing her first novel, *Mary, A Fiction*, an idealized autobiographical version of her childhood and youth.[20] By 1787, she and her employers had had enough of each other. She left the Kingsborough household, determined to earn her living as an author.[21]

In August 1787, Wollstonecraft located in London to work as a translator and an assistant editor of a new journal, the *Analytical Review*, published by Joseph Johnson, one of the United Kingdom's leading publishers of political, educational, literary, and children's books. Her work on the *Review*, which provided abstracts and reviews of recently published books, exposed Wollstonecraft to new vistas of knowledge. She became an expert reviewer, keen to provide her readers with clear summaries of books in their contexts.[22] Johnson, who accepted Wollstonecraft's *Mary* for publication, gave literary guidance and steadfast support. He introduced her to London's liberal literary circles, and she became acquainted with Tom Paine, the American revolutionary and author of *Common Sense;* Heinrich Fuseli, the Swiss painter; William Blake, the poet and engraver; Joseph Priestly, the natural scientist; and William Godwin, the influential political and social theorist, whom she would eventually wed.[23]

In 1788, Wollstonecraft's third book appeared, *Original Stories from Real Life, with Conversations, Calculated to Regulate the Affections, and Form the Mind to Truth and Goodness.*[24] In this book, Mary used her life experiences and those gleaned from her career as a governess to examine the relationships between mothers and daughters. Mrs. Mason, cast as the model of virtue, teaches two sisters the values of kindness, benevolence, and patience. The book demonstrated Wollstonecraft's growing interest in education and her recognition of the formative importance of early childhood.

The years 1789 and 1790 found Wollstonecraft actively participating in the ideological debates surrounding the French Revolution that pitted liberals and radicals against conservatives. Wollstonecraft, of course, was squarely committed to the revolution. Her friend Dr. Price in an address acclaimed revolutionary changes in France. Attacking Price, the conservative philosopher Edmund Burke wrote *Reflections on the Revolution in France* (1790), which became the classic statement of conservative ideology.[25] Burke assailed the revolutionaries for destroying the cultural connections that tradition gave to generations past, present, and future. For Burke, traditional institutions safeguarded human freedom against the violence of revolutionary excesses such as those in France. Wollstonecraft was quick to respond to Burke and the conservatives. Her *Vindication of the Rights of Men*, published in 1790, expressed her long-seething attitudes against the power of rank, aristocracy, privilege, and wealth in limiting human freedom.[26] She attacked the customs and laws that subordinated one part of humanity to another.[27]

Wollstonecraft was a recognized writer when her next publication, *A Vindication of the Rights of Woman*, appeared in 1792. In it she argued against Rousseau's portrayal of Sophie in *Emile*, which she considered denigrating to women.[28] Also, the dramatic course of events in revolutionary France motivated her to appeal for women's rights and education. Wollstonecraft dedicated *A Vindication of the Rights of Woman* to Talleyrand, whose plan for a national system of male education for was being debated in the French National Assembly. Objecting to the exclusion of women from Talleyrand's proposal, Wollstonecraft tried to persuade him to include girls in the schools. Arguing that women possessed the same intellectual powers as men, she asserted that they should enjoy the same educational opportunities, enroll in the same programs, and attend the same schools as boys.[29] The exclusion of girls from schools would deny the new French republic the talent of its women in creating a new social and political order.

In December 1792, Wollstonecraft journeyed to France to experience the revolutionary events firsthand. When she arrived in Paris, the more moderate Girondin faction was in control of the National Assembly. The Girondins, seeking to implement Enlightenment concepts into law, had established several committees to draft proposed legislation. Wollstonecraft was delighted with the Legal Committee's proposals to recognize the rights of women and children. She was invited to work on an educational plan for the government's consideration.[30]

By the spring of 1793, the revolution had grown increasingly radical. The moderate Girondins lost power and revolutionary impetus passed to the Paris commune and the Montagnards, or Mountain faction, led by Robespierre, Danton, and Marat. Political prisoners had been massacred, and King Louis XVI had been arrested, tried for treason, and executed on January 21, 1793. Robespierre, heading the Committee of Public Safety, began a dictatorship, designed to purge France of its internal enemies. Wollstonecraft witnessed the rise and subsequent dictatorship of Robespierre and the Reign of Terror. Many of her more moderate French friends, especially the Girondins, were victims of the Terror. Distressed by the revolution's turn to violence and repression, Wollstonecraft wrote a "Letter on the Present Character of the French Nation." She revealed in it her temporarily lost faith in the power of human rationality to shape events. Her doubts were transitory, however. Recovering her belief in humanity's inevitable progress, her *An Historical and Moral View of the Origin and Progress of the French Revolution* (1794) emphasized the need to interpret the momentous revolutionary events objectively.

While in France, Wollstonecraft fell in love and had an affair with Gilbert Imlay, an American financial speculator engaged in the import-export trade. On May 14, 1794, Mary and Imlay's daughter, Fanny Imlay, was born. Although they were not married, Imlay registered Mary as his wife at the American Embassy. In April 1795, she and her daughter returned to England, where the unfaithful Imlay was now residing. Abandoned by Imlay, Wollstonecraft attempted suicide by taking laudanum. Imlay, hoping to divert her, proposed that she travel to Scandinavia, accompanied by the baby and a nursemaid, to act as his business agent in an effort to recover cargo that had been diverted there. Accepting his offer, she left on June 21, 1795, for Sweden, Norway, and Denmark. Following her pattern, she wrote about her experiences in *Letters Written During a Short Residence in Sweden, Norway, and Denmark*, published in 1796.[31] The letters, part travel narrative and part introspection, reveal a lonely and rejected, depressed but romantic wanderer through foreign lands. Returning to England in 1795, she discovered that Imlay had again been unfaithful to her. Again she attempted suicide, by throwing herself in the Thames, but was rescued by boatmen. In the spring of 1797 she abandoned her obsessive love and parted with Imlay and determined to raise her daughter and support herself as an independent woman.[32]

Wollstonecraft resumed her work with the *Analytical Review*. In her association with England's liberal thinkers, she met William Godwin, a noted political theorist. An intellectual leader of Britain's radical reformers and author of *Enquiry Concerning Political Justice* (1793), Godwin stressed the power of human reason to improve society. Godwin and Mary became close friends and then fell in love. He wrote of their relationship, "no two persons ever found in each other's society, a satisfaction more pure and refined."[33] When Mary became pregnant, she and Godwin were privately married.

Wollstonecraft continued to work on her novel, *The Wrongs of Women; or Maria*, which realistically described the degradation of middle- and lower-class women in a male-dominated society. The novel, like most of her writing, was semiautobiographical. Maria's family was a fictional replica of Wollstonecraft's, consisting of a tyrannical father, a submissive mother, and four siblings.[34] Further, the heroine, Maria, like Wollstonecraft, is victimized by an unfaithful lover.

On August 30, 1797, Wollstonecraft gave birth to a daughter, Mary. The delivery had complications, which led to puerperal infection that claimed her life on September 10, 1797.

Godwin edited and published Wollstonecraft's *Posthumous Works* in 1798, and wrote *Memoirs of the Author of A Vindication of the Rights of Woman* (1798), which expressed his affection and esteem of his wife.

Mary Wollstonecraft's literary legacy was carried on by her daughter, Mary Wollstonecraft Shelley, a prolific author in her own right. Like her mother, she wrote about her travels through a Europe recovering from the Napoleonic wars in *A Six Weeks Tour* (1817). Mary Wollstonecraft Shelley's most famous novel is *Frankenstein, or, the Modern Prometheus*, published in 1818. In this work she poses an issue of profound moral import: Will the new age of science and technology improve human character and values? Or are there weaknesses in human nature that will pervert the new science and technology? In the novel, Dr. Frankenstein, a well-educated physician from a respected family, embarks on a quest to conquer humankind's greatest and most feared enemy, death. By using parts of bodies, he hopes to create a new and deathless man, a new creature for a new age. Using medical science and the new technological power of electricity, he creates a new person out of the old. At first the new creature is a child-like giant figure, a noble savage. However, the creature encounters human cruelty, which turns him into a monster. Dr. Frankenstein's quest to have power over human nature leads to his own and his creature's destruction.[35]

Wollstonecraft's Major Social and Educational Themes

Mary Wollstonecraft's essays and novels pursue a persistent theme: How can people, both women and men, create a personal state of being and a society based on love, respect for nature, and education rather than on power, control, and domination? In particular, she was concerned with securing women's rights in a male-dominated society in which fathers, husbands, and elder brothers dominated daughters, wives, and sisters. She extended her intellectual compass to include the broader issues of how to reform society, indeed how to revolutionize it.

Wollstonecraft's *Thoughts on the Education of Daughters* (1787) was one of her early works that dealt with education. Many of its insights, though of a general nature, were remarkable for the period of its publication. Her *Original Stories from Real Life* (1788) presented a series of moral episodes designed to illustrate the proper values for young women. *A Vindication of the Rights of Men* (1790), her rebuttal to Edmund Burke's conservatism, was a strong defense of human rights. *A Vindication of the Rights of Woman* (1792) was her most powerful statement on women's rights. The following sections examine her educational ideas as expressed in these four publications.

Thoughts on the Education of Daughters

Wollstonecraft's *Thoughts on the Education of Daughters* focuses on women's upbringing and education. However, many of her comments are applicable to both sexes. Wollstonecraft begins with marriage and family. Her own family life was made insecure by frequent moves as her alcoholic and domineering father unsuccessfully tried to improve his income. She regarded her mother as passive and unsupportive. Further, her sister Eliza had been pressed into what was an unhappy marriage by her father and eldest brother. Finally, Mary herself had suffered an unhappy love affair with Gilbert Imlay.[36] With this background, she advised her readers that the education of a daughter began with her parents' marriage and family life. Warning about the negative consequences that unhappy marriages have on children's formative development, she cautioned that the most dysfunctional parent had the power to jeopardize the welfare of the entire household and cause lifelong emotional injury to his or her children.

Based on her reminiscences of her own unhappy childhood and feelings of rejection by her mother, Wollstonecraft called attention to the crucial importance of early childhood experiences in forming a daughter's character. She maintained the need for a close, intimate relationship between mother and daughter during infancy. Giving practical advice, she counseled mothers to nurse their infant daughters rather than employing wet nurses.

Turning to a young woman's intellectual and moral development, Wollstonecraft affirmed her belief that human beings are born with an innate sense of truth, the power of rationality. This innate power can be either stimulated and developed or it can be dulled by miseducation. Like Locke and Pestalozzi, she was a proponent of learning through sensory experience in interaction with the environment. Experience of the natural environment can stimulate a love of nature, build the stock of ideas, and exercise critical thinking. Children can be encouraged to observe natural phenomena. In Lockean fashion, Wollstonecraft examined the process by which ideas are acquired and formed. She said it is important that children learn to build compound and complex ideas by comparing and contrasting the creatures and objects that they observe. Recognizing the basic principles of natural education, she advised that "intellectual improvements, like the growth and formation of the body, must be gradual."[37]

Wollstonecraft believed that children were keen observers of their surroundings. In particular, small animals were likely to capture their attention. She recommended that children be told stories about animals, then learn to read little stories about them in which the animals illustrated human virtues and vices.

Disputing the adage that children should be seen but not heard, Wollstonecraft encouraged adults to invite them to enter into conversations and to express their ideas and feelings. It was important for children to develop ease with the art of conversation. When children ask questions, adults should take their queries seriously and answer them reasonably.

Unlike Rousseau, who argued against the premature introduction of books, Wollstonecraft, a prolific author who expressed her ideas and sentiments in writing, emphasized reading. She argued that a "relish for reading, or any of the fine arts, should be cultivated very early in life." Although holding the senses to be the primary source of ideas, she theorized that the individual should not be "entirely dependent on the senses for employment and amusement."[38] Her opinion of the value of reading differed, however, from the conventional schoolroom wisdom of the eighteenth century. For Wollstonecraft, reading's primary purpose was for enlightenment and to cultivate the understanding of life, nature, and society. It was not to require children to memorize passages they did not comprehend, nor was it to provide a stock of quotations from celebrated authors.

Wollstonecraft was concerned that girls and young women not be indoctrinated by the so-called "women's literature" of the period, romances and stories that gave a false but conventional portrayal of love and marriage. Many of the books written for women trivialized women's experience. It was especially important that the young woman's judgment and experience be such that she could establish a true perspective on women and not be deluded by novelists who cast them in roles of superficiality and sentimentality.

Although Wollstonecraft was reared in a household without servants and had been in service herself as a governess, she directed her writing to families of wealth and status. She advised mothers to be closely involved in the upbringing of daughters and not to leave them in the care of servants. If so left, they would be prone to acquiring habits of cunning and deceit, which would distort their innate sense of truth. Wollstonecraft, who believed individuals were born with an innate sense of truth, argued that it was highly important that this sense be developed into the capacity for critical thinking. Despite her later emphasis on human rights, she asserted in her early works on education that daughters should acquire "a proper submission to superiors; and condescension to inferiors."[39]

Wollstonecraft, who had to fight against the imposition of the expectations of others, advocated that young women be educated to be, and to fulfill, themselves rather than conform to what others wanted them to be. In conventional eighteenth-century society, young women were conditioned to be what others—fathers, then husbands—wanted them to be. The "art" of pleasing others often led to artificiality and insincerity in which the young woman hid or masked her true thoughts and emotions. For example, women were judged to be incapable of abstract thought and were therefore thought to be uninterested in intellectual and political issues.

In *Thoughts on the Education of Daughters*, Wollstonecraft was frequently autobiographical, translating her own experiences into admonitions. In her novels, she was likewise autobiographical, using episodes in her own life to develop her characters. She had been a companion to an older wealthy woman and had worked as a governess for the daughters of a titled family. Finding both of these situations unsatisfactory, she strongly reacted against being in a subservient role. In advising on the education of young women, she was most attentive to middle-class women, who while educated lacked financial means and needed employment. In eighteenth-century England, the few occupations open to educated middle-class women were serving as companions, governesses, or teachers. Commenting on being a companion or governess, she wrote of the humiliation of living with and depending on "intolerably tyrannical" strangers who constantly reminded their employees of their "subordinate state."[40]

Although she sought independence from the conventions of her day, Wollstonecraft was involved in several intense and stormy love affairs. She was infatuated with and pursued Fuseli, a Swiss painter who rejected her. She had an obsessive affair with the unfaithful American financier, Imlay. It was William Godwin in whom she found true love and affection. In *Thoughts*, written before these relationships, she counseled on love and marriage, commenting that "people of sense and reflection" are subject to "violent and constant passions."[41] Their strong emotions may cause them to be attracted to a person their reason would reject. Passion without mutual esteem, she warns, will be temporary or will lead to depravity. However, love of a worthy person, rationally considered, was the surest guide to one's own happiness and intellectual and moral improvement.

Cautioning young women against early marriage, Wollstonecraft advised that education, experience, and reflection should be personal guides for deferred but happy marriages. Young women who married before 20 often were wed to men they would reject if they were older and more experienced. Properly educated women, she predicted, were more likely to marry men of principle.

Original Stories

Mary Wollstonecraft's *Original Stories from Real Life, with Conversations, Calculated to Regulate the Affections, and Form the Mind to Truth and Goodness* was first published in 1788 and reissued by Joseph Johnston in 1791. These stories were designed to be morally instructive for young women. Wollstonecraft assumed that all humans possess the God-given power to reason that leads to intelligent behavior. Due to errors in their early education, a young woman may acquire some character defects. The book, of the eighteenth-century educational "rescue" literature genre, is intended to provide guidance in freeing a person from moral weakness. Among its educational principles are (1) the senses need to be exercised and developed, (2) moral virtues can be cultivated in the young by teaching them to care for animals and to provide charity for the dependent poor, and (3) teachers must emphasize the importance of truly constructive activities.

The principal characters are the governess, Mrs. Mason, the narrator, who is a moral exemplar, and two sisters, Mary and Caroline, in her care. Mrs. Mason, a widow, epitomizes kindness, patience, and experience. As an independent woman, Mrs. Mason seeks to instill both a sense of morality as well as critical thinking in the girls. The sisters, having been brought up largely by servants, have acquired some undesirable behaviors. Mary, age 14, has a "turn for ridicule," and Caroline, age 12, is "vain of her person."[42]

A typical moral lesson in *Original Stories* is provided by the story of "Jane Fretful," a selfish and continually angry young woman. As a child, Jane's mother was unwilling to set limits on the little girl's demanding behavior. Trying to calm Jane's temper, she let Jane have her own way and tried to satisfy every childish whim. Although Jane had some "tenderness of heart," this virtue was stunted by her constant appeasement. Jane grew to believe that the "world was made only for her." If her friends had a toy she wanted, she would cry and demand it. Instead of "being a comfort to her tender, though mistaken mother," Jane caused her the anxiety of having to appease an unappeasable child. When she was given a dog that she wanted, Jane in a fit of rage gave it such a severe blow that she killed it. As a young woman, Jane continued to rage, demand, cajole and threaten, driving her mother to an early death. When Jane herself died, "no one shed a tear" and she was "soon forgotten."[43]

A Vindication of the Rights of Men

Wollstonecraft's noted entry into political theory came with her *Vindication of the Rights of Men*, a rebuke to Edmund Burke's *Reflections on the Revolution in France*.[44] Both works are highly significant in that Burke's *Reflections* became the oft-quoted classic statement of conservative ideology and Wollstonecraft's *Vindication*, though written to defend human rights, generally did so from a feminist perspective. Not only were these opposing treatises political statements, they carried important implications for education. Burke saw the ideal polity resting on an ancient foundational chain of traditional institutions—monarchy, church, and family—that, creating historical continuity, contributed to enduring social stability and tranquility. Most unfortunately, Burke argued, the French Revolution, with its violent excesses, destabilizing this ordered continuity, had wrought social chaos. Stressing the traditional family and home, Burke saw women's femininity as a "littleness" and a "weakness" that was a gentle civilizing force.[45] In strong contrast, Wollstonecraft saw the existing order as based on an engrained partiality that subordinated commoner to aristocrat, poor to rich, and women to men. Rather than conserving the exploitative existing social order, Wollstonecraft contended that it needed reforming and improving. Human beings, both women and men, she argued, were not to be prisoners in the Bastille of tradition but were to create a more egalitarian and open society. Educationally, Burke's conservatism saw education as transmitting tradition to reinforce allegiance to existing institutions and values. For Wollstonecraft, education should awaken and sharpen human intelligence so that it became an instrument of society's improvement.

A Vindication of the Rights of Woman

Wollstonecraft's *A Vindication of the Rights of Woman*, her most famous book, is widely recognized as a pioneering work in feminist educational theory. In it she refutes the authors of books on education such as Rousseau, arguing they were written by men who were "more anxious to make" women into "alluring mistresses than affectionate wives and rational mothers."[46] (For Rousseau's educational ideas, see Chapter 10). Though Rousseau was inconsistent in his ideas on women, his portrayal of the education of Sophie, who would be Emile's wife, was to make her attractive and pleasing for her husband. Rousseau contended that men and women should have a different education because they are endowed with complementary but opposing natures. Wollstonecraft, arguing for social and educational equality between the sexes, challenged Rousseau. For her, both women and men share the same rational nature and should, therefore, have the same education. Although men and women differ in physical strength, Wollstonecraft contended that all other distinctions were but social constructions, designed to reinforce male dominion over women.[47] She rejected Rousseau's portrayal of Sophie's education as a miseducative prescription for dependency rather than a genuinely rational education for self-definition and independence.

Convinced that knowledge was power, Wollstonecraft concluded that both parenting and schooling had failed to give women the education that would fully develop their intellectual power. Indeed, conventional women's education had deliberately dulled women's intellectual proclivities, miseducating them. As both women and men possessed the same intellectual powers, she argued that women should not be limited in their educational opportunities. Wollstonecraft argued that a truly liberating education for both women and men would develop the intellect and lead to mental independence rather than subordination.

Wollstonecraft argued that women should reject the stereotypes that reinforced their subordination. Perpetual subordination had made them into childlike creatures who were trained to amuse and please others rather than realize their own potentialities as independent people. A conventional upper- and middle-class young woman's education was often given over to pursuits considered suited for minds that were not to be taxed intellectually. The young women's curriculum of the time consisted of needlework, embroidery, novels, romances, poetry, and music designed to amuse rather than instruct.

Wollstonecraft did not deny that women, if they so chose, were to be wives and mothers. Rather she challenged the notion that they were to have an education so appropriate to these roles that it denied the knowledge that informed and exercised their rationality. In no way did the differences in male and female sexuality have any bearing on their reasoning to the same truths.

Wollstonecraft rejected the customary view that the most socially appropriate roles for women were to be wives and mothers and that the socially approved occupations were to be midwives, teachers of small children, or governesses. She argued that women should pursue the whole of knowledge and a range of occupations and professions. They might study medicine and be physicians as well as nurses. They might study political science and history and the various lines of business and take their full place in society.

For Wollstonecraft, women's education, going far beyond schooling, had serious social, economic, and political ramifications. Women, whether married or single, could escape dependency on men only when they were educated to support themselves economically. Wollstonecraft, who had struggled mightily to support herself, believed that professional careers in law, medicine, and business would be opened to educated women. Economic independence would lead to the right to vote and to actively participate in politics.[48]

Influenced by events in revolutionary France, Wollstonecraft developed a plan for a national system of education modeled on Talleyrand's proposal in the French National Assembly. In her plan, she advocated the establishment of government-sponsored co-educational day schools for the compulsory education of children from 5 to 9 years of age. These schools were to be completely free and open to all children regardless of class. Like Robert Owen (see Chapter 15), she believed that primary schooling, from ages 5 through 9, should foster a sense of equality. Therefore, children were to wear the same type of clothing and receive the same kind of instruction. The school was to be located in a large area of land in which the children could play, exercise, and engage in gymnastics. The curriculum was to include reading, writing, arithmetic, natural science, and some simple experiments in physical science. Elements of religion, history, and politics were to be taught by way of teacher–student conversations.

Although Wollstonecraft leaned toward political and gender egalitarianism, her plan for national education nevertheless retained some socioeconomic class distinctions. At age 9, students, both boys and girls, were streamed into different schools according to their intellectual abilities and anticipated vocations. Children intended for domestic employment or mechanical trades were to receive vocational instruction. Boys and girls were to be taught together in the morning. In the afternoons, girls were to attend a separate school where they learned such traditional gender-specific skills as needlework, sewing, and millinery. Again, it is interesting to note that Wollstonecraft, despite her liberal feminism, continued to apply the traditional gender-specific curriculum to lower–socioeconomic status girls. After completing this instruction both boys and girls would enter the workforce.

While lower-achieving and lower–socioeconomic status children attended vocational schools, those of superior intellect or economic fortune attended an academic school where they studied classical and modern languages, science, history, politics, and literature. Wollstonecraft firmly recommended that their education should be coeducational and that talented young women should have the same opportunities as men. Believing that human progress depended on the education of both men and women, she made a strong case for coeducation based on the Enlightenment premise that human progress depended on knowledge and science.[49]

The Wrongs of Women; or Maria

Wollstonecraft was steadfast and committed to the cause of women's liberation from the conditions that subordinated them in the late eighteenth and nineteenth centuries. At the time of her death, she was working on a novel, *The Wrongs of Women; or Maria*, which was published posthumously. Using the theme of a common sisterhood of all women, she intertwined the life stories of three women from different social classes: one from the impoverished working class, one from the middle class, and one a wealthy aristocrat. However, the oppressive male-dominated society had brought them all to the same destination, an insane asylum. Though not mentally ill, all three were confined because of a social and legal system over which they were powerless. Wollstonecraft had returned to her persistent theme—the need for women to be united in their struggle for empowerment. All three women, though in ways particular to their social class and status, were the hapless victims of a patriarchal society. Maria, the central figure, has been confined by her brutish and domineering husband who has taken her freedom and child from her.[50] The book is intended to emphasize the point that all women, regardless of socioeconomic class, are victims of the same system and need to unite to oppose it.

Conclusion: An Assessment

Mary Wollstonecraft's life was extraordinary for an eighteenth-century woman. She broke the bonds of the limited expectations to which women, especially those of the middle class, were tied. Her own life was a dramatic series of traumas and triumphs.

Wollstonecraft was not afraid to challenge traditional institutions and conventional thinking. She contested the writings of two of the leading theorists of the period, Jean-Jacques Rousseau and Edmund Burke. While Rousseau was a champion of child freedom and political equality, he believed women's education should be designed to make them pleasing and attractive to men. Wollstonecraft challenged Rousseau's view, which she believed contributed to women's unequal education and subordination. She also disputed Burke, the champion of British conservatism. Burke's condemnation of the French Revolution and his arguments for preservation of the class-based status quo were repugnant to her. She believed that women's rights and equality were part of a movement of general revolutionary change that would liberate human beings from the tyranny of the past.

Wollstonecraft must be counted among the early leaders for women's rights and feminine equality. Not exclusively a feminist writer, she also was an educational theorist. Wollstonecraft rebelled against the then-dominant educational theory of an appropriate education for women that defined them as obedient wives, childbearers, and caregivers. She argued resolutely against the idea that social class and gender predetermined a person's life. Rather every person, endowed with the power of reason, had the right to an education that would open rather than close their human possibilities. Although she concentrated on women's education, many of her ideas applied to both genders. Mary Wollstonecraft's works have won a significant place in literature, the history of feminism, and educational thought. Wollstonecraft's work is testimony to what remains an unfinished agenda in women's rights and education.

Questions for Reflection and Dialogue

1. Compare and contrast Rousseau and Wollstonecraft on women's education. Can you identify examples of their positions in contemporary education?
2. Why and how did Wollstonecraft rebel against the social and educational conventions of her times? Can you identify similar reactions regarding the contemporary education of women?

3. Identify and analyze the early childhood experiences that shaped Wollstonecraft's personality and career. What are the effects of dysfunctional families on children that continue into adulthood?
4. Identify and analyze the knowledge and values that Wollstonecraft regarded as most important in a woman's education. Are her views still valid today?
5. How do you think Wollstonecraft would react to the contemporary American family or families?
6. Do you think Wollstonecraft was a pioneering figure in feminism and women's rights? Why or why not?

Projects for Deepening Your Understanding

1. Do some research on the effects of dysfunctional families, especially that of alcoholics, on children. Then relate your findings to the life of Mary Wollstonecraft.
2. Read one of Wollstonecraft's books and write a review that highlights her ideas on education.
3. Read a biography of Wollstonecraft and write a review that highlights the events that shaped her ideas on education.
4. Consider Wollstonecraft's ideas on women's education in relationship to contemporary multicultural education. Are there groups today who suffer the same biases as women did during Wollstonecraft's life?
5. In an essay, compare and contrast Wollstonecraft's ideas with those of contemporary feminist education.
6. Consult the syllabi and suggested readings for courses in women's history at your college or university. Determine if Wollstonecraft is included in these courses, and how she is presented.
7. Interview a professor on women's history at your college and institution regarding her or his interpretation of Wollstonecraft's contributions and significance.

Notes

1. Louise Byer Miller, "Wollstonecraft, Gender Equality, and the Supreme Court," in Maria J. Falco, ed., *Feminist Interpretations of Mary Wollstonecraft* (University Park: PA.: The Pennsylvania State University Press, 1996), 152.
2. Virginia L. Muller, "What Can Liberals Learn from Mary Wollstonecraft?" in Falco, ed., *Feminist Interpretations of Mary Wollstonecraft*, 48.
3. Virginia Sapiro, "Wollstonecraft, Feminism, and Democracy: 'Being Bastilled,'" in Falco, ed., *Feminist Interpretations of Mary Wollstonecraft*, 38.
4. Moira Ferguson, "Introduction," to Mary Wollstonecraft, *The Wrongs of Women; or Maria* (New York: W. W. Norton, 1975), 10.

5. Maria J. Falco, "Introduction: Who Was Mary Wollstonecraft?" in Falco, ed., *Feminist Interpretations of Mary Wollstonecraft*, 2.
6. Carol H. Poston, "Mary Wollstonecraft and 'The Body Politic,'" Maria J. Falco, ed., *Feminist Interpretations of Mary Wollstonecraft*, 88–89.
7. Ferguson, "Introduction," 7.
8. Jennifer Lorch, *Mary Wollstonecraft: The Making of a Radical Feminist* (New York and Oxford: Berg, 1990), 3.
9. Janet M. Todd, ed., *A Wollstonecraft Anthology* (Bloomington, IN: Indiana University Press, 1977), 2.
10. Lorch, *Mary Wollstonecraft*, 8.
11. Lorch, *Mary Wollstonecraft*, 12–13.

12. Lorch, *Mary Wollstonecraft*, 16.

13. Todd, *A Wollstonecraft Anthology*, 3–4.

14. Mary Wollstonecraft, *Original Stories from Real Life, with Conversations, Calculated to Regulate the Affections, and Form the Mind to Truth and Goodness* (Oxford, UK, and New York: Woodstock, 1990), ii.

15. Todd, *A Wollstonecraft Anthology*, 4.

16. Lorch, *Mary Wollstonecraft*, 21.

17. Mary Wollstonecraft, *Thoughts on the Education of Daughters with Reflections on Female Conduct, in the More Important Duties of Life* (London: Joseph Johnson, 1787; reprint, Clifton, NJ: A. M. Kelley, 1972).

18. Lorch, *Mary Wollstonecraft*, 23–25.

19. Miriam Brody, "The Vindication of the Writes of Woman: Mary Wollstonecraft and Enlightenment Rhetoric," in Falco, ed., *Feminist Interpretations of Mary Wollstonecraft*, 115–16.

20. Mary Wollstonecraft, *Mary, A Fiction* (London: Joseph Johnson, 1787; reprint, New York: Garland, 1974).

21. Todd, *A Wollstonecraft Anthology*, 5–6.

22. Lorch, *Mary Wollstonecraft*, 29–31.

23. Todd, *A Wollstonecraft Anthology*, 6–7.

24. Wollstonecraft, *Original Stories*.

25. Edmund Burke, *Reflections on the Revolution in France*, Conor Cruise O'Brien, ed. (Harmondsworth, UK: Penguin, 1986).

26. Mary Wollstonecraft, *A Vindication of the Rights of Men* (London: Joseph Johnson, 1790; Gainesville, FL: Scholars' Facsimiles & Reprints, 1960).

27. Todd, *A Wollstonecraft Anthology*, 8–9.

28. Mary Wollstonecraft, *A Vindication of the Rights of Woman* (London: Joseph Johnson, 1792; New York: W. W. Norton, 1975).

29. Maria J. Falco, "Introduction: Who Was Mary Wollstonecraft?" in Falco, ed., *Feminist Interpretations of Mary Wollstonecraft*, 2–3. Also, see Gerald L. Gutek, *A History of the Western Educational Experience*, 2d ed. (Prospect Heights, IL: Waveland Press, 1995), 184–87.

30. Lorch, *Mary Wollstonecraft*, 39.

31. Mary Wollstonecraft, *Letters Written During a Short Residence in Sweden, Norway, and Denmark* (London: Joseph Johnson, 1796; Lincoln, NE: University of Nebraska Press, 1976).

32. Todd, *A Wollstonecraft Anthology*, 14–15.

33. William Godwin, *Memoirs of the Author of A Vindication of the Rights of Woman* (London: Joseph Johnson, 1798, 165), cited in Todd, *A Wollstonecraft Anthology*, 15.

34. Ferguson, "Introduction," 13.

35. Betty T. Bennett and Charles E. Robinson, eds., *The Mary Shelley Reader* (New York and Oxford: Oxford University Press), 3.

36. Ferguson, "Introduction," 13.

37. Wollstonecraft, *Thoughts on the Education of Daughters*, 17.

38. Wollstonecraft, *Thoughts on the Education of Daughters*, 48.

39. Mary Wollstonecraft, "Thoughts on the Education of Daughters," in Todd, *A Wollstonecraft Anthology*, 29.

40. Wollstonecraft, "Thoughts on the Education of Daughters," in Todd, *A Wollstonecraft Anthology*, 33.

41. Wollstonecraft, "Thoughts on the Education of Daughters," in Todd, *A Wollstonecraft Anthology*, 29.

42. Wollstonecraft, *Original Stories*, iii.

43. Wollstonecraft, *Original Stories*, 31–36.

44. For Burke's position, see Edmund Burke, *A Philosophical Enquiry into the Origin of Our Ideas of the Sublime and the Beautiful* (1757), ed. James T. Boulton (London: Routledge & Kegan Paul, 1958); and his *Reflections on the Revolution in France*. For Wollstonecraft's rebuttal, see her *Vindication of the Rights of Men*.

45. Lorch, *Mary Wollstonecraft*, 78.

46. Mary Wollstonecraft, "A Vindication of the Rights of Woman," in Todd, *A Wollstonecraft Anthology*, 85.

47. Wendy Gunther-Canada, "Mary Wollstonecraft's 'Wild Wish': Confounding Sex in the Discourse on Political Right," in Falco, ed., *Feminist Interpretations of Mary Wollstonecraft*, 72–73.

48. Maria J. Falco, "Introduction: Who Was Mary Wollstonecraft?" in Falco, ed., *Feminist Interpretations of Mary Wollstonecraft*, 3.

49. Wollstonecraft, "A Vindication of the Rights of Woman," in Todd, *A Wollstonecraft Anthology*, 106–11.

50. Virginia Sapiro, "Wollstonecraft, Feminism, and Democracy: 'Being Bastilled,'" in Falco, ed., *Feminist Interpretations of Mary Wollstonecraft*, 40.

Suggestions for Further Reading

Alexander, Meena. *Women in Romanticism: Mary Wollstonecraft, Dorothy Wordsworth, and Mary Shelley.* Savage, MD: Barnes & Noble, 1989.

Detre, Jean. *A Most Extraordinary Pair: Mary Wollstonecraft and William Godwin.* New York: Doubleday, 1975.

Falco, Maria J., ed. *Feminist Interpretations of Mary Wollstonecraft.* University Park, PA: The Pennsylvania State University Press, 1996.

Ferguson, Moira. *Mary Wollstonecraft.* Boston: Twayne, 1984.

Flexner, Eleanor. *Mary Wollstonecraft: A Biography.* New York: Coward, McCann & Geoghegan, 1972.

George, Margaret. *One Woman's "Situation": A Study of Mary Wollstonecraft.* Urbana, IL: University of Illinois Press, 1970.

Jump, Harriet D. *Mary Wollstonecraft: Writer.* Hertfordshire, UK: Harvester/Wheatsheaf, 1994.

Kelly, Gary. *Revolutionary Feminism: The Mind and Career of Mary Wollstonecraft.* New York: St. Martin's, 1992.

Lorch, Jennifer. *Mary Wollstonecraft: The Making of a Radical Feminist.* New York: Berg, 1990.

Martin, Jane Roland. *Reclaiming a Conversation: The Ideal of the Educated Woman.* New Haven: Yale University Press, 1985.

Mazel, Ella. *Ahead of Her Time: A Sampler of the Life and Thought of Mary Wollstonecraft.* Larchmont, NY; New York: Bernel Books, 1995.

Nixon, Edna. *Mary Wollstonecraft: Her Life and Times.* London: J. M. Dent & Sons, 1971.

Poovey, Mary. *The Proper Lady and the Woman Writer: Ideology as Style in the Works of Mary Wollstonecraft, Mary Shelley, and Jane Austen.* Chicago: University of Chicago Press, 1984.

Sapiro, Virginia. *A Vindication of Political Virtue: The Political Theory of Mary Wollstonecraft.* Chicago: University of Chicago Press, 1992.

Sunstein, Emily W. *A Different Face: The Life of Mary Wollstonecraft.* Boston: Little, Brown, 1975.

Todd, Janet M., ed. *A Wollstonecraft Anthology.* Bloomington, IN: Indiana University Press, 1977.

Todd, Janet. *Mary Wollstonecraft: A Revolutionary Life.* New York: Columbia University Press, 2000.

Tomalin, Claire. *The Life and Death of Mary Wollstonecraft.* Harmondsworth, UK: Penguin, 1974.

Wardle, Ralph M., ed. *Godwin and Mary: Letters.* Lawrence, KS: University of Kansas Press, 1967.

Wardle, Ralph M. *Mary Wollstonecraft: A Critical Biography.* Lincoln, NE: University of Nebraska Press, 1967.

Wollstonecraft, Mary. *Collected Letters of Mary Wollstonecraft.* Ralph M. Wardle, ed. Ithaca, NY: Cornell University Press, 1979.

———. *The Collected Letters of Mary Wollstonecraft.* Janet Todd, ed. New York: Columbia University Press, 2003.

———. *An Historical and Moral Overview of the Origin and Progress of the French Revolution and the Effect It Has Produced in Europe.* In *The Works of Mary Wollstonecraft.* Janet Todd and Marilyn Butler, eds. Vol. 6. New York: New York University Press, 1989.

———. *Of the Importance of Religious Opinions.* Janet M. Todd and Marilyn Butler, eds. New York: New York University Press, 1989.

———. *Mary, A Fiction.* In *The Works of Mary Wollstonecraft.* Janet Todd and Marilyn Butler, eds. Vol. 1. New York: New York University Press, 1989.

———. *Mary Wollstonecraft: Political Writings.* Janet M. Todd, ed. London: W. Pickering, 1993.

———. *Thoughts on the Education of Daughters.* In *The Works of Mary Wollstonecraft.* Janet Todd and Marilyn Butler, eds. Vol. 1. New York: New York University Press, 1989.

———. *A Vindication of the Rights of Men.* In *The Works of Mary Wollstonecraft.* Janet Todd and Marilyn Butler, eds. Vol. 1. New York: New York University Press, 1989.

———. *A Vindication of the Rights of Woman.* Carol H. Poston, ed. New York: Norton, 1988.

———. *The Wrongs of Women; or Maria.* ed. Mary Ferguson. New York: Norton, 1975.

———. *Original Stories from Real Life, with Conversations, Calculated to Regulate the Affections, and Form the Mind to Truth and Goodness.* Oxford, UK, and New York: Woodstock, 1990.

———. *Political Writings.* London: W. Pickering, 1993.

CHAPTER 14

Horace Mann: Leader of the Common School Movement

This chapter examines the life, educational philosophy, and contributions of Horace Mann (1796–1859), a leader in the United States's common school movement, which was the forerunner of today's public school system. Mann's policies as secretary of the Board of Education in Massachusetts in the first half of the nineteenth century have significantly shaped U.S. education.

We discuss Mann's influence on U.S. education in its historical context and in terms of its enduring effect on educational philosophy and policy. First, we describe the social, political, and economic context in which Mann lived and worked. Second, we analyze Mann's biography, his education and career, to determine the evolution of his ideas. Third, we examine the continuing effect of Mann's contributions on U.S. education. By this analysis, we shall see the interrelated dynamics of educational history and philosophy. Mann's educational philosophy emerged as he confronted the issues facing the United States in the early nineteenth century. Although originating in that historical context, his concepts of the nature of common schooling and of the relationship of public education to U.S. society have endured as sustaining elements of the "public school philosophy."

To organize your thoughts as you read this chapter, focus on the following questions:

1. What were the major trends in the historical context in which Mann lived?
2. How did Mann's educational biography shape his philosophy of education?

3. How did Mann's educational philosophy determine his educational policies and practices?
4. What is the enduring impact of Mann's contributions to U.S. education?

The Historical Context of Mann's Life

The first half of the nineteenth century was a time in which the United States, still a young and developing country, was seeking to establish its identity among the nations of the earth. The representative political institutions of life in the United States were still in their early stages of development. The U.S. Constitution had been in effect only eight years in 1796, the year of Mann's birth. As the nineteenth century began, the proper kind of education for a republic such as the United States was still being debated. For such a new nation, it was important that education contribute to a sense of national identity. This feeling of group identity or social consensus is also referred to as an *ideology*. Underlying school systems and their curricula is a sense of agreement on what knowledge is most worthwhile and what values are most important. As yet the cultural sense of U.S. identity was still underdeveloped. The context into which Mann was born and grew to adulthood coincided with the United States's beginnings as a young and aspiring nation.

The historical context of Mann's life included the ideas of the revolutionary generation who, with the Declaration of Independence in 1776, proclaimed the 13 colonies' determination to be a free and independent nation and who, with the adoption of the Constitution in 1788, created the institutions to govern the new republic. In 1796 John Adams succeeded George Washington as the second president. Four years later, Thomas Jefferson became president. During Mann's childhood, the republic's founders were not remote historic figures but were still at the helm of the ship of state. Although the revolutionary generation gained political independence for the colonies, many of America's educational ideas and institutions were remnants of the era before independence. Educational institutions had to be created that would fulfill the new nation's political, social, and economic needs. The role education would play in shaping the new U.S. consciousness was yet to be determined.

The ideas of the republic's founding statesmen, especially those of Benjamin Franklin and Thomas Jefferson, were part of the optimistic philosophical outlook of the eighteenth century's Age of Reason. Reflecting the milieu of political and scientific enlightenment present at the republic's birth, a new kind of education was needed to create American cultural identity and to apply scientific knowledge to develop the continent's vast natural resources. Benjamin Franklin, proponent of practicality and invention; Thomas Jefferson, proponent of an enlightened and scientific citizenship; and Noah Webster, proponent of American language and cultural identity, each contributed ideas to Horace Mann's philosophy of education.

The revolutionary impulse, a strong ideological factor in the new republic, posed issues that Mann and those to follow him would face as leaders of public education. What kind of schooling would prepare responsible citizens to participate in elections, serve on juries, and contribute to an enlightened public opinion? What kind of education would cultivate a common cultural identity, a sense of belonging to a people who shared a common language, goals, institutions, and procedures? What kind of education would develop the wilderness beyond the frontier?

Along with the Enlightenment's revolutionary impulses, still another key element in the historical context of Mann's life was the revival of Evangelical Protestantism. This religious movement shaped the moral milieu of the common schools founded from 1830 to 1860. Many clergy who led the Evangelical Protestant revival also supported *common*, or public, schools. They were active in the common school movement as authors of textbooks, founders of teacher education institutes, and as school administrators.[1] Their essential rationale was that U.S. institutions, including schools, should reflect the beliefs and values of the dominant Protestant culture. Schools in particular should stress the literacy needed for Bible reading, and the school milieu should reflect Protestant values. Industriousness, frugality, and punctuality, central values in the Protestant ethic, were regarded as virtues that promoted economic success as well as social and political order. Together with the Evangelical Protestant moral code, some Americans, fearful of cultural change, developed a nativism that stereotyped non-Protestants, especially Roman Catholics and Jews, as people to be absorbed into a general Protestant culture.[2]

The desire to model U.S. institutions, especially schools, on the design of Evangelical Protestantism revealed a long-standing tension in American life. Although the Enlightenment influence on the U.S. tradition, especially on Jeffersonianism, emphasized separation of church and state and corresponding separation of public schools and denominational religion, Evangelical Protestantism identified U.S. institutions with a generalized Protestant cultural ethos. Just as religious issues were a part of Mann's historical context, they raise serious questions in contemporary American society, politics, and education. The religious issues that Mann faced can be found in today's controversies over prayer and the posting of the Ten Commandments in public schools and controversies over the teaching of creationism and evolution in the curriculum.

The religious context in which Mann lived was growing more complex as immigration accelerated the growth of non-Protestant sectors of the U.S. population, especially the Roman Catholic and Jewish. Seeds of cultural and religious pluralism had been planted and were germinating in the soil. Just as the strategy for absorbing new immigrants into American society was debated in Mann's day, it continues to be an issue for contemporary society. Today's new immigrants tend to be from Asia, Africa, Mexico, and South America. The debates over the strategy for bringing the new immigrants into American culture today are waged by proponents of assimilation and those who favor multicultural and bilingual and bicultural education.

During Horace Mann's career, he and other common school leaders faced the issue of religion in the schools. Should schools be separated completely from sectarian religion, as Jefferson had prescribed? Or might the emerging common schools reflect an interdenominational Protestant ethos? Should the state support denominational schools?

Although political ideology and religious revival were important forces in the context of the common school movement, other social and economic realities also influenced the development of education. From the older New England states of Connecticut, New Hampshire, Vermont, and Massachusetts—Mann's home state—to the newer states of Ohio, Indiana, and Illinois, which had been part of the Northwest Territory, Americans were pushing the frontier westward. By 1850, the United States had been settled up to the Mississippi River.

The majority of Americans lived in rural areas, on farms and in small towns. Indeed, until 1860, 80 percent of the population of the United States lived in rural areas. This rural and small-town population needed basic education for literacy—reading, writing, and simple arithmetic. Although there was general agreement on the need for basic literacy and numeracy, schooling beyond these educational essentials was debated. Common school leaders such as Mann developed the curriculum by adding subjects they believed would meet civic needs.

Horace Mann witnessed the beginning stages of the industrialization that would transform the United States from an agrarian and rural society into an urban, industrial, and modern nation. For example, his hometown of Franklin, Massachusetts, which had been primarily agricultural when Mann was born in 1796, had by the 1820s become a center for textile manufacturing.[3] Throughout the country, cities and factories were growing and creating urban areas. New York City, Philadelphia, and Mann's own Boston, with their large populations, had educational needs and expectations that differed from those of rural areas.

Together with industrialization and urbanization, different ethnic and language patterns were beginning to change U.S. society from a predominantly English culture to an ethnically, linguistically, and culturally pluralistic one. At the beginning of the nineteenth century, most immigrants were northern Europeans, from Great Britain and the Scandinavian countries. During the 1830s and 1840s, immigration patterns changed as large numbers of immigrants came from Ireland and Germany. In the last two decades of the nineteenth century, another shift would occur as immigrants came from southern and eastern Europe. Of importance was the fact that the United States was becoming culturally pluralistic rather than a nation dominated by English-speaking Protestants. Because many immigrants were Roman Catholics, religious tensions were felt in the schools.

Social and economic changes that began in 1800 and continued throughout the nineteenth century raised a number of questions for Mann and other common school leaders. Among them were

1. What kinds of schools and curricula should be designed for the children of the growing urban population?
2. What kind of education was needed to prepare workers and managers for the factories, mills, and business enterprises of an industrializing society?
3. How could schools create a civic consensus for a society that was becoming ethnically, linguistically, and culturally diverse?
4. What moral and ethical values should be emphasized as tensions mounted between the Protestant majority and the Roman Catholic minority?

To a degree, all education reflects its political context. The effort to create common schools was part of the political life of the United States. Horace Mann's life, beginning with the last year of George Washington's presidency, spanned the administrations of 12 other U.S. presidents. This half-century, characterized as the Age of Jackson, was an era of national expansion and growing sectional controversy between North and South over the slavery issue. This period also saw the United States as a combatant in two wars, that of 1812 against Great Britain and the Mexican War of 1846–1848.

The Age of Jackson, dominated by Andrew Jackson, president from 1829 to 1837, had a pronounced impact on American politics. Jackson, a Democrat from Tennessee and a hero of the War of 1812, represented the growing power of the recently admitted frontier states. Historians see the Jacksonian era as the period when the common man began to play a larger political role through the doctrine of popular sovereignty, which asserted that one man equals one vote. Jackson's political appointees were drawn from his political supporters rather than from high-social status groups. Leadership was no longer limited to a financial oligarchy as envisioned by the Federalist Alexander Hamilton. Nor were the republic's leaders to be drawn from Jefferson's proposed "aristocracy of intellect." Rather, national as well as state and local offices would go to the victors of the election process. The common man's political ascendancy occurred as many states, especially those on the frontier, reduced or eliminated property requirements for voting. Only 365,000 people had voted in 1824 when John Quincy Adams was elected president. Four years later, the number of voters swelled to 1,155,340, and had elected Jackson to the presidency.[4]

Fearful of social disorder and mob rule, Horace Mann feared Jackson's rise to political power. He had supported John Quincy Adams in 1824 and by 1830 was drawn to the newly formed Whig party, an often-fragile coalition of Jackson opponents. Just as the opponents to George III in England were called Whigs, Jackson's opposition, who derisively dubbed him "King Andrew," took that name. The leading Whig spokesmen were senators Henry Clay of Kentucky and Daniel Webster of Massachusetts.

In terms of educational attitudes, Jacksonian democracy implied a broader conception of education in which the common man would be prepared not only to vote in elections but to seek public office as well. Challenging the notion that educational opportunity should be limited to the well-educated upper classes, Jacksonian democracy went hand in hand with universal education. Despite their egalitarian preferences, Jacksonian Democrats generally saw schooling in limited and local terms rather than as a national priority.

The development of statewide educational policy was more of Whig concern. For the Whigs, the development of common schools as an internal improvement would aid economic development, and as a means of social control would check social disorder. Public education, though a more general internal improvement, was similar to state-subsidized canals and roads, which contributed to a national transportation system that carried agricultural products and raw materials from the western frontier states and territories to the eastern states for manufacturing or export to European markets. As an internal improvement, investments in public schooling would pay the social dividends of preparing an educated leadership group and the trained workforce needed for national economic development.

Whig politicians, such as Mann, supported common schools because they believed that representative political institutions required literate and educated citizens. Beyond this commitment to general literacy, however, Whigs feared that Jacksonian democracy could easily degenerate into "mobocracy," or rule by uneducated, unlettered, ignorant frontiersmen and immigrants. Whigs feared that the growing number of immigrants from Ireland and Germany would become pawns of political bosses or "papist" priests. Common schools, reasoned the Whigs, could instill the "right attitudes and values" into the young and make them orderly, civil, and industrious citizens in a nation modeled on the mores of upper middle-class, English-speaking Protestants. According to this strategy, the dominant socioeconomic classes would use public schooling to mold the outlook and values of the lower classes and control the nation socially.

Still another important impulse running through U.S. thought, especially in New England, was humanitarian reformism. Concurrent with the general reform influence, the movement for common schooling originated in the New England states of Massachusetts, Connecticut, New Hampshire, and Vermont, where Puritanism's gloomy moral prescriptions were being reshaped, especially among intellectuals, into humanistic sentiments seeking to uplift individuals by educating them. Stimulated by Ralph Waldo Emerson's liberal philosophical transcendentalism, ideas for reform found their way into town meetings and state legislative chambers. Like-minded reformers argued for a range of humanitarian improvements including the abolition of slavery, recognition of women's rights, public schooling, and prohibition of alcoholic drink. Common school advocates saw public education as an agency for personal and societal moral regeneration.

Mann's life was a drama portrayed against the backdrop of a nation seeking to define its national character. The forces that moved across this backdrop represented the ideology of republican American exceptionalism, the rising tide of frontier democracy, new waves of immigration, and an emerging industrial economy. In the next section, we turn to Mann's life and career to see how one of the nation's leading educators helped to shape the national character through common schools.

Horace Mann: Leader of the Common School Movement

Although many people supported public education, Mann is generally acclaimed as the common school movement's foremost statesman. This lawyer, politician, and educator popularized and established the philosophical and organizational foundations of public schooling through his position as secretary of the Massachusetts Board of Education.[5]

Horace Mann, descended from old Massachusetts stock, was born on May 4, 1796, at Franklin, one of five children of Thomas and Rebecca Stanley Mann. The Manns were a farming family and the children at an early age were expected to perform chores.

The town of Franklin was named for Benjamin Franklin, the self-made inventor and statesman of the revolutionary generation, whose practicality appealed to the frugality and industriousness of the New England temperament. Responding to the honor of having the town named for him, Franklin donated a collection of books to the community library. These books would be read by the earnestly studious young Horace Mann.[6]

Franklin during Mann's childhood was a tightly knit community characterized by a deep consensus about politics and religion that bordered on conformity. Later in his life, Mann recalled a childhood dominated by hard work and regular church attendance. At the end of the eighteenth century, society and morality in rural Massachusetts were heavily influenced by the religious creed of orthodox Calvinism, which in Franklin was preached by the imposing and severe "fire and brimstone" clergyman, Reverend Nathanael Emmons (1773–1827). Mann remembered Emmons as

> a man of pure intellect, whose logic was never softened in its severity by the infu-
> sion of any kindliness of sentiment. He expounded all the doctrines of total de-
> pravity, election, and reprobation and not only the eternity but the extremity of hell

torments, unflinchingly and in their most terrible significance, while he rarely if ever descanted upon the joys of heaven, and never, to my recollection, upon the essential and necessary happiness of virtuous life.[7]

Mann, like other children in early nineteenth-century New England, was expected to attend church services regularly, where sermons emphasizing punishment and guilt were part of growing up.[8] Emmons preached that children, like a fallen humanity, were innately depraved. Their own escape from the fires of hell, the preacher warned, would be repentance of sin and submission to God's laws.[9] Mann's schooling, too, especially the required books the *New England Primer* and the *Westminster Assembly Shorter Catechism*, reinforced the culture of Calvinism. As an educator, Mann, rebelling against the emphasis on human depravity, developed his own, more sympathetic version of child development. However, the impressions of childhood remain, as Freud later noted, to shape a person's psychological outlook.

Emmons, determined to supervise the life of the residents of Franklin, held strictly to Calvinist values, especially the sanctity of the religious observance of the Sabbath.[10]. After Mann's brother, Stephen, had drowned while swimming on Sunday, Emmons preached about the damnation of those who died unconverted, strongly suggesting that Stephen was among the damned. This event had a lasting effect on the 14-year-old Horace. As he grew to adulthood, orthodox Calvinism's austere proscriptions lessened their grip on Mann, who eventually became a convert to the more liberal Unitarianism. However, the religious perceptions of his childhood remained rooted in him throughout his life.[11] He continued to believe that a good life must be purposeful and conform to the divine plan. Further, a good life must be strenuously devoted to humanitarian reforms that would elevate humanity. These values, which guided Mann as a common school leader, entered into the moral code of the common school philosophy.

Growing up in rural Massachusetts also had a formative effect on Mann. Convinced of the values of hard work, diligence, and seriousness, he exemplified the Protestant work ethic, which saw industriousness and productivity as positive moral values. His educational philosophy would emphasize that children should be educated to respect ethical values and that schools had a duty to "train up" hardworking men and women. The common school philosophy that Mann did so much to form was exemplified in the McGuffey *Readers'* portrayal of good little boys and girls who were always truthful, diligent, and obedient. The McGuffey syndrome would be revitalized later in the nineteenth century in Horatio Alger's many novels, which told of how industrious youths triumphed over adversity.

Along with the Protestant ethic, Mann's formative years took place in a time of intense patriotism. Mann learned to read by studying the grammar of Noah Webster, an exponent of American cultural nationalism.[12] Like most of his peers, he believed that the United States was a divinely favored nation with a special manifest destiny. This sense of an American destiny would lead to the American exceptionalism that entered his political and educational philosophy. According to American exceptionalism, Americans, different from the inhabitants of other countries, were a chosen people who dwelt in an exceptional and providentially blessed nation.

If there is a strong force that shapes a person's educational attitudes, it is one's school experiences. Memories of good teachers and bad ones, no matter how unsophisticated and childlike, always return to the mind to influence a person's educational opinions.

Mann was no exception to this tendency. Those school days that he fondly recalled and those that still provoked anxiety affected his educational philosophy.

Mann attended Franklin's local school, a remnant of the old district schools inherited from colonial days. The town paid less than $100 annually for the teacher's salary and for heating and maintaining the one-room schoolhouse. Mann remembered a drafty building, a leaking roof, and uncomfortable benches. The school year was brief, limited to about 10 weeks. The widely used *New England Primer* was employed to teach the alphabet, reading, and moral instruction. In addition to the *Primer*, students memorized the *Westminster Assembly Shorter Catechism*.

Mann's education at the Franklin town school was typical for the period. Poorly prepared teachers, often young men who were temporarily working at school keeping on their way to more prestigious careers in law or religion, taught classes. They used corporal punishment to keep their classes in order and heard memorized recitations.

Recalling his school days in Franklin, Mann assessed the quality of the instruction that he had received. Evaluating teachers was something he would often do in his later career. His teachers, he wrote, were "very good people" but poor instructors. Neglecting children's interests and their sensory experience, his teachers did nothing to develop aesthetic sensitivity through art and music. He recalled that "the memory for words was the only" faculty the teachers sought to develop in their students. Ignoring the realities of their environment, Mann's teachers emphasized only the information that came from books.[13]

As a common school leader, Mann persistently advocated a broadened curriculum that went beyond the basics of reading, writing, arithmetic, and the catechism. He urged curricular enrichment that included history, geography, health, and music. He also recognized that the school's physical plant was important. He would argue for increased taxation to provide sturdier, more comfortable schools than the one he had attended in Franklin.

In addition to the basic skills learned at the town school, Horace Mann's early education was shaped by two powerful informal educational forces: his family and the town library. Formal schooling is only one part of a person's total education. Informal agencies also are important in that they either supplement and reinforce or they negate what goes on at school.

Mann's parents created a home environment that stimulated his interest in learning and motivated his thirst for knowledge. Respecting learning, his parents encouraged him to read the books that belonged to the family. Emulating Ben Franklin, Mann frequented the library that Franklin had given to the community and eagerly read works on history and biography.[14]

After his father's death in 1809, it seemed likely that Mann because of a reduced family income would have to limit his education to primary schooling. However, his desire for further education remained unabated and, supported by his mother, he sought admission to Brown University in Providence, Rhode Island. Brown attracted students such as Mann because of its more open Baptist theology and modest tuition fees.[15] He prepared for the entrance examinations by studying the Latin and Greek classics and mathematics with private tutors. Passing examinations in these subjects, he was admitted as a student to Brown in 1816.

Mann's classmates at Brown were primarily from the middle and lower middle socioeconomic classes. Their choice of Brown was often economically motivated as tuition, room, and board came to the modest amount of $100 per year. The students lived plainly and generally devoted themselves to their academic programs. Brown at that time lacked the prestige of Harvard and Yale.

Mann's academic program at Brown was typical for students of that era. He studied the classical Latin and Greek languages and literatures, geometry, geography, English, logic, and public speaking. Like others of his generation, he especially valued Euclid's geometry, believing it would sharpen his powers of logic. He attended lectures in the required moral philosophy, delivered by Brown's president, Asa Messer. He especially benefited from his study of English, which gave him a literary style that he used to embellish his essays and speeches. His interest in public speaking led him to join the university's literary and debating society, the United Brothers. Frequently appearing on its programs, his favorite topics, anticipating those he would continue to address after college graduation, were politics, philosophy, science, and ethics. Of these, he most enjoyed addressing political issues, in which he stressed responsible republicanism, humanitarianism, and social reform.

Mann's undergraduate speeches and essays embodied a firmly held American exceptionalism that he would reiterate in his later arguments for common schools. He regarded the old European political order to be in decline. The United States, an exceptional nation, free of aristocratic decadence, was destined to be the world's republican beacon.[16]

Mann developed into a master of the spoken and written word, which he used for exhortation, inspiration, and persuasion. His speeches and compositions showed him to be an advocate of gradual reform within the system rather than a proponent of radical change. His annual reports, written when he was secretary of the Massachusetts Board of Education, were cogently and effectively written and remain impressive statements of the public school philosophy. His oratorical abilities made him a popular speaker on public platforms, using his eloquence to further the arguments for publicly supported schooling.

Mann, an ambitious student driven by the need to excel, graduated first in his class from Brown University in 1819. As class valedictorian, he was selected to give the commencement address. His speech, "The Gradual Advancement of the Human Species in Dignity and Happiness," affirmed his steadfast belief in human progress and in the role of science and education in creating a better future.[17] Mann's valedictory revealed what would be a persistent theme in the public school philosophy he later developed. Harkening back to the Enlightenment belief in progress, Mann looked optimistically forward to a better society. Never utopian, however, this promise of a better life would be redeemed by applying intelligence diligently. Unlike revolution, education would gradually and nonviolently improve the human condition.

After graduating from Brown, Mann read law in the office of Josiah J. Fiske, an attorney in Wrentham, Massachusetts. Like other ambitious young men, he saw the legal profession as a means of entering political and public life. He interrupted his legal study to accept a teaching position at his alma mater in 1820. For a salary of $375 per year, he was a Latin and Greek tutor and a librarian. Two years later, in 1819, he returned to legal studies, this time at Litchfield, Connecticut, with Judge James Gould, a noted attorney. Completing his legal studies, Mann moved to Dedham, Massachusetts, where he was admitted to the bar in 1823.

From 1823 to 1837, Mann successfully practiced law, earned a reputation as an outstanding orator and lawyer, made many prominent friends, and prepared for a political career. He married Charlotte Messer on September 30, 1830. He was devoted to his wife, who was in ill health, suffering from consumption during much of their brief marriage. Charlotte died on August 1, 1832.[18] For years after Charlotte's death, Mann suffered from severe depression, grieving for his deceased young wife. In 1843, he married Mary Peabody who, actively interested in social and educational reform, encouraged her husband's work. From a distinguished New England family, Mary was a sister of Elizabeth Peabody, a pioneer of the kindergarten, and Sophia, the wife of author Nathaniel Hawthorne. Horace and Mary Mann had three sons, Horace, Jr., George Combe, and Benjamin Pickman.

Mann was elected as a Whig to the Massachusetts General Court, the state's house of representatives, in 1827, serving until 1833, when he was elected to the state Senate for a four-year term. From 1836 to 1837, he served as the Senate's president.[19] With other Whigs, Mann supported internal improvements such as state support for railroad, road, and canal construction. Using an ideology of positive republicanism, he argued that the people would benefit from using tax revenues for internal improvements. All members of society, he reasoned, would benefit from improved transportation and communication.[20] Similar reasoning would lead him to support public education as a kind of social internal improvement.

While in the state legislature, Mann devoted himself to reform causes. In the early nineteenth century, reforms such as temperance, penal reform, women's rights, abolition of slavery, care for the mentally ill, and support of common schools were part of the general cultural climate. Early in his career Mann supported temperance, the restriction of the sale of alcoholic drinks, as a way to reduce pauperism and crime. He favored both formation of voluntary societies that would work for reform and for legislative action to eradicate the conditions that led to what he regarded as a social evil.[21]

As a legislator, Mann developed a concept of public service that was also to provide the ideological orientation for his civic education. Citizens, like those whom they elected as representatives, should be "principled men who would rise above sectarian and political biases" to determine their political destiny in an enlightened and disinterested fashion.[22] Using this model, Mann acquired a record as an effective advocate of social improvement. His reform proposals were carefully researched and supported by statistics. His humanitarian efforts led to an investigation by the legislature of conditions in prisons and in asylums for the mentally ill. Mann sponsored legislation to improve the care of the mentally ill and his efforts contributed to the establishment in 1833 of the Worcester Asylum, a model institution.

In the late 1830s, the Massachusetts legislature addressed several important educational issues. In 1834, Massachusetts received federal funds to compensate the state for the services of its militia in the War of 1812. Part of the funds were deposited in an interest-earning common school fund. To share in the funds, each town in Massachusetts had to levy taxes to be used for education. This legislation used a matching formula in which both the state and the local town would contribute to education.[23] Mann strenuously supported "An Act Relating to Common Schools," introduced by James G. Carter, which passed in 1837. The Act established a State Board of Education to collect and disseminate information about schools and to make recommendations for their improvement. Horace Mann, named as the board's first secretary, left the state senate to take up his educational responsibilities.[24]

With his appointment, Mann, always the diligent public servant, prepared for his new position by poring over educational literature, such as Victor Cousin's report on Prussian schools. He traveled throughout the state, giving speeches and meeting with people, to build an informal infrastructure of voluntary supporters for common schools. He showed himself to be a consensus builder intent on motivating people of diverse backgrounds and interests to enlist in a common cause. Further, he pressed the cause of public education by journalism, establishing and editing the *Common School Journal*.

As secretary of the Board of Education, his duties included compiling educational statistics and dispensing educational information. The secretary was also to prepare printed abstracts based on the data collected, to guide the state legislature in drafting school laws. These abstracts formed the basis of Mann's celebrated annual reports to the board. The collection and publication of information, however, also carried with it the possibility of influencing educational legislation. For example, Mann was to survey the condition of schools throughout the state in order to recommend policies for improving them and the instruction that their teachers provided.[25]

To gather information firsthand, Mann visited schools throughout Massachusetts. His findings, documented in his first annual report of 1838, revealed that many of the shoddily constructed school buildings were in a dilapidated condition and that the district school committees, which were responsible for education in their localities, exercising little supervision, did little to improve instruction.[26] Further, Mann found that employment of inadequately prepared teachers had lowered the quality of instruction. Commenting on the low economic and social status of teachers in the district schools, he found their salaries hovering at 5 to 8 dollars per month for women and 10 to 16 dollars for men.[27] Finding much to be done to improve education, Mann affirmed his conviction that the state should take greater responsibility in educating its children:

> The theory of our laws and institutions undoubtedly is, first, that in every district of every town of the Commonwealth, there should be a free district school, sufficiently safe, and sufficiently good, for all the children within its territory, where they may be well instructed in the rudiments of knowledge, formed to the propriety of demeanor, and imbued with the principles of duty.[28]

Like Jefferson before him, Mann insisted that the state had primary responsibility for supporting and governing public education. He consistently argued that state-supported schools should be available to all children and that their quality should exceed that of private schools. A skilled lawyer and eloquent orator, Mann devised what amounted to a legal brief for common schools, which he argued would (1) educate for responsible citizenship in a republic, (2) provide the knowledge needed for national economic development and prosperity, (3) serve as the great economic equalizer that would reduce class conflicts, and (4) instill moral and ethical values in the young.[29]

Mann's first annual report was followed by 11 more reports that addressed education in Massachusetts. His comments in these reports were applicable to schools throughout the United States. Among Mann's frequent themes were the policies needed to improve common schools, and the schools' role in preparing a trained and literate workforce and in educating a responsible citizenry. Additionally, Mann addressed the more specific need to improve school buildings, curriculum, reading, penmanship, and other more immediate problems. To improve the physical plant of schools, he argued for improved ventilation, lighting, and heating. He recommended more windows, ceiling vents, the installation of desks with back supports to replace the crude backless benches currently used, and the need for playgrounds. To improve the teaching of reading, he urged teachers to abandon the conventional "a-b-c" method in favor of learning whole words, and then sounding them out phonetically. He wrote in his second annual report:

> Perhaps the best way of inspiring a young child with a desire of learning to read is, to read to him, with proper intervals, some interesting story, perfectly intelligible, yet as full of suggestion as of communication; for the pleasure of discovering is always greater than that of perceiving.[30]

Mann's annual reports revealed a philosophy of education concerned both with general national purposes and with specific curricular objectives directly related to schooling. In terms of its social significance, Mann wrote, "Education, then, beyond all other devices of human origin, is the great equalizer of the conditions of men—the balance-wheel of the social machinery."[31] While setting general goals, Mann ensured that specific curricular and instructional objectives were consistent with his overall philosophy.

To improve schools in Massachusetts, Mann carefully developed a strategy to revitalize the deteriorating district schools into an effective system of publicly supported and controlled schools. Strategically, he defined the nature, purpose, and function of common schools. He skillfully created a coalition of diverse groups that supported tax-supported schools. Pragmatically, as a former legislator, he effectively worked with many of his colleagues in the state legislature, winning their support for increased taxation and the creation of normal schools.

While identified in history as the "father of America's public education," Mann also made contributions to national politics and higher education. As abolitionism grew in Massachusetts and other Northern states, Mann, a consistent reformer, began to focus more attention on slavery. From the 1830s until the Civil War's beginning in 1861, the enslavement of Africans became an increasingly divisive sectional issue, pitting the Southern slave states against the Northern free states. At first, Mann supported the American Colonization Society's program to gradually emancipate and resettle former slaves in Africa.[32] After the Mexican War, he grew increasingly antislavery, opposing slavery's extension into the western territories. In his own personal actions, he worked to have African Americans admitted to both common and normal schools. When an African American student, Chloe Lee, could not find lodging to attend normal school at West Newton, Mann made room for her in his own house.[33] He also represented several individuals accused of aiding the escape of fugitive slaves.

In 1848, Mann was elected to the U.S. House of Representatives as a Whig, to complete the remainder of the term of the deceased distinguished former president John Quincy Adams; he then, backed by both the Whigs and the new Free Soil Party, won a full term in the general elections of that year. In Congress, opposing the Compromise of 1850, he argued against the extension of slavery to the western territories that were annexed to the United States and voted against the Fugitive Slave Law, which allowed federal marshals to recapture and return escaped slaves to their masters. When the Whig Party refused to renominate him because of his opposition to the Compromise of 1850, Mann nevertheless won reelection that year as a Free Soil candidate.

In 1852, Mann, leaving politics, accepted the presidency of Antioch College, a new institution in Yellow Springs, Ohio, being established by the Christian Connexion. As the college's first president, Mann had to supervise its buildings' construction and create its curriculum. Mann's principles of higher education, consistent with his general educational philosophy, emphasized (1) personal morality and a commitment to social uplift and reform but not indoctrination in any specific religious dogma, (2) intrinsic individual achievement rather than competition, and (3) coeducation, to further gender equality. The curriculum Mann devised consisted of Latin, Greek, mathematics, English, history, philosophy, and natural science as required subjects. It reflected his own favorite subjects that he used so well: composition and public speaking. An innovation was electives, which students could choose in modern languages, art, and the methods of teaching.[34] Mann's tenure as a college president was extremely difficult and challenging. Not only did he have to build, staff, and attract students to the new institution, he had to raise the funds to keep it operating. Mann made frequent desperate fundraising trips to keep the nearly bankrupt institution afloat. Worn out by a life given to reform, Horace Mann died on August 2, 1859.

Mann's Concept of the Common School

Mann's career as a lawyer and politician shaped his belief that the common school was directly related to civic competency and to public service. He subscribed to the Whig ideology that public education, like other internal improvements, could be an agency for national economic development and civic order. His ideology, however, did not seek to merely preserve the socioeconomic status quo but saw education as a means of effecting the gradual, nonrevolutionary, transformative improvement of society. He believed that a representative republican government, through state-supported education, could increase social intelligence in the general population and bring about needed social reform.[35] As indicated earlier, Mann's ideal of the good society was not an open-ended experimental one but was shaped by definite views of what made individuals good persons and citizens.

Mann's concept of the common school rested on the republican ideal that the best society was one in which people governed themselves through elected officials and representative institutions. The well-being of society depended, he believed, on literate, diligent, productive, and responsible citizens.[36] Inextricably related to the political order, common schools were to educate responsible leaders and citizens who would not be beguiled by demagogues or join irresponsible mobs. A proper civic education, Mann argued, should teach basic principles of government, provide insights into representative institutions, and generally form good citizens. The common school would be a cultural agency that transmitted the U.S. cultural heritage to young people through literature and history.

Mann believed the common school could perform its civic, political, and cultural roles in a nonpartisan way. The public school, although performing a political role, should not be tied to any political party. Mann wanted the common schools to do a delicate political balancing act. He wanted them to cultivate a general political consciousness but not indoctrinate students in a partisan political ideology. What Mann saw as the desirable civic role of public schools in the nineteenth century still challenges public schools today.

Mann's concept of the common school differed from that of the two-track system of schools in Europe, especially in England and France. European primary schools educated lower-socioeconomic status children in reading, writing, and religion, but upper-class males attended preparatory schools that readied them to enter selective secondary schools and colleges. In 1843, on a trip to Europe, Mann visited educational institutions in the United Kingdom, France, and the German states and kingdoms. He was especially interested the schools of Prussia, the largest German kingdom. Many educators, including Victor Cousin, had lauded the efficiency and systematization of the Prussian schools as agencies other countries might well emulate. What Mann saw on his visit were national schools that, while orderly and efficient, reinforced Prussian absolutism and militarism. Mann concluded that America's schools, too, could be orderly and efficient, working not for absolutism but rather for republicanism.[37]

Instead of segregating students according to socioeconomic class as in Europe, Mann saw the U.S. common school as an integrative social agency for bringing children of different social and economic classes and religions together in one institution. Mann's emphasis on the integrative role of common schools stemmed from his fear that the divisiveness of partisan politics, ethnic differences, and religious sectarianism would impair the nation's domestic tranquility and weaken the impulse for social reform.[38] Mann's common school was also a completely public institution, supported by public taxation, governed by publicly elected officials, and responsible to the community that it served. Mann's concept of the common school embraced two principles enshrined in the public school philosophy: common schools should be socially integrative and should be publicly controlled, supported, and governed.

Public schools today are seen as agencies that should include rather than exclude different groups of people. Although Mann was primarily concerned about segregation on the basis of socioeconomic class, contemporary policies have made schools inclusive in many other areas. For example, the U.S. Supreme Court in *Brown v. Board of Education* in 1954 struck down laws that justified and supported racially segregated schools. By ending racial segregation, public schools became instruments to help create a racially integrated society. In similar fashion, legislation pertaining to the education of handicapped persons created the movement for mainstreaming handicapped children in regular classrooms whenever possible. These recent trends reflect the integrationist theme in Mann's common school philosophy.

Mann's philosophical consistency was evident in how he based the common school curriculum on broad social and political goals. To create a common civic community that included diverse social, economic, ethnic, and religious groups, Mann believed the common school curriculum should provide the same basic knowledge and skills equally to all its students. It should provide the elementary subjects and skills that prepared persons to function successfully as responsible citizens of the community, as economically productive managers and workers, and as ethical persons who shared common values.[39] The common school curriculum, designed to prepare people for everyday life, included reading, writing, spelling, arithmetic, history, geography, health, music, and art—the skills and subjects needed by practical businessmen, skilled workers, and competent citizens alike.

In the first half of the nineteenth century the United States, in its early stages of industrial transformation, was a developing country. Although incomplete by today's standards, the common school curriculum was the forerunner of the contemporary elementary school program. The common school curriculum stressed reading, writing, spelling, and speaking, which today are included in the language arts. Similar to the contemporary curriculum, the nineteenth-century common school stressed mathematics. History and geography, which were introduced into the common school curriculum, remain key elements in the contemporary social studies program. Mann's emphasis on health, music, and art remains with us today. Although much has changed in the history of elementary schooling, particularly in the areas of teaching methods, textbooks, and materials, the line of curriculum development can be traced to the skills and subjects that formed a common school education.

The values Mann wanted common schools to implant in the young originated in his own moral upbringing in rural Massachusetts, from his exposure to Emerson's transcendentalism, and from his persistent commitment to republican government. Essentially, he believed common schools should prepare individuals who would and could earn a living, pay taxes, and support their families and their communities. Mann's paramount moral values were those of hard work, effort, honesty, diligence, thrift, literacy, respect for property, and respect for reason. His economic ideas, valuing private property and encouraging individual initiative, were those of an emerging free-enterprise capitalism. Reflecting the Calvinism of his youth, Mann believed that men of property and position had a special responsibility to be the stewards of society. They were to support schools, improve living and working conditions, and be agents of moral regeneration.

Mann's own values reflected residues of the Calvinism of his childhood and the more liberal impulses of Unitarianism and transcendentalism. As secretary of the Board of Education, his actions were governed by the Massachusetts School Law of 1827, which required that teachers should impress on children "the principles of piety, justice and sacred regard for truth" but not use any book that favored "any religious sect."[40] Mann found himself walking a delicate tightrope on the issue of values in the school. He firmly believed that the schools should instill a basic morality, but equally opposed the entry of religious sectarianism into the public schools. Using the same style of consensus building that had served him in the past, Mann sought to allay the attacks of orthodox Congregationalists by contending that the common schools could cultivate the values common to Christians. His religious compromise on the ethical principles of a common Christianity satisfied many, but not all, of the Protestant clergy. However, Roman Catholics, especially the Irish, who were immigrating in large numbers to Massachusetts, found that Mann's common Christianity turned out to be a common Protestantism. Of his various consensus-building compromises that of a common Christianity was the most fragile. To avoid the "Protestant orientation" of the common schools, Roman Catholics created their own separate parochial school systems independent of public schools. Others who believed that common schooling should be religiously neutral later achieved a secular public school system separate from religious denominationalism.

Mann's concept of the common school with its strong emphasis on the cultivation of values was still another element that would shape the institution's development. Mann's emphasis on the moral mission of public education was also influenced by his association with George Combe, a proponent of phrenology, a psychological theory that held that the mind was composed of faculties such as "combativeness," "benevolence," and "self-esteem." Mann accepted Combe's arguments that human character could be improved by exercising the positive faculties and allowing the negative ones to atrophy.[41] Americans expect public schools to shape and encourage certain values and behavior. Value formation remains today an important charge of public schooling along with its more academic function.

Although even in Horace Mann's day the question of what values should be cultivated was intensely debated, the value orientation of today's public schools is even more controversial. The religious value issues that provoked controversy in the nineteenth century still remain. For example, religious differences are part of the context of the debate over the teaching of creationism and evolution in schools. The schools are now involved in many areas of life that used to be dealt with by the church and the family. Questions of the proper kind of sex education, for example, provoke value conflicts in schools.

Although many issues related to common schooling generated controversy, Mann was a skilled educational leader who was generally able to develop a climate of opinion supportive of public education. For Mann, educational administration was a form of political leadership. It was necessary for him to do the following:

1. Define and explain the purposes of common schooling in terms that appealed to diverse groups.
2. Persuade conflicting groups that it was in their interest to support common schools.
3. Mobilize these groups to campaign actively for and support legislation and taxation for public schools.

Among the key groups whose support he needed were the clergy of the major Protestant churches, the businessmen who controlled the economic sector, and the farmers and tradesmen who constituted the majority of the population.

The Protestant clergy were often leaders who could shape public opinion in their communities. Initially, some clergy favored schools that were church affiliated. Mann argued that common schools could cultivate values derived from a generalized interdenominational Protestantism. The Protestant clergy were generally receptive to Mann's compromise of a common Christianity and provided much-needed support for public schools.[42]

Mann also needed the support of the business community—the owners of industrial and commercial enterprises. Using the full extent of his persuasive powers, he convinced them that it served their best interests to have their property taxed to support common schools to educate children other than their own. Using the Calvinist argument of stewardship, he referred to Them as responsible agents, or stewards, of the nation's economy. It was their responsibility to invest a part of their profits in society's proper education. In turn, education, in the form of common schooling, would pay the dividend of providing a supply of competent managers, skilled workers, and citizens who respected private property. These trained, orderly, and industrious workers would further increase profits that could then stimulate an ever-expanding economy.

Mann realized that the majority of people were neither religious nor business leaders. They were the common people of the day, the farmers and tradespeople of modest incomes. With this group, he used an argument still used to win support for increased taxation for public schools. Public schools, he told this group, was their best means for social and economic mobility. Public schools would make it possible for their sons and daughters to gain better jobs and improve their socioeconomic status. Mann claimed that the common schools would be the "great leveler," the social agency that would provide an equal opportunity. With an equal educational start, those who succeeded socially, economically, and politically would do so not because they were born into socially prominent families but because of their own merit and achievement.

Mann developed and perfected a consensus style of leadership. Groups that had different interests could unite in a common cause. Although their motives for entering into this common coalition were different, the result was the same—a climate of public opinion that supported the common schools.

Mann's strategy for creating a system of public education in Massachusetts required that public opinion be favorably inclined and that the necessary legislation be passed. He realized, however, that the success of the common schools needed more than public and legislative approval. It needed well-prepared teachers who implemented the common school philosophy in their classroom practices. To implement his philosophy of education in public school policy, curriculum, and instruction, Mann sought to professionalize teachers by improving their qualifications. In this way, Mann became a significant leader in American teacher education.

Teachers, Mann believed, should have expert knowledge of the skills and subjects they teach, be competent in methods of instruction, be skilled classroom managers, and be role models, exemplars of moral, civic, and ethical behavior for their students.[43] Mann's ideal of the well-prepared teacher differed significantly from the earlier model of the teacher. In the colonial period, elementary school teachers were primarily school keepers. Often, they were young men who, preparing for the law or ministry, used teaching as a temporary occupation until they could enter higher status and salaried careers. In contrast, Mann believed that those who became teachers should make it their primary career. As a major career commitment, the prospective teacher was to be prepared as a professional educator. To bring about the professionalization of teachers, Mann advocated more humane and efficient methods of instruction and the creation of normal schools to improve teacher education.

Mann in his speeches and writing, especially in his seventh annual report, urged teachers to be more humane and efficient in their methods of instruction and classroom management. Believing that children's interest was a better motivator than fear, Mann wanted to eliminate psychological fear and corporal punishment from the classroom. In 1844, a group of 31 Boston schoolmasters publicly challenged Mann, contending that the abolition of corporal punishment would lead to anarchy in schools. The debate between the masters and the secretary continued for several months in the press and at the podium, with Mann the apparent but not uncontested victor.

Mann's major effort in professionalizing teacher preparation rested on the concept of the *normal school*, which came originally from France, where it was used to prepare primary school teachers. The "*école normale*" or model school provided preparation for teaching, which included practice teaching in a demonstration school. Mann, James Carter, and other common school leaders believed normal schools could prepare the teachers needed for the public school system. In the United States, the normal school was a two-year institution, specifically designed to prepare prospective teachers.

Convinced by Mann's persuasive arguments for improving teacher qualifications, the Massachusetts legislature authorized the Board of Education to establish normal schools at Lexington, Barre, and Bridgewater. To be admitted to a normal school, applicants had to be 16 years old, have completed a common school education, be in good health, and sign a declaration of intention to teach. The normal school curriculum omitted the Latin and Greek classics that had dominated secondary and higher education since the colonial period. Normal school students instead studied English composition and grammar, spelling, geography, arithmetic, health, and history, the essential subjects taught in common schools. The normal school curriculum also emphasized the history and philosophy of education, the principles and methods of teaching, and clinical experience, which involved teaching in a model or demonstration school. The early normal schools, like the common schools, also emphasized the ethics and values of a common Christianity. Daily Bible reading was also required.

The common school and the normal school were related institutions in that the latter prepared the teachers for the former. An important trend was set in motion in these institutions in that elementary school teaching became an occupation that shifted from male to female dominance; the majority of the students who attended the normal schools and went on to become common school teachers were young women. Although they were underpaid and subjected to many restrictions on their personal freedom, the entry of women into teaching was a first stage in their movement into other occupations and professions.

The normal schools were also the initial institutional development in the professionalization of teacher education. They were institutions in which educational ideas were developed and innovative methods such as those devised by Johann Heinrich Pestalozzi, Friedrich Froebel, and Johann Herbart were introduced to the United States from Europe. Eventually, many normal schools became four-year, degree-granting teachers' colleges. In the mid-twentieth century, many of these teachers' colleges became all-purpose colleges and universities that continued to have as part of their mission preparing teachers.

The normal school program was the forerunner of contemporary teacher education programs. The preparation of prospective teachers in the skills and subjects they were to teach in the common schools resembles the preparation of contemporary teachers in the methods and materials related to language arts, social studies, sciences, and mathematics. The contemporary cultural foundations of education—history of education, philosophy of education, comparative education, and sociology of education—originated in the normal schools. The very important area of clinical experience and practice teaching also originated in the nineteenth-century normal schools.

Conclusion: An Assessment

In conclusion, we assess Horace Mann's influence on U.S. education in four key areas:

1. His role in articulating and explaining the relationship of public education to the U.S. political and socioeconomic order.
2. His effort in defining the concept of the common school and developing the procedures by which it would be governed, supported, and controlled.

3. His effort to emphasize a particular set of values that common schools were to cultivate.
4. His work in designing a strategy to improve the preparation and status of teachers.

Mann's conception of the public school's relationship to the U.S. political and socioeconomic social order was based on an ideology that combined the diverse but related strands of American exceptionalism, development theory, and social reform. Because of his pioneering work for common schools, public education in the United States came to reflect these strands. Inspired by revolutionary republican ideology, Mann believed that the United States as a nation above all others had a moral mission to play in the world. Historically, the public schools were to prepare patriotic citizens who held their country and schools in the highest regard. This exceptionalist impulse was more than a mere celebration of the nation; it was a dedication to patriotism as a commanding value. As a Whig politician, Mann endorsed fully his party's commitment to economic development through government-sponsored internal improvements. Thus, public schooling was tied to the country's industrial and technological development, often referred to as the diffusion of science among the general population. Mann, who lived in an era of reform, was a social reformer. Public schooling was seen as an essential reform that was foundational to all other reforms in that it would create an enlightened citizenry who altruistically would overcome special interests to work for the good of the commonwealth.

Mann developed a concept of civic education in which individuals put aside their special interests and unite for the common good. Indeed, the term *common school* implied that, by generating a shared community of mutual interest, people of diverse backgrounds could live peacefully and productivity in common society.

Some contemporary critics of Mann's concept of civic education see him not as the disinterested and objective legislator and educator that he appeared to be. These critics contend that Mann was really advocating imposition of a political and social order based on the Whig ideology of civic order and neo-Evangelical Protestant preconceptions of the nature of a good society. For those who did not share these this Whiggish and Evangelical orientation, the common school ideology really was a form of social imposition and control.

Even if one accepts Mann's concept of disinterested civic education as arising from political objectivity, questions can be asked about its adequacy for our times. Modern U.S. society is characterized by competing special interest lobbies that pursue their own agendas rather than the common good. Is it possible to recreate a sense of commonality and mutuality?

Mann enlisted support for public education by building a large constituency for it. He did this by building a consensus that brought different groups to enlist in a common cause. His style was to maximize areas of agreement and minimize differences. The concept of consensus based on the "great middle" of the population marked the origins of what would become the public school lobby in the United States, a coalition of parents, teachers, school administrators, and board members.

In informing the public about the role and meaning of education, Mann moved thinking about education into the channels of formal instruction. Creating a concept of education that took place primarily in schools, the role of formal institutions was exalted over informal means of education such as the home, neighborhood, and church. He introduced the concept of the "residual function" of the school, namely that functions once performed informally by other institutions were now the province of the school.

In the public schools' institutionalization and governance, Mann took a middle ground between local control and a larger state role. While seeking to revitalize the New England tradition of local support of schools, he also wanted the state to exercise a larger encouraging, supervising, and supporting role. What he effectively did was to create a state system of schools that was more than a collection of semiautonomous little school districts. Anticipating the twentieth century's consolidation movement, he urged the state to consolidate the many small districts into larger ones. Important for the course of public education was Mann's belief that common schools should be governed and supported by a state and local partnership. This policy remains a prominent feature of contemporary public education.

The pattern of public education in the United States that developed from the common school movement combines local and state control and support. This pattern, which reflects the political ideology of Mann and others, governs U.S. public education today. It should be pointed out that, during Mann's career, it was only one of many alternatives that might have been used. Other possibilities for the development of education in the United States include the following:

1. Schools could have followed a pattern of denominational religious control as they did in other Western countries.
2. Schools could have been organized on the Lancastrian monitorial model in which private philanthropists funded mass educational endeavors.
3. Schools might have been linked to definite communitarian efforts designed to transform society radically, as attempted by Robert Owen at New Harmony, Indiana (see Chapter 15).

Instead of these alternatives, the public schools became agencies transmitting a view of society and politics that was stable and orderly rather than socially or culturally reconstructive. Further, public education as state and local functions corresponded to other dominant trends in the United States, such as westward settlement and capitalism.

In terms of their value orientation, Mann's common schools reflected the dominant Protestant ethos of the time. Public schools were not exclusively academic but were also expected to develop the morals and ethics of the young. The ethical system that Mann embraced merged the values of the Protestant ethic with those of an emergent capitalism. Diligence, hard work, industriousness, punctuality, respect for private property, and an almost habitual tendency to orderly procedures became the creed of public schooling at the time of its origin, and continue to dominate it today. Although successful in imposing this generalized value orientation on the public schools, Mann was less successful with his compromise that common schools could cultivate a common Christianity. The increasingly pluralistic religious climate in the United States during the mid- and late nineteenth century eroded that fragile compromise.

Although Mann was astute in recognizing the common schools' power as an agency of ethical and moral values, the value creed and cultural ethos that he stressed reflected the dominant social, political, and economic group in American society. In his desire to create a consensus climate for the common schools, he also helped to create a view of public education that was culturally monolithic. The school's values reflected a white,

English-speaking, Protestant, upper middle-class orientation. With the value presuppositions that Mann helped to create at work throughout the rest of the nineteenth and the early twentieth century, the public schools did not reflect the United States's growing ethnic, linguistic, and cultural diversity. Only in the mid- and late twentieth century was the public school philosophy sufficiently enlarged to reflect the diversity of a culturally pluralistic society.

Finally, Horace Mann contributed the notion that teaching needs professionalization. The professional preparation Mann inaugurated with the normal schools was a significant point of departure for today's teacher education programs. Because of his efforts, teaching became more than a temporary occupation that a person did on the way to something better. Teaching became a career that required commitment and preparation.

Questions for Reflection and Dialogue

1. Analyze Horace Mann's conception of *civic education* and indicate whether it encouraged social continuity or change.
2. Identify the values that Mann believed should be cultivated in the common schools. Are these values similar to or different from those emphasized in public education today?
3. Analyze the consensus style of leadership developed by Mann. Is this style of leadership adequate for today's educational leaders and administrators?
4. Analyze the common Christianity compromise developed by Mann. What, if any, possibilities exist for a common ethical creed in today's schools?
5. Consider the contemporary movement toward educational standards and their verification by standardized testing. Do you think Mann would support or oppose the standards movements?
6. Reflect on the purposes and strategies of multicultural education. Do you think Mann would support or oppose multicultural education?
7. Reflect on the disparities between the varying resources of school districts. How do you think Mann would react to these disparities?
8. Consider the teacher preparation program at your college or university. How do you think Mann would evaluate this program?

Projects for Deepening Your Understanding

1. Review the goals of the Education Act of 2002, No Child Left Behind. Then suppose that you are Horace Mann and write a report on the act from his point of view.
2. Identify some of the religious controversies that relate to public schools. Then suppose that you are Horace Mann and write a reaction from his point of view.
3. Review the current status of public school funding in your state. Then suppose that you are Horace Mann and write a report on the adequacy of your state's funding from his point of view.
4. Using Mann's annual reports as a source, prepare a paper that describes his idea of the elementary school curriculum.

5. Using the McGuffey *Reader* or other books of the period of the 1830s to 1860s, identify and analyze the values conveyed in these reading series or materials.

6. Identify a college that originated as a normal school in your state or region. If a history of that institution is available, write a paper that describes its history as a teacher education institution.

Notes

1. Lloyd P. Jorgenson, *The State and the Non-Public School, 1825–1925* (Columbia, MO: University of Missouri Press, 1987), 31–54.

2. Jorgenson, *The State and the Non-Public School,* 69–72.

3. Jonathan Messerli, *Horace Mann: A Biography* (New York: Alfred A. Knopf, 1972), 22–23.

4. Frederick M. Binder, *The Age of the Common School, 1830–1865* (New York: John Wiley & Sons, 1974), 7–21.

5. The definitive biography of Horace Mann is Messerli, *Horace Mann.*

6. Robert B. Downs, *Horace Mann: Champion of Public Schools* (New York: Twayne, 1974), 11.

7. Mary Mann, *Life of Horace Mann* (Boston: Walker Fuller, 1865), 11–12.

8. N. Ray Hiner and Joseph M. Hawes, *Growing up in America: Children in Historical Perspective* (Urbana, IL: University of Illinois Press, 1986).

9. Messerli, *Horace Mann,* 18.

10. Messerli, *Horace Mann,* 10–11.

11. Lawrence Cremin, ed., *The Republic and the School: Horace Mann on the Education of Free Men* (New York: Teachers College Press, 1957), 4.

12. Messerli, *Horace Mann,* 12.

13. Mann, *Life of Horace Mann,* 11–12.

14. Downs, *Horace Mann,* 14.

15. Messerli, *Horace Mann,* 29–31.

16. Messerli, *Horace Mann,* 35.

17. Downs, *Horace Mann,* 17.

18. Messerli, *Horace Mann,* 160.

19. Downs, *Horace Mann,* 20.

20. Messerli, *Horace Mann,* 105–7.

21. Messerli, *Horace Mann,* 117–21.

22. Messerli, *Horace Mann,* 119.

23. Messerli, *Horace Mann,* 223.

24. Downs, *Horace Mann,* 27–29.

25. Downs, *Horace Mann,* 29–30.

26. Cremin, *The Republic and the School,* 29–33.

27. Messerli, *Horace Mann,* 254.

28. Cremin, *The Republic and the School,* 32.

29. Messerli, *Horace Mann,* 263–64.

30. Cremin, *The Republic and the School,* 39.

31. Cremin, *The Republic and the School,* 87.

32. Messerli, *Horace Mann,* 210.

33. Messerli, *Horace Mann,* 446–47.

34. Messerli, *Horace Mann,* 543–44.

35. Messerli, *Horace Mann,* 108–9.

36. Merle Curti, *The Social Ideas of American Educators* (Peterson, NJ: Littlefield, Adams, 1959), 101–38.

37. Messerli, *Horace Mann,* 392–93.

38. Messerli, *Horace Mann,* 346.

39. Lawrence A. Cremin, *The American Common School: An Historic Conception* (New York: Teachers College Press, 1951), 62–63.

40. Messerli, *Horace Mann,* 310.

41. Messerli, *Horace Mann,* 350.

42. Jorgenson, *The State and the Non-Public School,* 31–54.

43. Downs, *Horace Mann,* 39–41.

Suggestions for Further Reading

Binder, Frederick M. *The Age of the Common School, 1830–1865.* New York: John Wiley & Sons, 1974.

Cremin, Lawrence A. *The American Common School: An Historic Conception.* New York: Teachers College Press, 1951.

———, ed. *The Republic and the School: Horace Mann on the Education of Free Men.* New York: Teachers College Press, 1957.

Downs, Robert B. *Horace Mann: Champion of Public Schools.* New York: Twayne, 1974.

Eimon, Pan. *Triumphant Teacher Triad: the Story of Domingo Faustino Sarmiento of Argentina, and of his Boston, USA Colleagues Horace Mann and Mary Peabody Mann.* Amarillo, TX: Amarillo Branch, American Association of University Women, 1994.

Hiner, N. Ray, and Hawes, Joseph M. *Growing up in America: Children in Historical Perspective.* Urbana, IL: University of Illinois Press, 1986.

Jorgenson, Lloyd P. *The State and the Non-Public School, 1825–1925.* Columbia, MO: University of Missouri Press, 1987.

Mann, Horace. *Lectures on Education.* New York: Arno, 1969.

Messerli, Jonathan. *Horace Mann: A Biography.* New York: Alfred A. Knopf, 1972.

Sawyer, Kem Knapp. *Horace Mann.* New York: Chelsea House Publishers, 1993.

C H A P T E R

15

Robert Owen: Utopian Theorist and Communitarian Educator

In this chapter we examine the life, educational philosophy, and contributions of Robert Owen (1771–1858), utopian theorist, proponent of communitarianism, social planner, and educational innovator. Owen's emphasis on developing planned communities and his stress on the formative effect of the social environment on human beings anticipated contemporary programs of community development and early childhood education. Owen's development of planned communities at New Lanark, Scotland, and New Harmony, Indiana, have intrigued social and educational historians over the years. His many publications on society and education examined the interconnections of school and society.

We discuss Owen's influence on Western educational theory and practice in its historical context and in terms of its effect on educational philosophy and policy. First, we examine the historical context of the industrializing, early nineteenth-century United Kingdom as the situation against which Owen reacted. Second, we look at Owen's biography, his education and career as an industrialist and utopian theorist, to determine the evolution of his ideas. Third, we analyze Owen's theory of human nature and society. Fourth, we explore his experiment in schooling at New Lanark. Last, we assess Owen's significance as an educator.

To help you organize your thoughts as you read this chapter, focus on the following questions:

1. How did Owen react to the major trends of his historical context?
2. How did Owen's life, his educational biography, shape his philosophy of education?

3. How did Owen's theories about human nature, community, and society shape his educational theories and practices?
4. What is the significance of Owen's contributions to education?

The Historical Context of Owen's Life

Robert Owen's work as a social and educational theorist can be viewed in many dimensions. He was a utopian thinker, a social theorist, and an educational practitioner. We will look at all these dimensions of his life, but his use of social imaging is most interesting. By using their social imagination, utopian thinkers project human nature, culture, and community into the future and try to imagine the contours of a new and better society.[1] Utopian thinkers such as Owen use their historical context—its social, economic, and educational conditions—as a point of departure for their futuristic projections. They often transpose the repressive conditions of their society and, in their opposites, seek to create a better social order. Thus, in place of the injustices found in their present situation, they conjecture an improved place on Earth, free of the obstacles that impede human happiness. Studying these utopian theorists, it is possible to engage in the educational uses of social imagination and project how a perfect system of education could help to create a better world. From such flights of imagination, future realities may come.

As a utopian thinker, Owen's ideas on education arose from the existing social and economic conditions of early nineteenth-century Great Britain. Seeking to create a new sociology, Owen believed many of the exploitative circumstances of the early Industrial Revolution resulted from misreading and misinterpreting events.

For Owen, the classical economic theorists such as Adam Smith, David Ricardo, and Thomas Malthus had drawn erroneous conclusions about the effects of the Industrial Revolution. Owen regarded their theories as misleading rationales for the competition, exploitation, and unhappiness that many people, particularly the working classes, were experiencing in the nineteenth century. Classical economists had provided early liberal politicians with a justification for laissez-faire policies that left undone desperately needed social and educational reforms. Owen sought to create a new social and economic theory that would counteract and replace laissez-faire economics.

A prosperous mill owner, Owen was well versed in the factory system's new and efficient modes of industrial production. In no way did he oppose industrialization; rather, he wanted to humanize it by eliminating its negative consequences on people's health and welfare. He believed that machine power had the potential of creating a new and more equitable society. The industrial system made it possible to mass produce goods more efficiently and generate material abundance. What was wrong, in Owen's opinion, was that the wealth produced by industrialism benefits only a few. He found the cause of the malaise to be an archaic system of private property. From his utopian perspective, Owen projected a better future if private ownership was abolished and a cooperative economy and society created.

According to Owen's analysis of early nineteenth-century industrialism, private property led to human exploitation and socioeconomic class conflicts. The upper and middle classes of owners, managers, and professionals were locked in an inexorable struggle against the laborers who worked in the factories, mines, and mills. Class antagonisms, based on economic divisions, would generate social tensions and violence. In the utopia of his dreams, violence would have no place. However, to end the hatred that led to violence, it was necessary to eradicate its cause—the desire for economic gain at other people's expense.

Although David Ricardo argued that economic prosperity required that profits be reinvested in capital expansion to earn still more profits, Owen claimed that the goods and services of the industrial order should be shared equally by all.[2] Equal sharing would reduce class antagonism, and ownership of property by communities rather than individuals would end class divisions altogether. Completely rejecting the concept of class struggle and antagonism, Owen believed that his projected new community would be classless.

On the issue of class conflict Owen showed himself to be an educator and propagandist rather than the organizer of a political movement as such. He believed that his persuasive abilities would convince the wealthy classes to give up their privileges and property voluntarily for the common good. He also believed he could educate workers to abandon their feelings of antagonism toward their economic oppressors. Peaceful persuasion and education based on his social science would create human harmony and do away with class hatred. By the mid-nineteenth century, scientific socialists—as Karl Marx and Friedrich Engels styled themselves—would praise Owen's assessment of economic conditions as laudable but would condemn the nonviolent social change that he envisioned as unrealistic.

The scientific socialism of Karl Marx (1818–1883) was a rival ideology to Owen's utopian communitarianism. Educated as a philosopher in Germany, Marx spent much of his life in exile in the United Kingdom, where with his chief collaborator, he formulated his ideology in such works as *Das Kapital* and the *Communist Manifesto*. Marx developed a materialist and economic interpretation of history. Most significant, for him, is control of the means and modes of production—the ownership, production, distribution, and consumption of goods. The means and modes of production are the economic foundation upon which rests the social structure—institutions such as the family, state, church, school, law court, police force, and army, for example. Whoever controls the economic foundation will also control these social institutions. In the modern industrial age, society is divided into two conflicting classes: the capitalists, who own the factories—the means and modes of production—and the proletariat, the workers who produce goods but who do not own the machines with which they work. The capitalist exploiters have created a false ideology to mislead and miseducate the workers so they are not conscious of their true situation as victims of exploitation. (See Chapter 24 for the Marxist element in Freire's view of ideology.) Capitalism, with its insatiable appetite for profits, is destined to sow the seeds of its own destruction. Its demands for more market and more consumer goods will lead to spirals of overproduction, which will lead to reoccurring economic crises, recession, and depression. Unemployment, once periodic, will become chronic, and conditions will grow ripe for revolution. Marx predicted that workers, because of their exploitation and repression, would organize, revolt, and overthrow their capitalist exploiters.

Marx reasoned that a small intellectual elite of dedicated revolutionaries who knew history's true course would lead the inevitable revolution. The vanguard of the proletariat would organize the workers and raise their consciousness about the true conditions of their exploitation, thus creating a new classless society destined to replace the capitalist economic order.

After the revolution, all instruments of production would be centralized in the proletarian state created by the victorious workers. A dictatorship established by the proletariat would bring about the reforms needed. The state apparatus would be taken over and redirected to ensure the working class consolidation of power and control. When the remnants of the old capitalist regime had been obliterated, a classless society would appear, in utopian fashion, in which there would be no repression. When everyone was a member of one class—the working class—the state, as an instrument of the domination of one class over another, would wither away.

Although he rejected Marxist class warfare, Owen was dismayed by the lack of economic and social planning and coordination he saw in early nineteenth-century Britain. Nowhere was the absence of coordinated planning more evident than in the mushrooming growth of Britain's cities. The migration of rural agricultural workers to the cities to become factory workers had been unplanned, haphazard, and without consideration of the social and educational consequences that followed in its wake. Masses of people had crowded into sadly deficient tenements that were ill heated, poorly ventilated, and infested with vermin. The absence of sanitary facilities, supplies of pure water, and adequate sewage disposal made the urban areas inhabited by the working classes ripe for the spread of diseases.

Government services such as hospitals, schools, and police were rudimentary at best and unable to cope with the problems created by a burgeoning population. In Owen's reading of events, classical liberal ideology, buttressed by the theories of the Manchester school of economics, further aggravated the situation by endorsing a hands-off, laissez-faire policy. The antidote that Owen developed in his utopian vision of the new social order was one of total involvement by community agencies in human life.

Further, the migration of rural people to the cities produced social changes that affected living conditions and styles of life. The factory system's appetite for cheap labor, especially that of women and children, changed the pattern of family life and early educational practices. The parenting function exercised by both parents, but especially by mothers, changed. Women worked in the factories for long hours, often from early morning to late at night. Children, too, toiled at the monotonous routines of tending the machinery of factory and mill. Education, which had been extremely limited for the children of the working poor, was rendered even more inadequate. In the new social order of Owen's dreams, the situation of women and children was to be greatly improved, and education would be the remedy.

Owen was especially concerned about the stereotyped and limited role of women in the social and economic context of early nineteenth-century England. By law, custom, and social convention, women were held to be unequal and subordinate to men. Women could not legally hold property in their own names. Their property was that of their fathers, husbands, or guardians. Courtship and marriage in the early nineteenth century were based on property and its control. For the members of a society to be truly free and equal, women had to have equality of educational opportunity and be free to choose their social relationships. In his new world, Owen saw women as equal participants, free from the old gender-defined tasks of cooking, cleaning, and childrearing that had limited them in the past. In the new society, social agencies would perform these functions.

As he surveyed the cultural conditions of the early nineteenth century, Owen believed that unregulated and exploitative industrialism produced a sense of alienation in workers that separated them from involvement with the product they were manufacturing. Unlike the older form of workmanship in which the craftsperson had pride in the product being made, the worker on the factory assembly line made only one part of the finished item. The worker's alienation from the process and the product was further aggravated, Owen believed, by the fact that the economic profit was expropriated completely by the factory owner. Also, the worker performed his or her labor in social isolation. Thus, in terms of identifying the worker with the product, of providing an economic incentive, and in bringing about societal involvement, the industrial system was lacking.

Although the sense of community was declining, the leading apologists of the classical school of economics and their associates in liberal politics were following the ideological line of Smith, Ricardo, and Malthus that nature should be allowed to take its inexorable course without interference by human planning. Smith argued that government should not interfere with the natural laws of supply and demand; Ricardo argued that profits needed to be maximized even at the expense of workers; and Malthus suggested that plague, famine, or war would check the burgeoning growth of population and that if these natural processes were interfered with, the population would exceed the Earth's potential for feeding it.

Owen believed that conditions of scarcity, unemployment, and economic boom or bust could be altered. To replace the alienation and class antagonism of an exploitative industrial system, it was imperative that a viable sense of community be restored. This could best be developed in villages of mutual cooperation in which the enterprise of the inhabitants was balanced between agriculture and industry. In these villages the inhabitants would come to know each other directly, as in an extended family, although the ties would be based on sociality rather than kinship. The theme of the "machine in the garden" would characterize Owen's utopian plans.

Owen's Life: The Biography of a Utopian

Robert Owen was born in Newtown, a small town in Wales. In his autobiography, Owen, who identified his father, Robert, as an ironmonger and saddler, claimed to be influenced by his parents' habits of hard work, industriousness, and thrift.[3] By all indications, Owen was altruistic but also paternalistic. His autobiography reveals a person with strong self-esteem that his critics claimed bordered on egotism. He took keen delight in hearing his own voice and reading his own words.

Owen's reflections on his childhood are full of self-praise and reveal the confidence of a self-made and mostly self-educated man.[4] He was, he asserts, the fastest runner, the best dancer, the most popular young man, and the most gifted scholar in Newtown. Because of his academic accomplishments, the village schoolmaster relied on Owen to instruct the other children in the school. Imbued with a confidence that he carried throughout his life, Owen's self-generated enthusiasm for his own ideas, words, and plans caused him to operate in a reality of his own making. The eternal optimist, Owen often had difficulty distinguishing between his successes and his failures.

At the age of 10, Owen left Newtown to seek fame and fortune, returning 77 years later, in 1858, to die in the place of his birth. After spending some time in Stamford and London, he took a position as an apprentice in a draper's shop in Manchester, a rapidly growing city in the throes of England's Industrial Revolution.[5] By age 18, Owen, who had worked at various jobs after completing his apprenticeship, had accumulated enough money to invest in a partnership in a firm manufacturing cotton-spinning ma-chinery. He was an ambitious young man intent on making his way up the economic lad-der during a time when fortunes could be quickly made and as quickly lost. His next venture, in 1792, saw him managing a mechanized cotton mill owned by Peter Drinkwater. Commenting that his business career was an educational experience, Owen noted that he improved the technique of cotton manufacturing, gained expertise in fac-tory management, and was stimulated by association with Manchester's leading entre-preneurs and intellectuals.[6] Owen was quite successful in the profit-making he would later see as exploitative.

In 1799, Owen and several associates formed the Chorlton Twist Company, which raised sufficient capital to purchase control of David Dale's New Lanark mills. Cotton manufacturing was then a leading industry in Britain, and Dale's mills, situated in the valley near the falls of the River Clyde at New Lanark, Scotland, were among the most prosperous. While negotiating for the properties, Owen met Dale's daughter, Caroline, and fell in love with her. When they married, Owen had not only made a business arrangement but had also married into one of nineteenth-century England's leading industrial families.

New Lanark, the scene of Owen's social and educational experimentation from 1799 to 1824, was an industrial village, a mill town. Located halfway between Scotland's large cities of Glasgow and Edinburgh, New Lanark consisted of mill buildings where cot-ton cloth was manufactured by water power–driven machinery, many large apartment or row houses for the workers, a company store, and the mansion of the owner.

When he took charge of the mills in 1799, Owen found that he was responsible for managing more than 1,000 workers, including men, women, and children. Surveying the living and working conditions at New Lanark, Owen was disturbed by his findings. The town, he observed, was ridden with delinquency, vice, drunkenness, theft, and ver-min. The firsthand encounter with these conditions started the young businessman down the path to utopianism, to communitarianism, and to a life dedicated to social re-form. Consistent with the character that he would exhibit throughout his career as a so-cial reformer, Owen acted in the paternalistic fashion that earned him the title of the "benevolent Mr. Owen." His reforms were based on what he claimed to be his great philosophical discovery, that "Man's character is made for and not by him."[7] Rejecting the conventional wisdom that poverty and vice were caused by the innate depravity of the human character, Owen argued that human behavior was shaped by the environ-mental circumstances in which people lived. Better housing, food, clothing, and edu-cation would improve the social environment and reform the character of its inhabitants.

Owen had not yet determined that communal ownership of property was a neces-sary condition for social reform. Still committed to private ownership at New Lanark, he believed that a businessman could earn profits without exploiting his workers. Initially suspicious of Owen's promises to improve their living and working conditions, the New Lanark workers feared that Owen was trying to guile them into working harder and pro-ducing more profits for the company. Nevertheless, Owen inaugurated his reform pro-gram there.

Under Owen's direction, a concerted program of social reform and community re-newal was instituted in the Scottish mill town. One set of reforms had to do with the working conditions in the mills. The hours of labor were reduced for all, and children under the age of 10 were not permitted to work in the mills. Owen also ended the practice of wholesale employment of orphan children that had characterized the previous management of the mills. Further, he introduced a system whereby every employee's efficiency was rated daily. Next, he turned to reforming living conditions. The streets were swept, debris was removed, and the mill village generally improved in physical appearance. Inspection teams visited workers' apartments to make sure that they were kept clean. The company store was stocked with fairly priced items.

High on Owen's agenda for the social improvement of New Lanark was education. He established a general school for the education of the town's children, which was characterized by its progressive methods. He founded an infant school for the early education of children ages 2 to 6, after which they entered the general school. Believing that education was a lifelong undertaking, Owen also established the Institute for the Formation of Character, which featured adult education, afterwork lectures, and concerts. Under his direction, New Lanark became a total educational environment.

Word of Owen's reforms at New Lanark traveled widely throughout Europe and the Americas. His fame as a prosperous factory owner and a paternalistic reformer attracted a steady stream of visitors to observe the work in the mills, instruction in the schools, and the general atmosphere of reform. Indeed, New Lanark stood out as a place apart in an era that was content to rely on so-called natural forces of supply and demand rather than on social imagination. Owen spent more time guiding visiting notables around New Lanark than on managing the mills. He began to write tracts describing his reforms and was a frequent speaker to groups throughout England.

Thoroughly enjoying his reputation as a philanthropist and social reformer, Owen decided that his plans for reform should not be limited to New Lanark but should be disseminated throughout the British Isles, through Europe, to the Americas, and even perhaps to the rest of the world. He moved from local reform to projects of world renewal. Owen's *Report to the Committee of the Association for the Relief of the Manufacturing and Labouring Poor* (1817) and his *Report to the County of Lanark* (1820) reflect his movement to the larger role of social critic and reformer.[8] At this stage in his career, his communitarian ideology began to take shape.

Owen believed that problems of periodic unemployment and inadequate poor relief could not be dealt with in a piecemeal fashion. These issues, he believed, were part of a larger and more pervasive social crisis. Owen believed the Industrial Revolution not only changed economic modes of life, but transformed civilization itself. Industrialization increased productivity and stimulated economic growth, but these benefits were unequally distributed because of an archaic and irrational individualism based on private property. Periodic unemployment, Owen reasoned, was not an inevitable result of industrial modernization as Adam Smith and David Ricardo had argued, but was rather the unnecessary baggage of a competitive and exploitative economy.

In his *Report to the County of Lanark*, Owen, now a full-fledged communitarian socialist, called for the creation of self-supporting "villages of unity and mutual cooperation," not only for the poor but for all classes and all persons. In these villages, where all property would be owned communally, all residential accommodations would be arranged in a parallelogram of connected buildings that would also house schools, apartments, factories, libraries, kitchens, hospitals, dining rooms, and lecture halls. His concept of the "village of unity" quickly developed into a comprehensive communitarian ideology that Owen tried to implement at New Harmony, Indiana, from 1825 to 1828. The Scottish factory town of New Lanark and the frontier village in Indiana became linked by the transatlantic bonds of Owen's communitarian ideology.[9]

Owen's experiences from 1799 to 1824 at New Lanark produced the underlying concepts of his communitarian ideology. He had, largely through his own imaginative efforts, taken a typical factory village and transformed it into a model community. In contrast to the grime, crime, vice, and exploitation that characterized the life of the working class in the early nineteenth century, Owen had brought cleanliness, order, and education to the mill workers of New Lanark, whether they wanted it or not.

In 1824, Owen left New Lanark and came to the United States. For the next four years, Owen sought to establish his new communitarian vision of society and education in New Harmony, which he purchased from the Harmonists, a sect of German religious pietists who also lived a communitarian lifestyle. Attracted to the United States as an open society, Owen believed that the American frontier was the ideal locale for his social experiment. The United States, the New World, was free of the class-conscious prejudices and irrational traditions of Europe—the Old World—and would be the place for what he called his "new moral world."

After speaking to sessions of the U.S. Congress attended by the president and members of the Supreme Court, Owen extended his open invitation to all interested parties to join him at New Harmony. One thousand people came. It was an uneven assortment of humanity that ventured to the Indiana frontier. Some of the United States's leading scholars and scientists came with William Maclure, the pioneer geologist and philanthropist, to establish a center for scientific and educational research and dissemination. Among them were Thomas Say and Gerard Troost, both eminent natural scientists, and Joseph Neef, who had been trained by Pestalozzi at Burgdorf. Others were inspired by Owen's vision of a new society in a new land. Some had continually failed and were looking for one last chance to begin again. Still others were opportunists who saw Owen as a naive do-gooder whom they could divest of funds.[10]

Owen planned to create a community of equality at New Harmony in which the town's property would be owned in common by the residents. Education would play a central role in the community, which was to develop a comprehensive set of educational institutions, ranging from nursery schools for children to lectures for adults. Owen predicted that the Indiana community would be so successful and prosperous that other communities would organize to imitate it. With New Harmony at the center of a new communitarian world, Owen envisioned a comprehensive network of satellite cities that would encircle the Earth. Once the parent community had been established, it would serve as the model city. For Owen, communitarian education would create and sustain his envisioned new moral world:

> The world will thus be governed by education alone, since all other governments will then become useless and unnecessary. To train and educate the rising generation will at all times be the first object of society, to which every other will be subordinate.[11]

Owen's educational program at New Harmony was closely related to his communitarian ideology. He believed the small, voluntary, experimental community would quickly reform the behavior and character of its residents. Because social regeneration was to be accomplished peacefully, education was to be the primary instrument of reform. In his insightful commentary on early nineteenth-century education, Arthur Bestor writes that for the educationists of the era, "the relationship between school and society appeared a reciprocal one." According to Bestor,

> The school should respond to social change, they held, but it should also be an instrument for effecting desirable alterations in society. In their hands educational reform became a branch of social reform.[12]

Conceiving of social reform as a total process, Owen believed the reformed community itself, as an informal educational agency, would be a potent force for societal reform. Schooling would reflect and maintain the values that existed within the community. Although the school alone could not create a new society, it could perpetuate the new social design by transmitting communitarian knowledge, skills, and values to young New Harmonists.

Schooling at New Harmony represented a shift in educational theory and practice from ancient classical languages and literature to utilitarianism. For Owen and his chief associate, William Maclure, the Greek and Latin language curriculum was archaic, a pedagogical residue that was irrelevant to scientific and industrial progress. Based on his experiences at New Lanark, Owen's educational program at New Harmony was designed to serve practical and utilitarian goals as well as contribute to fundamental social reconstruction.

A key provision in Owen's New Harmony plan was the abolition of private property, which he had earlier identified as the primary cause of human and social evils. Common property, supported by common education, would be the "great equalizers" that would end class conflict and violence. On May 1, 1825, the "preliminary society of New Harmony" was organized "to improve the character and conditions of its own members, and to prepare them to become associates in independent communities, having common property."[13]

Ten months later, on February 5, 1826, an overly optimistic Robert Owen proclaimed that New Harmony was now the "community of equality." New Harmony's constitution committed its members to "equality of rights" and "equality of duties" within a society of "cooperative union" and a "community of property." Clearly reflecting Owen's conceptions of character formation, cooperation, and education, the constitution stated that "man's character, mental, moral, and physical, is the result of his formation, his location, and . . . the circumstances within which he exists."[14]

Further, the constitution proclaimed that "all members of the community" were to be "one family." There was to be "similar food, clothing, and education." All were to "live in similar houses" and "be accommodated alike." Restating the importance of education, the document read, "It shall always remain a primary object of the community to give the best physical, moral, and intellectual education to all its members."[15]

Unfortunately for Owen, his ambitious plan for a new social order did not succeed. Displaying a chronic tendency to disharmony, the inhabitants of New Harmony endlessly debated with each other over the constitution and its revisions, quarreled over the division of property that Owen continually postponed, and disputed social and educational theories and practices.

With the community in the throes of disintegration, Owen and William Maclure quarreled. After litigation, they divided what was left of the community. In 1828, Owen left New Harmony and returned to England, remaining confident that the new world he envisioned was merely postponed. Convinced of the inevitability of the new social order, Owen continued to write, lecture, and organize societies to promote communitarianism. In the United Kingdom, he organized workers' cooperatives. Some see him as contributing the ideas of what would become one of Britain's major political parties, the Labour party. He continued to work for communitarianism, women's rights, improvement of working conditions, and universal education until his death in 1858.

Owen's Social and Educational Theory

Robert Owen's plan for creating the new moral world was based on his conception of human nature. His oft-repeated dictum that "man's character was made for and not by him" expressed his belief that he had made a fundamental and revolutionary discovery that previous generations had ignored. In his "Essays on the Formation of Character," from his *New View of Society*, Owen argued that human character was formed by the interaction of the person's original or germinal nature with environmental circumstances. In Owen's communitarian view of progress, the controlled communitarian environment was the most efficacious setting in which to perfect the human personality. His key beliefs were that character development was completely plastic and that whoever controlled the environment would be able to produce the kind of human character they wanted. Thus, Owen gave himself a great power over human destiny. Although his intentions were benevolent, the same doctrine of total control could have malevolent effects in the hands of a dictator.

For Owen, individuals were not responsible for their behavior because they had no control over their origins or their early childhood experiences. Human beings, however, were not fated to be hapless victims of accidents of birth and a disordered environment. Given the correct environment, which Owen believed he could establish, the human being could be formed into a good, kind, sharing person. However, it was crucial that character formation begin as early as possible, even in infancy. Owen's emphasis on early childhood education both at New Lanark and New Harmony have made him one of the pioneering theorists in this field.

Owen saw himself as a behavioral and social engineer and believed that he had discovered the laws of human development. He gave his greatest attention to plans to restructure the environment so that human development followed its proper social course. The communitarian environment was Owen's prescribed setting for character formation and personal socialization. Owen clearly pointed to the importance of the communitarian environment in shaping character when he stated,

> It having been discovered that man at birth is wholly formed by the power which creates him, and that his subsequent character is determined by the circumstances which surround him, acting upon his original or created nature—that does not in any degree form himself, physically or mentally, and therefore cannot be a free or responsible agent: the first practical effects of this knowledge must be, to banish from the mind of man all ideas or merit or demerit in any created object or being—to extirpate from his constitution all the feeling to which such ideas give rise; and thus at once to reconcile him to human nature, to himself, and to all his fellow creatures.[16]

Like Rousseau, Owen rejected views of human nature that asserted that individuals entered life with a depraved character. In contrast, Owen wrote that the human being is "a delightful compound, containing the germs of unalloyed excellence, and which require for their due development, only a kindly soil and a careful cultivation."[17] Evil came not from human nature but from ignorance.

Based on his principle of human character, Owen specified a range or continuum of human behaviors. At one end of the continuum was bad behavior, which was caused by evil surroundings. At the other end was superior character, which resulted from favorable conditions where institutions, laws, and customs conformed to the laws of human nature.

To develop superior character, Owen argued, a favorable environment had to be created and those who resided in it needed the right kind of education. The proper environment was one that had been converted from private to social production, distribution, and communal consumption of goods and services. The right kind of education dispelled the ignorance that came from erroneous education. The vague and mysterious strictures that originated with mythology, found in the classics; and theology, which had dominated education, needed to be displaced by a new worldview based on the laws of human nature and social development.

Owen's social theory closely corresponded to his view of human nature. His theory of society and social change, in turn, was heavily influenced by his economic ideas. As a social theorist, Owen began his career as a critic of the capitalist system that had earned him wealth and fame. From the negative role of social critic, he advanced to a proactive role as the prophet of a new social and economic system. Moving beyond its initial economic perspective, Owen's system grew into a comprehensive ideology that rested on the community of equality as the dynamic change agency.

Owen's theory of social change was precipitated by his experiences at New Lanark and by his observations of nineteenth-century English society. Continually reiterating that man's character was formed for and not by him, Owen stressed the environment's role in shaping human behavior. If the environment were properly organized, then those who interacted with it would be shaped by its wholesome stimuli. Owen regarded the cooperative community as the ideal environment for shaping the morality of the inhabitants who would dwell in peace and harmony in the new social order.

Believing that the new moral world would come about by peaceful and nonviolent means, Owen relied on education, both formal and informal, as the instrument to create the new society. Through his own polemical tracts, lectures, and books, Owen displayed a missionary zeal and worked to gain converts for his new secular religion. He used informal education to disseminate information of his vision of the new society and recruit converts for his cooperative commonwealth. He saw his communities of cooperation as educative environments that would form the new moral order by educating moral citizens. Schools in these egalitarian communities, as formal educational agencies, would train later communitarian generations.

Owen's theory of social change was charged with a secular millennialism that convinced him that the new moral world would, like Marx's classless society, come as a result of historical inevitability. His conviction that the new society was inevitable caused him to discount political organization and revolutionary tactics as necessary means of social change. Although he sought to convert heads of state, monarchs, presidents, and politically influential people to his ideology, Owen did not seek to head an organized political movement.

Because of his rejection of revolutionary violence and class warfare, Owen was condemned as a utopian by the Marxists. Holding that social change could be achieved without violence, Owen believed that when people had been educated to recognize the injustice of the old system they would replace it with his envisioned humane society. Because Owen held that individuals were not responsible for forming their own character, he regarded class hatred as irrational and irrelevant in achieving the new society.[18]

Owen's rejection of class conflict and revolutionary violence led Marx and Engels to condemn Owenism as utopian socialism—a soft-headed and soft-hearted, muddled approach to the class struggle that misled the working classes from their true revolutionary role. Although Engels commended Owen for his analysis of the economic woes of the existing society, he condemned his failure to recognize the revolutionary nature of economic class conflict. Unlike Marx, who believed that the proletariat would be led by an elite vanguard, Owen held that all properly educated people could contribute to establishing the cooperative commonwealth.

Convinced that his social science explained the laws governing the universe, Owen believed that he had discovered the natural laws of human and social development. Owen was certain that he had correctly formulated a new social science. For the Owenites, social science, which was synonymous with the ideology of communitarian socialism, was the method of studying society to discover the laws that governed it and formed human character.[19] Following his premise that a controlled environment would produce the desired personality type, Owen was a convinced social engineer. He believed that the social scientist, informed by the laws of social organization and human development, could construct the planned environment—the community of equality—so that its residents would develop according to a societal blueprint. Because social engineering was a way of creating the new person who would inhabit the world, Owen saw himself in the role of the chief engineer who would create such a reconstructed social order.

Owen's planned reconstruction of the social environment was to lead to a fundamental reshaping of human behavior. By living in an environment based on the laws of social science, the new person would be a moral member of society. Within the context of Owenite social science, education was broadly viewed as a total process of communitarian enculturation, which included but was not limited to schooling. In the past, the old, immoral, and discordant modes of thought of the individualistic society were transmitted to the young both by the culture and by schooling that was dominated by the classics. In the new society, a new form of schooling based on social science would help to create a new form of community. In the next section we describe Owen's actual conduct of schools at New Lanark.

Owen's Schools at New Lanark

Along with socially controlled general reform, Owen emphasized that education, especially for children, was a key element in improving human character. In *An Outline of the System of Education at New Lanark* (1825), Robert Dale Owen, Owen's eldest son, provides a detailed account of schooling in that industrial village.

Robert Dale Owen describes the school as a two-story building, constructed of gray stone, as were the other structures at New Lanark. The first story was divided into three large rooms where classes were scheduled on reading, natural science, history, geography, and other subjects. After attempting to teach large classes of 100 pupils, Owen decided instruction would be more effective in smaller classes and limited enrollment to 50 pupils.

The school's second story uniquely reflected Owen's educational philosophy. It was divided into two classrooms: The principal schoolroom was 90 feet long, 40 feet wide, and 20 feet high; the second classroom was somewhat smaller. Its unique feature was that "the walls are hung round with representations of the most striking zoological and mineralogical specimens, including quadrupeds, birds, fishes, reptiles, insects, shells, minerals, &c."[20] At one end of the room was an upper story gallery for the orchestra; at the other end were hung representations of the hemispheres with the countries and seas indicated by various colors but otherwise unidentified.[21] This room also served as a lecture hall and a ballroom.

The school's physical design and its furnishings reflected Owen's educational theory. Large rooms made it possible for children to move from area to area, depending on the subject being taught. Owen stressed using objects or their representations in the form of drawings and models in instruction. In view of the importance Owen gave to music and dancing, the school had an orchestra platform, a rare feature for a nineteenth-century school.

Frequently called the "father of infant education," Owen was a convinced proponent of early childhood education. His emphasis on the importance of early learning experiences rested on his communitarian ideology that reform required children to be educated in a controlled environment away from socially corrupting influences. At New Lanark, the ages of the children attending school ranged from 18 months to 12 years, with some children leaving school at age 10 to work in the mills. Although he wanted to restrict child labor and keep the New Lanark children in school until age 12, Owen yielded to parental demands that they be allowed to work in the mill at age 10. In the early nineteenth century, children's labor and the wages they earned were regarded as needed contributions to a family's income.

The school day began at 7:30 A.M. and ended at 5 P.M., with long breaks or intervals during the day ranging from one to two hours. Owen believed that instruction was more effective and efficient if interspersed with periods of relaxation. The infant classes, enrolling children from age 2 to 6, were in session for only half of that time.[22] In addition to the day classes, the school was open at night and instruction was provided for older children and adults.

For infants and older children, instruction was free. For children between the ages of 6 and 10, a small fee was charged. Owen's rationale for charging this fee was that its payment would prevent parents from negatively regarding the school as a charity institution. In early nineteenth-century England, charity schools were conducted for some children of the dependent poor.

Both boys and girls wore a similar uniform, a white Roman-style cotton tunic. The boy's tunic came to the knee, and the girl's tunic reached the ankle.[23] The uniform dress reflected Owen's belief that schooling should foster a sense of equality.

Within the school, Owen sought to create a permissive but controlled environment in which learning would be a pleasurable experience for the children. Extrinsic rewards and punishments that Owen regarded as contributing to an artificial character were abolished. Owen believed that extrinsic incentives, which substituted false goals for the natural consequences of action, produced people with weak and unstable characters. At New Lanark, no rewards were given for outstanding scholarship or good conduct nor were children punished for idleness or disobedience. The motivation for learning was to come from the child's interests. Good conduct would result from the spirit of amiable cooperation engendered by group membership. Teachers were to treat all children with kindness and use restraint only to protect young children from physical harm.[24]

Owen's emphasis on a child-centered classroom climate was a radical change from the conventional teaching style of the early nineteenth century, which included corporal punishment. Given these guidelines for school management, Owen had difficulty finding properly trained teachers. Because he opposed religious and classical education, he did not want to employ teachers who stressed either catechetical instruction or Latin and Greek. In many British primary schools, conventional teaching practices called for strongly domineering teachers who, with the rod, demanded and obtained strict discipline and rigid conformity. In contrast to teachers trained according to conventional practices, Owen wanted patient teachers who loved children and related to them easily and naturally.

In hiring the first teachers in the New Lanark schools, Owen sought people with the right disposition and attitude toward children rather than pedagogical training or previous teaching experience. Owen identified two individuals who met his requirements: John Buchanan, a local weaver, and Molly Young, a 17-year-old mill employee. He regarded these two as unspoiled and sufficiently flexible to teach according to his pedagogical design.[25] As Owen hired other teachers, he selected those with backgrounds and personalities similar to Buchanan and Young. Unfortunately, unlike Pestalozzi and other educational innovators, Owen did not institutionalize his pedagogical style by developing teacher education programs. An exception to his use of untrained teachers were the music and dancing teachers, who were skilled in their arts.

Although Owen based instruction on children's interests and emphasized using object lessons, the New Lanark curriculum was more subject centered than was the case with either Pestalozzi or Froebel. The curriculum for the 6- to 10-year-olds consisted of reading, writing, arithmetic, natural science, geography, history, singing, and dancing. In addition, girls were taught sewing and needlework.

In teaching reading, Owen's principle was that "children should never be directed to read what they cannot understand."[26] The method was to have a child read aloud and then have other pupils in the class question her or him about the content. Understanding was emphasized rather than mimicry of the author's language and style.

Owen anticipated what has come to be called the "broad fields curriculum" in that he stressed that natural science, geography, and history be taught in a correlated manner. The method was for the teacher to present an outline of the topic, which was then slowly filled in with supporting details.[27] According to Robert Dale Owen,

> In . . . Natural History, the division of Nature into the Animal, Vegetable, and Mineral Kingdoms, is first explained to them, and in a very short time they learn at once to distinguish to which of these any object which may be presented to them belongs. The teacher then proceeds to details of the most interesting objects furnished by each of these kingdoms, including descriptions of quadrupeds, birds, fishes, reptiles, and insects—and of the most interesting botanical and mineralogical specimens.

The details are illustrated by representations of objects, drawn on a large scale and as correctly as possible.[28]

Owen, who personally enjoyed music and dancing, included art and aesthetic appreciation in the New Lanark school program. Children were instructed in singing by both ear and notes. Dancing, which Owen claimed was a pleasant, natural, and social exercise that improved carriage and deportment and "increased cheerfulness and hilarity," was taught through varied Scotch reels, country dances, and quadrilles.[29] Both boys and girls performed military drill. They were formed into divisions led by young drummers and fifers and moved in unison from place to place in the industrial village.

In addition to the school, Owen designed and constructed a three-storied, multifunctional educational and cultural center, which opened in January 1816 as the Institute for the Formation of Character. It was here that Owen's concept of infant education was more fully implemented. The curriculum and methods in the infant school were child centered, play oriented, and aimed to stimulate children to use their senses to develop skills of careful observation. Teachers placed objects in strategic locations throughout the building to stimulate children's curiosity and observation. Resistant to book-centered education, Owen wanted children to be taught the nature, qualities, and uses of common objects by direct, exploratory activities and by casual conversation between teacher and child. Teachers were to use natural objects found within the immediate location of the village to excite children's curiosity. This initial interest was to be reinforced by animated conversation between the youngsters and their teachers, who in turn gained new knowledge about the objects and their pupils.[30] Anticipating the British primary method, Owen developed a method of early childhood education in which children moved about freely and learned by pursuing activities that stimulated their interests.

In his commentary, Robert Dale Owen identified several factors that limited the school's effectiveness. First, the children were in school for only five hours each day. The remaining time was spent with parents and others who lacked the proper disposition to the knowledge and values emphasized in Owen's schools. (Later, Owen recommended that children be separated from their parents, raised in communal dormitories and educated in communal boarding schools.) Second, it was difficult to locate teachers who shared Owen's educational philosophy. Third, parents did not support certain features of Owenite education. For example, they wanted their children to read at an age earlier than Owen prescribed. They also wanted them to leave school at age 10 rather than 12 as Owen recommended. Finally, parents wanted religious instruction, which Owen believed was harmful. Throughout his career Owen met opposition from religious educators. Owen argued that emphasis on religion produced prejudicial attitudes rather than egalitarian values.

When Owen came to New Harmony, Indiana, he already had firm opinions about the conduct of schools based on his experience at New Lanark. At New Lanark, Owen had exclusive control of the schools. At New Harmony, in contrast, educational arrangements were controlled by William Maclure, Owen's partner in the communitarian venture.[31] Maclure, who sought to integrate basic scientific research with Pestalozzian pedagogy, had a different educational philosophy from Owen. Differences between Owen and Maclure, and the presence of other educators such as Joseph Neef and Marie Duclos Fretageot, made education at New Harmony a much more complex and often controversial undertaking than at New Lanark.

Conclusion: An Assessment

Owen's significance needs to be assessed in terms of his contributions to social and educational theory. Too often, historians have viewed him only as a utopian socialist and have not seen him as the creator of a comprehensive social and educational theory. To assess Owen's importance to modern education, he must be viewed as a theorist who recognized that education was inextricably related to society. As a pioneer in the sociology of education, he was not content merely to theorize but rather wanted to use education as an instrument to create a new society.

Owen anticipated in his social theory the very modern proposition that model cities can be designed and that they will, in turn, produce model men and women. His designs to create planned communities anticipated the essential strategies used by contemporary urbanologists and community planners. Corrupt, degenerative, and polluted environments, Owen said, create selfish, sick, and sluggish human beings. Clean, attractive, and wholesome social environments, conversely, would create harmoniously integrated members of society. Although using more sophisticated designs, today's advocates of socially engineered model cities, who regard the social environment as the key to reforming human behavior, still follow many of Owen's premises.

By attacking the traditional schools of the early nineteenth century, Owen rejected and sought to discredit inherited educational practices that he believed retarded children's social development. His concept of early childhood education emphasized, as did the ideas of the later progressive educators, children's interests and experiences.

Without doubt, Owen's intentions as a social reformer were altruistic and humanitarian. At the same time, he was a benevolent paternalist who invaded the individual's right to privacy. A sociological and pedagogical busybody, Owen's planned society interfered with the individual's personal freedom to choose her or his own course of self-development. As a self-anointed prophet and social engineer, Owen sought to shape people according to what he believed was in their best interest. In many respects, Owen was the unwitting predecessor of the molders of public opinion and even of the totalitarians, who regard humanity as clay to be molded as they see fit.

Perhaps the most useful legacy that Robert Owen left to education was that of the utopian thinker who used social imagination to project a vision of a better world. As such a thinker, he provided a useful critique of his times. He also demonstrated how utopian conjectures can lead to social and educational change.

Questions for Reflection and Dialogue

1. Identify some of the changes that have taken place in family life in the United States. How do you think Owen would react to these changes?
2. Reflect on the idea of social and economic conflict from an Owenite and a Marxist perspective.
3. Reflect on the uses of educational technology. Does this technology lead to more personal freedom or control? How would Owen use this technology?
4. Analyze the concept of *social imagination*. How can the theory of social imagination be applied to conjecturing new educational designs and futures? Use your social imagination to envision and describe an ideal school of the future.

5. What are the educational uses of studying utopian theories? Can you identify any contemporary utopian theories?
6. How was Owen's communitarian socialism a reaction against the existing socio-economic conditions of early nineteenth-century England? Identify conditions in the contemporary United States that you believe need reforming.
7. How was Owen's school at New Lanark a departure from existing approaches to schooling? How would Owen's New Lanark school fit contemporary versions of schooling?
8. Did Owen develop a useable strategy for dealing with social class, racial, ethnic, and religious conflicts?

Projects for Deepening Your Understanding

1. Using the concept of social imagination, write a utopian essay that describes a community and its schools as you would envision them in the future.
2. Select and review a book written by a utopian thinker.
3. In an essay, analyze Robert Owen's character as a social theorist and educator.
4. In a position paper, either support or attack the proposition that Owen's plan for creating moral character was designed to liberate people.
5. In an essay, profile the kind of teacher who would be suited to teach in a school conducted by Owen.
6. In an essay, assess the significance of Owen's educational ideas for contemporary education.

Notes

1. Elise Boulding, *Building a Global Civic Culture: Education for an Interdependent World* (New York: Teachers College Press, 1988), 108–17.
2. Michael J. Gootzeit, *David Ricardo* (New York: Columbia University Press, 1975).
3. Robert Owen, *The Life of Robert Owen Written by Himself With Selections from His Writings and Correspondence*, vol. 1 (London: Effingham Wilson, 1857–1858; reprint, New York: Augustus M. Kelley, 1967), 1–2.
4. Gerald L. Gutek, "Education and Reform at Robert Owen's New Lanark," *Journal of the Midwest History of Education Society* 17 (1989), 164–71.
5. Margaret Cole, "Robert Owen Until New Lanark," in *Robert Owen: Industrialist, Reformer, Visionary, 1771–1858* (London: Robert Owen Bicentenary Association, 1971), 4–14.
6. Robert Owen, *Life*, 34–38.
7. Harold Silver, "Owen's Reputation As an Educationist," in *Robert Owen: Prophet of the Poor,*

ed. Sidney Pollard and John Salt (Lewisburg, PA: Bucknell University Press, 1971), 65.
8. Robert Owen, *A Supplementary Appendix to the First Volume of the Life of Robert Owen* (London: Effingham Wilson, 1858; reprint, New York: Augustus M. Kelley, 1967). See Appendix I, "Report to the Committee of the Association for the Relief of the Manufacturing and Labouring Poor, 1817," 53–54; and Appendix S, "Report to the County of Lanark, 1820," 263–320.
9. The definitive treatment of Owenism as a transatlantic movement is John F. C. Harrison, *Quest for the New Moral World: Robert Owen and the Owenites in Britain and America* (New York: Scribner's, 1969).
10. Gerald L. Gutek, "New Harmony: An Example of Communitarian Education," *Educational Theory* 22 (winter 1972), 34–36.
11. Robert Owen, "The New Social System," *The New Harmony Gazette* 2 (January 10, 1827), 113.

12. Arthur E. Bestor, Jr., *Backwoods Utopias: The Sectarian and Owenite Phases of Communitarian Socialism in America, 1663–1829* (Philadelphia: University of Pennsylvania Press, 1950), 134–35.

13. George B. Lockwood, *The New Harmony Movement* (New York: D. Appleton, 1905), 84.

14. Lockwood, *The New Harmony Movement*, 105–6.

15. Lockwood, *The New Harmony Movement*, 107–8.

16. Robert Owen, "The New Social System," 113.

17. Robert Owen, "The New Social System," 113.

18. Harrison, *Quest for the New Moral World*, 81.

19. Harrison, *Quest for the New Moral World*, 79.

20. Robert Dale Owen, *An Outline of the System of Education at New Lanark* (Cincinnati: Deming & Wood, 1825), 11.

21. Robert Dale Owen, *Outline of the System of Education*, 13.

22. Robert Dale Owen, *Outline of the System of Education*, 12–13.

23. Robert Dale Owen, *Outline of the System of Education*, 13.

24. Frank Podmore, *Robert Owen* (London: Hutchinson, 1906), 136–37.

25. Robert Owen, *Life*, 140.

26. Robert Dale Owen, *Outline of the System of Education*, 14.

27. Robert Dale Owen, *Outline of the System of Education*, 16.

28. Robert Dale Owen, *Outline of the System of Education*, 17.

29. Robert Dale Owen, *Outline of the System of Education*, 25–26.

30. Robert Owen, *Life*, 140–41.

31. Paul K. Bernard, "Irreconcilable Opinions: The Social and Educational Theories of Robert Owen and William Maclure," *Journal of the Early Republic* 8 (Spring 1988), 21–44.

Suggestions for Further Reading

Bestor, Arthur E., Jr. *Backwoods Utopias: The Sectarian and Owenite Phases of Communitarian Socialism in America, 1663–1829*. Philadelphia: University of Pennsylvania Press, 1950.

Boulding, Elise. *Building a Global Civic Culture: Education for an Interdependent World*. New York: Teachers College Press, 1988.

Butt, John, ed. *Robert Owen: Aspects of His Life and Work*. New York: Humanities Press, 1971.

Elliott, Josephine M., ed. *Partnership for Posterity: The Correspondence of William Maclure and Marie Duclos Fretageot, 1820–1833*. Indianapolis: Indiana Historical Society, 1994.

Francis, Richard. *Transcendental Utopias: Individual and Community at Brook Farm, Fruitlands, and Walden*. Ithaca, NY: Cornell University Press, 1997.

Harrison, John F. C. *Quest for the New Moral World: Robert Owen and the Owenites in Britain and America*. New York: Scribner's, 1969.

———. *Utopianism and Education: Robert Owen and the Owenites*. New York: Teachers College Press, 1968.

Kolmerten, Carol A. *Women in Utopias: The Ideology of Gender in the American Owenite Communities*. Bloomington, IN: Indiana University Press, 1990.

Lockwood, George B. *The New Harmony Movement*. New York: D. Appleton, 1905.

Owen, Robert. *Selected Works of Robert Owen. Volume 1, Early Writings*. Gregory Claeys, ed. London: W. Pickering, 1993.

———. *Selected Works of Robert Owen. Volume 2, The Development of Socialism*. Gregory Claeys, ed. London: W. Pickering, 1993.

———. *Selected Works of Robert Owen. Volume 3, The Book of the New Moral World*. Gregory Claeys, ed. London: W. Pickering, 1993.

———. *Selected Works of Robert Owen. Volume 4, The Life of Robert Owen*. Gregory Claeys, ed. London: W. Pickering, 1993.

Owen, Robert Dale. *An Outline of the System of Education at New Lanark*. Cincinnati: Deming & Wood, 1825.

———. *Threading My Way: Twenty-seven Years of Autobiography*. New York: G. W. Carleton, 1874. Reprint, New York: Augustus M. Kelley, 1967.

Pitzer, Donald E. *Robert Owen's American Legacy*. Indianapolis: Indiana State Historical Society, 1972.

Podmore, Frank. *Robert Owen: A Biography*. London: Hutchinson, 1906. Reprint, New York: Augustus M. Kelley, 1968.

Pollard, Sidney, and Salt, John, eds. *Robert Owen: Prophet of the Poor*. Lewisburg, PA: Bucknell University Press, 1971.

Silver, Harold, ed. *Robert Owen on Education*. Cambridge, UK: Cambridge University Press, 1969.

Sutton, Robert P. *Les Icariens: The Utopian Dream in Europe and America*. Urbana, IL: University of Illinois Press, 1994.

Tsuzuki, Chushichi. *Robert Owen and the World of Co-operation*. Tokyo: The Association, 1992.

CHAPTER 16

Friedrich Froebel: Founder of the Kindergarten

In this chapter we discuss the life, educational philosophy, and contributions of Friedrich Froebel (1782–1852), a German educator whose pioneering efforts in early childhood education led him to establish the kindergarten. Froebel's innovative experiments in educating young children, conducted originally in Germany, contributed to an enlightened concept of childhood and had a worldwide influence on early childhood education.

In this chapter, we discuss Froebel's role in reshaping early childhood education in its historical context and in terms of its enduring effect on educational philosophy and policy. First, we describe the general social, political, religious, and intellectual context in which Froebel lived and worked. Second, we analyze Froebel's biography, his education and career, to identify the events that shaped his ideas. Third, we examine the continuing effect of Froebel's contributions on early childhood education. By this analysis, we shall see how the events of nineteenth-century Germany worked to shape both Froebel as a person and his philosophy as an educator. For example, philosophical idealism, the dominant philosophy in nineteenth-century Germany, had a pronounced influence on how Froebel viewed human growth and development.

To organize your thoughts as you read this chapter, focus on the following questions:

1. What were the major trends in the historical context of nineteenth-century Germany, in which Froebel lived?

2. How did Froebel's educational biography shape his philosophy of education?
3. How did Froebel's educational philosophy determine his educational policies and practices?
4. What is the enduring impact of Froebel's contributions to education?

The Historical Context of Froebel's Life

Friedrich Froebel, a complex and eccentric personality, was born in 1782 in the small town of Oberweissbach in the German state of Thuringia. The political weakness and disunity of the various German states had an impact on Froebel as well as on many young people who believed Germans should be united in one nation. The year of Froebel's birth saw Germans living in 300 separate sovereign states or principalities. Although by 1806 the number of German states had been reduced to 100, Germans were still disunited politically. Although Froebel was an educational rather than a political theorist, his philosophy of education, stressing themes of interrelationship and interconnection, reflected his wish for German unification. Other German politicians and philosophers would echo the theme of Germanic unity and the encompassing role of the nation-state in a more nationalistic manner than Froebel, but nonetheless the spirit of German nationalism was present in his philosophy.

From 1800 to 1815, Napoleon, the forceful emperor of France, dominated Europe. Until his defeat in Russia in 1812, Napoleon, a consummate military strategist, led the French armies in vanquishing Europe's great powers on the battlefield. In 1806, Napoleon defeated Prussia and its kindred German allies. Froebel, then age 24, served with the German army that was soundly defeated at the battles of Jena and Auerstadt. Since the days of Frederick the Great, the Prussians had taken pride in their army. Now, defeated by their ancient French adversary, the humbled Prussian King Frederick Wilhelm had to watch Bonaparte's triumphal entry into Berlin, his capital. Prussians had a feeling of inferiority and a desire for revenge. Throughout Prussia and the German states allied with it, there was a sense of need to rebuild not only the army but the morale of the German people.

After the 1806 defeat, the Prussians set to work rebuilding their military forces and recouping their fortunes. The major leader of the effort to regenerate Prussia was Heinrich Friedrich Karl von Stein (1757–1831). Von Stein embarked on a defensive reform program designed to strengthen the basically conservative and autocratic Prussian state, seeking to instill in the Prussian people the will to resist the French by fostering community spirit and commitment to the nation. He streamlined the Prussian administrative and military systems to make them more efficient.[1] Led by the patriotic Baron von Stein and Chancellor Karl August Hardenberg, the Prussians prepared themselves for revenge on Napoleon. Weakened by his Russian disaster in 1812, Napoleon's army was defeated by the combined forces of England, Austria, Russia, and Prussia in the four-day "Battle of Nations" at Leipzig, October 16–19, 1813. For Prussia and its other German states allies, this was a war of liberation. After Napoleon's final defeat at Waterloo, Prussia emerged as the most powerful German state. These military events shaped the context in which Froebel developed his educational ideas.

The years after Napoleon's defeat and exile to St. Helena saw the restoration of monarchies and the assertion of conservative political ideologies in Europe. Conservative forces, led by the Austrian foreign minister Klemens von Metternich, suppressed liberal intellectual and educational ideas. For example, in the German states, the fraternities that students had organized in the universities to promote German liberalism and nationalism were suppressed. The Carlsbad decrees of 1819 banned liberal-minded professors from teaching in universities as well.

By 1848, the suppression of nationalism and liberalism by European conservative governments was challenged dramatically by a series of popular revolutions in France, Austria, Hungary, Italy, Prussia, and several of the smaller German states. In March 1848, liberals and nationalists in Prussia and other German states took to the streets in demonstrations for reform. The Prussian king Frederick Wilhelm IV responded by abolishing censorship and summoning a constituent assembly. Simultaneously, liberal leaders called an assembly at Frankfurt to prepare a constitution for a united and federated German nation. However, internal disagreements about the form of government for the proposed German confederation deadlocked the Frankfurt assembly. Regaining their strength, the conservative forces in the Prussian government rallied and the liberal assembly was disbanded without accomplishing its goal. It was not until January 18, 1871, that a united German empire would be proclaimed in the Hall of Mirrors at Versailles as a consequence of the victory over France in the Franco-Prussian War.

Froebel's life coincided with a period of rich intellectual development in Germany. Among those who contributed to this flowering of German intellectualism was Johann Gottfried Herder (1744–1803). Herder's multivolume *Ideas on the Philosophy of History of Humanity* combined biological, ethnographical, and literary insights into a philosophical treatise. His broad view of history and philosophy contributed to philosophical idealism and to the sense of nationalism. Johann Wolfgang von Goethe (1749–1832) was also among the major contributors to early nineteenth-century German intellectual life. The renowned author of *Faust* and *Werther,* Goethe wrote on such sciences as anatomy, mineralogy, meteorology, botany, and zoology. Still another intellectual of the period was the scientist and educator Wilhelm von Humboldt (1767–1835). A pioneering anthropologist and linguist, von Humboldt studied the languages of aboriginal groups such as Native Americans and classical languages such as the Sanskrit of the ancient Indians of Vedic times.[2]

Philosophy in the Western world as well as in Germany was being recast in an idealist framework by the intellectual giant Immanuel Kant (1724–1804), a professor at the University of Königsberg. Kant's *Critique of Pure Reason* (1781) challenged Locke's empiricist view that ideas originated with sensation. In contrast, Kant argued that the mind possesses categories such as space and time that are *a priori* "modes of perception" or mental structures by which we organize our experience in the real world.[3] According to Kant, these necessary mental structures, existing in the mind prior to sensation, make experience coherent and intelligible. Kant argued that universal moral laws exist that are independent of changing times and circumstances.[4]

Other philosophers who promoted idealism in Germany were Johann Gottlieb Fichte (1762–1814) and Georg Wilhelm Hegel (1770–1831). Like Plato in ancient Greece, these idealists saw reality in nonmaterialist terms. For them, reality was the unfolding of the absolute idea, the perfect all-encompassing form of the good on Earth. Fichte, a university professor and rector of the University of Berlin, in a series of lectures to the German people urged the regeneration of German culture through a revitalized form of education.

Intellectual life in early nineteenth-century Germany was especially dominated by Hegel, a professor at the University of Berlin and author of many tomes extolling idealism.[5] Like Fichte, Hegel stressed the power of ideas and the mind. The great spiritual force, which is the origin and the culmination of the universe, functions in the individual human mind and is manifested in human cultural and social institutions such as law, education, and art. The highest embodiment of the absolute on Earth was the state, which encompassed all other institutions.

For Hegel, the nature of thought and history occurred through the dialectical process. Thought in the mind of God—the absolute idea—and in the human mind begins with an idea, which is a thesis, and continues with its opposite, an antithesis. The mind then recognizes the positive or related elements in both the thesis and the antithesis and combines them in a synthesis. The synthesis, in turn, is a new idea that contains its antithesis and thus the process is ongoing. Through the dialectical process, ideas are ever expanding and related to each other in an evolving sense of intellectual wholeness or completeness. The result is that all ideas, through this dialectical process, lead to and are derived from the all-encompassing idea. Hegel believed the absolute mind, God's mind, functioned dialectically. Because the absolute mind contains and encompasses all ideas, history was the unfolding of God's mind to human beings over time.

As described by Hegel, the dialectical process held great appeal for many of nineteenth-century Germany's intellectuals. In his own way, Froebel incorporated the dialectic in his theory of human growth. Karl Marx would recast Hegel's nonmaterialist propositions into dialectical materialism. The regnant idealist philosophy produced an intellectual climate of opinion that shaped Froebel's ideas on education.

In addition to the idealist philosophical milieu in Germany, Froebel's formative years, especially as a university student, coincided with new scientific discoveries and theories. Influenced by the idealist frame of reference, the German scientific perspective saw all living things interrelated by a great chain of being rising from lower to higher forms of life. The biologists of the day were laboring to identify the essential structures of plants and animals so they could classify them in such a comprehensive ordering. While seeking an encyclopedic schema of classification, many scientists believed that every living thing developed according to an archetypal plan common to members of that particular genus or species. Operating in a pre-Darwinian mode, they did not see the species undergoing evolutionary change. Rather, creatures had been created by God to fill an assigned rung on a complex hierarchical ladder of being.

Just as Froebel was influenced by philosophical idealism, so were his ideas shaped by the dominant trends in science. When he developed his educational theory, Froebel continually referred to doctrines of interconnectedness in which all creatures and all ideas were part of a grand, ordered, and systematic universe. Such a universal design had no room for change or accident. Everything had a place and everything was to be in its place.

Froebel's philosophy of early childhood education was filled with religious language, symbolism, and meaning. The son of a Lutheran clergyman, he was born into and came to maturity in an environment permeated by Lutheran Christianity.

In the late eighteenth and early nineteenth centuries, Lutheranism was experiencing some religious tensions. Most Lutheran synods and congregations, following the

creed established by Martin Luther in the Protestant Reformation, adhered to orthodox theology and practices. There were those who felt a need, however, for a more
personal and mystical mode of religious experience than that offered by the official
Lutheran establishment. Froebel and others seeking a more personal religious experience found it in the theology of Jacob Böhme (1575–1624), a seventeenth-century
Silesian mystic. Böhme, who claimed to have experienced a mystical state, criticized
the formalism of the Lutheran church. Among Böhme's writings were *Aurora, or The
Dawn* (1612), *The Three Principles of Divine Being* (1619), and *The Signature of All Things*
(1622). His stress on personal religious experience influenced both pietism in religion
and romanticism in literature and philosophy. Froebel's kindergarten used a great deal
of semireligious symbolism. It is believed his tendency to express himself through symbolic language and metaphors was influenced by Böhme. The emphasis on a more per-
sonalized and pietistical form of religious experience had an effect in Germany where
new sects such as the True Inspirationists emerged, and in Sweden where Erik Jansson
led dissenters who departed from official Lutheranism's orthodoxy.

It was this combination of political, philosophical, scientific, and religious events
and movements that formed the historical context in which Froebel lived and that influenced his formulation of a philosophy of early childhood education.

Friedrich Froebel: Pioneer Early Childhood Educator

In this section, we turn to Froebel's life and career.[6] Young Froebel, christened Friedrich
Wilhelm August, was born on April 21, 1782. He was the youngest of five sons of
Johann Jacob Froebel, the Lutheran pastor of the church at Oberweissbach.[7] The vil-
lage was located in the Thuringian forests of the small principality of Schwarzburg-
Rudolfstadt, one of the many independent states that were part of a fragmented
Germany in the early nineteenth century. Today, the village lies about 100 miles south-
west of Leipzig.

Froebel's mother died when he was 9 months old. When he was 4 years old, his father remarried. Froebel disliked his stepmother, whom he believed neglected him to devote her affection to her own child. This feeling of rejection was so intense that as an
adult he still complained, "Love was not only withdrawn entirely from me and transferred to her own child, but I was treated with worse than indifference . . . by word and
deed, I was made to feel an utter stranger." Froebel felt increasingly alienated from his
father, whom he recalled considered him to be "stupid, mischievous, and untrustwor-
thy."[8] Lonely, rejected, and isolated as a child, Froebel's feeling of low self-esteem stayed
with him throughout his life.

Froebel's memories of an unhappy early childhood had a pronounced effect on the
theory of kindergarten education that he developed later in his life. It is interesting to
note that Froebel, like Rousseau, lost his mother to death when he was so young that
he could not have had a clear memory of her. He also had a stepmother whom he disliked intensely. When he developed his theory of early childhood education, he, like
Pestalozzi, created a version of the teacher who was a loving, kindly, and gentle moth-
erlike figure. His concept of the kindergarten teacher undoubtedly came from his idealized affection for his own lost mother (see Chapters 10 and 11).

During his own childhood, Froebel had an uneasy and unsatisfying relationship with his father. He was not a particularly attractive child physically and his social relationships with children other than his siblings were rare. These negative experiences caused him to be shy, introspective, and socially inept. When he created his kindergarten, he wanted his school to foster a sense of emotional security and self-esteem in children.

As a young child, Froebel was fascinated with the woodlands, plants, and animals near his home. He found a particular pleasure in gardening. The images of blooming flowers in his own small garden abound in the prose he used to express his educational philosophy.

Young Friedrich Froebel's first educational experience was in Oberweissbach's primary school for girls. His father regarded the village boys as ruffians and determined that Friedrich, whom he apparently regarded as a slow child, should be sent to the more protected environment of the girls' school. This school followed the conventional curriculum of Bible study, catechism, reading, writing, and arithmetic. With the exception of arithmetic, his favorite subject, Friedrich had difficulty in school. Attendance at his father's church also affected him; he found solace in the hymns, an important feature in the Lutheran religious service.

When Froebel was 10 years old, his maternal uncle, Herr Hoffman, decided to intervene in his nephew's unhappy situation. Hoffman invited the youngster to stay with him at Stadt-Ulm, where he was a Lutheran archdeacon. Stadt-Ulm was about 20 miles from Froebel's family home at Oberweissbach. Froebel's father agreed and Friedrich spent his next five years at his uncle's home. Froebel described his uncle as a "loving father" who was "mild, gentle, and kind-hearted."[9] Friedrich made a good adjustment to Stadt-Ulm's town school, where he studied reading, writing, arithmetic, religion, Latin, and geography, and began to make his first friendships with other children.

Froebel's next educational experience came as an apprentice to a forester and surveyor in the town of Neuhaus. Froebel's apprenticeship, which began when he was 15, lasted two years. This experience was disappointing to him. He believed that the forester, though expert in his field, had difficulty in teaching him the necessary information and practical skills.[10] During this time, the adolescent Froebel read widely in the areas of forestry, geometry, and botany. Spending his free time taking long walks in the Thuringian forests, the highly introspective youth developed a deep reverence for nature.[11] His outlook grew more and more mystical. Common objects, especially plants, took on a double meaning—one of their outward physical appearance and another symbolic of their underlying spiritual reality.

At 17, Froebel was admitted to the University of Jena. Here, his academic interests expanded as he attended lectures in mathematics, geometry, natural history, mineralogy, physics, chemistry, forestry, architecture, surveying, drawing, botany, and other subjects. In his studies, Froebel enjoyed geometry and proved skilled in drawing geometrical forms. His adeptness in the use of forms would shape his later development of the kindergarten gifts (discussed later in this chapter). Courses in such natural sciences as mineralogy, biology, and botany, which emphasized classification of plants and animals into a great chain of creation, also intrigued him.[12] Searching for the universal key to knowledge, he wanted to discover the interconnecting relationships of the various subjects he studied. Either because of his own inability to integrate a variety of subjects or because of the disconnected teaching that he encountered, his goal eluded him. He was a student at Jena for two years, ending his study at age 19.[13]

Froebel, never comfortable with his father, experienced more difficulties with him. Because of a loan he made to his brother, Friedrich could not pay his own tuition bills and was confined to the university's debtor's prison. Agreeing to pay his bills, Froebel's father secured his release but only with the condition that Friedrich officially renounce any future claims to an inheritance from the family estate. Froebel signed the document of agreement. His father died the next year, in 1802, and Friedrich never again set foot in his family home.

After ending his university studies at Jena without completing a degree, Froebel tried to find a suitable career. For a time he worked in the Office of Woods and Forests, then was a secretary to an estate owner, but his work at these positions was unsatisfactory to both Froebel and his employers.

In 1805, Froebel received an inheritance from his Uncle Hoffman that enabled him to go to Frankfurt to study architecture. Although he pursued architecture for only a brief period, he developed a sense of perspective and proportion that he later transferred to his design of the kindergarten's gifts and occupations. In his kindergarten, Froebel saw children working, like little architects, with building materials to design and construct their own structures. Following his philosophical idealism, he developed the principle that children in their activities should always integrate existing structures into new ones in a synthetic whole.

While in Frankfurt, Froebel met Anton Gruener, the headmaster of the Frankfurt Model School, a Pestalozzian school. Gruener, who sensed that Froebel would make a good teacher, hired him as a teacher in the school.

To prepare him as a teacher, Gruener arranged for Froebel, now 24, to spend two weeks at Johann Henrich Pestalozzi's educational institution at Yverdon. Pestalozzi's method of instruction emphasized the use of objects. Rejecting the corporal punishment and psychological coercion used in traditional classroom management, Pestalozzi argued that cognitive learning was most effective in schools where children were emotionally secure (for Pestalozzi's educational method, see Chapter 11).

Froebel was impressed with Pestalozzi. He believed Pestalozzi's respect for the dignity of children and creation of a learning environment of love and emotional security were valuable educational elements that he wanted to incorporate in his own teaching. Although Froebel saw the value of using objects in instruction, he believed the Pestalozzian object lesson was too empirical and needed a more philosophical foundation. Froebel would recast Pestalozzi's object lesson into a more symbolic version that gave objects double meanings. Using his philosophical idealism, Froebel devised object lessons in which objects had both the meaning of everyday experience as well the more symbolic significance of the spiritual sphere.

After his work with Pestalozzi, Froebel returned to Frankfurt and assumed his position as a teacher at the Model School, where he taught a class of 40 boys, ranging in age from 9 to 11.[14] Froebel at last had found his true vocation. Teaching gave him a sense of personal meaning and fulfillment. He taught at the Model School for three years. In 1808, he resigned his position to return to Yverdon for two years of study with Pestalozzi. He learned much from the master Swiss educator but also identified areas that he wanted to improve upon. Convinced that play was a crucial activity in child development, he began to study and search for the meaning of play. Play would become an important foundation in kindergarten education. Froebel also became intrigued with studying how children developed their use of language. To find answers to these questions, Froebel was convinced that he needed further study.

In 1810, Froebel returned to Germany where for two years he attended the University of Gottingen, studying Persian, Hebrew, Arabic, and Greek. Again his idealism convinced him that the various human languages were somehow related and interconnected. If he could find how these various languages were connected to each other by their structure, he believed he could apply his finding to language development and teaching. Along with his language studies, Froebel attended lectures in physics, chemistry, mineralogy, geology, history, and economics. He was especially drawn to geology and mineralogy, which in the early nineteenth century attracted the serious attention of both academic and amateur scientists. Like his previous university experience, Froebel was a wide-ranging rather than an in-depth student.

Froebel's studies were interrupted in 1812, when he enlisted in the Lutzow Jagers, an infantry division that fought with the German forces against Napoleon's invading French army. Froebel's military service brought him into contact with other young men who shared an interest in education. For example, he became friends with Wilhelm Middendorf and Heinrich Langethal, two soldiers who would later work with him in the kindergarten.[15]

From 1812 to 1816, Froebel served as assistant to Professor Christian Samuel Weiss (1780–1856), director of the University of Berlin's mineralogical museum. Recognized as an expert in physics and quantitative mineral analysis, Weiss held the university's chair of mineralogy. While Froebel was his assistant, Weiss was engaged in establishing the scientific foundations and techniques of crystallography.[16] Crystals, Weiss concluded, resulted from the uniform arrangement of minuscule particles into three-dimensional grids. Weiss believed that crystallization, in which crystals developed from very simple forms into highly complex structures, was the key to understanding the process of natural growth. Froebel, who enjoyed studying and drawing geometrical forms, was fascinated by the many shapes of crystals as combinations of squares, cubes, triangles, and tetrahedrons.[17] Froebel, already steeped in philosophical idealism and religious symbolism, believed crystallization manifested God's geometrical handiwork and revealed the divine universal laws governing human growth and development. The universal process, Froebel now believed, followed a pattern that moved from simple to complex. Although Pestalozzi, too, had stressed movement from simple to complex in his teaching method, Froebel believed the process of ever-increasing complexity was a cosmic law that encompassed all existence. Froebel's attraction to crystallization fitted nicely with his philosophical idealism in which ideas, as Hegel wrote, were embedded in an unfolding and ever-enlarging universal synthesis. Later in his career, Froebel, using the forms of crystals, created his kindergarten gifts, which in wood and cardboard expressed the divine geometric forms that children could touch and manipulate.

In 1816, ready to implement his ideas, Froebel established a school at Griesheim, a small town near Darmstadt, which he called the Universal German Educational Institute. The next year he moved the school to Keilhau. His school, which enrolled students aged 7 or older, was not yet a kindergarten. The school struggled with enrollments. At its peak, it enrolled 60 students. With only 5 students enrolled in 1829, Froebel was forced to close the school. Froebel's former army comrades Middendorf and Langethal taught at the school. During the 13 years that the institute functioned, Froebel was able to test some of his educational ideas and develop new insights into child nature and the learning process.

Froebel wrote about his educational ideas and work in *Principles, Aims, and Inner Life of the Universal German Educational Institute in Keilhau* (1826). Foremost among his principles was that each child should be respected as an individual and be educated according to his or her own needs and interests. At the same time that children's individual differences were recognized, Froebel believed that general, universal laws governed their growth and development. He sought to develop a method of instruction that encompassed both the universal laws of child development and ways in which each child could express herself or himself creatively according to individual needs. Froebel and his staff maintained an individualized lesson plan for each child that identified needs and indicated achievement.

Though his first effort to operate his own school succeeded educationally, Froebel had serious difficulties as an administrator in terms of funding and public relations, and proved inept as a manager. Throughout its 13-year history, the institute was frequently on the edge of bankruptcy. Although Froebel's educational philosophy rested on a spiritual frame of reference, he was accused of deviating from orthodox Lutheran doctrine. This religious issue generated some hostility in the community.

Despite opposition from her father, an official in the Prussian War Ministry, Froebel in 1818 married Henrietta Wilhelmine Hoffmeister (1780–1839), a young lady he had met in Berlin. Henrietta, a well-educated woman who had studied with the idealist philosopher Fichte, shared her husband's love of children and of nature. She assisted him in his educational work until her death.[18]

In 1831, Froebel was ready to leave his faltering institute at Keilhau. He accepted the Swiss composer Xavier Schnyder's invitation to establish an educational institute at his castle at Wartensee on Lake Sempach in the Lucerne Canton. Schnyder, who had taught music at Pestalozzi's institute at Yverdon, had an interest in education. With approval from the Swiss Ministry of Education, Froebel opened his school in Schnyder's castle. Some 30 students enrolled in his school, which offered lessons in arithmetic, languages, history, and gymnastics. The castle's physical environment was not satisfactory for a school, and Froebel moved the school to Willisau. Here, the school prospered, and Froebel gained a reputation as a capable educator.

Froebel next accepted an invitation to establish an orphanage at Burgdorf, a town where Pestalozzi had once operated an educational institute. At Burgdorf, Froebel became involved in several educational endeavors. He conducted a school for the town children and a boarding school for those who lived a distance from the town. He began to train teachers. Significantly for his later career, Froebel, growing increasingly committed to early childhood education, established a nursery school for 3- and 4-year-old children. He wrote rhymes and songs and devised physical exercises, activities, and games for use in the nursery school. He began experimenting with the objects and other materials that would become his kindergarten gifts. True to his emphasis on play, he stressed play's educative role in the school.[19] When his wife became seriously ill, Froebel returned to Germany in 1836. In 1837 the couple located in the town of Blankenburg, location of a spa, where Henrietta was to recuperate. Her health instead deteriorated and she died in 1838.

At Blankenburg, Froebel in 1837 opened an institute for the early education of children. In 1840, the institute was renamed the Universal German Kindergarten. The kindergarten provided a milieu in which children could develop freely and naturally. Children's play was emphasized as a natural activity in which they acted out their interests and satisfied their needs. Here Froebel designed his unique kindergarten materials of gifts and occupations. *Gifts* were objects Froebel believed had a special symbolic potential. *Occupations* were the raw materials children could use in drawing and building activities that allowed them to concretize their ideas. Importantly, songs, stories, and games would introduce children to their culture and socialize them. The institute prospered and Froebel's fame spread. By 1848, 44 kindergartens were functioning in the German states. He began to train a number of young women as kindergarten teachers. Froebel's book, *Mother-Play and Nursery Songs*, which appeared in 1844, had a favorable reception. He founded his *Weekly Journal of Education* in 1850 and the *Journal for Friedrich Froebel's Educational Aims* in 1851.[20] In 1851, Froebel married Luise Leven, a protege. Among his dedicated followers was Baroness Bertha von Marenholtz-Bulow, who worked to gain support for Froebel's educational work.

In August 1851, a strange controversy developed surrounding the kindergarten in Prussia. Karl von Raumer, the Prussian minister of education, accused kindergartens of undermining traditional Prussian values by spreading atheism and socialism. Based on unfounded information, von Raumer had attributed a revolutionary tract to Friedrich Froebel. The pamphlet's author, however, was Karl Froebel, Friedrich's nephew. Although Friedrich Froebel denied the charges, von Raumer, who refused to acknowledge his error, banned kindergartens in Prussia. In the midst of the controversy, Froebel died on June 21, 1852. Although kindergartens existed in the other German states, they were not permitted in Prussia until 1860. By the end of the nineteenth century, Froebelian kindergartens existed throughout Europe, North America, and even in Japan.

Froebel's Kindergarten Philosophy

In this section, we shall examine Froebel's kindergarten philosophy, which was most fully expressed his *The Education of Man* (1826).[21] Written in Froebel's obscure prose, he attempted to weave often diverse strands of philosophical idealism, Christian mysticism, romanticism, and science into a coherent educational philosophy.

Froebel began his philosophical commentary by asserting that all existence, including human existence, originates in and with God. His conception of God combined the traditional Lutheran theology of a personal creator with the Hegelian view of the all-encompassing absolute idea. All creatures great and small have the same spiritual source. Human beings are endowed by their creator with a divine or spiritual essence and, at the same time, have a body that makes them part of the natural and physical order. Thus, Froebel saw human beings as composed of both a spiritual and a physical dimension. It is the spiritual essence, however, that by vitalizing and motivating humans leads to their development. In terms of children's nature, Froebel asserts that each child at birth has within her or him a spiritual essence, a life force, that seeks to be externalized. Through the child's own activity, the inner spiritual essence is externalized. The kindergarten's gifts, occupations, and activities, especially play, are designed to ensure that children's development follows the correct pathway, which is both God's and nature's plan. Human destiny, said Froebel, is to become conscious of this spiritual essence and to reveal it by externalizing it. In this process of leading the spiritual essence outward, the human being is really growing nearer to God.

Following the idealism that dominated German intellectual thought in the early nineteenth century, Froebel construed ultimate reality to be spiritual rather than physical. All that existed was based on an ideational prototype that existed as a concept in the divine mind, in the absolute. According to this metaphysical view, all ideas were related to and interconnected with each other and culminated in the great all-encompassing idea that was God. All existence was united and related in a great chain of being, a universal unity. Although nature appeared to exhibit diversity and individualization, it was in reality one great coherent spiritual unity. In children's education, the principle of interconnectedness was to be observed. Nothing should remain in isolation. In the kindergarten, children were to learn that they were members of a great, universal, spiritual community. Froebel saw no conflict between the individual and group or between individual needs and differences and a universal theory of human development. Each individual child was active and autonomous but also associated spiritually with every other person and thing.

For Froebel, children's growth and development was essentially based on the doctrine of preformation, the unfolding of what is present latently. All the child would become as a man or woman was already present at birth. Using an analogy from the plant world, Froebel reasoned that as a seed contains the roots, stalk, leaves, and blossoms of the mature plant, so does the human embryo possess all that the adult will become. Just as the seed requires a garden with proper soil, moisture, light, and nutrients to grow in the right direction, the child needs a special educative environment for growth—the kindergarten. Just as the plant needs the cultivation of a gardener, children need the care of a loving and kindly teacher.

Like Pestalozzi, Froebel used the concept of an idealized loving mother as his ideal kindergarten teacher. The kindergarten teacher was to be an agent who cooperated with God and nature in facilitating children's growth and development. Teaching was similar to a religious vocation. To prepare for this vocation, kindergarten teachers were to engage in introspective reflection on their own childhood experiences. By this self-analysis, they were to rediscover the hidden clues about childhood that were locked in their memories. Froebel, who often reflected on his unhappy and melancholy childhood, found in his memories ways to make the early experiences of other children happier than his own.

Kindergarten teachers were also to be observers of child life, games, play, and activities. Through such observations, they could identify patterns in children's behavior and use them to structure learning activities. Froebel strongly advised teachers to have a strong philosophical foundation for their instruction. True to idealism, the activities of teaching and learning were not separate and disconnected episodes, but part of a whole that reflected the divine plan.

With a philosophy and attitude conducive to working with children, teachers could proceed to implement the kindergarten's distinctive educational features. As they prepared the kindergarten as a special environment for children's growth and development, teachers had to pay special attention to the elements of space and time. *Space* referred to the kindergarten's physical setting and layout; *time* referred to the sequencing of activities children would experience.

In structuring the kindergarten, Froebel was convinced that its primary focus should be directed toward play. In terms of his idealist symbolism, play was the means that stimulated children to express their innermost thoughts, needs, and desires in external actions. Froebel's exaltation of the role of play was a strikingly different from that of many conventional educators up to the nineteenth century. With the exception of Comenius and Pestalozzi, play was regarded as an unworthy element of human life. In the strictly interpreted Calvinist theology, play, a form of idleness, contributed to social disorder and moral laxity. For Froebel, however, play was a natural part of living. Its nonserious mode permitted children to act on their thoughts without the consequences that work entailed. Froebel should be recognized as one of the pioneers in legitimizing the concept of play in Western educational history.[22]

In Froebelian terms, the concept of play can be analyzed further as a means of cultural recapitulation, imitation of adult vocational activities, and socialization. Froebel believed the human race could be viewed both in its racial, ethnic, and linguistic diversity and as a unity. He believed the human race, in its collective history, had experienced major periods of cultural development. For example, humans had once lived in caves, then in tents or other temporary dwellings as nomadic hunters, then in permanent houses as an agricultural people, and so on. During each of these major epochs, humans added to and refined their culture, moving generally from the simple to the complex. In Froebel's theory of cultural recapitulation, each individual human being repeated the general cultural epoch in his or her own growth and development. Although the human race had taken centuries to go through these cultural epochs, the individual did so in a time span of a few years.

In the kindergarten, children's play provided the means of living through and experiencing cultural recapitulation. For example, children enjoy drawing and often draw pictures on walls. Their drawings are simple and primitive and resemble those of ancient cave dwellers. Thus, in Froebelian terms, children are living through a particular cultural epoch of the human race. Children like to play hunting and gathering games; in this activity, they too are repeating a particular cultural epoch. The recapitulation process was aided in the kindergarten by the introduction of certain songs and stories with cultural significance.

In play, children imitate adult society, particularly its social and economic activities. Froebel encouraged children to act out in play such activities as cleaning rooms, serving food, and gardening. These and other activities were a means of expressing their perceptions of adult vocations.

The process of playing at adult vocations took on a highly symbolic religious and philosophical aspect in Froebel's kindergarten. In Lutheran theology and religious practice, the practice of vocations was a form of human industriousness that had been ordained by God. Martin Luther, for example, had admonished parents to make certain that their children learned useful vocations. As an idealist educator, Froebel believed that human vocations represented the thoughts of God on earth. Just as God's thoughts had taken on physical shape and substance in the sensory world, so should human beings give expression to their ideas by transforming thought and raw materials into finished products.

By connecting play with vocations, one can observe the complexity of Froebel's philosophy of early childhood education. If one considers the human vocation of agriculture as an example, it can be recognized as one of humanity's major economic occupations. Children enjoy planting seeds in their gardens and observing the phenomenon of the seeds sprouting, growing, and developing as plants. The raw materials of seeds, soil, water, and fertilizer culminate in products: flowers, vegetables, or fruit. At the same time these obvious physical happenings are transpiring in the garden and are perceived by the children's senses, Froebel construed that other events are occurring in their spiritual world. The children are recapitulating a major epoch of human culture and are acting out their internal impressions of a most significant adult activity. To give gardening a greater cultural significance, the teacher introduces songs and stories that relate to planting and harvesting.

Play also was the means for children's socialization. Through the kindergarten's activities, each individual child was led into the larger world of group life. Froebel regarded his own childhood as a time of isolation, rejection, and loneliness. His kindergarten was designed to encourage children to play and interact with each other under the guidance of a loving teacher. Again, socialization as a part of play had a broader symbolic meaning for Froebel. In his idealist view, the world and its beings were members of an all-encompassing spiritual community that came from the mind of God, the absolute, and sought to return and be reunited with their divine source. Children were born and nurtured in their immediate families. These families were part of a larger village or town community. The town in turn was part of a national community. The next stage in human history would be an international or world community. Although such a worldwide ecumenical vision was broad and grandiose, its beginnings could be found in the kindergarten.

The Kindergarten Curriculum: Gifts and Occupations

A unique feature of Froebel's kindergarten curriculum was the series of gifts and occupations he developed as teaching and learning materials. The *gifts* were objects that represented what Froebel defined as *fundamental forms*. Recall that Pestalozzi had developed an object lesson based on form, number, and sound or name. Congruent with Froebel's philosophy, the gifts had two meanings: their actual physical appearance and also a symbolic meaning. Symbolically, they were intended to stimulate children to bring the fundamental concept they suggested into mental consciousness. The following are Froebel's gifts:[23]

1. Six soft balls, colored red, blue, yellow, violet, green, and orange
2. A wooden sphere, cube, and cylinder to illustrate the concept of unity in that the cylinder contains a sphere and the cube contains a cylinder
3. A large cube divided into eight smaller cubes
4. A large cube divided into eight oblong blocks
5. A large cube divided into twenty-one whole, six half, and twelve quarter cubes
6. A large cube divided into eighteen whole oblongs, with three divided lengthwise and three divided breadthwise (Gifts 3 through 6 could be used for construction and building activity, for measurement and geometry, and to develop the sense of pattern, balance, and symmetry.)

7. Quadrangular and triangular tiles used to arrange figures and make patterns
8. Sticks for outlining figures
9. Whole and half wire rings for outlining figures

The Froebelian kindergarten gifts followed the order of beginning with the simple undifferentiated sphere or circle, which Froebel saw as a fundamental structure, and moving to more complex objects. Froebel believed each gift led children to the next in the series. He attached great symbolic meaning to the sphere. For example, the Earth, the sun, the moon, and other planets were spheres. In the kindergarten, a large number of activities and games were played with the balls. Many kindergartens featured a large circle painted on the floor. Children would join hands around the circle and move in one direction, then the next. The symbolism of this activity represented the unity of all human beings.

Following the idealist predilection for synthesis of opposites, Froebel used cylinders that represented the integration or fusion of the sphere and the cube. The various cubes and their subdivisions were building blocks designed to illustrate the relationships between the whole and the part. Children could use them to create geometrical designs or fashion buildings. Children could use the sticks and rings to trace designs on paper. This activity exercised the small muscles of the hand, developed coordination between hand and eye, and was a first step toward the skill of writing.

Although the gifts were objects given in fixed form to children, the *occupations* were items children could use in making and constructing activities. Among the occupations were paper, pencils, wood, sand, clay, straw, sticks, and other items children could work on or with to create a picture, an object, or some product.

In addition to the gifts and occupations, the kindergarten repertoire of activities included games, songs, and stories. Froebel would observe children engaged in free play and then from his observation design a game based on what he had observed. His aim was to organize games that would enlist children in social activities, exercise their bodies, and train their powers of observation. He published a collection of kindergarten songs in 1843 under the title *Mutter-und-Kose-lieder*, or *Mother's Songs, Games, and Stories*.[24] Each song had a motto designed to stress a particular value.

Conclusion: An Assessment

In this section we assess the diffusion and significance of Friedrich Froebel's educational contributions. The kindergarten has been among the most successful of nineteenth- and twentieth-century educational innovations, especially in worldwide diffusion. After Froebel's death in 1852, the kindergarten philosophy was carried throughout Europe and North America by his devoted disciples.

Among Froebel's most energetic disciples was Baroness Bertha von Marenholtz-Bulow, author of *A Woman's Educational Mission, Being an Explanation of Friedrich Froebel's System of Infant Gardens* (1855).[25] The Baroness traveled throughout Europe encouraging the kindergarten movement. Aided by Elise van Calcar, she established Froebel Societies in the Netherlands and in Belgium, which led to the opening of a kindergarten in Leiden in 1860. By 1872, von Marenholtz's efforts led to the creation of kindergartens in the Austro-Hungarian empire, with a large number located in Vienna. She also was influential in initiating kindergartens in Italy.[26]

The kindergarten became popular in Japan, where it was introduced during the Meiji restoration. In 1876, the first kindergarten in Japan was established at the Female Normal School as part of the teacher education program. By 1911, 497 kindergartens were operating in Japan.[27]

Two sisters, Bertha and Margarethe Meyer, natives of Hamburg, Germany, were noteworthy for their efforts in establishing kindergartens in the United Kingdom and the United States. Bertha Meyer Ronge established kindergartens at Manchester and Leeds in the United Kingdom. As immigrants came to the United States from Germany after the failed revolution of 1848, they brought the kindergarten idea with them. In Watertown, Wisconsin, Margarethe Meyer Schurz, the wife of future U.S. senator Karl Schurz, established a kindergarten for German-speaking children in 1856. In New York, Matilda H. Kriege established a kindergarten as part of a German school. She also imported kindergarten materials from Germany to the United States and convinced U.S. manufacturers to produce and market them.

The kindergarten idea gained support among leading proponents such as Henry Barnard, the first U.S. commissioner of education, who popularized Froebel's educational ideas in his *Common School Journal*. In 1860, Elizabeth Palmer Peabody (1804–1894), the sister of Horace Mann's wife, Mary, established an English-language kindergarten in Boston in 1860. Committed to popularizing the kindergarten, in 1867 she embarked on an educational tour of Europe to visit kindergartens. On her return she translated several of Froebel's books into English, formed a kindergarten association called the Froebel Union, and established an institute to train kindergarten teachers. Among her books on the kindergarten are *Moral Culture and Kindergarten Guide* (1864), *Kindergarten in Italy* (1872), and *Letters to Kindergartners* (1886).[28]

A significant event in making the kindergarten part of the public school system occurred in St. Louis, Missouri, in 1873, when a kindergarten was established at the Des Peres School. Superintendent of Schools William Torrey Harris (1835–1909), a philosophical idealist like Froebel, incorporated it into the public school system. St. Louis, with its large German population, proved a congenial environment for transplanting Froebel's institution. In his efforts to establish the kindergarten in the public school system, Harris enlisted Susan Elizabeth Blow (1843–1916), a dedicated proponent of Froebel's work. Blow wrote *Symbolic Education* (1894), *Letters to a Mother on the Philosophy of Froebel* (1899), and *Kindergarten Education* (1900). Together, Blow and Harris made St. Louis a center of kindergarten activity. When Harris became the U.S. commissioner of education, he continued to press for the kindergarten's incorporation into the public school system. Today, the kindergarten is a part of almost all public school systems in the United States.

Still another influence of Froebel was on art and architecture and art education. Froebel's kindergarten emphasized the development of conceptualization through symbols, especially as portrayed in the gifts. Norman Brosterman, in his *Inventing Kindergarten*, suggests the possible influence of Froebelianism and the kindergarten on such modern movements in abstract art as Cubism and Neoplasticism.[29] The handicraft aspects of Froebel's work made an impact on art education and handicraft programs. The geometrical designs of the arts and crafts movement also reveal a possible Froebelian influence. Frank Lloyd Wright, the brilliant American architect, credited his child-hood experience with Froebel's kindergarten gifts as the foundation of his innovative architectural designs.[30]

Froebel's great contribution was to give us a version of childhood that exalted the dignity of children and their right to be children rather than miniature adults. For him, childhood had a spiritual quality that needed to be recognized and nurtured. Froebel contributed to legitimizing play at a time when children were often exploited as laborers and play was disdainfully rejected as idleness.

Today, kindergarten teachers continue to emphasize Froebel's ideas of developing the social side of children's nature and a sense of readiness for learning. The important outcome for kindergarten children is readiness for the intellectual learning that will come later on in their educational careers.

The aspect of Froebel's work that has largely disappeared is the mysterious symbolism that clouded much of his philosophy of education. When considered in the context of Froebel's life, when idealism was in vogue in his native Germany, it is not difficult to see why his philosophy contained large allegorical and symbolic elements. For today's teacher, Froebel's message of liberating children and allowing them to develop according to their needs and nature remains of vital significance.

Questions for Reflection and Dialogue

1. Reflect on current proposals for making early childhood education more academic, such as having Head Start programs emphasize literacy. How do you think Froebel would react to these proposals?
2. Reflect on your attitude about play for both children and adults. How do you think Froebel might react to your concept of play?
3. How was philosophical idealism a factor in Froebel's kindergarten theory?
4. Describe Froebel's educational method as a strategy in externalizing the interior or inner qualities of the human being.
5. What is the role of gifts and occupations in Froebel's kindergarten?
6. How was the kindergarten brought to the United States?

Projects for Deepening Your Understanding

1. Visit several kindergartens. Do you find any evidence of Froebel's philosophy and method?
2. Interview several kindergarten teachers about their philosophy of education, especially their views of child nature, aims, activities, and the general role of the kindergarten in education. Report your findings to the class.
3. Interview professors who teach early childhood education courses at your college or university. Try to determine their attitude about the role and place of the kindergarten in contemporary education. Share your findings with the other members of the course.

4. Visit several kindergarten and Montessori classes. Compare and contrast the kindergarten and the Montessori prepared environment as learning environments. (Montessori education is treated in Chapter 21. You might want to read ahead or defer this activity until you examine Montessori education.)
5. In a paper, develop a character sketch of Friedrich Froebel.
6. Design a lesson plan that follows the Froebelian approach.

Notes

1. C. W. Crawley, ed., *War and Peace in an Age of Upheaval, 1793–1850* (Cambridge, UK: Cambridge University Press, 1963), 376–82.
2. Bertrand Russell, *A History of Western Philosophy* (New York: Simon & Schuster, 1967), 701–13.
3. Roland N. Stromberg, *European Intellectual History Since 1789* (Upper Saddle River, NJ: Prentice Hall, 1981), 28–29.
4. Immanuel Kant, *Prolegomena to Any Future Metaphysics* (Indianapolis: Bobbs-Merrill, 1950).
5. J. Loewenberg, *Hegel Selections* (New York: Scribner's, 1959).
6. For his autobiography, see Friedrich Froebel, *Autobiography*, trans. Emilie Michaelis and H. Keatley Moore (Syracuse, NY: C. W. Bardeen, 1889). A useful biography is Robert B. Downs, *Friedrich Froebel* (Boston: Twayne, 1978).
7. Froebel, *Autobiography*, 3–4.
8. Downs, *Friedrich Froebel*, 11–12.
9. Froebel, *Autobiography*, 20–21.
10. Froebel, *Autobiography*, 24.
11. Norman Brosterman, *Inventing Kindergarten* (New York: Harry N. Abrams, 1997), 17.
12. Brosterman, *Inventing Kindergarten*, 17.
13. Downs, *Friedrich Froebel*, 16–17.
14. Downs, *Friedrich Froebel*, 19.
15. Downs, *Friedrich Froebel*, 25–26.
16. John C. Greene and John G. Burke, *The Science of Minerals in the Age of Jefferson, Transactions of the American Philosophical Society*, vol. 68 (Philadelphia: American Philosophical Society,

1978), 16–19. Also see John G. Burke, *Origins of the Science of Crystals* (Berkeley, CA: University of California Press, 1966).
17. Brosterman, *Inventing Kindergarten*, 22–25.
18. Froebel, *Autobiography*, 123.
19. Downs, *Friedrich Froebel*, 34–39.
20. Brosterman, *Inventing Kindergarten*, 28.
21. Friedrich Froebel, *The Education of Man*, trans. W. H. Hailman (New York: D. Appleton, 1896).
22. Gerald L. Gutek, *A History of the Western Educational Experience* (Prospect Heights, IL: Waveland, 1995), 255–69.
23. The gifts are beautifully illustrated in Brosterman, *Inventing Kindergarten*, 42–70. Also see Downs, *Friedrich Froebel*, 47–50.
24. Friedrich Froebel, *Mother's Songs, Games, and Stories*, trans. Francis and Emily Lord (London: W. Rice, 1910).
25. Bertha von Marenholtz-Bulow, *A Woman's Educational Mission, Being An Explanation of Friedrich Frobel's System of Infant Gardens* (London: Darton, 1855).
26. Brosterman, *Inventing Kindergarten*, 94–97.
27. Brosterman, *Inventing Kindergarten*, 97–98.
28. For the history of the kindergarten in America, see Nina C. Vandewalker, *The Kindergarten in American Education* (New York: Arno/New York Times, 1971).
29. Brosterman, *Inventing Kindergarten*, 104–53.
30. Brosterman, *Inventing Kindergarten*, 10–11.

Suggestions for Further Reading

Blow, Susan E., *Letters to a Mother on the Philosophy of Froebel*. Bristol: Thoemmes Press, 2000.

Brehony, Kevin, ed. *Evolution of English Nursery Education*. London: Routledge, 2001.

Brehony, Kevin, ed. *Friedrich Froebel's Pedagogics of the Kindergarten*. London: Routledge, 2001.

Brehony, Kevin, ed. *The Origins of Nursery Education: Friedrich Froebel and the English System*. London, New York: Routledge, 2001.

Brehony, Kevin, and Hailmann, W. N., eds. *Friedrich Froebel's The Education of Man*. London: Routledge, 2001.

Brehony, Kevin, and Jarvis, Josephine, eds. *Friedrich Froebel's Education by Development*. London: Routledge, 2001.

Brehony, Kevin, Michaelis, Emilie, et al., eds. *Froebel's Letters on the Kindergarten*. London: Routledge, 2001.

Brosterman, Norman. *Inventing Kindergarten*. New York: Harry N. Abrams, 1997.

Bultman, Scott. *The Froebel Gifts 2000: the Building Gifts 2–6, Ages 3 & Up*. Grand Rapids, MI: Kindergarten Messenger, 2000.

Compayre, Gabriel. *Development of the Child in Later Infancy*. Bristol: Thoemmes Press, 2000.

Downs, Robert B. *Friedrich Froebel*. Boston: Twayne, 1978.

Froebel, Friedrich. *Autobiography*. Trans. Emilie Michaelis and H. Keatley Moore. Syracuse, NY: C. W. Bardeen, 1889.

———. *Mother's Songs, Games, and Stories*. Trans. Francis and Emily Lord. London: W. Rice, 1910.

Eliot, Henrietta Robins Mack, and Blow, Susan E. *The Mottoes and Commentaries of Friedrich Froebel's Mother Play*. Bristol: Thoemmes Press, 2000.

Hayward, Frank H. *The Educational Ideas of Pestalozzi and Froebel*. Westport, CT: Greenwood, 1979.

Headley, Neith. *Education in the Kindergarten*. New York: American Book Co., 1966.

Hewes, Dorothy W. *W. N. Hailmann: Defender of Froebel*. Grand Rapids, MI: The Froebel Foundation, 2001.

Hughes, James L. *Froebel's Educational Laws for All Teachers*. Bristol: Thoemmes Press, 2000.

Lawrence, Evelyn, ed. *Froebel and English Education*. New York: Schocken, 1969.

Liebschner, Joachim. *A Child's Work: Freedom and Play in Froebel's Educational Theory and Practice*. Cambridge: Lutterworth, 2001.

Lilley, Irene M. *Friedrich Froebel: A Selection from His Writings*. Cambridge, UK: Cambridge University Press, 1967.

Ross, Elizabeth D. *The Kindergarten Crusade: The Establishment of Preschool Education in the United States*. Athens, OH: Ohio University Press, 1976.

Rubin, Jeanne Spielman. *Intimate Triangle: Architecture of Crystals, Frank Lloyd Wright, and the Froebel Kindergarten*. Huntsville, AL: Polycrystal Book Service, 2003.

Vandewalker, Nina C. *The Kindergarten in American Education*. New York: Arno/New York Times, 1971.

Weber, Evelyn. *The Kindergarten: Its Encounter with Educational Thought in America*. New York: Teachers College Press, 1969.

CHAPTER 17

John Stuart Mill: Proponent of Liberalism

In this chapter we explore the life, educational philosophy and contributions of John Stuart Mill (1806–1873), a proponent of liberalism in philosophy, social policy, and education. Mill's reconceptualization of liberal ideology, which revised Jeremy Bentham's Utilitarianism, moved liberalism from a natural rights, laissez-faire position to one of humanitarian social reform. As a writer on education, Mill is best known for his strong defense of human rights and freedom.

We examine here the course of Mill's life, expressed in his *Autobiography*, and his significant work on social and educational philosophy. First, we look at the general social and intellectual context in nineteenth-century England, which influenced and shaped Mill, placing particular emphasis on the intellectual context, especially the philosophical ideas of James Mill and Jeremy Bentham. Second, we examine Mill's biography, including his education—which was planned and implemented by James Mill and Bentham—and his career as a writer on society and education themes. Third, we identify and discuss key elements in Mill's social and educational philosophy. Fourth, we assess the continuing effect of Mill's concepts of human freedom and disinterested participation in social life and issues.

Mill's own educational experience illustrates the need in contemporary education for the harmonious integration of the intellectual and emotional dimensions of life. We also examine the evolution of liberalism as a social and political theory for its long-term educational implications.

To organize your thoughts as you read this chapter, focus on the following questions:

1. What were the major trends, especially those of an intellectual nature, in the historical context in which Mill lived?
2. How did Mill's life, particularly his educational biography, shape his philosophy of education?
3. How did Mill's social and political philosophy with its emphasis on human freedom and liberty determine his educational policies and practices?
4. What has been the enduring impact of Mill's contributions to educational theory and practice?

The Historical Context of Mill's Life

In this section, we survey the historical context of nineteenth-century England, in which John Stuart Mill lived. When Mill was born, in 1806, the United Kingdom had a rapidly growing population of slightly more than 9 million people. This population growth was a by-product of British industrialization. As the nation that gave birth to the Industrial Revolution, Great Britain was well on the way to becoming the factory of the world. Along with its industrial primacy, England had been a leader in the coalition of European nations that had finally vanquished Napoleon at Waterloo in 1815 and exiled him on the island of St. Helena.

Britain's industrialization produced important socioeconomic changes. It created both an economic elite of industrial capitalists who garnered great profits and a large and growing industrial working class. Workers—men, women, and children—were massed in huge factories to tend machines on assembly lines. For many laborers, the working day was long, sometimes lasting 14 to 15 hours. Workers lived in crowded and dirty tenements.

Such pronounced social change and the pressures of debilitating working conditions caused unrest that sometimes broke into rioting and violence, but most often the victims of unregulated and exploitative industrialism found succor in bottles of cheap gin. Only a very few industrialists, such as the utopian socialist Robert Owen, experimented with communitarian planning and education to remedy the plight of the working class. (See Chapter 15 for a discussion of Robert Owen as a communitarian reformer.) The prevalent opinion of the early nineteenth century, especially among liberal ideologists, was that economic prosperity and human progress depended on the free operations of the market with no government regulation.

Economic theory in early nineteenth-century Britain was dominated by the Manchester school's free-market ideologues.[1] Adam Smith, the preeminent economist, argued that not only business but the nation itself prospered when free from government's regulatory interference. For Smith's classical liberal followers, a noninterventionist policy without tariffs, trade barriers, and other restrictions was the best.[2] As the Reverend Thomas Malthus asserted in his influential *Essay on the Principle of Population as It Affects the Future Improvement of Society* (1798), population has a constant tendency to increase beyond the food supply. If war or disease did not check population growth, then famine would reduce it to manageable levels. David Ricardo, proponent of the iron law of wages, provided industrialists with an economic rationale for low wages and long hours of work. If wages rose above the subsistence level, workers would use their increased income to bear more children. More children meant a labor surplus in which workers would be forced to work for reduced wages. A far better use of profits was capital investment in more factories and machinery.[3] The best economic minds of the early nineteenth century were resolutely against government intervention and regulation. Let the market work its natural course.

At the same time that laissez-faire economic policy was a standard feature of liberalism, its politics continued to stress Locke's freedoms of speech, press, assembly, and religion against a powerful state's interference. The doctrine of the natural rights of human beings, expressed in Locke's *Second Treatise of Government* (1689), proclaimed the inviolability of the innate and inherent right to life, liberty, and property. Economically, socially, politically, and educationally, liberal ideology asserted the inviolability of individual rights and safeguarded the property rights and interests of the rising middle classes.

Despite liberalism's ascendancy in nineteenth-century Britain, liberals were dissatisfied with their country's inherited political, religious, and social structures. For them, too much of the aristocratic past remained in the control that the Tories, or conservatives, had over many electoral districts (the so-called "rotten boroughs"), which with populations much smaller than the growing industrial cities still elected defenders of the old aristocratic status quo to the House of Commons. They were also dissatisfied with the power of the established Church of England over schools and universities. For liberals, these institutional residues of an archaic and aristocratic past were obstacles to society's progress. Although generally believing that institutions needed to be changed to function effectively, the issue of how to bring about such change divided liberals.

Liberals also were beginning to feel an internal tension about government's role in reforming institutions and shaping the future. For classical liberals—the followers of Locke, Smith, Malthus, and Ricardo—the future would be better if government were absent from social and economic affairs. They believed the old order's overripe fruit was already spoiling and would fall from the vine of its own internal rot. Other liberals, the Utilitarian disciples of Jeremy Bentham, believing it possible to improve individuals and society, advocated a limited government role in social reform.[4] The Benthamite Utilitarians developed a program of social, economic, and political action to reform British life and institutions. Bentham devised a philosophical methodology to bring about reform according to rational calculations that estimated the consequences of action in terms of pleasure and pain. Such a program, Utilitarians argued, would generate the "greatest good for the greatest number" of people. One of the leading associates of Bentham was James Mill, John Stuart Mill's father. Because of their powerful shaping influence on John Stuart Mill, Bentham's and the senior Mill's ideas were an important part of the context of his life.

Jeremy Bentham (1748–1832), the son of a wealthy London lawyer, described as a "bookish child" of "dwarfish" appearance, was an intellectually precocious child who was studying Latin at age 4 and French at 7. Fond of books, he was nicknamed "the philosopher." In 1755, he was enrolled in Westminster, a venerable English public school designed to educate well-rounded gentlemen. Bentham detested the classical preparatory curriculum and the regimen that required boys to enthusiastically participate in team sports. In 1760, he was admitted to Queen's College at Oxford University, a highly prestigious institution that educated England's future leaders. Though he once again found little of interest in his collegiate studies, he completed his academic program and received his bachelor of arts degree in 1763 and his master of arts degree in 1766. He then studied law and was admitted to the bar in 1769. Although he never practiced law, his legal studies were a foundation for his developing social philosophy, Utilitarianism. Bentham came away from his formal education with a deep antagonism toward the institutions and the teachers who had educated him. He detested what he regarded as a rigidly prescribed classical curriculum and the reactionary attitudes of his professors. He considered the English legal system a "jungle of unintelligible distinctions, contradictions, and cumbrous methods through which no man could find his way without the guidance of the initiated, and in which a long purse and unscrupulous trickery gave the advantage over the poor to the rich, and to the knave over the honest man."[5]

Bentham's critique of English law illustrates the Utilitarian predilection to reform an institution according to rational principles. The legal system was cluttered and the process was riddled with archaic residues that blocked its efficient functioning. Bentham's *Rationale of Judicial Evidence* (1827), advocating reform of the archaic legal system, recommended establishing a code of a few easily applied rules with cases decided on logic rather than custom.

Concurrent with his plan for judicial reform, Bentham proposed prison reform. He designed a model for a new kind of prison that would rehabilitate rather than punish prisoners. His new prison, called a "panopticon," placed the warden in a vantage point from which he could observe all inmates and prescribe a specific program for improving their behavior.[6]

Bentham's proposals illustrate the Utilitarian liberals' reformist ideology. They were researchers who, like the later U.S. progressives, carefully studied institutions and their functions to make them operate more effectively, fairly, and efficiently. They were not activists who took the reform cause into the streets or organized demonstrations or protests. Rather, they wrote proposals that put forth the design of reformed institutions. Though they ventured into politics as did John Stuart Mill, their essential methodology for reform was philosophical and educational rather than directly activist. When James Mill sought Bentham's advice in educating his son, John Stuart, the boy's learning plan resembled Bentham's panopticon for rehabilitating prisoners through total social control. The two elder Utilitarians planned to control completely John's behavior and create a perfect model of their philosophy.

Providing a complete rendition of his philosophy in *Introduction to the Principles of Morals and Legislation* (1789), Bentham challenged Locke's theory of the existence of inherent human rights that primitive humans possessed in the state of nature. Likewise, he rejected the Lockean idea that government was created as a social contract between the governors and the governed to protect and maintain these natural rights of life, liberty, and property. Bentham insisted that the fundamental principle governing human life, which he called the principle of utility, was the desire to experience pleasure and to avoid pain. As individuals estimated pain and pleasure, the ultimate criterion for human choice and action was the degree to which the action's consequences added to pleasure and diminished pain. In society and politics, the principle of utility prescribed that legislation and its implementation should bring the greatest good for the greatest number of people.

Although moving away from Lockean and Jeffersonian natural rights doctrines, Bentham's principle of utility still proclaimed the liberal's emphasis on the individual. He asserted that individuals were goal directed as they asserted their self-interests.

These goals, based on maximizing pleasure and minimizing pain, were best determined by the individual. However, Bentham's reformist agenda opened the way for regulations that might limit individual freedom. Arguing that some freedoms might need to be curtailed to expand other freedoms, the Benthamite Utilitarians initiated, perhaps unwittingly, the movement to social welfare state liberalism.

For Bentham, pleasure and pain could be estimated with almost mathematical precision. Happiness, a pervasive feeling of comfort, was produced by measurable material consequences of action. Pleasure and pain could be calculated by asking such questions as, How intense was the pleasure or pain? How long did it last? How many people were affected by the pleasure or pain? Thus, Bentham proposed reducing questions of individual choice and social policy making to adding and subtracting.

Bentham's view of mathematical decision making may sound simplistic and mechanical, but it anticipated the proposition that everything that exists can be measured. It anticipated the opinion of some modern educators that all education can be reduced to stated and measurable behavioral objectives. Bentham's view of ethics by estimation was an important influence on John Stuart Mill's education.

Bentham's Utilitarian principle of the "greatest happiness or greatest good for the greatest number of people" began the liberal split into two factions—the strict classical liberals who wanted a very limited role for the state in social policy and those who saw the state as the appropriate agency for social reform. (Chapter 18, on Herbert Spencer, discusses the resurgence of classical liberalism. Chapters 19 and 20, on Jane Addams and John Dewey, examine U.S. progressives who were liberal proponents of an enlarged government role.)

Bentham's Utilitarianism signaled the transition of the social reformist wing of liberalism from preoccupation with individualism to broader social issues. Bentham faced the theoretical challenge of how to transform individual self-interest into a social good. Using mathematical estimation to formulate policy, Bentham concluded that the public interest was the sum of the interests of all individuals who composed society.[7] Further, his Utilitarianism was highly egalitarian. As all humans share the same kind of psychology, they experience roughly the same amount of pleasure and pain. On such an egalitarian scale, the inherited conservative social order, resting on an aristocracy of blood and breeding, made no sense. On a scale of calculated happiness, all existing institutions, laws, customs, traditions, and conventions could be weighed whatever their social origin. If not producing the greatest good for the greatest number, they could be abolished or reformed.

Basic to social reform for Bentham and his followers was parliamentary or political reform. Following the principle of utility, legislators were to ask, What use is the institution or law in maximizing the greatest happiness for the greatest number? Through legislation, not revolution, a reformed environment would be created inhabited by individuals who rationally calculated the consequences of their actions. Underlying Bentham's concept of legislated reform was the liberal's commitment to gradual change that, while eliminating feudal aristocratic privileges, would not jeopardize the middle-class values of individual freedom and the sanctity of private property.

As part of a nonrevolutionary philosophy for gradual and limited social change, the Utilitarians relied heavily on education. Like the later U.S. progressives, they had a journalist's way of educating people. Through tracts, periodicals, pamphlets, and books, they sought to create an informed public opinion. Such an informed opinion required a literate population, which meant creating a system of popular education. Bentham saw popular education as the means by which individuals would know their true self-interests and participate intelligently in forming the public interest. Here, the Utilitarians faced an educational dilemma in that they wanted widespread popular education, but not a state-controlled school system.

Like the legal system, Bentham and his associate James Mill found the existing educational system to be a hodgepodge of malfunctioning institutions. In the early nineteenth century, the growing British population was seriously undereducated. The elite minority—the children of the landed aristocracy and the new industrialists—attended primary schools that prepared them for college-preparatory secondary schools, either grammar schools or the prestigious "public schools" of Eton, Westminster, Rugby, Charterhouse, and Harrow. Despite their misleading name, these actually private schools catered to the rich and well born. Their stuffy curriculum of Latin and Greek, taught by semireligious clerics, did not provide the kind of education needed by Utilitarian reformers. The leading universities, Oxford and Cambridge, also perpetuated the status quo. Bentham and his associates were unrelenting opponents of these bastions of traditional classical higher education. To create an educational alternative, Bentham and other Utilitarians established the University of London in 1828 to promote the new social philosophy and social science needed to educate reformers.

If the education of the upper classes was of the wrong sort, that of the working classes was either nonexistent or piecemeal and sporadic. The development of a system of primary and secondary schools was retarded by the Church of England's attitude, shared by Tory conservatives, that education was largely a private matter. Only for the dependent poor should charity be provided to educate their children. Neither, however, did the liberal stance of little or no government interference encourage establishing a popular school system.

In the early nineteenth century, a small number of church-supported, endowed primary schools enrolled a limited number of children, estimated to be about 150,000 students. Another 50,000 children were enrolled in makeshift "dame schools," reading and writing schools conducted for profit by enterprising women. In addition to these primary schools, a few factories provided some primary education for their child laborers. Overall, only a minority of the primary school–age children were attending some sort of school.[8]

With such educational underdevelopment, the Utilitarians faced the dilemma of encouraging educational reform without creating state-supported schools. In typical liberal fashion, they cautiously sought to deal with the problem gradually and incrementally. Bentham himself was concerned with educating both the middle and working classes. Like other middle-class reformers, he wanted to improve the condition of the working classes by educating their children. Motivated by both humanitarian altruism and fearing the potential threat posed by a large, discontented, and illiterate working class to middle-class security, Bentham's *A Scheme for Improved Pauper Management* (1797), included educational provisions. He called for establishing "Houses of Industry," which would provide basic literacy, moral instruction, and vocational training. Like other middle-class reformers, Bentham thought he knew what was best for the British underclass. With a large measure of social control, he recommended training the will of the poor to resist vices, such as endemic consumption of alcohol. Among the moral values that would be stressed were punctuality, honesty, thrift, self-control especially in terms of sexuality, and respect for private property.[9] Bentham believed that his plan for educating the poor could be self-supporting, paid primarily by the industries that employed the children or their parents. Government assistance would be limited to the unemployed. One important aspect of Bentham's plan was that it would be compulsory.

James Mill (1773–1836), John Stuart's father, was among Bentham's most steadfast disciples. As James Mill determined he would educate his son according to Bentham's Utilitarianism, a brief commentary on the senior Mill explains the intellectual context that shaped John Stuart Mill's upbringing.

James Mill was born at Northwater Bridge, in the parish of Logie Port, in Forfarshire in Scotland, where his father, James Mill, Sr., was village shoemaker. His mother, Isabel Fenton, from a family of higher social status, determined that young James would enjoy the advantages that education could bring. Through his mother's efforts, James, who attended the local parish school, proved to be an academically gifted pupil. The village minister, Reverend Peters, noticing James's academic acumen, encouraged his enrollment at Montrose Academy, a preparatory school. He also attracted the support of Sir John and Lady Stuart, who helped subsidize his higher education at the University of Edinburgh. At the university he completed divinity studies and, after graduation in 1798, was licensed as a Presbyterian preacher.[10]

In 1802, James Mill, seeking to improve his economic opportunities, moved to London to pursue a career as a journalist. He continued to enjoy the patronage of Sir John Stuart, who introduced him to some of Britain's leading public figures. Succeeding as a writer, Mill contributed articles to such respected journals as the *Literary Journal*, the *British Review*, and the *Philanthropist*. Mill's associates included David Ricardo, the influential economist, and Jeremy Bentham, the well-known philosopher. The Bentham–Mill alliance would have important consequences, not only for the development of Utilitarian philosophy and liberal ideology, but for the education of John Stuart Mill, whom they planned to fashion into the perfect Utilitarian.

In 1805, James Mill married Harriet Burrow. Nine children were born to the couple, the eldest of whom was John Stuart. In 1818, James Mill secured employment as examiner of correspondence in the East India Company's London office. His access to records and correspondence furnished the material for his multivolume *History of British India* (1817–1818). James Mill's other books were *Elements of Political Economy* (1821–1822), *Analysis of the Phenomena of the Human Mind* (1829), and *A Fragment on Mackintosh* (1835).

James Mill's "Essay on Education" delineated his educational philosophy.[11] Like Bentham, his Utilitarian mentor, James Mill believed a proper education should aid in securing the greatest happiness for the greatest number of people. Although Mill was influenced by Bentham's philosophy, he also made his own contribution to Utilitarianism and to liberal ideology. According to Mill, an individual can bring happiness to others "either by abstaining from doing harm, or by doing them positive good." For Mill, abstention from doing harm was the principle of "Justice," and doing "positive good" was that of "Generosity." Accordingly, education's overarching goals were to ensure justice and generosity.[12] These goals required individuals to weigh personal pleasures against the consequences that actions have on other people.

Using a Utilitarian rationale, James Mill saw education as an agent for cultivating individual and social happiness. For Mill, human happiness was not a hedonistic pursuit of sensual pleasures or appetites. Rather, measured on a Benthamite calculus, actions had to be meticulously weighed in terms of their long-run individual and social benefits. Genuine happiness involved controlling human appetites and rejecting short-run pleasures for long-range human happiness. Mill's properly educated person based decisions on a careful and temperate estimate of pleasure and pain.

According to Mill, a child's education required some adult imposition so the youngster would learn to reject fulfilling impulsive desires and direct his or her energy toward goals that would improve both him or her as an individual and society as well. As his son's tutor, James Mill was a highly directive instructor who completely controlled John Stuart's environment—limiting peer association and determining goals for him.

John Stuart Mill: Autobiography and Education

In this section we examine the life, education, and career of John Stuart Mill, a determined advocate of human freedom.[13] Born on May 20, 1806, in Yorkshire, England, the eldest son of James Mill, his life coincided with the evolution of liberalism, which was both a philosophy and an ideology of political and social reform. The maturation in liberal thought is evident in Mill's own education and career. When he was born in 1806, the classical liberal position that restricted government to a circumscribed laissez-faire position of noninterference in social and economic life was challenged by Utilitarianism, the internal reform movement within liberalism led by Bentham and John's father, James.

Like Herbert Spencer's father (see Chapter 18), James Mill dominated his family. Mill's mother, a quiet and unassuming woman, appears as a minor character in his childhood and education. She apparently devoted her energies to caring for her husband and children. As an adult, John Stuart said little about his mother but much about his father. He wrote that if his mother had been more assertive she might have brought a more emotional and humane atmosphere to a household dominated by the icy rationalism and cool logic of James Mill, who saw even family life and childrearing in Utilitarian terms.[14]

John Stuart's childhood was dominated by Bentham and his father. The two anointed John Stuart as their philosophical heir and eventual leader of Utilitarianism. Bentham eagerly used the opportunity to test his educational theories on young Mill.[15]

When John Stuart was 3, James Mill moved his family into Bentham's home so that Bentham could directly supervise the educational experiment. Leaving nothing to chance in John Stuart's education, James Mill and Bentham set a rigid schedule of lessons and activities. Bentham, believing human happiness could be mathematically calculated, had decided that thorough scheduling would reduce the chance element, the unplanned and spontaneous happening. A completely scheduled education would use time efficiently and effectively.

James Mill and Bentham determined John Stuart's curriculum. He would learn ancient Greek and Latin, literature, mathematics, history, and the physical and natural sciences, with an emphasis on chemistry. After John Stuart had mastered these subjects, he would then study logic and philosophy, areas in which the two senior Utilitarians had a keen interest. As his Utilitarian instructors saw little use in art, music, and poetry, these were absent from their pupil's schedule.

The two philosophers devised a daily routine for their young pupil. John Stuart arose at six every morning and studied 3 hours before taking a half-hour break for breakfast. Then, he had a concentrated block of 5 hours of study with an emphasis on applying his lessons to problems given to him by his father and Bentham. After dinner, he studied for an additional 3 hours. Thus, a typical day consisted of 11 hours of lessons and study. His only breaks from this academic routine were discussions with his father on the books assigned as readings. John and his father also took a daily walk through nearby woods and gardens during which they pursued an intellectual topic.[16]

John Stuart studied ancient Greek and Latin languages and literature, then considered essential in the education of upper-class males. However, James Mill's method in teaching languages differed from how they were taught in nineteenth-century grammar and preparatory schools where students memorized vocabulary from a *nomenclature*, a book of Latin or Greek words, and studied grammar. After they had mastered the rules of grammar and had acquired an adequate vocabulary, students in conventional schools began translating the classics. Memorization rather than comprehension was often the goal.

James Mill began teaching his son Greek when John Stuart was 3; Latin instruction began when he was 8. Mill devised a set of flash cards with important Greek and Latin words on them so that John learned the essential vocabulary. He seated John in his library and had him read the classical texts, beginning with *Aesop's Fables*. When John came upon a word or phrase he did not know, he asked his father, who was busily working on his multivolume *History of British India*. The senior Mill would supply the needed word or phrase and the youngster would continue his lesson. John Stuart later commented that his father, who usually would not tolerate interruptions, accepted them in such instances.[17]

The relationship between James Mill and his son was primarily intellectual, with little feeling or emotion. In his *Autobiography*, Mill reflected on his education, which he believed was overly intellectual and without opportunities for association and play with other children, or for enjoying nature, art, or poetry. Although he was an intellectually gifted and precocious child, Mill considered his education uneven and his own academic performance to be average. He believed that it left him deficient in physical dexterity, intellectual creativity, and public speaking. These feelings of inadequacy were reinforced by his father, who, rather than praising his son's achievements, was a critical tutor who consistently heaped on the young boy more academic assignments and challenges. John Stuart Mill later wrote:

> I was constantly meriting reproof by inattention, in observance, and general slackness of mind in matters of daily life. My father was the extreme opposite in these particulars: his senses and mental faculties were always on the alert; he carried decision and energy of character in his whole manner and into every action of life.[18]

John Stuart Mill's memory of his father was one of intellectual awe. His most enjoyable memory was of their daily walks, which provided rare opportunities for observing and enjoying nature. However, even on these walks his father, always driven by efficiency, questioned his son about the day's lessons.

As the foremost disciple of Bentham, James Mill wanted his son to continue in philosophical lineage and become the philosophical leader of his generation.[19] He wanted

John Stuart to develop a critical mind that challenged conventional ways of thinking. However, by concentrating on languages, mathematics, and the sciences to the exclusion of poetry, music, art, and literature, the senior Mill deprived his son of the means for aesthetic appreciation and enjoyment. The daily regimen imposed on the youngster deprived him of the children's play and spontaneity that made for an emotionally healthy adulthood.

As a child and youth, John Stuart did not rebel against the regimen his father and Bentham imposed on him. He tried to emulate his father, a distinguished author, by writing his own essays. At an early age, John Stuart wrote a history of the Roman republic. In his *Autobiography* he recalled,

> In my eleventh and twelfth year I occupied myself writing what I flattered myself was something serious. This was no less than a history of the Roman Government . . . My father encouraged me in this useful amusement, though . . . he never asked to see what I wrote; so that I did not feel that in writing it I was accountable to any one, nor had the chilling sensation of being under a critical eye.[20]

When he was 12, John Stuart Mill's education became increasingly focused on philosophy. With the object of sharpening his logical thinking, John Stuart was to analyze philosophical works, identify their major premises, and examine the consistency of the particular philosopher's arguments.[21] The daily walks of the father-tutor and pupil-son now became Socratic dialogues in which John Stuart was to analyze his reading and defend his conclusions. John Stuart commented that this rigorous analytical training served him well in his later career as a philosopher and spokesman for the cause of reform. In particular, he believed he learned to avoid fallacious reasoning and ambiguous expression and how to formulate his ideas logically and clearly.

In reflecting on his own education, Mill claimed it had the power of forming "exact thinkers, who attach a precise meaning to words and propositions, and are not imposed on by vague, loose or ambiguous terms," and had trained him with the skill of "disentangling the intricacies of confused and self-contradictory thought."[22]

When he was 14, John Stuart's education became somewhat independent of his father's supervision. He was permitted to take a long study and travel tour of France, where he encountered the social, political, and educational philosophies current on the European continent. During his sojourn in France, he began to change from a "little Englander" who glimpsed life through strictly British lenses to a person of wider perspectives.

When he returned to England to begin his career, John Stuart Mill's life was still being controlled by his father. In 1823, James Mill secured a clerical position for his son with the East India Company, a private stock company that controlled large areas of India. John Stuart worked for the East India Company for the next 35 years, being eventually promoted to the rather prestigious position of Examiner of Correspondence with the Native States. As had been true of his father's career, his job with the East India Company provided an income while allowing sufficient time to pursue his real interest in philosophical writing and editing.

John Stuart Mill was now actively involved in the Utilitarian cause. With Bentham and his father, he was engaged in publishing *The Westminster Review*, the official Utilitarian journal. John Stuart served as editor of the *Review* and contributed frequent essays. His articles challenged the philosophical and political opposition, the conservatives who wanted to retain the old order and the Owenite Socialists who wanted to build a new social order but one of common property. During his childhood and youth, Mill had been socially isolated but now he was making acquaintances in the Utilitarian circle.

Outwardly, John Stuart Mill appeared to be the perfect Utilitarian, formed in the image and likeness of his father. Inwardly, however, he experienced an anxiety that sought freedom from his father's tight control. Despite his efforts to repress his feelings, his emotions struggled to the surface. In 1826, at age 20, John Stuart began to experience bouts of psychological depression, accompanied by symptoms of physical fatigue and exhaustion, loss of interest, and anxiety. Continuing to work at the East India Company, he found himself unable to carry on his philosophical activities—the writing and editing—that had so engaged him. He now began to probe his psyche in introspective self-analysis. Plagued by severe self-doubts, he questioned the purpose of his life. In his *Autobiography*, Mill recounted that the reform cause that had motivated him in the past was losing its meaning. He stated that "the whole foundation on which my life was constructed fell down. . . . I seemed to have nothing left to live for."[23]

Mill's severe psychological crisis actually turned out to be the beginning of a recovery that would lead him to a more balanced life. Although the precise precipitating cause of Mill's psychological depression has intrigued psychobiographers, it is clear that he was no longer able to repress his frustration and resentment against an overly controlling but highly admired father. During his exclusively intellectual education in the formative years of childhood, he had little involvement with peers. As a young adult, his emotional and social life was severely underdeveloped. During his period of mental and emotional storm and stress, Mill realized that Bentham's Utilitarian philosophy, while highly useful, was by itself incomplete.

As he struggled with the inner demons of psychological depression, John Stuart Mill slowly began to feel as well as to think about life. As his feelings surfaced, he began to search for new creative outlets. He now felt free to enjoy music, art, and poetry. These aesthetic dimensions of life were true joys to be experienced.

As he worked his way through his psychological crisis, he began to place his educational past into perspective. He found that his exposure to Bentham's Utilitarianism could be a philosophical point of departure rather than a dogma to be blindly accepted. He found that he could make good use of his father's exacting training in philosophy while he did his own thinking. He realized that human happiness was not determined by keeping a ledger-like account of credits and debits of pain and pleasure. Rather, human happiness was a whole—the integrating of life's intellectual, emotional, cognitive, and affective dimensions of life—not something to analyze and dissect into bits and pieces. As he created a revised Utilitarianism, Mill sought to make seemingly opposing views fit together. He did not approach philosophy through intellectual dissection but rather attempted to construct a revised edifice from existing strands of thought.

Recovering from his psychological depression, Mill began to seek and experience what had been absent in his education—aesthetic appreciation and emotional feelings. Continuing to value intellectual and logical thought, Mill broadened and integrated his view of life. At this phase in his life he became romantically involved with Harriet Taylor, who became his confidant and companion and later his wife.

When Mill met Taylor, Harriet was in her early twenties, the wife of John Taylor and mother of two children. She was a member of a Utilitarian group that included some of Mill's friends. John Stuart was drawn to the opinionated young woman who firmly advocated women's rights, and Harriet, in turn, was equally attracted to the reserved young intellectual. In nineteenth-century Victorian England, divorce was out of the question. However, Harriet's husband did not oppose their association, which appeared to be a platonic relationship. Mill continued to live with his mother and Harriet with her husband. It was not until 1851, two years after John Taylor's death, that John Stuart Mill and Harriet Taylor were married. In 1858, Harriet died and was buried near Avignon in southern France. Mill built a small cottage near the cemetery where she was buried and would retreat there to contemplate and write.[24]

There has been much speculation by historians as to the extent to which Harriet Taylor influenced John Stuart Mill's later philosophical thought. Without doubt, she had a salutary effect on liberating his pent-up emotions. In many respects, she was a psychological counterforce to the intellectual control that James Mill had exercised on his son. She was a gentling influence who allowed him to show his feelings and emotions. In any event, Harriet Taylor was a confidant with whom John Stuart Mill shared his ideas. Harriet, who had strong views about women's rights in society, politics, and education, most likely influenced Mill's support of women's equality. When elected to the House of Commons, he introduced a bill for women's suffrage, which was defeated. Harriet Taylor also may have helped push Mill from the laissez-faire liberal social and economic position in the direction of reformist humanitarian liberalism. However, Benthamite Utilitarianism had already moved him in this direction.

Mill, in his *Autobiography*, praised Harriet for her intellectual vitality and her compassionate nature. He wrote that her mind was a "perfect instrument, piercing to the very heart and marrow of the matter; always seizing the essential idea or principle." He praised her sensitivity and "her gifts of feeling and imagination."[25]

Mill devoted the rest of his life to philosophical writing. One of his most influential books, *On Liberty* (1859), expressed his fear of a coming mass society, characterized by a conformity that would stifle individual freedom. His *Utilitarianism* (1863) sought to revise and revitalize the philosophy on which he had been nurtured and educated. Here, he amended ethical theories based on Bentham's principle of utility, which asserted that human happiness could be measured quantitatively. While Bentham contended that all categories of human pleasure were at the same level, Mill found them to be more complex and qualitative. Pleasures could be placed on scale, with intellectual pleasures ranking higher than physical ones. Defending Utilitarianism against critics who attacked it as a selfish ethical theory, Mill argued that it had an altruistic dimension in seeking to increase pleasure for all human beings. He also sought to redefine the role of the state. Government, he said, should ensure that citizens had equal access to the sources of happiness but maintained that it remained the individual's right to choose the happiness desired.

In addition to his writing, Mill made a brief foray into active politics and was elected to one term in the House of Commons, serving from 1865 to 1868. Although elected as an independent from the district of Westminster, Mill supported the Liberal party on most votes. He supported extending suffrage to those disenfranchised because of property restrictions. He had earlier supported the "great reform" bill of 1832, which reduced property qualifications. As an advocate of universal suffrage, he also supported the reform bill of 1867, which passed while he was in Parliament. He introduced a bill that would have given the vote to women but failed in his efforts.

In 1867, he was appointed rector of St. Andrews University in Scotland. In his inaugural address at St. Andrews, Mill expressed his views on higher education and the proper role of the university. The university, he said, should devote itself to the cultivation of the intellect and not become a professional training school. He defined education in broad terms. In addition to formal schooling that involves books and lectures, Mill said that education was part of a large informal process that provided the knowledge of how to care for property, do one's daily work, and participate in social and political life.

Mill died in 1873 at Avignon and was buried next to his beloved Harriet.

Mill's Social and Educational Philosophy

John Stuart Mill, the product of an unusual but carefully directed education, was recognized by the end of his life as the foremost theoretician of the new humanitarian liberalism. Although he retained his commitment to Bentham's principle that social policy should seek to secure the "greatest happiness for the greatest number," he rejected the Benthamite methodology that happiness could be calculated with mathematical precision. Mill, in his creation of humanitarian liberalism from his revision of Utilitarianism, came to see human happiness in qualitative rather than strictly quantitative terms, which had definite political and educational implications.

For Mill, human beings possessed a potential for sympathy to others that could be developed by education. This human tendency to altruism, he believed, along with knowledge of the principle of utility, would generate an ethical disposition. People so educated would choose the higher-order pleasures that maximized not only their own pleasure but created the greatest good for the greatest number. Educated in the Utilitarian philosophy, people would be able to resolve their moral dilemmas by judging the consequences of their actions in both their personal lives and in society's institutional arrangements. Mill's consequentialism, the judging of actions by their consequences, was a movement away from a metaphysically based ethics to one that was empirical and psychological.

Underlying Mill's political and educational philosophy was an affirmation of individual liberty and freedom. For him, personal freedom and the free circulation of ideas were necessary conditions for political and social progress. In his much-quoted *On Liberty*, Mill expressed his belief in human progress through freedom of thought. He asserted that no person or group was infallible or had a monopoly on truth. Individuals had the right to develop new ideas even as they challenged existing ones. The freedom of thought and expression enabled individuals to examine their own beliefs and the conventions and institutions of society.

Mill was firmly convinced "the only purpose for which power can be rightfully exercised over any member of a civilized community, against his will, is to prevent harm to others. His own good, either physical or moral, is not a sufficient warrant."[26] Mill's determination that social reform be accomplished without jeopardizing individual freedom differed by degree from the position of latter-day humanitarian liberals, especially the progressives in the United States, who believed some degree of social control was needed to regulate society and its institutions. For Mill, social control was permissible only to stop individuals from coercing each other.[27] He would have rejected progressive social controls that attempted to coerce people into becoming better citizens, however the word "better" might be defined. (An example of such a government-imposed social control was the prohibition of alcoholic beverages in the United States in the 1920s.) For him, the search for the good life was an individual project, not one determined by consensus, no matter how democratic the process used to reach it.

Mill's emphasis on individual liberty was based on his belief that a society benefited from the presence of critically minded individuals who challenged conventional wisdom and originated new ideas. Liberty and criticism were utilitarian or useful to a society because they created an environment in which new ideas could be expressed and tested in the court of human opinion. Along with political authoritarianism and despotic government, the greatest obstacle to the freedom to originate and circulate ideas was the restraining power of the status quo and the willingness to accept whatever existed as right and true.

The freedom to hold ideas had a corollary freedom in that individuals should be free to express and communicate their ideas in speech and in print. It was of crucial importance that there be freedom of speech, press, and assembly. It was of equal importance that teachers be free to teach and students be free to learn. This meant that the school should not be an agency to impress conventional wisdom and the status quo on the young but rather an agency to foster individual intellectual initiative, especially critical thinking.

Mill's political philosophy rested on the liberal ideological commitment to an elected representative government in which legislators were responsible to the electorate. A strong defender of civil liberties, Mill believed such freedoms were best secured and maintained under a representative self-government. However, representative institutions required that the people, the electorate, have a civic education that made them conscious of the need to protect their liberties and to elect officials who would act in liberty's name. The view that civic education is necessary for the functioning of representative institutions is also found in the ideas of Thomas Jefferson (see Chapter 12) and Horace Mann (see Chapter 14).

For Mill, there was a more subtle kind of tyranny. Less obvious than dictatorship, the tyranny of the majority was just as pernicious to human freedom. With such tyranny the majority imposed prevailing opinions on the minority. His well-founded fears anticipated the modern tendency to a mass society fed information by a mass media that forms a public, but conformist, mass opinion. In a parliamentary system of government, legislators are elected by the majority of voters. Mill feared that an uneducated mass of voters might be swayed by demagogues who, despite their popular appeal, would repress human rights and freedom if elected. (For example, in the 1930s, Adolf Hitler, who established a ruthless totalitarian state, determined to gain power in Germany by popular election.)

Although there is danger that the majority of voters might elect demagogues, there was also the threat that modern society might generate a mass mind. The Industrial Revolution had made it possible to mass produce goods that were cheap but uniform. On the assembly line, standardized machines produced standardized products. For example, a shoemaking factory could produce thousands of shoes of the same width, length, and color. If the shoes fit the majority of consumers, the volume of sales would be large. However, the mass-produced shoe might not fit the feet of the minority.

Further, the cheapness of the shoes would tend to drive the individual shoemaker with a small shop out of business or force him to restrict his trade to wealthier customers who could afford his services.

The mass production of the industrial factory system had not only economic consequences but threatened to have similar effects on public opinion. Mill feared that mass conformity was a formidable threat to human freedom because it was so socially pervasive. He wrote that it left the individual with "fewer means of escape, penetrating much more deeply into the details of life, and enslaving the soul itself."[28]

A trend in the nineteenth century that escalated in the twentieth was gearing information and entertainment to the interests of the majority. In Mill's day, the cheaply produced newspaper appeared. The newspaper sold for a few pennies and made its income by large readership. The larger the circulation and sales, the greater the profits. The newspapers that dominated the scene were those that appealed to the largest readership. To attract this readership, the reporting of news and human interest features was geared to the widest possible audience, a mass audience whose taste was based on the average person. As there is no average person in reality, this fictional character is a composite of individuals. The average implies a sameness that comes from reducing to a common mold people who do not fit the composite. The consequence of such reductionism is that personal uniqueness, individuality, and eccentricity become regarded almost as abnormalities.

While the popular press of the nineteenth century catered to the average person, as a force of informal education it also molded popular opinions, tastes, and values. If Mill were alive today, he would recognize in the mass media—newspapers, magazines, radio, and especially television—new dangers to individuality. To capture the largest possible audience, the media gear their reporting of information and presenting of entertainment to what the majority wants. Once again, the fictional but powerful average person's taste sets the standard. However, in the modern mass society, the average person is computed by sophisticated samplings and public opinion polls. The result is a sameness, a conformity that, while popularly based, restricts ideas, opinions, and tastes that deviate from the average. Unless the proper educational checks were established, Mill feared that the future might be one of the conformism of the mass society and the mass mind— a worldview based on the average.

Just as Mill feared that the tyranny of the majority might reduce standards to averages, he was concerned that representative institutions might become places where special interest groups secured legislation to advance their causes rather than those of the greatest number of persons.

At the time that Mill dealt with the question of special interest groups the contending parties were the industrial employers and the working-class employees. Throughout the nineteenth century in the United Kingdom, industrial employers held the advantage. However, in the twentieth century, with the rise of large industrial unions and the British Labour party, the tide would shift. In the Marxist view, the interests of capitalist and worker were irreconcilable and would bring about class conflict, revolution, and the eventual but inevitable triumph of the proletariat.

Mill, raised on Bentham's theory of rational decision making and committed to liberal principles of nonviolent social change, took a moderate position. Committed to private property, he opposed the exploitation of workers by capitalist industrialists. Although a humanitarian, he feared that undereducated workers could degenerate into a mob that would destroy liberty. Again, Mill looked to education, especially the education of a disinterested group of citizens who could resolve the dilemma of special interests.

In his *Dissertations and Discussion* (1867), Mill argued for the value of disinterested participation in society. For Mill, a group of well-educated persons, or "disinterested participants," might be able to stem the tide of the tyranny of the majority as well as reconcile the contentions of conflicting special interest groups. A *disinterested* person was one who was neither biased by personal interests nor motivated by the desire for personal profit. While disinterested persons were unprejudiced, they were nonetheless participants in the social and political processes and not aloof from them. Unlike members of special interest groups, disinterested persons would not be motivated to seek special privileges or advantages. The quality of disinterestedness implied having an educated perspective that made it possible to evaluate an issue objectively.

For Mill, education had the potential of being the great solvent of a free society. Educated people, Mill reasoned, would be concerned with the general good rather than with special class interests. Disinterested, critically minded, well-educated people could act as the lever of social policy—a kind of swing vote. As a social voice of criticism, they might exercise the important role of objective decision making. Mill had a vision of a new kind of scholar—a person disinterested in special gain but a critical thinker—in preparing and advancing legislation in the general and public interest.

Mill's argument in *On Liberty* stated that

- The individual is interested in advancing his or her own welfare.
- The individual's welfare is intimately related to promoting the public good.
- New ideas that express human inventiveness and creativity advance both individual and social progress.
- New ideas are generated by individuals or by members of minorities.
- In a social and political climate of freedom of thought and opinion, alternative ideas will be expressed and compete with each other.
- From the competition of ideas, truth will emerge and new policies will be formulated.

Conclusion: An Assessment

John Stuart Mill's life, education, and philosophy are instructive for educators. His *Autobiography* is itself an analysis of educational theory. Like autobiography and biography in general, it is an account of the effects of persons, situations, and ideas in shaping a life. John Stuart Mill's education at the hands of his Utilitarian tutors, Jeremy Bentham and James Mill, is an account of education that was purposeful but out of balance. It produced a critically minded intellectual who, while skilled in analyzing political and philosophical works, was awkwardly prepared for the totality of life. While Mill's mind was intellectually honed to precision, his education was so one sided that he was stunted emotionally. What is instructive about studying Mill's life and education for today's teachers is the lesson that it is necessary for a person to have an education that harmoniously blends the intellectual or cognitive dimension of humanness with the emotional or affective dimension.

In terms of social and educational policy, the educational implications of Mill's stress on individual freedom are clear. In the educative process, the learner is to be appreciated as an individual personality who has her or his own interests, needs, values, and most importantly, ideas. Attention needs to be focused constantly and consistently on the learner, who possesses unique potentialities to achieve fulfillment as a human being and to contribute from this unique individuality to the happiness and welfare of others.

In a mass society such as ours, Mill's call to preserve individuality suggests many educational implications. Educational institutions in the United States, like other social institutions, have become large, massive, complex, and bureaucratic places. This massiveness produces a numbing effect on individuality. In corporate education, as well as corporate society, there is the danger that in the desire for efficient programming of instruction, individual students will have their behavior so modified that uniqueness is ground out of the human character. When individuals are lost in the mass and become blurs in the faceless crowd of the statistically standardized average, they are reduced to impersonal statistics. In the mass school system as in the mass society, individuals become increasingly subject to what Mill called the conformity of the mass. In U.S. schools, the danger to individuality comes also from the pressures to quantify and standardize all modes of education. If massive schools bring about a condition of educational conformity and oppressive impersonality, they need to be redesigned according to individual needs rather than reduce individuals to fit institutional requirements.

An educational institution that encourages the development of diverse ideas, in Mill's perspective, is one that is characterized by a pervasive academic freedom. In such schools, teachers are free to teach and students are free to learn. As liberty in the larger society is jeopardized by coercion, bureaucracy, authoritarianism, violence, conformity, and anarchy, these same forces limit academic freedom in schools.

According to Mill, it is possible and desirable to frame social, political, and educational policies that advance the interest of both the individual and society. The kind of society that Mill advocated would recognize the values of individual freedom of thought and expression and encourage disinterested and objective examination and action on social issues. Mill's preferred kind of individualism looks beyond special interests to social progress.

Finally, Mill's modified Utilitarianism was an important stage in the history of liberalism. Although original liberalism was still alive and laissez-faire liberalism would be revived by Herbert Spencer, Mill's emphasis on social policy with a humanitarian conscience was a step toward John Dewey's new liberalism. Utilitarianism's emphasis on how to promote desirable and avoid undesirable consequences would find a congenial home in Dewey's experimentalism.[29] Mill, however, who opposed all forms of coercion, unlike Dewey, was concerned that the group could be an instrument of mass coercion. Mill's liberal ideology pointed up the importance of the individual and of personal liberty. It raised the liberal's dilemma that recognizes the need of regulation to protect the interests of society's members, especially those in disadvantaged situations, but also recognizes in such regulation the beginning of controls on human freedom.

Questions for Reflection and Dialogue

1. Reflect on how James Mill sought to eliminate "chance," the unplanned and spontaneous occurrence, in John Stuart Mill's education. Why did James Mill attempt to do this? Consider the role that chance has played in your life and education.

2. Reflect on how Jeremy Bentham's and James Mill's interests and needs determined John Stuart Mill's education. Cite some examples in which adults' rather than children's interests and needs determine what is taught in schools.
3. Reflect on the meaning of Mill's concept of disinterested participation. Have you ever been a disinterested participant? Identify some current issues in which you might be a disinterested participant.
4. Describe the liberal orientation to life, politics, society, and education.
5. What is the "tyranny of the majority"? Identify at least three symptoms of the tyranny of the majority in contemporary U.S. life and education.
6. How might Mill react to such issues in American society as prayer in public schools, gun control, and limiting the access of children and adolescents to television and Internet content considered to be pornographic?

Projects for Deepening Your Understanding

1. Arrange the members of your class into a focus group that is reviewing the current season's television programs, determining those that should be retained and those that should be eliminated. What group processes emerge? How would Mill react to the role of focus groups in contemporary society?
2. What does a public opinion poll tell us? How would Mill react to the power of public opinion polls in modern American society?
3. Examine candidate positions in campaigns for public office. How do candidates take on or avoid dealing with unpopular subjects?
4. Review the literature on the standards movement in education and the role of standardized tests in setting and determining student achievement. How do you think Mill would react to the use of standardized testing in the standards movement?
5. In an interpretive essay, analyze the relationship between John Stuart Mill and James Mill.
6. In a paper, examine the proposition that John Stuart Mill was an intellectual genius.
7. In an essay, describe an educational situation that exemplifies Mill's concept of the freedom of ideas.

Notes

1. W. D. Grampp, *The Manchester School of Economics* (Stanford, CA: Stanford University Press, 1975).
2. J. Salwyn Schapiro, *Liberalism: Its Meaning and History* (New York: Van Nostrand, 1958), 112–14.
3. Michael J. Gootzeit, *David Ricardo* (New York: Columbia University Press, 1975).
4. J. Salwyn Schapiro, *Liberalism and the Challenge of Fascism: Social Forces in England and France* (New York: McGraw-Hill, 1949), 43–59.
5. Schapiro, *Liberalism and the Challenge of Fascism*, 44.
6. Schapiro, *Liberalism and the Challenge of Fascism*, 44–45.
7. Schapiro, *Liberalism and the Challenge of Fascism*, 51–55.
8. Elie Halevy, *England in 1815* (New York: Barnes & Noble, 1961), 526–32.
9. Brian W. Taylor, "Useful Education for the Poor: A Benthamite Perspective," paper presented at the annual meeting of the Midwest History of Education Society, 1979, 10.
10. Alexander Bain, *James Mill: A Biography* (London: Longmans, Green, 1892), 23.

11. W. H. Burton, ed., *James Mill on Education* (London: Cambridge University Press, 1969), 41.

12. Burton, *James Mill on Education*, 64–65.

13. For his autobiography, see John Stuart Mill, *The Autobiography of John Stuart Mill*, ed. John J. Coss (New York: Columbia University Press, 1944). Biographies of Mill include Alan Ryan, *John Stuart Mill* (New York: Pantheon, 1970); Peter J. Glassman, *J. S. Mill: The Evolution of a Genius* (Gainesville, FL: University of Florida Press, 1985); and Richard J. Halliday, *John Stuart Mill* (London: Allan & Unwin, 1976).

14. Mill, *Autobiography*, 2.

15. John B. Ellery, *John Stuart Mill* (New York: Twayne, 1964), 19.

16. Mill, *Autobiography*, 21.

17. Mill, *Autobiography*, 4.

18. Mill, *Autobiography*, 25–26.

19. William J. Baker, "Grandgrindery and the Education of John Stuart Mill: A Clarification," *Western Humanities Review* 24 (Winter 1970), 51.

20. Mill, *Autobiography*, 9–10.

21. Mill, *Autobiography*, 12.

22. Mill, *Autobiography*, 14.

23. Mill, *Autobiography*, 94.

24. John Stuart Mill and Harriet Taylor Mill, *Essays on Sex Equality*, ed. Alice S. Rossi (Chicago: University of Chicago Press, 1971), 6.

25. Mill, *Autobiography*, 121.

26. Schapiro, *Liberalism and the Challenge of Fascism*, 281.

27. Alan Ryan, *John Dewey and the High Tide of American Liberalism* (New York: W. W. Norton, 1995), 105.

28. Ryan, *Dewey and the High Tide of American Liberalism*, 282.

29. Ryan, *Dewey and the High Tide of American Liberalism*, 90.

Suggestions for Further Reading

Atkinson, Charles. *Jeremy Bentham: His Life and Work*. New York: AMS, 1971.

Burston, W. H. *James Mill on Education*. London: Cambridge University Press, 1969.

Carlisle, Janice. *John Stuart Mill and the Writing of Character*. Athens, GA: University of Georgia Press, 1991.

Cohen, Marshall, ed. *The Philosophy of John Stuart Mill*. New York: Modern Library, 1961.

Donner, Wendy. *The Liberal Self: John Stuart Mill's Moral and Political Philosophy*. Ithaca, NY: Cornell University Press, 1991.

Ellery, John B. *John Stuart Mill*. New York: Twayne, 1964.

Garforth, Francis W. *Educative Democracy: John Stuart Mill on Education in Society*. Oxford, UK: Oxford University Press, 1980.

———, ed. *John Stuart Mill on Education*. New York: Teachers College Press, 1971.

Glassman, Peter J. *J. S. Mill: The Evolution of a Genius*. Gainseville, FL: University of Florida Press, 1985.

Grote, John. *An Examination of the Utilitarian Philosophy*. Bristol, UK: Thoemmes, 1990.

Jackson, Julius. *A Guided Tour of John Stuart Mill's Utilitarianism*. Mountain View, CA: Mayfield, 1993.

Kahan, Alan S. *Aristocratic Liberalism: The Social and Political Thought of Jacob Burckhardt, John Stuart Mill, and Alexis de Tocqueville*. New York: Oxford University Press, 1992.

Kerner, George C. *Three Philosophical Moralists: Mill, Kant, and Sartre*. New York: Oxford University Press, 1990.

Kinser, Bruce A. *A Moralist In and Out of Parliament: John Stuart Mill at Westminster, 1865–1868*. Toronto: University of Toronto Press, 1992.

Kurer, Oskar. *John Stuart Mill: The Politics of Progress*. New York: Garland, 1991.

Mazlish, Bruce. *James and John Stuart Mill*. New York: Basic Books, 1975.

Mill, John Stuart. *Autobiography and Literary Essays*. London: Routledge, 1996.

———. *The Basic Writings of John Stuart Mill: on Liberty, the Subjection of Women, and Utilitarianism*. New York: Modern Library, 2002.

———. *Essays on Equality, Law, and Education*. London: Routledge, 1996.

———. *Essays on Ethics, Religion and Society.* London: Routledge, 1996.

———. *John Mill's Boyhood Visit to France: Being a Journal and Notebook.* Toronto: University of Toronto Press, 1992.

———. *On Liberty.* Peterborough, Ont.: Broadview Press, 1999.

———. *A System of Logic.* London: Longmans, Green, 1952.

———. *Utilitarianism and On Liberty: Including "Essay on Bentham" and Selections from the Writings of Jeremy Bentham and John Austin.* Oxford: Blackwell, 2002.

Mill, John Stuart, and Mill, Harriet Taylor. *Essays on Sex Equality.* Ed. Alice S. Rossi. Chicago: University of Chicago Press, 1970.

Ryan, Alan. *John Stuart Mill.* New York: Pantheon, 1970.

Smart, Paul. *Mill and Marx: Individual Liberty and the Roads to Freedom.* Manchester, UK: Manchester University Press, 1991.

Steintrager, James. *Bentham.* Ithaca, NY: Cornell University Press, 1977.

Stephens, Leslie. *The English Utilitarians.* New York: August M. Kelley, 1978.

Strasser, Mark P. *The Moral Philosophy of John Stuart Mill: Toward Modifications of Contemporary Utilitarianism.* Wakefield, NH: Longwood, 1991.

Thomas, William. *Mill.* Oxford, UK: Oxford University Press, 1985.

Zastoupil, Lynn. *John Stuart Mill and India.* Stanford, CA: Stanford University Press, 1994.

Zerilli, Linda M. G. *Signifying Woman: Culture and Chaos in Rousseau, Burke, and Mill.* Ithaca, NY: Cornell University Press, 1994.

CHAPTER 18

Herbert Spencer: Advocate of Individualism, Science, and Social Darwinism

This chapter analyzes the life, social theory, and educational philosophy of Herbert Spencer (1820–1903), a proponent of science in the curriculum and social Darwinism in society. Spencer, an eminent British intellectual of the Victorian era, developed socioeducational theories that exerted an important transatlantic influence. Spencer, who developed a naturalistic approach to education, also developed the social implications of Charles Darwin's theory of biological evolution.

In this chapter we look at Spencer's influence on educational theory in general and on U.S. society and education in particular. First, we describe the social, political, and economic context, the historical milieu in which Spencer lived and worked. Second, we analyze Spencer's biography, his education and career, to determine the evolution of his ideas. Third, we address the effect of Spencer's educational ideas and of social Darwinism. By this analysis, it is possible to see the interworkings of ideology and education in society. For example, Spencer's social Darwinism was a potent ideology that provided a rationale for industrialization and modernization in the United States. Although his reputation is inextricably linked to social Darwinism, Spencer also was a major force for educational change, especially in curriculum.

To organize your thoughts as you read this chapter, focus on the following questions:

1. What were the major trends in the historical context in which Spencer lived?
2. How did Spencer's life, his educational biography, shape his educational theory?

3. How did Spencer's "sociology of knowledge" influence his educational philosophy and policies?
4. What is the enduring significance of Spencer's educational contributions?

The Historical Context of Spencer's Life

Herbert Spencer's life coincided with the period when Western nations, especially the United Kingdom, the United States, and Germany, were being profoundly changed by industrial modernization.[1] The harnessing of science and engineering to achieve the mass production of the factory system brought about change not only in the economic system but in society as well. Spencer, an engineer and sociologist, sought to understand the new industrial situation by studying technological change from a variety of perspectives—economic, biological, sociological, political, and educational. From his analysis, he hoped to predict how social change occurs.

Although the processes of industrial and technological change were affecting both the United Kingdom and the United States, they took somewhat different courses in the two nations most influenced by Spencer's ideology. In the United Kingdom, industrialization began in the early nineteenth century with the Industrial Revolution. Water, steam, and then other forces of energy drove the machinery of Britain's mills and factories. Early textile mills were joined by iron and steel foundries to make England the "workshop of the world."

Control of British political life alternated between the Conservative party, largely composed of old aristocracy, landed gentry, small landowners, and supporters of the Church of England, and the Liberal party, composed of industrialists, middle-class businessmen, tradesmen, and Nonconformist Protestant dissenters from the established Anglican Church. In the Victorian age, named after the long-reigning Queen Victoria, British politics were dominated by Benjamin Disraeli, the Conservative leader, and William Ewart Gladstone, leader of the Liberals.

Conservatives took a largely gentleman's stance to the profound changes sweeping the British Isles, emphasizing the importance of the crown, the church, the aristocracy, and tradition. Early in the nineteenth century, the Liberals, supported by the new money of the rising middle classes, had challenged the traditional Tory, or Conservative party, establishment. Liberals sought to advance the interests of the new middle classes by rolling back the privileges of the old aristocracy. Liberals espoused a number of reforms that extended the right to vote to more members of the lower classes, restricted child labor, and encouraged greater individual freedom. If the Conservatives were defenders of the great traditions of Britain, the Liberals were the proponents of gradual change and moderate reform.

Industrialization also brought changes in British class structure. The upper rungs of society were still occupied by the landed aristocracy—the great families of England—and the landed gentry. Their offspring attended the famous "public schools," actually prestigious and exclusive preparatory schools that readied them for entry into the venerable universities of Oxford and Cambridge. By birth, breeding, and education, the privileged classes continued to dominate the upper echelons of the Church of England, the officer corps of the military services, and the imperial civil service.

The British middle classes, ranging from small shopkeepers to large industrialists, challenged the older Tory aristocracy. The "new money" of the middle classes, made in trade and commerce, was earning the power that wealth brought to its possessors in a free enterprise society. Many Liberal-sponsored reforms sought to give the middle classes political power commensurate with their economic power. Wealth brought some power but did not immediately alter the social status quo. Although a number of industrialists' sons entered the great public schools and universities, the middle class established grammar schools and new, practically inclined institutes and universities to educate their children.

Industrialization created a new class, the working class of miners and factory workers. By various reform acts, larger numbers of the working class gained the right to vote. Workers began to organize trade unions to improve working conditions and earn higher wages. For most of the nineteenth century, Conservatives and Liberals vied for the increasing number of working-class voters. Neither party, however, truly represented working-class interests.

Liberalism, in particular, faced a dilemma that would split it after World War I and severely diminish it as a force in British political life. Originally, the ideology espoused freedom of speech, press, assembly, religion, and trade, opposing any restrictions by government on these Lockean "negative" freedoms. However, if government were to be an agency of reform directed to ameliorating the harsh and exploitative conditions of nineteenth-century industrialism such as squalid tenements, unsafe working conditions, and child labor, then it would have to take on regulatory powers that limited the freedom of some to exploit others. Although some liberal purists, called "classical liberals," adhered to the socioeconomic doctrines of their founding fathers—John Locke, Adam Smith, David Ricardo, and Thomas Malthus—others, the "new or modern liberals," advocated in the Utilitarian fashion of Jeremy Bentham and John Stuart Mill gradual reforms to ameliorate exploitative conditions and bring about by legislation the "greatest good for the greatest number."

Within this context of an industrializing British society with its tension between tradition and change, Herbert Spencer, a child of a Nonconformist Protestant middle-class family, lived and worked. By family and class, Spencer was on the side of British liberalism. Resenting the privileged position enjoyed by the officially established Church of England, he wanted the Anglican Church's educational role diminished. Largely a self-educated person, Spencer did not value the classically oriented traditional education that characterized the public schools and the older, prestigious universities. Spencer criticized this traditional education as ornamental and of little practical use. England's prestigious secondary and higher educational institutions resisted attempts to add scientific and technological studies to their curricula. For Spencer, securing the entry of new studies that would modernize the economy and production was a determined educational crusade.

Ideologically, Spencer was associated with classical liberalism rather than its more modern socially reformist Utilitarian wing. This was not because he was a person of wealth but because his ideological convictions led him to oppose any restrictions on individual freedom. Social reformist efforts, regardless of their humanitarian intentions, would inevitably lead to more government regulation. The result would be a super welfare state that intruded into areas of private life. Spencer believed that government involvement in housing, education, and medicine would create inefficient and costly state monopolies. He believed in a government with very limited and specified powers.

In 1859, Charles Darwin (1809–1882) published *The Origin of Species by Means of Natural Selection*, a book that provoked a revolution in biological thinking.[2] Darwin's evolutionary thesis was an important part of the intellectual context of Spencer's world and exerted a powerful influence on his social thinking. Darwin, the official naturalist on an English surveying ship, the *Beagle*, had observed and collected plant and animal specimens that caused him to postulate an evolutionary theory of the origin of species. Hypothesizing that plants and animals had slowly evolved as a result of a process of natural selection, Darwin concluded that all forms of organic life were descended from a small number of primitive prototypes. Existing plants and animals, as well as extinct ones, were descendants of ancestral prototypes that had experienced slow and gradual modifications that, if they enhanced survival, were transmitted to their offspring as inherited characteristics.

In summary, Darwin's thesis held that

- More individuals of each species were born than could survive.
- There is a struggle, or intense competition, among these individuals to obtain what they need to survive.
- Those individuals who vary in a profitable way enhance their chances for survival and thus are naturally selected.
- Naturally selected individuals perpetuate themselves by passing on their advantage to their offspring.

Although some scientists disputed Darwin's evolutionary thesis, it received support from such academicians as Joseph Hooker, Charles Lyell, and Thomas Huxley in England, Asa Gray in the United States, and Ernest Haeckel in Germany. Such publications as Lyell's *Antiquity of Man* (1863) and Huxley's *Man's Place in Nature* (1863) paved the way for a more general application of evolutionary theory to human society.[3]

Charles Darwin's theory of evolution was located in the natural sciences of biology, botany, and zoology, but it also produced dramatic controversies in theology, philosophy, and education. Orthodox theologians, Catholic and Protestant alike, argued that Darwin's theory of changing and evolving species directly contradicted the literal account of creation in the Bible's book of Genesis, which said that species had been created in their fixed and final form.[4] Later, other theologians would find an accommodation to Darwin's evolutionary theory by reading Genesis in an allegorical way. For religious literalists, there was and continues to be no compromise with evolutionary theory. Spencer, who was not strongly committed to religious doctrine, readily accepted Darwin's theory.

It was neither biology nor religion that attracted Spencer to Darwin's evolutionary theory. He was most intrigued by its social implications. If the natural world of plants and animals followed nature's unyielding evolutionary laws, did not the same laws apply to human society and its institutions? Social Darwinism, the body of social theories emerging from the effect of Darwin's theory of evolution, found a staunch and leading advocate in Herbert Spencer.

Spencer's identification with social Darwinism made him a popular and highly respected theorist in the United States. Like the United Kingdom, the United States after the Civil War was in the throes of industrial and technological change. In the second half of the nineteenth century, the United States was most receptive to social Darwinism and to Spencer's ideas, even more so than his native England.

In the United States, social Darwinism provided an ideological rationale for a public policy that supported the business activities of powerful industrialists such as Andrew Carnegie and John D. Rockefeller, and the trend to industrial modernization. At the same time, social Darwinism could be used to repress the counteractions of discontented agrarian populists and the embryonic trade union movement.[5] After the Civil War, heavy industries—coal, oil, iron, and steel—enjoyed a tremendous expansion with the support of political allies, primarily in the Republican party. Raw materials such as oil, iron ore, and coal were exploited with little concern for environmental protection and human rights. A transcontinental network of railroads was constructed with subsidies from the federal government to link growing cities with the sources of raw materials needed to manufacture products for national and international markets. The leaders of the dominant political party, the Republicans, allied with the "captains of industry" to oppose regulatory legislation. The emergence of social Darwinism as a gospel of economic progress and prosperity provided a useful and apparently coherent "scientific" rationale for these industry leaders and their social, political, and educational allies in the United States.

The attempt of the social Darwinists to use science as a basis for social policy was not new. Since the eighteenth-century Enlightenment, theorists had sought to create a science of society that was analogous and parallel to the discoveries and formulations of the physical sciences. Spencer saw physics and chemistry as key subjects in moving humankind along a progressive course. For Spencer and other social theorists, such as William Graham Sumner, Darwin's evolutionary view of biology could be adapted to society, politics, and education.

Ideologically, the United States was a more receptive home for social Darwinism than was England. In 1869, Darwin had been honored with membership in the prestigious American Philosophical Society, an organization founded by Benjamin Franklin that numbered Thomas Jefferson as one of its presidents.[6] Herbert Spencer was the favorite philosopher of Carnegie and other industrialists. In the name of freedom of competition, the advocates of a basically unregulated but growing economy found social Darwinism to be a scientifically based rationale for the following policy assumptions:

- The captains of industry were providing great service to the country by exploiting its resources and establishing an industrial economic base.
- There should be no interference or regulation by either government or misguided social planners and reformers.
- An economy that followed natural principles of supply and demand and encouraged the initiative that came from free enterprise would enjoy progress and economic prosperity.

Herbert Spencer's theories on the evolutionary development of society, private enterprise, and a free and unregulated economy fit well into the cultural milieu of the second half of the nineteenth century. In the following section, we look at the life of Herbert Spencer, the nineteenth century's leading apologist for social Darwinism.

Herbert Spencer

Herbert Spencer was born on April 17, 1820, in Derby, England.[7] His father, William George Spencer, an educator and writer, was the author of *Inventional Geometry*, a textbook on the basic principles of geometry. William, the dominant member of the family, had definite opinions about what was wrong and right about English society, politics, economics, and religion. Outspoken, highly opinionated but coolly rational, William Spencer had a strong influence on his son's education and intellectual outlook. The elder Spencer encouraged his son to think for himself, stand up for his ideas, and be critical of the conventional wisdom of the day. Spencer's mother appears to have been a rather passive person who devoted herself to satisfying the needs of her husband and son. The Spencer household was characterized by the spirit of nonconformity in religion, politics, and social life. Spencer's childhood produced in him an attitude of the strongest kind of individualism and a resistance to infringements on freedom of choice by church or state.[8]

As a child, Herbert attended school for only a short time. His father regarded the schools as inadequate and ineffective and took charge of his son's education.[9] From his father, Herbert learned the basics of reading, writing, arithmetic, literature, and science, with the greatest stress on mathematics and science. Commenting on his early education, Spencer wrote that he knew virtually nothing of Latin, Greek, ancient history, and literature.[10] Note that these subjects were regarded at the time as forming the necessary education of the English gentleman. William Spencer regarded the study of ancient languages and literature to be a waste of time that could be more efficiently spent on a practical education grounded in mathematics and science.

Of equal importance with the subjects he studied with his father was the style and method of the father–son tutorial relationship. They questioned all existing knowledge, especially assumptions resting on the ancient classics and philosophy. They approached existing beliefs with the skeptic's critical perspective. No philosophical first principles were taken on face value. Nor did they value the Greek and Latin classics. Departing from the Victorian adage that "children should be seen but not heard," William Spencer expected and encouraged his intellectually precocious and highly verbal son to engage adult guests in the Spencer home in discussions of current issues. Spencer's childhood was a prelude to his adult career as a social theorist rather than an opportunity for association with other children and participation in their play, games, and activities. Despite his suffering of periodic episodes of "mental fatigue," Spencer professed gratitude to his father for developing his skills of intellectual analysis and synthesis. Of his father's educational method, Spencer wrote,

> Concerning things . . . and their properties, I knew a good deal more than is known by most boys. My conceptions of physical principles and processes had considerable clearness; and I had a fair acquaintance with sundry special phenomena in physics and chemistry. I had also acquired both in personal observation and by reading, some knowledge of animal life, and especially of insect life. . . . By miscellaneous reading a little mechanical, medical, anatomical, and physiological information had been gained; as also a good deal of information about the various parts of the world and their inhabitants.[11]

In 1832, William Spencer decided that his son would benefit from exposure to the ideas of his brother, the Reverend Spencer. At age 13, Herbert began three years of study with his uncle. He learned small amounts of Latin and Greek but his more formal studies once again gravitated to mathematics and the natural and physical sciences. Young Spencer particularly enjoyed Euclid's geometry and trigonometry. History, literature, and languages, which the Spencers regarded as ornamental, were purposefully neglected.

After completing his studies, Herbert Spencer pursued a career in civil engineering from age 17 to 27. As an engineer, he applied mathematics and science to practical matters. Increasingly, however, his mind went from specific engineering projects to the consideration of larger matters. How had humankind reached its current state of social development? How did social change occur? How should people be educated in a world that was growing steadily more industrial and technological? True to the education that he had received from his father and uncle, Herbert Spencer rejected much of the wisdom of the day and set out on a single-minded intellectual odyssey to find the answers to these questions. He read widely in the sciences, especially the works of Lyell on geology and Lamarck on biology.

In 1842, Spencer began a career as a writer and critic for *The Economist*, a leading periodical. His articles espoused the classical liberal ideology that stressed personal liberty, rugged individualism, and freedom from government interference, themes that concerned him throughout his life.

Spencer's journalistic career was secondary to his primary interest in creating a comprehensive body of knowledge, a sociology of knowledge based on science, that would dethrone theology and metaphysics from their preeminent positions in the intellectual world. He spent his time writing and publishing a large number of essays and books. In 1860, he began work on *The Synthetic Philosophy*, the name he gave to his sociology of knowledge. His work was interrupted by bouts of ill health caused by a regimen of research and writing that left little time for recreation. He regarded many of the recreational outlets that art, literature, drama, and music provided as merely distractions from science. Despite self-diagnosed nervous exhaustion, insomnia, and digestive problems, Spencer continued to labor on his monumental *Synthetic Philosophy*, completing it 36 years later.[12]

Spencer's career as an author rather than his personal life stands out in his biography (and in his autobiography). He was a tireless and ambitious writer. His method of research was more journalistic than scholarly. He claimed that his ideas were his own rather than borrowed from others. His method was to skim articles that appeared in the leading journals and periodicals. Historical and biographical articles received a quick perusal. When he encountered an article on science, engineering, or technology he would study it thoroughly and absorb it.

Spencer's writings would first appear as lectures, articles, and essays. Then, they would be collected, and perhaps be reorganized, into books. His total output was voluminous. Among his most widely read books was *First Principles of a New System of Philosophy* (1862), which stated his application of evolutionary theory to society. It was a pioneering contribution to sociology. In *First Principles*, Spencer examined the structure and function of social institutions. His *Social Statics; or the Conditions Essential to Human Happiness Specified, and the First of Them Developed* (1850) was a strong statement for individualism, human freedom, and the need to keep state and church from interfering in human affairs. *Essays: Scientific, Political, and Speculative* (1860) was a collection of Spencer's ideas on the importance of science and the need to limit government power and regulation. Although his books contained commentaries on education,

Spencer addressed education specifically in *Education: Intellectual, Moral, and Physical* (1855), which grew out of his influential essay, "What Knowledge Is of Most Worth?"

Spencer's Social Theory

Spencer's self-determined lifelong task was to create a comprehensive sociology of knowledge capable of explaining the evolution of society and of predicting social change. The study of theories of social change, such as Spencer's, raises the following important questions for educational policy makers:

- Does education, especially schooling, reflect current social conditions and values or can it bring about changes in these conditions and values?
- If one can determine the essential processes that generate social change, is it not possible to formulate educational policies that either accelerate or retard such change?
- Is social change a process that occurs because of natural laws or can it result from deliberate human planning?

Spencer's opinion about social change was based on a worldview that saw the universe in materialistic terms. Essentially, the matter of the universe was being constantly redistributed by incessant motion. The characteristics of this cosmic redistribution were evolution and dissolution. Evolution, accompanied by the dissipation of motion, resulted in the progressive integration of matter. Dissolution, accompanied by the absorption of motion, brought about the disorganization of matter.[13]

Life itself was inherently an evolutionary process. Organisms, including human beings, were part of an evolutionary chain that went from the very simple, characterized by an incoherent homogeneity, to the complex, characterized by a coherent heterogeneity. That which is homogeneous is unstable because the "persistent force" of motion will cause differences to arise in the course of future development. Simple and homogeneous organisms will eventually become complex and heterogeneous.

Societies, like biological organisms, experience the process of evolution from the simple and primitive to the complex, heterogeneous, and specialized. In the future, advanced societies will reach a state of equilibrium, or perfect balance, that will be stable, harmonious, and capable of providing the greatest happiness to the greatest number.

Although he held a materialistic view of the universe, Spencer believed that true religion dealt with the worship of the "unknowable." In life, decisions had to be made and policies formulated on what could be known empirically. The guide to the operations of the knowable was science. The surest way of creating a complex and specialized society was by the application of science to the activities that sustained life.

For Spencer, the dynamic process that affected both natural and social phenomena was evolution. According to Spencer, it would be folly to attempt deliberately to change society by either revolution, legislation, or education. The prudent and effective policy was efficient adjustment to the environment. The most able individuals would adjust quickly and intelligently to the circumstances and situations that the natural and social environment posed. The educational policy Spencer endorsed would incorporate and emphasize the scientific method for such efficient adjustment. It would educate scientists, technologists, and specialists who would make their way up the rungs of society by their skill, endurance, and innovation. The fittest of each generation would survive by skill, scientific intelligence, self-control, discipline, and the ability to adapt.

It was crucial that the fittest individuals be not only permitted but also encouraged to excel. For Spencer, ethics meant that the fittest were allowed to compete. The government's role was strictly negative—to make sure that individual freedom was not curtailed. Every person had the right to do as she or he pleased provided that their actions did not violate the natural rights of others to pursue their own self-interests. Government aid, "wars against poverty," and welfare programs were doomed to failure. Not only did they maintain the unfit, they limited the freedom of the fittest. Further, they were not in tune with the natural process of evolution. Driven by competition and the desire to survive, the fittest by their inventiveness and innovation would create a better and more progressive society.

Spencer's Rationale for Curriculum Construction

In addition to being a leading proponent of social Darwinism, Spencer also should be seen as a pioneering educational theorist. Even before the publication of Darwin's evolutionary theory, Spencer was using naturalistic and scientific principles to urge a more practical and utilitarian curriculum. As a proponent of the principle of naturalism in education, Spencer followed in the tradition of Rousseau and Pestalozzi. (See Chapters 10 and 11.)

Spencer's advocacy of scientific study anticipated the modern school curriculum. Because he is so closely identified with social Darwinism and its highly individualistic and competitive ethic, Spencer has often been cited as representing the kind of social and educational theory that reformers such as Jane Addams (see Chapter 19) and John Dewey (see Chapter 20) opposed. Indeed, many of Addams's and Dewey's socioeducational theories need to be seen as important counterarguments against Spencerianism.

To see what Spencer was advocating in education, it is useful to examine what he was against. Spencer opposed the "public school" education that he neither experienced nor wanted to experience as a child. In these selective preparatory schools, boys were drilled in Latin and Greek grammar and literature. Advancing to Oxford and Cambridge, they continued to study the classics, literature, philosophy, and history. In the British educational tradition, this kind of study was supplemented by the milieu of living at the preparatory school. Here, one learned to play the game, develop the social graces, and become devoted to the school, a kind of preparatory social club for the larger gentlemen's network that controlled much of British life.

Herbert Spencer, educated by father and self, was not part of the educational milieu that produced cultivated English gentlemen, nor did he want to be part of what he regarded as an obsolete class. The liberally educated gentleman was, in Spencer's opinion, a superfluous person. The modern world, marked by science, technology, and engineering, needed specialists rather than generalists. Just as he opposed the dominant forms of secondary and higher education, Spencer also opposed primary and elementary schooling geared to memorization of textbooks and instilling religious dogmas. The education that he proposed brought together principles of naturalism and of science.

Spencer's best-known work on education is his rationale for a new scientific curriculum, titled "What Knowledge Is of Most Worth?" published in 1855.[14] Spencer began by examining the historical conditions that had shaped education. He believed that schooling, from the primary level through higher education, was determined largely by tradition and routine. For example, the dominance of the Latin and Greek classics in the curriculum was largely a matter of tradition. These languages, useful in the theological and philosophical education of the Medieval scholastics, no longer served a purpose in a modern industrial society. However, the social and educational establishments, wedded to the past, continued to refer to the ancient classics as the "mark of the educated man" and required them for admission to university study and for entry into governmental positions. Not only were the classical languages obsolete, they also took up time, money, and energy that could be better directed to the study of science, technology, and engineering.

Schooling, controlled by the vested interests of the landed aristocracy and established church, was also a means of social control. In schools, students were taught to conform to, not challenge, traditional expectations and roles. Individual initiative was repressed rather than liberated creatively. Spencer was a determined proponent of liberating individuals from social control, including that fostered by formal education.

Spencer observed that educational attainments such as certificates, diplomas, and degrees had become a kind of "paper chase" used to gain social status and prestige rather than coveted for any instrumental value. The old form of classical education, monopolized by the upper classes, became the educational prize that the new middle class desired.

Rather than relying on tradition, custom, routine, and the desire for social status, Spencer argued there were important questions to be answered in establishing a curriculum:

1. Were not some subjects more important than others in generating added knowledge that was useful?
2. Should not the subjects be taught according to their importance?
3. Might not time be spent more effectively on some subjects than on others?

Using his engineer's mind, Spencer believed curriculum should be determined by estimating the time, money, and energy spent in teaching a subject and the consequences derived from its study: Did the particular subject pay its way?

To answer his overarching question, "What knowledge is of most worth?" Spencer raised a number of related questions to guide curriculum construction:

1. How should the human body be treated to maintain its health?
2. How should the human mind, the source of our rational powers, be treated?
3. How should our economic, social, political, and educational affairs be managed?
4. How should our children be reared and educated?
5. How should responsible citizens act?
6. What is the best use of natural resources?

Spencer's focusing questions provided a new rationale for constructing the curriculum that would have a decided influence on U.S. educators, especially those who believed that schooling should be responsive to human needs and should produce economically and socially efficient persons.

To answer his own questions, Spencer began to categorize human activities into clusters that could be used as the basis for arranging the curriculum. He identified the following clusters of activities:

1. Self-preservation—the physical health—of the human body
2. The self-preservation of human life by providing the necessities of life such as earning a living
3. Rearing and educating children
4. Maintaining proper social and political relationships such as civic education
5. Making time for miscellaneous leisure activities that provide enjoyment and satisfaction such as art, literature, drama, poetry, and music

Like modern curriculum specialists, Spencer began the task of curriculum construction by identifying important human activities rather than subject matters. Once these activities had been identified, appropriate skills and subjects could be designed to prepare individuals to perform them. In examining Spencer's list, note that he established a priority based on their relationship to each other. The first activity, self-preservation, is necessary for the second, earning a living, and so on. The knowledge that was most useful in performing the first four categories of activities was scientific. The last category, miscellaneous activities, required physical health, economic security, and political order provided by categories one, two, and four.

Spencer answered his query on knowledge with a resounding endorsement of the importance of science. Indeed, scientific knowledge could be applied to all the activities that human beings needed to perform. For example, knowledge from anatomy and physiology could be used to enhance physical health. Productivity in an industrial society required knowledge of the properties of raw materials that came from chemistry, botany, and zoology. In a technological society characterized by the application of scientific information to industrial processes, mathematics was indispensable. In a society of mass production and consumption, mathematics was a necessary tool for business—for estimating supply and demand, for conducting trade, and for accounting purposes. Spencer's arguments for a curriculum oriented to mathematics and science may seem commonplace today; however, in the second half of the nineteenth century it was a bold proposal that challenged traditional education's emphasis on the classics, philosophy, theology, and literature.

In his argument for parenting education, Herbert Spencer was a modernist who anticipated an important contemporary trend. Spencer considered rearing and educating children to be one of the most important but seriously neglected human activities. In this category, Spencer addressed themes related to women's education and to general education.

At the time that Spencer wrote, working-class women in England received little education beyond primary schooling. Middle- and upper-class women enjoyed more educational opportunities but Spencer considered them misguided and misdirected. Women's finishing schools emphasized memorizing "dead languages, reading romantic novels, reciting poetry, and doing needlework," not the practical matters of life, especially child care and education.

In his commentary on the education of children, Spencer shows himself to be in the tradition of such naturalists in education as Rousseau and Pestalozzi. Just as natural laws govern nature and society, they determine patterns of human growth and development. Rather than relying on convention and custom, Spencer advised educators to base instruction on the laws of psychology. Psychology, according to Spencer, tells us that instruction is more effective when it is based on direct experience in the real world rather than on the abstract verbalism of books. Children need a store of experience before they can truly understand what they read.

Spencer recommended that parents and teachers follow a method that emphasized the following:

1. Begin with children's immediate and direct experience.
2. Use concrete situations before moving to more abstract problems.
3. Let children learn from the natural consequences of their actions rather than from artificial rewards and punishments.
4. Avoid the rote memorization of highly verbal lessons.
5. Impress on children the practical application of what they are learning.

These principles of instruction, Spencer reasoned, constituted the best preparation for dealing with life's real problems and for the later study of advanced mathematics and sciences.

Spencer had specific recommendations related to the proper education for citizens. Civic education, he advised, should be based on the principles of sociology rather than on history. History was too focused on the study of kings and queens, the lives of great men, and battles and military campaigns. Studying history filled the mind with irrelevant and isolated facts that had little value in explaining society and predicting the course of social change. Spencer advised educators to look to social science for the materials of civic education. Sociology, properly organized and taught, could inform us about how human societies had evolved, how institutions functioned, and how individuals related to the social whole. The same laws of change that governed the evolution of species also governed the evolution of society. Social change came about as the fittest individuals made efficient functional adaptations to a changing environment. The proper civic education, like education in general, would encourage the fittest to excel in the race of life. Such a civic education would convince individuals to avoid what Spencer regarded as the false promises of "do-gooders," socialists, and would-be reformers. If nature took its course as it was bound to do, the future would be a progressive and prosperous one for those persons who really mattered in the natural order of things.

Although Spencer must be recognized as a contributor to the natural and scientific education of children and as a pioneering figure in the study and organization of the curriculum, his educational goals were so precise and single minded that he spent little time discussing the humanities, art, literature, and music. He recognized that arts and letters held potential for aesthetic experience, for recreation, and for leisure but did not see them to be instructive of human behavior. As science, industry, and technology advanced, more time would be available for leisure and recreation, he believed, but the arts and letters were not his major concern.

Conclusion: An Assessment

Herbert Spencer's theories need to be assessed in two dimensions, as social theory and as educational theory. As social theory, Spencer's social Darwinism appeared obsolete and irrelevant in the post-Depression and post–World War II eras. In the United Kingdom, the policies of the British Labour party created a welfare state in the decade and a half after World War II. In the United States, Franklin Roosevelt's New Deal policies, designed to alleviate the unemployment of the Great Depression of the 1930s, established a policy of government intervention in the economy that was imitated by subsequent administrations, particularly in Truman's Fair Deal, Kennedy's New Frontier, and Johnson's Great Society. In the western European democracies, especially in the Scandinavian nations, the social welfare state was firmly established. The Soviet Union, the socialist states of eastern Europe, and the People's Republic of China were following Marxist policies of total social planning and control. Indeed, Spencerianism and its emphasis on individualism and resistance to state regulation seemed a historical anachronism that was best suited to be an academic counterfoil to the modern state with its regulation, planning, and welfare programs.

In educational philosophy and theory, too, Spencer's social theory appeared an anachronism. The socially oriented wing of progressive education led by John Dewey appeared to have won the battle against Spencer's rugged individualism. Dewey's stress on cooperation, echoed by William H. Kilpatrick, rejected individualistic competition as socially unintelligent and economically wasteful. George Counts and other social reconstructionists argued that the school ought to take the lead, or at least join with progressive forces, in creating a new social order. In many respects, progressive social theory, politics, and education formed a direct attack against Spencerian social Darwinism.

Since the 1980s, however, certain Spencerian themes resurfaced. The neoconservatives in the United States stressed the need for a resurgent individualism and for the deregulation of the economy. Ronald Reagan's presidency called for a return to self-reliant individualism, inventiveness, and innovation. The social welfare programs in the United Kingdom were reduced by Prime Minister Margaret Thatcher.

The state-run economies in the Soviet Union and its eastern European satellite states, controlled by bureaucrats steeped in Marxist ideology, grew increasingly unproductive. At the beginning of the 1990s, the Soviet system had collapsed completely. Even in Communist China, more sectors of the economy were open to privatization. In the world economy, promoters of democratic capitalism called for deregulation and the operation of the free market. It seemed that Spencer's ideas of economic individualism and competition had taken on a new relevance.

Apart from the political relevance that Spencer may have today, his ideas exerted an important formative influence on U.S. educational theory. Perhaps it is more accurate to say that his ideas paralleled and theoretically reinforced some important shifts taking place in education in the United States. Spencer's appeal to educators was not unlike his popularity with industrialists and businessmen in the latter half of the nineteenth century.

Spencerianism affected U.S. education in its curricular and value emphasis. Spencer's arguments for a revised curriculum with the physical and natural sciences appealed to educators, particularly those who rebelled against the classically dominated curriculum. Concurrently, Spencer's social Darwinist ideology, with its emphasis on individual initiative, scientific inventiveness, and unregulated competition was congenial to the national mood of industrial expansion. Thus, in terms of its reliance on scientific subject matter and competitive values, Spencer's educational doctrines found a home in U.S. schooling.

Since the United States in the late nineteenth century was still a bastion of Evangelical Protestant religion, the same people who rejected Darwin's theory of evolution supported the competitive ethics of social Darwinism. In many respects, the values of social Darwinism were a modernized version of the older Protestant ethic of hard work, perseverance, diligence, and orderliness that was part of the public school's orientation.

Social Darwinism functioned as a kind of naturalistic Calvinism. The human relationship to nature was similar to the human condition in a predestined theology. Meant to be a time of testing, life was hard and demanding. Life's hardships were a means of developing and encouraging morality and character. In the theological sense, punishment was meted out to the negligent, the shiftless, the wasteful, and the inefficient. In the social Darwinism sense, economic punishment was the deserved consequence of such behavior. Poverty was a sign of personal irresponsibility, not of social conditions beyond the control of the individual.

The United States in the late nineteenth century seemed to many to be a nation enjoying economic prosperity because of individual inventiveness and competitive effort. This economic development occurred because of a government that allowed it to happen rather than trying to regulate it. If individuals were left to compete, then progress would occur. Although there might be immediate hardship for some, in the long run individual and social progress was made inevitable by the course of natural evolution. As Richard Hofstadter suggests, the reigning public policy assumption was that "all attempts to reform social processes were efforts to remedy the irremediable . . . that interfered with the wisdom of nature" and that would "lead only to degeneration."[15]

Spencer's emphasis on slow, gradual, and unhurried evolutionary social development found a parallel in his educational thinking. Spencer argued that learning, too, was a process of gradual and cumulative growth. In this regard, the hard-minded and seemingly hard-hearted evolutionary thinker was in agreement with the romantic Rousseau and the child-centered Pestalozzi and Froebel. Although they might vehemently reject Spencer's rugged individualism and highly competitive ethics, progressive educators in the United States could easily concur with his child-centered view of unhurried, gradual, and direct learning.

The Spencerian concept of unhurried evolutionary development carried immense educational implications. First, it argued for change in the curriculum and methods and challenged the verbalism of schools dominated by rote, routine, and custom. Second, in terms of broad educational policy and social goals, Spencer's evolutionary concept placed the school on the side of the socioeconomic status quo. Because deliberate efforts to bring about social change were not only ill advised but pernicious, the school should be a reflective agency rather than an agency of social change. The school functioned most efficiently when it identified the fittest and provided the educational challenges that caused them to rise to the upper socioeconomic echelons.

In another respect, the vogue of Spencerianism also affected how schools were run. Because the captain of industry was the dominant role model, industrial efficiency became a style for educational administrators. The phrase "run schools like a business" summed up the administrative style. Efficiency and effectiveness were prized by those who would try to create a science of education. Because science had the power to explain nature's fundamental law of evolution and social science explained how society functioned, they felt the same kind of science could be applied to education.

Questions for Reflection and Dialogue

1. Reflect on Spencer's analysis of the relationship of technological innovation to social and educational change. How do you think he would react to new educational technologies, especially electronic data retrieval, computers, and the Internet?
2. Reflect on Spencer's argument that education should promote the "fittest," the most able persons in society. How do you think Spencer would react to social promotion policies in public schools?
3. Reflect on Spencer's arguments for little or no government regulation of social and economic life. What kind of response would his arguments have in contemporary American society?
4. Reflect on Spencer's position on the government's role in education. How do you think he would react to proposals for aid to nonpublic schools and vouchers to enhance parental choice?
5. Reflect on Spencer's attempt to apply a biological theory, such as Darwin's evolution, to society and education. Are there similar attempts today?
6. In a class dialogue, consider Spencer's question—What knowledge is of most worth?—for contemporary American society. Attempt to arrive at some statement, or identification of the skills and subjects, that answers the question. Would Spencer agree or disagree with your answer?
7. Why was the United States an especially receptive country for Spencer's ideas? Does it remain a receptive environment for contemporary ideas on utility and competition?
8. Analyze Spencer's strategy for curriculum construction based on basic human activities. Do you find these ideas still current in American curricula?

Projects for Deepening Your Understanding

1. Review the literature on the standards movement in education and the role of standardized tests in setting and determining student achievement. How do you think Spencer would react to the use of standardized testing in the standards movement?
2. Review the literature on home schooling. Both John Stuart Mill and Herbert Spencer were home-schooled. Consider the impact of their fathers on their education. How might advocates and opponents of home schooling assess the educational experiences of Mill and Spencer?
3. Review the required subjects in your college or university curriculum—those needed to meet general education requirements. Then evaluate these requirements

according to Spencer's assertions: (1) some subjects are more important than others in generating useful knowledge; (2) subjects should be taught according to their importance; and (3) time and resources should be spent on some but not other subjects. (Note that the same assertions can be applied to the elementary and secondary school curriculum.)

4. In an outline form, sketch out a curriculum for secondary education based on Spencer's theory.

5. Prepare a lesson plan for use in an elementary class that reflects Spencer's educational ideas.

6. In a position paper, either defend or attack the following statement: Spencer's views on society and education are irrelevant for contemporary U.S. education.

7. In an essay, consider the following statement: Spencer's theory was socially conservative and educationally innovative.

Notes

1. C. E. Black, *The Dynamics of Modernization: A Study in Comparative History* (New York: Harper & Row, 1966).

2. Jonathan Howard, *Darwin* (New York: Oxford University Press, 1982). Also see Michael Ruse, *The Darwinian Revolution* (Chicago: University of Chicago Press, 1979).

3. Carlton J. H. Hayes, *A Generation of Materialism: 1871–1900* (New York: Harper & Row, 1941), 9–13.

4. Neil C. Gillespie, *Charles Darwin and the Problem of Creation* (Chicago: University of Chicago Press, 1979).

5. Richard Hofstadter, *Social Darwinism in American Thought* (Boston: Beacon, 1958), 3–12.

6. George Daniels, ed., *Darwinism Comes to America* (Waltham, MA: Blaisdell, 1968).

7. For biographical information on Spencer, see *Herbert Spencer, An Autobiography*, 2 vols. (New York: D. Appleton, 1904); David Duncan, *Life and Letters of Herbert Spencer*, 2 vols. (New York: D. Appleton, 1908); William H. Hudson,

Herbert Spencer (London: Archibald & Constable, 1908); John D. Y. Peel, *Herbert Spencer: The Evolution of a Sociologist* (New York: Basic Books, 1971); and Josiah Royce, *Herbert Spencer: An Estimate and Review* (New York: Fox, Duffield, 1904).

8. Andreas M. Kazamias, ed., *Herbert Spencer on Education* (New York: Teachers College Press, 1966), 3.

9. Hudson, *Herbert Spencer*, 3–12.

10. Spencer, *Autobiography*, vol. 1, 100.

11. Spencer, *Autobiography*, vol. 1, 100.

12. Spencer, *Autobiography*, vol. 2, 203.

13. Hofstadter, *Social Darwinism in American Thought*, 36–38.

14. There are many editions of Spencer's "What Knowledge Is of Most Worth?" In this section I rely heavily on Kazamias, *Herbert Spencer on Education*, 121–59.

15. Hofstadter, *Social Darwinism in American Thought*, 6–7.

Suggestions for Further Reading

Carnegie, Andrew. *Autobiography*. New York: Houghton Mifflin, 1920.

———. *The Gospel of Wealth and other Timely Essays*. Cambridge, MA: Harvard University Press, 1962.

Cashman, Sean D. *America in the Gilded Age*. New York: New York University Press, 1988.

Daniels, George, ed. *Darwinism Comes to America*. Waltham, MA: Blaisdell, 1968.

Egan, Kieran. *Getting It Wrong from the Beginning: Our Progressivist Inheritance from Herbert Spencer, John Dewey, and Jean Piaget*. New Haven: Yale University Press, 2002.

Gray, Tim. *The Political Philosophy of Herbert Spencer: Individualism and Organicism*. Aldershot, England; Brookfield, VT: Avebury, 1996.

Hacker, Louis. *The World of Andrew Carnegie, 1865–1901*. New York: J. B. Lippincott, 1968.

Hofstadter, Richard. *Social Darwinism in American Thought*. Boston: Beacon, 1958.

Kazamias, Andreas M., ed. *Herbert Spencer on Education*. New York: Teachers College Press, 1966.

Kennedy, James G. *Herbert Spencer*. Boston: G. K. Hall, 1978.

Offer, John. *Herbert Spencer: Critical Assessments*. London; New York: Routledge, 2000.

Paxton, Nancy L. *George Eliot and Herbert Spencer: Feminism, Evolutionism, and the Reconstruction of Gender*. Princeton, NJ: Princeton University Press, 1991.

Peel, J. D. Y. *Herbert Spencer: the Evolution of a Sociologist*. Aldershot, England; Brookfield, VT: Gregg Revivals, 1992.

Rumney, Jay. *Herbert Spencer's Sociology: A Study in the History of Social Theory*. New York: Atherton, 1966.

Spencer, Herbert. *Essays: Scientific, Political and Speculative*. London: Routledge/Thoemmes, 1996.

———. *First Principles*. London: Routledge/Thoemmes, 1996.

———. *Political Writings*. Cambridge, UK: Cambridge University Press, 1993.

———. *The Principles of Psychology*. London: Routledge/Thoemmes, 1996.

———. *Social Statics*. London: Routledge/Thoemmes, 1996.

———. *The Study of Sociology*. London: Routledge/Thoemmes, 1996.

———. *Herbert Spencer, Collected Writings*. William Henry Hudson et al., eds. London: Routledge/Thoemmes Press, 1996.

Taylor, M. W. *Herbert Spencer and the Limits of the State: the Late Nineteenth-Century Debate Between Individualism and Collectivism*. Bristol, England; Dulles, VA: Thoemmes Press, 1996.

———. *Men Versus the State: Herbert Spencer and Late Victorian Individualism*. Oxford, England; New York: Clarendon Press; Oxford University Press, 1992.

Weinstein, D., *Equal Freedom and Utility: Herbert Spencer's Liberal Utilitarianism*. Cambridge; New York: Cambridge University Press, 1998.

PART
IV

CHAPTER 19

Jane Addams:
Advocate of
Socialized Education

In this chapter, we examine the life, educational philosophy, and contributions of Jane Addams (1860–1935), a pioneer in settlement house and social work and the women's rights and peace movements. Addams was a leader in immigrant and urban education. She developed the philosophy of "socialized education," which resembled John Dewey's experimentalism and progressivism (discussed in Chapter 20).

We discuss Addams's influence on U.S. education in its historical context and in terms of its continuing effects on educational philosophy and policy. First, we describe the general social, political, and economic context in which Addams lived and worked. Second, we analyze Addams's biography, her education and career in settlement house and social work, to determine the evolution of her ideas. Third, we assess the continuing effect of Addams's contributions to social and educational ideas in the United States. Through this analysis of context and biography we shall see how the interrelated dynamics of educational history and philosophy shaped Addams's actions in the big-city, urban melting pot of late nineteenth- and early twentieth-century America.

To organize your thoughts as you read this chapter, focus on the following questions:

1. What was the historical context in which Jane Addams worked?
2. How did she interpret the major forces of immigration and urbanization that were transforming U.S. life?
3. How did Addams's educational biography shape her social and educational philosophy?

4. How did Addams's educational philosophy determine her social and educational policies and practices?
5. What is the continuing impact of Addams's contributions to U.S. social and educational ideas?

The Historical Context of Addams's Life

Jane Addams was born in 1860, the year of Abraham Lincoln's election as president, and she died in 1935 during the middle year of the Great Depression when Franklin D. Roosevelt was in the White House. During the 75 years of her life, the United States was transformed from a predominantly rural and agricultural society to an urban and industrial nation. Addams's work as the founder of Hull House, a settlement house in Chicago, was centered in the vortex of this transformation of U.S. life. Her work can be interpreted in light of urbanization and immigration. For the U.S. economy, society, and schools, the shift to an urban and industrial socioeconomic order posed serious policy issues.

After the Civil War ended in 1865, the process of urbanization accelerated and metropolitan New York, Chicago, Philadelphia, Boston, Detroit, and Cleveland grew into major population centers. New York City's population growth dramatically demonstrates the phenomenon of urbanization. In 1860, New York's population was 1,174,000; it had reached 4,766,000 by 1910. Philadelphia, the third-largest city, had a population of 1,549,000. By 1930, more than 25 percent of the population of the United States was living in the seven urban areas of New York, Chicago, Philadelphia, Boston, Detroit, Los Angeles, and Cleveland.[1]

Chicago, the second-largest city in the United States and the one to which Addams would give acclaim as founder of Hull House, in particular experienced phenomenal growth. In 1870, five years after the end of the Civil War and one year after the great fire, Chicago's population was 298,977. In 1880, its population was 503,185. By 1900, the population had tripled, to 1,698,575. In 1910, it had reached 2,185,283. Twenty years later, in 1930, Chicago had grown to 3,376,438.[2] Like the rest of urban America, Chicago was experiencing a continuing upward cycle of population growth.

Urban America's growth was accelerated by the process of industrialization begun in the mid-nineteenth century. Stimulated by the Civil War, industrialization accelerated throughout the rest of the 1800s and reached its peak in the early twentieth century. The factories and mills that produced iron, steel, textiles, and other products were located throughout the United States, but were especially concentrated in the large urban areas.

Large cities attracted new residents who, searching for a better economic position and style of life, came from several locales. From 1860 to 1935, the number of Americans engaged in agriculture slowly declined while the industrial workforce grew. There was a general migration of Americans from farm to city, especially among the young. Jane Addams was particularly concerned not only with the economic placement of these young people but with their moral and social adjustment as well. There was also a movement of African Americans from the rural South to the urban North. No longer did young blacks heed Booker T. Washington's admonition to "cast down your buckets where you are" but instead, leaving the racially segregated South, migrated to the

North's large cities in search of better jobs and education. In addition there were the hundreds of thousands of immigrants, primarily from southern and eastern Europe, who left their native lands hoping to share in America's promise.

In the expanding big cities, recent immigrants from Europe made up a large proportion of the population. Between 1870 and 1920, some 26,277,000 immigrants entered the United States. As of 1910, one-third of the population of America's eight largest cities were immigrants.[3]

A noticeable shift in immigration patterns occurred after 1890. Until that date, 85 percent of European immigrants had come from northern and western Europe, especially from Germany, the United Kingdom, Ireland, and Scandinavia. After 1890, the great majority of immigrants came from southern and eastern Europe, from Italy, Russia, Austria-Hungary, and Greece. From the Hapsburg empire of Austria-Hungary came a variety of ethnic and linguistic groups—Czechs, Slovaks, Slovenes, Croats, and Hungarians. Poles came from their native land, which was then subdivided and ruled by Austria-Hungary, Germany, and Russia. In addition to Russians, Ukranians, and Belorussians, there was a large immigration of Jews from Russia who sought to escape from the tsarist government's anti-Semitic policies. To this complex ethnic mix were added Armenians, Assyrians, Syrians, and others from the Ottoman Empire. Serbians, Romanians, and Bulgarians came from the small independent Balkan monarchies. In the 1890s, 1,914,000 people immigrated from southern and eastern Europe. The next decade saw a virtual tidal wave as their numbers swelled to 6,224,000. During the next decade, marked by World War I, the number of southern and eastern European immigrants declined to 2,370,000. After Congress enacted legislation to restrict immigration, the numbers declined severely.[4]

In 1910, Chicago had a total population of 2,185,000, of whom 1,693,918 were either "foreign born" or classified as "white foreign stock."[5] The massive influx of immigrants to cities such as Chicago produced serious social and educational change and tension. First, there was the effect of demographic changes produced by the entry and location of large numbers of new residents in the cities. As is true of most social change of this magnitude, there was virtually little or no planning to accommodate the increasing population. Municipal governments faced added demands for more public health, sanitation, police and fire protection, public transportation, and educational services.

Public school systems in large urban areas, in particular, responded to an increased population of school-age children by becoming larger, more standardized, and often more bureaucratic. Using the model of efficient centralization developed by William Torrey Harris, the superintendent of schools in St. Louis, large city systems turned to standardization to solve problems of organization, staffing, attendance, and instruction.[6] The corporate model of organization, used in business, was imitated in schools where the general superintendent became the chief organizational officer of the school district and the building principal became the system's middle manager. To move large numbers of children through the system with some measure of efficiency, students were organized on an age-specific graded pattern. Textbooks were standardized into series that corresponded to the prevailing graded pattern. Though more efficient than the old ungraded one-room schools, the corporate urban schools tended to function in a lock-step pattern.

Professionally trained school administrators, seeking to use the corporate model in the large urban districts, often encountered obstacles that left the results of their labors uneven. Entrenched political machines, often supported by immigrant voting blocs, manipulated or controlled school boards. Machine politicians continued to place political patronage appointees in schools. Often, schools were scenes where corporate professionalism was locked in combat with political patronage over appointments and appropriations. Not only did professional administrators face machine politicians but they encountered the distrust of many immigrants who found the public schools to be hostile environments for their children. In her work at Hull House, Jane Addams was often at odds with the powerful ward boss, Johnny Powers. As a member of the Board of Education of the Chicago public schools, she encountered the tensions between professional educators and machine politicians.

Although the weight of sheer numbers had its effect, there were also myriad social and psychological tensions caused by the immigrants' relocation to a new environment and the often antagonistic reaction of the older stock of Americans to the newcomers. The population of the large cities lived in residential areas that were segregated according to income, language, ethnicity, race, and often religion. In contrast to the *de jure*, state-sanctioned racial segregation in the South, that of the northern big city was *de facto*, a consequence of residence. Usually following a grid pattern, neighborhoods might be upper socioeconomic class, middle class, working class, or strictly ethnic. The first generation of immigrants tended to locate in neighborhoods where the residents were members of their own ethnic group. Such ethnic enclaves or urban ghettos were known as "Little Italy," "Greektown," "Polonia," or "Chinatown." There was little assimilation in these neighborhoods, with the exception of the workplace and the public school, because the residents spoke the same language, attended the same church, read the same foreign-language newspaper, and were members of the same fraternal societies and recreational organizations.

By settling in ethnic enclaves, new immigrants gained a sense of security in a strange land. In part, the settlement in ethnic ghettos was self-imposed as the newly arriving immigrants clustered together to find a sense of psychological security with their own. The ethnic areas, typically located in crowded areas of the city with housing in overcrowded substandard tenements, were also a means by which the older stock of white, English-speaking Protestants isolated themselves from the immigrants. In part, the social isolation of the new immigrants was imposed by the dominant social and economic classes.

Progressives such as Jane Addams feared that the division of American society into ethnic and class enclaves was eroding the sense of community that sustained a shared commitment to democratic institutions and processes.[7] Although progressives opposed the domination of the U.S. economy by big business monopolies and trusts, they also were concerned that the representative political processes and a sense of community had been jeopardized by the profound social changes taking place in the United States at the turn of the century. They feared that the new immigrant masses, inexperienced in exercising the vote and unfamiliar with the processes of representative government, would become pawns of the big-city political bosses. Ethnic voting blocs could give the political machines pluralities over reform-minded progressives. They also feared that the division of society into ethnic and language blocs would reduce commitment to the common sense of community. In her work at Hull House and in her public speaking and writing, Addams attempted to find solutions to the problems of ethnic, class, and language divisiveness. She sought to find a way that would preserve the best that each unique ethnic heritage had to offer to America while uniting all Americans in a shared vision of the nation's meaning, purpose, and mission. Her search for a middle way between doctrinaire assimilation and ethnically generated divisiveness is not unlike the current search for ways to meld a common cultural core and multiculturalism in contemporary American society and education.

Jane Addams pondered the vision of what the pattern of American life would be in the twentieth century, and many of these same issues face American society and education in the twenty-first century. For Addams, the question was, Would American society be based on a uniform version of "Americanism" that stressed the values of white, Anglo-Saxon, English-speaking Protestants? Or was it possible to devise culturally pluralistic alternatives to such a monocultural version of the American heritage? As will be seen later in the chapter, Addams found a middle path that avoided an either-or position between unbridled assimilation and ethnic divisiveness.

Ellwood P. Cubberley, one of the country's most respected educators in the early twentieth century, believed that the pattern of national life already had been established along the lines of an English-speaking and English-behaving society. The task that Cubberley gave to the country's teachers was to assimilate immigrants into a monocultural version of American life. In his widely used book, *Changing Conceptions of Education* (1909), Cubberley contrasted the old and new immigrants. Finding the older western and northern European immigrants easy to assimilate, Cubberley wrote, "All except the Irish came from countries where general education prevailed and where progressive methods of agriculture, trade, and manufacturing had begun to supersede primitive methods." Favorably stereotyping the older immigrants, Cubberley said, "All were from race stock not very different from our own" and possessed a large degree of "courage, initiative, intelligence, adaptability and self-reliance." He praised as good additions to American life the "good nature of the Irish, the intellectual thoroughness of the German, the respect for law and order of the English, and the thrift of the Scandinavian." In contrast, Cubberley depicted the newer southern and eastern European immigrants as "illiterate, docile, lacking in self-reliance and initiative, and not possessing the Anglo-Teutonic conceptions of law, order, and government." Their entry to the United States, he wrote, has diluted "tremendously our national stock" and corrupted "our civic life."[8] Unequivocally propounding assimilation by Americanization, Cubberley advised teachers,

> The great bulk of these people have settled in the cities of the North Atlantic and North Central states, and the problems of proper housing and living, moral and sanitary conditions, honest and decent government, and proper education have everywhere been made more difficult by their presence. Everywhere these people tend to settle in groups or settlements, and to set up here their national manners, customs, and observances. Our task is to break up these groups of people as a part of our American race, and to implant in their children, so far as it can be done, the Anglo-Saxon conception of righteousness, law and order, and popular government, and to awaken in them a reverence for our democratic institutions and for those things in our national life which we as a people hold to be of abiding worth.[9]

The Americanization process of assimilating immigrants that educators such as Cubberley prescribed began generally with the immigrants' children rather than with the adults themselves. Although the children of many Roman Catholic immigrants attended bilingual and bicultural parochial schools that often followed ethnic lines, the children of immigrants who attended public schools were indoctrinated according to the Americanization ideology. With a few exceptions, instruction was generally in English in most school districts. Immigrant children either learned English or failed. The issue of the primary language of instruction still remains at the core of contemporary debates over bilingual and bicultural education.

Along with the formal curriculum, the school milieu, or the "hidden curriculum," reinforced the ethos and values of the dominant culture so revered by Cubberley. Success in school and in the larger society, immigrant children were told, depended on their conformity to the behavior of the dominant group. These children learned that using a foreign language, speaking with an accent, observing different customs and holidays—the things that keep an ethnic heritage alive—were deviations that marked one as belonging to an inferior group.[10] Leonardo Covello, recalling his school days in the New York public schools, reminisced that "throughout my whole elementary school career, I do not recall one mention of Italy or the Italian language or what famous Italians had done in the world, with the possible exception of Columbus."[11] Covello, who attended a public school in a predominantly Italian neighborhood, recalled childhood's bitter memories:

> We soon got the idea that "Italian" meant something inferior, and a barrier was erected between children of Italian origin and their parents. This was the accepted process of Americanization. We were becoming Americans by learning how to be ashamed of our parents.[12]

Although educators such as Cubberley set forth the ideology of Americanization that dominated public school policy on education of immigrants, other voices proposed alternative patterns. One articulate spokesperson for cultural pluralism was Horace Kallen, who defined the pursuit of happiness as "the creation of cultures and the sporting union of their diversities as peers and equals; it is the endeavor after culture as each communion and each community . . . envisions its own cultural individuality and struggles to preserve, enrich, and perfect it by means of a free commerce . . . with all mankind."[13]

The America into which Jane Addams was born was also a society of limited and well-defined roles for women. She was born into the strictures of the Victorian era, which restricted the public life of women and largely confined them to the traditionally ascribed roles of wife, homemaker, and mother. Despite the campaigns of the suffragettes, only slight progress had been made. Although more women were attending college than in earlier decades, their roles on graduation remained limited to the traditional ones. For those who worked, careers were still largely limited to elementary school teaching and to nursing. It was a rare and courageous woman who chose a different path. Jane Addams was such a woman.

The United States in which Jane Addams lived and worked was a nation undergoing fundamental transformation. It was a country experiencing the change from rural to urban, from agricultural to industrial, and from monocultural to more pluralistic patterns of life. It was in this cultural context that Addams sought to devise a strategy to restore a sense of shared community that embraced diversity.

Jane Addams: Educator of Immigrants

Jane Addams, who would found Hull House and become a pioneer in social settlement work, was born on September 6, 1860, in Cedarville, a small Illinois town located in the northern section of state near the larger cities of Freeport and Rockford. She was the daughter of John Huy Addams, a prominent local businessman and Republican party leader, and Sarah Weber Addams. Sarah, descended from German ancestors, had attended a woman's boarding school where she had studied languages, literature, and music. John was born of English settlers who had located originally in Pennsylvania.[14] In addition to Jane, the Addamses had seven children.

An attractive but delicate and wistful little girl, Jane Addams was diagnosed as having Potts' disease, an illness that caused a curvature of the spine. Throughout her life, Jane would experience back pain, especially aggravated by emotional stress and depression.[15] Jane's mother died on January 14, 1863, when Jane was 2 years old. Her mother's death caused Jane to experience a fear of separation that made her reserved in social relationships. In the absence of her mother, Jane's formative years were profoundly influenced by her father, especially by his strong ethical sense and his dedication to public service.

Jane Addams was the daughter of a highly successful father, a man who was Cedarville's wealthiest and most important person. John Huy Addams owned the local flour mill, was president of Second National Bank of Freeport, and owned two Freeport insurance companies.[16] John Addams was respected for his community efforts. He opposed slavery, supported education, and helped raise funds to build Cedarville's Methodist church, library, and school. Attracted to politics, John Addams, a friend of Abraham Lincoln, helped to organize the Republican party and was elected to the Illinois state senate. One of Jane's early recollections, when she was four, was of American flags, with black bunting, fixed on the gate posts leading to her home. When she asked why, her father, in tears, told her that Lincoln, the greatest man in the world, had died. Throughout her life, her father was Addams's model for a life of public service and ethical behavior.[17]

In 1867, when Jane was 8, John Addams married Anna Hostetter Haldeman, a widow, whose two sons joined the Addams household. Although she had little formal education, Anna, a talented musician and avid reader, regarded herself to be a woman of culture and bearing. Unlike Jane, who would challenge the traditional Victorian role of women as devoted wives and mothers, Anna relished the security and position it provided.[18] When it came time for higher education, Jane wanted to attend Smith College, a new women's college, located in Northampton, Massachusetts, but instead agreed to her father's wish that she stay close to home. On September 3, 1877, 17-year-old Jane entered Rockford Female Seminary, a women's college founded in 1847 by Anna Peck Sill under Presbyterian and Congregational auspices. Jane was one of 180 students, most of whom were the daughters of white, middle-class, Protestant families. The atmosphere at the school was morally strict and semireligious.[19]

An eager student, Addams enrolled in a range of courses such as Greek, Latin, German, geology, astronomy, botany, Medieval history, civil government, music, literature, Bible studies, and moral philosophy. She read widely and was especially attracted to books by George Eliot, Victor Hugo, John Ruskin, Thomas Carlyle, and Matthew Arnold. She showed her talent for journalism, contributing essays to the *Rockford*

Seminary Magazine. Jane's leadership qualities attracted other students to her and led to her being elected class president.[20] She became a close friend of Ellen Gates Starr, who would join her in founding Hull House. Jane's propensity to leadership would be repeated as she attracted other young women as settlement workers at Hull House. She grew increasingly interested in defining a career for herself that went beyond the traditional Victorian roles of wife and mother. She began to experience the inner tensions of her own personal desires for self-definition and the conventional demands of the "family claims" of her parents.[21] Completing her program at Rockford Seminary, she was valedictorian of her graduating class in 1881. She received her bachelor of arts degree in 1882, when Rockford Seminary was authorized to award degrees.[22]

On August 17, 1881, when Jane was 21, her father died. She deeply missed his counsel and strong guiding influence. She began to experience psychological depression and symptoms of ill health that plagued her periodically for the next eight years. Feeling trapped by the conventional definition of the role deemed appropriate for a middle-class young woman in the late nineteenth century, she sought to develop a self-definition that would give purpose to her life.

In the fall of 1881, Addams, accompanied by her stepmother, moved to Philadelphia to enroll at the Women's Medical College. She found that medical study did not really interest her. Suffering from psychological depression and severe back pains, she dropped out of medical school. After taking a "rest cure," she returned to Cedarville where she managed the family business.[23] She slowly regained her health but had not yet found the meaningful career for which she was searching.

Wandering both physically and intellectually, Addams took two extended tours of Europe, one in 1883 and the other in 1888, where she studied art, architecture, and German.[24] Her second tour was especially significant in bringing her to a career decision. For many young American women, traveling in Europe was a "grand tour." For Addams, however, the time away from her native land gave her a clearer cross-cultural perspective into her life and possibilities.[25]

While in Spain, Jane and her friends attended a bullfight. Witnessing what she regarded a disgusting spectacle, she experienced a profound insight. She wanted a life in which she could work to improve the human condition.[26] Her insight took the form of a definite plan when she was in the United Kingdom. She became keenly interested in the social settlement work of Canon Samuel A. Barnett, a Church of England clergyman. In 1872, Barnett was appointed vicar of St. Jude's, one of the poorest parishes, in the Whitechapel district in London's impoverished West End. Enlisting the aid of Oxford University students, Barnett embarked on a program to improve the conditions of his parishioners and other poverty-stricken residents. He established an evening school, a fund to support children's excursions in the country, and an art gallery. After Arnold Toynbee, the famous British historian, visited St. Jude's in 1875, a settlement building was named Toynbee Hall in his honor. Addams was a frequent visitor at Toynbee Hall, which became the prototype for her own settlement, Hull House, in Chicago.

Between 1881 and 1889 Addams went through a process of existentialist self-definition. She realized that as a young woman she could either conform to the expectations of others or define herself through her own choices. She began to resolve the conflicts of being a progressively inclined young woman with the demands of conformity in Victorian society. After a period of self-centered introspection, she came to the realization that to define herself she needed to recognize and do battle with the confining structures of sexism and elitism that permeated American society during the Gilded Age.[27]

When Jane Addams resolved her search for a meaningful career, she determined to work among the disadvantaged in the United States in the same way that the young men of Oxford were aiding London's poor and indigent. She and her longtime friend Ellen Gates Starr established Hull House, named for Charles J. Hull, its former owner, on Halsted and Polk streets on Chicago's near west side in 1889. Addams had a twofold mission: providing a meaningful career of service for college-educated, middle-class young women and aiding the urban poor, especially immigrants, in improving themselves and their situation in America. To create the possibility of useful careers for young women satisfied her long personal search for a life of fulfillment. She would share the answer to her long quest with other young women.

Initially, she approached the polyglot ethnic immigrants of Chicago's west side—the Italians, Bohemians, Poles, and Russian Jews—as a middle-class reforming progressive who had benefited from being a child of the dominant group. She would share the middle-class behaviors and values of a well-educated and traveled young lady with the less fortunate immigrants who came to Hull House. By her knowledge and example, she would uplift them intellectually, morally, and spiritually. She and her associates designed a rather formal curriculum to educate those who came to the new settlement house.

Just as Addams planned to educate the immigrants, she in turn was educated by them. Although moral uplift might be the ideal, the immigrants had practical needs. They needed to find jobs, pay rent, obtain basic municipal services such as garbage removal, find health care, and learn to educate their children. Could the genteel and idealistic young lady from Rockford Seminary help them to met the challenges of survival as strangers in a new land? A quick learner, Addams redesigned her strategy to settlement house work and the urban education of immigrants. Those she would teach became her teachers. Hull House's mission was revised to meet the practical needs of those who came there for help. Classes became more informal and eventually became a mutual sharing of information, ideas, and skills.

Under Addams's leadership, Hull House became a multipurpose settlement house. Although its adult education courses resembled formal schooling, most instruction was informal or nonformal as individuals joined in learning particular subjects or skills—the applied knowledge—they needed to survive in the new world. Because many of the neighborhood women needed child care services, Hull House added a kindergarten, a nursery school, and a playground. Classes and clubs were established for older children. Because many had no experience with U.S. finance, Addams established a savings bank. Hull House had a medical dispensary for health care. Because its neighborhood was a working-class area, trade unions frequently met at Hull House. In addition to its many informal educational activities, Hull House offered adult education and college extension courses to those who sought to improve their situation through continuing education. Within two years of its founding, Hull House's 50 clubs and many classes were serving 1,000 people who came there every week.[28]

In her work at Hull House, Addams, who had been nurtured by her father to respect politics as a call to service, ran into the realities of Chicago-style politics, personified by the Nineteenth Ward's political boss, Johnny Powers. An immigrant himself, Powers had clawed his way to power in Chicago's local government. He controlled services and also jobs. For many immigrant voters, the way to a job was to vote as directed by the political machine. Addams, the progressive reformer, found herself locked in conflict with Powers, the boss. She sponsored and organized the Nineteenth Ward Improvement Club to aid immigrants in gaining needed municipal services such as garbage collection. The struggle between Addams and Powers was never resolved. Despite her opposition, Powers continually won at the polls.

Hull House was a place where women could create their own self-identity and give meaning to their lives by pursuing careers of useful service. Addams and Starr were joined by other educated young women, such as Julia Lathrop, who would become the first chief of the Federal Children's Bureau, and Florence Kelley, who would become the chief factory inspector for the Illinois Bureau of Labor Statistics.[29] Addams and her associates at Hull House effectively lobbied for the establishment of the nation's first juvenile court.[30] An important feature of Hull House was that Addams and her colleagues added expertise to their enthusiasm for personal and social reform. They were advised by some of the leading academicians of the progressive era. Richard T. Ely, professor of economics at the University of Wisconsin, provided guidance on the strategies needed to make the new settlement house an effective agency for reform. John Dewey, then a professor of philosophy, psychology, and pedagogy at the University of Chicago, became a trustee of Hull House and close adviser to Addams. Sociologists and educators from the University of Chicago were frequent visitors to Hull House, where they conducted research and lectured. Thus, Addams moved her work at Hull House from that of the well-intentioned amateur philanthropist to that of the social worker who used social science knowledge and philosophical pragmatism as foundations for her work.[31]

Jane Addams made Hull House into a recognized institution, not only in Chicago, but in the United States. The single building that housed the settlement had grown, by 1910, into a complex of 13 brick buildings. Addams herself was recognized as a national advocate for child labor legislation, housing and sanitation reform, vocational and immigrant education, women's suffrage, and international peace.[32] Jane Addams's pioneering work, her articles and books, and her public speaking attracted an international audience. She was a prolific author. Her autobiography, *Twenty Tears at Hull-House* (1910), and *The Spirit of Youth & the City Streets* (1909) were well received and widely read.[33] In 1912, she had the distinction of seconding the nomination of Theodore Roosevelt as the Progressive party candidate for president. In 1919, she was elected president of the Women's International League for Peace and in 1931 was awarded the Nobel Peace Prize.[34] She died on May 21, 1935.

Jane Addams as an Educational Theorist

Jane Addams developed a philosophy of education called "socialized education" that reflected her experiences at Hull House as an urban educator and an educator of immigrants. Although rooted in her immediate experiences, her ideas had a broader relevance for the greater society. In this section of the chapter, we identify and examine some of Addams's ideas on education.

Addams's socialized education was a multidimensional theory that related to the broad needs of American society. Her philosophy of education addressed the need to restore a sense of community to a society gripped by a profound transformation from a rural to an urban economy. In particular, she found the sense of shared common experience disintegrating as the inherited beliefs and values that had originated in rural America were losing their meaning for the growing urban population, especially for new immigrants from southern and eastern Europe. Although the settlement house, a society in microcosm, might bring together working-class immigrants with educated middle-class reformers, such social integration was needed nationally.

For Addams, the settlement house, like the progressive school, was an experimental setting for solving the social, economic, psychological, and political problems of modern urban life. It was a place in which knowledge, based on social science, could be applied to solving practical problems. Importantly, it also introduced both the settlement house workers and their clients to the method needed to apply knowledge to life.

Although Addams conceived of the settlement house as a social and educational institution, she envisioned it in a collaborative relationship to schools and universities rather than as a rival or alternative to them. For her, the public school that provided basic skills and subjects was age specific to children and adolescents and also time specific to the instructional day and place. In contrast, the education provided by the settlement house was for adults and well as children and not limited by age, time, or place. The settlement house's educational program reached out from its location into the community—into its housing, work, politics, businesses, churches, and recreation. Its hours of operation were flexibly arranged to meet the needs of its people rather than organized around time and cost-efficient management prescriptions.

Addams, like Dewey and other progressives, believed that many schools of the time had become isolated from the realities and issues of a changing society. The schools' formalism and cultural remoteness often made them and their teachers alien intruders into the ethnic and immigrant community rather than full participants in the total educational process.[35]

Although professors such as Dewey, the philosopher and educator; Albion Small, the sociologist; and Richard Ely, the economist, advised Addams and participated in Hull House's educational program, they saw the university in a special and supportive but distinctive relationship to the settlement house. The settlement house and its population were not to be used for solely academic research. However, it provided a setting and a population that yielded data that could be used as evidence for reform legislation to improve health care, working conditions, safety, and housing. Following the progressive model, the findings of sociological and demographic research supplied progressive legislators with the data needed to support reforms.

Jane Addams's concept of socialized education related to conditions of work in an urban and industrialized society. Industrialization, relying heavily on machines and assembly lines for mass production, had radically altered the nature of work and its relationships to education. Quickly and cheaply made in comparison with handicraft production, modern industrial manufacturing made a mass supply of goods available to a mass market of consumers. Work on the factory's assembly line was standardized and routine in that each worker repeated the same task throughout the day. The factory employee worked in isolation on only a part, rather than on the whole product as did the craftsperson.

Industrialization also altered the concept and process of vocational education. Until the Industrial Revolution, vocational education—largely geared to handicraft production—was based on apprenticeship in which the apprentice, the young person learning the trade, studied with a craftsperson who had mastery of the needed skills. With the exception of youngsters growing up on farms, industrialization also changed children's perceptions of work. Often, handicraft production was done in the home with children involved in the process. Seeing their parents working and earning, children had had direct experience with work and income. In an industrial society, work, done away from the home and usually out of the child's neighborhood environment, became a remote concept for many children.

Well aware that modern industrial processes of production tended to alienate workers socially, Addams believed that industrial occupations needed to be infused with social purpose. Industrial workers needed the kind of education that would explore social relationships and connections and forge the interconnections needed to recreate a sense of community. Industrial education, as a integral component of socialized education, should do the following:[36]

1. Examine the history of industrial development in terms of the individual's relationship to it.
2. Develop a historical perspective in which industrial machines and processes were viewed as products in a long line of evolutionary development.
3. Identify the economic and social interrelationships between workers and their common endeavors.
4. Develop the interconnections that enabled workers to see their specialized efforts within a larger holistic framework.

Addams, like Dewey, believed children as a part of their education should be introduced to a range of vocations. However, she steadfastly opposed child labor and premature vocational education. Like other progressives, she condemned child labor in factories, mills, and mines as a national disgrace. She lobbied for the enactment of compulsory school attendance regulations and laws restricting child labor. In her struggle, she organized the National Child Labor Committee as a lobbying organization.

Addams's opposition to child labor rested on her ideas of progressive reform and on her belief that childhood was a crucial stage of human growth and development. She was always interested in educational theory and like Rousseau, Pestalozzi, and Froebel believed that play was a key factor in a healthy child's development. Further, elementary education, with its emphasis on basic skills, was a necessary precondition for subsequent education. Children who were deprived of the opportunities for play and schooling and put to work in factories were deprived of the childhood experiences that contributed to their growth and development. Further, it was unjust and undemocratic that upper- and middle-class children could enjoy childhood's benefits, while working-class children were made to work as laborers.

Addams firmly believed that all children, regardless of socioeconomic class or ethnicity, should develop an understanding of life in an industrialized and urban society. Educators should consciously work to surmount the schools' predilection toward formalism and isolation from social issues. The school curriculum should be redesigned to provide youngsters with broadened experiences that explored children's immediate environment in a way that highlighted connections with an industrial society. For example, the curriculum might include projects on the manual arts and industrial history and encourage pupils to build small-scale reproductions of the industrial system.[37]

An important part of Addams's work at Hull House related to the education of immigrants, both adults and children. Just as she was concerned about encouraging relationships between the individual and industrial society, Addams also was attentive to the need to develop connections between the immigrant family and the larger society. Hull House was to be a cultural bridge between immigrants' Old World experiences and the challenges of acclimation to the New World environment. Addams anticipated contemporary multicultural education. She argued that there were reciprocal and mutual benefits for those who participated in multicultural education. While immigrants could learn from the middle class, the middle class, in return, would learn from immigrants. Her brand of multiculturalism sought to preserve the immigrant cultures and to develop in the dominant group an appreciation for the skills and experiences of immigrants.[38]

Addams structured immigrants' adjustment to modern American urban and industrial society through a continuum of experiences that connected the customs, traditions, and values of Europe with those of the United States. She feared that a sharp break between the European cultural context and the new conditions of life might lead to isolation, alienation, or cultural shock. Unlike those who taught immigrant children to become Americans by first becoming ashamed of their parents and their inherited culture, Jane Addams wanted to give value to the inherited and the new and to reduce intergenerational conflict.

Addams was sensitive to the ethnic cultures of those who used Hull House's facilities. She organized special events that celebrated Italian, German, Greek, Russian, French, and other cultural heritages. To demonstrate in a concrete way the value of Old World culture, Addams created the Hull House Labor Museum. Museum exhibits featured the handicraft skills and artifacts that characterized life in Europe, and in this setting, the young could experience through demonstrations and displays the artistry and handicrafts of their parents.[39] The Labor Museum was also a vehicle for interethnic and intercultural sharing and dialogue because not only did immigrants face hostility from members of the dominant culture, but also they often encountered antagonism from members of other ethnic and language groups. Finally, the exhibits and demonstrations in the museum illustrated the evolution and progress of industrialization in a way that linked the European handicraft past with the industrial present.

As a member of the Chicago Board of Education and as a writer and speaker on educational reform, Addams urged the public schools to create a closer relationship with the immigrant family. Encouraging a more culturally pluralistic perspective, she opposed the policy of Americanization into the dominant white, Anglo-Saxon, Protestant culture urged by Cubberley and others. Anticipating contemporary programs of multicultural education, Addams wanted the schools to incorporate the history, customs, traditions, songs, crafts, and stories of the various ethnic groups into the curriculum.[40] She wanted schools to emphasize the ecumenical values that ethnic and racial groups contributed to human civilization. Such a perspective would overcome, she believed, the narrow monoculturalism that tended to stereotype those of other languages and cultures.

As a young woman who overcame the gender restrictions of Victorian society, Jane Addams was a committed proponent of women's education. She was a prophet of the feminist revolution that occurred in the second half of the twentieth century. No longer were daughters and wives of the upper middle class to be social ornaments polished at finishing schools. The modern woman, Addams wrote, was a person who possessed a sense of social commitment and obligation to make the world a better place.[41]

As a young woman, Addams had to free herself from the constraints of family expectations and social restrictions. Daughters of middle-class families, she wrote, often found themselves in conflict between family claims and their own sense of social responsibility. Although she did not forsake the importance of the family, Addams argued that modern women needed to participate in social life and help solve society's problems. To Addams and her associates, women needed the kind of education that equipped them to be full participants in modern life. Such an education involved not only knowledge but a sense of social obligation.

Conclusion: An Assessment

Jane Addams's biography reveals her transformation from the reserved graduate of a small women's college into an internationally recognized social reformer and pioneer of the settlement house movement. She created her own self-definition by serving others, not as a well-intentioned do-gooder, but with a keen recognition that she and other women had a special mission in a country undergoing fundamental changes.

Like Theodore Roosevelt and John Dewey, Addams was a progressive thinker and doer. She was not a revolutionary who wanted a radical transformation of the fundamental political, social, and educational institutions of the United States. Rather, she sought to preserve America's essential institutional framework by creating new collaborative agencies such as the settlement house and by extending the social functions of existing ones such as schools. For her, America's central need in the early twentieth century was to meet the challenges that a once-agrarian nation faced in the light of the powerful forces of industrialization and urbanization.

In her work at Hull House, Addams demonstrated that knowledge should be applied in the service of persons. Like Dewey, she wanted to instrumentalize knowledge by using it to solve political, social, and economic problems.

Addams's philosophy of socialized education reflected her thoroughgoing progressivism. Her conception of education was an urban *paedeia* encompassing a range of educational agencies. It encompassed informal education related to the education of immigrants as well as more formal agencies such as schools and universities. It was designed to create more extensive relationships between human experience and the emergent industrial society. Socialized education had a special reference to the industrial and urban forces at work in the late nineteenth- and early twentieth-century United States. Large cities such as Chicago needed a renascent sense of community based on the realities of industrial society. Socialized education, both in and out of school, was to examine the history, processes, and consequences of industrialism. Above all, it was to reduce the isolation that industrial workers experienced when they were seen as mere appendages of machines.

At Hull House, Addams grew sensitive to the educational and social problems faced by immigrants and their children. Immigrant education was an important corollary of socialized education. In Addams's opinion, public schooling frequently separated immigrant children both emotionally and culturally from their families. Addams sought to redress this tendency by urging public schools to encourage appreciation for the history, culture, traditions, and arts and crafts of immigrants' native countries. Contrary to the rigid Americanist ideology, Addams believed that valuing the immigrant contribution would not only reunite immigrant children with their families and their ethnic heritage but also would integrate them into American life.

In many ways, Jane Addams was as much a product of her past as she was the prophet of a new social order. The immigrants who were flocking to the United States's growing cities were to be schooled in the participatory political processes of the small-town Midwest that Addams saw as a child in Cedarville. Through the process of a growing network of interconnections and interrelationships, the new community, the great society of an industrialized but still democratic America would arise. Jane Addams's life and work affirms the progressive belief in the possibilities of human personal and social improvement.

Questions for Reflection and Dialogue

1. How did Jane Addams's search for a purposeful and meaningful life reflect the situation of women in late nineteenth- and early twentieth-century America? Compare and contrast the contemporary situation of women with that of women of Addams's time.
2. How was Jane Addams's work at Hull House a response to the challenges of social, economic, and demographic change in the United States? How do you think she might react to social changes in the contemporary United States, especially in urban areas?
3. Compare and contrast the Americanist, assimilationist, and cultural pluralist positions toward the education of immigrants. Reflect on how these positions relate to contemporary issues regarding multicultural and bilingual education.
4. What were the progressives' concerns about the nature of the American community? In your opinion is there a strong sense of community in the United States today?
5. How was Jane Addams's work at Hull House a response to the changing economic and demographic conditions of the United States?
6. What were the major ideas in Addams's philosophy of socialized education?
7. Assess Jane Addams's contributions to U.S. social and educational ideas.

Projects for Deepening Your Understanding

1. Review the recent literature in the debate over multiculturalism and political correctness. Can you detect any aspects of the Americanist, assimilationist, and cultural pluralist in the contemporary viewpoints?
2. In an opinion piece, compare and contrast the career options of contemporary women with those who lived at Jane Addams's time.

3. How did Addams seek to make connections between the immigrants and the then existing American culture and society? Do you think that her approach is relevant to contemporary multicultural education?

4. Review the literature on service-oriented education. Is the work of the women of Hull House relevant to contemporary service education?

5. Identify the ethnic and national origins of the most recent immigrants to the United States. Are their problems similar to or different from those faced by the people in the Hull House neighborhood?

6. In a position paper, either defend or attack the following statement: Jane Addams was a proponent of an assimilationist policy regarding the education of immigrants.

7. In an essay, examine Hull House as both an informal and formal educational institution.

Notes

1. Oscar Handlin, "The Immigrant Contribution," in Richard Leopold and Arthur Link, eds., *Problems in American History* (New York: Prentice Hall, 1952), 643–90.

2. *Population Abstract of the United States* (Washington, DC: U.S. Government Printing Office, 1980), 199.

3. Oscar Handlin, *Immigration as a Factor in American History* (Upper Saddle River, NJ: Prentice Hall, 1959), 14–15.

4. Handlin, *Immigration as a Factor in American History*, 14–15, 199.

5. *The People of Chicago* (Chicago: Department of Development and Planning, 1976), 27.

6. Salwyn E. Troen, *The Public and the Schools: Shaping the St. Louis System, 1838–1920* (Columbia, MO: University of Missouri Press, 1975).

7. Robert M. Crunden, *Ministers of Reform: The Progressives' Achievement in American Civilization, 1889–1920* (Urbana, IL: University of Illinois Press, 1984).

8. Ellwood P. Cubberley, *Changing Conceptions of Education* (Boston: Houghton-Mifflin, 1909), 13–15.

9. Cubberley, *Changing Conceptions of Education*, 15–16.

10. For a historical perspective on the education of immigrants, see Selma Cantor Berrol, *Growing Up American: Immigrant Children in America, Then and Now* (New York: Twayne, 1995).

11. Leonard Covello, with Guido D'Agostino, *The Teacher in the Urban Community: A Half Century in City Schools* (Totowa, NJ: Littlefield, Adams, 1970), 44.

12. Covello, *The Teacher in the Urban Community*, 45.

13. Horace M. Kallen, *Cultural Pluralism and the American Idea: An Essay in Social Philosophy* (Philadelphia: University of Pennsylvania Press, 1956), 100.

14. Gioia Dilberto, *A Useful Woman: The Early Life of Jane Addams* (New York: Scribner's/Lisa Drew, 1999), 25.

15. Dilberto, *A Useful Woman*, 31–32.

16. Jane Addams, *Twenty Years at Hull House with Autobiographical Notes*, edited with introduction by Victoria Bissel Brown (Boston and New York: Bedford/St. Martins, 1999), 2–3.

17. Jane Addams, *Twenty Years at Hull House with Autobiographical Notes*, 4–6.

18. Allen F. Davis, *American Heroine: The Life and Legend of Jane Addams* (New York: Oxford University Press, 1975), 6–7.

19. Dilberto, *A Useful Woman*, 62–66.

20. Dilberto, *A Useful Woman*, 70–72.

21. Dilberto, *A Useful Woman*, 16.

22. Winifred E. Wise, *Jane Addams of Hull-House* (New York: Harcourt Brace Jovanovich, 1935), 61–74, 77–80.

23. Dilberto, *A Useful Woman*, 84–97.

24. Ellen Condliffe Lagemann, ed., *Jane Addams on Education* (New York: Teachers College Press, 1985), 16–17.

25. Daniel T. Rodgers, *Atlantic Crossings: Social Politics in a Progressive Age* (Cambridge, MA: Belknap/Harvard University Press, 1998).

26. Dilberto, *A Useful Woman*, 125–26.

27. Jane Addams, *Twenty Years at Hull House with Autobiographical Notes*, 8–9.

28. Dilberto, *A Useful Woman*, 161.

29. Lagemann, *Jane Addams on Education*, 25–26.
30. For the progressive women's efforts for juvenile courts, see Elizabeth J. Clapp, *Mothers of All Children: Women Reformers and the Rise of Juvenile Courts in Progressive Era America* (University Park, PA: Pennsylvania State University Press, 1998).
31. Helene Silverberg, ed., *Gender and American Social Science: The Formative Years* (Princeton, NJ: Princeton University Press, 1998), 252.
32. Jane Addams, *Twenty Years at Hull House with Autobiographical Notes*, 23–24.
33. Jane Addams, *Twenty Years at Hull-House* (New York: Macmillan, 1910); and Addams, *The Spirit of Youth & the City Streets* (New York: Macmillan, 1909).
34. For the women's peace movement, see Leila J. Rupp, *World of Women: The Making of an International Women's Movement* (Princeton, NJ:

Princeton University Press, 1997); and Frances H. Early, *A World without War: How U.S. Feminists and Pacifists Resisted World War I* (Syracuse, NY: Syracuse University Press, 1997).
35. Jane Addams, "A Function of the Social Settlement," *Annals of the American Academy of Political and Social Science* 13 (1899), 323–45.
36. Jane Addams, *Democracy and Social Ethics*, ed. Anne F. Scott (Cambridge MA: Harvard University Press, 1964), 178–220.
37. Addams, *Democracy and Social Ethics*, 178–220.
38. Addams, *Twenty Years at Hull House with Autobiographical Notes*, 51.
39. Addams, *Twenty Years at Hull-House*, 136–44.
40. Jane Addams, in Lagemann, *Jane Addams on Education*, 136–42.
41. Addams, in Lagemann, *Jane Addams on Education*, 64–73.

Suggestions for Further Reading

Addams, Jane. *Democracy and Social Ethics*. Urbana; Chicago: University of Illinois Press, 2002.

———. *Excellent Becomes the Permanent*. New York: Macmillan, 1932.

———. *My Friend, Julia Lathrop*. New York: Macmillan, 1935.

———. *The Long Road of Woman's Memory*. Urbana; Chicago: University of Illinois Press, 2002.

———. *A New Conscience and an Ancient Evil*. Urbana; Chicago: University of Illinois Press, 2002.

———. *Newer Ideals of Peace*. New York: Macmillan, 1907.

———. *Peace & Bread in Time of War*. Urbana; Chicago: University of Illinois Press, 2002.

———. *Philanthropy & Social Progress*. New York: Thomas Y. Crowell, 1893.

———. *The Second Twenty Years at Hull-House*. New York: Macmillan, 1930.

———. *The Spirit of Youth & the City Streets*. Urbana; Chicago: University of Illinois Press, 1972.

———. *The Jane Addams Reader*. Jean Bethke Elshtain, ed. New York: Basic Books, 2002.

———. *On Education*. Ellen Condliffe Lagemann, ed. New Brunswick, NJ: Transaction Publishers, 1994.

———. *The Selected Papers of Jane Addams*. Mary Lynn McCree Bryan, Barbara Bair, and Maree

de Angury, eds. Urbana; Chicago: University of Illinois Press, 2003.

———. *The Selected Papers of Jane Addams. Volume 1, Preparing to Lead, 1860–81*. Mary Lynn McCree Bryan, Barbara Bair, et al., eds. Urbana; Chicago: University of Illinois Press, 2003.

———. *The Social Thought of Jane Addams*. Christopher Lasch, ed. New York: Irvington, 1997.

———. *Twenty Years at Hull-House with Autobiographical Notes*. Victoria Brown, ed. Boston: Bedford/St. Martin's, 1999.

Balch, Emily Greene, and Alice Hamilton. *Women at The Hague: The International Congress of Women and its Results*. Urbana; Chicago: University of Illinois Press, 2003.

Berrol, Selma Cantor. *Growing Up American: Immigrant Children in America, Then and Now*. New York: Twayne, 1995.

Clapp, Elizabeth J. *Mothers of All Children: Women Reformers and the Rise of Juvenile Courts in Progressive Era America*. University Park, PA: Pennsylvania State University Press, 1998.

Crunden, Robert M. *Ministers of Reform: The Progressives' Achievement in American Civilization, 1889–1920*. Urbana, IL: University of Illinois Press, 1984.

Davis, Allen F. *American Heroine: The Life and Legend of Jane Addams.* Chicago: Ivan R. Dee, 2000.

———. *Spearheads for Reform: The Social Settlements and the Progressive Movement, 1890–1914.* New York: Oxford University Press, 1967.

Dilberto, Gioia. *A Useful Woman: The Early Life of Jane Addams.* New York: Scribner, 1999.

Diner, Steven J. *A Very Different Age: Americans of the Progressive Era.* New York: Hill & Wang, 1998.

Early, Frances H. *A World without War: How U.S. Feminists and Pacifists Resisted World War I.* Syracuse, NY: Syracuse University Press, 1997.

Edwards, Rebecca. *Angels in the Machinery: Gender in American Party Politics from the Civil War to the Progressive Era.* New York: Oxford University Press, 1997.

Elshtain, Jean Bethke. *Jane Addams and the Dream of American Democracy.* New York: Basic Books, 2002.

Farrell, John C. *Beloved Lady: A History of Jane Addams's Ideas on Reform and Peace.* Baltimore: Johns Hopkins University Press, 1967.

Jackson, Robert M. *Destined for Equality: The Inevitable Rise of Women's Status.* Cambridge, MA: Harvard University Press, 1998.

Lagemann, Ellen Condliffe. *A Generation of Women: Education in the Lives of the Progressive Reformers.* Cambridge, MA: Harvard University Press, 1979.

———, ed. *Jane Addams on Education.* New York: Teachers College Press, 1985.

Linn, James W. *Jane Addams: A Biography.* Urbana; Chicago: University of Illinois Press, 2000.

Polikoff, Barbara Garland. *With One Bold Act: The Story of Jane Addams.* Chicago: Boswell Books, 1999.

Rodgers, Daniel T. *Atlantic Crossings: Social Politics in a Progressive Age.* Cambridge, MA: Belknap/Harvard University Press, 1998.

Rupp, Leila J. *Worlds of Women: The Making of an International Women's Movement.* Princeton, NJ: Princeton University Press, 1997.

Schott, Linda K. *Reconstructing Women's Thoughts: The Women's International League for Peace and Freedom before World War II.* Stanford, CA: Stanford University Press, 1997.

Silverberg, Helene, ed. *Gender and American Social Science: The Formative Years.* Princeton, NJ: Princeton University Press, 1998.

John Dewey: Pragmatist Philosopher and Progressive Educator

Chapter 20 examines the life, career, and educational contributions of John Dewey (1859–1952), one of America's most influential philosophers and educators. To approach Dewey biographically, we need to examine not only the events that shaped his life but also how he reflected on, interpreted, and participated in these events. Dewey's 93 years spanned a series of momentous events that shaped modern society. Darwin's *On the Origin of Species*, published in 1859, the year of Dewey's birth, generated bitter controversy between those who defended the literal truth of the Bible's book of Genesis and the proponents of the new theory of evolution and natural selection. Two years later, the U.S. Civil War, beginning in 1861, saw Dewey's father fighting with the Vermont cavalry to preserve the Union. One of Dewey's earliest memories was seeing the buildings of his hometown, Burlington, Vermont, draped in black bunting to mark Lincoln's death.[1] He would see the United States transformed by science and technology from a predominantly rural and agricultural economy and society to an industrial and technological one. He would experience and actively participate in the major social, economic, and political changes caused by the progressive movement, the Great Depression, the New Deal, and two world wars. At the end of his life the United States, a global power, was locked in the Cold War with the Soviet Union. The science that Dewey so prized had brought humankind into the nuclear age and exploration in outer space. The compelling power of Dewey's achievements derived from his acumen in examining and reflecting on the dynamics of change and incorporating his observations into his philosophy of education.

Just as the United States and the world were changing during Dewey's life, relationships between society and schools were also being reconstructed. Dewey's pragmatic educational philosophy, experimentalism, sought to integrate the larger context of a changing world with the smaller settings of changing communities, neighborhoods, and schools.

In this chapter we examine Dewey's influence on U.S. society, philosophy, and education in its historical context and in terms of its persisting social and intellectual effects. First, we describe the general social, intellectual, political, and economic context in which Dewey lived and worked. Second, we analyze Dewey's biography, especially his education and career, to determine how his ideas evolved. Third, we explore Dewey's legacy of continuing contributions to U.S. education. By this analysis, we shall see how the sweep of significant historical events worked to shape a notable thinker's educational philosophy. Dewey developed his educational philosophy as he experienced the great transformation of U.S. life that occurred as the nation moved from the nineteenth into and through the twentieth century. Originating in that historical context, Dewey's philosophy has left an enduring effect on Pragmatism as an educational philosophy and on how we view the role of experience in education.

To help organize your thoughts as you read this chapter, focus on the following questions:

1. What were the major trends in the historical context, the time and situation, in which Dewey lived?
2. How did Dewey's educational biography shape his philosophy of education?
3. How did Dewey's Pragmatic philosophy influence his educational policies and practices?
4. What is the continuing impact of Dewey's contributions to U.S. education?

The Historical Context of Dewey's Life

During John Dewey's long life, politics, economics, society, and education experienced a great transformation in the United States and the world.[2] Rather than reciting the record of these events chronologically, we focus here on three major themes that shaped Dewey's worldview and philosophy of education:

1. The American temperament, especially the images of the frontier, individualism, and community
2. Selected U.S. political, social, and economic developments, such as the progressive movement and the Great Depression of the 1930s
3. Educational developments related to the school and society, such as progressive innovations in curriculum and administration

To argue that a people in the course of their historical experience develop a national character is a much-debated issue in anthropology and sociology. However, historically, groups of people over time do develop a sense of identity that creates a feeling of belonging. For the people of nations such as the United States, beliefs arise about the past and its meaning for a national identity. At times, these beliefs are based on real historical events and at other times they reside in cherished myths. Although these myths may not be true historically, neither are they false. Such myths may be powerful in creating the national ideology, those commonly shared ideas that vivify a feeling of identity, unity, and purpose.

In the American experience, a cluster of shared ideas has contributed to the national ideology of what has been called "American Exceptionalism," that which Americans believe makes them a unique people. Prominent among them are images of the westward-moving frontier, rugged individualism and entrepreneurship, and the role of the small-town community. While there are other important popular images in the American temperament, these three, which embrace both history and myth, are most significant in interpreting Dewey's work.

Although there were early Spanish settlements in what are now the southwestern states, the basic pattern of settlement in the United States moved from east to west. The conventional history textbook relates that settlers, first locating along the Atlantic coast in the 13 original colonies, moved relentlessly westward, establishing a series of settlements in the north and southwest territories east of the Mississippi River and then crossing into the trans-Mississippi west.

Based on a demographic account of settlement, a historical interpretation of the frontier's effect on American culture has developed. In *The Impact of the Frontier,* progressive historian Frederick Jackson Turner crafts an interpretation that was long regarded as the definitive explanation of the rise of U.S. culture and character.[3] His thesis of the formative influence of the frontier is that the westward movement through a succession of differing natural environments—coastal regions, forests, plains, deserts, and mountains—created a flexible, egalitarian, and uniquely American character. Settlers in the western regions often found themselves in a wilderness environment. Free of the inherited mental residues of European traditionalism, Americans changed this environment, established farms and towns, and introduced their culture and institutions. As these westward-moving pioneers settled in new habitats, they too were changed by a series of interactive episodes with the environment. Consequently, the American character became flexible, resourceful, and open to change. In creating his experimentalist philosophy, Dewey appropriated this perceived American propensity for change and incorporated it into his theoretical outlook.

A second element in the American temperament is rugged individualism. This concept grew out of the myth that the frontier was settled by daring individuals and their families who fearlessly established homesteads in the wilderness. American individualism, often personified by the "mountain man," trapper, homesteader, and cowboy, referred to fiercely independent persons who "did their own thing." The concept of frontier individualism was then blurred into that of the "captain of industry," whose entrepreneurial skills and competitive resourcefulness promoted U.S. industrialization while he often amassed a huge private fortune. The mythic conception of rugged frontier individualism was reinterpreted to mean that success required the free rein of individual initiative, unfettered by government constraints or regulation.

Throughout his career but especially during the Great Depression of the 1930s, Dewey challenged what he regarded as the myth of rugged individualism. In *Individualism Old and New* (1929) he argued that special interests were using the old concept of rugged individualism to block reform and that the culture needed a new, socially responsible version of individualism compatible with the reality of an interdependent industrial and technological society.[4] To help create this new version of individualism, Dewey, in developing his educational philosophy, emphasized the crucial importance of the collaborative group and shared activities and experiences in creating social intelligence.

Running through the American temperament also has been a vision of community. Originating in the New England town, there emerged an idyllic Norman Rockwell–like portrait of "Our Town," a place that was a home where everyone knew each other, shared joys and sorrows, and cared about one another. Important in the small town's daily life were the grocery store on Main Street, the church, and the school. Perhaps young John Dewey experienced such a version of small-town America in the Burlington, Vermont, of his childhood and youth. To Dewey, who rejected dualisms and contradictions, it probably seemed incongruous that the American temperament valued both rugged individualism and small-town togetherness.

In Dewey's thought, the themes of community, togetherness, collaboration, and sharing were ever present. Like the *polis* of ancient Athens, the town hall was truly the cradle of U.S. democracy. Industrialization, technology, and the irresistible forces of modernization had weakened the older version of the small-town American community. The need for community was too important to be abandoned, however. When Dewey developed his philosophical agenda for a renascent America, he incorporated a revitalized sense of community. It was one that retained the essence of face-to-face sharing but in the context of interdependency, industrialization, and technology. He envisioned the school as a miniature society that would be the catalyst for creating a new sense of community.

The principal events of the late nineteenth and early twentieth centuries that affected American and global society also shaped Dewey's worldview and philosophy. Although he lived through two world wars and a great economic depression, Dewey's emergence on the philosophical and educational scene coincided with the progressive movement in American life.[5]

A multifaceted social, political, and educational phenomenon, the progressive movement's high tide in the United States was from 1890 to the country's entry into World War I in 1917. Because Dewey was positioned squarely within progressivism, especially in education, we shall examine the progressive movement and its effect on his philosophy and activities.

The longstanding historical interpretation of progressivism is that it was a movement to reform and revitalize U.S. life and institutions. By the 1880s and 1890s, reform-minded individuals realized that the United States faced a multitude of crucial issues. For example, a few large business corporations, especially in iron and steel, petroleum, and railroads, had secured virtually monopolistic control of the nation's economy and were influencing legislation at the local, state, and national levels at the expense of the public good. Progressive reformers sought to limit the power of these giant corporations by enacting and enforcing antitrust legislation.

Progressives were also concerned that certain businesses, such as the meatpacking industry and the drug and medicine industry, were selling products that were either unsanitary or dangerous to an individual's health. Upton Sinclair's exposé of the meatpacking industry in Chicago is an example of progressive investigative journalism. Progressive forces in the U.S. Congress, encouraged by President Theodore Roosevelt, enacted the Pure Food and Drug Act, which regulated these industries for the public health and welfare.

In U.S. political life, national progressivism was identified with such reformist presidents as Theodore Roosevelt and Woodrow Wilson. At the state level, it was often associated with leaders such as Governor Robert M. La Follette of Wisconsin, who worked to curb special business interests and control by political bosses. Progressives sought to revitalize representative political processes by campaigning against corrupt politicians. In some states, they enacted referenda laws, which enabled citizens to place items on the ballot to be decided by popular vote. At the national level, progressives in both the Republican and Democratic parties sought to control trusts and monopolies, promote civil service reform, encourage conservation of natural resources, and enact other reforms.

In a broad sense, the progressive impulse was educational. Progressivism meant the general populace had to be instilled with political consciousness and activism on behalf of reform. For example, President Woodrow Wilson, a former political science professor and president of Princeton University, believed the nation's chief executive had an educational duty to inform and instruct its citizens.

At heart, progressivism was not a revolutionary movement that sought to radically transform the U.S. economic and political system. It did not reject private enterprise but rather sought to ensure that the economic system was truly competitive. Neither did it challenge the essential framework of republican political institutions but wanted to ensure that they were genuinely representative and followed established constitutional processes.

Applied to institutions, progressivism was highly procedural and process oriented. Its essential strategy was as follows:

1. Identify instances where economic, political, and educational institutions were not functioning properly and efficiently.
2. Investigate and research these problem areas with the assumption that information could be used to structure solutions.
3. Develop and enact legislation to remedy the problem and provide the needed regulation to ensure the problem would not recur.
4. Enact the needed legislation so that it now became part of the general policies that governed the particular area in which the problem had initially occurred.

Progressive procedures essentially affirmed Jefferson's belief that informed and enlightened citizens were capable of self-government.

The progressive ranks were dominated by white, middle-class Protestants of northern European, particularly English, ethnicity. Generally, they were well-educated men and women, willing to devote time and energy to organizing and promoting reform causes. John Dewey, Jane Addams, and Woodrow Wilson fit this model well.[6] Often missing from the progressive profile were immigrants from southern and eastern Europe, African Americans, and Hispanics.

Although conventionally viewed as promoting needed reforms of U.S. life, some recent interpretations portray them as agents of social control. Based on their white, Anglo-Saxon, middle-class ideology, they are seen as trying to impose their values on the rest of the population, especially new immigrants and first-generation ethnics. In particular, they are seen as using settlement houses and schools to impose the information, work skills, and values that would make working-class immigrants happily subordinate to the dominant, middle-class group. Critics of the group-centered education that John Dewey developed see it as a form of middle-class control by consensus. In other words, the progressives had a particular notion of what the U.S. community should be, based on their own experiences. Revisionist historians contend that progressives were too myopic to permit the emergence of a genuine culturally, ethnically, linguistically, and racially pluralistic society.

Together with the progressive movement, the Great Depression of the 1930s shaped Dewey's outlook on life, society, and schools. Dewey, noted as a "frontier thinker" in education, contributed to and was associated with an important journal, *The Social Frontier*, edited by George S. Counts.[7] Dewey and the other frontier educators believed that U.S. political, social, economic, and educational institutions were in a profound crisis and needed to be reconstructed in the light of the great technological changes that had taken place in U.S. and Western society. Examining key themes of the American temperament identified earlier—frontier, individualism, and community—they sought to reconceptualize them to meet the needs of a modern interdependent technological society. The frontier, they claimed, no longer meant the settlement of Americans on territory in the west. No longer confined to occupying geographical space, it now meant that the American people needed to create new frontiers in politics, society, the economy, and education. For them, the inherited myth of rugged individualism was wasteful, inefficient, and counterproductive in an interdependent society and economy. Rather, it was crucial that the modern individual, while retaining personal freedom, be eager and ready to cooperate in social, economic, and educational planning and implementation for the common good. From this needed social reconstruction would be born a revitalized American community that was no longer defined in terms of geographical setting but would rest on an ever-expanding network of human interrelationships.

Dewey's philosophy also needs to be examined in terms of the major trends that were affecting U.S. education, particularly schools, during his lifetime. His persistent opposition to the dichotomy that separated the school from society runs consistently throughout Dewey's ideas on education. For him, schools were embedded in society, not isolated from it.

By 1880, America's public school system was institutionally and structurally in place. Horace Mann's vision of a system of locally controlled and publicly supported schools, providing all the children of the community with a basic education, had been realized. However, many schools, like other institutions, had problems that reduced their effectiveness. For example, instruction had become very formal, often consisting of memorized recitations. In some cities, progressive investigative journalists found that key appointments in schools were based on political patronage rather than educational qualifications.[8]

Progressive educational reformers sought to address these school-based problems by curricular innovation and by educational expertise. Progressive curricular reformers sought to improve the school's educational effectiveness by introducing methodological innovations into the classroom. For example, Colonel Francis Parker, a leading progressive educator, emphasized activity-based "learning by doing," a theme that strongly appealed to Dewey. Rather than relying on teacher-directed recitations, curricular progressives introduced such innovations as relating instruction to children's experience and needs; using the laboratory or experimental method as an instructional strategy; using field trips and excursions that involved visits to zoos, art galleries, parks, and museums; creating learning situations that encouraged collaborative social interaction; and relating instruction to broad social, political, and economic issues and problems. These progressive innovations were embodied in Dewey's educational philosophy and practice.

Some progressive educators concentrated their efforts on reforming curriculum and instruction; others, especially administrators, sought to make schools more effective and efficient.[9] These administrative progressives believed that professional educators, not amateurs or politicians, should operate schools. They asserted that professionally prepared administrators, superintendents, and principals could use scientific management techniques to make operating schools more efficient and businesslike. Additionally, there were educators who concluded that a science of education could be devised and applied to instruction. Educators such as E. L. Thorndike argued that educational outcomes could and should be specified and measured.[10]

In addition to these social, political, and educational forces that were part of the context of Dewey's emergence on the American scene, there was also an intellectual ferment in the land caused by a new philosophical way of looking at the world called pragmatism. The pragmatist thinkers Oliver Wendell Holmes, Jr., Charles S. Peirce, and William James challenged the traditional philosophical assumptions of a completed and perfect universe that could be approached, if at all, through metaphysical speculation into the nature of ultimate reality. Rejecting the philosophical security provided by absolute truth and values, the new philosophers saw the world as pluralistic, tentative, open, and changing. Human beings were engaged in interactions with the environment and in relationships with each other that were flexible, malleable, and always in need of reappraisal and readjustment. The pragmatist philosophers saw ideas not as the reflection of ultimate and unalterable truths as the Platonic and Hegelian idealists professed but rather as humanly arrived–at instruments, hypotheses, to be devised, acted on, and tested in the reality of experience.[11] John Dewey would enter the ranks of the new philosophers to create his own version of pragmatism.

It was against this backdrop of social, political, economic, and educational developments that John Dewey developed his educational ideas and practices.

Dewey as a Pragmatist Philosopher and Progressive Educator

John Dewey was born in Burlington, Vermont, on October 20, 1859, the third son of Archibald Sprague Dewey, a Civil War veteran, and Lucina Artemisia Rich Dewey.[12] Descended from rural families, the Deweys decided to leave farming and moved to Burlington to operate a family-owned grocery store. Dewey's mother, 20 years younger than her husband, came from a well-respected and public-spirited Vermont family. Her grandfather, Charles Rich, served 10 years in the U.S. House of Representatives and her father, Davis Rich, served in Vermont's General Assembly. Lucina, committed to social service and reform, impressed the values of responsibility and purpose on her children, especially John. Dewey's father, Archibald, however, with a quite different temperament, was an energetic entrepreneurial businessman.[13] Small-town grocery stores, like the Deweys', were often centers of community life, where customers met, exchanged pleasantries, gossiped, and discussed local issues.

John was the third of four sons born to the Deweys. His older brother John Archibald died in a tragic accident at age 2. He had been critically scalded when he fell into a pail of boiling water; then, as he was being wrapped in oil and bandages to ease his torment, the bandages caught fire and the little boy suffered a painful death. Forty weeks later, John Dewey, named after his deceased brother, was born. Jay Martin, a biographer of Dewey, calls him a "replacement" child who had to live not only for himself but for his departed brother as well.[14] John had two other brothers, Davis Rich Dewey, who became a distinguished economist, and Charles Miner Dewey.[15]

John Dewey grew up in a formative moral climate of community participation and service. The Dewey family, inspired and directed by Mrs. Dewey, were active members of Burlington's First Congregational Church. Guided by his mother, John developed his early religious ideas—a sense of personal responsibility for one's actions and a need to do good for others—through social service.[16]

Life in small-town Vermont had an important effect on young John Dewey. Throughout his life, Dewey cherished a vision of the face-to-face, New England town meeting–type of community that shaped his emphasis on community's role in forming social consciousness and participation.

Dewey began his formal education in September 1867, entering District School No. 3, the local public elementary school. He studied the usual elementary subjects—reading, writing, spelling, rhetoric, arithmetic, history, and geography.[17] Shy and socially reserved, he pursued his studies earnestly. By skipping some grades, he was able to complete his elementary education in five years. When he developed his own philosophy of education, Dewey would reject the compartmentalized curriculum and emphasis on recitations that he had experienced in elementary school in favor of experienced-based active learning.

In 1872, Dewey began his secondary education in the Burlington high school. Enrolled in the college preparatory curriculum, he took courses in Latin, Greek, French, English grammar, literature, and mathematics.[18] He read widely on his own and became a polished writer. Completing the four-year high school program in three years, the 15-year-old Dewey graduated in 1875.

In 1875 shortly before his sixteenth birthday, Dewey entered the University of Vermont. Still a relatively small institution, the faculty of eight instructed a student body of 100. The college curriculum, like that of the high school, was heavily prescribed and oriented toward the classics. Dewey enrolled in such courses as Greek, Latin, rhetoric, English literature, history, philosophy, political economy, and psychology. Often in the library, he continued his lifelong habit of wide and extensive reading, especially in his favorite subjects of history, literature, and philosophy. As an undergraduate, Dewey made his first foray into philosophy, the discipline that would engage him throughout his life. H. A. P. Torrey, his professor of philosophy, led Dewey to the leading German idealist philosophers Kant, Hegel, and Schelling. Dewey felt a special attraction to the philosophers of science such as Auguste Comte, the positivist, T. H. Huxley, the evolutionist, and Herbert Spencer, the social Darwinist. Ranking second in a class of 18, he received his bachelor of arts degree in 1879.[19]

Dewey, at age 19, took his first teaching position in the high school at Oil City, Pennsylvania. East of Pittsburgh on the Allegheny River, Oil City, with a population of 8,000, was an important center in the petroleum industry. Here, for two years, Dewey, earning a salary of $40 a month, taught Latin, algebra, and natural science. He left Oil

City in 1881, to return to Vermont as a teacher at the Lake View Seminary in Charlotte, near Burlington. Located near the University of Vermont, Dewey enrolled as a graduate student in philosophy. He was awarded his master's degree in 1881.[20]

In 1882, Dewey entered the new graduate institution, Johns Hopkins University, to pursue advanced study in philosophy. Created by Daniel Coit Gilman in 1876, Johns Hopkins enjoyed recognition as one of the premier research institutions in the United States. Gilman had imported the German research model in which a select group of graduate students worked in small seminars on specialized topics under the direction of a distinguished professor who was a recognized expert in the field. The goal of the seminar method was the discovery and dissemination or original knowledge. The seminar method had a profound effect on Dewey, who came to see education as the means of creating knowledge through inquiry rather than the transmission of extant information.

Dewey was a student at Johns Hopkins during a very exciting period in American higher education. He had the rare opportunity to study with some of the country's leading scholars who were pioneers in their fields. Dewey's major professor and program direction was George Sylvester Morris, a highly regarded interpreter of the German idealist philosopher Georg Wilhelm Hegel. Professing a philosophy of dynamic idealism, Morris wrote *A History of Philosophy from Thales to the Present* (1874) and *Hegel's Philosophy of the State and of History* (1887). Although Dewey would later abandon Hegel's abstract metaphysics for his own experimentalism, his thinking retained a Hegelian tendency to reconcile apparent contradictions, or dualisms, into unified broad concepts such as experience, democracy, and community. The Hegelian theme of a unifying "great community" exerted continuing appeal for Dewey. For him, the Hegelian ethical accentuation of human self-realization remained a guiding prospect but no longer one to be reached spiritually.[21] Dewey came to see personal self-realization as a goal to be achieved in human experiences that were enlarged by social transactions as individuals engaged in democratic participation in community.[22]

Dewey enrolled in Charles S. Peirce's course in mathematical logic. A somewhat erratic and difficult person and teacher, Peirce was engaged in groundbreaking work in mathematical logic and logical analysis. His new method of doing philosophy, called Pragmaticism, unlike Hegelian metaphysics, emphasized the use of statistical probability in framing hypotheses for action. Dewey did not enjoy Peirce's style of teaching and judged Peirce's approach to logic to be too mathematical. When Dewey was working toward his own version of Pragmatism and pursuing his own special interests in logic and science, he gained a greater respect for Peirce's highly original contributions to philosophy.[23]

Dewey enlarged his academic interests by taking courses in psychology with G. Stanley Hall, a pioneer in child and adolescent psychology. Hall, who had introduced the psychological laboratory method at Johns Hopkins, took an interdisciplinary approach to philosophy, psychology, physiology, and education that resonated well with Dewey.[24]

Believing that the philosopher had to go beyond the study of philosophy itself and reach out to other disciplines, Dewey took courses outside of his field. He studied world history and political science with the gifted historian Herbert Baxter Adams. In Adams's course, he met and had discussions with his fellow student, Woodrow Wilson, the future U.S. president.[25] In addition to his own graduate study, Dewey taught an undergraduate course in the history of philosophy. Dewey successfully defended his dissertation on "The Psychology of Kant" and received his Ph.D. in 1884.

In 1884, Dewey's long career in higher education began as an instructor in philosophy at the University of Michigan in Ann Arbor. He lectured in psychology and on the British philosophers Herbert Spencer and John Stuart Mill. At Ann Arbor, he met and fell in love with Harriet Alice Chipman, a junior majoring in philosophy at the university. Alice, who was preparing for a teaching career, engaged him in lively discussions about education. Alice and John were married on July 28, 1886.[26] They had six children: Frederick Archibald, born in 1887, Evelyn in 1889, Morris in 1892, Gordon in 1896, Lucy in 1897, and Jane in 1900. Dewey's intense involvement with his children further stimulated his interest in education, especially child development and learning. When the Deweys were on a European trip in 1896, Morris, aged 2½, died of diphtheria. Tragedy struck a second time, again on a European trip in 1904, when their son Gordon, aged 8, died from typhoid fever. While in Europe, the Deweys adopted an 8-year-old Italian boy, Sabino. Harriet died in 1927. In 1946 Dewey remarried, to Roberta Lowitz Grant.

In 1888, Dewey, now a recognized philosopher, left Michigan to accept a position as a full professor of mental and moral philosophy at the University of Minnesota. He stayed at Minnesota for only one year. In 1889, he returned to the University of Michigan as head of the philosophy department. These career moves show that he was a sought-after professor who was using his prominence to rise up the academic ladder.

As university professor, Dewey earned a reputation as a serious, demanding, and well-prepared lecturer. At the beginning of a course, he provided his students with a summary of the content for each class session, the required readings, a detailed digest of each subject to be covered in the course, and a bibliography of further readings.[27] Because of his exacting preparation, Dewey was able to rewrite his lecture notes as articles and books. He published *Outlines of a Critical Theory of Ethics* (1891) and *The Study of Ethics: A Syllabus* (1894).

In 1894, Dewey was on the move again, accepting an appointment as chairman of the Department of Philosophy, Psychology, and Pedagogy at the University of Chicago. A new institution, the University of Chicago had been established only four years earlier with funds provided by the oil baron John D. Rockefeller, Sr. The founding president of the University of Chicago, William Rainey Harper, energetically recruited a faculty of distinguished professors to make his institution a leader in academic research and scholarly publication.[28]

The composition of Dewey's department at the University of Chicago was interesting in that by including professors of philosophy, psychology, and pedagogy, it brought together in one unit those disciplines with which Dewey would be involved for the rest of his career. The study of education as a university subject was still new. From the parent discipline, philosophy, would come the knowledge and insight needed for the philosophy of education. From psychology would come valuable contributions to educational psychology, child and adolescent development, and learning theory. Pedagogy—the traditional name given to principles of instruction—would become, with the foundations of philosophy and psychology, a broadened and enriched field of inquiry and application.

Dewey was invigorated by Chicago's lively and enlivening atmosphere. He was a frequent regular visitor and lecturer at Jane Addams's Hull House. (Addams is discussed in Chapter 19.) Addams's philosophy of socialized education with its emphasis on community resonated well with Dewey's emerging experimentalism. His conversations with

Addams helped Dewey to clarify his thinking. Dewey came to Chicago with a Hegelian outlook on social conflict based on the idea that some institutions and people were locked in inevitable conflict. Disagreeing, Addams convinced him that conflict was unnecessary and occurred when individuals interjected their personal biases into a situation. The genuine resolution of conflict, Addams advised Dewey, came when a person acted out of a unified striving to resolve a problem or issue.[29]

While in Chicago, Dewey broadened his insights into the relationships between schools and children's learning. He met with Colonel Francis Parker, the champion of progressive education, and lectured at Parker's Cook County Normal School. Using his theory on "The Reflex Arc Concept in Psychology," Dewey shared his ideas on learning with the prospective teachers. The mind, Dewey argued, was not a preformed structure but rather an organic functioning process in which interests led to action. Learning was a continuing process of adjustment and readjustment to changing circumstances that expands a person's interests and judgments.[30]

Dewey established his famous University of Chicago Laboratory School in 1896 as an experimental setting to test his ideas on child psychology and learning. Dewey's view of the school is elaborated on in his widely read *The School and Society* (1899). Emphasizing the vital link between school and society, Dewey called his laboratory school a "miniature society," an "embryonic community," in which children learned collaboratively by working together to solve problems. Through group-based process learning, children developed their mutual relations and learned to become participants in the larger society. The school was organized according to activities that centered on the "methods of life," human occupations, in relationship to their social use. Based on the methods of life, children would be brought gradually to subjects that arose from these methods. For example, the activities of producing items, "making and doing," would lead to economics. Learning to cooperate in democratic decision-making would lead to citizenship and politics.[31]

For Dewey, a laboratory school was an experimental school in which educational theories were to be tested. If validated in the actual experience of teaching and learning, those theories could be disseminated to a larger educational audience. Dewey's school attracted the attention of educators during the years of its operation, 1896 to 1904, and his work continues to intrigue educational historians, philosophers, and curricular specialists.[32] Disagreements between Dewey and President Harper about the administration of the Laboratory School led to Dewey's resignation in 1904 and his departure from the University of Chicago.

In 1905, Dewey accepted a professorship in Columbia University's Department of Philosophy, which he held until he retired in 1930. It was at Columbia that Dewey wrote *Democracy and Education* (1916), *Reconstruction in Philosophy* (1920), *Human Nature and Conduct* (1922), *Experience and Nature* (1925), *The Public and Its Problems* (1927), *Individualism Old and New* (1929), *The Quest for Certainty* (1929), *Art as Experience* (1934), *A Common Faith* (1934), *Liberalism and Social Action* (1935), and *Freedom and Culture* (1939). At Columbia, Dewey formed a close association with a number of professors of education, including William Heard Kilpatrick, George S. Counts, and Harold Rugg, who were leading progressive educational theorists. Through his association with these professors, Dewey's ideas on education, already well known, reached an even larger audience of teachers.

Enjoying an international reputation as a distinguished philosopher and educator, Dewey lectured to audiences in several foreign countries. From 1919 through 1921, when the political map of the world was being reshaped after World War I, Dewey delivered lectures in major Japanese and Chinese cities. At the time of Dewey's lectures at the National University in Beijing, China was struggling to become a democratic republic based on the principles of Sun Yat-sen. In 1924, Dewey consulted with the government of Turkey, a country pursuing a course of modernization. In 1928, Dewey visited the Soviet Union, which only 11 years earlier had overthrown its tsar and established a Communist regime based on Marx's dialectical materialism. When Dewey was in the Soviet Union, its founder, Nikolai Lenin, had been dead four years and Joseph Stalin was consolidating his power in what later became a despotic tyranny. Dewey was a popular figure in the Soviet Union, which in seeking new patterns of education had experimented with some of his ideas. When he spoke out against Stalinism a few years later, however, Dewey and his books were banned there. Throughout his public life, Dewey, though decidedly to the left of the political center, was a convinced anti-Communist. In 1936–1937, he chaired a commission of inquiry that determined that Stalin's allegations against Leon Trotsky, a prominent Bolshevik leader, lacked credibility.

Dewey participated in and often led liberal and reformist political movements. Seeking to protect the freedom to teach and the freedom to learn in higher education, Dewey was a founder of the American Association of University Professors (AAUP). He served as the association's first president in 1915. He was a founding member of the National Association for the Advancement of Colored People (NAACP) and was active in the American Civil Liberties Union (ACLU) and the New York City Teachers Union.

For 22 years after his retirement from Columbia University, until his death on June 1, 1952, Dewey continued to speak for social and educational reform and renewal. His reputation remains that of a man committed to Pragmatism and progressivism.

Dewey's Experimentalism

In this section, we examine Dewey's key ideas on educational philosophy. Philosophically, Dewey is associated with the group of U.S. philosophers including Charles S. Peirce, William James, and George H. Mead, who developed Pragmatism. Breaking with Western philosophy's traditional preoccupation with speculative metaphysics, these Pragmatists asserted that the philosopher's genuine enterprise was to work to define and solve human problems. Pragmatists contend that truth is tentative, a warranted assertion, rather than universal, eternal, and absolute. Based on human experience, truth involves testing or verifying an idea by acting on it and determining if the consequences of such action resolve the particular problem. The Pragmatist predilection to tentativeness, empiricism, and change stands in opposition to Plato's metaphysics (see Chapter 3). According to Platonic idealism, truth reflects unchanging, perfect, universal, and eternal ideas to which human behavior should conform. In contrast, Pragmatism fits the American temperament, perhaps derived from the frontier experience, that sees human behavior as the interaction of people with changing environmental situations. Educationally, a goal based on Pragmatism would encourage learners to be open and willing to accept the challenge of change.

Our analysis of Dewey's philosophy of human life within an ever-changing environment begins with comments on his book *The Quest for Certainty* (1929).[33] Here, Dewey critiqued Western philosophers' tendency to hypothesize that the world existed in two dimensions—one perfect and unchanging and the other imperfect and changing. Philosophers such as Plato, arguing that reality was based on the form of the good, concentrated on a perfect world but neglected human experience. Christian theologians, such as Aquinas and Calvin, emphasized the soul's eternal spiritual afterlife in heaven. According to Dewey, this Western philosophical and theological tradition reflected the individual's attempt to deny death and disappearance by believing that a part of the human being, a spiritual essence or soul, would live forever. Thus, Western philosophy, emphasizing a perfect world beyond human experience, had misrepresented the issues of everyday life. Grounded in the empirical world, Dewey's experimentalism advised people to solve the problems of life intelligently and reflectively.

According to Dewey, the quest for certainty resulted in a belief in two worlds and two dimensions of human nature—the physical, bodily nature and the spiritual or rational nature. What some philosophers called the higher and lower orders of human nature, Dewey rejected as a harmful dualism that separated mind and body and theory and practice. Dewey believed that mind and body together created human experience and that theory and practice also united to solve the problems people encountered in their experience. Rejecting dualistic philosophies, Dewey devised a theory of knowledge based on a continuum of human experience that integrated rather than separated thinking and acting, fact and value, and intellect and emotion.[34]

The mind-body and theory-practice dualisms that Dewey sought to resolve had significant consequences for educational practice, especially for curriculum. Traditional philosophers asserted that the mind and the pure theory derived from it were superior to practice in solving the problems of life. According to this view, thinking was best when it stayed at the higher speculative plane. Pure theory was preferred to actually doing and making things, to discovering and inventing, and to resolving problems of politics, health, peace, and society. In such a traditional outlook, the fine arts were better than the practical arts, liberal education was superior to vocational education, and so on. For Dewey, the challenge was to reconcile these longstanding dualisms into a unified flow of experience. The kind of education that emerged for him was unified and not segmented into separate categories. Based on and related to human experience in the real world of the person interacting with the environment, it did not promise certainty. Rather, it pointed the way to chart one's course in an uncertain and changing world.

Dewey's abandoning of a certain and static world for an open universe of constant change was influenced by Charles Darwin's theory of evolution. Darwin's *Origin of Species by Means of Natural Selection* was published in 1859, the year of Dewey's birth. Darwin's theory of evolution postulated that the different species of plant and animal life had evolved slowly over the course of time by successful adaptation to changing environments. Darwin's theory contrasted with the literal view in the Bible's book of Genesis that all species had been created by God in fixed and final form. Darwin's theory of evolution made an impression on Dewey, especially the emphasis on the adaptation of the species as a response to changing environmental conditions.

For Dewey, the concepts of organism and environment were significant in formulating an experimentalist *epistemology*, or how we think, and an educational method based on it.[35] Similar to other, simpler organisms, the human being was a living organism, physiologically composed of living tissue and possessing life-sustaining drives and impulses. The human organism, however, with its highly developed brain, was a reflective creature who could hypothetically conjecture the consequences of a projected action and create plans of actions that enhanced life. Further, the human organism, with its opposable thumb and fingers, could make and use instruments. Importantly, the human as a vocal creature could form sounds and communicate through speech. Every organism, including the human one, lived in an environment, a habitat, containing conditions that both supported and threatened life. For Dewey, life was a series of connected and related interactive episodes between the human organism and its environment.

As Dewey saw it, human life was sustained through successful interactions with this environment. Instead of being pitted in an inexorable struggle with nature as the social Darwinist claimed, Dewey advised human beings to instrumentally use nature to transform parts of the environment to increase life-sustaining possibilities. Through the use of scientific intelligence and collaborative social activity, people possess the possibility of using selected natural elements to solve problems caused by other aspects of the natural environment.[36]

Along with his definition of experience as the interaction of the person with the environment, Dewey's theory of learning also emphasized the psychological principle of the "reflex arc." Instead of construing the "arc" as a series of actions by which a person reacted to a stimulus in the environment, Dewey redefined activity as an organic whole in which a person acted with knowledge of the results of the activity. Learning, thus, became an activity by which a person adapted to the environment in a unified way instead of in a series of disconnected reactions. By this kind of unified, purposeful action, learning took place.[37]

Dewey called these interactive episodes "experience." Educational practice, influenced by Dewey's Pragmatism, emphasizes the experience-based curriculum. In the interactive episode between the person and the environment, thinking occurs and from it learning takes place. When the person encounters an obstacle or impediment to activity, a problematic situation arises. For Dewey, life itself was problematic. Interaction with the environment alters both the individual and the society so that new problems arise. It is by resolving these problems that thinking occurs and human growth, or progress, takes place.[38]

Dewey designed a series of problem-solving steps that approximate what he considered to be the scientific method, broadly construed. Referred to as the "complete act of thought," Dewey's experimental or process-oriented method consisted of the following phases:

1. The person encounters something different, a new experience or deviant particular, that stops the flow of ongoing activity. It is in the context of this new element that the person finds herself or himself in a problematic situation. Note that the problematic situation can be used educationally when a student or group of students encounters a problem needing to be solved.

2. For the person to solve the problem, the element that is blocking activity must be located and defined. The question needs to be asked, "What is causing the problem?" Once a definition is posed, the person can begin to locate and solve the problem. In the educational situation, the ability to define the problem correctly

is an important skill. The definitional phase of problem solving, if correctly done, will point the learner to the resources needed to solve the problem.

3. After the problem has been located and defined, it is then possible to gather information, do research, and consult previous experience that will shed light on the problem and point to its resolution. In the educational situation, this phase may involve researching in the library, conducting interviews, and collecting information. In this stage, the teacher functions as a resource person who facilitates students' research activities.

4. Now comes the conjectural stage, in which tentative hypotheses of possible action are structured. The person or group reflects on the possible actions and mentally explores the consequences of each. Now the question becomes, "If I do this, what is likely to result?" In the educational situation, the goal is to develop reflective attitudes that contribute to planning skills. Such plans, called "ends in view," give direction to experience.

5. The last stage involves acting on the tentative hypothesis that is likely to resolve the problem by effecting the projected and desired consequences. If the problem is solved, the procedures of the complete act of thought have been followed correctly. If it is not resolved, the process needs to be reexamined to identify mistakes that may have interfered with its solution. If the problem is solved, the person resumes activity and adds the particular problem-solving episode to her or his network of experience. In the educational situation, the final step of the problem-solving sequence is of crucial importance. Unlike many conventional school situations where problem solving stays strictly academic, Dewey's process requires action, an empirical test. It is this stage that avoids the dualism of theory and practice and integrates them into complete thinking.

For Dewey, the complete act of thought, or problem solving according to the scientific method, is the proper way to think and also the most effective strategy for teaching and learning. Because of his emphasis on the scientific method, Dewey's version of Pragmatism is called *experimentalism*. Life and learning involve a series of experiments by which human beings seek to gain control and direction of their interactions with their environment. This process is an active, ongoing, cumulative flow of human experience that unites the episodes of the past with those of the present to give direction and control over the future. Dewey emphasized that human beings had the possibility of directing and controlling the course of change by using the scientific method. When an individual faces a personal problem or the group faces a social, political, or economic problem, the scientific method should be used to solve that problem and obtain the desired consequences. Dewey's concept of the scientific method was a broadly conceived procedure of scientific intelligence that was applicable to human affairs.[39]

In addition to emphasizing the scientific method, Dewey's experimentalism also accentuates the person as a member of society. Indeed, education is a process of socialization that brings one into participation in associative life. For Dewey, human intelligence is socially acquired as people interact with each other in solving problems in their environment. The social environment contains all of the sociocultural dimensions that the human race has created over time—political, economic, and educational infrastructures and processes as well as artistic, philosophical, and religious forms. The human group possesses the possibilities for developing and enriching shared intelligence.

As indicated earlier, Dewey and other progressives were searching to develop strategies to revitalize the American conception of the community. In particular, Dewey's emphasis on communal cooperation challenged the then-prevalent theory of social Darwinism, championed by Herbert Spencer and his American disciple, William Graham Sumner. Rejecting the competitive ethic of social Darwinism's rugged individualism, Dewey and the other progressives wanted to revitalize the face-to-face, shared experiences they believed had once characterized small-town America. However, they realized that the sense of community needed to be reconstructed to meet the requirements of an interdependent, technological, and industrial society.

For Dewey, a genuine sense of community arose through three stages: common sharing, communication, and community itself. In the first stage, the group shares common objects and pursues common activities. This is the beginning of a sense of "we feeling" or group identification. Because they use common instruments to attain common goals, the members of the group develop ways of talking about their common endeavors. When individuals communicate, they assume the perspective of the other person in developing their own understanding and behavior. Communication thus develops a commonly shared context; this context, in turn, frames the basis of community.[40] This sense of mutuality and reciprocity in making and doing, in planning and implementing, leads to a sense of full sharing in the community.

Just as he opposed metaphysically based value criteria, Dewey disputed the prevalent classical liberal orientation in U.S. society that argued that values were based on individual self-interest. He also combated the trend in which the general community was fractured into contentious special interest groups. He saw human beings as communal participants who defined and tested collective goals. In U.S. political life, Dewey was a proponent of grassroots, face-to-face, participatory democracy.

For Dewey, the United States was unique in its commitment to national democratic processes and to its respect for cultural diversity and pluralism. Its myriad smaller communities were integrated within the democratic procedures of the broader encompassing community, the great society. Each of the smaller communities—racial, ethnic, gender—has its own identifying context, communication, and sense of membership. Each has a potentially enriching contribution to make to the greater community. While the smaller cultural communities could be expected to differ with each other on some matters, it was crucial to the welfare of the larger community, especially to its democratic processes and values, that these disagreements occur within a communal framework and not degenerate into noncommunal conflict. The resolution of communal conflicts meant that they could be resolved in a procedural, nonviolent, nondestructive way. The larger community, the greater society, was one governed by commonly shared processes of conflict resolution. For Dewey, there was a communal, or communitarian, core of beliefs and values. This core, however, rested on commonly agreed-to and shared democratic procedures.

In applying Dewey's general theory of community to schooling, the group should be envisioned as possessing immense educational potential. Collaborative group problem solving, planning, and implementation reduces the isolation of the individual from others and through mutual activities produces an enriched social intelligence. Barriers to full human association block free interaction. They impede the possibilities of individuals and groups to contribute to cultural growth by mutually sharing experience.[41]

Dewey's emphasis on the group of learners is revealed in his early work at the University of Chicago Laboratory School, which he called a "free and informal community."[42]

As a true progressive, Dewey advocated a democratic society as the environment most conducive to applying the scientific method and creating a truly sharing community. In fact, his choice of title—*Democracy and Education*—for his most complete rendition of his philosophy of education reveals his emphasis on democratic processes. Although his view of democracy was undoubtedly shaped by his life and education in the United States, democracy for Dewey was more than political institutions. Democracy was a way of life, a culture, free of those absolutes that blocked truly experimental inquiry. No subject, custom, or value was so sacrosanct that it was to escape inquiry. Further, the social setting was to be free of coercive and authoritarian persons who would jeopardize freedom of thought, inquiry, and experimentation.

Dewey's conception of the school curriculum integrated both the experimental qualities of the scientific method and the educative role of the group. Unlike the conventional curriculum, which was organized around tool skills such as reading, writing, arithmetic, and academic subject matter disciplines such as history, mathematics, and chemistry, Dewey structured the school's program around three broad focusing sets of activities: making and doing, history and geography, and science. The scientific method, broadly conceived as the complete act of thought, was used throughout these sets of activities.

Making and doing referred to the kinds of activities that children did in their first years of school. These activities led children from their immediate families and homes into the larger society. At school, children might sweep the floor, water plants, set the table for lunch, and go on shopping trips. Working together in these collaborative activities, which were similar to the kinds of things they did at home, created a school community. Home experiences led easily into school experiences without isolating either from each other. The activities related to making and doing were intended to bring children into touch with how life was sustained.[43] The stage of making and doing was followed by history and geography. These areas of inquiry were not taught as conventional academic subjects but rather were designed to expand children's perspective into time and space. The third stage of curriculum, science, was broadly construed to mean the investigation of the various subject matter disciplines, not in isolation from each other, but in terms of what they could provide to solve problems.

In *Experience and Education*, Dewey reiterated the theme that genuine education is based on the experience of the learner. Warning against an "either-or" posture, he challenged Robert Hutchin's idea that education should reflect the enduring ideas of the great books of Western civilization as a surrender to the old forms of the past. He also warned his progressive followers that merely opposing traditionalism was an inadequate foundation for a democratic philosophy of education. What true progressivism needed was a criterion of experience that promoted human growth through the intelligent activity of problem solving.

By having students solve problems using the scientific method and group processes, Dewey believed they would gain a sense of reflective inquiry and practical intelligence. Dewey's experimentalism also carried the values that would underlie the new and still undefined, reconstructed U.S. community. Experimentalist ethics, free of fixed regulations, were to be worked out in the situations and contexts that called for choice among competing values. Those who experienced an experimentalist education were to be eager to direct the course of change, flexible in their attitudes and dispositions, willing to experiment and to question inherited traditions and values, and socially involved and tolerant of others—participants in formulating a broad social consensus.

Conclusion: An Assessment

John Dewey's experimentalism has exercised a shaping influence on U.S. society and education. In its origins, he developed his philosophy of education during the progressive era that engendered a pragmatic outlook on politics, law, art, and education. His philosophical inquiries examined institutions and values in the light of the changing circumstances of life in the United States. For those who accepted the experimental mode, the question was, How well does this institution or value satisfy the needs of a rapidly changing society? No longer could institutions and values rest on maintaining the traditional status quo.

In the twenty-first century, Dewey's emphasis on social intelligence and community has again elicited a favorable response. Dewey's emphasis that individuals create meaning through their associative participation in community has struck a resonant chord within the contemporary communitarian movement. The contemporary search for a revitalized liberalism as a consensual middle ground between the extremes of neoconservatism and neo-Marxist critical theory also is inspired by Dewey's political philosophy. Dewey's call for education based on and tested in experience is being reasserted by some educational policy makers.

In education and in schools, Dewey's influence has had far-reaching significance. His emphasis on the vital importance of children's interests and needs in shaping curriculum worked to change the meaning of schooling. Through his work, education was construed as a process of using the scientific method to intelligently solve problems rather than transmitting bodies of information. In teacher education, Dewey and his educational disciples, many of whom were graduates of Columbia University's Teachers College, had their greatest effect. From these experimentalist educators, prospective teachers learned about the importance of collaborative group projects; using inquiry methods; and the need for process-based learning activities. Dewey-inspired elements can be easily detected in such contemporary educational movements as constructivism, whole language learning, and authentic assessment.

Though Dewey enjoyed a reputation as an eminent philosopher of education, his experimentalism has produced ongoing debate in American society and education. Although many educators have been inspired by Dewey's philosophy, his experimentalism also generated strong opposition. Those who see the curriculum as a stable body of academic subjects and values that is constant rather than relative have been antagonistic to Dewey's pragmatic cultural relativism.

Many teachers selectively borrowed and designed lessons around such key Deweyan phrases as "learning by doing," "the activity method," "problem solving," and "children's interests and needs." Some of these educators found a liberating appeal in these specific parts of Dewey's work without accepting his relativistic view of knowledge and values. As selective users of Dewey's philosophy, they wanted to preserve their allegiance to what they believed were timeless standards of academic integrity and patriotism. They held back from examining those values that made their lives and work intellectually and emotionally secure.

Others opposed Dewey's philosophy because of their own strongly differing philosophical convictions. To those who saw Western civilization as derived from and resting on the universals of Judeo-Christian culture, Dewey's philosophy encouraged a dangerous relativism. Regardless of changing times and circumstances, they believed that certain truths would be forever valid and that certain values would be universally applicable. For them, good and bad and right and wrong did not depend on changing circumstances but were the moral standards that schools should perennially convey to each new generation.

Educators—especially the essentialists such as William Bagley in the 1930s, Arthur Bestor in the 1950s, and William Bennett in the 1990s—argued that Dewey's educational philosophy was weakening the schools' primary academic purpose. For them, the school was to teach the basic skills of reading, writing, and arithmetic, and the fundamental intellectual disciplines of English and foreign languages, history, mathematics, and science.[44] Anything else would dilute the school's primary mission.

In a time when fear of terrorism has generated suspicion and limitations on difference and dissent, Dewey's arguments for an open universe and an open society take on a renewed importance. His arguments for a pluralist conception of culture and for expanded freedoms of inquiry, dissent, and expression are significant for American society. As Louis Menand so simply but eloquently states about Dewey and the pragmatists' conception of democracy: ". . . democracy . . . isn't just about letting the right people have their say; it's also about letting the wrong people have their say. It is about giving space to minority and dissenting views so that, at the end of the day, the interests of the majority may prevail."[45]

Although his philosophy differed in many fundamental ways from Plato, it can be said that Dewey shared some things with the ancient Greek philosopher. Education was so powerful and so potent a force that it could not be relegated to the school's four walls. It was, after all, the great cultural force that had the possibility of creating the new American *paedeia*, the great society of a renascent democratic community. For Dewey, the quest to realize the promise of democracy was never finished but like experience was an ongoing challenge.

Questions for Reflection and Dialogue

1. Why was the American culture and society a likely environment for the development of Pragmatism?
2. What was the progressive agenda and method for reforming U.S. society and education?
3. Why and how did Dewey seek to reconstruct and redefine the concept of individualism in modern society?
4. Why was Dewey so opposed to philosophical and educational dualism? Can you identify any forms of dualism in contemporary American society and education?
5. What is Dewey's complete act of thought? Do you think it is a useful method of inquiry and instruction?
6. How were Dewey and other progressive theorists trying to create a new concept of community? In your opinion, what is the current status of community in American society?

7. Describe Dewey's work at the University of Chicago Laboratory School. Do you think schools should be educational laboratories?

8. Apply Dewey's concepts of the common, communication, and community to the current debates over multiculturalism and bilingualism in education.

Projects for Deepening Your Understanding

1. In an opinion paper, present your views on the question, Is the U.S. character pragmatic and experimental?

2. Develop a character analysis of John Dewey.

3. In an opinion paper, react to such trends in education as portfolios and authentic assessment, constructivism, character education, and standards based on standardized testing from the perspective of Dewey's experimentalist philosophy.

4. In an essay, identify and comment on the evidences of dualism in contemporary education. For example, do you find evidence of a separation between theory and practice?

5. Prepare an extended review of Dewey's *Democracy and Education*.

6. Design a lesson plan that follows Dewey's complete act of thought of problem solving.

7. In an opinion paper, answer the question: Are American society and culture pluralistic?

Notes

1. Jay Martin, *The Education of John Dewey: A Biography* (New York: Columbia University Press, 2002), 13.

2. For a useful treatment of the United States when Dewey began his career, see David Traxel, *1898: The Birth of the American Century* (New York: Alfred A. Knopf, 1998).

3. Frederick Jackson Turner, "The Significance of History," *Wisconsin Journal of Education* (October 1891), 230–34.

4. John Dewey, *Individualism Old and New* (1929; reprint, New York: Capricorn, 1962), 74–100.

5. Lawrence A. Cremin, *The Transformation of the School: Progressivism in American Education, 1876–1975* (New York: Alfred A. Knopf, 1962).

6. Robert M. Crunden, *Ministers of Reform: The Progressive's Achievement in American Civilization, 1889–1920* (Urbana, IL: University of Illinois Press, 1984), 3–15, 94–96.

7. Lawrence J. Dennis, *George S. Counts and Charles A. Beard: Collaborators for Change* (Albany, NY: State University of New York Press, 1989), 117–21.

8. Cremin, *Transformation of the School*, 3–7.

9. Raymond E. Callahan, *Cult of Efficiency* (Chicago: University of Chicago Press, 1962), 55–67, 126–29, 144–59.

10. Geraldine M. Joncich, ed., *Psychology and the Science of Education: Selected Writings of Edward L. Thorndike* (New York: Teachers College Press, 1962).

11. Louis Menand, *The Metaphysical Club: A Story of Ideas in America* (New York: Farrar, Straus and Giroux, 2001), ix–xii.

12. Biographical studies of Dewey are George Dykhuizen, *The Life and Mind of John Dewey* (Carbondale: Southern Illinois University Press, 1973); Neil Coughlan, *Young John Dewey: An Essay in American Intellectual History* (Chicago: University of Chicago Press, 1975); Robert B. Westbrook, *John Dewey and American Democracy* (Ithaca, NY: Cornell University Press, 1991); Jay Martin, *The Education of John Dewey: A Biography* (New York: Columbia University Press, 2002).

13. Martin, *The Education of John Dewey*, 14–15.

14. Martin, *The Education of John Dewey*, 5–6.
15. Alan Ryan, *John Dewey and the High Tide of American Liberalism* (New York: W. W. Norton, 1995), 41–42.
16. Martin, *The Education of John Dewey*, 20–21.
17. Ryan, *John Dewey and the High Tide of American Liberalism*, 41.
18. George Dykhuizen, *The Life and Mind of John Dewey* (Carbondale, IL: Southern Illinois University Press, 1973), 4–9.
19. Ryan, *John Dewey and the High Tide of American Liberalism*, 11–18.
20. Ryan, *John Dewey and the High Tide of American Liberalism*, 19–25.
21. Robert B. Westbrook, *John Dewey and American Democracy* (Ithaca, NY: Cornell University Press, 1991), 42–43.
22. Walter Feinberg, "Dewey and Democracy at the Dawn of the Twenty-first Century," *Educational Theory* 43, No. 2 (1993), 199.
23. Martin, *The Education of John Dewey*, 73–74.
24. Martin, *The Education of John Dewey*, 71–72.
25. Martin, *The Education of John Dewey*, 76.
26. Westbrook, *John Dewey and American Democracy*, 77.
27. Martin, *The Education of John Dewey*, 106.
28. Ryan, *John Dewey and the High Tide of American Liberalism*, 42.
29. Menand, *The Metaphysical Club*, 313.
30. Martin, *The Education of John Dewey*, 186–94.
31. Martin, *The Education of John Dewey*, 199–200.
32. For Dewey's Laboratory School, see Arthur G. Wirth, *John Dewey as Educator: His Design For Working in Education (1894–1904)* (New York: John Wiley & Sons, 1966); Herbert M. Kliebard, *The Struggle for the American Curriculum 1893–1958* (Boston and London: Routledge & Kegan Paul, 1986); and Laurel N. Tanner, *Dewey's Laboratory School: Lessons for Today* (New York: Teachers College Press, 1997).
33. John Dewey, *The Quest for Certainty: A Study of the Relation of Knowledge and Action* (1929; reprint, New York: Putnam, 1960).
34. Hilary Putnam and Ruth Anna Putnam, "Education for Democracy," *Educational Theory* 43, No. 4 (1993), 364.
35. John Dewey, *How We Think* (Boston: D. C. Heath, 1910).
36. Feinberg, "Dewey and Democracy," 204–5.
37. Menand, *The Metaphysical Club*, 328–30.
38. Ryan, *Dewey and the High Tide*, 28.
39. Westbrook, *John Dewey and American Democracy*, 141.
40. Sandra Rosenthal, "Democracy and Education, A Deweyan Approach," *Educational Theory* 43, No. 4 (1993), 377.
41. Putnam and Putnam, "Education for Democracy," 196.
42. John Dewey, quoted in Wirth, *John Dewey as Educator*, 125.
43. Ryan, *Dewey and the High Tide*, 173.
44. The case against certain progressive educational reforms is made in Diane Ravitch, *Left Back: A Century of Failed School Reforms* (New York: Simon and Schuster, 2000).
45. Menand, *The Metaphysical Club*, 440–41.

Suggestions for Further Reading

Berube, Maurice R. *American School Reform: Progressive, Equity, and Excellence Movements, 1883–1993*. Westport, CT: Praeger, 1994.

Cambell, James. *The Community Reconstructs: The Meaning of Pragmatic Social Thought*. Urbana, IL: University of Illinois Press, 1992.

Chambliss, Joseph J. *The Influence of Plato and Aristotle on John Dewey's Philosophy*. Lewiston, NY: E. Mellen, 1990.

Coughlan, Neil. *Young John Dewey: An Essay in American Intellectual History*. Chicago: University of Chicago Press, 1975.

Dewey, John. *A Common Faith*. New Haven, CT: Yale University Press, 1934.

———. *Democracy and Education: An Introduction to the Philosophy of Education*. 1916. Reprint, New York: Macmillan, 1964.

———. *Experience and Education*. New York: Collier, 1963.

———. *Individualism Old and New*. 1929. Reprint, New York: Capricorn, 1962.

———. *Lectures on Ethics, 1900–1901*. Carbondale, IL: Southern Illinois University Press, 1991.

———. *Liberalism and Social Action*. 1935. Reprint, New York: Capricorn, 1963.

———. *Philosophy & Education in Their Historic Relations*. Boulder, CO: Westview, 1993.

CHAPTER 20

———. *The Political Writings.* Indianapolis: Hackett, 1993.

———. *The Quest for Certainty: A Study of the Relation of Knowledge and Action.* 1929. Reprint, New York: Putnam, 1960.

———. *The Later Works, 1925–1953.* Jo Ann Boydston and Anne Sharpe, eds. Carbondale, IL: Southern Illinois University Press, 1989.

———. *The Middle Works, 1899–1924.* Jo Ann Boydston, ed. Carbondale, IL: Southern Illinois University Press, 1985.

———. *The School and Society.* Jo Ann Boydston, ed. Carbondale, IL; London: Southern Illinois University Press; Fiffer & Simons, 1980.

———. *The Moral Writings of John Dewey.* James Gouinlock, ed. Amherst, NY: Prometheus Books, 1994.

———. *Reconstruction in Philosophy and Essays, 1920.* Jo Ann Boydston and Ralph Ross, eds. Carbondale, IL: Southern Illinois University Press, 1988.

Dewey, John, and Tufts, James H. *Ethics.* Rev. ed. New York: Henry Holt, 1932.

Diggins, John P. *The Promise of Pragmatism: Modernism and the Crisis of Knowledge and Authority.* Chicago: University of Chicago Press, 1994.

Dykhuizen, George. *The Life and Mind of John Dewey.* Carbondale, IL: Southern Illinois University Press, 1973.

Feffer, Andrew. *The Chicago Pragmatists and American Progressivism.* Ithaca, NY: Cornell University Press, 1993.

Gunn, Giles B. *Thinking Across the American Grain: Ideology, Intellect, and the New Pragmatism.* Chicago: University of Chicago Press, 1992.

Hendley, Brian P. *Dewey, Russell, Whitehead: Philosophers as Educators.* Carbondale, IL: Southern Illinois University Press, 1986.

Hickman, Larry A. *John Dewey's Pragmatic Technology.* Bloomington, IN: Indiana University Press, 1990.

Hook, Sidney. *John Dewey: An Intellectual Portrait.* Westport, CT: Greenwood, 1971.

Hoy, Terry. *The Political Philosophy of John Dewey: Towards a Constructive Renewal.* Westport, CT: Praeger, 1998.

Kliebard, Herbart M. *The Struggle for the American Curriculum 1893–1958.* Boston and London: Routledge & Kegan Paul, 1986.

Kulp, Christoper B. *The End of Epistemology: Dewey and His Current Allies on the Spectator Theory of Knowledge.* Westport, CT: Greenwood, 1992.

Kurtz, Paul. *Philosophical Essays in Pragmatic Naturalism.* Buffalo, NY: Prometheus, 1990.

Martin, Jay. *The Education of John Dewey: A Biography.* New York: Columbia University Press, 2002.

Paringer, William A. *John Dewey and the Paradox of Liberal Reform.* Albany, NY: State University of New York Press, 1990.

Putnam, Hilary. *Pragmatism: An Open Question.* Cambridge, MA: Blackwell, 1995.

Rawls, John. *Political Liberalism.* New York: Columbia University Press, 1993.

Rice, Daniel F. *Reinhold Niebuhr and John Dewey: An American Odyssey.* Albany, NY: State University of New York Press, 1992.

Rockefeller, Steven C. *John Dewey: Religious Faith and Democratic Humanism.* New York: Columbia University Press, 1991.

Ryan, Alan. *John Dewey and the High Tide of American Liberalism.* New York: W. W. Norton, 1995.

Shusterman, Richard. *Pragmatic Aesthetics: Living Beauty, Rethinking Art.* Cambridge, MA: Blackwell, 1992.

Sleeper, R. W. *The Necessity of Pragmatism: John Dewey's Conception of Philosophy.* New Haven, CT: Yale University Press, 1986.

Stein, Jerome Abraham. *John Dewey and Adult Education.* Ann Arbor, MI: U.M.I., 1995.

Stuhr, John J., ed. *Philosophy and the Reconstruction of Culture: Pragmatic Essays After Dewey.* Albany, NY: State University of New York Press, 1993.

Tanner, Laurel N. *Dewey's Laboratory School. Lessons for Today.* New York: Teachers College Press, 1997.

Traxel, David. *1898: The Birth of the American Century.* New York: Alfred A. Knopf, 1998.

Welchman, Jennifer. *Dewey's Ethical Thought.* Ithaca, NY: Cornell University Press, 1995.

West, Cornel. *The American Evasion of Philosophy: A Genealogy of Pragmatism.* Madison, WI: University of Wisconsin Press, 1989.

Westbrook, Robert B. *John Dewey and American Democracy.* Ithaca, NY: Cornell University Press, 1991.

Wirth, Arthur G. *John Dewey as Educator: His Design for Work in Education (1894–1904).* New York: John Wiley & Sons, 1966.

21

Maria Montessori: Proponent of Early Childhood Education

In this chapter we examine the life, educational philosophy, instructional methods, and contributions of Maria Montessori (1870–1952), a commanding leader in early childhood education. Montessori developed a distinctive method of education that enjoys implementation in countries around the world. She was a highly motivated person who successfully broke through many of the barriers limiting educational opportunities for women in the late nineteenth and early twentieth centuries.

We discuss Montessori's influence on early childhood education in its historical context and in terms of its enduring effect on educational philosophy, policy, and practice. First, we describe the general social, political, economic, intellectual, and educational milieu of postrisorgimento Italy, in which Montessori lived and worked. Many of the conditions that affected the lives of women in late nineteenth-century Italy were also found in other western European nations and in the United States. Second, we analyze Montessori's biography, her background and career, to determine the forces that contributed to shaping her educational ideas. Third, we consider the Montessori method in terms of its foundations and its implications for teaching and learning. Fourth, we assess the continuing effect of Montessori's contributions. This analysis of the life, times, and contributions of Maria Montessori illustrates the interaction of a leading educator's biography with the development of her educational theory. For example, Montessori's educational philosophy and method emerged as she gained insights from her work in medicine, anthropology, and pedagogy. Her multidisciplinary approach to education led her to develop an educational method designed to educate the whole child—physically, mentally, and emotionally.

To organize your thoughts as you read this chapter, focus on the following questions:

1. What were the major trends in the historical context, the culture of postrisorgimento Italy, in which Montessori lived and worked?
2. How did Montessori's background, education, and career shape her philosophy and method of education?
3. How did Montessori's educational philosophy influence her educational policies and practices?
4. What is Montessori's enduring influence on education in general and on early childhood education in particular?

The Historical Context of Montessori's Life

Maria Montessori was born only 10 years after Italy became a united nation. Italian unification, under the royal House of Savoy, came as a result of the movement known as the *risorgimento*. Spokesmen for the risorgimento, such as Camillo Cavour and Giuseppe Garibaldi, although from opposite ends of the political spectrum, were united in their desire that the various small states and principalities on the Italian peninsula should form one country. By 1860, the political goals of the risorgimento had been accomplished. Garibaldi's volunteer army, the Carbonari, had toppled the old Bourbon kingdom of the two Sicilies and the armies of Piedmont-Sardinia had brought Victor Emmanuel to the throne of Italy as a constitutional monarch.

Essentially, the new Italy was a product of the forces of liberalism and nationalism. Nationalists like Garibaldi wanted Italy to take its place in the political sun. Liberals such as Cavour wanted an Italy that would industrialize and modernize its economy. Although these forces enjoyed political success, there were strong conservative pockets of opinion that were uneasy about the new Italy. Serious opposition came from the pope, who opposed the annexation of the papal states to Italy, refusing to acknowledge the political reality that a united Italy presented. The pope regarded himself as a prisoner of the Vatican. This created a dilemma for Roman Catholics in Italy, such as the Montessori family, who wanted to remain loyal to the pope, the head of their church, and to their king, the head of their state. Maria Montessori's uncle, Antonio Stoppani, a noted Roman Catholic priest, called for reconciliation between church and state. Maria's father, Alessandro Montessori, although remaining a committed Catholic, took a position in the new state's civil service.

Postrisorgimento Italy experienced the processes of modernization and development. Strong regional differences remained, especially the tension between the slowly industrializing north and the strongly agricultural and traditional south. Internal migration brought large numbers of former peasants to cities such as Milan and Rome to find better jobs and improve their economic conditions. In these cities, tenement districts arose to house the industrial underclass. It would be in one of these poverty-stricken districts of Rome, San Lorenzo, that Montessori would establish her first Casa dei Bambini, or Children's House. Anticipating by nearly 100 years such contemporary approaches to early childhood education as Operation Head Start in the United States, Montessori realized the crucial importance that the child's early years held for later success.

The Italy in which Montessori was born was still a very traditional, conservative country. In such a society, the roles that one would play were inherited across time and generations. *La famiglia*, the family, was a paramount institution that was often the Italians' primary source of identification, loyalty, and commitment. To family was added the determining factor of socioeconomic class. Although industrialization and modernization were bringing change to Italian society, a person's education and career remained largely determined by family background and social status. The children of peasants were destined to take their parents' place on the farms and landed estates of Italy. The sons of the middle class were likely to become overseers of estates, managers of businesses, or engaged in commerce. Children of the landed aristocracy would continue to enjoy the benefits of inherited wealth that made them a leisure class.

If the positions of the males in Italian society were determined by family and class, the roles of women were even more fixed by custom and tradition. Although membership in a particular class was a conditioning factor, women were expected to become the central sustaining force in their families as wives and mothers. With their roles so determined, higher and professional education were closed to them. Indeed, social sanctions were an even more potent factor in limiting women's career choices. Society allowed and economic necessity required women of the lower socioeconomic classes to work as agricultural, domestic, or factory laborers. Daughters of the lower middle class might become elementary school teachers or nurses. Young women of the aristocracy might attend finishing schools or convent schools to learn art, music, and literature. However, Maria Montessori would challenge nineteenth-century Italy's social and educational conventions. She would enter a technical secondary school to study engineering and the University of Rome's Medical School to become a doctor.

The Italian educational system in the late nineteenth century followed the continental European pattern of being heavily class determined. The Cassati Law provided for the establishment of primary or elementary schools. Compulsory education laws were not rigorously enforced, however. Italy, especially in the southern regions, had a high rate of illiteracy. At the secondary level, the schools were specialized into the highly academic college preparatory school, the *liceo*, and into a range of technical and vocational schools. Only a very small number were admitted to university studies. As a member of the middle class, Montessori had the opportunity to complete elementary school. Her determination to pursue a technical secondary education and medical school, however, was a radical departure from the educational expectations of young women at the time.

In addition to the socioeducational milieu of late nineteenth-century Italy, an important aspect of the general historical context in which Montessori worked relates to the conditions and development of early childhood education. At the time that she developed her educational philosophy, conventional schooling, especially at the primary level, was dominated by the classroom teacher as the central instructional agent. Under the direction of the teacher, children followed instructional routines centered on the study and usually memorization of textbooks, recitation, and dictation. In Italian schools, children often used a single textbook that combined in one volume all the subjects taught—reading, writing, arithmetic, history, and geography. Like schools throughout the Western world, recitation was the favored method of instruction. Children stood when questioned by the teacher and provided accurately memorized responses from the textbook. Italian schools, in particular, featured dictation, in which students would copy word for word statements made by the teacher. Each letter of the alphabet had to be placed squarely in a small box marked on a copy book. This was the kind of elementary school Montessori attended as a child. Although it provided basic literary and mathematical skills, it stressed routine and discouraged spontaneity and creativity. When Montessori devised her unique approach to education, she developed a new pattern for schools that, although not sacrificing order and structure, did encourage the joy of spontaneous learning.

In addition to the political and social patterns of Italian life, Montessori's context included the developments that were taking place at the beginning of the twentieth century in psychology and education. While recitations from textbooks still dominated classroom instruction, educational pioneers such as Rousseau, Pestalozzi, and Froebel had contributed new insights into children's nature and education. Jean-Jacques Rousseau's *Emile* had portrayed how education, based on natural principles, could free children from restrictive social conventions. Although she commended Rousseau's emphasis on child freedom, Montessori was skeptical about his proposal that children learn best by following their instincts and impulses in an unstructured natural environment. Pestalozzi had developed a theory of education that urged the reform of schools into homelike places where children felt emotionally secure and learned by using their senses in specially designed object lessons. Pestalozzi's emphasis on learning through sensation and working with objects was an antecedent of Montessori's own accentuation of sensory training. Of these three educators, Montessori was most often compared and contrasted with Froebel, the kindergarten's founder. Like Montessori, Froebel wanted early childhood education to take place in a specially created environment, the kindergarten, or child's garden. For Froebel, a philosophical idealist, children's innate inner spiritual powers would be developed most effectively in an educational environment where they learned through self activity and by using specially designed materials such as gifts and occupations. (For Rousseau, see Chapter 10; for Pestalozzi, Chapter 11; for Froebel, Chapter 16.)

As she became more knowledgeable about these important educational theories, Montessori recognized their value but also found them inadequate scientifically. Though promoting child dignity and freedom, she found that Rousseau, Pestalozzi, and Froebel had relied too much on philosophical speculation rather than a scientific understanding of children based on clinical observation. By introspecting on their own childhoods, they had proclaimed what purported to be universal principles of human growth and development. Rousseau's wild romantic flights of imagination, Montessori believed, had ignored children's need to learn in a structured environment. Pestalozzi's object lessons, though moving in the right direction, was just a crude beginning. Froebel's kindergarten was so steeped in abstract idealist imagery that it lacked a genuine foundation in modern science and psychology. Though recognizing her pedagogical predecessors' contributions, Montessori would remedy their deficiencies by turning to the actual observation of children, in clinical fashion, for her ideas on educational method. She would observe children and then create an educational method that responded to their behavior.

At the same time that Montessori had determined to create a scientifically based pedagogy in Italy, educators elsewhere in the world, too, were arriving at new insights into education. In the United States, progressive educators were working out new methods. At the Cook County Normal School in Chicago, Colonel Francis Parker (1837–1902) stressed experienced-based learning activities such as nature studies and field trips.[1] John Dewey, the experimentalist philosopher, was using his University of Chicago Laboratory School to test his theory of learning through experience, activities, and problem solving. (For Dewey, see Chapter 20.) Though both Montessori and Dewey called for the application of science to education, their views of science were sharply different. While Dewey's view stressed tentativeness and openness, Montessori saw science leading to universal principles. William Heard Kilpatrick (1871–1965), a leading progressive who would become an early and severe critic of Montessori, was developing his own method of education based on children's involvement in group-centered projects.[2] Kilpatrick would attack Montessori's method as out-of-date and inadequate in the areas of the children's socialization and creativity. These progressive educators—Parker, Dewey, Kilpatrick—who would become dominant figures in American educational theory were on a different path than the one that Montessori took. The progressives saw the school as a socially oriented embryonic society in which children learned by using the scientific method in a permissive environment. Enthusiastically calling for democracy in education, the progressives replaced universal principles with freedom and activity. Montessori's emphasis on learning in a structured environment and using didactic apparatus would differ from the American progressives.

Still yet another highly significant way of looking at childhood was emerging in Europe. In Vienna, Sigmund Freud (1856–1939) in his psychoanalytic psychology was coming to recognize the role of the irrational in human growth and development.[3] For Freud, early childhood was a time of sexual feelings and societal repression that shaped the child's psyche and had long-term consequences for the adult personality. Freud believed that children experience a sequence of psychosexual developmental stages. If the child was overgratified or repressed during any particular stage, the personality might become fixated at that stage.

The careers of Montessori and Freud revealed some interesting parallels. Both, attracted to science, became physicians and both studied psychology. However, they developed very different ideas about child development. Montessori rejected Freud's ideas on infant sexuality and the long-term significance of emotional conflict on later development.[4]

Montessori's attraction to physiological anthropology was part of a more general movement taking place in Italian social science in which Cesare Lombroso and Giuseppe Sergi developed the field of physical anthropology. Montessori was familiar with Lombroso's research in criminal anthropology, which involved taking the physical measurements of criminals, especially the size and shape of the head and face and trying to generalize about the characteristics of the criminal type. She was most influenced by Sergi, the founder of the University of Rome's Institute of Experimental Psychology, with whom she had studied. Physical anthropology, which Montessori would apply to education, focused on the scientific study of the human being as a physiological organism. It used empirical means to measure, record, and quantify the anatomical and morphological variations in humans. The use of measurements became an important part of Montessori's educational method.

It was in this context of a new political Italy, changing but still retaining much of the binding force of custom and tradition, that Montessori was born and educated. It was in this era of changing ideas on education that she made her mark. We now turn to her biography.

Maria Montessori: Pioneer in Early Childhood Education

Maria Montessori was born on August 31, 1870, in Chiaravalle, a hill town on the Adriatic seacoast in Italy's Ancona province. She was the only child of Alessandro Montessori, a business manager in the state-run tobacco monopoly, and Renilde Stoppani, the well-educated daughter of a highly respected family.[5]

Signor Montessori's position in the Italian civil service gave his family a secure income and comfortable social status in the Italian middle class. Signor Montessori, a decorated veteran of the war for Italian unification in 1848, retained his military bearing throughout his life. Despite the social and economic changes taking place in the new Italy, he held to the attitudes and values of an Italian-style Victorian respectability. His strong-willed daughter, Maria, however, like Jane Addams in the United States, would break with many of these traditional expectations about a young woman's proper role. (For Addams, see Chapter 19.)

Renilde, Alessandro's wife, was a niece of Father Antonio Stoppani, a scholar-priest, who was known for his work in science and geology. Though a traditionally educated middle-class woman, Renilde was more willing to break with tradition than her husband. At certain crucial times, she supported her daughter's challenges to convention. Alessandro would initially resist his daughter's career plans, then yield to his wife's and daughter's wishes.

In 1875, Alessandro was reassigned to Rome and the Montessori family moved to the eternal city, Italy's capital. Maria attended the state primary school on the Via di San Nicolo da Tolentino. Her primary schooling followed the traditional approach: pupils were expected to learn from the teacher's transmission of information and textbooks. Instruction relied heavily on the memorization of textbooks, recitation, and dictation. Though providing basic literacy, these traditional methods were indifferent to children's creativity and often looked on spontaneity as a challenge to authority. Later educators such as Paulo Freire would call this storage and retrieval approach to learning the "banking" method of education in which information was deposited and stored for later use.[6] (See Chapter 24.) When she created her own method of education, Montessori would emphasize children's freedom to explore their environment and spontaneously discover knowledge.

After completing her elementary education, Maria—displaying her independent nature—announced to her parents her plan to enroll in a technical secondary school. This was a radical deviation from the general Italian educational pattern in which middle-class girls might attend a normal or a finishing school.

In 1883, 13-year-old Maria Montessori enrolled in the Regia Scuola Technica Michelangelo Buonarroti, a state technical school. Following the continental European pattern, Italian secondary schools were arranged into a variety of specialized institutions such as the classical college preparatory school, the *liceo*, or technical institutes for technology, engineering, art, agriculture, and commerce. At the Scuola Technica, Maria pursued a seven-year curriculum, approved by the national ministry, that included Italian literature, French, mathematics such as algebra and geometry, sciences such as chemistry and physics, history, and geography. Instruction followed the conventional pattern of attending lectures, memorizing textbooks, and responding to the instructors' questions with structured recitations. Montessori graduated from the technical school in the spring of 1886 with a high academic ranking, having earned a cumulative grade of 137 out of a possible 150 points.[7]

Maria Montessori, again flaunting educational convention, next enrolled in the Regio Istituto Technico Leonardo da Vinci, where, from 1886 to 1890, she studied subjects related to engineering. In 1890, in a momentous career change, she decided to leave engineering for medicine. Initially, the all-male faculty of the University of Rome's School of Medicine rejected her application. Montessori, showing her usual determination, persisted and reapplied. The reluctant medical faculty admitted her in the fall of 1890, giving her the distinction of being the first woman to attend. After studying physics, mathematics, and natural sciences, she passed the examinations for the *diploma di licenza* in 1892, earning a final grade of 8 out of a possible 10 points. Now, she was academically eligible to begin the study of medicine, anatomy, and pathology, and to do clinical laboratory work.[8]

Since medical studies, like medicine itself, were bastions of male domination, Montessori encountered regulations and practices that discriminated against women. The male medical students deliberately shunned her and devised ways to humiliate and isolate her. She could not enter a classroom until all the male students had taken their seats. Since dissection of a naked cadaver was deemed highly improper for a woman, she was permitted in the anatomy laboratory only in the evenings when male students were absent. Surmounting such discouraging obstacles, Montessori earned scholarships in surgery, pathology, and medicine.[9]

During her last two years of medical school, Montessori studied pediatrics at the Children's Pediatric Hospital, an experience that moved her in the direction of a career in early childhood education. In 1896, Montessori claimed still another distinction, becoming the first Italian woman to earn the degree of Doctor of Medicine. At age 26, Dr. Maria Montessori joined the staff of the university's San Giovanni Hospital and also began private practice.

Recognized for her distinctive achievements in education, Montessori played an active role in the European women's movement. As a member of the Italian delegation to the International Women's Congress in Berlin in September 1896, Montessori spoke out for the improvement of women's social and economic status and sponsored a resolution demanding equal pay for equal work for women.[10] She urged women to take a leading role in educational reform and to work as literacy volunteers among the poor. In 1899, Montessori lectured on the "New Woman" of the twentieth century. Challenging traditional stereotypes of women's intellectual inferiority to men, she predicted that science and technology would liberate women of the future from gender-designated careers, especially the drudgery of domestic work.

Montessori volunteered as an assistant physician at the University of Rome's Clinica Psichiatrica, where she was researching her thesis, "A Clinical Contribution to the Study of Delusions of Persecution." Her in-depth research on mental illnesses and psychological disorders was moving her closer to a lifelong commitment to children's psychology and education.[11] As she investigated mental retardation and other psychological disorders in children, she came upon the accomplishments of Jean-Marc Gaspard Itard (1774–1838) and Edouard Seguin (1812–1880), two French physicians and psychologists. Montessori's study of Itard and Seguin would prove to be highly significant in the development of her educational method.

Itard, a specialist in otiatria, had worked with deaf and hearing-impaired children. He modeled his observation of hearing-impaired children on the method of clinical observation that physicians used with their patients. Itard's most famous case was his well-publicized treatment of the "wild boy of Aveyron," a feral youth apparently abandoned or lost as a child who was found living with animals in the forests. The boy, about age 12, did not speak and had no practical skills. Itard attempted to train the boy to speak and learn the skills needed to care for himself.[12]

Itard's experiment with the "wild boy" and his work with mentally impaired children led him to postulate that human beings went through specific, definite, and necessary developmental stages. He hypothesized that children experienced their stages of development by engaging in activities for which they were physiologically and psychologically ready and that were appropriate to the particular period. Abnormal children, especially those severely physically or mentally impaired, however, tended to miss the full potential of the development stage and were left with deficits that diminished their further growth.[13] He concluded that children needed to experience the activities appropriate to their stage of development at the right time, or suffer the consequence of continual and cumulative impairment.[14] As a physician, Montessori was favorably impressed by Itard's use of empirical observation and hailed his efforts as "the first attempts at experimental psychology."[15]

Seguin worked with mentally impaired children at the Hospice de Bicetre, a training school for children from the insane asylums of Paris.[16] Seguin believed that institutions for handicapped children should be centers of training and education and that both medical and pedagogical knowledge should be used in treating the handicapping condition. He used physiological measurement and clinical observation to diagnose the condition and to prescribe remedial treatment. Seguin devised didactic apparatus and materials to train the senses and improve the physical skills of children with mental handicaps. In working with these children, Seguin devised several techniques that Montessori would later adopt, such as aligning instruction to particular developmental stages, using didactic materials, and training children to perform practical skills so that they could achieve some degree of independence.[17] From the work of Itard and Seguin, Montessori developed two principles: (1) mental deficiency required a special kind of education as well as medical treatment; (2) this special kind of education was facilitated by using didactic materials and apparatus.

In September 1898, Montessori presented her ideas on the education of mentally retarded children to the Pedagogical Congress in Turin. At that time, mental retardation was not categorically defined and often included children who were physiologically impaired as well as those labeled as "laggards" and delinquents. Rather than confining mentally impaired children to insane asylums with adults, Montessori urged that they be housed in educational institutions. These institutions were to have the services of a psychiatrist and pediatrician as well as educational specialists who could diagnosis each child's problem and design an individualized learning prescription for each child.[18]

In 1900, the Scuola Magistrale Ortofrenica, the Orthophrenic School, opened with Montessori and Dr. Giuseppe Montesano as codirectors. Training hearing-impaired and mentally deficient children, the school served as a training school for teachers who were prepared to educate children with handicapping conditions. Montessori directed the Orthophrenic School for two years (1900–1901).

At the Orthophrenic School, Montessori and Dr. Montesano developed an intimate personal relationship. Montessori became pregnant and bore Montesano's son, named Mario. After his birth, Mario was sent to live with a wet nurse in the country. Montesano's family, especially his mother, opposed a marriage. Montesano made it a condition of legally granting the child his name that the birth remain secret, except for family members. Montessori, who seemed to have her way on so many other decisions, apparently acquiesced. Shortly afterward, Montesano married another woman and Montessori left the Orthophrenic School. Mario was raised by others and at seven went to a boarding school near Florence.[19] When he was 15, after the death of Montessori's mother, Mario came to live with Maria. He was first presented as Montessori's nephew and then as her adopted son.[20] Over time, Mario Montessori would become his mother's closest associate in publicizing and implementing the Montessori method and in founding and administrating the Association Montessori Internationale.

Between 1904 and 1908, Montessori lectured at the University of Rome's Pedagogical School on the application of anthropology and biology to education.[21] She especially emphasized the importance of taking exact physical measurements of children's height and weight, size of head, pelvis, limbs, and types of malformations. These measurements were to be systematically recorded in an individualized biographical empirical record for each child.[22] Montessori's lectures were published as *L'Antropolgia Pedagogica*, (*Pedagogical Anthropology*), a book that brought together her insights from pediatric medicine, child psychology, and cultural anthropology and applied them to children's development and education.[23]

An important opportunity took place for Montessori in 1907 when Eduoardo Talamo, director-general of the Istituto Romano di Beni Stabili (the Roman Good Building Association), a philanthropic society engaged in improving housing conditions of the poor, asked her to establish a school in a slum area in Rome. The association was rehabilitating housing in Rome's San Lorenzo Quarter, a desperately poor area that Montessori described as a miserable "world of shadows."[24]

Talamo wanted Montessori to help solve an urgent practical problem. When their parents went to work, preschool-age children living in the remodeled housing development were left unattended, the forerunners of today's latchkey children. The association wanted Montessori to establish a day care center for these children. She, however, had more ambitious plans, and seized an opportunity to create a school that also could serve as a laboratory to test her ideas. Under much more favorable circumstances, John Dewey, too, was testing his educational ideas at the University of Chicago Laboratory School. (See Chapter 20.)

Montessori's first school, the *Casa dei Bambini*, or Children's House, opened in a large tenement at *Via dei Marsi* 58 on January 6, 1907. Her first pupils were 50 children, from ages 3 to 7, whose families lived in the tenement. She saw the Children's House as a school-home, an educational agency that was part of the children's family life.

Though an educational institution, Montessori also saw her new kind of school in broad social terms that related to her concept of the twentieth-century's "new woman." The Casa dei Bambini was located in a working-class area where many mothers worked away from home in Italy's developing industries. Montessori believed that in the future more women of all socioeconomic classes would join the workforce. Schools, as educational institutions, needed to recognize this technologically generated change and provide for the children of working mothers. Schools like the Casa dei Bambini would make it possible for mothers to safely leave their children and "proceed with a feeling of great relief and freedom to their own work."[25]

Montessori applied one of her basic principles at the Casa—children's maximum development and most effective learning takes place in a structured and orderly environment. She required that the parents of children attending her school follow some regulations. Children were to come to school with clean bodies and clothing. Parents were expected to be interested in and support their children's education and to attend frequent parent-directress conferences.

Like John Dewey at the University of Chicago Laboratory School, Montessori made sure the school's physical arrangements, the tables, chairs, and apparatus, were fitted to children's sizes and needs. She did not want the classroom's physical arrangements to restrict the children's freedom of movement as it did in traditional schools. Tables and chairs were sized according to children's heights and weights. Washstands were accessible for younger children. Classrooms were lined with low cupboards where children could easily reach didactic materials and when finished return them to their proper place. Montessori created a school that would develop children's sensory and motor abilities, give them freedom of choice within a structured environment, and encourage their independence and self-confidence.

Montessori's idea of the role of the teacher was very different from that of traditional schools. While traditional teachers typically took center stage in the classroom, Montessori renamed her teacher a "directress." The directress, an educator properly trained in the Montessori method, was to guide children in their own self-development.[26] Trained in the clinical observation of children and scientific pedagogy, the directress needed to be sensitive to children's readiness and stages of development. She was to establish the prepared environment, with its appropriate apparatus and materials, and to cooperate in the children's own self-education.

The curriculum of the Casa dei Bambini was based on Montessori's principle that children experience crucial times in their development called "sensitive periods." During these sensitive periods, children are in a high state of readiness for particular learning activities such as sensory training, exercising motor skills, language learning, and social adaptation. To aid their development during these sensitive periods, the children are provided with self-correcting didactic materials and apparatus that they themselves select. Montessori skillfully solved the problem of motivating children that teachers face in group learning situations in traditional schools. Since the children in Montessori schools choose their own activities and materials, they are self-motivated. Since the materials are self-correcting, children work at their own pace, requiring little teacher intervention. Montessori relied heavily on self-correcting educational materials because she believed that children acquire self-discipline and self-reliance by recognizing their own mistakes and repeating a particular task until it is done correctly.

Montessori's curriculum at the Casa dei Bambini aimed to develop competencies in three broad areas: practical life skills, motor and sensory training, and more formal literary and computational skills and subjects. The practical exercises developed skills needed in everyday life such as serving food, washing one's hands and face, tying a shoelace, or buttoning a shirt or blouse. These exercises aimed to make children less dependent on help from adults and able to perform needed skills on their own. The practical skills were generic in that once a child had mastered a particular skill such as tying or buttoning, it could be transferred to the many occurrences when it was needed in daily life. Designed to exercise and develop motor, muscular, and coordination skills, the practice life skills gave children a sense of independence and a self-confidence that they could do things without adult assistance. The everyday life activities included washing and dressing oneself, setting tables and serving meals, housekeeping, gardening, gymnastic activities, and rhythmic movements. Using framed pieces of cloth with buttons, laces, and hooks, the children practiced so that they could transfer to buttoning and hooking their own clothing and tying their shoes. There were also ordinary household objects—washbasins, dishes, silverware, and gardening tools. Washstands and tables were child-sized so that children could easily reach them. Cabinets to store materials were accessible so that children could reach and return materials to their proper location.

Montessori's materials and activities for sensory education aimed to develop children's competency in perceiving distinctions in color and hue, smell, touch, and sound and tone as well as the skills necessary to maneuver various objects. Montessori developed an order in using the materials. First came a series of solid insets—wooden cylinders of different sizes to be inserted in holes of the same size in a wooden block. Next came 10 pink wooden cubes of graduated size with which the child built a tower, then knocked it down, and rebuilt it. There were 10 brown wooden prisms and 10 red rods used to build a broad and long stair. There were geometric solids (pyramid, sphere, cone), little boards with rough and smooth surfaces and others of different weights and colors, and pieces of fabric of different textures. There were wooden plane insets, a little cabinet of drawers, each containing framed geometrical figures—blue triangles, circles, squares of different sizes—to be taken out and replaced correctly in their frames. There were cards with paper geometrical shapes pasted on them and a series of cylindrical boxes filled with different materials that produced different sounds when shaken. A series of musical tone bells was used together with a wooden board that had musical staff lines and a set of wooden disks to represent the notes. The tone bells were used to develop the child's ability to discriminate between various tones. Sensory boxes included those filled with spices with distinctive odors. As the child worked with the didactic materials, he or she learned to recognize, group, and compare similar objects and to contrast them with dissimilar ones.

Montessori faced the common problem of primary school teachers—how to teach reading and writing. Rejecting the idea that reading and writing needed to be imposed on children, Montessori believed that they would learn to read and write when they were ready to do so. She created materials that developed this kind of readiness: sandpaper letters, boxes of colored cardboard letters and numbers, and counting rods.[27]

Montessori's claim that children of four and five years "burst spontaneously into writing" was met with considerable attention as well as skepticism. To create readiness for writing and reading, two skills Montessori saw as closely related, she used cardboard letters covered with sandpaper. As the children touched and traced these letters, the directress sounded them out. At the same time that the children were being prepared for writing the letter by tracing it, they learned to recognize the sound it represented. Children discovered reading as they understood that the sounds of the letters they were tracing and then writing formed words. After enough practice, the children were able to compose words without assistance. They learned to count by arranging objects according to their number and measuring them by using colored rods of varying lengths.

Children learned about the natural environment by planting and cultivating gardens; Montessori believed this established the intellectual connection between seeds sprouting and plants growing and the larger world of nature. The keeping of small animals in the school introduced children to the beginnings of zoology and developed a sense of responsibility in caring for them.

By 1910, Montessori's success at the Casa dei Bambini led to the establishment of additional schools in Rome and other Italian cities. She had established a model school and a training institute for directresses. Her growing reputation attracted attention in Europe and North America, especially in the United States. As her method grew in popularity, Montessori decided to keep control firmly in her own hands. She would control the training of Montessori directresses and production and distribution of Montessori materials and apparatus to prevent any deviation from her method.

Montessori described her work at the Casa dei Bambini in *The Method of Scientific Pedagogy Applied to Infant Education in the Children's Houses* in 1910. *Scientific Pedagogy,* retitled *The Montessori Method* (1912), was published in 11 languages. *The Montessori Method* was followed by *Dr. Montessori's Own Handbook* (1914) as an official guide to the method to distinguish it from imitators. Her two-volume work, *The Advanced Montessori Method,* appeared in 1918–1919.[28]

Educators came to Rome from other countries, including the United States, to attend her lectures, interview her, and observe her schools. Some visitors became dedicated disciples who imported the Montessori method to their own countries. Ruth French, an American disciple, lauded Montessori as a "magical personality that makes her words seem winged messengers of light and the mighty fever of enthusiasm is amazing to the beholder."[29] Journalists like the American publisher S. S. McClure publicized the Montessori method. Still others, like the Teachers College professor William H. Kilpatrick, became severe critics.

The United States, with over 100 Montessori schools operating in 1913, appeared especially propitious for Montessorian education. The Montessori Educational Association had been organized to promote Montessorianism. The association's board of directors, with Mrs. Alexander Graham Bell as president, listed such prominent individuals as Margaret Wilson, the president's daughter, Philander P. Claxton, the U.S. Commissioner of Education, Samuel S. McClure, publisher of the widely read *McClure's Magazine,* and Dorothy Canfield Fisher, a well-known writer on education.[30] Fisher's book, *A Montessori Mother* (1912) enthusiastically acclaimed the Montessori school as a place where "children acquire intellectual vigor, independence, and initiative as spontaneously, joyfully, and tirelessly as they acquire physical independence and vigor as a by-product of physical play."[31]

Among Montessori's dedicated American disciples was Anne E. George who, in 1910, had been the first American to be prepared by Montessori as a directress. George established the first Montessori school in the United States at Tarrytown, New York. George, in 1913, established another Montessori school, the Children's House, in Washington, D.C.

Montessori's leading promoter in the United States was the publisher and editor Samuel S. McClure. McClure, an enthusiastic and opportunistic promoter of the Montessori method, envisioned himself as the leader of the movement in the United States. He hoped not only to contribute to American education by his promotion of Montessorianism but also to make a financial profit by publicizing Montessori and sharing in the sale of Montessori publications and apparatus. *McClure's Magazine* ran a series of laudatory articles on Montessori and her method that featured Montessori as an "educational wonder worker."

A highly energetic promoter, McClure developed an ambitious plan to bring Montessori to lecture in the United States under the auspices of the American Montessori Association. Montessori arrived in 1913 and spoke to overflow audiences in Washington, D.C., New York City, Philadelphia, Boston, Chicago, and San Francisco. Since she did not speak English, Montessori delivered her lectures in Italian; they were translated into English by Anne E. George. The lectures, which attracted a favorable response, were seen as a prelude to a concerted Montessorian presence in American education.

In 1915, Montessori returned to the United States for a second visit, under the auspices of the National Education Association (NEA). Her lectures and demonstration classes coincided with the meetings of the NEA and the International Kindergarten Union. Montessori arranged a model school at the Panama-Pacific International Exposition in San Francisco where the children could be observed through glass walls.[32]

Montessori's lecture tours and the growing number of Montessori schools established between 1910 and 1920 constitute the first wave of Montessorianism in the United States. This initial wave of enthusiasm, however, failed to firmly establish Montessori education in the United States. American educators began to criticize her method and its applicability to American children. Her critics were generally Froebelian kindergarten advocates and progressive educators. (For the kindergarten, see Chapter 16.) Since the kindergarten and the Montessori school served the same age group, they were frequently compared.

Both Froebel and Montessori believed that children possessed an interior spiritual force that stimulated their self-active development, and emphasized that early childhood education needed a specially prepared environment. Montessori had criticized Froebel's gifts and occupations as often being misaligned with children's readiness. She contended that while her didactic materials were self-correcting, kindergarten teachers had to intervene in using Froebel's objects to make sure children were using them correctly.[33]

While some cooperation took place between Froebelians and Montessorians, many kindergarten proponents were suspicious about the newer Montessori method. Elizabeth Harrison, a national authority on the kindergarten, stated that, despite some positive features, the Montessori method overemphasized individual work to the detriment of group work and failed to cultivate children's imaginative, dramatic, and poetic activities.[34]

Another highly important group of Montessori critics were some university professors of education, particularly progressive followers of John Dewey. (See Chapter 20.) Some leading progressive educators argued that Montessorianism was not a genuinely progressive method. University of Omaha professor Walter Halsey labeled the Montessori method a mere "fad promoted and advertised by a shrewd commercial spirit" that was being enthusiastically accepted by the "novelty loving American public."[35]

A serious critique came from William Heard Kilpatrick, a prominent professor at Columbia University's Teachers College. Kilpatrick, unleashing his attack in *The Montessori System Examined* (1914), disparaged the Montessori method as a mid-nineteenth century period piece that was "fifty years behind" modern educational thought.[36] Kilpatrick, who himself had designed the collaborative project method, alleged that Montessori did not encourage the group work necessary for developing social intelligence and problem-solving skills.[37]

The entry of the United States into World War I caused a shift in interest from European educational ideas to ways to mobilize the country for victory against the German kaiser. By 1917, the first wave of enthusiasm for Montessorianism was ebbing severely. Thus the Montessori method did not make significant inroads into colleges of education at leading universities at the very time when education was being firmly established as a field in American universities. Neither did it enter in any significant way into public schools in the United States. The Montessori school was located at the periphery of the public educational system; later it would come to occupy a major sector of the private part of that periphery. It would not be until the 1950s that a second and much more substantial wave of Montessorianism occurred in the United States. This second American Montessori movement would lead to the establishment of hundreds of Montessori schools throughout the United States.

In the United Kingdom, Montessorianism fared better than in the United States. As in the case of Americans, a number of British teachers journeyed to Rome to be trained as directresses by Montessori. A British Montessori Society was established to promote the method in 1912. Montessori made an extended trip to the United Kingdom in 1919, where she supervised a training course, lectured, and attended numerous receptions and meetings in her honor. English-language translations of Montessori's books attracted a wide readership. By the 1920s, a large number of Montessori schools and classes were functioning in the United Kingdom.

As in the United States, a number of British critics appeared after the initial enthusiasm had waned. While some British educators remained committed to Montessori disciples, others attacked her method as culturally and aesthetically deficient. However, the Montessori method persisted as a force in British early childhood education, especially in the private sector.

On the European continent, the Montessori method enjoyed more substantial gains than in the United Kingdom and the United States. Municipal officials in Barcelona, Spain, supported by the Catalan regional government, invited Montessori, in 1916, to lecture and establish schools. The Escola Montessori, with infant and primary departments for three- to ten-year-olds and the Seminari Laboratori de Pedagogia, an institute for teaching, research, and training in the Montessori method, was established and supported by the Catalan government.[38] Spain was Montessori's principal base of operations from 1916 to 1927. In 1924, the authoritarian government of Primo de Rivera, seeking to suppress the Catalan autonomy, closed the model Montessori school in Barcelona. When the second republic was established in 1932, the new government sponsored a Montessori international training course in Barcelona. When the Spanish Civil War broke out in 1936, Montessori, generally a nonpolitical person, left Spain.

In 1917, Montessori presented a lecture to the Pedagogical Society of Amsterdam, her first visit to the Netherlands. This was followed by the establishment of the Netherlands Montessori Society in 1917. In 1920, she lectured at the University of Amsterdam. She later made the Netherlands the center for Montessori education and established the headquarters of the Association Montessori Internationale in Amsterdam.

In 1922, Benito Mussolini and his Fascists marched on Rome and established a Fascist regime in Italy. Mussolini's intense Italian nationalism drew the support of some leading Italian intellectuals such as the idealist philosopher Giovanni Gentile

(1875–1944). Mussolini appointed Gentile Minister of Education in 1923. Gentile's emphasis on children's self- or auto-education caused him to look favorably on the Montessori method. Gentile, along with Queen Margherita, were interested in promoting the Montessori method in Italy.

Through the auspices of Gentile, Mussolini and Montessori had a meeting in 1924 at which *il Duce* expressed an interest in establishing Montessori schools. Mussolini was interested in a method that he believed instilled discipline and order and in which children learned to read and write at age 4. He also wanted to use Montessori's name and her associations in other countries to popularize his Fascist ideology. Montessori, in turn, was initially receptive to receiving official government support for her schools. In 1926, Montessori was officially recognized by the Tessera Fascista, the Fascist women's organization, and was made an honorary party member.[39] The Ministry of Education officially endorsed the Montessori training program for Italian teachers in Milan. In March 1927, Montessori and Mussolini met again and there was more cooperation between Montessori and the Fascist government. The government helped to subsidize a publication, *L'Idea Montessori.* By 1929, the Italian government was sponsoring several Montessori enterprises such as the training college, the Regia Scuola Magistrale di Metodo Montessori in Rome, a Montessori training course in Milan, and 70 infant and elementary classes in schools throughout Italy.[40]

The years 1929 to 1930 marked the high point of Montessori's educational work in Italy with the support of Mussolini's Fascist state. Mussolini intended to use the international Montessori movement to showcase modern Italian education under Fascism.[41] However, Mussolini met Maria Montessori's firm resolve to control her own method of education and keep it as she had designed it.

In 1929, Montessori and her son, Mario, established the Association Montessori Internationale (AMI) to control and supervise Montessori activities, including training programs, throughout the world. With Maria Montessori as its president, the AMI controlled rights to the publication of Montessori's books and the manufacture and sale of the materials and training course fees. Mario became her agent, protector, and representative. Both she and Mario insisted that there be no deviation from the approved pedagogical line that Montessori had instituted.[42]

Mussolini, whose slogan was "Everything in the State, nothing against the State, nothing outside the State," was growing steadily more totalitarian, crushing opposition and coercing those suspected of dissent. He was determined to spread Fascist ideology throughout Italy, instilling it in schools and youth organizations.[43] The regime established a number of Fascist youth organizations such as the *Balilla* for boys from 8 to 14 and the *Avanguardisti* for youth from 14 to 18. Girls were enlisted in the *Piccole Italiane.* Dressed in uniforms, like the national Fascist militia, the children drilled and paraded through the streets of Italy's cities and villages. The Fascist regime was also tightening its control of Italy's schools with all teachers required to take a loyalty oath.[44]

Cooperation between Mussolini's Fascist government and Montessori was always uneasy. Mussolini wanted to make political capital out of Montessori. Montessori, however, did not accept the Fascist ideology and viewed her role to be that of an international educator rather than a promoter of Italian nationalism. In fact, she believed that the child's nature and stages of development were universal and not determined by national, racial, or ethnic origins. In 1934, the Italian government, seeking to capture publicity, wanted to name Montessori as Italy's children's ambassador to the world.

Montessori refused to accept the appointment unless the Italian government recognized her as the sole authority and spokesperson for the AMI. The Fascist government responded to Montessori's intransigence by closing Montessori schools and suppressing the movement.[45] Maria Montessori left Italy as an exile.

In 1936, Montessori, accompanied by her son, Mario, located her educational activities in the Netherlands, making Amsterdam the headquarters of the AMI. From this location she continued her worldwide activities. Believing that she had developed a truly global method of education, Montessori traveled the world to promote her philosophy. She conducted training classes and addressed conferences in Italy, the United States, the Netherlands, Spain, France, the United Kingdom, Ireland, India, and other countries.

In October 1939, Montessori, at age 69, traveled to India conduct a training school, sponsored by the Theosophical Society at Adyar in Madras. When Italy, a member of the Axis, invaded France and entered World War II in 1940 on the side of Germany, Italian nationals in Great Britain and its colonies were interned. Montessori, an Italian national, was not actually interned by the British authorities in India, but she was confined to the Theosophical Society's compound. The British easily decided that Montessori posed no security threat and released her to carry on her educational activities in India, where she spent the war years.

When World War II ended, Montessori returned to Europe, arriving on July 30, 1946, at the AMI headquarters in Amsterdam to resume her worldwide activities. In 1947 she returned to Italy, at the invitation of the government, to reestablish the Opera Montessori and help reopen Montessori schools. The aging Montessori delegated many administrative responsibilities of the international society to Mario Montessori, her trusted confidant and aide. Maria Montessori died on May 6, 1952, in Noorwijk aan Zee, a small village near the Hague, and was buried in the local Catholic cemetery.

The Montessori Philosophy and Method

Montessori's philosophy of education was based on her conception of science, her observations of children, and on her extensive research in anthropology, psychology, and pedagogy. Her method mixed elements that were derived from her "scientific pedagogy" and others from her spiritual insights. All children, she claimed, at birth possess a psychic power, an inner self-teacher, that stimulates their own self-directed learning.[46]

For Montessori, the educational process involves two necessary elements: the child and the environment. The individual child's physiological and mental constitution endows her or him with the power to learn. The environment provides the necessary milieu in which human development takes place.[47] By interacting and being involved with the objects and situations in their environment, children actively engage in their own auto-education. Their physiological and psychic powers move them to freely explore the environment. These interactions and the information elicited are then incorporated into the child's emerging self—her or his network of experience-based concepts.[48]

Montessori believed that it was absolutely imperative for children to be free to explore and interact with their environment. Her fundamental principle was that children need the freedom to act to bring about their own growth and development. She called this principle "the liberty of the pupils in their spontaneous manifestations."[49] Although she emphasized children's liberty, Montessori did not construe freedom to mean "doing your own thing" but rather the freedom to act within a structured environment. Montessori claimed that children desired order and strongly preferred the security of a structured environment. In a structured learning environment where everything has its place and time, behaviors and expectations are clearly known and there are minimal ambiguous, anxiety-provoking, unknown situations.

Montessori believed children naturally possess a strong capacity for mental concentration. If genuinely interested in an activity, they will willingly expend their attention and energy on it, staying with it, until mastering the skill or task it involves. Further, children are eager to try and master new skills. On their own initiative, they will keep at a task, repeating it until they know how to do it. Children realize that learning practical skills such as tying a shoelace without adult help gives them independence. When given a choice between work and play, Montessori claimed they will choose work.

Children, Montessori asserted, are naturally and energetically working to achieve functional independence. An innate drive, which Montessori called a "divine urge," stimulates their self-activity to perform actions that promote growth that leads to further development and greater independence.[50] For the child, independence simply means being able to "do it all by myself." Montessori realized that appropriate adult intervention is needed at certain times but should decrease steadily as children learn how to do things for themselves. Independence, based on the freedom to be self-active, lays the foundation for the values of perseverance at a task, persistence in doing something until it is done correctly, and satisfaction at a job well done—all desirable qualities in the independent adult with a sense of high self-esteem.

Montessori redefined the school as a prepared environment in which children are able to develop freely at their own pace, unimpeded in the spontaneous unfolding of their natural capacities. The school's prepared environment enables children, through the manipulation of a graded series of self-correcting didactic materials, to exercise and develop their senses and thinking as they gain greater independence.[51] According to Montessori, "A room in which all the children move about usefully, intelligently, and voluntarily, without committing any rough or rude act, would seem to be a classroom very well disciplined indeed."[52] To maximize the opportunities for children's freedom within a prepared environment, Montessori developed a new kind of school in which children were grouped in a multiage arrangement rather than chronologically as found in many schools. She replaced the conventional classroom's rows of immovable standardized desks with lightweight, child-sized tables and chairs that the children themselves could move. To store materials, there were easily accessible cupboards the children could reach.

Montessori's new school required a new conception of what it meant to be a teacher. She designated her new kind of teacher a "directress," who directs, or guides, children's learning without interfering with it. She contrasted the directress with teachers in conventional schools who, at the center of the classroom, struggle to motivate and engage a group of children with different levels of readiness and ability. Such teachers search unceasingly for the magic method that will entice children to learn as a group. Montessori believed that these various strategies to gain the attention and to engage a group of children often had the unintended consequence of confusing and distracting them from their own interior self-motivated desire to learn. Montessori minimized "collective" or group simultaneous instruction of a class or pupils. She believed that an overemphasis on group instruction forced the teacher to act as a drill sergeant who issued commands to get all the individuals in a class to act as a unit. Montessori solved the problem by individualizing learning so that each child could follow her or his interests by choosing from a variety of educational materials and working at her or his own pace.[53]

The directress, using clinical observation of children, acts as a diagnostician who creates an educational profile, a biography, for each child. She notes the child's physical development, previous learning, readiness for new learning experiences, and individual interests and needs. She prepares the environment so that it contains the materials and opportunities that excite children's desire to learn. She then guides but does not push each child to the appropriate activity, material, or apparatus.

Montessori's method rested on her principle that children's education should grow out of and coincide with the child's own stages of development. She was convinced that children progressed through a series of developmental stages, each of which required an appropriate and specifically designed kind of learning. For Montessori, each stage of human development was a psychic "rebirth," with one phase of the sequence dramatically flowing into the next. She identified three major developmental periods: (1) birth to age 6; (2) ages 6 to 12; (3) ages 12 to 18. The first stage, the period of the "absorbent mind," is subdivided into two phases, from birth to 3 and 3 to 6. During the first stage, children, by their environmental explorations, absorb information, construct their concepts about reality, begin to use language, and enter the larger world of their group's culture. During the second period, from 6 to 12, the skills and powers that surfaced and were developed in the first period are exercised, reinforced, polished, and expanded. The third period, from 12 to 18, coinciding with adolescence, is a time of great physical change with the individual striving to reach full maturity. The third period is subdivided into two phases, 12 to 15 and 15 to 18.[54] During the third period, adolescents work to understand social and economic roles and find their place in society.

For early childhood education, Montessori's emphasis on "sensitive periods" during the "absorbent mind" stage is most important. During the sensitive period from birth to age 6, children work at exploring their environment, develop motor skills such as walking, and are eager to touch and feel small objects. Montessori's choice of the word *absorbent* reflected her belief that children at this stage are engaged primarily in absorbing sensory impressions and information from their environment. The impulse for this absorption was driven by the child's interior impulse to acquire this knowledge for self-development and eventual independence. Since the content of the knowledge absorbed depends on the learning possibilities present in the child's environment, it is crucial that the environment be prepared so it contains the maximum appropriate possibilities for exploration and absorption. The information the children absorb clusters in the mind around points of sensitivity that pertain to such powers as judging distances, making comparisons, and developing language skills, for example. These sensitive points stimulate the children to choose a task or a particular apparatus and then work with it until they master it.[55]

Until age 3, the child's mind functions unconsciously as she or he begins to construct personality and intelligence through environmental explorations. Children also start to acquire their group's language and culture. From ages 3 to 6, children consciously direct their environmental explorations. Children are especially drawn to manipulative tasks—how to do things—which satisfies their need to coordinate and control their own physical movements and bodily development.

Involved in a piece of work, a child will repeat the same series of movements over and over until a task is mastered. This repetition, Montessori asserted, is the means of establishing the new learning into the network of previous experience and to coordinate motor activity with the idea of doing the task correctly and bringing it to a successful completion. This repertoire of skills and information about the world lays the foundation for future learning.[56]

The period of the "absorbent mind" is not only crucial for motor, skill, and cognitive development but also for establishing patterns for early socialization and acculturation. Montessori believed that children during early childhood absorb the distinctive linguistic and cultural patterns of their cultural group. As they absorb their group's language by hearing it spoken, they simultaneously absorb its values, customs, morals, and religion. These cultural patterns, according to Montessori, represent the summarized part, the collective memory, that is repeated in the habitual life—the traditions and customs—of a particular people. As individuals grow and mature, they will continue to develop and will make cultural and social adaptations and revisions to the patterns acquired in early childhood. However, any future changes will occur in alignment with the network of earlier learning already established in early childhood.[57]

In summary, based on her concepts of sensitive periods, Montessori developed four operational principles that govern learning in the prepared environment:

1. The principle of freedom to explore the environment in order to gain greater independence.
2. The development of will—the moral sense—by choosing the material with which one will be engaged and by respecting the rights of other children to work with the material of their own choice.
3. The power of attention in which a child concentrates on accomplishing a task.
4. The principle of work by which a child stays at a task, often performing repetitive actions, until it is mastered.

The curriculum that Montessori established for early childhood education included practical life skills, sensory education, language and mathematics, and more general physical, social, and cultural development. The first educational activities leading to greater independence for children are skills related to practical life. The aims of these activities are that children succeed in learning: (1) to care for their own bodies; (2) to respect and care for the environment; (3) proper social relationships; (4) how to control and direct their physical movements to accomplish specific tasks. These activities include tasks that are part of living as a member of a family in a home—setting the table, serving food, doing dishes, cleaning up after a meal. They include skills required for personal cleanliness and hygiene—washing the face and hands, brushing teeth, and so on. They are abilities needed to dress oneself—buttoning clothes and tying shoes. Special didactic apparatus—lacing and tying frames—give children an opportunity to practice a particular skill. Included in the practical life skills are muscular exercises to develop and exercise motor coordination, walking, and respiratory skills.

The Montessori curriculum's sensory materials and activities are designed to develop the child's sensory acuity and ability. Children learn to order, classify, and compare sensory impressions by touching, seeing, smelling, tasting, listening, and feeling the physical properties of the objects in the environment and by using specially designed apparatus and materials. Sensory skills include those related to sound and the ability to distinguish between tones. Those related to sight exercise the ability to recognize and distinguish color, hue, and shading. Those related to touch involve the ability to feel texture, softness, hardness, cold, and warmth. Specialized didactic apparatus and materials are used, such as cylinders, tone bells, stacking blocks, materials of various colors and so on.[58]

According to Montessori, language development is a spontaneous creation of the child. Children develop their vocabulary by learning the names of objects in their environment; then they learn to classify the objects into categories: living or nonliving, plant or animal, flower or tree, vertebrate or invertebrate, and so on. Language acquisition proceeds to learning the alphabet and phonetic sounds. This leads to working with letters mounted on sandpaper outlines that children can trace. Children compose words by using the letters of a movable alphabet. Montessori claimed that children burst spontaneously into writing and reading.

Arithmetic is taught by the manipulation of geometrically shaped objects, by using rods of various lengths, and by organizing quantities of objects in counting boxes. The materials include numbers, rods, and objects arranged in tens. As in learning letters, children trace sandpaper-covered numbers.

More general physical, social, and cultural skills are learned through the children's individualized physical activities, their responsibilities in caring for plants and animals, and their mutual respect for their own work and that of their peers.

Montessori believed that moral development, or character education, like cognitive and skill development, arises from the child's free engagement with the environment. In developing their willpower, children freely choose a task and learn to control their action by directing it to the requirements needed to complete it. The moral sense develops according to the successes experienced in surmounting obstacles and mastering challenges that occur in this interaction. As children learn to take control over their actions, they build their own sense of self-discipline. During this crucial period, children undergo experiences that shape their personalities and their character. If they have been injured, experienced cruelty and violence, or faced obstacles beyond their readiness to deal with them, negative personality deviations may result. If they meet challenges appropriate to their development and have the freedom provided by the structured learning environment, they are likely to develop positive self-esteem and healthy personalities.[59] Montessori argued that her prepared environment is especially conducive for intellectual and moral development in that it encourages the child to act spontaneously and freely, to select the task, and to build self-esteem by meeting and mastering the challenges found in a safe learning setting.

Conclusion: An Assessment

From the 1920s until the 1950s, Montessori education declined in the United States. Then in the mid-1950s, the Montessori method enjoyed a significant revival. Montessori's method was rediscovered by parents seeking a more academically oriented early childhood school than available in many public school kindergartens or progressive private schools. Indeed, by the mid-1950s, progressive education, which had eclipsed the first attempt to introduce the Montessori method from 1914 to 1918, was, itself, declining. A major leader in launching the American Montessori revival was Nancy McCormick Rambusch, founder of the Whitby School in Greenwich, Connecticut. Although deeply committed to Montessori's philosophy, Rambusch believed the method needed to incorporate new developments in education. Those who wanted a more up-to-date Americanized version of Montessorianism organized the American Montessori Society in 1960. By the end of the 1950s, over two hundred Montessori schools and several large training schools were functioning.[60]

In the second wave of Montessori education in the United States, the demand for schools exceeded the supply of trained Montessori teachers. As a result, schools and teacher preparation programs proliferated without a consistent set of accreditation standards. While some schools held closely to Montessori's original method, others were more flexible. In the 1960s, the Montessori method gained a further impetus during President Lyndon Johnson's "Great Society" initiative in the "war against poverty." Part of the antipoverty legislation was directed toward providing compensatory education programs for poverty-impacted children. Some Operation Head Start programs, designed to provide early learning experiences for socially and culturally disadvantaged children, adopted the Montessori approach. This use of the Montessori method marked a return to its original purpose at the first Casa dei Bambini in Rome.

Currently, approximately 6,000 Montessori schools are operating in the United States. Most of these schools are nonpublic institutions and primarily enroll children between the ages of two and six. The majority of schools offer early childhood and primary programs. A few schools offer programs for intermediate and upper-grade pupils. There has been a recent but still limited movement of the Montessori method into the public school sector, with some 500 Montessori magnet schools or divisions operating.[61]

Maria Montessori made a significant contribution to educational theory and practice, especially to early childhood education. In particular, she called attention to the formative significance of the early years of childhood on later development. She anticipated and led what is now the current movement to provide more and earlier educational opportunities for children. Montessori's work provided new insights and stimulated research into child nature, stages of development, and the educative role of the environment, and stimulated the growing worldwide interest in early childhood education. Among Maria Montessori's enduring contributions to education were: (1) the clear recognition of the significance of early stimulation on later learning, especially its implications for socially and economically disadvantaged children; (2) the concept of sensitive periods, phases of development, when certain activities and materials are appropriate to learning specific motor and cognitive skills; (3) the recognition that learning is complex and multifaceted and involves a variety of experiences; (4) the recognition that the school must be part of the community and must involve parents if instruction is to be most effective.

Maria Montessori was a woman who wanted to shape her own destiny and life. Like Jane Addams, she lived at a time when women's careers were largely other-determined, either by custom and tradition or the prescriptions of a male-defined society. Montessori determined early in her life that she would be a self- rather than an other-determined person. As a student of medicine and as a world-famous educator, she broke new pathways not only for herself but for other women as well.

Questions for Reflection and Dialogue

1. How did Montessori react to the social and educational conventions of her time? Do you know of individuals today who react in a fashion similar to Montessori?

2. Compare and contrast how Jane Addams and Maria Montessori overcame the gender restrictions during their time. Were their reactions and actions similar or different? Which one do you think is the most appropriate model for contemporary women?

3. Reflect on Montessori's concept of the structured environment and her belief that children learn most effectively in a structured environment. Recall your own early childhood educational experiences. Do you agree or disagree with Montessori?

4. Why do you think Montessori education enjoys such popularity as a method of earlier childhood education?

5. Examine the Montessori method as an example of the transference of an educational innovation from one country to another.

Projects for Deepening Your Understanding

1. Review the current literature in child psychology and development. Compare and contrast your findings with Montessori's concept of the child and children's learning.

2. If you have completed a methods course, reflect on how the classroom as a learning environment and the role of the teacher were presented. Compare and contrast that presentation with Montessori's concept of the directress and the prepared environment.

3. Visit the following websites: http://www.montessori_ami.org.htm, the site of the Association Montessori Internationale established by Maria Montessori and Mario Montessori, and http://www.amshq.org.html, the site of the American Montessori Society. Do some research on these organizations and how they present Montessori's philosophy and method of education.

4. Visit a Montessori school. Observe a classroom. Identify those aspects of Montessori's method that are evident in the classroom. If you are engaged in clinical experience or student teaching, compare and contrast your classroom situation with that of the Montessori school.

5. Interview the parents of children who attend Montessori schools. Present your findings in a report to the students in this course.

6. The kindergarten and the Montessori school are often compared and contrasted. Visit a kindergarten and a Montessori school. What similarities and differences do you find in these two school settings?

Notes

1. For Parker's philosophy of education, see Francis W. Parker, *Talks on Pedagogics* (New York: E. L. Kellogg & Co., 1894). For a biography, see Jack K. Campbell, *Colonel Francis W. Parker: The Children's Crusader* (New York: Teachers College Press, 1967)

2. For a biography of Kilpatrick, see Samuel Tenebaum, *William Heard Kilpatrick: Trail Blazer in Education* (New York: Harper and Brothers, 1951).

3. For Freud's psychoanalytic theory, see Sigmund Freud, *An Outline of Psychoanalysis.* Trans. James Strachey. (New York: W. W. Norton, 1949). For a biography of Freud, see Peter Gay, *Freud: A Life for Our Time* (New York: W. W. Norton, 1988).

4. Rita Kramer, *Maria Montessori: A Biography* (Reading, MA.: Perseus Books, 1988), 320–21.

5. Kramer, *Maria Montessori,* 22–24.

6. Paulo Freire, *Pedagogy of Freedom: Ethics, Democracy, and Civic Courage* (Lanham, MD.: Rowman & Littlefield Publishers, 1998), 32–33.

7. Kramer, *Maria Montessori,* 33.

8. Kramer, *Maria Montessori,* 34–35.

9. Lena L. Gitter, *The Montessori Way* (Seattle, WA: Special Child Publications, 1978), 7.

10. Kramer, *Maria Montessori,* 55.

11. Kramer, *Maria Montessori,* 48.

12. Itard published two accounts of his experiment with the wild boy of Aveyron: *De l'éducation d'un homme sauvage ou des premiers développements physiques et moraux du jeune sauvage de l'Aveyron* and *Rapport sur les nouveaux développements et l'état actuel du sauvage de l'Aveyron* (1807). For an English version, see Jean Marc Gaspard Itard, *The Wild Boy of Aveyron* (New York: McGraw-Hill/Appleton & Lange, 1962).

13. Itard's major work was the two-volume *Traite des maladies de l'oreille et de l'audition* (1821).

14. Timothy D. Seldin, "Montessori," James Guthrie, ed. *Encyclopedia of Education,* 2d ed. (New York: Macmillan Reference USA/Thomson Gale, 2003), 1676.

15. Maria Montessori, *The Montessori Method,* trans. Anne E. George (New York: Frederick A. Stokes Co., 1912), 33–34.

16. Seguin's major work was *Traitement Moral, Hygiène et Education des Idiots,* which was published in France in 1846. After his immigration to the United States, it was republished in English in 1886 as *Idiocy and its Treatment by the Physiological Method.*

17. Katherina Myers, "Seguin's Principles of Education as Related to the Montessori Method," *Journal of Education* 77 (May 1913), 538–41.

18. Kramer, *Maria Montessori,* 73–76.

19. Kramer, *Maria Montessori,* 92–93.

20. Kramer, *Maria Montessori,* 185.

21. Kramer, *Maria Montessori,* 68–69.

22. Kramer, *Maria Montessori,* 96–97.

23. Maria Montessori, *Pedagogical Anthropology* (New York: Frederick A. Stokes, 1913).

24. Maria Montessori, *The Montessori Method* (New York: Frederick A. Stokes, 1912), 51.

25. Montessori, *The Montessori Method,* 60–61.

26. Florence Wade, *The Montessori Method and the American School* (New York: Macmillan, 1913), 31.

27. Kramer, *Maria Montessori,* 209–10.

28. Maria Montessori, *The Advanced Montessori Method,* trans. F. Simmonds and I. Hutchinson (London: Heinemann, 1919).

29. Ruth M. French, "The Working of the Montessori Method," *Journal of Education* LXXVII (October 1913), 423.

30. E. M. Standing, *Maria Montessori* (Fresno, CA.: Academy Library Guild, 1957), 42–44.

31. Dorothy Canfield Fisher, *A Montessori Mother* (New York: Henry Holt and Co., 1912), 21.

32. Kramer, *Maria Montessori,* 212–16.

33. Montessori, *The Montessori Method,* 171.

34. Elizabeth Harrison, "The Montessori Method and the Kindergarten," U.S. Bureau of Education *Bulletin,* 1914, No. 28.

35. Walter N. Halsey, "A Valuation of the Montessori Experiments," *Journal of Education* 77 (January 1913), 63.

36. William H. Kilpatrick, *The Montessori System Examined* (New York: 1914).

37. Kilpatrick, *The Montessori Method Examined,* 20.

38. Kramer, *Maria Montessori,* 249.

39. Kramer, *Maria Montessori,* 300.

40. Kramer, *Maria Montessori,* 302–4.

41. Kramer, *Maria Montessori,* 311–12.

42. Kramer, *Maria Montessori,* 317.

43. Benito Mussolini, *Fascism: Doctrine and Institution* (Rome: Ardita, 1935), 40.

44. W. F. Connell, *A History of Education in the Twentieth Century World* (New York: Teachers College Press, 1980), 250–54.
45. Kramer, *Maria Montessori*, 326–27.
46. Maria Montessori, *The Absorbent Mind* (New York: Henry Holt and Co., 1995), 7.
47. Montessori, *The Absorbent Mind*, 89.
48. Montessori, *The Absorbent Mind*, 102.
49. Montessori, *The Montessori Method*, 80.
50. Montessori, *The Absorbent Mind*, 83.
51. Kramer, *Maria Montessori*, 373.
52. Montessori, *The Montessori Method*, 93.
53. J. McV. Hunt, "Introduction," in Maria Montessori, *The Montessori Method* (New York: Schocken Books, 1964), xxviii–xxix.
54. Montessori, *The Absorbent Mind*, 19–20.
55. Montessori, *The Absorbent Mind*, 51.
56. Kramer, *Maria Montessori*, 180–81.
57. Montessori, *The Absorbent Mind*, 189.
58. Connell, *A History of Education in the Twentieth Century*, 135.
59. Montessori, *The Absorbent Mind*, 195.
60. Kathy Ahlfeld, "The Montessori Revival: How Far Will It Go?" *Nation's Schools* 85 (January 1970), 75–80.
61. Timothy D. Seldin, "Montessori," 1697.

Suggestions for Further Reading

Fisher, Dorothy Canfield. *A Montessori Mother*. New York: Henry Holt and Co., 1912.
———. *Montessori for Parents*. Cambridge: Robert Bentley, Inc., 1965.
———. *The Montessori Manual*. Cambridge: Robert Bentley, Inc., 1964.
Gitter, Lena L. *Montessori's Legacy to Children*. Johnstown, PA: Farew Associates, 1970.
———. *The Montessori Way*. Seattle: Special Child Publications, Inc., 1970.
Gutek, Gerald L. "Maria Montessori: Contributions to Educational Psychology," in Barry J. Zimmerman and Dale H. Schunk (eds.), *Educational Psychology: A Century of Contributions*. New York: Lawrence Erlbaum Associations, Publishers, 2003, 171–86.
Hainstock, Elizabeth G. *The Essential Montessori*. New York: New American Library, 1978.
Hall, Vernon C. "Educational Psychology From 1800 to 1920," in Barry J. Zimmerman and Dale H. Schunk (eds.), *Educational Psychology: A Century of Contributions*. New York: Lawrence Erlbaum Associations, Publishers, 2003, 3–39.
Hunt, J. McV. "Introduction: Revisiting Montessori," in Maria Montessori, *The Montessori Method*. New York: Schocken Books, 1964.
Kilpatrick, William H. *The Montessori System Examined*. Boston: Houghton Mifflin, 1914. Reprint, New York: Arno/New York Times, 1971.
Lillard, Paula P. *Montessori: A Modern Approach*. New York: Schocken, 1972.

Montessori, Maria. *The Absorbent Mind*. Oxford: Clio Press, 1989.
———. *The Child in the Family*. Trans. Nancy Rockmore Cirillo. Chicago: Henry Regnery, 1970.
———. *Childhood Education*. Trans. A. M. Joosten. Chicago: Henry Regnery, 1949.
———. *The Discovery of the Child*. Trans. Mary A. Johnstone. Madras, India: Theosophical Press, 1948.
———. *Dr. Montessori's Own Handbook*. New York: Frederick A. Stokes, 1914. Reprint, Cambridge, MA: Robert Bentley, 1967.
———. *Education and Peace*. Trans. Helen R. Lane. Chicago: Henry Regnery, 1949.
———. *From Childhood to Adolescence*. New York: Schocken, 1948.
———. *From Childhood to Adolescence: Including Erdkinder and the Function of the University*. Oxford: Clio Press, 1994.
———. *The Montessori Method*. Trans. Anne E. George. New York: Frederick A. Stokes, 1912. Reprint, Cambridge, MA: Robert Bentley, 1967.
———. *Pedagogical Anthropology*. Trans. Frederick T. Cooper. New York: Frederick A. Stokes, 1913.
———. *The Secret of Childhood*. Trans. Barbara Barclay Carter. New York: Frederick A. Stokes, 1939.
———. *Spontaneous Activity in Education*. Trans. Florence Simmonds. New York: Frederick A.

Stokes, 1917. Reprint, Cambridge, MA: Robert Bentley, 1967.

———. *Basic Ideas of Montessori's Educational Theory: Extracts from Maria Montessori's Writings and Teachings.* Paul Oswald and Gunter Schultz-Benesch, eds. Oxford: Clio Press, 1997.

———. *The California Lectures of Maria Montessori; Collected Speeches and Writings.* Robert G. Buckenmeyer, ed. Oxford: Clio Press, 1997.

Oren, R. C. *Montessori: Her Method and the Movement—What You Need to Know.* New York: Putnam, 1974.

———. *Montessori Today.* New York: Putnam, 1971.

———, ed. *Montessori for the Disadvantaged.* New York: Capricorn, 1968.

Rambusch, Nancy McCormick. *Learning How to Learn.* Baltimore: Helicon, 1962.

Standing, E. M. *Maria Montessori: Her Life and Work.* Fresno, CA: Academy Library Guild, 1957. Reprint, New York: New American Library, 1962.

Ward, Florence E. *The Montessori Method and the American School.* New York: Macmillan, 1913. Reprint, New York: Arno/New York Times, 1971.

CHAPTER 22

Mohandas Gandhi: Father of Indian Independence

This chapter examines the life and social and educational philosophy of Mohandas K. Gandhi (1869–1948), the father of Indian independence. Although he did not seek personal power or acclaim, Gandhi was a commanding presence on the world scene. By force of his spiritual and ethical convictions and his philosophy of nonviolent social and political change, Gandhi became a respected and influential world figure. His broadly construed educational ideas were designed to kindle sentiments of mutual respect and cooperation. His message of nonviolence is much needed in the contemporary world, which faces the threats of violence by terrorist groups and increasing hatred between ethnic and religious factions. Gandhi's lesson was that one could love one's own people and simultaneously love all humankind. In addition to his philosophy of nonviolent social change, Gandhi also designed a plan of basic education for the small-scale and sustainable development of India's villages.

We discuss Gandhi's effect on world education in its historical context and in terms of its significance on educational philosophy and policy. First, we describe the general social, political, and economic context in which Gandhi lived and worked. A major characteristic of this context was the end of European imperialism and colonialism—in India's case, British colonialism. For students of educational policy, colonialism's effect and its decline and demise are significant trends that shaped the course of human history. Second, we analyze Gandhi's biography, his education and career as an independence leader, to determine the evolution of his social and educational ideas. Third, we explore these ideas, particularly his policy for basic education. Fourth, we assess Gandhi's contributions to world education. Our discussion illustrates the process of change caused by the interaction of a leading and forceful personality such as Gandhi with momentous world forces such as the decline of imperialism. Not only was he a force for change in his native India, but Gandhi's ideas of nonviolent protest and passive resistance influenced the strategy that Dr. Martin Luther King, Jr., used in the Civil Rights Movement in the United States in the 1950s and 1960s and that Nelson Mandela used in South Africa in the 1970s and 1980s.

To help you organize your thoughts as you read the chapter, focus on the following questions:

1. What were the major trends in the historical context in which Gandhi lived?
2. How did Gandhi's educational biography shape his social and educational philosophy?
3. How did Gandhi's social and educational philosophy shape his educational policies and programs?
4. What is the enduring effect of Gandhi's contributions to world education?

The Historical Context of Gandhi's Life

Mohandas Gandhi's life coincided with important worldwide trends that transformed the old order and brought a new social and political world into being. Gandhi was born in an India that was part of the British Empire—on which, according to the slogan, "the sun never set." His death by an assassin's bullet came when India had gained its independence as a sovereign and independent nation. Although the struggle for Indian independence has elements that are unique to that subcontinent's history and culture, it was also part of the epic story of the decline of imperialism and the liberation of colonial peoples from foreign domination. By the end of the nineteenth century, India—divided into British India, which was ruled directly by Great Britain, and the many princely states indirectly under English rule—was regarded as the crown jewel of Britain's far-flung empire. The history of British rule in India, which began in 1639 when the Mughal rulers ceded a tract of land to the English near Madras, was part of the larger story of Western imperialism. The European nations of Great Britain, France, Spain, Portugal, the Netherlands, and Germany until its defeat in World War I had carved out colonies primarily in Africa and Asia. Great Britain controlled India, Burma, and Malaya in Asia and Nigeria, Ghana, Rhodesia, and South Africa in Africa; France controlled Morocco, Algeria, and Equatorial Africa in Africa and Indochina in Asia; and the Netherlands controlled the Dutch East Indies.

The pattern of imperialism was for a European power such as Great Britain to claim an African or Asian territory by virtue of discovery and exploration and to establish settlements of missionaries, civil servants, soldiers, and merchants in the colony. In the case of India, the British defeated their Portuguese and French rivals and then subjugated the subcontinent either militarily or through diplomacy. Once control was established, Great Britain took over the politics and economy of the subject colony. A colonial possession such as India was the source of raw materials such as cotton, tea, and hemp, which were sent to England to be manufactured into finished products. The colony was a market for the imperial nation's manufactured products. In other words, the imperial relationship worked to the diplomatic, political, and economic benefit of Great Britain and to the disadvantage of the subject colony.

Gandhi argued that British economic policy had exploited the Indian people, especially the 75 percent of the then–500 million who inhabited India's thousands of small villages. In the past, the villagers had grown and spun cotton cloth as an indigenous local industry, but this was no longer done under British rule. The British commercial policy had idled village handicraft industries, and the villagers had to purchase from British merchants the cloth they once made themselves.

The policy of imperialism had important educational consequences throughout the colonial world. Europeans generally exported their educational philosophies, institutions, and policies to their colonial subjects. The educational policy practiced by the imperial nation related directly to its rule over and governance of the subject colony. In the colonies, direct rule relied on the presence of a military force. In India, the British army maintained garrisons that suppressed insurrection and revolt.

To govern a colony, especially one as vast in territory and diverse in population as India, the British brought civil servants and educators from Great Britain to staff the upper positions in the colonial government. These English administrators tended to live in enclaves that were socially isolated from the indigenous population. The role of such officials was to protect British imperial interests, which meant establishing and maintaining a British version of law and order. In India, the British constructed a great railway network that facilitated transportation and a telegraph system that facilitated communication and also served British interests. To pay the costs of the transplanted civil service, taxes were levied and collected from the indigenous population. (A similar pattern of imperial-colonial rule had been played out in North America in the eighteenth century, resulting in the American Revolution.)

To consolidate their control in the colony, the officials of the European nation typically trained a small portion of the indigenous population for subordinate civil service and administrative posts. For example, a British administrator would generally have an Indian deputy and staff working under his supervision. A small group of Indians, usually from the upper castes, were educated in preparatory schools, secondary schools, and universities in the English language and style. This small elite of English-speaking Indians, never more than about 2 percent of the population, then entered the administration.

For a time, the British debated how to educate this Indian elite. Should its education be in the indigenous or in the English language, literature, and culture? Some English policy makers, called "orientalists," argued for the indigenous language and culture. However, a more powerful group of British policy makers called "anglicists," headed by Lord Macaulay, decided that education in India should be on the British or western European model. India's educational situation was complicated by the existence of seventeen major languages spoken in various regions of the subcontinent. The language issue would remain a complicating factor in Indian politics and education.

The decision to impose the British language and Western attitudes on the educated elite in India had serious educational consequences. First, the education of the vast majority of the population—the millions of children who lived in thousands of villages—was neglected. Village India remained a backwater of pervasive illiteracy and ignorance. For Gandhi, the illiteracy, grinding poverty, and ignorance of the underemployed and undernourished Indian villager was one of the nation's most serious problems. His policy of basic education was designed to renew village life and economy.

A second consequence of the British educational policy was that the educated elite of English-speaking Indians tended to be separated from the main problems of Indian life. Although the British intended to Westernize this elite, the education they received was, in the British tradition, highly literary. According to the British civil service tradition, the best preparation for administrative duties was to study the classics, ancient history and literature, and British history and literature. This education lacked scientific, technological, engineering, and managerial knowledge and skills. The result was that the elite in India was educated like the English but considered inferior by their British supervisors. Further, they were culturally divorced from their own heritage.

When Gandhi returned to India from South Africa, he, too, was a product of a British education. He deliberately immersed himself in Indian culture and problems so that he could rediscover his roots. Many of his associates in the Congress party, the principal movement for Indian independence, were anglicized Indians who had to recapture their cultural identity before they could reach the masses and persuade them to join the independence movement.

There was still another factor operating in the educational situation in India. A unique feature of Indian society was the cultural-social-religious caste system. An individual was born into a *caste*, an ascribed status, and remained in it throughout life. Although anthropologists and sociologists debate the origins of the caste system, it had a definite social and economic influence not only on Gandhi's life but on contemporary India as well. Reinforced by Hindu theology, the dominant religiocultural system of India, Indian society was rigidly segregated by caste membership. The original four great castes were the following:

1. *brahmans*, scholars and priests
2. *khasatriyas*, warriors
3. *vaishyas*, merchants
4. *shudras*, farmers

These castes were further subdivided into hundreds of *jatis*, or subcastes, which minutely and rigidly defined a person's status, role, and function. Occupation, associates, and marriage were determined by and within the confines of a given caste. In addition to the social rigidity imposed by the four major castes and their many subdivisions, there remained a large part of the Indian population known as the *outcastes*, or *untouchables*, regarded as the dregs of Indian society. They were relegated to the most burdensome jobs—often as sweepers and scavengers—and confined to the poorest and most squalid sections of cities and villages. Indeed, if even the shadow of an untouchable fell upon a member of an upper caste, that person would have to undergo ritual purification to remove the stain of untouchability. Although Gandhi did not challenge the caste system itself, he strongly opposed untouchability. He renamed the untouchables the *harijans*, or people of God, and argued for the removal of disabilities because of caste. It should be noted that the Indian constitution, which was adopted after independence, outlaws disability because of caste and provides some compensatory assistance to untouchables. Such was not the case, however, when Gandhi assumed leadership of the Indian independence movement.

Because of both ingrained Indian traditions and British policy, members of the upper castes tended to be those who were educated and gained entry into the administrative structure in imperial India. At that time, the concept of social mobility was both nonexistent and incompatible with caste. Further, upper-caste Indians had strong inherited conceptions about the nature of work and the status of workers. The Brahman caste were intellectuals who did not do manual work. Physical labor was the task of other, lower castes. Indian society had a strong dichotomy between intellectual and physical work. An educational goal was to escape physical labor. In his educational philosophy, Gandhi regarded the dichotomy to be a characteristic that had to be undone in the new India of his dreams. His educational policy was designed to emphasize the importance and dignity of physical labor.

The country that Gandhi wanted to become free and independent was a mosaic of races, languages, and ethnic groups. Although the vast majority of the population were Hindus, other religious groups were the Muslims, Sikhs, Jains, Pharsees, and Christians. Antagonism was strong between Hindus and Muslims. When the British left India, the subcontinent was divided into India, with a predominantly Hindu population, and Pakistan, with a largely Muslim population. At the time of independence, bloody religious and communal rioting and disorders occurred that prompted Gandhi to go on a hunger strike until the religious factions laid down their arms.

Still another problem was divisiveness over language. The Aryan population of the northern states of India spoke Hindi, which was derived from the ancient Sanskrit, and the people of the southern states, descended from Dravidian ethnic stock, spoke a variety of languages. In the face of such language divisions, English was the link language of government, commerce, and communication.

If it faced problems of great magnitude, India also had rich cultural and spiritual resources that would nourish Gandhi's passion for freedom. Hinduism, the dominant religion, seems to mean many things to many people. Although it appears to be a polytheistic religion of many deities and cults, there is an underlying spiritual thread. Atman, or Brahma, is the spiritual source of all life and to which all life sought to return. According to the Hindu belief in reincarnation, a person undergoes a series of births, deaths, and rebirths until *karma*, the force determined by a person's actions and their ethical consequences, is freed from the appetites and desires of earthly existence. When the soul achieves this level of earthly detachment, then the person is freed from the cycle of birth and death.

In this cosmology what is important is eternity, not the moment. Although such a worldview may carry a fatalism that diminishes individual ambition, it brings a perspective that focuses on the eternal rather than the transitory. Gandhi was willing to discipline himself, to overcome the desires that might divert him from his goal, and to work patiently for his cause. As a child, he was inspired by stories about Rama, the Hindu deity of doing one's duty in life. As an adult, his study of the *Bhagavad Gita* led him to the concepts of *aparigraha*, the nonpossession of material wealth, and to *samabhava*, equability.[1]

Gandhi was a proponent and disciple of nonviolence. Orthodox Hinduism, as well as Buddhism, which was originally a reform movement within Hinduism, stresses that no harm should be done to any living creature—person or animal or insect. All creatures are part of the cosmic drama and are seeking reunification in Brahma. Of all the leaders of great revolutions, Gandhi must be considered the most unusual. He proposed to free his people from British rule without violence—without guns and bombs. Those who joined his movement had to be self-disciplined followers who would not take up arms, engage in terrorism, nor inflict harm on their adversaries. Gandhi forged the weapon of passive resistance and of peaceful boycotts to persuade the British their day was finished in India and that they should quit the subcontinent.

Finally, still another aspect of Hinduism shaped Gandhi's outlook. In Hinduism, the highest state of life is free of worldly concerns and passions. This detachment from the world enables the person to contemplate the meaning of life and the greatness of the universe. Although Gandhi was certainly an activist for Indian independence and for human rights, he incorporated an aspect of personal detachment in his life. To free India, Gandhi determined that he had to be free from the desire for personal glory and power. He was a leader of the most unusual kind—devoid of personal egotism. It is from this general examination of the context of Indian life and society that we now turn to the life of Mohandas Gandhi, the Mahatma, or great soul.

Mohandas Gandhi: Father of Indian Independence

Mohandas Karamchand Gandhi was born on October 2, 1869, at Porbandar, the capital of a small princely state, on the peninsula of Kathiawad, in India. The fourth child of Karmachand and Puthabai Gandhi, he was born into the Modh Bania *jati*, a subdivision of the commercial trading Vaisya caste. His father, Karamchand Gandhi, had served as prime minister to the prince of Porbandar. Gandhi was influenced by his father, who was known as an honest and practical politician and by his mother's religious belief in the sacredness of all life.[2]

Gandhi began his primary education in Porbandar at the local school, where he began his study of Gujarati, the language of the region. After the family moved to Rajkot, he then attended the local primary school. His secondary education was at the Alfred High School, a college preparatory institution. He began the study of English and completed courses in mathematics, chemistry, astronomy, history, and geography.[3]

Following the Hindu custom, Gandhi's marriage was arranged by his parents and the parents of his fiancée. He was betrothed at age 7 to Kasturbai, daughter of the merchant Kokuldas Makanji. In 1883, Mohandas and Kasturbai, both 13, were married. Although Kasturbai remained virtually illiterate throughout her life, she and Gandhi shared a lasting mutual affection and she joined him in his work. Later, Gandhi condemned what he called "the cruel custom of child marriage."[4]

In 1887, Gandhi enrolled in Sarmaldas College in Bhavnager but left after a semester to go to England, in 1888, to study law. His wife and son remained in India. Gandhi stayed in England for three years. Like other Indian students in England, Gandhi modeled himself on what he thought was the ideal English gentleman. After completing his legal studies and begin admitted to the bar, he returned to India in 1891 to begin practicing law in Bombay, India's bustling, large port city.[5]

Gandhi's career next took him to South Africa as legal counsel for Dada Abdulla and Company, a large Indian commercial firm. From 1893 to 1901, except for brief visits to India, he and his family lived in South Africa. The country had a sizable Indian population consisting of many who had come as laborers and others as small shopkeepers.

Gandhi soon discovered that the South African government had enacted restrictive policies against the Indian population that severely limited their personal freedom and economic opportunities. For example, in the South African state of Transvaal, Indians could not own property, except in a few designated areas. Nor could they vote or travel without an identity pass. Gandhi, increasingly sensitive to violations of human rights, organized and led the Natal Indian Congress, which sought to remove the discriminatory laws against the Indian population. During the time Gandhi lived in South Africa, he developed his strategies of nonviolent passive resistance.

In 1901, Gandhi and his family returned to India. He opened a law office in Bombay but soon his attention was diverted to the Indian independence movement, which was in its early stages. Because of his British education and long absences from India, Gandhi believed he no longer knew the real India. He determined to renew his cultural roots and embarked on a rail tour, traveling third class across India, observing local conditions and meeting local leaders of the Indian National Congress party.

In 1902 Gandhi received an urgent message from the Indian community in South Africa, pleading with him to represent them against new discriminatory laws being enacted by the South African government. The government announced a program that required every Indian over age 8 to be fingerprinted and to carry a registration certificate. Those who failed to do so would be summarily deported.[6] From 1902 until 1915, Gandhi was in South Africa, representing the Indian minority and organizing them against the government's repressive policy. In 1903, Gandhi began publishing *Indian Opinion*, a journal, as a vehicle of communication for the Indian community and to inform others about the situation in South Africa.

Gandhi began to form a plan of action for his movement to alleviate the conditions of the oppressed South African Indians. He was inspired by John Ruskin (1819–1900), the English writer, moralist, and critic, and Leo Tolstoy (1828–1910), the Russian novelist. Both Ruskin and Tolstoy had decided ideas on social justice and education that Gandhi incorporated into his own philosophy. From Ruskin, Gandhi took the ideal of "human companionship" as an agency of individual and social reform. From Tolstoy, he took the ideal of the need to disobey evil power structures, including those of the government.[7]

Gandhi was convinced that he and his followers had to become morally prepared for the coming struggle. To train his associates in the rationale and methods of nonviolent resistance, Gandhi established Phoenix Farm, near Durban. Phoenix Farm, Tolstoy Farm, and other centers for social and moral education that Gandhi later established integrated Ruskin's and Tolstoy's ideas with the Indian concept of the *ashram*, a school in which disciples studied the way of life presented to them by an enlightened teacher or guru.

Gandhi's educational experiment at Tolstoy Farm, an *ashram* located in the Transvaal in South Africa, is especially illustrative of his educational philosophy and methods. The various schools Gandhi would establish when he returned to India essentially followed the pattern used at Tolstoy Farm. Located on 1,100 acres, it was an experiment in agriculturally based communal living. The residents of the farm were primarily Indians of different religions, languages, and castes. Gandhi hoped to demonstrate that a commonly practiced mutuality of interests would be stronger than the forces that traditionally had divided Indians. The school, attended by the community's children, was a focal point of the experiment. Gandhi taught in the school. Of his experiences at Tolstoy Farm, he wrote, "Tolstoy Farm was a family in which I occupied the place of the father, and that I should so far as possible shoulder the responsibility for the training of the young."[8]

Gandhi based his conduct of the school on his philosophy of the well-rounded intellectual, moral, and physical development of the whole person. In both the traditional Indian and the British systems of education, Gandhi believed that moral and physical development had been sacrificed to an exclusive emphasis on intellectual development. Unfortunately, in the conventional schools, intellectual education had further deteriorated, he believed, into a highly literary, verbal, and bookish method that stressed rote memorization. At Tolstoy Farm, Gandhi sought to undo the exaggerated literary bent of conventional education and emphasize total development.

Gandhi believed that all education should rest on a moral-spiritual foundation. He commented,

> I had always given the first place to the culture of the heart or the building of character, and as I felt confident that a moral training could be given to all alike, no matter how different their ages and their upbringing, I decided to live amongst them all the twenty-four hours of the day as their father.[9]

A deeply religious person, Gandhi believed moral development needed a spiritual foundation. Tending to see the expression of God's truth in the principles of the world's great religions, Gandhi's approach to spirituality was universalist rather than sectarian. However, each child was also to understand the principles of his or her particular religion. To do this, Gandhi encouraged each child to read and study the scriptures appropriate to his or her religious creed.

Within the general moral climate of the school, Gandhi believed that the subject-oriented phase of education should take place. Whenever possible, children were instructed in the language they spoke in their family. They learned the primary tool skills of reading, writing, and arithmetic in addition to studying English, history, geography, and singing.

Gandhi included vocational education both at Tolstoy Farm and in his philosophy of basic education. Vocational education was designed to emphasize the dignity of work and to teach individuals employable skills. Gandhi believed that the ancient Indian scholarly tradition, the British educational system, and the caste system all worked to diminish the importance of physical and manual labor and to relegate those who did such labor to the lower rungs of society. Further, Gandhi recognized that unemployment was a pervasive problem, especially in the Indian villages. Gandhi's emphasis on physical work and vocational education was therefore a persistent theme in his educational philosophy. At Tolstoy Farm, the teachers, including Gandhi, worked among the children, who were engaged in gardening, performing agricultural chores, cleaning the school and its playground, and learning crafts. When he returned to India, Gandhi took up spinning cotton and making cotton cloth, which became a part of the school routine. Thus, his educational work in South Africa became the experience-tested background for his philosophy of basic education.

An unusual blending of the contemplative and activist personality, Gandhi was heavily involved in developing a political movement to redress the injuries inflicted by the restrictive laws of the South African government. Between 1905 and 1910, Gandhi was instrumental in mobilizing the Indian community against a series of repressive South

African acts. His strategy involved the use of the *satyagraha*, an all-encompassing Hindi word that means awareness of the "soul force" or truth that is in each person. The person who practiced *satyagraha* was to use that spiritual force against ill-directed police, military, political, and economic pressure by engaging in nonviolent civil disobedience, passive resistance, and noncooperation against unjust laws. Although the concept of *satyagraha* was rooted in Indian philosophy, it also was expressed in Western thought by civil disobedience based on the higher law concept developed by Henry David Thoreau at Walden Pond. Similar ideas were expressed by Tolstoy in his pacifist stage. Dr. Martin Luther King, Jr., drew on similar sources of moral and political philosophy during the Civil Rights Movement.

The development of the concept of *satyagraha* by Gandhi for use against South African authorities and its later use throughout the struggle for Indian independence has important educational as well as moral implications. First, Gandhi believed that all people had the moral force or power to resist social injustice within them but that it needed to be raised to consciousness. Second, the use of "soul power" or moral force had to be disciplined by training that involved curbing the emotions so that the protester would not respond to violence with counterviolence. Gandhi recognized that the use of violence was a kind of terror that spawned further acts of terror, which dehumanized both the victimized person and the perpetrator of the violent action. Third, by a complete spiritual formation that led to nonviolent action the person could be prepared to participate in the movement of liberation.

Between 1906 and 1914, Gandhi organized three major *satyagraha* campaigns against the South African government. He was jailed on several occasions for inciting public unrest but always renewed his efforts on being released. His campaign was directed against an ordinance that restricted the entry of Indians into South Africa, the registration act that compelled Indians to carry identification papers that restricted their freedom of movement, and a law that held that non-Christian marriages were invalid. Because South Africa was a member of the British Commonwealth, Gandhi's activities reached the British government and he was called to London several times as the British government attempted to mediate the impasse in South Africa. In 1914, passage of the Indian Relief Act eliminated some of the restrictions against the Indian population.

In 1915, Gandhi returned to India and began the movement to secure Indian independence, which would occupy the rest of his life. In many ways, Gandhi's nonviolent passive resistance campaigns in South Africa prepared him for the next 33 years. He again established an *ashram*, Satyagraha Ashram, to prepare a core of his followers for the long campaign ahead. From 1915 to 1920, he helped organize local *satyagraha* campaigns against specific injustices. As he had done in South Africa, he also turned to journalism, assuming the editorship of *Young India*, an English-language weekly, and *Navajivan*, a weekly published in Gujarati, one of the Indian languages.

For the next 20 years, Gandhi was the leading voice calling for an independent India. His movement for independence involved a multidimensional strategy against British rule. First, he had to unite the various ethnic, language, and religious groups that divided India into often contentious factions. His greatest difficulty in presenting a united front against the British came from the Muslim minority, who feared that they would be dominated by the Hindu majority in an independent India. His ability to keep the Muslims in his movement was always shaky and broke down when India received independence in 1947. At that time, Pakistan was established as an independent Muslim state, headed by Mohammed Ali Jinnah. At various times, there were also outbreaks of communal disorders between the Hindus and Muslims that caused great distress for the proponent of nonviolence. When such outbreaks occurred, Gandhi would suspend his activities for independence and go on a fast, which on several occasions was life threatening, until the communal rioting and violence had ended.

A second part of Gandhi's strategy for independence was to enlist those who would become the leaders of an independent India to follow his policies of nonviolence and revitalization of village life. The major leaders of the independence movement were in the National Congress party, and Gandhi formed a close association with such promising figures as Jawaharal Nehru, Sarder Patel, and others. Although Gandhi was the undisputed moral leader of the movement, not all of the Congress party leadership believed that his nonviolent strategy would be effective. In numerous meetings Gandhi had to persuade them to accept his strategy.

Gandhi also had to deal with the British authorities. His campaign was really directed at persuading the British to voluntarily leave the subcontinent. It was a long process that took more than 30 years and a Britain that was worn out by World War II to accept. Gandhi would call for an all-India *satyagraha*, a campaign of massive civil disobedience, often accompanied by a cessation of work and transportation. The British would respond, often arresting Gandhi and the Congress party leaders. Gandhi would be released and the scenario would be repeated. During his lifetime, Gandhi spent a total of 2,338 days in prison. As a result of his patient but persistent strategy, India became independent in 1947 when the British voluntarily left.

Although independence was won, the process of achieving freedom was a traumatic one. Even though Gandhi opposed the division of India, two independent nations, India and Pakistan, were created. The Hindu and Sikh religious groups that were living in the Muslim nation of Pakistan began a painful exodus to India. Many of the Muslims living in India migrated to Pakistan. In the midst of the relocation and resettlement of these millions of displaced persons, communal rioting broke out between the religious factions, resulting in massacres and pillaging. Gandhi began a fast that lasted until the rioting subsided. On January 30, 1948, Gandhi was assassinated by Vinayak Godse, a fanatical Hindu nationalist. The man who preached and practiced nonviolence was a victim of the violence he so deplored.

Gandhi's Social and Educational Theory

Gandhi's social and educational theory integrated spiritual, political, economic, and educational elements. Gandhi had no pretensions of being an original thinker or a systematic philosopher. He saw himself, rather, as implementing in daily life the eternal truths that governed the universe. He stated, "I do not claim to have originated any new principle or doctrine. I have simply tried in my own way to apply the eternal truths of our daily life and problems."[10]

Gandhi's religious ideas came from but were not a rigidly orthodox interpretation of Hindu theology. He shared the Hindu metaphysical view that the universe was inherently spiritual or nonmaterial. This spiritual perspective, also found in philosophical idealism, stresses the importance of the inner self, the spiritual essence or force, that is at the heart of human nature. In this view, the universe is the creation and the manifestation of God, a supreme spiritual presence. Following philosophical idealism, Gandhi believed that the entire universe was governed by unalterable laws. He stated that "there is an orderliness in the universe; there is an unalterable law governing everything and every being that exists or lives."[11]

In the Hindu cosmology, the purpose of human existence is to be reabsorbed into God and to end the tribulations of life. Unlike the Christian conception of salvation as an act that brings the person into the presence of God, the Hindu view was rather that of becoming part of God and being absorbed within divinity itself. The Hindu concept of *reincarnation*—successive births and deaths in either higher or lower orders of life depending on one's performance in the previous existence—emphasized the sacredness of all life. Along with his acceptance of the spiritual nature of the universe, Gandhi also accepted the inherent dignity of life.

With its cosmology of absorption of all life into its spiritual source, Hinduism in India was a highly syncretistic religion. It was not creedal and dogmatic as were the various Christian denominations but was more the expression of a total way of life. Thus, Christianity in its Catholic and Protestant forms and other religions such as Buddhism and Islam could be seen as manifestations of the divine will rather than as distinctive religions. In his social and educational theory, Gandhi talked about the universal principles and truths of all the great religions. Although immersed in the Hindu reli-giocultural ethic, Gandhi found worth and value in all of the world's great religions. He stated, "All religions are founded on the same moral laws. My ethical religion is made up of laws which bind men all over the world."[12]

Although Gandhi was deeply impressed by the spiritual meaning of human life, he also believed that human beings, for the perfection of their own nature and for the contribution they were to make in the perfection of others, should be developed intellectually and physically as well as spiritually. According to Gandhi, the education that brought this development about involved the harmonious cultivation of the heart, or will; the mind, or intellect; and the body. For him, "man is neither mere intellect, nor the gross animal body, nor the heart or soul alone. A proper and harmonious combination of all the three is required for the making of the whole man."[13] Although each person should seek the perfection of his or her own mind, will, and body, human perfection could not be achieved in isolation but only in the cooperative mutuality of human community. The moral person, living within the moral society, lived a life of service to others. Such a moral society rested on love, the fundamental spiritual force that united individuals into a common humanity. According to Gandhi:

> Scientists tell us that without the cohesive force amongst the atoms that comprise this globe of ours, it would crumble to pieces and we would cease to exist. As even there is a cohesive force in blind matter so must there be in all things animate; and the name of that cohesive force among animate beings is love. We notice it between father and son, between brother and sister, friend and friend. But we have to learn to use that force among all that lives, and in the use of it consists our knowledge of God. Where there is love there is life; hatred leads to destruction.[14]

Gandhi then was essentially a spiritual and moral leader who became involved in politics and education to remedy what he regarded to be immoral conditions that violated the spiritual dignity of persons. His philosophy, stressing personal development through social service, had a unique spiritual base. He stated that all "social, political, and religious" activities had to be guided "by the ultimate aim of the vision of God. The immediate service of all human beings becomes a necessary part of the endeavour . . . because the only way to find God is to see Him in His creation and be one with it. This can only be done by service to all."[15]

Gandhi's emphasis on community service anticipated the contemporary trend in American education for the inclusion of service-oriented education in the school curriculum. Similar to Gandhi's concept, service-oriented education enables students to be involved and engage in constructive projects in their local community such as assisting in day care and early childhood education, visiting and helping at senior care facilities, and engaging in environmental cleanup projects. Gandhi would have applauded this recent trend in American schools.

Although based on these general philosophical considerations, several elements in Gandhi's thought rose out of the Indian context, although their significance was larger than that context:

- The right of people to political self-determination
- The removal of prejudices that were either customary or statutory and that denied people opportunities for self-development
- The emphasis of a strategy of national development located at the grassroots level
- The use of nonviolent passive resistance as a strategy for bringing about social and political change

As a world figure, Gandhi's efforts to win independence for India was part of the tide of anti-imperialism and anticolonialism that swept Asia and Africa after World War II. As an advocate of human freedom, Gandhi believed that people had the right to political self-determination, which was a means to personal self-determination. If the people of Asia and Africa were forced to live in childlike submission to European overlords, their personal development would be impossible.

Gandhi's campaign for an independent India carried obvious political implications but had educational implications as well. The kind of education the European imperial powers imposed on colonial peoples was one that fitted them for dependency rather than for self-reliance. Education for freedom needed to awaken a sense of cultural and national identity by studying the history, language, and literature indigenous to the country. Gandhi believed that studying one's own cultural heritage, however, must not lead to a nationalist chauvinism against other nations.

In South Africa and in India, Gandhi opposed discrimination based on either custom or law. In South Africa, the government had discriminated against the Indian minority through restrictive statutes. In India, the caste system was the source of customary discrimination against members of lower castes and the untouchables. Gandhi took a stand against prejudice and discrimination by associating with the untouchables, working with them, and including them in his movement. His teachings and writings consistently opposed discrimination.

In addition to his political and social philosophies, Gandhi also had an economic theory that he hoped would revitalize the Indian economy. Gandhi believed the revival of Indian life had to begin in the villages where the great mass of the population lived. He saw small-scale industries that centered on handicraft production as the key element in such an economic revitalization. In the decade after Indian independence, government planners—although paying lip service to Gandhi's theory of small-scale local economic development—concentrated on large-scale projects designed to bring about a modern industrial economy. Since the 1980s, however, on the world scene, the trend has been to small-scale, locally initiated grassroots development such as Gandhi proposed. Gandhi's strategy of civil disobedience involved strong educational components. Participants in such nonviolent activity had to be spiritually prepared for the struggle and trained in the tactics of passive resistance.

Gandhi's Theory of Basic Education

Mohandas Gandhi developed a theory of education designed to aid in the reconstruction of India. Gandhi's rejection of the British-imposed pattern of education as well as his desire to revitalize village life prompted his plan of basic education.[16] The ignorance, illiteracy, and poverty of the Indian masses, especially in the villages, both depressed and challenged Gandhi. He recognized that the colonial system of education, separated from the day-to-day life of the common people, had created an intellectual elite of an educated minority. The ambitions of this group had to be redirected from the security of service to the British to the uncertain but necessary campaign of creating a revitalized and independent India. For India, the Indian people, regardless of religion or caste, had to be united, massive illiteracy combated, and popular education integrated into the mainstream of Indian life. In addition to its direct educational consequences, Gandhi believed that his projected policy of basic education had political and economic implications for an independent India. It would realize the creative and economically productive capacity of the Indian people and eventually free them from economic exploitation by a foreign power.

In expressing his educational philosophy, Gandhi defined *education* as the "all-round drawing out of the best in child and man—body, mind, and spirit." Concerned with the holistic and harmonious development of the human being, Gandhi, in *India of My Dreams*, expressed his vision of the new India:

> I hold that the true education of the intellect can only come through a proper exercise and training of the bodily organs, e.g. hands, feet, eyes, ears, nose, etc. In other words, an intelligent use of the bodily organs in a child provides the best and quickest way of developing his intellect. But unless the development of the mind and body goes hand in hand with a corresponding awakening of the soul, the former alone would prove to be a poor lop-sided affair. By spiritual training I mean education of the heart. A proper and all-round development of the mind, therefore, can take place only when it proceeds...with the education of the physical and spiritual faculties of the child. They constitute an indivisible whole.[17]

For Gandhi, an education that integrated and harmonized the human faculties should be craft centered. Gandhi said he would "begin the child's education by teaching it a useful craft and enabling it to produce from the moment it begins its training."[18] Accordingly, in Gandhi's plan of basic education, primary schooling was compulsory for all children between the ages of 7 and 14 and was conducted in the child's own language. The craft used in the particular school was to be one of the major occupations found in India and all instruction was to be correlated to the particular craft. Further,

Gandhi believed the sale of the items produced in the schools would make education productive and self-supporting.

In 1937, an all-India conference of educators met at Wardha to consider Gandhi's educational proposals. The Wardha Conference adopted a three-point resolution in support of Gandhian basic education that was also endorsed by the Indian National Congress party. According to the party,

1. Free and compulsory education should be provided for seven years throughout India.
2. The language of instruction at the primary level should be the child's mother tongue, the vernacular spoken in her or his home.
3. The entire educational process should be craft centered and instruction should be integrally related to the central craft taught in the school.[19]

By 1939, the political and educational leaders in the independence movement strongly endorsed Gandhi's plan of basic education. However, World War II and the intensification of the independence struggle pushed educational matters into the background. It was not until 1946, on the eve of independence, that Gandhi again turned his attention to education.

He called for "education for life, through life" and once again urged the implementation of his plan for basic education. His proposals now went beyond those that had been endorsed by the Wardha Conference. The scope of basic education had been extended to cover ages 6 to 14. An educational agency, the Hindustani Talimi Sangh located at Wardha, was established to disseminate and prepare materials for the implementation of the plan. In particular, a comprehensive syllabus was prepared to guide and correlate instruction.[20]

Gandhi's philosophy of basic education was also an element in his design for a new India. Like other social reformers, Gandhi saw education as a method of social reconstruction that would improve both individuals and their society.[21] He saw basic education as the means to a cooperative human commonwealth. By involving children as participants in an interacting educational and productive group, basic education would counteract the ingrained Indian attitude that relegated physical labor to lower castes and also the modern tendency to antisocial individualism. Basic education, according to Gandhi, would inculcate a spirit of cooperation, unity, and group responsibility. It would be one of the agencies for regenerating the sense of community. Like John Dewey, Gandhi also conceived of the school as a miniature society where children as social participants had rights and responsibilities. Gandhi saw basic education as providing a common educational foundation that would reduce the gap between urban and rural India. He stated,

> Craft education will provide a healthy and moral basis of relationship between the city and the village and thus go a long way towards eradicating some of the worst evils of the present social insecurity and poisoned relationship between the classes.[22]

Believing both traditional Indian education and British education to be too verbal and passive, Gandhi advocated learning through active participation in productive occupations that had educative potentialities. For example, the craft might be cotton spinning and manufacturing. Handicraft production centering on the production of cotton cloth had a number of correlated educational possibilities. It was related to botany and to agriculture in that children could observe and participate in planting, cultivating, and harvesting cotton. It was related to small-scale industry in that children could observe and participate in ginning cotton—separating the fiber from the seeds and spinning the fiber into thread.

They could also participate in weaving the thread into cloth. Further, the cloth could be made into clothing. Thus, children's participation in craft education—in the case of cotton, from planting the seed to manufacturing the clothing—would enable them to understand the full process of production. Further, the finished product was something they could see and appreciate as the tangible manifestation of their work. Thus, in Gandhi's mind, craft education satisfied a material need of society and served as the basis for purposeful, creative, and socially useful education.

As an educational method, Gandhi's proposed craft-centered basic education bore some resemblance to Pestalozzi's object lesson and to the efforts of such progressive educators as William H. Kilpatrick in making projects the focus of learning. There is a similarity between Gandhi's relationship of craft-centered education to economic development and to Booker T. Washington's work at Tuskegee Institute, where he saw vocational, trade, and agricultural education as the means to improving the economic status of blacks in the United States (Chapter 23, on W. E. B. Du Bois, contains a discussion of Washington's educational philosophy and practices). Like these educational reformers in Europe and the United States, Gandhi had in mind a curricular and instructional reform that would make schooling an interesting and challenging experience for children.

Gandhi's proposed educational program was designed to liberate children's creative impulses by providing them with opportunities for purposeful and meaningful activity. Craft instruction was to make the school more vital and interesting to children by freeing them from routine and boredom.[23] Craft-centered education would provide children with a sense of accomplishment, dignity, and purpose. Because it was centered on making a tangible product, craft education would provide children with the opportunity to appreciate their accomplishments. Students would take pride in their work, develop self-confidence, and come to recognize the dignity of labor. By correlating instruction with meaningful work, basic education would break down old prejudices and socially integrate those of different castes.

Although resting on a vocational core, Gandhi's basic education plan also contained a cultural element. Craft instruction would break down the aesthetic separation between fine and applied art. Both dimensions of aesthetic experience would merge into an integrated flow of human activity and a correlated educational process.

Although Gandhi's life and presence on the world scene was of immense educational value to those he encountered personally and through his autobiography and writings, he also should be seen as definitely contributing to educational philosophy and policy formulation. Although his general philosophy involving the affirmation of the spiritual dimension of human behavior and a strategy of nonviolent social change are large elements of the Gandhian worldview, he left a contribution to the educational heritage in his plan of basic education.

Conclusion: An Assessment

It is not easy to assess the life of a person such as Gandhi, who was such a moral force on the global scene. His role of educational theorist, although important to him, was but one of the many dimensions of his life and personality. To assess Gandhi's contribution, we shall comment on him as a world leader, a planner for national development, and an educational theorist.

Gandhi was a moral force, a spiritual leader rather than a political figure. He quickly learned, however, that, although moral principles can be stated in abstract documents, the ethical applications of such principles take place in political, social, and economic contexts. When Gandhi became involved in the politics of South Africa and India, struggling against unjust laws and arbitrary officials bent on enforcing them, he developed his strategy for social and political change. Rooted deeply in the spiritual dimension of life, Gandhi developed strategies for dealing with injustice, such as nonviolent passive resistance. To use nonviolent tactics, Gandhi's followers had to be brought to a state of moral readiness for engaging in passive resistance and schooled in the appropriate behavioral response to violence when it came from those in authority. Gandhi's strategy, one of the factors persuading the British to leave India, inspired the nonviolent campaign for civil rights that Dr. Martin Luther King, Jr., led in the United States.

In his own historical period, Gandhi stands out as a leader against imperialism. The late 1940s, the 1950s, and 1960s marked the end of European imperialism in Africa and Asia, and new nations arose. Gandhi holds a place of significance in world history along with Nehru, Sukarno, Nkrumah, and other leaders of anticolonialism. As indicated in this chapter, the changes that resulted from the end of colonialism and the gaining of independence held tremendous educational implications. Education, in the form of schooling, became a force for nation building.

In terms of the implementation of Gandhi's plan for basic education in India, the results have been mixed. Less than 20 percent of Indian schoolchildren of primary age attend basic education schools. The majority attend more conventional schools. Although government authorities comment favorably on basic education, resources in India have been directed by central government planners to higher education of a scientific nature. Instead of encouraging "bottom up" development education originating in the villages as Gandhi urged, government strategy generally has been to modernize the nation from the top downward by training scientific and technological elites.

Gandhi's plan for the reconstruction of India with its basic education component was a theory of national development. From the end of World War II to the present, an important world trend has been the desire of economically underdeveloped nations in Africa, Asia, and South America to improve their economies. Such economic development is regarded as the key to improving the standard of living and providing increased social, health care, and educational opportunities.

In *India of My Dreams,* Gandhi describes national development that would begin at the grassroots level. According to such a strategy, planning would be done by the local people who would create their own small-scale industries. As indicated, basic education was the educational component of such locally directed development activities. If local people had direct input into planning and running their economic affairs, Gandhi reasoned, they would believe themselves to be part of the process and be highly motivated to improve their economic condition.

The 1950s and 1960s, however, did not follow the pattern that Gandhi had urged. Instead of grassroots development, the strategy that was used in the newly independent, "third-world" nations was based on projects planned by their central governments, with the assistance of developed nations such as the United States, and imposed on local communities. These projects were generally large scale in scope, such as the construction of large dams, the change in agricultural production from subsistence farming to cash export crops, or the industrialization of the economy. Although the intention of these projects was economic growth, at times the projects actually worked against the economic interests of the lower socioeconomic classes and to the advantage of the upper classes. Further, the projects often disrupted traditional values.

In the late 1980s, there was a revitalization of interest in grassroots development efforts such as those suggested by Gandhi. In Central and South America, Africa, and Asia, voluntary organizations and governments as well began to follow policies that encouraged projects for small-scale sustainable development planned and implemented at the grassroots level. Gandhi's approach to small-scale development has renewed possibilities in the contemporary world.

Finally, as an educational theorist, Gandhi is significant for the relationship that he made between education and social change. His plan struck parallels with other approaches to education developed in Western educational thought. For example, Gandhi's theory of education that would develop the well-rounded person intellectually, morally, and physically was similar to Pestalozzi's method of education that emphasized training the senses through object lessons in homelike educational environments. There is a similarity between Gandhi's theory of basic education and Booker T. Washington's Tuskegee Institute in Alabama. Washington believed that the education of blacks in the United States should concentrate on vocational, trade, and agricultural education that could provide essential skills useful in establishing an economic base. Similarly, Gandhi believed that craft-centered education could provide an economic basis to revitalize India's villages. There is also a parallel between Gandhi's stress on craft-centered activities and progressive educators' emphasis on project-centered activities in the United States. Despite their metaphysical differences, Gandhi and Dewey concurred that education should be a force to build socially integrated communities.

The first decade of the twenty-first century, marred with violence, desperately calls for a rekindling of Gandhi's philosophy of nonviolence. Terrorist acts on September 11, 2001, claimed 3,000 innocent lives when hijacked passenger jets were deliberately crashed into the twin towers of the World Trade Center in New York City. Television carries daily accounts of terrorism and counteraction on the part of Arabs and Israelis. Occupied by the United States, Iraq is a country in turmoil. Civil war and tribal conflicts still grip many countries in Africa. Some extremists call for holy wars against their adversaries. A strong moral voice such as Gandhi's appears to be missing from the world scene. One can recall the words uttered by Prime Minister Nehru at Gandhi's death: Gandhi's light "was no ordinary light"—"...a thousand years later that light will still be seen...and the world will see it and it will give solace to innumerable hearts."[24] There is a desperate need for Gandhi's moral voice and nonviolent persuasion.

Questions for Reflection and Dialogue

1. How did Gandhi seek to revitalize village India? Is his plan relevant to modern society, especially to economically depressed inner cities and rural areas in the United States?
2. What were the major elements in Gandhi's theory of basic education? In your opinion, are any of these elements applicable to American education?
3. Reflect on Gandhi's opposition to "untouchability." Does American society have its own form of "untouchability"?
4. Identify the key events in Gandhi's life. Indicate how these events contributed to shaping his character.
5. Analyze nonviolent passive resistance as an instrument of social change. Provide examples of how others have used this approach to peaceful protest.
6. Today, there are many instances of racial, ethnic, and religious violence throughout the world. If Gandhi were with us today, how would he react to such violence and seek to bring about conflict resolution?
7. Contemporary American society has had many incidences of violence in and around schools, often inflicted by students on each other. How would Gandhi analyze this violence and what might he suggest to end it?

Projects for Deepening Your Understanding

1. In a research paper, examine an aspect of the imposition of British educational structures on India during the colonial era. Are there instances, today, in which one country seeks to impose its political and educational structures on another?
2. Review a biography of Gandhi (see Suggestions for Further Reading for choices).
3. Prepare a research paper that compares Gandhi and Martin Luther King, Jr. on the use of nonviolent passive resistance. How acceptable do you think this approach might be in the contemporary United States?
4. Review the literature on service-oriented education. Then, design a project that uses Gandhian principles to carry out service education.
5. Maintain a clippings file of newspaper accounts of violence in the world. Analyze these articles and seek to identify the reasons for such acts of violence. How do you think Gandhi would react to these instances of contemporary violence?
6. Review the literature that favors and opposes multiculturalism and bilingual instruction in American education. Then, write a paper that indicates what you believe would be Gandhi's position in this controversy.
7. Review the literature on separation of church and state in American society and education. Then, write a paper that indicates what you believe would be Gandhi's position on this issue.
8. Schools, especially secondary schools, often have much conflict between "in groups" and "out groups." Provide a plan to reduce this conflict based on Gandhi's principles.

Notes

1. Yogesh Chadha, *Gandhi: A Life* (New York: John Wiley & Sons, 1997), 100.
2. Chadha, *Gandhi: A Life*, 1–5.
3. Chadha, *Gandhi: A Life*, 7–8.
4. Chadha, *Gandhi: A Life*, 10–12.
5. Chadha, *Gandhi: A Life*, 30, 41.
6. Chadha, *Gandhi: A Life*, 114.
7. Chadha, *Gandhi: A Life*, 155.
8. Shriman Narayan, ed., *The Selected Works of Mahatma Gandhi*, vol. 2 (Ahmedabad: Navajivan, 1968), 496.
9. Narayan, *Selected Works of Mahatma Gandhi*, vol. 2, 499.
10. Narayan, *Selected Works of Mahatma Gandhi*, vol. 6, 94.
11. Narayan, *Selected Works of Mahatma Gandhi*, vol. 6, 104.
12. S. P. Chaube, *Recent Educational Philosophies in India* (Agra: Ram Pradad & Sons, 1967), 116.
13. Narayan, *Selected Works of Mahatma Gandhi*, vol. 6, 104.
14. M. K. Gandhi, *My Philosophy of Life* (Bombay: Pearl, 1961), 27–28.
15. Narayan, *Selected Works of Mahatma Gandhi*, vol. 6, 114.
16. K. G. Saiyidain, *The Humanist Tradition in Modern Indian Educational Thought* (Madison, WI: Dembar Educational Research Services, 1967), 89.
17. M. K. Gandhi, *India of My Dreams* (Ahmedabad: Navajivan, 1947), 185.
18. Gandhi, *India of My Dreams*, 186.
19. G. Ramanathan, *Education from Dewey to Gandhi* (London: Asia, 1965), 4–5.
20. Ramanathan, *Education from Dewey to Gandhi*, 4–5.
21. Humayun Kabir, *Indian Philosophy of Education* (New York: Asia, 1961), 22.
22. Gandhi, *India of My Dreams*, 187.
23. M. Patel, *The Educational Philosophy of Mahatma Gandhi* (Ahmedabad: Navajivan, 1953), 198.
24. Prime Minister Nehru quoted in Yogesh Chadha, *Gandhi: A Life*, 464.

Suggestions for Further Reading

Arnold, David. *Gandhi*. Harlow, England; New York: Longman, 2001.

Attenborough, Richard. *Gandhi: In My Own Words*. London: Hodder & Stoughton, 2002.

Barraclough, John. *Mohandas Gandhi*. Oxford: Heinemann Library, 1997.

Brown, Judith M. *Gandhi: Prisoner of Hope*. New Haven: Yale University Press, 1998.

Brotherton, Julian. *Gandhi and Western Education Today*. London: Gandhi Foundation, 1993.

Burke, S. M., and Quraishi, Salim Al-Din. *The British Raj in India: An Historical Review*. New York: Oxford University Press, 1995.

Chadha, Yogesh, *Gandhi: A Life*. New York: John Wiley & Sons, 1997.

Clement, Catherine. *Gandhi: Father of a Nation*. London: Thames and Hudson, 1996.

Clymer, Kenton J. *Quest for Freedom: The United States and India's Independence*. New York: Columbia University Press, 1995.

Copley, A. R. H. *Gandhi: Against the Tide*. Calcutta; New York: Oxford University Press, 1993.

Dastur, Aloo J., and Mehta, Usha. *Gandhi's Contribution to the Emancipation of Women*. London: Sangam, 1993.

Fischer, Louis. *The Life of Mahatma Gandhi*. London: HarperCollins, 1997.

Furbee, Mary R., and Furbee, Mike. *Mohandas Gandhi*. San Diego, CA: Lucent Books, 2000.

Gandhi, Ela. *Mohandas Gandhi: the South Africa Years*. Cape Town; Johannesburg: Maskew Miller Longman, 1994.

Gandhi, M. K. *An Autobiography: or the Story of My Experiments with Truth*. London: Penguin, 2001.

———. *India of My Dreams*. Ahmedabad: Navajivan, 1947.

———. *Mohandas Gandhi: Essential Writings*. John. Dear, ed. New York; Edinburgh: Alban, 2003.

Iver, Raghavan. *The Moral and Political Writings of Mahatma Gandhi*. Oxford, UK: Clarendon, 1986.

Juergensmeyer, Mark. *Gandhi's Way: a Handbook of Conflict Resolution*. Berkeley, CA; London: University of California Press, 2002.

Martin, Christopher. *Mohandas Gandhi.* Minneapolis: Lerner Publications Co., 2000.

Parekh, Bhikhu C. *Gandhi.* Oxford: Oxford University Press, 2001.

———. *Gandhi: a Very Short Introduction.* Oxford; New York: Oxford University Press, 2001.

Ruhe, Peter. *Gandhi.* London: Phaidon, 2001.

Settel, Trudy S., *The Wisdom of Gandhi.* New York: Citadel; Partridge Green: Biblios, 2001.

Steger, Manfred B., *Gandhi's Dilemma: Nonviolent Principles and Nationalist Power.* Basingstoke: Macmillan, 2000.

Veerraju, Gummadi. *Gandhian Philosophy: Its Relevance Today.* New Delhi: Borehamwood: D.K. Printworld; Motilat, 2002.

Wolpert, Stanley. *Gandhi's Passion: the Life and Legacy of Mahatma Gandhi.* Oxford: Oxford University Press, 2001.

C H A P T E R 23

W. E. B. Du Bois: Scholar and Activist for African American Rights

This chapter analyzes the life, educational philosophy, and contributions of William E. B. Du Bois (1868–1963), a distinguished sociologist and historian who was a leader of the movement to raise black consciousness and win full equality for African Americans. Du Bois's 16 pioneering books on sociology, history, and race relations established the scholarly foundations for the study of the African American experience.[1] He also wrote two autobiographies, several novels, and a play. Scholar and activist, Du Bois's editorship of *The Crisis*, the journal of the National Association for the Advancement of Colored People (NAACP), contributed to the momentum that led to the Civil Rights Movement of the 1950s and 1960s.

In this chapter we examine Du Bois's influence as an informal educator as well as his ideas on formal education. First, we discuss the general social, political, and economic context—especially how this context had an effect on African Americans. Second, we analyze Du Bois's biography, his education and career, to determine the evolution of his social and educational ideas. Third, we identify and examine Du Bois's major social, political, and educational ideas. Fourth, we assess the continuing effect of Du Bois's contributions to U.S. education. This analysis is designed to identify the forces that shaped Du Bois's life and to illustrate how his ideas and activities influenced the recent history of ethnic and cultural relations in the United States.

To organize your thoughts as you read this chapter, focus on the following questions:

1. What were the major trends, especially in the relationships between blacks and whites in the United States, in the historical context in which Du Bois lived?
2. How did Du Bois's life, education, and career shape his social and educational philosophy?
3. How did Du Bois's philosophy shape his social and educational policies?
4. What was the crux of the educational controversy between Du Bois and Booker T. Washington?
5. What is the enduring effect of Du Bois's contributions on U.S. education?

The Historical Context of Du Bois's Life

The 95 years of W. E. B. Du Bois's life were of significant consequence to the history of African Americans in the United States. Though the Civil War had ended three years before Du Bois's birth, sectional feelings between the victorious Union and the defeated 11 states of the Confederacy remained strained. The years from 1865 until 1877, when federal troops were withdrawn from the South, marked the Reconstruction of the former secessionist states into the Union.

During Reconstruction, most African Americans, with the exception of a small minority residing in northern cities, still lived in the rural areas of southern and border states. Du Bois, born in Massachusetts, was a child of parents who had been free long before the Emancipation Proclamation of President Lincoln in 1863 and the ratification of the 13th amendment to the Constitution, which ended slavery in the United States. This was not the case with Booker T. Washington, who would eventually become Du Bois's antagonist. Washington had been born into slavery in the rural South.

The Reconstruction and post-Reconstruction eras, from 1877 to 1910, were crucial decades in establishing the social, political, economic, and educational patterns that governed racial relations in the South. Despite the efforts of Lincoln's successor, Andrew Johnson, to weaken Reconstruction policies, the Republican party's dominant wing, known as "Radical Republicans," determined federal policies in the South. Former Confederate leaders were disenfranchised and prevented from regaining political power. The Radical Republicans, led by the dedicated abolitionists Senator Charles Sumner and Representative Thaddeus Stevens, worked passionately to guarantee the voting and civil rights of the recently freed former slaves. In 1868, the 14th amendment to the Constitution, conferring citizenship and rights on the former slaves, was ratified. Two years later, the ratification of the 15th amendment confirmed the rights of formerly enslaved black males, the freedmen, to vote.

A coalition of Northern politicians, philanthropists, religious missionaries, and educators cooperated in advancing the civil and educational rights of blacks in the South. Although the Democratic party in the South was still regarded as the party that represented the old antebellum social order, the Republican party was regarded as the party of Lincoln and of freedom, particularly by blacks. Republican politicians, especially those affiliated with the party's radical wing, endeavored to organize southern blacks as a voting bloc. If the Republicans could carry the southern states in national elections, the party could maintain its control of the presidency and Congress. With federal troops safeguarding African Americans' right to vote, the Radical Republicans, supported by black voters, gained control of legislatures throughout the South.

The interpretations of political reconstruction have generated controversy in American historiography. The older interpretation, advanced by historians sympathetic to the "old South," was that the politics of the Reconstruction era were corrupt. According to this rendition of history, opportunistic Northern politicians, the "carpetbaggers," descended on the South, carrying all they owned in a single carpetbag, determined to make their fortune in corrupt schemes. These carpetbaggers, supported by white Southern turncoats, the "scalawags," used the politically unsophisticated black voters to win elections. They then manipulated African Americans elected to the state legislatures to secure power and make profits.

In contrast to the older historiography, more recent interpretations of Reconstruction view the period as an era of substantial achievement in building an economic and educational infrastructure in the South that benefited both whites and blacks. According to this view of history, Reconstruction legislatures embarked on internal improvement programs for the war-devastated South that involved road and railway building. These improvements laid the needed foundations for industrializing the "new South." Further, Reconstruction legislatures enacted the first levies of a fairer and more uniform taxation system. In education, the legislatures enacted laws that extended the common school system to the South, which hitherto had generally failed to maintain public schools. As a historian, Du Bois wrote a history of the Reconstruction that challenged and corrected stereotypic fallacies about the role of African Americans.

If the South's political reconstruction left its impact on white–black racial relationships and attitudes, educational reconstruction, too, was an equally potent factor. This educational reconstruction shaped the ideas of Booker T. Washington, the leading African American spokesman through the rest of the nineteenth century and until his death in 1915. It also influenced Du Bois's rejection of Washington's philosophy of industrial education for African Americans and shaped his own vision of black education.

The initial efforts to educate former slaves came from Northern educators, many of whom had been enthused by New England's abolitionist ideology and ideal of common schooling. Often supported by Protestant denominations in the North, these educators also received financial aid from philanthropists who wanted to improve the condition of blacks and from the Freedmen's Bureau, a federal agency established to facilitate their transition from slavery to citizenship. Northern schoolmasters and school "marms," as they were called, labored with a missionarylike zeal to educate African American children. They emphasized a latter-day version of Puritanism that specified such educational goals as developing diligence, orderliness, and punctuality—the old New England virtues—along with basic literacy's reading, writing, and computation.[2]

The New England version of education made a profound impression on the South's recently emancipated blacks. The foundation of literacy and morality was further reconstituted into what was called "industrial education." Institutes such as the Hampton Institute, founded in 1868 and operated by Colonel Samuel Chapman Armstrong, implemented the philosophy of industrial education. Armstrong, who asserted that his black students needed to be "trained before they could be educated," believed that the inculcation of moral values preceded intellectual education. Emphasizing the "Yankee values of industriousness and thrift," Colonel Armstrong developed a thoroughly practical curriculum of vocational training.[3]

Booker T. Washington, a student at Hampton Institute, captured the attention of Colonel Armstrong, who made the industrious young man his secretary. Washington went on to endorse and implement industrial education at Tuskegee Institute in Alabama and then disseminate its doctrines throughout the South. Indeed, Washington's endorsement of industrial education extended this philosophy throughout the nation as the most suitable educational program for African Americans as well as Native Americans.

Industrial education was virtually synonymous with vocational training. Although the word *industrial* was used, the underlying philosophy was more general in content. It meant that males were to learn such trades as brickmaking and bricklaying, shoemaking, carpentry, blacksmithing, and so on and that females were to learn the domestic skills of cooking, sewing, food preservation, and child care. Because most African Americans then were farmers in the rural South, industrial training also involved learning techniques that would increase agricultural productivity. It was also intended to prepare African American youth, especially young women, in teacher education programs for black elementary schools.

Under Armstrong's tutelage, Washington became a leading proponent of industrial education. When the Alabama legislature approved and funded an African American training school at Tuskegee, Alabama, in 1881, Washington, bearing Armstrong's strong endorsement, was appointed the institute's headmaster, or principal. In his numerous speeches, essays, and books, the eloquent Washington recounted the story of his success that made Tuskegee the leading educational institution for blacks in the United States. Washington began his work at Tuskegee on July 4, 1881. Using an old church building as a school, Washington himself taught the 37 students enrolled in the institute's first class. Within a decade, Washington had built the institute into a nationally recognized institution with 100 buildings, a student enrollment of 1,200, and a faculty of 88.[4] Just as Hampton had been the paradigm for Tuskegee, Washington's Tuskegee Institute became the model for other black colleges throughout the country.

While Du Bois was growing up in Great Barrington, Massachusetts, and attending that community's elementary and high schools, Washington had made Tuskegee into a national educational force. While Du Bois was pursuing advanced degrees at Harvard and the University of Berlin, Washington was gaining acknowledgment as the spokesman of black America. Although both Washington and Du Bois sought to advance the cause of African Americans in the United States, they developed very different strategies. To understand the context that shaped Du Bois's ideology, we must examine Washington's work at Tuskegee and his educational philosophy of industrial education.

Washington first became recognized as an educator and then, because of his success in education, attracted a receptive audience for his socioeconomic and political doctrines. At Tuskegee, Washington concentrated on basic rather than higher education. Perhaps his decision was largely made for him by the conditions he faced. With minimal funding from the Alabama legislature, now in white control, Washington had to build the institute with his own labor and that of his first students.

Washington theorized that what the South's rural black population needed most was a basic education that, following the philosophy of industrial education, stressed health principles, literacy, and fundamental skills. He explained his use of industrial education at Tuskegee:

First, we have found the industrial teaching useful in giving the student a chance to work out a portion of his expenses while in school. Second, the school furnishes labour that has an economic value and at the same time gives the student a chance to acquire knowledge and skill while performing the labour. Most of all, we find the industrial system valuable in teaching economy, thrift, and the dignity of labour and in giving moral backbone to students.[5]

After inculcating basic skills and the "right" moral values, this fundamental curriculum would be followed by more specialized programs: For young men, there would be vocational education in the various trades or agricultural education based on the climate, topography, and crops of the southern region; for young women, domestic education and normal training—teacher preparation—to become elementary school teachers. Washington's students learned brickmaking, bricklaying, and carpentry by constructing their own classroom buildings and dormitories. Agricultural education meant raising the crops grown in Alabama—corn, cotton, and peanuts. Washington encouraged the research of George Washington Carver, a professor at Tuskegee, to find new uses for those crops that would improve the economy for rural blacks. Washington believed that improvement in agricultural techniques would increase the income of black farmers, many of whom were caught in the sharecrop system. *Sharecroppers* were tenant farmers who cultivated land owned by someone else, usually a white landowner. In return for their use of a home and land, the tenant farmer would pay rent by turning over to the landowner a large part of the crops produced. Washington, who discouraged migration from the South, believed blacks should remain in the South and become a class of independent landowning farmers. He stated,

To . . . our aspiring youth, seeking an opening in life, to me but two alternatives present themselves, as matters now stand—to live a menial in the North, or a semi-freeman in the South. This brings us face to face with Northern competition and Southern prejudice, and between them I have no hesitancy in saying that the Negro can find his way to the front sooner through Southern prejudice than through Northern competition. The one decreases, the other increases.[6]

Washington's Tuskegee program was nonthreatening to the Southern white power structure that, with the removal of federal troops in 1877, had regained political power and was now disenfranchising African American voters. Further, it was providing a small but trained force of black craftsmen for what was being proclaimed as the industrial "new South." Washington's educational program, though socially and politically conservative, contained some progressive aspects in students' learning by doing in the trades and in agriculture. However, unlike educational progressivism, Tuskegee's vocational training program was so specific that it limited further educational progress and mobility, especially into higher and professional education. When Du Bois challenged Washington's leadership, he criticized the restrictiveness of the Tuskegee educational philosophy.

As Washington's fame spread, industrial education for African Americans was endorsed by many educators in both South and North. For example, many of the nation's leading educators met at the Monhonk conferences of 1890 and 1891 in New York to consider the issue of African American education. After being lectured by General Armstrong that blacks needed to be instilled with a sense of the dignity of work and to learn solid industrial and agricultural trades, the conference attendees voted over-whelmingly to support industrial education.

Washington's rise to prominence took place during the time when there was an intense Southern white reaction against the earlier Reconstruction period. From the end of Reconstruction through the First World War, the politics of the South created a rigid, racially segregated society. During the 1880s and 1890s, the populist movement gained political momentum in the South as disgruntled and economically hard-pressed white and black farmers challenged the rule of conservative white "bourbon" Democrats. White Farmers' Alliances and Black Farmers' Alliances were organized, and some cooperation occurred between the two. Blacks had a short-lived opportunity to act as the balance of power between contending factions of white voters.

The first signs of political alliance between the economically struggling farmers were wrecked, however, by the barrier of racism. So-called poor white farmers, who tilled small farms, had in their background an intense fear of blacks as economic competitors. Using arguments of white supremacy, some populist leaders challenged the conservative white politicians in the Democratic party primaries that nominated candidates for office. Because the South was then a virtually one-party section of the country, winning the Democratic party nomination carried with it the certainty of victory in the general election. Until the 1950s, the Republican party was a negligible force in the South.

The gaining of power by the populist-inclined, agrarian Democrats over the conservative "bourbon" Democrats proved disastrous for black interests in the South. During the period from 1880 to 1910 the most severe restrictions were enacted against African Americans in the South. By the 1880s, blacks had few friends in the national Republican party who were willing to take up their cause. The generation of Radical Republicans had now passed from the political scene, and party leaders were more preoccupied with courting the "captains of industry" in the growing corporate sector. Further, the social Darwinist ideology was in vogue both in popular and academic circles. Some social Darwinists portrayed the struggle for survival as a racial combat in which the fittest race was the white race (see Chapter 18). Added to these factors was the accommodationist strategy of Booker T. Washington, who decided to go along with rather than resist the prevailing ideology.

In the late 1880s and 1890s, the Southern states enacted laws to limit and then virtually eliminate an African American political role. For example, Mississippi passed a poll tax that required a fee to vote. The poll tax eliminated many black voters from the voter registration lists. In addition, Mississippi passed a law that required voters to explain selected provisions of the state and national constitutions before they could vote. The election officials, who were white, asked complicated questions and then disqualified black voters. In Louisiana, for example, there were 130,344 registered black voters in 1896; by 1900, only 5,320 remained on the voting lists.[7] In addition to the statutory limitations on black suffrage, the Ku Klux Klan used intimidation and terror against African Americans who challenged the system. The 1890s were a time of virulent racism. What took shape in the South was a rigid racial segregation system of separate schools and transportation facilities that, with the force of state law, relegated blacks to second-class citizenship.[8]

While strict segregation laws were enacted throughout the South, Booker T. Washington, continuing to hold to his philosophy of industrial education, took an accommodationist line. Speaking on September 28, 1895, to a large audience at the Atlanta

Cotton Exposition, Washington made a highly significant and often-quoted pronouncement on white–black racial relations in the South. The Tuskegee president told his listeners,

> No race can prosper till it learns that there is as much dignity in tilling a field as in writing a poem. It is at the bottom of life we must begin, and not at the top. The wisest among my race understand that the agitation of questions of social equality is the extremist folly, and that progress in the enjoyment of all the privileges that will come to us must be the result of severe and constant struggle rather than of artificial forcing.[9]

In 1896, the U.S. Supreme Court's landmark decision in *Plessy v. Ferguson* gave federal constitutional sanction to *de jure* segregation in Southern and border states. At issue was the constitutionality of an Alabama law that required separate railway carriages for white and "colored" passengers. The case arose when Homer A. Plessy, an African American, boarded an East Louisiana Railway train as a passenger from New Orleans to Covington. Taking a seat reserved for whites, Plessy refused to move to the black section when ordered to do so by the conductor. Plessy was arrested and brought before Judge John H. Ferguson of the Criminal District Court of New Orleans. Ferguson rejected Plessy's lawyer's argument that his arrest violated the Constitution's 14th amendment. The precedent-setting case reached the U.S. Supreme Court.

Justice Henry Brown, speaking for the majority of the justices of the Supreme Court in *Plessy*, established the precedent of "separate but equal," which would stand until overturned in the *Brown v. Board of Education of Topeka* decision in 1954 that ended *de jure* racial segregation in the United States. In 1896, however, the Court, ruling that segregation was not discriminatory against blacks, stated that racially separate facilities, as long as they were equal, could be ordered legally by the states. According to the Court's decision, the object of the 14th amendment

> . . . was undoubtedly to enforce the absolute equality of the two races before the law, but in the nature of things it could not have been intended to abolish distinction based upon color, or to enforce social, as distinguished from political equality, or a commingling of the two races upon terms unsatisfactory to either.[10]

The political and economic reality, however, was that these separate facilities, particularly schools, were not equal. By 1900, the Southern states, which lagged seriously behind the other states in educational funding, were spending twice as much to educate white than black children.

This was the historical context that shaped the background of W. E. B. Du Bois's struggle for African American freedom and civil, political, and educational rights in the United States. The context involved longstanding racist attitudes in the South that were given the sanction of law. It involved a Northern attitude in which racism was real but covert. It involved an attitude on the part of politicians, including progressives, to avoid entanglement in the race question. It involved the existence of segregated institutions, especially schools, for a large part of the nation's population of children and youth.

W. E. B. Du Bois: Activist for African American Civil and Educational Rights

William E. B. Du Bois was born on February 23, 1868, in Great Barrington, Massachusetts, a New England town nestled in the Berkshire hills. His ancestry was of mixed African and European descent. Alfred Du Bois, his father, a grandson of James Du Bois, a white plantation owner in the Bahamas, was born in Haiti. Mary Silvina Burghardt, his mother, was descended from Africans who had been brought by force to the United States by William Coenraet Burghardt, a Dutch slave trader. The Burghardt family, which dated to the prerevolutionary period, had long-established roots in Great Barrington. Alfred and Mary were married in 1867 and William was born a year later. Du Bois's father left Great Barrington in search of work when William was a year old and never returned to the family. William was raised by his mother, who, although suffering from depression and the effects of a stroke, supported the household and encouraged her son's educational ambitions.[11]

William Du Bois's life as a youngster growing up in a New England town differed radically from that of Booker T. Washington in the South. Unlike Washington, who was born into slavery, Du Bois's ancestors had been free since the American Revolution. He was a member of a small African American community, a minority of 25 families in a town of 3,920 inhabitants that included descendants of the founding Dutch and English settlers as well as newly arriving Irish and Czech immigrants.[12]

Du Bois's early religious convictions were Calvinist, the bedrock theology of the Puritans that flowed into New England Congregationalism. He and his mother attended the First Congregational Church and William participated in its Sunday school. Congregationalism had been a significant force in the pre–Civil War abolitionist movement. In addition, many teachers who went to the South after the Civil War to teach in Freedmen's Bureau schools had been nurtured in Congregationalism's Calvinist theological foundations. This religious predilection would be a powerful force in the "black Puritanism" that shaped the religious outlook of many African Americans.

In a community where blacks and whites coexisted civilly, Du Bois, though conscious that he was different, appears to have been accepted socially by his white classmates. Unlike Washington, who had to struggle against great odds to obtain an education, Du Bois attended his local elementary school, enrolling at age 6. A serious student, he was a favorite pupil of his teachers. He then enrolled in Great Barrington's high school. Frank Hosmer, the high school principal, noticing Du Bois's academic talent, encouraged him to enroll in the college preparatory curriculum, which included algebra, geometry, Latin, and Greek.[13] After reading Macaulay's *History of England*, Du Bois, seeking to emulate the noted historian's style, became keenly interested in history, which would become his major field at Harvard.

Du Bois also benefited from Great Barrington's informal educational agencies. Because his mother was the family's sole support, Du Bois worked at a variety of jobs to supplement her income as a maid in white households. He took part-time jobs while in high school doing chores for senior citizens, working as a clerk in a local grocery store, and delivering newspapers. An avid reader, Du Bois was befriended by the owner of the local bookstore, who permitted him to read the newspapers, magazines, and books that he stocked. Showing a talent for writing, young Du Bois became the Great Barrington reporter for the *Springfield Republican*.[14] The fledgling reporter covered the town meetings, which in the New England tradition of local control set the budget for the schools, roads, and other community responsibilities.

In addition to pursuing the rigorously academic college preparatory curriculum, Du Bois was active in cocurricular activities at the high school. He was coeditor of the high school newspaper, *The Howler*, and organized a literary society, the "Sons of Freedom," which worked on projects to assist Great Barrington's African American population.[15] Already as a high school student, Du Bois exhibited adeptness as a journalist, editor, and organizer—abilities he would employ later as one of the founders of the Niagara Movement and the NAACP.

In 1884, Du Bois graduated from high school with high honors. He was the school's first African American graduate. Du Bois delivered a commencement oration on Wendell Phillips, the New England abolitionist.[16] Encouraged by his mother and the Burghardt family, he applied for admission to Harvard University. However, his mother's death in March 1885 and insufficient funds made it highly unlikely that he would be able to attend college. At this point, Frank Hosmer and several other community leaders created a fund to send William to college. Du Bois's white benefactors decided that he should attend Fisk University, a Congregational institution for African Americans in Nashville, Tennessee, rather than Harvard, however.[17]

Du Bois, age 17, left Great Barrington in 1885 and made his first journey to the South to enroll at Fisk University, an institution of 450 students that had been founded in 1866 by the American Missionary Society. The faculty of 15, 14 white and 1 black, were dedicated Congregationalists who were still motivated by the spirit of New England abolitionism. Unlike Hampton and Tuskegee's industrial training programs, Fisk's curriculum was academic in the classical sense. It included Greek, Latin, French, German, theology, natural sciences, music, moral philosophy, and history, subjects Booker T. Washington would disdain as ornamental.[18] Although Du Bois found himself well prepared for college, he noted that many of the other students, graduates of segregated Southern black secondary schools, were ill-prepared for higher education. At Fisk, Du Bois excelled in Latin, Greek, French, rhetoric, botany, and calculus. Pursuing his love of history, he read Carlyle's *On Heroes, Hero-Worship, and the Heroic in History*, which advanced the thesis that great men were the principal agents in history.[19] Like Hosmer, Du Bois's professors at Fisk recognized his academic talent and saw him as one likely to achieve distinction in scholarship.

As in high school, Du Bois was attracted to journalism and editing. He worked on the staff of the *Fisk Herald*, the university newspaper, and became editor-in-chief in his senior year. He made his first sortie into fiction, writing "Tom Brown at Fisk," which was serialized in the *Herald*.[20] Attracted to cultural activities, he joined the Mozart Society, a choral group.[21] As a student at Fisk, he came face to face with the South's racial segregation. The New England native's confrontations with racism were turning him into an activist who would battle segregation.

In 1886, Du Bois, deciding not to spend summer vacation in Great Barrington, determined to learn firsthand about the lives and situations of rural southern African Americans. After taking education courses at the Lebanon Teachers's Institute, he passed the elementary teachers' examination and was issued a teaching certificate.

In the summers of 1886 and 1887, Du Bois taught in a small rural black elementary school near Alexandria in east Tennessee for a salary of 28 dollars per month. Housed in an abandoned log storage barn, the school enrolled 15 students, ranging in age from

6 to 20.[22] While teaching rural black children in this dilapidated school, Du Bois had a graphic exposure to the consequences of racism and segregation and debilitating rural poverty.[23] Du Bois's attendance at Fisk University and his teaching experience made him conscious of his race and its condition in a South that was erecting rigid walls of segregation.

In June 1888, Du Bois graduated from Fisk University. His commencement address was an oration on Otto von Bismarck, the "Iron Chancellor," who had unified Germany through a policy of diplomacy and military force. African Americans, Du Bois argued, needed leaders like the German chancellor who could raise consciousness and create a mobilized and disciplined people.[24] Even at this early stage in his academic career, Du Bois was moving in the direction of the need for a highly educated black vanguard, the "talented tenth."

Du Bois had not abandoned his high school dream of earning a degree from Harvard University. He was convinced, contrary to Booker T. Washington's doctrine of the need to create a class of black tradesmen and farmers, that an important road to black equality would be through higher and professional education. In 1888, Du Bois, the sixth African American to be enrolled up to that time at Harvard, was admitted with junior standing and awarded a scholarship to support his study.[25]

As a Harvard student, Du Bois encountered a generation of professors who were luminaries in their academic disciplines. He studied philosophy with George Santayana. He was particularly impressed by William James, who was propounding his own version of Pragmatic philosophy and psychology in his books, *Principles of Psychology* (1890) and *The Will to Believe* (1897). James became a personal friend and provided sound academic counsel to the aspiring Du Bois. Du Bois also came to incorporate an element of Pragmatism into his emerging outlook. His study of economics under Charles Dunbar and Frank Taussig made him a devotee of laissez-faire economic theory, a commitment he later abandoned for Marxism. Once again, Du Bois impressed his professors with his academic talents. He graduated *cum laude* on June 25, 1890, earning his bachelor's degree with a concentration in philosophy.[26]

Du Bois now began his graduate study at Harvard. After some hesitation between philosophy and history as a career choice, Du Bois decided on history, a subject he pursued under Professor Albert Bushnell Hart's direction. Hart was noted for his emphasis on basing interpretation on solid original primary sources. Du Bois's work with Hart was particularly useful in developing an historical competency that he would combine with sociology. Du Bois's expertise in historical sociology was particularly effective in his research on Philadelphia's black community, which would later earn him academic fame.[27]

From 1890 to 1892, Du Bois pursued graduate studies in history as well as taking courses in economics and political science. In 1891, he was awarded his master of arts degree in history and was admitted to the doctoral program in social science. He also began research on his dissertation, "The Suppression of the African Slave-Trade to the United States of America, 1638–1870."[28]

As was then the academic custom, Du Bois went to Germany to complete his higher academic studies. German universities were preeminent in the new scholarship, in which a small number of carefully selected graduate students worked in seminars with distinguished professors who were specialists in their academic disciplines. Young Americans aspiring to be professors would travel to Germany, seek admission to a leading research university, and then import the new scholarship to U.S. higher education. The German universities emphasized research and publication, two activities in which Du Bois would excel as a university professor. Supported by the Slater Fund, Du Bois traveled in 1892 to Europe with the goal of enrolling at a German university.[29]

After traveling through western Europe and intensively studying the German language, Du Bois enrolled at Berlin's premier Friedrich Wilhelm University. Here, until 1894, he studied the social sciences with such leading experts as Gustav Schmoller, the economist, Rudolph von Gneist and Heinrich von Treitschke, the political scientists, and Max Weber, the sociologist. His studies in Berlin reinforced what Hart had emphasized in historiography. Theoretical hypotheses were to be formulated only after completing very meticulous research into actual social, political, and economic phenomena. When Du Bois was in Berlin, German philosophy was dominated by Hegelian idealism, which exalted the nation-state as the earthly embodiment of the Absolute. Captivated by the Hegelian dialectical process, Du Bois began to interpret race relations as a clash of thesis, the former slave master, and the antithesis, the freed slave.

Despite his excellent academic record at the Friedrich Wilhelm University, Du Bois confronted the academic obstacles that blocked the careers of many graduate students. The majority of the faculty voted that Du Bois was ineligible for doctoral examinations because he had not satisfied residency requirements. Du Bois's scholarship support ended and economic circumstances forced his return to the United States to complete a Harvard doctorate rather than one in Berlin. Apparently, the administrative decision at Berlin was based on academic rigidity rather than racial prejudice. Du Bois encountered little antiblack discrimination in Europe. However, he was stunned by the degree of nationalism and ethnic hostility, especially the strong undercurrent of anti-Semitism.[30] Du Bois's European venture broadened his intellectual worldview so that he came to see racial relations in an international and pan-African perspective that included the African American experience in the United States. Long before Alex Haley gained prominence as the author of *Roots*, Du Bois saw connections between the struggle of blacks in the United States against racial segregation and black Africans against an exploitative European colonialism. Du Bois believed that black people in the United States needed to become conscious and proud of their African heritage. Such heightened consciousness would be an asset in the coming struggle for civil and educational rights. Blacks in Africa, too, needed to draw on the resources of their cultural heritage in the coming struggle against colonial rule.

While in Europe, Du Bois encountered the theories of Karl Marx, which were popular in Socialist and Communist circles. His later attraction to Marxism and his international orientation brought a new dimension to his views of the black situation in the United States, to his scholarship, and to his social activism. He came to believe that blacks were victims, as were working-class whites, of an exploitative capitalism. Once again, Du Bois's background deviated from that of Booker T. Washington, whose life, with the exception of some European travel late in his career, was based largely in the American South.

Du Bois returned to the United States in 1894 and completed his doctoral studies at Harvard. In 1895, Harvard University accepted his doctoral dissertation, which was subsequently published as a book in the Harvard Historical Studies Series.[31]

From 1894 through 1896, Du Bois was professor of classics at Wilberforce University, an institution affiliated with the African Methodist Episcopal Church, in Xenia, Ohio. Assigned a heavy teaching load in Latin, Greek, and German, Du Bois missed teaching history and sociology, his areas of specialization. He was a rigorous, demanding, and somewhat aloof teacher. He disliked the paternalistic administration and atmosphere of religious conformity at Wilberforce University. While at Wilberforce, the young professor married Nina Gomer, an undergraduate student from Cedar Rapids, Iowa. After their marriage in Iowa, the couple returned to Wilberforce to live in a small two-room apartment in the men's dormitory.

In 1896, a research opportunity enabled Du Bois and his wife to leave Wilberforce. The University of Pennsylvania was conducting a comprehensive historical and sociological study of Philadelphia's African American population, which at 40,000 was the nation's largest northern black community. As the project's research director, Du Bois conducted a monumental and often-cited sociological study of the black community. Pioneering in sociological survey methods, his detailed study examined family structure, neighborhoods, social organizations, educational institutions, political involvement, and economic roles. Du Bois's *The Philadelphia Negro*, published in 1899, provided significant generalizations about the development and problems of Philadelphia's African American community.[32]

Though not the sole cause of disadvantagement, Du Bois established that racial discrimination was a powerful determinant in limiting African American socioeconomic and educational opportunities. African Americans were still the historic victims of slavery, which continued to affect their family structure, work ethic, and class behavior. Du Bois also discerned an evolving class structure within the Philadelphia black community: a small elite, a moderate-size middle class, a large strata of working poor, and those lowest on the socioeconomic scale, the "submerged tenth." His findings in the Philadelphia study contributed to his evolving strategy of racial change. He believed that a well-educated elite, the "talented tenth," would lead the African American advance.[33]

Du Bois's Philadelphia study made him a recognized scholar in sociology, especially in the subfield of historical sociology. In addition to using archival documents, Du Bois had taken his study into Philadelphia's streets. He surveyed several thousand members of the community and interviewed several hundred of them. He visited their institutions, homes, schools, and other agencies of community life.[34] Du Bois generated a massive database and reached significant conclusions that could be used in later reform efforts.

In 1897, Du Bois accepted a position as a professor of economics and history at Atlanta University in Georgia. Established by Congregationalists after the Civil War, Atlanta University, an African American institution of higher learning, offered both a traditional academic curriculum as well as some vocational programs. For 13 years, Du Bois taught history, sociology, and economics at Atlanta University. As a teacher, Du Bois, a "no-nonsense" instructor, appealed most to bright, academically talented students. Others tended to be intimidated by his erudition and demanding course requirements.

Du Bois coordinated the annual Atlanta University Conference on Negro Problems. The conference's proceedings, a knowledge base on African American culture, documented significant changes in black communities. Important shifts were taking place in African American demographics as large-scale migration was under way from rural to urban areas and from South to North. Using an extensive survey method,

Du Bois documented growing educational disparities between the schooling of black and white children.

While at Atlanta Du Bois articulated his educational concept of the "talented tenth." Although all blacks should enjoy the equality of educational opportunity denied them by the institutionalized racism of a segregated society, Du Bois argued that all races, including blacks, had an intellectually gifted elite. This elite—the talented tenth—should have the advantage of higher and professional education. As African Americans struggled for equal rights, the talented tenth would be the leadership vanguard of the movement.

While a professor at Atlanta University, Du Bois continued to write and publish. His *The Souls of Black Folk*, a collection of essays on African American life and culture, was published in 1903.[35] *Souls of Black Folk* added a new dimension to the literature on African Americans as it examined the social and cultural psyches of people of African descent in the Americas. In 1909 he published *John Brown*, his biography of the radical abolitionist who led an abortive attempt at Harper's Ferry to free the slaves.[36] Du Bois also served as a consultant for the U.S. Department of Labor.

Booker T. Washington, often called the "Wizard" because of his adroit political sagacity, began to feel threatened by Du Bois's rising star. For a time, these two very different men had cooperated. Washington had even offered Du Bois a position at Tuskegee, which Du Bois declined. Washington had become a recognized leader of African Americans. What was called the Tuskegee Machine controlled the appointment of many African Americans to political and educational positions. Du Bois had become convinced that Washington's accommodationist policy had to be challenged and discredited so that African Americans would pursue a more militant and activist course.

Du Bois's relationship with Washington had begun as admiration for the Tuskegee educator but it had turned to apprehension that Washington was leading African Americans down a disastrous path. Finally, it deteriorated into open antagonism. Du Bois accused Washington of encouraging African Americans to renounce three necessary means of empowerment: political organization, the legal pursuit of civil rights, and participation in higher education.[37]

Washington and Du Bois had different origins, temperaments, and ideologies. Washington's origins and attitudes were of the rural South; Du Bois was a cosmopolitan scholar. While both were skilled speakers, Washington, the educator-politician, was expert in using crowd psychology to assess his audience and use anecdotes and humor in winning it to his point of view. The scholarly Du Bois was more of a cool intellectual who used logical argument to put forth his agenda. For Du Bois, the higher education of able African Americans was necessary for black empowerment. For Washington, industrial education and the ownership of small businesses were the more realistic course. In his masterful biography of Du Bois, David Levering Lewis finds that Washington and Du Bois were addressing "two dissimilar socioeconomic orders" and "speaking past each other" rather than analyzing the same racial issues. Washington's impoverished agricultural rural South with its racism, embedded from slavery, was unready for the Du Bois's agenda. Conversely, Washington's passive accommodationism was not a viable program for racial progress in the "urban, industrial, multiethnic North." While Washington's ideology was rooted in the South's past, Du Bois spoke for a more national, indeed global, future.[38]

By 1905, Du Bois, with a like-minded group of blacks and whites, met at Fort Erie, Ontario, on the Canadian side of Niagara Falls, to form an organization and develop a strategy to advance African American civil rights. Taking a proactive stance that ran counter to Booker T. Washington's gradualism, the group, organized as the "Niagara Movement," named Du Bois its general secretary, a position he held until 1910.

In 1910, the National Negro Committee, an interracial group that included Du Bois and others of the Niagara Movement, officially reorganized as the National Association for the Advancement of Colored People (NAACP). The new organization united leading blacks and whites to work for the civil, social, and educational progress of African Americans. The NAACP elected Moorfield Storey, a past president of the American Bar Association, as its president. With Du Bois, the other leaders of the NAACP were Mary Ovington, a progressive organizer, Rabbi Stephen Wise, Oswald Garrison Villard, and other national figures. Two prominent black ministers, Bishop Alexander Walters and the Reverend William Brooks, were among the founders. In contrast to Washington's accommodationism, the NAACP developed the following strategy:

- Raise black consciousness and act as a unified voice for African Americans.
- Embark on a general educational program to inform both blacks and whites about the condition of African Americans in the United States.
- Begin the legal battle to end legally sanctioned racial segregation in the United States. (This battle eventually led to victory in the *Brown* decision in that 1954 overturned *Plessy v. Ferguson*.)

In 1910, Du Bois was appointed the NAACP's director of publicity and research, made a member of its board of directors, and named editor of *The Crisis*, the association's official journal. He was ideally suited for the position of editor. Since his high school days in Great Barrington and as an undergraduate at Fisk University, he had been involved in journalism as a writer and an editor. A first-rate scholar with proven academic credentials, Du Bois, a gifted editorialist, was adept at drafting a readable argument for a wide audience. Under his editorship, *The Crisis* addressed a range of issues relating to the black situation in the United States. Despite opposition from the conservative Booker T. Washington and his Tuskegee Machine, *The Crisis* was becoming a force in raising black consciousness from passive accommodation to activism.[39]

Under Du Bois's editorship, *The Crisis*'s circulation steadily increased. Its subscribers, numbering 3,000 in 1911, reached 22,500 by 1912, 33,000 by 1914, and 45,000 by 1916.[40] Despite his success with *The Crisis*, Du Bois, a demanding personality, was often in conflict with the other trustees.

In addition to his work in the NAACP, Du Bois continued as scholar, historian, sociologist, and writer. In 1911, his book *The Quest for the Silver Fleece* appeared. It was followed by *The Negro* (1915), *Darkwater: Voices from Within the Veil* (1920), and *The Gift of Black Folk* (1924).[41]

From 1910 onward, the years in which Du Bois labored to establish and give momentum to the NAACP, especially in the period between World Wars I and II, momentous changes were occurring among the African American population. First, blacks were no longer concentrated in the rural South. The wars generated employment needs and had expanded the job market in the United States. By the thousands, blacks migrated from the rural South to Northern cities to take jobs and improve their economic condition. Large black communities developed in the cities of New York, Philadelphia,

Boston, Chicago, Detroit, and Cleveland. Blacks joined labor unions and a new spirit of activism was born.

Second, the condition of African Americans had grown more complex and varied than it had been in the days of Booker T. Washington. An urban black community now existed along with the Southern rural and agricultural community. Further, Washington's death in 1915 left a leadership void among more conservative and accommodationist blacks. Three, a new attitude was emerging among African Americans, especially the young. Soldiers who had fought for democracy abroad in both world wars were no longer willing to accept oppression in their native land. These factors gave a new momentum to the movement for civil rights and educational opportunities.

Although Du Bois never gained the prominence that Washington had enjoyed, he was nonetheless one of the leaders of the rising black movement in the United States. Along with his important role in the NAACP, he was involved in cultural, educational, and political affairs and was especially interested in helping aspiring young black artists, writers, and poets in their careers. Achievement in the arts by African Americans was both a way of contributing to U.S. and world culture generally and of raising black consciousness and self-esteem particularly. In the 1920s and early 1930s, he encouraged African American writers, artists, poets, and actors who were part of the Harlem Renaissance, such as Countee Cullen, Jean Toomer, Langston Hughes, and Claude McKay. Du Bois helped arrange conferences, performances, and concerts as well as meetings and appointments with publishers and sponsors.

Throughout his life, Du Bois was involved in education. His articles and books were important sources on African American history and culture. In addition to these formal educational activities, Du Bois was an important informal educator as editor of *The Crisis*. Along with the law and political organization, Du Bois saw education as an important instrument in the struggle for equality. His theory of the talented tenth was intended to create a leadership elite. However, he was also concerned that blacks receive the best elementary and secondary education their talents would allow. To this end, he joined Jessie Redmond Fauset, a teacher in the New York City public schools, to publish *The Brownies' Book*, a children's monthly magazine. Designed to stimulate black children's early learning and to provide them with models, *The Brownies' Book* contained stories, legends, and poems.[42]

Ideologically, Du Bois felt a growing attraction to Marxism. In 1911, Du Bois, who believed that blacks in the United States were victims of capitalist exploitation, joined the American Socialist party, then led by Eugene V. Debs. During World War I, however, Du Bois supported the war effort, unlike the Socialist party, which opposed American intervention. In the later part of his life, Du Bois joined and participated in left-wing political organizations and movements. He saw both Republicans and Democrats as unwilling to take the necessary political risks to support full civil rights for blacks and other minority groups.

During the Great Depression of the 1930s, Du Bois proposed organizing black-run cooperatives to ease the economic plight of African Americans. His proposal was not supported by the NAACP's board of directors, who believed it might encourage racial separatism rather than integration. Du Bois, a person of strong opinions, became embroiled in disputes with the more conservative members of the association. In 1934, he resigned from NAACP's board of directors and as editor of *The Crisis*. He returned to Atlanta University as professor and chairman of the Department of Sociology. For the next 10 years, he remained at Atlanta University, until he was reconciled with the leadership of the NAACP and returned to work for that organization. During this time, he wrote several important books. His *Black Reconstruction: An Essay Toward a History of the Part Which Black Folk Played in the Attempt to Reconstruct Democracy in America, 1860–1880*, appearing in 1935, was a formidable scholarly work in the revisionist movement in interpreting the crucial reconstructionist period.[43] This book was followed by *Black Folk Then and Now* (1939) and *Dusk of Dawn: An Essay Toward an Autobiography of a Race Concept* (1940).[44]

In 1944, Du Bois returned to the NAACP's national staff as director of special research. When World War II ended, his activities began to shift to the international scene. He was particularly interested that postwar reconstruction would end colonialism and bring political independence to the European powers' colonies in Africa and Asia. He was a leader in the pan-African conferences that were held periodically. In 1945, he was a consultant to the U.S. delegation at the founding of the United Nations. His global interests were reflected in his books, *Color and Democracy: Colonies and Peace* (1945) and *The World and Africa: An Inquiry into the Part Which Africa Has Played in World History* (1947).[45]

In the early stages of the Cold War when the general political mood in the United States was becoming more anti-Communist, Du Bois moved steadily toward the left. As Cold War tensions deepened between the United States and the Soviet Union, Du Bois was accused of being a Soviet sympathizer and a member of Communist front organizations.

As a result of internal tensions in the NAACP, in 1949 Du Bois was dismissed from his position in the organization. Moving steadily to the left in his thinking, Du Bois believed that the Soviet Union was one of the few nations that practiced genuine racial equality. In 1950, he attended the All-Union Conference of Peace Proponents in Moscow. He either did not understand or misinterpreted the effects of Stalinism in the Soviet Union and the totalitarian police state over which the Soviet dictator had presided since the 1930s. As Khrushchev revealed in the early 1960s, the tyrannical Stalin had engineered the mass extermination of millions of Soviet citizens.

In the early 1950s, the United States was undergoing anti-Communist investigations against alleged subversives in the U.S. government and in educational institutions, especially colleges and universities. The country was in the grip of the "witch hunting" inquisition carried on by Senator Joseph McCarthy, who recklessly exploited the highly charged atmosphere for political advantage. Du Bois, who did not conceal his Marxist ideology or his positive attitude toward the Soviet Union, was especially suspect during this period. An official of the Peace Information Center, Du Bois was investigated as a member of what was alleged to be a Communist "front organization." When the U.S. Justice Department required Du Bois and the Peace Information Center to register as agents of a foreign government in 1951, Du Bois refused to comply. Du Bois and other officers of the center were indicted and brought to trial. The case eventually reached the U.S. Supreme Court, where Du Bois and his associates were acquitted on the grounds that the Justice Department had failed to prove its allegations. In 1952, Du Bois wrote about the trial and his work for international peace, *In Battle for Peace: The Story of My 83rd Birthday.*[46]

Nina Du Bois, his wife of 54 years, died on July 1, 1950. She had been an invalid since suffering a stroke five years earlier. In February 1951, the 83-year-old Du Bois married Shirley Graham, a close friend and coworker from the Peace Information Center.

From 1952 to 1958, the U.S. government refused to issue a passport to Du Bois, who had received invitations to visit many of the newly independent African nations. He again turned to writing and produced a trilogy—*The Ordeal of Mansart* (1957), *Mansart Builds a School* (1959), and *The Worlds of Color* (1961).[47]

In 1958, passports were finally issued to Du Bois and his second wife, who embarked on a world tour. In the Soviet Union, he was awarded the Lenin Peace Prize. In 1961, dissatisfied with the slow pace of racial change and the political situation in the United States, Du Bois accepted the invitation of President Kwame Nkrumah of Ghana to direct a massive research project designed to produce an African encyclopedia. In 1963, he became a Ghanese citizen. On August 27, 1963, Du Bois died at the age of 95. The former professor, editor, and activist was accorded a state funeral on August 29, 1963, symbolizing his role as a pan-African leader.

The Social and Educational Ideas of W. E. B. Du Bois

During Du Bois's life of nearly a century, the conditions of African Americans in the United States went through many changes. Through these various alterations, Du Bois consistently advocated civil rights and equality of educational opportunity for blacks and other members of U.S. society denied these rights. His philosophy of education, reflecting his scholarly work in history and sociology, contained a Pragmatic bent in that scholarly research was to be used for social and economic improvement. In the later phase of his career, he placed his ideas and insights into a Marxist frame of interpretation that saw social and racial relations in the larger framework of dialectical materialism and class struggle.[48]

Among Du Bois's most insightful books on African American culture in the United States is *Souls of Black Folk* (1903), which is his own autobiography as well as a panoramic historical, sociological, and philosophical commentary on black culture in America. In it, he examines what it means for him and other African Americans to be regarded as a "problem" by whites. He explores the idea that African Americans live with a double consciousness—a sense of being black and also of being members of a larger white-dominated culture. The book deals with history, education, social relations and also with an important aspect of African American heritage—the Sorrow Songs. The Sorrow Songs conveyed the hope that slavery will end and that blacks will be set free in the "promised land." Using religious images from the Old Testament, such songs as "Go Down Moses" and "Swing Low, Sweet Chariot" expressed the desire for freedom in a way that could be hidden from the slave owners. In some ways, Du Bois's search for meaning in the Sorrow Songs was an attempt to find the soul of African Americans in their musical heritage. In the book, Du Bois identified the "color line" that separated white and black Americans as the nation's most pressing problem.

Du Bois's social and educational ideas can be examined first in terms of his strategy to further African American progress, especially his opposition to Booker T. Washington's accommodationism. Though both Washington and Du Bois agreed on the need to improve the economic conditions of African Americans and foster self-sufficiency, they took different paths.[49] As indicated earlier, Washington's strategy was based on building an economic base for blacks in a gradual and incremental way that did not challenge the existing white power structure. Du Bois challenged Washington, and the president of Tuskegee Institute responded by opposing Du Bois.

To organize and mobilize African Americans, Du Bois believed that Washington had to be displaced as the spokesman of black America. This task, however, was formidable. Du Bois basically argued that Washington's political passivity, gradualism, and philosophy of industrial education would perpetuate a racially based caste system in the United States. Du Bois judged Washington as an accomplice in maintaining a system that relegated blacks to second-class citizenship and a subordinate economic and educational position.

In *The Souls of Black Folk*, Du Bois examined the social, cultural, and educational aspects of black life in America. He appealed to African American intellectuals to take the initiative in working for voting rights, civil rights, and equal access to colleges and universities. His essay, "Booker T. Washington and Others," attacked the senior black leader for weakening African American political power, for jeopardizing their civil rights, and for discouraging the entry of black youth into higher education. Because of Washington's accommodationist strategy, blacks had been politically disenfranchised. The laws of many states, especially in the South, had legally relegated African Americans to an inferior civil and educational position.[50] In a stinging rebuke of Washington's philosophy of industrial education, Du Bois wrote,

1. He is striving to make Negro artisans businessmen and property-owners; but it is utterly impossible, under modern competitive methods, for workingmen and property-owners to defend their rights and exist without the right of suffrage.
2. He insists on thrift and self-respect, but at the same time counsels a silent submission to civic inferiority such as is bound to sap the manhood of any race in the long run.
3. He advocates common-school and industrial training, and depreciates institutions of higher learning; but neither the Negro common-schools, nor Tuskegee itself, could remain open a day were it not for teachers trained in Negro colleges, or trained by their graduates.[51]

In contrast to Washington's industrial education, Du Bois made higher education a key plank in his educational philosophy. It was in colleges, universities, and professional schools that the African American intellectual elite, the vanguard of the movement, the talented tenth, would be educated. Again opposing Washington's strategy that the process of educational and social change for blacks should work its way upward from the bottom, Du Bois believed it should be led from the top by African Americans with higher and professional educations. For Du Bois, social progress came as "more often a pull than a push" as an exceptional leader lifted "his duller brethren slowly and painfully to his vantage-ground."[52]

Du Bois accorded higher education a highly important cultural significance in his educational philosophy. Although often associated with the history of African Americans in higher education, Du Bois's academic work exercised a more general impact on scholarship, especially in history and sociology.[53] This cultural perspective on higher education was already evident in 1903 when Du Bois wrote:

The function of the Negro college, then is clear: it must maintain the standards of popular education, it must seek the social regeneration of the Negro, and it must help in the solution of problems of race contact and co-operation. And finally, beyond all this, it must develop men.[54]

Although he was most concerned with higher education, Du Bois had opinions about elementary and secondary education. He took a broad view of education, defining it as all that shapes a person's outlook and behavior. In commenting on children's education, he wrote,

Children must be trained in a knowledge of what the world is and what it knows and how it does its daily work. These things cannot be separated: we cannot teach pure knowledge apart from actual facts, or separate truth from the human mind. Above all we must not forget that the object of all education is the child itself and not what it does or makes.[55]

For Du Bois, the first years of public schooling, regardless of the child's race or class, should cultivate basic literacy and communication skills. It should also broaden children's horizons of space, time, and events by introducing them to the "extraordinary multiplicity of the world's things."[56] Like John Dewey, Du Bois recognized the educative value of a learning environment that was rich in objects that could stimulate children's interests and curiosity. The poverty-ridden neighborhood and the ramshackle school had little of the "things" that enriched a child's experience.

Differing from Washington's emphasis on vocational education, Du Bois opposed early or premature vocational education that turned children's early education into training for the trades, farming, or domestic service. Although the world of work might be introduced to students, who could study the major human occupations and professions, this introduction should be educational in the broad sense rather than be specific training. Premature vocational training tended to limit children's general education and future career choice. Du Bois believed black children, like all children, should learn to read, write, calculate, and broaden their horizons by studying history, geography, and literature rather than being trained for particular jobs. Du Bois did not oppose technical education but he did not want it to come too early, nor to be a substitute for general education.

An early pioneer of the contemporary Afrocentric curriculum, Du Bois was concerned many textbook accounts of American history and world civilization were biased by a distorted interpretation of history, a "miseducation," and were Eurocentric and ignored the contributions of African and Asians. Du Bois's *Black Reconstruction* sought to correct the version of Reconstruction that portrayed it as an economically unproductive and politically corrupt era. Du Bois and the African American historian Carter G. Woodson sought to correct the historical record by pointing to the important achievements of the Reconstruction legislatures in establishing an economic and educational infrastructure in the South.[57] To correct the Eurocentric version of world history, Du Bois's *The Negro* (1915), a seminal work in Afrocentric scholarship, examined the cultural and political sophistication and complexity of precolonial Africa.[58] In it, Du Bois explored the development of ancient African cultures in the Neolithic age and, like the modern scholar Bernal, the Hamitic foundations of ancient civilizations.[59] Du Bois's books *Africa: Its Place in Modern History* (1930); *Africa: Its Geography, People, and Products* (1930); and *The World and Africa: An Inquiry into the Part Which Africa Has Played in World History* (1947) provided a knowledge base that helped bring the study of Africa into the curriculum.[60] Rather than being a historical "add on," Du Bois sought to infuse African history into the general narrative of world history. Although Du Bois, as a historian, was interested in tracing African American roots to Africa, his pan-African studies laid foundations of a worldwide black activism. According to Du Bois,

> There has been consistent effort to rationalize Negro slavery by omitting Africa from world history, so that today it is almost universally assumed that history can be truly written without reference to Negroid peoples. I believe this to be scientifically unsound and also dangerous for logical social conclusions.[61]

An African perspective was especially important for African Americans who, living in two worlds—that of the black community and that of the white-dominated society—developed a "double-consciousness."[62] Knowledge of their African roots and heritage could provide a psychic foundation on which to create an African American identity within the larger American society.

In addition to his pan-Africanism, Du Bois developed an international perspective that stressed the reality of a multicultural world society and the importance of education in a multicultural context. He advised African Americans to overcome their cultural isolation and to become reunited with their African origins and roots. Through his travel and education, Du Bois had become a citizen of the world. For him, it was particularly important that African Americans become multilingual. He urged African Americans to improve their foreign language abilities in order to communicate with black people throughout the world. Outside of the United States, many black people in Africa, South America, and the Caribbean spoke either French, Spanish, or Portuguese. American blacks should study these modern languages rather than the ancient Greek, Latin, and Hebrew languages. In every black community in the United States there should be classes in the modern languages that blacks speak in other countries and libraries that feature magazines and books in these languages. While having personal self-esteem and pride in their African heritage, African American children should learn they are inhabitants of a multicultural and multiracial world.

Conclusion: An Assessment

As a leader in the movement for African American civil rights and equality, W. E. B. Du Bois was of a different character, disposition, and background from others such as Dr. Martin Luther King, Jr. Whereas King had Southern roots, was immersed in black Christianity, and practiced nonviolent, Gandhi-inspired passive resistance, Du Bois combined scholarship with activism. He was a consummate researcher, historian, and sociologist as well as political strategist. A person of firmly held beliefs, Du Bois had little patience with those who could not fashion a clear and logical argument.

Du Bois's work moved history forward and contributed to the coming struggle for civil rights. After a long series of court cases, the strategy of the NAACP was fulfilled in 1954 in the case of *Brown v. The Board of Education of Topeka, Kansas*. Using sociological and psychological evidence, the NAACP sought successfully to overturn the earlier *Plessy v. Ferguson* decision, which had established the "separate but equal" precedent. Thurgood Marshall and the attorneys representing the plaintiffs in *Brown*, Oliver Brown and his daughter Linda, argued that segregated schools had a negative effect on the social and psychological development of black children. Speaking for the Supreme Court, Chief Justice Earl Warren answered the question, "Does segregation of children in public schools solely on the basis of race, even though the physical facilities and other 'tangible' factors may be equal, deprive the children of the minority group of equal education opportunities? We believe that it does." Warren went on:

> In the field of public education the doctrine of "separate but equal" has no place. Separate educational facilities are inherently unequal. Therefore, we hold the plaintiffs and others similarly situated for whom the actions have been brought are, by reason of the segregation complained of, deprived of the equal protection of the laws guaranteed by the Fourteenth Amendment.[63]

The Supreme Court's desegregation decision in *Brown* was but another phase in the Civil Rights Movement in the United States. The efforts of Dr. Martin Luther King, Jr., to organize a campaign against *de facto* segregation were just starting. Racial conflicts such as those that would occur at Little Rock, Arkansas, and the University of Mississippi were still ahead.

Although the African American struggle for civil and educational rights had enlisted Du Bois's attention for most of his life, he is also important because of his scholarly contributions in sociology and history, which examined the black experience in the United States and in the world. Du Bois's books were important sources that anticipated the African American and black studies programs that developed at many colleges and universities. Du Bois, always concerned with historical accuracy and sociological validity in his research and writing, made valuable contributions to these disciplines.

Questions for Reflection and Dialogue

1. Reflect on DuBois's concept of "double consciousness." What does it mean for African Americans? Consider your own experience. Have you ever felt that you were living with a double consciousness in two worlds? What problems does that feeling create?
2. What was the general social, economic, and educational condition of African Americans at the end of the Reconstruction period?
3. Describe the major features of Booker T. Washington's philosophy of education.
4. How did the contexts differ in which Booker T. Washington and W. E. B. Du Bois lived and worked?
5. How did the key events in Du Bois's life shape his social and educational perspective?

6. What were the key points in Du Bois's criticism of Washington?
7. How did Du Bois contribute to Afrocentric scholarship and curriculum?

Projects for Deepening Your Understanding

1. For a period of time, such as two weeks, watch the news on television. Keep a log on how much of the coverage is devoted to Africa and what is featured. How do you think Du Bois would react to this coverage?
2. Review the literature on multicultural education. How do you think Du Bois would react to the movement for multicultural education?
3. Read and review one of Du Bois's books (see Suggestions for Further Reading).
4. In a research paper, examine Du Bois as a pan-Africanist.
5. In a paper, assess Du Bois's contributions and significance in U.S. social and educational thought.
6. Examine the African American studies program at your college or university and determine if it has been influenced by Du Bois's ideas and scholarship.

Notes

1. David Levering Lewis, *W. E. B. Du Bois: Biography of a Race, 1868–1919* (New York: Henry Holt, 1993), 3.
2. The interplay of race and religion in the new common schools in the South is examined in Ward M. McAfee, *Religion, Race, and Reconstruction: The Public Schools in the Politics of the 1870s* (Albany, NY: State University of New York Press, 1998).
3. Louis Harlan, *Booker T. Washington: The Making of a Black Leader, 1856–1901* (New York: Oxford University Press, 1972), 61–64.
4. Booker T. Washington, ed., *Tuskegee and Its People: Their Ideals and Achievements* (New York: Appleton, 1905); and Washington, *The Future of the American Negro* (Boston: Small, Maynard, 1900), 108–10.
5. Washington, *The Future of the American Negro*, 111–12.
6. Victoria E. Matthews, *Black-Belt Diamonds: Gems from the Speeches, Addresses, and Talks to Students of Booker T. Washington* (New York: Fortune & Scott, 1989), 8.
7. Lewis, *Du Bois: Biography of a Race*, 260.
8. For the repression of African Americans in the South, see Leon F. Litwack, *Trouble in Mind: Black Southerners in the Age of Jim Crow* (New York: Alfred A. Knopf, 1998).

9. Booker T. Washington, "The Atlanta Exposition Address," quoted in *Booker T. Washington and His Critics*, ed. Hugh Hawkins (Boston: D. C. Heath, 1962), 17.
10. Richard Kluger, *Simple Justice* (New York: Alfred A. Knopf, 1976), 73–74.
11. Manning Marable, *W. E. B. Du Bois: Black Radical Democrat* (Boston: Twayne, 1986), 2–3.
12. Lewis, *Du Bois: Biography of a Race*, 15.
13. Virginia Hamilton, *W. E. B. Du Bois: A Biography* (New York: Thomas Y. Crowell, 1972), 15.
14. Marable, *Du Bois: Black Radical Democrat*, 4.
15. Marable, *Du Bois: Black Radical Democrat*, 4–6.
16. Lewis, *Du Bois: Biography of a Race*, 50.
17. Marable, *Du Bois: Black Radical Democrat*, 7.
18. Lewis, *Du Bois: Biography of a Race*, 58–59.
19. Lewis, *Du Bois: Biography of a Race*, 75.
20. Lewis, *Du Bois: Biography of a Race*, 74.
21. Marable, *Du Bois: Black Radical Democrat*, 9.
22. Lewis, *Du Bois: Biography of a Race*, 68–69.
23. Marable, *Du Bois: Black Radical Democrat*, 9–10.
24. Lewis, *Du Bois: Biography of a Race*, 77.
25. W. E. B. Du Bois, *The Autobiography of W. E. B. Du Bois: A Soliloquy on Viewing My Life from the Last Decade of its First Century*, ed. Herbert Aptheker (New York: International, 1968), 107.
26. Lewis, *Du Bois: Biography of a Race*, 84–88.
27. Hamilton, *Du Bois: A Biography*, 15.

28. Marable, *Du Bois: Black Radical Democrat*, 15.
29. Lewis, *Du Bois: Biography of a Race*, 117.
30. Marable, *Du Bois: Black Radical Democrat*, 17–20.
31. W. E. B. Du Bois, *The Suppression of the African Slave-Trade to the United States of America, 1638–1870* (New York: Longmans, Green, 1896).
32. W. E. B. Du Bois, *The Philadelphia Negro: A Social Study* (Philadelphia: University of Pennsylvania Press, 1899).
33. Lewis, *Du Bois: Biography of a Race*, 206.
34. For a reappraisal of Du Bois's research, see Michael B. Katz and Thomas J. Sugrue, eds., *W. E. B. Du Bois, Race, and the City:* The Philadelphia Negro *and Its Legacy* (Philadelphia: University of Pennsylvania Press, 1998).
35. W. E. B. Du Bois, *The Souls of Black Folk: Essays and Sketches* (Chicago: A. C. McClurg, 1903).
36. W. E. B. Du Bois, *John Brown* (Philadelphia: George W. Jacobs, 1909).
37. Lewis, *Du Bois: Biography of a Race*, 288.
38. Lewis, *Du Bois: Biography of a Race*, 502.
39. Hamilton, *Du Bois: A Biography*, 104.
40. Lewis, *Du Bois: Biography of a Race*, 416, 474, 514.
41. W. E. B. Du Bois, *The Quest of the Silver Fleece: A Novel* (Chicago: A. C. McClurg, 1911); Du Bois, *The Negro* (New York: Henry Holt, 1915); Du Bois, *Darkwater: Voices from Within the Veil* (New York: Harcourt Brace Jovanovich, 1920); Du Bois, *The Gift of Black Folk: Negroes in the Making of America* (Boston: Stratford, 1924).
42. Hamilton, *Du Bois: A Biography*, 133.
43. W. E. B. Du Bois, *Black Reconstruction: An Essay Toward a History of the Part Which Black Folk Played in the Attempt to Reconstruct Democracy in America, 1860–1880* (New York: Harcourt Brace Jovanovich, 1935).
44. W. E. B. Du Bois, *Black Folk Then and Now: An Essay on the History and Sociology of the Negro Race* (New York: Henry Holt, 1939); Du Bois, *Dusk of Dawn: An Essay toward an Autobiography of a Race Concept* (New York: Harcourt Brace Jovanovich, 1940).
45. W. E. B. Du Bois, *Color and Democracy: Colonies and Peace* (New York: Harcourt Brace Jovanovich, 1945); Du Bois, *The World and Africa: An Inquiry into the Part Which Africa Has Played in World History* (New York: Viking, 1947).
46. W. E. B. Du Bois, *In Battle for Peace: The Story of My 83rd Birthday* (New York: Masses and Mainstream, 1952).
47. W. E. B. Du Bois, *The Ordeal of Mansart* (New York: Masses and Mainstream, 1957); Du Bois, *Mansart Builds a School* (New York: Masses and Mainstream, 1959); Du Bois, *Worlds of Color* (New York: Masses and Mainstream, 1961).
48. For a highly useful discussion of Du Bois's educational philosophy, see Derrick P. Alridge, "Conceptualizing a Du Boisian Philosophy of Education: Toward A Model For African-American Education," *Educational Theory* 49, No. 3 (1999), 359–79.
49. Alridge, "Conceptualizing a Du Boisian Philosophy," 363.
50. Du Bois, *The Souls of Black Folk*, 15.
51. Du Bois, *The Souls of Black Folk*, 52.
52. Du Bois, *The Souls of Black Folk*, 84.
53. For Du Bois's impact on general scholarship, see Adolph L. Reed, Jr., *W. E. B. Du Bois and American Political Thought: Fabianism and the Color Line* (New York: Oxford University Press, 1997).
54. W. E. B. Du Bois, *The Souls of Black Folk*, ed. David W. Blight and Robert Gooding-Williams (Boston and New York: Bedford, 1997), 101.
55. Henry Lee Moon, *The Emerging Thought of W. E. B. Du Bois* (New York: Simon & Schuster, 1972), 125.
56. Moon, *The Emerging Thought of W. E. B. Du Bois*, 125.
57. Alridge, "Conceptualizing a Du Boisian Philosophy," 366–67.
58. Lewis, *Du Bois: Biography of a Race*, 462.
59. Martin Bernal, *Black Athena: The Afroasiatic Roots of Classical Civilization: The Fabrication of Ancient Greece 1785–1985* (New Brunswick, NJ: Rutgers University Press, 1987).
60. W. E. B. Du Bois, *Africa: Its Place in Modern History* (Girard, KS: Haldeman-Julius, 1930); Du Bois, *Africa: Its Geography, People and Products* (Girard, KS: Haldeman-Julius, 1930); Du Bois, *The World and Africa: An Inquiry into the Part Which Africa Has Played in World History* (New York: Viking, 1947).
61. Du Bois, *The World and Africa*, vii.
62. Alridge, "Conceptualizing a Du Boisian Philosophy," 370–71.
63. Chief Justice Earl Warren, quoted in Kluger, *Simple Justice*, 781–82.

Suggestions for Further Reading

Alridge, Derrick P. "Conceptualizing A Du Boisian Philosophy of Education: Toward a Model For African-American Education." *Educational Theory* 49, No. 3 (1999), 359–79.

Anderson, Elijah. *The Study of African American Problems: W. E. B. Du Bois's Agenda, Then and Now.* Thousand Oaks, CA: Sage Publications, 2000.

Anderson, James. *The Education of Blacks in the South, 1860–1935.* Chapel Hill, NC: University of North Carolina Press, 1988.

Andrews, William L., ed. *Critical Essays on W. E. B. Du Bois.* Boston: G. K. Hall, 1985.

Banks, William M. *Black Intellectuals: Race and Responsibility in American Life.* New York: Norton, 1996.

Cook, Robert. *Sweet Land of Liberty? The African-American Struggle for Civil Rights in the Twentieth Century.* New York: Longman, 1998.

Crouch, Stanley, and Benjamin Playthell. *Reconsidering the Souls of Black Folk.* Philadelphia; London: Running Press, 2002.

Du Bois, W. E. B. *Africa: Its Geography, People, and Products.* Girard, KS: Haldeman-Julius, 1930.

———. *Africa: Its Place in Modern History.* Girard, KS: Haldeman-Julius, 1930.

———. *The Autobiography of W. E. B. Du Bois: A Soliloquy on Viewing My Life from the Last Decade of its First Century.* Herbert Aptheker, ed. New York: International, 1968.

———. *Black Folk Then and Now: An Essay in the History and Sociology of the Negro Race.* New York: Henry Holt, 1939.

———. *Black Reconstruction: An Essay Toward a History of the Part Which Black Folk Played in the Attempt to Reconstruct Democracy in America, 1860–1880.* New York: Harcourt Brace Jovanovich, 1935.

———. *Color and Democracy: Colonies and Peace.* New York: Harcourt Brace Jovanovich, 1945.

———. *Darkwater: Voices from within the Veil.* Mineola, NY: Dover Publications, Inc., 1999.

———. *Du Bois on Education.* Lanham MD; Oxford: AltaMira; Oxford Publicity Partnership, 2002.

———. *Dusk of Dawn: An Essay Toward an Autobiography of a Race Concept.* New Brunswick: Transaction Books, 1992.

———. *The Gift of Black Folk: Negroes in the Making of America.* Boston: Stratford, 1924.

———. *In Battle for Peace: The Story of My 83rd Birthday.* New York: Masses and Mainstream, 1952.

———. *The Negro.* Mineola, NY: Dover Publications, Inc., 2001.

———. *The Philadelphia Negro: A Social Study.* Philadelphia: University of Pennsylvania Press, 1996.

———. *The Souls of Black Folk: Essays and Sketches.* Chicago: A. C. McClurg, 1903. Reprint, David W. Blight and Robert Gooding-Williams, eds. Boston and New York: Bedford, 1997.

———. *W. E. B. Du Bois Speaks: Speeches and Addresses, 1920–1963.* New York: Pathfinder Press, 2000.

———. *The World and Africa: An Inquiry into the Part Which Africa Has Played in World History.* New York: Viking, 1947.

———. *John Brown.* David R. Roediger, ed. New York: Modern Library, 2001.

Foner, Philip S. *W. E. B. Du Bois Speaks: Speeches and Addresses, 1920–1963.* New York: Pathfinder, 1970.

Gaines, Kevin K. *Uplifting the Race: Black Leadership, Politics, and Culture in the Twentieth Century.* Chapel Hill, NC: University of North Carolina Press, 1996.

Hamilton, Virginia. *W. E. B. Du Bois: A Biography.* New York: Thomas Y. Crowell, 1972.

Harlan, Louis. *Booker T. Washington: The Making of a Black Leader: 1856–1901.* New York: Oxford University Press, 1972.

Horne, Gerald. *Black and Red: W. E. B. Du Bois and the Afro-American Response to the Cold War.* Albany, NY: State University of New York Press, 1986.

James, Joy. *Transcending the Talented Tenth: Black Leaders and American Intellectuals.* New York: Routledge, 1997.

Katz, Michael B., and Sugrue, Thomas J., eds. *W. E. B. Du Bois, Race, and the City:* The Philadelphia Negro *and Its Legacy.* Philadelphia: University of Pennsylvania Press, 1998.

Lewis, David Levering. *W. E. B. Du Bois: Biography of a Race, 1868–1919.* New York: Henry Holt, 1993.

———. *W. E. B. Du Bois: The Fight for Equality and the American Century, 1919–1963.* New York: Henry Holt, 2000.

Litwack, Leon F. *Trouble in Mind: Black Southerners in the Age of Jim Crow.* New York: Alfred A. Knopf, 1998.

Marable, Manning. *W. E. B. Du Bois: Black Radical Democrat.* Boston: Twayne, 1986.

Matthews, Victoria E. *Black-Belt Diamonds: Gems from the Speeches, Addresses, and Talks to Students of Booker T. Washington.* New York: Fortune & Scott, 1989.

McAfee, Ward M. *Religion, Race, and Reconstruction: The Public School in the Politics of the 1870s.* Albany, NY: State University of New York Press, 1998.

Moore, Jacqueline M. *Booker T. Washington, W. E. B. Du Bois, and the Struggle for Racial Uplift.* Wilmington, Delaware: S. R. Books, 2003.

Rampersad, Arnold. *The Art and Imagination of W. E. B. Du Bois.* New York: Schocken, 1990.

Reed, Adolph L., Jr. *W. E. B. Du Bois and American Political Thought: Fabianism and the Color Line.* New York: Oxford University Press, 1997.

Washington, Booker T. *The Future of the American Negro.* Boston: Small, Maynard, 1900.

———. *Tuskegee and Its People: Their Ideals and Achievements.* New York: Appleton, 1905.

———. *Up from Slavery.* 1901. Reprint, New York: Bantam, 1967.

———. *Working with the Hands.* New York: Doubleday, Page, 1904.

Paulo Freire:
Advocate of
Liberation Pedagogy

This chapter examines the life and ideas of Paulo Freire (1921–1997), a Brazilian educator who developed his educational philosophy of liberation pedagogy while working to bring literacy to the impoverished illiterate peasants and urban poor of his native country. Freire developed his liberation pedagogy when he realized that literacy meant not only learning to read and write, but also helping people to form a social consciousness about the conditions of their lives. With such consciousness, the illiterate and uneducated could identify and seek to reform the economic, social, and political conditions that exploited them.[1]

In this chapter, we examine Freire's development of liberation pedagogy in its historical context and in terms of its influence on contemporary education. First, we examine the historical context of Freire's life in twentieth-century Brazil and how that country's social, economic, and political conditions shaped his ideas. We then consider Freire's life, especially his literacy work among Brazil's impoverished rural peasants, to see how he developed his method of consciousness-raising education and reform. Third, we identify and analyze the key elements of Freire's philosophy of education. Finally, we conclude by assessing Freire's influence on contemporary educational philosophy, especially Critical Theory.

To help you to organize your thoughts as you read the chapter, consider the following questions:

1. What were the major factors in Brazil's historical context influencing Freire?

2. How did Freire's life, his educational biography, shape his social, political, ideo-logical, and educational perspectives?
3. What are the key elements in Freire's philosophy of liberation pedagogy?
4. What has been the impact of Freire's educational ideas on contemporary educational theory and practice?

The Historical Context of Freire's Life

This section examines the historical context of Brazil, the setting in which Freire grew to maturity and formulated his educational ideas. It also analyzes the philosophical and ideological context in which Freire's philosophy of liberation pedagogy is situated. Our examination begins with a brief foray into Brazil's history.

Occupying a territory as large as the continental United States, Brazil is Latin America's largest country. In the sixteenth and seventeenth centuries, the Portuguese conquered the area that today constitutes Brazil. They settled parts of the vast region, coexisting with the indigenous Indian peoples. Like other colonial powers, the Portuguese exploited Brazil's vast natural resources—timber, gold, and other minerals. They also created a vast plantation system much like that of the American South. The Portuguese imported large numbers of enslaved Africans to work as laborers on the plantations. By the end of the nineteenth century, 50 percent of Brazil's population was descended from Africans, 25 percent from Europeans, primarily Portuguese ancestry, and the remaining 25 percent were Indians or *mamelucos*, people of mixed Indian and European ancestry.[2] The Portuguese were more open to racial diversity than the North American English colonists and settlers. Modern Brazil today has a rich cultural and racial diversity. Freire was born and educated in a largely multicultural nation that was united by the Portuguese language and a general allegiance to Roman Catholicism.

Brazil, like most of the South American countries, won its independence from colonial rule in the nineteenth century. Dom Pedro, the son of John VI, King of Portugal, led a successful independence movement and was installed as Brazil's emperor in 1822.

Dom Pedro was succeeded as emperor by his son, Pedro II, a capable and effective ruler. Unlike some of the South American nations that have a politically unstable history of recurrent military coup d'états, Brazil enjoyed relative social and political stability and economic prosperity throughout much of the nineteenth century. Though ruled by an emperor, its liberal constitution guaranteed the freedoms of speech, press, and religion and provided for a representative assembly. Pedro II reigned for 49 years, from 1840 to 1889. Among his notable achievements was the peaceful abolition of slavery in 1888. However, it should be noted that Brazil was the last western nation to end slavery, abolishing it 23 years after the Civil War did so in the United States. In 1889, a coup ended the monarchy and Brazil became a republic.

While its colonial history provides a backdrop for his work in education, Brazil's twentieth-century history sets the stage for Freire's career. Brazil engaged in a program of concerted industrialization and modernization that had uneven social and economic consequences. While its large cities became modern and sophisticated, its rural regions remained stagnant, poverty-ridden backwaters. The modern central cities of Rio de Janeiro and Sao Paulo, with avant-garde architecture, were ringed by urban sprawling slums with poor sanitation, grossly inadequate school and social services, and general lawlessness. Brazil's inherited hierarchical social structure, like that of other Latin American countries, exacerbated gross economic disparities. A very small but powerful ruling elite, with less than 5 percent of the population, controlled half of the nation's wealth. According to a 1985 report, 65 percent of Brazil's 45 million people suffered from malnutrition.[3] Brazil, during Freire's life, was marked by these dramatic contradictions between extreme wealth and dire poverty, abundance and near starvation, modernism and stark underdevelopment.

With such extreme economic and social contradictions, Brazil's political fortunes veered, in the twentieth century, from repressive, authoritarian military regimes to movements for representative democracy and social equality. Although the constitution of 1934 gave the secret ballot to both men and women, literacy tests were used to keep many poorer people from voting. Getulio Vargas, a long-term fixture in Brazilian politics, was president for 18 years, from 1930 to 1945 and from 1951 to 1954. A virtual dictator, Vargas's regime kept a tight rein on Brazil by censoring the media, proscribing rival political parties, and increasing the central executive's power. After Vargas was dismissed from office by the army in 1954, a power struggle developed between the political factions on the left and the right.[4]

In the late 1950s and early 1960s, President Juscelino Kubitschek implemented a program of concerted industrialization and modernization. Brasilia, the highly modern new capital, was constructed in the interior. Brazil's port city of Sao Paulo grew into South America's largest industrial city. Industrialization expanded and diversified Brazil's economy from a reliance on coffee to new manufacturing sectors, especially in steel-making, shipbuilding, and automobile and precision instrument production. Though still an important source of income, dependence on coffee, the major traditional export crop, lessened. The industrialization program, however, carried with it some serious weakness, and imbalances would threaten Brazil's economy in the future. The government policy of massive spending, without tax increases, generated a high rate of inflation that wreaked havoc on the middle classes. Further, much of the industrialization program was underwritten by foreign investments, chiefly from the United States, Canada, Japan, and Germany.

Most of the financial profits of industrialization remained in the hands of the ruling elite at the top of the economic and social hierarchy, with few benefits trickling down to the lower socioeconomic classes. The trade unions, the parties of the political left, the Catholic Action Movement, and some Catholic bishops and priests began to press for reforms to bring about an equitable distribution of wealth and to increase social welfare and educational programs to aid the poor. The reformist groups concentrated their efforts on Brazil's most severely depressed section—the large rural area of northeastern Brazil. Here, they conducted an adult literacy campaign, established schools and health clinics, and encouraged grassroots small-scale development programs. Freire, associated with the Catholic Action Movement, worked in the literacy campaign, organizing literacy circles that developed into his pedagogy of the oppressed. The reformist efforts to uplift the rural peasantry met strong opposition from the entrenched economic oligarchy of large landowners and industrialists who influenced the army. On March 31, 1964, President Joao Goulart, the Labor Party leader, was deposed by a military coup d'état. A repressive military dictatorship ruled Brazil for the next 21 years until 1985.[5]

The rapid drive for industrialization coupled with the repressive dictatorial rule of the military regime put a heavy strain on the already unbalanced economy. While national income rose, it was not equitably distributed. During the mid-1970s, Brazil's economy suffered from "stagflation," a slow growth rate of 5 percent and soaring inflation rates. Workers' real wages declined, 20 percent of the workforce was unemployed, and the annual inflation rate exceeded 200 percent. A severe drought in the large, impoverished northeast brought two million people to the edge of starvation.

The military regime responded to Brazil's economic and social ills by suppressing civil liberties, banning political opposition parties, and imposing strict censorship on the press. It imprisoned citizens suspected of reformist sympathies without trial. It tortured and killed some of its most noted opponents, among whom were rural social workers, civil rights lawyers, and priests and nuns involved with the Catholic Action Movement. Freire, known for his literacy work, was jailed and then forcibly deported from Brazil. During his exile, he continued his education work in Chile and then taught in the United States.

Throughout the 1980s, Brazil's economy and society showed great social strains. In 1982, inflation reached a monthly rate of 100 percent and the government issued a new currency. The foreign debt reached $120 billion, the debt of any developed country. Growing political unrest in Brazil and mounting international pressure forced the military regime to allow the restoration of representative government in 1985, when a freely chosen president was elected. The return of democratic government did not end the economic problems, however. By 1989, inflation had skyrocketed to 1,800 percent.[6]

In 1990, the government of President Fernando Color de Mello took action to bring the economy under control. Color de Mello imposed wage and price controls and froze bank accounts so that money would not leave the country. These stringent economic measures had popular support and brought about a semblance of economic stability. Since then, the Brazilian economy has improved. Despite more social and education programs, the country still is beset by social strains and class divisions.

One aspect of the Brazilian situation that affects the entire world is the threatened destruction of the Amazon Basin rain forests, which contain one-third of the earth's remaining tropical forests. This rich, biodiverse region plays a necessary role in replenishing the earth's oxygen and in combating the "greenhouse effect" caused by industrial emissions and pollutants in the atmosphere. The Amazon Basin's richness in natural resources, especially timber and minerals, has led to its exploitation. Logging, mining, farming, and ranching threaten the continued existence of the rain forests and of the indigenous people who live there. Freire's support of small-scale sustainable development represents an alternative to the massive exploitation of the region.

With this examination of the historical context of Freire's work in Brazil, we turn to situating his theory of liberation pedagogy in the larger framework of educational philosophy. In the late 1960s, Freire worked with Ivan Illich, who developed a theory of de-institutionalizing and deschooling society at Illich's Center for Information and Documentation (CIDOC) in Cuernavaca, Mexico. Although Freire did not endorse deschooling, a brief analysis of Illich's educational ideas helps explain their mutual antagonism to what they regarded as exploitative conditions and how people can be empowered through education. Illich believed that technologically advanced, modern nations, such as the United States, were imposing their institutions, technologies, and processes on the peoples of less technologically developed countries, especially in Latin America, Asia, and Africa.[7] Geared to advance a consumer-oriented, materialistic, exploitative society and economy that favored controlling economic elites, modern western nations, pursuing multinational globalization, imposed large industrial and agricultural corporations on less-developed countries. These modern corporations, driven by profit-making, ignored the social, health, and educational needs of the local people and exploited them as a cheap labor force. While these corporate institutions were being imposed, local needs, as found in the impoverished northeast region of Brazil and its big-city slums, were being ignored. Indeed, the problems of underemployment, illiteracy, and malnutrition were being exacerbated by an uneven form of modernization that benefited the rich to the detriment of the poor. For example, in Brazil, as in other South American and African countries, giant agribusiness corporations, aided by the inherited vested interests, have expropriated large tracts of land. Aided by their political allies in the developing country, these corporate giants expropriated the small farms of peasant families and reduced them to poorly paid workers or dispossessed landless peasants. Many of them left the rural areas to live at the margins of society as impoverished urban slum dwellers. The impoverished masses were too poor and undereducated to benefit from the modern institutions—the airports, hospitals, and universities—that served the elites. Much of Illich's socioeconomic analysis struck a responsive chord with Freire, who experienced poverty as a youth and who was devoting himself to raising the consciousness of dispossessed and marginalized people.

For Illich, the process of corporate modernization was reinforced by schooling. Schools in the modern sense, he argued, are age-specific institutions in which knowledge is packaged in a prescribed compulsory curriculum designed to indoctrinate a society of consumers of material goods.[8] Agreeing with Freire, Illich opposed what he called "educational banking," in which knowledge is defined as information to be deposited in mental banks for withdrawal at a later date. Instead of the school's imposed formal curriculum, Illich proposes that local people, in their grassroots settings, were to create their own knowledge base. Freire's literacy circles used in northeast Brazil, for example, were a grassroots voluntary organization of people who came together for the common purpose of learning to read. They learned by examining the actual conditions and situations of their lives, including those that exploited them. For Illich and Freire, the people at the local level were to create their own friendly, convivial, and humane ways to learn together.[9]

Illich argued that literacy and numeracy should be taught directly without the rigidity and conformity of the prepackaged school curriculum. Work skills could be learned through an apprenticeship. Other kinds of learning—about literature, history, the humanities, and the arts—could be acquired as persons interested in these areas met in voluntary, informal discussion groups. Instead of outside officials and experts determining how local people should live, the people themselves were to identify their needs, structure solutions, and work together to solve their problems. Freire agreed with Illich's premise that a genuine education should lead to raising the person's self- and social consciousness as a first step toward economic and political empowerment.

The educational philosophy developed by Illich and elaborated on by Freire rests on several agreed-upon principles: (1) modern global industrialization, though promising to benefit humankind, actually enriches ruling elites, and dehumanizes and impoverishes the multitudes; (2) education is never objective, nor neutral, politically but always involves ideological commitment and imposition; (3) it is possible, indeed necessary, to challenge the vested interests and ruling elites and to work for humanizing social change.

Philosophically, Freire was influenced by existentialism and Marxism. Like the existentialists, he rejects the view that the human being is defined as a predetermined general category prior to the individual person's existence. Drawing on existentialism, he sees the person as an incomplete and unfinished presence in the world. Consciousness-raising, in Freire's rendition of existentialism, means that individuals become fully aware that they are unfinished or indeterminate persons who are responsible for defining themselves through the actions they choose to perform. The ethical person consciously accepts this responsibility to create a future filled with promises and possibilities.[10] For Freire, a truly ethical person works to become conscious of the conditions in which she or he lives and works, and deliberately works to change those that are unjust or pernicious to human freedom. The ethical person consciously accepts this responsibility to create a future filled with promises and possibilities.[11]

Freire makes use of Marxism when he urges consciousness-raising in analyzing the contemporary situation, and when he urges an examination of the material conditions impacting a society.[12] These conditions of life and work—cultural, social, political, economic and educational—are historically derived and constitute the ongoing reality in which people find themselves. As they become conscious of social reality, individuals can understand their personal and social situations and the conditions that either repress or liberate them. Freire, though using Marxist concepts, rejects the Marxist determinism that our future, like our past, is a product of historical inevitability.

An important part of the intellectual context in which Freire worked and developed his philosophy of liberation pedagogy is his view of the role that ideology plays in educational policy-making. Ideology is the belief system—the core beliefs and values—that creates and maintains a group's identity. The core beliefs of a group—which may range in size from a nation-state to a racial, ethnic, or language group—often are expressed in a view of history and a political agenda. For example, ruling elites, such as landowners and industrialists that supported the military regime that imprisoned and exiled Freire from Brazil, have such an agenda. It is important in the struggle for liberation that marginalized groups—such as the landless peasants or oppressed minority groups—become conscious of the role that ideology plays in their lives and that they formulate their own ideological agendas. Freire sees all social and educational settings, including schools, as sites of ideological confrontation.

The concept of ideology is a major part of Freire's liberation pedagogy. As indicated, Freire considers all education to be conditioned by ideology. He distinguishes liberation pedagogy, as a radicalizing ideology, from rightist and leftist sectarian ideologies that distort history and rely on myths to create a sense of false consciousness. Freire, in his educational work in Latin America, was most engaged in opposition to rightist ideologies that rationalized the rule of reactionary, oligarchic, militarist regimes. He argues that rightist reactionary ideologies, such as conservatism, want to maintain the status quo that gives their members power. They want to "slow down the historical process" by constructing a protective historical interpretation that defends the ruling class's privileged position. This reactionary protectionism then is infused into the school curriculum and is used to indoctrinate the children of oppressed groups and minorities.

Liberalism, though promising equality of opportunity, establishes institutions and procedures that create bureaucratic and corporate elites that manage the system in such a way that it subtly disempowers the majority of people. For example, the bureaucratic control stemming from a central office, though promising educational resources, actually allocates them in a differential manner. Liberals, often intellectuals in the middle classes, tend to display a presumed benevolence toward subordinated groups but fail to acknowledge that they themselves enjoy a privileged status that makes them accomplices in repressive situations. Rather than acting directly to end the repression of marginalized people, liberals tend to skirt the main issues and implement piecemeal reforms that reinforce their own position rather than improve the situation of those they pretend to help. Even the liberal notion of welfare and assistance, benignly intended to aid the poor, creates a dependency that locks the dependents into the system rather than liberating them from it.[13]

Freire's philosophy of education was also influenced by liberation theology, a progressive and socially conscious movement in Roman Catholicism in Latin America. The Catholic Church in Central and South America was established as the official religion during the Spanish and Portuguese colonial eras. After the countries in the region gained independence, it continued to exercise a dominant cultural, social, and educational role. Throughout its history, the church in Central and South America generally took a conservative political stance supporting the forces who sought to maintain the status quo. In the late 1950s, however, a progressive movement, liberation theology, developed among some of the clergy and laity. According to the movement, which included the Catholic Action in Brazil, true Christianity included a program of social justice to improve the living and working conditions of the poor. Reformist Catholic efforts included the establishment of health clinics, small-scale enterprises, and educational and literacy work, such as that of Freire in Brazil.[14]

Paulo Freire: Biography of an Educator

Paulo Freire was born on September 19, 1921, in Recife, a port city in northeastern Brazil. His father served in the Brazilian army and then was an officer in the Perambuco state military police. Freire, who recognized the importance of reflecting on one's childhood to draw forth the formative experiences that established the foundations of personality, had fond memories of his father, and described him as "affectionate, intelligent, and open." Always willing to discuss and explore his interests with him, his father was an important educational influence. Freire said his first lessons in democracy came from his father's criticism of the arrogance, abuse of power, and corruption of Brazil's ruling classes. He remembered his parents as an "harmonious couple," who both kept their individuality. His mother was a Catholic and his father a spiritist. Paulo decided to take his mother's religion and Catholicism was an important influence on him. He said his parents taught him the letters of the alphabet by tracing them with a stick on the ground in the backyard.[15] After his forced retirement, Freire's father worked as a carpenter, doing odd jobs. He died in 1934.

Paulo began his formal education in a private school at age 8. He liked his first teacher, Eunice Vasconcelos. He especially enjoyed her relaxed teaching style and the exercise called "sentence forming" in which the pupils wrote the words they knew in a straight line and then formed sentences with the words. They then discussed the meaning of each sentence and gradually moved to those that were more complex.[16] However, he disliked many of his later elementary and secondary school experiences. Academic success in the classroom, he said, was largely based on a pupil's ability to memorize rather than understand. The ability to regurgitate memorized responses was regarded as a sign of intelligence. He recalled that the more he failed to memorize the more he regarded himself as insurmountably ignorant. In his educational writings, Freire would condemn the memorization and recitation approach as a "banking method" in which students stocked their minds with disconnected bits of information that were to be recalled at a later date.

The Great Depression of the 1930s brought economic hardship to Freire's middle-class family. His father had been forcibly retired and earned his living by doing odd jobs as a carpenter. Facing poverty, the Freires were forced to sell some of their prized possessions. They consciously struggled to retain the symbols of their former middle-class status; his father wore a tie and they kept the piano that dominated the living room. Freire recalled the ever-present problem he and his family faced was hunger.[17] He remembered his mother asking for credit at the local butcher shop, and being humiliated by the loud and sexist proprietor. Throughout his life, he was angered by the "disrespect of those in positions of power toward those who have none."[18]

Aided by the willingness of his family to sacrifice for his education and earning part of his tuition as a secondary school teacher, Freire was able to enroll in the University of Recife's Faculty of Law in 1941. In addition to his legal studies, he also took courses in philosophy and psychology. As a student, he paradoxically read the works of Marx and Catholic philosophers such as Jacques Maritain.[19]

In 1944, Freire married Elza Maia Costa Oliveira, a teacher in a Catholic primary school. The couple had three daughters and two sons.

He passed the bar examination but he left legal practice to devote himself to education, a field that held a stronger attraction for him. He went to work as a welfare official and rose to become director of the Department of Education and Culture of Social Services, from 1946 to 1954, in the state of Perambuco. His work brought him into contact with the poor. He began to experiment with a method of education for the poor, especially the illiterate masses. He also began studying and teaching the history and philosophy of education at the University of Recife. His doctoral dissertation, "Educacao e atualidade brasilirae" ("Education and the Present Moment in Brasil"), was accepted and he was awarded his doctoral degree in 1959.[20] In the early 1960s, Freire, as director of the University of Recife's Cultural Extension Service, launched a massive literacy campaign among the rural poor. Freire and his literacy teams taught reading to the peasants by focusing on the immediate situations that affected their everyday lives. He connected literacy directly to their economic and political situations. He was quickly labeled a dangerous radical by the reactionary Brazilian landowners and military. After a military coup took control of Brazil in 1964, all progressive movements, including Freire's literacy campaign, were suppressed. Freire was imprisoned for his subversive activities. After serving 70 days in prison, he was expelled from Brazil.

Freire took refuge in Chile where he worked in literacy programs for five years. He came to the United States in 1969 as a visiting professor at Harvard University and as a Fellow at the Center for the Study of Development and Social Change. It was during this time that Freire wrote *Pedagogy of the Oppressed* (1970), his groundbreaking introduction of liberation pedagogy, based on his grassroots work in literacy campaigns among Brazil's rural poor.[21] It was a well-reviewed, widely read, and influential book that challenged and transcended conventional thinking in educational philosophy and theory. *Pedagogy of the Oppressed* was followed by a series of books that elaborated on the themes of liberation pedagogy. Among them were *Education for Critical Consciousness* (1973), *Pedagogy in Process: The Letters to Guinea Bisseau* (1978), *Pedagogy of the City* (1993), and *Pedagogy of Hope* (1994).[22]

Freire left Harvard in the early 1970s to work as a consultant and eventually as Assistant Secretary of Education for the World Council of Churches. He lectured throughout the world on his philosophy of education.

In 1979, a more liberal regime was in place in Brazil and a political amnesty was declared that allowed exiles, such as Freire, to return to their native country. He was appointed to the faculty at the University of Sao Paulo. In 1988, he was appointed Minister of Education for the City of Sao Paulo, a position that made him responsible for guiding school reform in two-thirds of Brazil's schools.

Paulo Freire suffered a heart attack and died on May 2, 1997, at the age of 75.

Freire's Philosophy of Liberation Pedagogy

Freire initially developed his liberation pedagogy as a result of his literacy work with the impoverished, illiterate peasants in northeast Brazil. He also drew inspiration from the educational theories of Ivan Illich and from the liberation theology that was being applied by the Catholic Action Movement of which he was a member. Freire moved from the local context of Brazil and Latin America to a broader worldview. He broadened his outlook by reading and researching the foundations of education, delving into existentialism and Marxism, and he developed his philosophy of education from the local context to that of a global worldview.

Liberation pedagogy in Freire's philosophy of education refers to the power of education to liberate or free oppressed people from the social, economic, and political conditions that disempower and marginalize them. The word *pedagogy* comes from a Greek word meaning leading a person to knowledge; when linked with *liberation* the term refers to a transformative education that has the power to lead people to a raised consciousness or greater awareness of the realities of life. It is designed to empower people to resist and to reconstruct oppressive conditions and to create a more equitable, just, and humane society. The goal of liberation pedagogy is the creation of a new social order. Creating a new world comes from opening the self and society to new possibilities of leading a richer and fuller life.

A key concept in Freire's philosophy is *conscientizacao*, a Portuguese word that means to raise a person's consciousness; a critical awareness of the social, political, and economic conditions and contradictions of a person's life is necessary in order to identify those that are repressive or oppressive. The process of consciousness-raising is not intended to be an abstract academic exercise. Behind the conditions of exploitation are other people, usually members of powerful, favored economic or social elites; and equally present are members of marginalized groups, often minorities, women, the unemployed, the undereducated, and the poor. Consciousness-raising is to lead to "radicalization," a personal commitment to work for social change, reform, and a just and equitable society and economy.

In Freire's view, the study and role of history is important in leading to *conscientizacao*. This history, however, is not the chronological study of dynasties and wars, nor a congratulatory celebration or apology for the status quo. It is a personal autobiography, a self-study of a person's life or the collective life of a group. At this point, Freire makes use of the Marxist approach to analysis to identify which group controls the way in which wealth is produced and used. The critical study of history, Freire argues, reveals that some groups or classes have seized control of and expropriated wealth and used their power to control and subordinate others. Unlike the Marxists, however, Freire does not believe that our lives, our personal and collective group histories, are predetermined by the inexorable and inevitable laws of a universal dialectical process that is beyond our control. Instead, at this point he interjects insights from existentialism. Like the existentialists, he believes that our lives are indeterminate and open to our own self-determination rather than being determined in advance for us. To have a genuine awareness of the conditions in which we live marks the beginnings of our realization that we have the power to define ourselves and write our own history if we dare to seize the moment to do so.

Freire's view of consciousness-raising is highly contextual in that our lives take place in a concrete historical and geographical setting, in other words, at a particular time and place. The situations of our lives include our occupations, the partners we choose, and how we raise our children. We can provide for ourselves comfortably and enjoy life in a spiritual and cultural sense. Or, alternatively, we can face poverty, hunger, unemployment, repression, and exploitation. Freire developed his approach to literacy by teaching people to read about the realities they faced every day. For the illiterate person, learning to read decrees, deeds, laws, and the terms of loans and foreclosures was crucial. Such literacy led to greater awareness: What can I do about these conditions and situations? Am I powerless or can I empower myself? Freire, of course, argued that a person can take power if he or she recognizes who and what are behind the powerlessness. Though others—the generals, landlords, and politicians—may have been in control for a long time, it does not mean that we have to continue to surrender to their power. We do not have to abandon our choices to them. As we become conscious of the situations in which we live, we learn that we do not have to surrender to the forces of domination and to accept and adjust to the status quo. The conditions of our life situations can be viewed as starting points from which to begin the journey to self-definition.

For Freire, educational institutions and processes are never free of the conditions and situations—the contexts—of which they are a part. They are never ideologically neutral or scientifically objective. All educational systems, like all social, political, and economic systems, are ideologically conditioned. Education either teaches the younger generation to accept and conform to the power relationships of the existing system or it becomes a pedagogy of liberation. Education committed to liberation implies raising people's consciousness, encouraging them to reflect critically on social reality, and empowering them to transform the conditions that shape their lives.

For Freire, schools, curriculum and educational methods are intimately related to the social, political, and economic conditions and their contexts—the communities of which they are a part. Schools—like all social, political, and economic institutions—function in an ideologically charged society. The school's curriculum and instruction either transmit and condition students to conform to the official version of knowledge and values, or challenge them to become agents of their own humanization and liberation.

Consciousness-raising requires that the situations and actors that miseducate people, either unconsciously or deliberately, be exposed for what they are. Miseducation results from being indoctrinated in the officially approved knowledge and values. It produces a false consciousness, an inability or obstinacy to recognize historical truth and social reality. False consciousness, a concept Freire adopts from Marx, suggests its deluded victims have been indoctrinated into believing the rhetoric of those who control social institutions and economic processes, including schools. False consciousness results in a falsified history and distorted self-concept, often one of low self-esteem. A history that celebrates the achievements of the ruling class while ignoring the contributions of marginalized groups distorts the truth and provides a falsified record of the past. For example, a history that celebrates the victories and achievements of white Euro-American males and omits or minimizes the history of women, African Americans, Latinos, and other minority groups distorts the true historical record. An education that defines a person's values in terms of wealth and power and sees schooling as a ticket to success in an exploitative economic system cannot lead to true humanizing.[23]

Freire argues that all educational settings, especially schools, are impacted by politics, economics, and ideologies. He disparages the notion that teachers can and should be neutral, impartial, and uncommitted in the classroom on social, political, and economic issues.[24] For liberation pedagogy, such claims to objectivity mean the teacher is not conscious of the true conditions that affect education, or is engaged in a pretense that covers up hidden ideological commitments. He maintains that teachers need to develop a critical consciousness of the real power relationships in the schools in which they teach and of the social, economic, and political conditions in which their students live. For example, if they are teaching in an inner-city school, their students' lives are likely to be impacted by poverty, limited health care and recreational services, drug abuse, and the threats of gang violence. The teachers' own working conditions in such schools are likely to be impacted by decisions made by a remote bureaucracy, a lack of educational resources, and neglect from the more affluent sectors of society. When they understand the reality of their school situations, teachers can begin to resist these oppressive conditions and those who impose them. They can make determined efforts to become learners themselves—studying the lives, families, and groups whom they teach. With this kind of consciousness, teachers cannot remain neutral or hide behind a veil of objectivity. Claiming or feigning neutrality actually allies the teacher with the oppressors. Teachers have to confront and answer the question—do existing social, economic, and political conditions retard human liberation and freedom, or promote human self-fulfillment? The teacher either supports the oppressors, who have appropriated the material conditions of life—wealth, land, property—and constructed a social, cultural, and political system that justifies their exploitation of subordinated groups; or, the teacher acts to advance the liberation of the dispossessed.[25]

Freire urges that teaching be reconceptualized, that teachers take a critical and rigorous stance in examining the conditions of their school as a microcommunity of the larger society, and as a macrocosm that includes the more immediate and smaller segments of social reality. He also urges them to develop a sense of humility; they too are learners and have much to learn from their students. The rigorous critical attitude means that teachers need to understand that they work in an ideologically charged context of conflicting claims to knowledge, values, and power. Teachers may have to question the status quo, go against what is held to be conventional wisdom about how a school should be run, and take the risk of challenging the power structure both inside and outside of schools.

Freire's philosophical inclination toward existentialism contributed to shaping his concept of the human being as an "unfinished presence" in the world who is working out her or his own identity and purpose under real social, political, economic, and educational conditions. Not a mere abstraction, the idea of a person as unfinished or incomplete means that she or he is engaged in a process of self-identification. For students, it is important to learn to resist the forces that seek to define or categorize them as slow learners, unteachable, delinquent, and potential dropouts. These educational categories are actually social constructions imposed on people to define them as "others" that belong on the margins of school life. The raising of consciousness, through liberation pedagogy, means that students are engaged in studying their own autobiographies, their own life stories, and the collective history of their racial, ethnic, language, economic, and social groups. They are engaged in consciously examining the objective conditions and contexts of their lives, identifying those conditions, forces, and actors that diminish their opportunities for self-definition and self-fulfillment.[26]

In terms of educational method, Freire makes an important connection between thinking, or becoming conscious, and practice, or taking action. Critical thinking means that a person, a student, has learned how to examine the conditions of her or his life. She or he has learned how to cut through the fog of false consciousness—the histories, myths, and stories—that the oppressors have constructed as a rationale, the official school knowledge, to indoctrinate dominated groups. For example, the myth of America's wars as always just ignores the conquest of Mexican people in the Southwest. The Horatio Alger myth promises that every child, no matter how poor, can rise to the top of the economic and social ladder by working hard. These rationales, often found in the school's official knowledge, are based on the ruling group's ideology. They are used to indoctrinate the children of marginalized groups to accept uncritically the oppressive conditions in the social environment as being "right," "just," "the standard," or "in the nature of things." Thinking critically means that a student has acquired the skill to see these rationales for what they are—the constructions of an oppressive group that lead to their docile acceptance of a false ideology.

Freire makes a concerted attack on methods of instruction that lead to false rather than critical consciousness in students' perceptions of reality. Some conventional teaching methods contribute to false consciousness. For example, "teacher talk," which turns a teacher into a "talking head" or "talking text," implies that the teacher possesses knowledge and can transmit it to students by telling them what is true. It means that students attentively listen to, record, and memorize what the teacher is saying and passively deposit it in their minds to be recalled later for a test. Freire condemns the teacher talking–student listening method as educational "banking."[27] Each bit of information, transmitted by the teacher, is to be deposited in the student's mind, a mental bank. It is stored in a mental safety deposit box to be reclaimed and cashed in at some future date, usually for an examination. The standards movement that emphasizes determining student academic achievement by standardized testing is an example of assessment based on the banking model. The elaborate testing mechanisms, constructed from the officially transmitted knowledge, are used to sort students into groups, often isolating the marginalized students and thereby reproducing the social and economic inequalities of the existing system.[28]

Rather than the transmission of information by teacher talk, Friere argues that development of a critical consciousness comes from engaging in liberating dialogues, conversations between equals. In these dialogues, the students voice their self-perceptions, tell their own stories, identify their issues and problems, and examine the conditions that either restrict or expand their freedom. This free-ranging dialogue is owned by its participants and not imposed as discussions of the official knowledge deposited in the texts of a prescribed curriculum. Critical thinking and open dialogue facilitate the process of humanization and expression that makes it possible to identify, resist, and reject the rationales of the dominant ruling elites. It makes it possible for the community of learners to access knowledge that is true to them and that leads to a genuine consciousness of social reality.

For Freire, real learning takes place as teachers and students share engagement in an open and ongoing dialogue. The participants in the transformed school settings, like the peasants in rural Brazil, create meaningful knowledge that arises from their critical reflections on the experiences of their everyday life and situations. The moment of learning comes when the participants in the dialogue start to evaluate critically what they know, and trace the genealogy of this acquired knowledge that purports to be truth. At what time in their lives and under what conditions did they acquire their assumptions about what is true and good? Are these beliefs the results of their own freely made choices or do they represent the false ideologies of others? From these consciousness-raising questions arise the opportunities for critically examining, transforming, and humanizing life and society.[29] According to Macedo, a close friend and interpreter of Freire, genuine teaching: (1) recognizes the ideological nature of all social, political, economic, and educational constructs; (2) is committed ethically to resist and combat all racial, sexual, and class discrimination; and (3) requires a critical attitude, a rigorous stance to truth that is tempered by reflection and a sense of humility.[30]

For Freire, then, teaching is not collecting and transmitting knowledge; neither is learning the memorization of information to be retrieved in the future. Teaching and learning require that both the teacher and the students are mutually engaged in constructing knowledge through critical dialogue. Both participants in the educational dialogue—teacher and students—are reforming themselves. Freire's concept of teaching and learning as mutual reforming of the selves reflects his reliance on the existentialist theme that the human condition is one of incompleteness in which we act to bring our lives, through our own actions, to wholeness.

Critical thinking and engaged dialogue, however, are not just academic, schoolroom exercises. They are elements in what is a call to action—to organize and to develop a plan to change the system by eliminating the conditions of oppression. As individuals learn to think critically and to act on their ideas, they are engaged in the existential act of defining and recreating themselves and their social, political, economic, and educational context.

Freire sees ethical and aesthetic values, the true elements of character education, arising from the choices that people make in their own lives and society. He sees the contest in values coming from a conflict between conditions that humanize and dehumanize people. The question is—are values freely made and chosen by the person who embraces and is guided by them, or are they prescriptions imposed on the oppressed by those in positions of social and economic control? Freire argues that prescription "represents the imposition of one man's choice on another." Prescription, the countless "shoulds" and "should nots" of dominant groups, subverts the ethical and aesthetic sensibilities of marginalized people, imposing the dominant person's values on them. As Illich noted, many of the values transmitted as official character training in schools are really the disguised defenses of the ruling classes and groups. Those who rule often create a materialistic need for the products of a consumer-driven economy—designer jeans and athletic shoes, for example. Prescriptions of oppression—disguised as the "right way" to act or the "right" group to which to belong—are ingrained into the psyches of the oppressed. They are reinforced by rewards and threats or actual punishments. These prescriptions are enforced through the hidden curriculum as ways to isolate those who deviate from the prescribed officially sanctioned norms. Thus, the values of the oppressor become internalized in those whom they oppress.[31]

To become truly free to create one's own values, the ultimate kind of character education, means that one needs to recognize that the choice between contested values belongs to the individual person. The person's awareness of being "unfinished," in the existential sense, means that a person is free and responsible to make the choices and act on the decisions that lead to self-definition and self-fulfillment. This kind of authentic value creation does not mean, however, that a person is separate from others in creating self-definition. The project of self-completion is a social, political, economic, and educational one that takes place with others. Just as conditions and agents dispossess some, the reform and transformation of social reality by activated communities of those at the margins can remake the social order.

Conclusion: An Assessment

This chapter examined Freire's liberation pedagogy and explored the influences of Illich's theory of deinstitutionalization and of existentialism and Marxism on Freire's philosophy of education. It analyzed his opposition to false consciousness and his argument that a truly liberating education should lead to the construction of a true consciousness, based on a critical examination of the conditions that empower some and disempower others. It analyzed Freire's emphasis on the teacher as an ideologically committed person who, with students, engages in consciousness-raising educational dialogues.

Freire was a doer as well as a thinker, an activist as well as a theoretician, a practitioner as well as a philosopher. He developed his philosophy of liberation pedagogy as a result of teaching illiterate peasants to read. From this grassroots practice, he formulated his theory. He was a person who had a need to reflect and write. His articles and books gave a coherent, but poetical, rendition of theory born of practice to educators inspired by his words. Through his work, he created new and enlarged meanings. Dialogue was enlarged from discussion to an open and critical confrontation with one's life situation. Teaching was enlarged to mean being a searcher, along with students, on a risky but necessary path to become genuinely conscious of the conditions of reality. Learning was enlarged from simply taking in information to engaging in the project of completing one's identity and meaning in a world that needed to be made better, more humane, and more just. Schooling was taken out of its four walls and transformed into an education that opened the door to the actual world outside.

Questions for Reflection and Dialogue

1. Reflect on Freire's concept of human nature. Does it agree or disagree with the ideas of human identity, purpose, and learning that you generally have encountered in your courses in sociology and psychology?

2. Reflect on Freire's argument that education should stimulate a person's critical consciousness. What does it mean to have a critical consciousness? Has your education diminished or developed your critical consciousness?

3. How do the contexts in which we live shape our social, political, economic and educational beliefs about knowledge and values? Give some examples of how contexts have shaped your thinking.

4. Compare and contrast the concepts of being a "complete" or "finished" and an "incomplete" or "unfinished person." Explore what these concepts mean for education and for teaching and learning.

5. How does Freire's conception of the teacher–student relationship differ from conventional definitions?

6. What does Freire mean by the "banking" approach to curriculum and instruction? Provide examples of the "banking" approach to education.

7. Why does Freire oppose the conception of instruction as the transfer of knowledge from teachers to students?

8. What is the difference between "oppressed" and "oppressor" consciousness? Provide examples of these two forms of consciousness from your own education and experience.

9. Why is critical dialogue a crucial and necessary element in education based on liberation pedagogy?

Projects for Deepening Your Understanding

1. Conduct a critical dialogue, based on Freire's model, in which the participants examine the conditions of their current educational situation.

2. Consider the physical, social, political, and economic conditions of schools that you have attended or in which you are currently teaching. How do these local conditions influence what takes place in the school?

3. In a class discussion, identify what it means to have ideas based on "false" consciousness. During your discussion, develop a list of the factors that contribute to false consciousness in American society.

4. In a class discussion, identify those who are empowered and disempowered in American society, in general, and in your educational context, your school or college, in particular. What factors or conditions contribute to empowerment or disempowerment?

5. Visit classes in educational philosophy or the foundations of education. Do you find evidence of liberation pedagogy?

Notes

1. Richard Shaull, "Preface," in Paulo Freire, *Pedagogy of the Oppressed* (New York: Continuum, 1984), 9–11.

2. Philip L. Ralph, Robert E. Lerner, Standish Meacham, and Edward McNall Burns, *World Civilizations: Their History and Their Culture*, vol. II, 8th ed. (New York: W. W. Norton, 1991), 339.

3. Ralph et al. *World Civilizations*, 785.

4. Ralph et al. *World Civilizations*, 785.

5. Ralph et al. *World Civilizations*, 785.

6. Ralph et al. *World Civilizations*, 786–87.

7. Ivan Illich, *Deschooling Society* (New York: Harper & Row, 1971).

8. Illich, *Deschooling Society*, 37–38.

9. Ivan Illich, *Tools for Conviviality* (New York: Harper & Row, 1973), 10–45.

10. Paulo Freire, *Pedagogy of Freedom, Ethics, Democracy and Civic Courage* (Lanham, Maryland: Rowman and Littlefield, 1998), 25–26, 54.

11. Freire, *Pedagogy of Freedom, Ethics, Democracy and Civic Courage*, 25–26, 54.

12. Donaldo Macedo, "Foreword," in Paulo Freire, *Pedagogy of Freedom: Ethics, Democracy, and Civic Courage*, xxiv.

13. Macedo, "Foreword," in Freire, *Pedagogy of Freedom, Ethics, Democracy and Civic Courage*, xxviii.

14. For a treatment of the Catholic Action Movement, see Emanuel de Kadt's *Catholic Radicals in Brazil* (London: Oxford University Press, 1970).

15. Paulo Freire, *Letters to Cristina: Reflections on My Life and Work*. Donaldo Macedo, trans. (New York; London: Routledge, 1996), 28.

16. Freire, *Letters to Cristina*, 28.

17. Freire, *Letters to Cristina*, 15, 22.

18. Freire, *Letters to Cristina*, 41.

19. "People You Should Know: Freire," http://nlu.nl.edu/ace/Resources/Freire.html (August 11, 2003), 1.

20. "People You Should Know: Freire," 2.

21. Paulo Freire, *Pedagogy of the Oppressed* (1970) (New York: Continuum, 1996).

22. Paulo Freire, *Education for Critical Consciousness* (New York: Seabury, 1973); *Pedagogy in Process: The Letters to Guinea Bisseau* (New York: Seabury, 1978); *Pedagogy of the City* (New York: Continuum, 1993); *Pedagogy of Hope* (New York: Continuum, 1994).

23. Stanley Aronowitz, "Introduction," in Freire, *Pedagogy of Freedom: Ethics, Democracy, and Civic Courage*, 4.

24. Freire, *Pedagogy of Freedom, Ethics, Democracy and Civic Courage*, 22.

25. Aronowitz, "Introduction," in Freire, *Pedagogy of Freedom: Ethics, Democracy, and Civic Courage*, 11.

26. Freire, *Pedagogy of Freedom, Ethics, Democracy and Civic Courage*, 51.

27. Paulo Freire, *Pedagogy of the Oppressed*, trans. Myra Bergman Ramos (New York: Continuum, 1984), 57–59.

28. Aronowitz, "Introduction," in Freire, *Pedagogy of Freedom, Ethics, Democracy and Civic Courage*, 4–5.

29. Aronowitz, "Introduction," in Freire, *Pedagogy of Freedom, Ethics, Democracy and Civic Courage*, 8–9.

30. Macedo, "Foreword," in Freire, *Pedagogy of Freedom, Ethics, Democracy and Civic Courage*, xiii.

31. Freire, *Pedagogy of the Oppressed*, 31.

Suggestions for Further Reading

Darder, Antonia. *Reinventing Paulo Freire*. Boulder, Co.: Westview Press, 2002.

Freire, Paulo. *Conscientisation and Liberation: A Conversation with Paulo Freire*. Cuernavaca Centro Intercultural de Documentacion, 1973.

———. *Education for Critical Consciousness*. New York: Seabury, 1973.

———. *Letters to Cristina. Reflections on My Life and Work*. London: Routledge, 1996.

———. *Mentoring the Mentor: A Critical Dialogue with Paulo Freire*. New York: P. Lang, 1997.

———. *Pedagogy in Process: The Letters to Guinea Bisseau*. New York: Seabury, 1978.

———. *Pedagogy of the City*. New York: Continuum, 1993.

———. *Pedagogy of Freedom: Ethics, Democracy, and Civic Courage*. Lanham, Maryland: Rowman and Littlefield, 1998.

———. *Pedagogy of Hope.* New York: Continuum, 1994.

———. *Pedagogy of the Oppressed.* Myra Bergman Ramos, trans. New York: Continuum, 2000.

———. *Politics and Education.* Los Angeles: UCLA Latin American Center Publications, 1998.

———. *The Politics of Education: Culture, Power, and Liberation.* South Hadley, MA: Bergin & Garvey, 1985.

———. *Teachers as Cultural Workers: Letters to Those Who Dare Teach.* Boulder, CO: Westview Press, 1998.

———. *The Paulo Freire Reader.* Ana Maria Araujo Freire and Donaldo P. Macedo, eds. New York: Continuum, 2000.

———. *Pedagogy of Hope: Reliving Pedagogy of the Oppressed.* Ana Maria Araujo Freire, ed. New York: Continuum, 1999.

Gadotti, M. *Reading Paulo Freire: His Life and Work.* New York: SUNY Press, 1994.

Gartner, Alan, Greer, Colin, and Riessman, Frank. *After Deschooling, What?* New York: Harper & Row, 1973.

Horton, Myles, and Freire, Paulo. *We Make the Road by Walking: Conversations on Education and Social Change.* Philadelphia: Temple University Press, 1990.

Illich, Ivan D. *Celebration of Awareness: A Call for Institutional Revolution.* New York: Doubleday and Co., 1970.

———. *Deschooling Society.* New York: Harper & Row, 1971.

———. *Tools for Conviviality.* New York: Harper & Row, 1973.

McLaren, Peter. *Che Guevara, Paulo Freire, and the Pedagogy of Revolution.* Oxford: Rowman and Littlefield, 2000.

McLaren, Peter, and Leonard, Peter. *Paulo Freire: A Critical Encounter.* New York and London: Routledge, 1993.

Morrow, Raymond A., and Torres, Carlos Alberto. *Reading Freire and Habermas: Critical Pedagogy and Transformative Social Change.* New York: Teachers College Press, Columbia University, 2002.

Reimer, Everett. *School is Dead: Alternatives in Education.* Garden City, NY: Doubleday and Co., 1970.

Taylor, P. *The Texts of Paulo Freire.* Buckingham: Open University Press, 1993.

Shor, Ida, and Freire, Paulo. *A Pedagogy for Liberation: Dialogues on Transforming Education.* Boston. MA.: Bergin & Garvey, 1987.

INDEX